THE SOVIET UNION, 1922-1962
A Foreign Affairs Reader

THE
SOVIET UNION,
1922-1962
A FOREIGN AFFAIRS READER

Edited by

Philip E. Mosely

Foreword by

Hamilton Fish Armstrong

Published for the
COUNCIL ON FOREIGN RELATIONS
by
FREDERICK A. PRAEGER, *Publisher*
New York · London

Published in the United States of America in 1963 by
Frederick A. Praeger, Inc., Publisher
64 University Place, New York 3, N. Y.

Published in the United Kingdom in 1963 by
Frederick A. Praeger, Inc., Publisher
49 Great Ormond Street, London W.C. 1

THE SOVIET UNION, *1922-1962:* A FOREIGN AFFAIRS READER
is published in two editions:
  A Praeger Paperback (P-107)
  A clothbound edition

For information, address Council on Foreign Relations,
58 East 68th Street, New York 21

FIRST EDITION

Library of Congress catalog card number: 63-10826

Printed in the United States of America
by Quinn & Boden Company, Inc., Rahway, N. J.

The Council on Foreign Relations is a non-profit institution devoted to study of the international aspects of American political, economic and strategic problems. It takes no stand, expressed or implied, on American policy.

The authors of books published under the auspices of the Council are responsible for their statements of fact and expressions of opinion. The Council is responsible only for determining that they should be presented to the public.

For a list of Council publications see pages *496* and *497*.

FOREWORD

By Hamilton Fish Armstrong

From the start, *Foreign Affairs* has shown its deep concern with events in the Communist world. In particular, it has tried to give its readers a broad basis for understanding and appraising the fluctuations in Soviet relations with the Western civilization for which Soviet leaders express such antipathy and disdain at the same time that they envy and emulate its achievements. In its forty years, *Foreign Affairs* has published well over two hundred articles on aspects of Soviet life, ideology and foreign policy by a vast variety of writers, including not only Western authorities in the great majority but also a number of Soviet leaders from Bukharin to Khrushchev, as well as a rebel like Chernov and a fallen Olympian like Trotsky.

It is from a well-stocked storehouse, then, that Philip E. Mosely has selected the contents of this volume. Some of the articles are factual, some analytical, some philosophical; some argue a particular view (usually contrary to a view already expressed in an earlier issue, or to be expressed in a later one); some set forth what its author fancifully (or not) supposed to be effective propaganda. The reader will easily determine which are which. Together, they form a panorama of the past forty years in what was at first a special field but which then assumed global proportions and now is becoming universal as the competition between the two societies reaches out along the pathlessness of sidereal space.

The first issue of *Foreign Affairs,* published in the autumn of 1922, contained an article on Russia, signed with the anonymous letter "K," chosen as a pseudonym by Archibald Cary Coolidge, the first Editor of the review; he was willing to hint at his real name but not to reveal it for fear of seeming to commit a fledgling publication to a certain point of view, even on matters regarding which he was a recognized authority. The article was notable not only in its own right, as the reader even today will quickly discover, but because it attracted the interest of the Kremlin hierarchy. The story is perhaps worth recalling.

A representative in Russia of the American Relief Administration, Dr. F. A. Golder, found (as he wrote Coolidge) that when he returned to Moscow from Riga in the autumn of 1922 "our friends of the red calico"—Trotsky, Lenin, Bukharin, Radek "and the other Olympians," mentioned by Golder in that order—were very much occupied with the Fourth Congress of the Communist International. But not too occupied to be interested in the first issue of *Foreign Affairs,* a copy of which already had reached Moscow. Radek, wrote Golder, "assured me that he has read it from cover to cover and has made a review of it in the *Pravda.* . . . He is full of praise of the high standard and speaks in very high terms of the article on Russia. . . . I dare not guess who wrote it. Radek thinks you did. I hope he is right. . . . Radek gave the copy to Lenin who is reading it now."

The sequel, as told by Golder in a second letter, dated December 11, was as follows: "The other evening Radek came to the Pink House [headquarters of the American Relief Administration] to have dinner with me. He brought with him the copy of *Foreign Affairs* in order to point out in the bibliography some of the American books he would like to have. He offered to copy, but I proposed that he leave his copy and I give him mine. He agreed. When I looked into it I found that he and Lenin had marked up a number of passages in the Russian article as well as some of the other articles. You would give a good deal to see that, wouldn't you?"

Later Golder sent Coolidge the marked copy. Two sorts of pencils had been used, in two quite different methods of marking. Folded into it was a two-page handwritten memorandum summarizing the Allied debts as described by John Foster Dulles in an article in the same issue; it was in a similar handwriting to that used on the envelope in which Radek later sent an article to *Foreign Affairs,* and it contains words in Polish, Radek's native language. By elimination, the markings of a different sort from Radek's presumably are Lenin's—marginal marks or underscoring of words made by Lenin as he read Coolidge's article. They occur profusely, emphasizing in some cases cautionary phrases about the Soviet economy, in others particular difficulties in Soviet foreign relations.

The Bukharin article also has a little history that it may be amusing to recall. One of my chief reasons for visiting Moscow in 1928 was to obtain an article for *Foreign Affairs* from Bukharin, called by Lenin "the greatest and most valuable theoretician." I spent several weeks in Moscow, but although I talked with Litvinov, Lunacharsky and several other leaders I was unable to see Bukharin. Near the end of my stay I was told that if I could wait two weeks longer he would see me, as by then he would have received "permission" from other members of the Politbureau "to talk with a foreigner." I could not wait.

But while I was in Paris in April 1936 I heard a rumor that Bukharin was there, staying at the Hotel Lutétia (my guess was that he was on his way home from a secret visit to Spain). I went there, asked the number of his room, went up, knocked, and soon was sitting beside him on his bed while he showed off his command of several languages, of which I understood only French well and German but a little. Bukharin by now was at odds with Stalin but he was still editor of *Izvestia* and a revered Communist oracle. The burden of his talk was to explain how national rivalry between Communist states was "by definition an impossibility." What makes wars, he said, was the competition among monopolist capitalisms for raw materials and markets. Since capitalist society is made up of selfish and competing units it is "a world at war." As Communism spreads to other states, the new Communist society will be composed of unselfish and harmonious units, and therefore a world at peace. "Just as capitalism cannot live without war, so war cannot live with Communism." The unity and harmony of Communist society were not a theory but "a spontaneous fact"—*"eine spontane Realität."*

When after the Second World War an international Communist society came into existence, and Moscow established relations with brotherly Marxist states, the ideal imagined by Bukharin vanished. One Communist leader who felt that his state was being exploited was branded as reactionary and bourgeois and expelled from the fraternity. Other states that came into Soviet hands were provided with Communist governors who did not follow Tito's risky path (or like Nágy were shot). And now Red China, following its own way, claims that it alone (along with little Albania) is faithful to correct Communist practice and that Moscow itself has strayed into heresy. Bukharin was not there to explain these rude contradictions to his maxim that competition or rivalry between Communist states was "by definition an impossibility." In March 1938, two years after I saw him in Paris and persuaded him to write the article here reprinted, he was executed.

The prefatory notes which Mr. Mosely has written for the thirty articles in the present volume serve to give each its place in the main current of history and provide a pattern for the whole. Since Mr. Mosely does not write about himself in these notes, I should say for those who do

not already know it that he is one of a small group of experienced specialists on Russian history and Soviet affairs. He writes always with directness, without exaggeration, and with a firm determination to look at the
facts, pleasant or unpleasant. His command of the wide range of matters
covered in this volume has enabled him, I believe, to select the things that
have the most lasting importance from the long list of available materials
and to give them not new substance (for they appear as originally printed)
but new interest and current significance.

AN EDITOR'S NOTE

I was delighted when the Editorial Advisory Board of *Foreign Affairs* asked me to bring together a selection of articles from the first forty years of the journal for publication as a Reader on Soviet affairs. For one thing, this would serve as a modest tribute to its two Editors, Archibald Cary Coolidge and Hamilton Fish Armstrong. More important, I knew, as a faithful reader of *Foreign Affairs,* what a wealth of analysis and first-hand observation would thus be made available to all those who are concerned to understand Soviet Russia, its evolution and its role in world politics today.

I owe a great deal to both Professor Coolidge and Mr. Armstrong. I was an undergraduate student of Professor Coolidge in 1924-25. My first period of research in Russia, in 1930-32, was made possible by my appointment as the first Archibald Cary Coolidge Fellow in History, with a stipend endowed by Professor Coolidge's will.

I have been even more deeply indebted to Hamilton Fish Armstrong over the years since 1940, when I first came to work in the Council's War and Peace Studies Project. I feel myself fortunate to have been associated with him in many stages of my work during and since World War II. In many activities I have been guided and sustained by his wise counsel and his warm friendship.

In actuality I should prefer to be described as the compiler of this volume, for the creative labors of editorship have all been on Mr. Armstrong's side. To an unusual degree Mr. Armstrong has peered ahead and tried to define the issues, and has then enlisted highly competent authors to explain them or to discuss policies. Many articles in the Russian and other fields of foreign affairs have had approximately the following origin: "Don't you think the public should have this or that or the third problem explained?" Long discussion in person, by telephone, or by letter, ending with "I wish you'd try your hand at a piece on that for the readers of *Foreign Affairs.*"

One "disadvantage" in my task as compiler has been that the high level of analysis and prescience shown by the Editor and the authors has made it extremely difficult to narrow the selection of articles to a mere thirty. Frankly, my task would have been easier, and my conscience lighter, if I could have chosen many more. In narrowing down the selection of articles, I have been guided by only one test: Will the reader of *today* find the article interesting and enlightening? Many that I have passed over were extremely interesting and sometimes quite influential at the time they appeared. Yet, if what they had to say has been overtaken by history, I have had no choice but to omit them. Thus, many articles dealing with the origins and events of World War II have been omitted, even though they were highly informative at the time they were published. Similarly, the continuous interest of *Foreign Affairs* in the analysis of Soviet economic development is sadly under-represented in this volume. The supporting data have "aged," and many insights that were influential at the time of publication have now become a part of the stock-in-trade of informed opinion. It has been necessary, likewise, to select only one, two or no articles in such fields as strategy, cultural life, science and religion. I have also had to omit almost all articles dealing with border areas of Russia and also those that dealt in retrospect with important events of Russian history.

The articles have been reproduced exactly as in the original, with one minor exception, apart from correcting the rare typographical errors and a few inconsistencies of styling. In one case, "The Fate of Polish Socialism," by Richard T. Davies, the author has changed four or five words in the text, since circumstances had prevented him from proofreading the original article. Rather than attempting to regroup the articles by subjects, I have presented them in their chronological order. At Mr. Armstrong's suggestion I have supplied each with a brief commentary, designed to "place" it in the longer perspective of the development and policies of the Soviet Union.

In preparing the Reader for publication I have received unstinting assistance from Grace Darling and Robert Valkenier in planning the format, binding, dust cover; from Lorna Brennan in copy-editing; from Marguerite Freund, Mary E. Woodring, Lorna Brennan, Helen Balkin, Barbara Hanes, Marguerite Hatcher, and Henrietta Kolborg in typing drafts and reading proofs; and from Elizabeth Kridl Valkenier, who prepared the index with her usual intelligent care.

P. E. M.

CONTENTS

Part III

STALIN'S BID FOR WORLD POWER,
1945-1953

Part IV

KHRUSHCHEV'S RUSSIA:
OLD GOALS, NEW METHODS, SINCE 1953

Part I

REVOLUTIONARY RUSSIA
AT THE CROSSROADS

1922-1929

THE first issue of *Foreign Affairs* (September 1922) presented a comprehensive review of Soviet conditions, prospects and policies, entitled "Russia After Genoa and The Hague." In signing his article with the initial K, Archibald Cary Coolidge held, with characteristic modesty, that it was unseemly to present his name in the first issue of the new journal, which he had recently undertaken to guide with the aid of Hamilton Fish Armstrong.

The reprinting of this article forty years later is not an act of editorial piety, however justified that would be. "Russia After Genoa" sums up almost five years of the Soviet regime with an amazing grasp of the essential realities of the new Russian state and its role in world politics. Its judgments have proved sound, as the reader will see for himself.

Mr. Coolidge's interest in Russia had been awakened early in his career, certainly by 1890-91, when, as secretary of the American Legation at St. Petersburg, he observed Russian life at close range. His understanding of Russia was then nourished over several decades by the study and teaching of European history, and his critical judgment was to be ripened through periods of intensive participation in the conduct of foreign affairs.

Born in 1866, Archibald Cary Coolidge studied at Harvard, Berlin and Paris, and in 1892 won his doctorate at Freiburg-im-Breisgau. Through service as a beginning diplomat in Paris, St. Petersburg and Vienna, he received an early initiation into the world of affairs. A lifelong devotion to teaching linked him to Harvard from 1893 until his death in 1928, a happy career which was interrupted repeatedly by public service from 1918 to 1922.

After visiting Sweden and Northern Russia in 1918 on a special mission for the Department of State, Mr. Coolidge served as chief of mission at Vienna and as an adviser and negotiator at the Paris Peace Conference. In 1921-22, he spent five months in Moscow as an officer of the American Relief Administration; the fruits of his first-hand observation of the new Soviet state provided a strong foundation for "Russia After Genoa."

Professor Coolidge's most important works, in which historical imagination and foresight are intimately fused, are "The United States as a World Power" (1908) and "Ten Years of War and Peace" (1927).

RUSSIA AFTER GENOA AND THE HAGUE

By *Archibald Cary Coolidge*

NOW that the smoke of the verbal battles between the Russian and the non-Russian participants in the last two international conferences has lifted, we can begin to estimate what results have been attained by the many weeks of earnest, not to say acrimonious, discussion between the representatives of assembled Europe. Few will deny that these results have been meagre compared with the hopes entertained at the outset. Some will even declare that no progress whatever towards a reconstruction of the world has come from these meetings of "best minds." Others will take a rosier view, but it is too early yet to reach many definite conclusions about questions with such intricate and far-reaching ramifications. We can only distinguish certain immediate and obvious phenomena.

One of these is that there has been a clearing of the atmosphere. Europe may feel no nearer to seeing her way out of her difficulties, but she knows better where she stands and what are the circumstances with which she has to deal. This is particularly true in regard to Russia, the great mystery of the last four years. The Soviet republic has come out of its seclusion, it has shown itself willing, nay eager, to talk with other states. As yet it has been officially recognized by but few, but it has reassumed a position in the concert of the powers whether the others like it or not. Its present standing, its attitude and aims, should be clearly understood, for Russia is too large a part of the world to be ignored with impunity.

When in October last Chicherin sent out his first note proposing an international conference on Russian affairs and offering as a *quid pro quo* for assistance the recognition of Russian pre-war debts, not many people realized just what were the situation and reasoning of the Soviet Government. Their overture was generally regarded as the appeal of a hopeless bankrupt forced at last by desperate necessity to recognize the error of his ways and to beg for succor at the hands of those he had grievously

3

injured. Even if we admit that there was justification for this opinion it was at best only a half truth. It was equally true that the ruling Communists had never felt more firmly on their feet than they did at that very moment, and not without reason.

The Russian Socialist Federated Soviet Republic was just completing the fourth year of its stormy existence, during which it had had innumerable difficulties to overcome and obstacles to surmount. Although by its own admission it could count on the active support of only a minority of the population and had had arrayed against it the vast majority of those who had formerly been the leaders in every form of public life, private enterprise or intellectual activity, although it had been undermined by the plots of reactionaries, social revolutionists, even anarchists, it had survived. It had fought against Germans, English, French, Americans, Japanese, Poles, Czechoslovaks, against Cossacks and other discontented elements within led by thousands of trained officers and armed and provisioned from without; it had seen most of its territory overrun at one time or another; and yet it had emerged triumphant. By the autumn of 1921 every assault, native or foreign, had failed. Only in the Far East under Japanese protection there was still military opposition, but even there it was diminishing. Peace had been concluded with Poland and with the Baltic states, for these were alien elements in the body politic which Communist Russia let go with little apparent regret and in full conformity with her theories. She had regained control in the Caucasus, she had concluded political treaties and was on friendly terms with Persia, Afghanistan and Turkey. It is true she still professed to fear attack in the east from Japan and in the west from Poland and Rumania supported by France, her newspapers and orators still harped on the evil designs of her capitalistic foes, but such talk was chiefly intended to stimulate the patriotism of the masses and particularly of the army. In reality, never before had Soviet Russia been so free from the menace either of foreign invasion or of serious insurrection.

This last fact was not due to any marked increase in popularity of the Communist regime. There was scant evidence of anything of the sort. But all open opposition had been beaten down. Every conspiracy had been ruthlessly suppressed. The peasantry who formed the immense majority of the population no longer manifested active discontent. What they asked for was to be let alone, and the Soviet Government had learned the wisdom of respecting this wish. The remnants of the former upper and educated classes were now thoroughly cowed by the terror they had lived through. The hundreds of thousands of irreconcilable refugees abroad were innocuous and were getting more and more out of touch even with their like in their native land. The component parts of the loosely federated state acted together with sufficient unity of purpose and were under the same rigorous general control. Doubtless disorder still prevailed in outlying districts and little heed was paid in some regions to the writ of the central authorities, but these were but local manifestations which could be dealt with in time. Altogether, Soviet Moscow felt it had been victorious in both foreign and domestic affairs and it was as far as possible from any such sentiment as contrition.

On the other hand, there were two painful truths which the blindest adherent of Bolshevism could not deny or explain away. First, in spite of Communist propaganda, no other country as yet followed more than temporarily the Russian example; second, in Russia itself the economic situation was utterly disastrous. In the early days the hopes of the Communists had been high. The Bolshevik triumph was to be but a step in the world-wide revolution which should soon extend to all lands. For a space, especially in the year 1919, the outlook was promising. In Germany the Spartacus movement threatened the existence of the new republic. At Budapest the red terror was installed by Bela Kuhn, the disciple of Lenin. At Vienna the weak government seemed likely to collapse at any moment. If this happened the example of Hungary and Austria could not but affect Rumania and Jugoslavia. Italy was reported to be full of seething discontent and should Italy raise the red flag France with her traditions of the Paris commune, the precursor of the Moscow one, must surely follow. Then the turn of England would come and sooner or later that of the United States. This was the doctrine which Communist writers and speakers (and none others were allowed) preached to thousands of eager believers throughout Soviet Russia.

But the prophecies did not come true. Every one of the supposedly tottering bourgeois governments succeeded in maintaining itself, growing stronger rather than weaker as time went on. Worse still, the regime of Bela Kuhn was quickly overthrown in Hungary, to the intense disappointment of Moscow. Of course, the certainty of the ultimate triumph of Communistic ideas everywhere was still proclaimed, but as the months followed each other that triumph began to look discouragingly remote. All the strenuous efforts of Bolshevist propaganda had produced but meagre results, and the natural consequence was a feeling of disillusionment and lassitude. The official tone might remain the same, the more ardent spirits might continue to dream and to plot, but the abler and harder headed men at the helm, sobered by stern experience in facing the difficulties of actual administration, had been brought to see that their first task was to make the best of conditions as they were. The capitalistic states of the world existed; they were in no hurry to come to an end; they could help Russia as well as harm her. As they now seemed disposed at least to leave her alone, was it not wisdom to stop wasting efforts on their conversion and to find out on what terms it was possible to live with them?

These arguments were reinforced by the appalling nature of the economic situation in which Soviet Russia found herself. Such a colossal catastrophe the world had never witnessed. Not only had factories and mines almost ceased to produce, but transportation had broken down; tools, clothes, shoes and other necessities of decent life were becoming unprocurable. Vast masses of peasantry with no stocks in reserve were raising but a fraction of the crops they formerly had and were concealing and hoarding what they did raise. Thus the threat of famine on a gigantic scale needed only a single bad harvest to make it become a terrific reality.

Of course it was explained that these evils were due to the sins of the former tsarist regime and to bourgeois exploitation, to war, to insurrection, to the intervention of foreign armies, to the blockade which had been instituted against the Russian labor republic by its capitalist foes, and to their continued machinations without and within. But granting all this, though these explanations had been repeated so often that the effect was beginning to wear off, the fact remained that the Communist promised land was becoming a hell on earth, not only to such of the hated bourgeoisie as still managed to survive, but to pretty much everyone else within its borders. Something had to be done to remedy the situation, even if certain sacred principles of Communist theory went by the board.

Already by the end of the year 1920 the Soviet leaders and especially Lenin, who with his strange cynical frankness seems to take a positive delight in pointing out the errors which he and his have committed, had made up their minds that they must embark on a new policy. They had come to recognize that in a country where nine-tenths of the people were peasants it was impossible to maintain a government supported only by the factory population. It had become evident, too, that the peasants could not be won over unless they were assured not only of the practical possession of their land but of the right to dispose of its products. Experience had shown that if they were to be deprived of their surplus produce (theoretically in return for manufactured goods which the ruin of industry had rendered it impossible to supply) they would answer by raising only what food was requisite for their immediate needs. There was no escaping the conclusion that they did not appreciate the beauties of Communism and for the present at least were unteachable. Therefore, as the life of Russia depended upon them, their terms must be accepted. The system of compelling them to hand over to the state everything not needed for their own requirements and those of their families had to be given up. The government surrendered, and it was enacted that henceforth after paying a moderate tax in kind the peasant should be at liberty to sell whatever he had raised, which implied in practice a recognition of his ownership of the land.

This enactment made an irreparable breach in the system under which Soviet Russia had been administered since the winter of 1917. It meant the beginning of what was almost a new revolution, for it did not and could not stand by itself. If the peasant might own and sell, then others must be allowed to. Why should he be the only person allowed to dispose of the fruits of his labors, and if people were to sell they must also have the means to buy. The Soviet authorities had never been able really to put an end to all private trade, indeed, in the cities, they had often winked at the illicit sale of food without which there would have been much more actual starvation. They now proceeded to re-establish the right of private property and of buying and selling, the government reserving to itself only the making of regulations and also the monopoly of certain products and key industries, including export. This is the famous "new economic policy" or "strategic retreat," which was elaborated by a long series of decrees in 1921 and the first part of 1922.

Under this policy Russia has reverted to something like her former life. The markets and the business streets of Moscow are once more crowded; many shops have been opened though there is but little variety in the goods, largely second-hand, which they have to offer; tickets for railways, tramways and theatres again have to be paid for. All this is obviously in violation of the principles on which the Soviet republic was proclaimed and which it long tried to enforce, and the process has been watched with disapproval and alarm by the more uncompromising left wing of the Communist Party, who have asked where it was to end.

But the necessity of a change was so clear that it has been put through without open opposition.

But the "new economic policy" did not relate to internal affairs alone, for the need of assistance from abroad has likewise been urgent. It is true that the Soviet Government and its partisans declared that Russia, the land of boundless natural resources, was capable of recovering her prosperity unaided, yet even they did not profess that in that case her recovery could be other than a slow and painful one. If she wished to get quickly on her feet, to provide a new plant in place of what had been destroyed, to make a vast number of indispensable repairs and to procure necessary articles of many kinds, in order to set her industries going again on their former scale, not to speak of the tapping of new sources of wealth, she could do so only with the aid of a great amount of capital and that capital she could not furnish herself; she must turn to foreigners, however much she might condemn their principles. Foreign capital could be obtained only from loans or in return for concessions, foreign goods could come in only by trade and nothing of the sort could be hoped for as long as Soviet Russia remained an outcast among the nations. If she must get outside assistance from abroad, the sooner she entered into normal relations with the rest of the world the better. The capitalist states might be unregenerate but she could not afford to wait till they had learned the error of their ways. She required immediate help and as a first step to this she wanted recognition.

That this help must be paid for in some way was evident, but the Soviet leaders believed they were in a position to bargain. They too had heard the widespread cry that the peace and prosperity of the world could not be restored until Russia had been once more admitted into the comity of nations and should again contribute by her efforts and from her huge resources to the welfare of mankind. They also know that in the capitalistic countries there were men who hoped splendid things from a reopening of Russian trade. No wonder, then, that the Moscow papers asserted that "Europe needs Russia as much as Russia needs Europe." What they did not perhaps appreciate was that there were millions of good people all over the globe who regarded Bolsheviks as little better than wild beasts.

The Soviet Government itself was naturally well aware that it would be met at the outset of any negotiations by the question whether it was prepared to recognize the tremendous claims against it. It was ready with its reply. The claims of foreign states against Russia could be divided into two categories, first, pre-war debts, and, secondly, war debts and claims for reparation for the destruction and confiscation of foreign property. As an offset to this second class of demands the Russians could bring up their own counter claims which were even more tremendous than the claims of the Allies, or at any rate could be made so if the occasion required. And these counter claims could not be waived aside as midsummer madness. They were based on quite enough international law and precedent to offer a presentable case before an impartial tribunal, could such a one be conceived of. The Allied powers without formal declaration of war with Soviet Russia had for years not only abetted and fostered countless plots against her, and furnished openly or covertly weapons, munitions, military instructors to armed forces who were trying to overthrow her government, but had also actually sent their armies into her territory. If Great Britain had once had to pay more than fifteen million dollars damages (the case had been specially studied up in Moscow) for having allowed the *Alabama* to sail from England to prey on commerce during the American Civil War, how much did the Allied and Associated Powers owe for their continual intervention in the Russian one? To be sure, the Allies had never recognized the Soviet Government and if it had been overthrown their intervention would have been counted to them by its successor as righteousness. But it had not been overthrown. It had maintained itself and its claims could not be ignored. If the South had been victorious Great Britain would not have had to pay an indemnity for the exploits of the *Alabama*. As the North was, she did. The logic of facts has to be taken into consideration.

We need not, however, suppose that the Soviet Government has expected that its claims on this score will be satisfied. Their value consists in their capacity of being used as an offset to Allied claims for compensation or war debt. This applies to the United States as well as to Great Britain and France. Some day the Americans may have to charge off the couple of hundred millions Russia now owes them as war debt and put it down as part of the cost of their expeditions to Archangel and Vladivostok.

As to pre-war debts, although Soviet Russia demurred in theory at recognizing an obligation to repay sums which had served to strengthen the former oppressive autocracy and militarism, in practice she could hardly hope to obtain the new loans she so ardently desired if at the same time she calmly repudiated her old ones. Here was her chance to make a concession. While refusing to admit a moral liability for these debts, she would express a willingness to meet them, though just to what extent need not be specified but would depend on the bargain she could drive later.

The country which would profit the most by this concession was the one which had been the bitterest and most active enemy of the Bolshevik regime from the first, and was most cordially detested by Moscow in return, namely France. Her attitude was still one of uncompromising hostility, and crowned with victory she was now the predominant power on the European continent. But it was in France that by far the largest portion of Russian pre-war debt was held and that not by a few millionaires but by tens of thousands of small investors. In order to protect their interests France would have to put her pride in her pocket, forget past grievances and present antipathies and come down to business. If she continued aloof and hostile, she would be in danger of sacrificing what she had invested in the past, as well as the special opportunities now offered.

With England the situation was even simpler. English conservatives might dislike Bolshevism—and England had done much to aid the enemies of the Soviets, especially in the warfare of Denikin—but the English are a practical people who accept the decision of facts. The Soviet Government was now firmly established. As England lives by her exports, her millions of unemployed were a sufficient reason for her to make every effort to open up new markets and to re-establish old ones. Why should she not come to terms with Russia, especially as her holdings of pre-war debts were much less serious than those of France? Lloyd George had intermittently given encouragement to the idea. As early as March 16, 1921, an agreement had been concluded which not only permitted Anglo-Russian trade, but sanctioned the residence of a Russian commercial agent in London. So far this had not led to any particular results, but the ice was broken.

The attitude of the United States presented a peculiar problem. As the richest, most successful bourgeois capitalistic state of the day, the United States embodies the most advanced type of the form of society which Communists regard it as their chief object in life to destroy, but as it has the largest amount of available capital it is the country which can do the most to build up Russia and finally it is the one which has shown itself by far the most generous in relieving Russian distress. Whatever might be the differences in their social conceptions, the advantage to Moscow of cultivating friendly relations with Washington was indisputable. This ought not to be difficult. The Americans have the reputation of caring for the almighty dollar and here was Moscow willing to offer them special opportunities to obtain a great number of dollars by the exploitation of untapped Russian resources. Yet, strange to say, America, which had no particular quarrel with Russia, which had not been injured by the breaking of an alliance with her as had England and France, which had no conflicting ambitions and several common interests and which was showing herself such a friend in need to starving Russians, nevertheless remained coldly aloof, haughtily refusing to recognize the Soviet Government or to have any dealings with it except in dispensing charity. To be sure, President Wilson in a direct communication had urged it not to make peace with Germany and this might be regarded as a recognition of sorts, but his appeal had fallen on deaf ears, and there had been no further official intervention. Later the Bullitt mission had aroused Soviet hopes but it had led to nothing but controversy. Since then not only had the Wilson administration refused recognition but the Harding one, by Mr. Hughes' declaration of March 25, 1921, had taken an equally uncompromising stand, nay, it had gone further, for it had invited other powers to a conference in Washington to discuss questions of the Pacific and of the Far East without the participation of Russia, in flagrant disregard of the fact that she was one of those most interested in just such questions. Chicherin had protested in July and again in November in vigorous but dignified language and had declared that any decisions reached would be for her null and void. The statement that the United States would act as the "moral trustee" for Russia seemed like adding insult to injury, and it was freely asserted in Moscow that America at the Washington Conference would try to buy concessions from the Japanese in other places by giving them a free hand in Siberia. Instead she showed she took her trusteeship seriously and did what she could to get them out of there.

Some would say that a bond was created between Soviet Russia and the United States by their similar attitude towards the League of Nations. The reasons influencing the two might not be quite the same, but the tone in regard to it of, for instance, the Boston *Transcript* differed little from that of the *Pravda*. If a common dislike draws nations together, abstention of the United States and Russia from the League should help to bring them closer to each other and to Germany.

When in the summer of 1921 in answer to the appeal of Maxim Gorki the American Relief Administration, whose president is the Secretary of Commerce, consented to enter Russia, it was hard for the Communists to believe that these bourgeois dispensers of charity were without secret political aims, and when this became self-evident it was harder still for them to understand why if the American people were willing to feed the hungry they should not be willing to do lasting good in a form that would be advantageous to themselves also by accepting the hand that was proffered them, entering into cordial relations, and taking part in the work of Russian economic regeneration. It was work, too, such as ought to appeal irresistibly to the daring imagination so characteristic of Americans, for it was not a matter of slowly building up a trade or of petty concessions but of immediate enterprises on the grandest scale with the promise of marvelous results. Why then did they hold back? Verily these Americans were strange people.

In the above reasoning there were two flaws which the rulers of the Soviet state did not, indeed could not be expected to, appreciate in their full seriousness. To begin with, in all the states with which they now wished to deal public opinion, or a large part of it, looked on them with unaffected moral reprobation, not to say actual loathing. To recognize the regime they had established was to condone crime. The tales of atrocities they had committed had shocked the civilized world; their denials and countercharges had found little credence. Their machinations and their propaganda had spread alarm everywhere and their wild rantings as well as those of their controlled newspapers about the wickedness of the bourgeoisie and the necessity of wading through blood to a world revolution were not calculated to win them friends in countries where the bourgeoisie and capitalists were influential, not to say dominant. Secondly, even granting that a good many people were inclined to overlook the misdeeds credited to the Bolsheviks, the question still remained, were they to be trusted? What guarantee could they offer that they would keep their word? Was it not more than likely that after they had lured foreign capital by fair promises they would so hamper its operation that it could make no profit, and when they were ready they would end by confiscating it as they had done before? Was there anything in their character or record which entitled them to be trusted? The Russian answer to this, that decrees, laws, nay whole codes were being promulgated with bewildering activity, guaranteeing all sorts of rights to foreigners as well as to natives, was not wholly convincing. The Soviet Government in its administrative routine may vie with any other in its wilderness of red tape, but it can turn out as many laws as it wants with incomparable speed. By the same token it can repeal them with equal facility. A realization of this may even have lurked in the minds of the creators of the "new economic policy."

This policy having once been decided upon for foreign as well as for domestic affairs, the next question was that of procedure. The Soviet Government, however desirous of recognition and of financial help, and however prepared to make concessions in return, did not propose to appear as a suppliant, or to give up more than it had to. It trusted to its own wits and in Chicherin it possessed a spokesman who had already proved that he could hold his own in dialectics against any opponent he encountered. He opened his campaign with his note of October 29, 1921, in which while asserting that Soviet Russia was not legally or morally bound by the debts of the former regime, nevertheless in view of her need of immediate assistance he stated she would consent to see what she could do towards meeting foreign claims. He therefore proposed that an international congress should be called which should recognize her government and devise the means necessary to bring about her economic rehabilitation.

This overture met with a chilling reception. Such replies as were received were unfavorable. But Moscow went on its way and though within its borders famine and distress became ever more grievous, its international position continued to improve. German and Norwegian trade delegations arrived in Moscow, the frontier with Esthonia was finally settled and a treaty was signed with Austria. The meeting of the Ninth Soviet Congress showed that there was at least no open dissension in the ranks of the faithful. Trotsky's speech which was largely devoted to foreign affairs breathed confidence, and though sharp in its denunciations of the actions of certain other powers, it was not at bottom bellicose. And soon the much desired happened. On January 6, 1922, the meeting of premiers at Cannes invited Soviet Russia to attend a general European Conference at Genoa.

There was no hesitation shown about accepting and few attempts to conceal the satisfaction at what the newspapers called "our victory." A strong delegation was chosen, including in theory Lenin himself, though there can have been little serious intention of having him risk his health, not to say his life, merely to satisfy idle curiosity abroad. Chicherin was competent to conduct the Russian case, which had been carefully prepared long before. Meanwhile the making of reassuring laws continued. On February 6th the famous "Cheka," or Extraordinary Commission, whose ruthless exploits had rendered it a name of terror to millions, was formally abolished.

As a preliminary move, the Russian delegates to Genoa on their way through Riga signed an agreement with Poland, Esthonia and Latvia confirming existing treaties and promising to facilitate trade and communications between the two parties. The representatives of the other three states also officially expressed the opinion that a general recognition of the Soviet Government would be helpful to the reconstruction of Europe. In Berlin the Russian delegates carried on negotiations which were soon to have important results. All told, they were proceeding to a meeting at which they might gain a good deal and stood to lose but little, for if they could not obtain collective assistance they were confident that profiting by mutual jealousies they could make some satisfactory bargains with individual powers.

They had, however, met with one severe disappointment before they started. On March 8 Secretary Hughes definitely declined the invitation to the United States to take part in the Conference. This deprived it of half its value for Moscow. What Russia wanted was recognition and above all money. Without American recognition that of Europe was of less consequence, for only the United States was rich enough to lend on a large scale. We may well surmise, therefore, that the absence of American representatives seriously affected the conduct of the Russians both at Genoa and The Hague. They now felt they had less to gain by making concessions and accordingly less reason for making them. Even Lenin's defiant speech to the Congress of Metal Workers at Moscow on March 6th may have been so influenced, for by that time the American refusal could be foreseen. He declared that if need be Russia would say, "All attempts to impose upon us terms as if we were vanquished are outright nonsense to which it is not worth while to reply. We are entering into relations as merchants and we know what you owe us and we owe you, and what legitimate and even exorbitant profit you may extort from us. We have a great number of proposals, the number of agreements grows and will grow, whatever the relations between the three or four victorious powers; a postponement of this conference will be a loss for yourselves, because by postponing it you will prove to your own people that you do not know what you want and that you are suffering from disease of the will." Turning to internal politics he told his enemies, "You challenged us to a desperate fight in 1917, and in reply we took recourse to terror, and again to terror—and will use it still again if you try it again," and as for 'the new economic policy' "we can say now that this retreat as far as concessions made to the capitalists are concerned is now ended."

In Europe, on the other hand, even it would seem in government circles, there existed a widespread belief that the economic situation in Russia was such that however much her representatives might bluff and bluster at the outset, in the end they would have to submit to almost anything. It would therefore be possible, as well as desirable, to impose not only stringent terms for the repayment of old debts, but elaborate and humiliating conditions for future benefits.

We need not enter here into the story of the Genoa Conference. Both sides began by putting forward their demands in extreme form—the principal Allies in the report of the preliminary conference held in London, the Russians in a memorandum they drew up in reply stating counter claims which appeared to the Allied powers utterly extravagant, not to say impertinent. In the weeks of wrangling that followed both sides made concessions but they never were near real agreement. From the first the Russians made it plain that they meant to be treated as equals, not as culprits or supplicants. They took the tone that they came to offer as well as to ask and in debate they did not shrink from irritating their opponents by sharp rejoinders. Yet although their demands made Europe gasp they were quite ready to bargain, indeed it sometimes seemed that there was no principle they would not sacrifice if only they could make sure of a large loan. It is not surprising that the conference ended as it did; it could hardly have done otherwise.

But if, owing to the absence of the Americans, the Russians at Genoa had not expected real financial help, they had no cause to be disappointed with the outcome of the conference. For one thing, they had found what they had long desired, a platform from which they could speak with a certainty of being listened to. They did not particularly care if they were disapproved of and stirred up anger. They had not come for sympathy but to assert themselves, and to obtain practical if not formal recognition. This they had achieved. The recognition they had won might not be friendly but it was real. To pretend not to recognize a government after arguing and trying to reach an agreement with it for long weeks, with the whole world following every move in the game, was almost ludicrous. The Soviet republic had indeed won the *de facto* recognition of Europe. It could afford to wait a while for the *de jure,* especially as thanks to American assistance the horrors of the famine were being combatted with some measure of success.

At the same time, the Russian delegates had not forgotten the other string to their bow, the opportunity for conversations with separate powers. The situation was promising. France and of late even Italy, ordinarily the faithful henchman of England, had shown themselves willing, although still theoretically at war with the Ottoman Empire, to make pacts with the Turks at Angora behind the back of their British ally. The desire of the Italians for a commercial treaty with Russia was well known and negotiations were already well under way. There was nothing to hinder the Soviet delegates at Genoa or afterwards at The Hague from dealing secretly with single states as well as openly with a number. This they proceeded to do.

On April 15th the Genoa Conference and the world were astonished by the news that Germany and Russia had just signed a formal treaty at Rapallo a few miles away. In its terms it was sound and statesmanlike. The two countries entered once more into normal relations, granting each other equal rights and privileges. By a particularly sensible provision all the claims each might have against the other were swept away, thus disposing of a vast mass of complicated and contentious matter, which could be handled in no other fashion without endless difficulties and possibilities of trouble. The Treaty of Versailles had recognized the right of Russia to German reparation payments. But now bygones were to be bygones. The two mighty former empires had fallen and their old quarrels were but memories. The two new and struggling republics needed the help which each could give the other.

Later history will show some day whether in the long run Russia or Germany will have profited the more by the treaty of Rapallo. At the time it was signed there is no doubt as to which gained by it. However ultimately advantageous it might be to Germany, she ran just then all the risks and paid all the penalties. She doubtless had a theoretical right to conclude the agreement, which was not unlike the one made by Poland, Esthonia and Latvia with Russia a few weeks before, but she chose the worst moment to do it. She prejudiced her case by an appearance of double-dealing, and she heightened the alarm of France, which it was her interest to allay, as well as weakened the hands of Lloyd George, on whom she depended and who was trying to do what he could for her. As a punishment for putting this spoke in the Allied wheel she had to accept the humiliation of being excluded from all further meetings in which Russian affairs were debated.

But Russia received no punishment. If she had worried England and France, why so much the better. It would make them more amenable to reason by showing them she could turn elsewhere. At the dramatic moment she had won an advantage which not only strengthened her immediate position but laid the foundation for greater things in the future.

Towards the close of the conference the news of the Shell oil concession created another sensation, though of a milder sort. The relations between the Shell Company and the British Government were enough to make the transaction interesting. Presently, too, the conference woke up to the fact that the intention of the Russians to redivide their oil districts in such a manner as to exploit them in large concessions to the best advantage, though economically wise, conflicted hopelessly with the return of oil properties to their former foreign owners. All that the Russians were willing to do was to offer not compensation but a certain priority in new concessions. At the last, when the conference ended without agreement, they took back all offers of any kind they had made and rested on their original positions.

When the time came for fresh attempts at accord at The Hague, the prospect was discouraging from the start. The United States had again refused to take part and the tone of the Russian delegates was not conciliatory, nor did the fact that they were long held aloof by the non-Russians and invited only to meet sub-commissions improve their disposition. On the other hand they seemed ready to go on talking indefinitely, it was suspected with ulterior motives, and there was again the feeling that they might be willing to sacrifice many principles if only offered money enough. They boldly asked for a huge amount. But the uselessness of further discussion soon became so increasingly evident that the conference broke up, this time with complete acknowledgment of failure, as it made no suggestion of further meetings.

To the self denying ordinance of the non-Russians, adhered to by the United States, that they would frown upon any acquisition by their nationals of Russian concessions which included property that had once belonged to other foreigners, the Soviet Government replied soon after by granting an oil concession to Germans, Germany not having been invited to The Hague. Although this concession did not include any former foreign property the retort was unmistakable.

On June 5th a treaty was signed between Russia and Czechoslovakia. Some of the provisions are significant. Questions of indemnity or return of property are postponed. Also, although it is stated that the treaty is not meant to anticipate the recognition *de jure* of the Soviet republic, nevertheless the chiefs and two other members of the principal mission of each country in the territory of the other are to have diplomatic privileges, and local agents are to have consular ones. In other words there is recognition in all but the name.

Since the close of the Genoa Conference the attitude of Moscow has perceptibly stiffened, whether it be owing to favorable crop reports which make the Communist rulers feel more independent of outside help, as is shown in their hampering even the work of the American Relief Administration, or whether it be due to an increase of influence of the left wing of the party, thanks to the incapacitation of Lenin, or whether to some other cause. This has manifested itself in a refusal to ratify the treaty of commerce which Chicherin concluded with Italy just before his departure from there, and still more in the fresh contempt exhibited for the opinion of the outside world. The way in which the recent trial of social revolutionists has been conducted was enough to alienate the sympathies of all but the Communistic fraction of European and American socialists, and the treatment of the clergy accused of resistance to the law confiscating church property for famine relief has looked, in spite of the charitable purport of the measure itself, like odious religious persecution. On the credit side we note a proposition, with whatever intention, to discuss the reduction of armaments.

In her external relations, as in her internal conditions, Soviet Russia presents a changing picture. Predictions as to the future are hazardous. We can do little more than note a few salient facts and guess at certain tendencies.

In Europe Russia no longer borders on any state of the first rank, such as Germany and Austria, but on five smaller ones: Finland (which now separates her from Sweden and Norway), Esthonia, Latvia, Poland and Rumania. All of these are composed, wholly or in part, of territory which until recently was hers, or at least under her sovereignty. Today she has recognized their independence in accordance with the principles she professes, and she has been liberal in the drawing of frontier lines, notably in the case of Finland to whom she has made a pure gift of the district of Pechenga in the extreme north simply because it is of greater value to Finland, which thereby gains a port of access to the

Arctic Ocean, than it is to Russia, which has plenty of sea coast on the Arctic, though nowhere else. Examples of such generosity between nations are rare. Nevertheless, Russia's European neighbors are much afraid of her. She is still far larger and possesses far more ultimate resources than all of them put together; she still maintains on paper a standing army of over a million men. They fear that her renunciation of the former borderlands of the empire may have been due only to the necessities of the moment and might be taken back at the first convenient opportunity. There are enough Communists in these states to furnish Moscow with pretexts for interfering if it wishes to do so. They are aware, also, that not only have most of the Russians in exile refused to accept the shrinkage of their country as permanent but that Soviet policy itself seems to be inspired by more nationalistic sentiment than it was a while ago. The example of the way Soviet governments were established with the aid of Russian soldiers in the three republics of the Caucasus is not reassuring.

On the other hand, a policy of reconquest on the part of Russia would inevitably provoke a coalition against her. Poland and Rumania are bound together by an alliance which represents a population of over forty million people and a very considerable military strength. They would have allies and they could count on much indirect assistance and perhaps active support from France. The Baltic states are far weaker and more exposed and one of them, Lithuania, from hatred of Poland leans towards Russia. In their case the danger to their independence lies not so much in their having belonged to Russia for two centuries as in the fact that they constitute her natural sea coast on the Baltic. Many wiseacres declare that it is impossible for her to do without them. One may reply that Germans have held the same views about Belgium, Holland and Denmark, and that these views are today not generally accepted. But peril is there and will continue. To meet it the Baltic republics must rely not only on their own sturdy resistance but on outside aid. Poland, for instance, can hardly leave them to their fate, even if she does not covet them for herself as she is suspected of doing. The condition of the Russian army is not of the best, especially for an offensive campaign, and the difficulties of arming, supplying and handling large masses of men would be great just now. Finally, in fairness to the Soviet Government, one must admit that in spite of rude language and non-fulfillment of some of the minor provisions of its treaties, it has shown no serious signs of deliberate intent to violate them.

With one of her neighbors Russia still has unsettled questions of such importance that under other circumstances they might easily lead to war. Profiting by the Russian Revolution and the ensuing confusion, Rumania, on the ground of historical right and more or less with the consent of the inhabitants, about half of whom are Rumanians, has possessed herself of the former Russian province of Bessarabia. This annexation has never been recognized by Moscow. On the other hand, the Bolsheviks appropriated to their own use the Rumanian gold reserve which at the time of the war had been sent to Russia for greater security. Naturally Rumania claims it back. The Soviet Government probably cares no more for Bessarabia (except perhaps the Ukrainian part of it) than it did for other lands it has ceded, but as the Rumanian gold has long been spent and would be inconvenient to return, the obvious course to follow is to keep open the dispute. If Rumania would buy Russian recognition of the *fait accompli* by abandoning the demand for her stolen gold, Moscow would hardly object, and this may be the ultimate solution, but so far Rumania has been unwilling to accept it. Neither side, however, is ready to go to war over these questions.

The threat of an attack upon Russia herself, in her hour of weakness, by her neighbors, especially Poland and Rumania aided and abetted by France, has been a favorite theme of Bolshevik oratory. We may take it that most of this has been for popular consumption, though she has had some genuine grievances to complain of, for the territory of her neighbors has been used as a base of operations for insurrections in her own. Still, if she has entertained real apprehensions, as she seems to have, this betrays more weakness than she has usually been credited with. Some Communists may even desire foreign aggression, for it would once more rally disaffected elements to the support of the government. But these small states will hardly be foolish enough to molest their gigantic neighbor, weak as she now is, if she leaves them alone. They have already got in full the boundaries they are entitled to, and even the desire of Poland and Rumania to see a really independent Ukraine which shall serve as a buffer between them and Moscow is moderated by the knowledge that such a Ukraine would be more nationalistic in character and would demand from them their Ukrainian territories with more insistence and asperity than Moscow does.

Of the great powers France is the one whose relations with Soviet Russia are the worst and not improbably may remain so for a good while to come. Some Frenchmen, to be sure, think that it will be easier to reach an agreement by separate treaty than it has been by general international convention. They may be right, but France has much to claim from Russia and comparatively little to offer these days when she no longer has moneys to lend. This puts her at a disadvantage in negotiating with an adversary as unsentimental as the Bolsheviks. But neither country at this moment is in a position to do the other great harm. England has more to offer and fewer claims to present. She is less embittered, and is also in greater need of Russian trade and of tolerable political relations, for she is more vulnerable. Moscow has enough means of action in the Mohammedan and Asiatic world to make trouble for her in several countries, notably in Afghanistan and India.

Many people regard the recent treaty of Rapallo between Germany and Russia as only a first step towards closer relations and perhaps actual alliance. Some would say it existed already. There are indeed many ways in which the two countries might help one another. German industry could furnish Russia with the chief articles of which she is in pressing need; German science and technical skill could guide the upbuilding of her industries, the reopening and the administration of her mines, the construction of great public works and likewise the training of her armies, although at least Trotsky would assert they are trained already. The trouble is all these benefits have to be paid for in cash— paper roubles and other forms of Soviet credit will not do—and Russia has not the cash to pay for them. Besides, though she wishes to use the Germans and has a wholesome respect for their abilities, she does not intend to put herself into their hands for exploitation. For her part she cannot give them the thing they would value most, military security. Russian armies today could not keep the French out of Berlin. Even if they could they would not be welcome. It looks, accordingly, as if Moscow and Berlin will not become intimate; but, though they have little trust in each other, they will remain on friendly terms. They have one common bond, which has helped to keep them together in the past and may again, their deep dislike for Poland.

Although in principle the foreign policy of the Soviet republic is based on internationalism and in practice is dominated by the necessities of the moment, some of the traditions of the former empire have not been forgotten. The Russia of today declares she has renounced imperialistic ambitions but that this does not mean she is indifferent to legitimate national interests even if she is not now in a position to assert them effectively. This is true of her policy both in the Near and in the Far

East. She no longer menaces Turkey, indeed she is on excellent terms with the Angora Government, but she has not lost her right to be heard in questions regarding Constantinople and the Straits which will always remain of vital importance to her southern trade. She will therefore not accept as valid any international arrangements concerning them made without her participation.

The same principle holds in regard to the Far East. Russia has given fair warning that the agreements reached at the Washington Conference do not exist as far as she is concerned. Her right to take this stand is unquestionable but she will make no complaint if the policy of Mr. Hughes results in the evacuation of Siberia and northern Sakhalin by the Japanese, a thing she earnestly desires but is too weak to bring about unaided. At any rate, she means some day to assert herself once more in this part of the world, though she may do so in the name of the Far Eastern republic which, without being a Soviet state, is none the less in her eyes a member of the Russian Federation. If the Americans, in the meanwhile, are willing to pull her chestnuts out of the fire for her so much the better. And now Japan has just manifested a willingness to enter into conference with her.

In her future dealing with China, as with Turkey, she will have the considerable advantage that she alone of the great powers has agreed under certain conditions to surrender all claim to consular jurisdiction and other capitulations of the sort which have seemed so necessary for the protection of Europeans in the past, but which are so resented by Chinese and Turks today. She has also given back her share of the famous concession of special rights along the Manchurian railway, thereby ingratiating herself with the Chinese and making the position of the Japanese in South Manchuria more awkward.

And finally as to America, the self-appointed moral trustee, the benefactor who has dispensed such charity as no people ever before bestowed on another and at the same time the stern critic who declines to recognize the government she has been cooperating with in feeding millions of its people—what is she going to do? Her position is morally strong, for in her condemnation as in her charity she has been guided by unselfish considerations. In no other country is there more genuine horror of the Bolsheviks as men of blood without ruth or faith who have wrought a havoc unparalleled in history. Are they to be helped and comforted because they have got to the end of their rope and after limitless wanton destruction have shown themselves incapable of creating or rebuilding?

Their methods are still those of brutal terror under which no one but the ruling minority can feel secure. Of what value are the promises of men whose highest aim is to subvert the very basis of the society on which our civilization is founded and who believe that every means to this end is justified? Some of these men may be honest fanatics of a dangerous kind, others are mere criminals. To grasp their hand in friendship is to touch pitch and be defiled.

To this some reply denying the accusations or putting much of the blame elsewhere. Still others believe that even granting the truth of the charges it does not follow that because we disapprove of the rulers of a country we should have no dealings with the people who suffer most from their rule. The progress of mankind has come through intercourse, and if we wish to aid the unfortunate millions of Russia, the way to do so is not to leave them alone or even merely to pauperize them with charity, but to help them to get to their feet again. Free communications with the outside world would be an inestimable boon to many of them. Shall we refuse to sell sorely needed farm instruments to the Russian peasants because we dislike the Moscow Soviet? To recognize the government of a country does not imply that we admire it, it is merely to take note of an existing fact. If the crimes of Sultan Abdul Hamid were not deemed a bar to American commerce and to the necessary official relations with Turkey, why should trading with Russia make us responsible for the practices of Lenin and Trotsky?

But apart from ethical considerations there are other reasons which explain the hesitation felt by many governments, and notably the American, about recognizing officially the present regime. Among these is doubt as to its duration and to what may succeed it. This is no mere question of change of personnel such as has often occurred in Latin America and elsewhere, but of something much more fundamental. Today we can see four possibilities of development in the case of Russia, any one of which would be of world-wide importance and any one of which might be precipitated by the permanent disappearance from the scene of Lenin, an event which in view of the state of his health may occur at any time, if it has not occurred already. The part which he has played has been so great and the place which he has held has been so commanding that by his departure he would leave a gap difficult to fill. A struggle for power between those next in line, of whose relative strength we know almost nothing, might lead to far-reaching results.

These four obvious possibilities are, first, a counter revolution, though not necessarily in favor of monarchy, such a one as was attempted by Kolchak, Denikin, Wrangel and others. This is still the dream of hosts of Russian exiles and of an unknown proportion of the population of Russia itself. The previous attempts to bring it about have failed and there seems no particular reason for expecting that others would succeed now.

Second, the "new economic policy" may continue to spread and may take deep root, the new codes of law may supplant the arbitrary dictatorship of the proletariat, the bourgeoisie may be able to raise its head again, and the men directing the ship of state, taught by experience, may abandon in practice many of their previous theories and methods. In other words, the Russian Republic may undergo the same sort of transformation as did the first French republic after the reign of terror. Even now a few more changes would make Soviet legislation not very different from that of the other new socialistically inclined republics.

Third, there may be a reaction to the left. If, for instance, Trotsky or Zinoviev succeeds to the place of Lenin, we may witness a return to the attempt to govern on purely Communistic principles accompanied by increased activity in propaganda abroad.

Fourth, even without dissension in the Communist ranks or attack from without or within, the economic condition of Soviet Russia may become so deplorable and transportation break down to such an extent that the central government will lose its control and the country fall into anarchy, breaking up into fragments, each mindful only of its own wants. How far such a process of disruption might go and whither it would lead is beyond our ken, but of this we may be sure: it would mean confusion and misery such as would stagger the imagination.

It was through his dominating mind and will and his shrewd judgment of coming events that Lenin created a small but relatively disciplined party and then, using it as a fulcrum of power, seized the revolutionary opportunity of 1917. His interpretation of Marxism led him to a new type of state and a new type of international revolutionary general staff, both based on the concept of a "permanent civil war." The Russian movement of protest had thrown up a host of dedicated idealists, more than a few terrorists, and many martyrs. It was less notable for producing men of will and action. In this brief portrait, sketched just after Lenin's death, Victor Chernov (1873-1952) drew on a long, deep, but not personally intimate knowledge of his fellow revolutionary and bitter political rival.

Chernov was expelled from the university at 20 for his leading part in student protests against the Tsarist régime, and from then on he was a professional revolutionary. Drawing on Russian populist traditions, on Marxism, and on an extensive knowledge of Western economics and sociology, Chernov developed and propagated an eclectic but powerful concept of peasant revolution as Russia's future path. The Socialist Revolutionary Party, of which Chernov was a principal founder, called for a democratic republic, political freedom, and the free use of the land by those who till it. In 1917 he returned to Russia from long exile to find his followers sharply divided. Some wanted to continue the war to defend the achievements of the revolution; others demanded immediate peace at any price; still others, like Chernov, hoped to organize support in both warring camps for a negotiated peace. The SR ranks were also split on the question of whether to divide all the land immediately among the peasants by direct action, or to wait for the Constituent Assembly to act in an orderly way.

The elections to the Constituent Assembly gave the Socialist Revolutionaries and their allies a clear majority. On January 5, 1918, Chernov was elected President of the Assembly, which, after one day's session, was dispersed by force at Lenin's command. After continuing the underground struggle against Bolshevik rule for several years, Chernov was forced again to leave Russia and found refuge in the West. His one major work in English translation is "The Great Russian Revolution" (1936), an analysis of the failure of the democratic forces in the 1917 revolution.

LENIN

By Victor Chernov

LENIN is dead—this time dead physically, for spiritually and politically
he has been dead a year at least. We have got in the habit of speaking
of him as a thing of the past; and for that very reason it will not be
difficult now to write of him dispassionately.

Lenin was a great man. He was not merely the greatest man in his
party; he was its uncrowned king, and deservedly. He was its head, its
will, I should even say he was its heart were it not that both the man and
the party implied in themselves heartlessness as a duty. Lenin's intellect
was energetic but cold. It was above all an ironic, sarcastic, and cynical
intellect. Nothing to him was worse than sentimentality, a name he was
ready to apply to all moral and ethical considerations in politics. Such
things were to him trifles, hypocrisy, "parson's talk." Politics to him
meant strategy, pure and simple. Victory was the only commandment to
observe; the will to rule and to carry through a political program without compromise, that was the only virtue; hesitation, that was the only
crime.

It has been said that war is a continuation of politics, though employing
different means. Lenin would undoubtedly have reversed this dictum and
said that politics is the continuation of war under another guise. The
essential effect of war on a citizen's conscience is nothing but a legaliza-
tion and glorification of things that in times of peace constitute crime. In
war the turning of a flourishing country into a desert is a mere tactical
move; robbery is a "requisition," deceit a strategem, readiness to shed the
blood of one's brother military zeal; heartlessness towards one's victims
is laudable self-command; pitilessness and inhumanity are one's duty. In
war all means are good, and the best ones are precisely the things most
condemned in normal human intercourse. And as politics is disguised
war, the rules of war constitute its principles.

Lenin was often accused of not being and of not wanting to be an
"honest adversary." But then the very idea of an "honest adversary"

was to him an absurdity, a smug citizen's prejudice, something that might be made use of now and then jesuitically in one's own interest; but to take it seriously was silly. A defender of the proletariat is under an obligation to put aside all scruples in dealings with the foe. To deceive him intentionally, to calumniate him, to blacken his name, all this Lenin considered as normal. In fact, it would be hard to exceed the cynical brutality with which he proclaimed all this. Lenin's conscience consisted in putting himself outside the boundaries of human conscience in all dealings with his foes; and in thus rejecting all principles of honesty he remained honest with himself.

Being a Marxist, he was a believer in "class struggle." As an individual contribution to this theory he used to confess his belief that civil war was the unavoidable climax of class struggle. We may even say that to him class struggle was but the embryo of civil war. Dissent in the party, whether serious or merely trifling, he often tried to explain as an echo of class antagonisms. He would then proceed to eliminate the undesirable by cutting them off from the party, and in doing this he "honestly" resorted to the lowest means. After all, is not a non-homogeneous party an illegitimate conglomeration of antagonistic class-elements? And all antagonistic class-elements should be treated according to the precept "war is war."

His whole life was passed in schisms and factional fights within the party. From this resulted his incomparable perfection as a gladiator, as a professional fighter, in training every day of his life and constantly devising new tricks to trip up or knock out his adversary. It was this lifelong training that gave him his amazing cool-headedness, his presence of mind in any conceivable situation, his unflinching hope "to get out of it" somehow or other. By nature a man of single purpose and possessed of a powerful instinct of self-preservation, he had no difficulty in proclaiming *credo quia absurdum* and was much like that favorite Russian toy, the Van'ka-Vstan'ka boy, who has a piece of lead in his rounded bottom and bobs up again as fast as you knock him down. After every failure, no matter how shameful or humiliating, Lenin would instantly bob up and begin again from the beginning. His will was like a good steel spring which recoils the more powerfully the harder it is pressed. He was a hardy party leader of just the kind necessary to inspire and keep up the courage of his fellow fighters and to forestall panic by his personal example of unlimited self-confidence, as well as to bring them to their senses in periods of high exaltation when it would be extremely easy for them to become "a conceited party," as he used to say, resting on their laurels and overlooking the perils of the future.

This singleness of purpose was the thing that most imposed respect among his followers. Many a time when Lenin managed to survive, thanks only to some blunder of his foes, the credit for his survival was attributed to his unflinching optimism. Often it used to be mere blind luck—but then blind luck mostly comes to those who know how to hold out through a period of desperate ill-luck. Most persons soon give up. They do not care to sacrifice their strength in evidently futile attempts; they are sensible—and it is this good sense that precludes good luck. There is some supreme common sense, on the other hand, in a man who will spend his last ounce of energy in spite of all odds—in spite of logic, destiny and circumstance. And with such "unreasonable common sense" nature endowed Lenin to excess. Thanks to this tenacity he more than once salvaged his party from apparently inextricable straits, but to the masses at large such occurrences were miracles and were ascribed to his genius of foresight. Foresight on a large scale, however, was the very thing he lacked. He was a fencing master first of all, and a fencer needs only a little foresight and no complicated ideas. In fact, he must not think too much; he must concentrate on every movement of his adversary and master his own reflexes with the quickness of inborn instinct, so as to counter every hostile move without a trace of delay.

Lenin's intellect was penetrating but not broad, resourceful but not creative. A past master in estimating any political situation, he would become instantly at home with it, quickly perceive all that was new in it and exhibit great political and practical sagacity in forestalling its immediate political consequences. This perfect and immediate tactical sense formed a complete contrast to the absolutely unfounded and fantastic character of any more extensive historical prognosis he ever attempted—of any program that comprised more than today and tomorrow. The agrarian plan worked out by him in the nineties for the Social-Democratic Party, something he had been toiling over and digesting for ten years, met with complete failure, an accident which never prevented him subsequently from hastily borrowing from the Social-Revolutionaries agrarian slogans which he previously had spent much effort in combating. His concrete plans of attack were superbly practical; but his grandiose program of action after victory, which was to cover a whole historical period, went to pieces at the first touch of reality. His "nearer political outlook" was unexcelled; his "further political outlook" went permanently bankrupt.

As a man who already had the truth in his pocket he attached no value to the creative efforts of other seekers after truth. He had no respect for the convictions of anyone else, he had none of the enthusiastic love of liberty which marks the independent creative spirit. On the contrary, he was dominated by the purely Asiatic conception of a monopoly of press, speech, justice, and thought by a single ruling caste, agreeing therein with the alleged Moslem saying that if the library of Alexandria contained the same things as the Koran it was useless, and if it contained things contrary it was harmful.

Granting that Lenin was absolutely lacking in creative genius, that he was merely a skillful, forcible and indefatigable expounder of other thinkers' theories, that he was a man of such narrowness of mind that it could almost be called limited intelligence, nevertheless he was capable of greatness and originality within those limitations. His power lay in the extraordinary, absolute lucidity—one might almost say the transparency—of his propositions. He followed his logic unflinchingly even to an absurd conclusion, and left nothing diffuse and unexplained unless it were necessary to do so for tactical considerations. Ideas were made as concrete and simple as possible. This was most evident in Lenin's rhetoric. He never was a brilliant orator, an artist of beautiful speech. He would often be coarse and clumsy, especially in polemics, and he repeated himself continually. But these repetitions were his very system and his strength. Through the endless re-digesting, uncouth pounding and clumsy jokes there throbbed a live, indomitable will that would not be deviated by an inch from the appointed path; it was a steady, elemental pressure whose monotony hypnotized the audience. One and the same thought was expressed many times in many different shapes till finally in one way or another it penetrated each individual brain; then, as a drop of water perforates the rock, constant repetition was applied to implant the idea into the very essence of the hearer's intelligence. Few orators have known how to achieve such admirable results by dint of repetition. Besides, Lenin always *felt* his audience. He never rose too high above its level, nor did he ever omit to descend to it at just the necessary moment, in order not to break the continuity of the hypnosis which dominated the will of his flock; and more than any one he realized that a mob is like a horse that wants to be firmly bestrode and spurred, that wants to feel the hand of a master. When needed he spoke as a ruler, he denounced and whipped his audience. "He's not an orator—he's more than an orator," someone remarked about him, and the remark was a shrewd one.

The will of Lenin was stronger than his intellect, and the latter was everlastingly the servant of the former. Thus when victory was finally won after years of clandestine toil he did not embark upon the task of embodying his ideas as would a constructive socialist who had pondered over his creative work in advance; he merely applied to the new, creative phase of his life's program the same methods which had been used in his destructive struggle for power, "On s'engage et puis on voit"—he was very fond of these words of Napoleon's.

Lenin has often been painted as a blind dogmatist, but he never was such by nature. He was not the kind to become attached for better or worse to a symmetrically finished system, he merely set his mind on succeeding in his political and revolutionary gamble, where to catch the proper moment meant everything. This is how he often became a quack, an experimenter, a gambler; this is why he was an opportunist, which is something diametrically opposed to a dogmatist.

Many critics have thought Lenin greedy for power and honors. The fact is he was organically made to rule and simply could not help imposing his will on others, not because he longed for this but because it was as natural for him to do so as it is for a large astral body to influence the planets. As for honors, he disliked them. His heart never rejoiced in pomp. Plebeian in his tastes and by his inmost nature, he remained just as simple in his habits after the October revolution as he had been before. He has often been represented, too, as a heartless, dry fanatic. This heartlessness of his was purely intellectual and therefore directed against his enemies, that is, against the enemies of his party. To his friends he was amiable, good-natured, cheerful, and polite, as a good comrade should be; so it was that the affectionate, familar "Iliich" became his universally accepted name among his followers.

Yes, Lenin was good-natured. But good-natured does not mean good-hearted. It has been observed that physically strong people are usually good-natured, and the good nature of Lenin was of exactly the same description as the amiability of a huge Saint Bernard dog toward surrounding pups and mongrels. So far as we can guess, real good-heartedness most probably was considered by him one of the pettiest of human weaknesses. At least it is a fact that whenever he wanted to annihilate some Socialist adversary he never omitted to bestow upon him the epithet

of "a good fellow." He devoted his whole life to the interests of the
working class. Did he love those working people? Apparently he did,
although his love of the real, living workman was undoubtedly less
intense than his hatred of the workman's oppressor. His love of the
proletariat was the same despotic, exacting, and merciless love with
which, centuries ago, Torquemada burned people for their salvation.

To note another trait: Lenin, after his own manner, loved those whom
he valued as useful assistants. He readily forgave them mistakes, even
disloyalty, though once in a while calling them sternly to task. Rancor
or vengefulness were alien to him. Even his foes were not live, personal
enemies but certain abstract factors to be eliminated. They could not
possibly excite his human interest, being simply mathematically determined points where destructive force was to be applied. Mere passive
opposition to his party at a critical moment was a sufficient reason for
him to have scores and hundreds of persons shot without a moment's
consideration; and with all this he was fond of playing and laughing
heartily with children, kittens and dogs.

It has been said that what the style is the man is. It would be even
truer to say that what the thought is the man is. If it has been given to
Lenin to leave any imprint of himself upon the doctrine of class struggle
it is to be found in his interpretation of the dictatorship of the proletariat,
an interpretation permeated with the conception of that will which was
the essence of his own personality. Socialism means the enfranchisement of
labor; and the proletariat is the warp and woof of the working mass.
In the proletariat itself, however, there are purer and less pure strains
of proletarians. Now if a dictatorship of the proletariat over the working
masses is required there must be, on the same principles, within the
proletariat itself a vanguard-dictatorship over the proletarian rank and
file. This must be a kind of quintessence, a true Proletarian Party.
Within this Proletarian Party there must likewise be an inner dictatorship
of the sterner elements over the more yielding ones. We have thus an as-
cending system of dictatorships, which culminates and could not help culminating in a personal dictator. Such Lenin came to be.

His theory of concentric dictatorships—which reminds one of the
concentric circles of Dante's Inferno—thus developed into a universally
applicable theory of Socialist dictatorial guardianship over the people,
that is, into the very antithesis of true Socialism as a system of economic
democracy. This favorite and most intimate conception of Lenin—and
the only one really his own—was a *contradictio in adjecto*. Such an

inner contradiction could not help but become, ultimately, a source of disintegration inside the party he had created.

He is dead. His party is now headed by men whom for a long period of years he moulded after his own image, who found it easy to imitate him but who are finding it extremely difficult to continue his policy. That party as a whole is now beginning to experience the fate of its supreme leader: gradually it is becoming a living corpse. Lenin is no longer there to galvanize it with his surplus energy; he spent himself to the dregs— spent himself on a party which is now, in its turn, exhausted. Over his freshly made grave it may for a moment draw closer together and pronounce vows of fidelity to the revered teacher who has told it so much in the past, but who today is telling it no more, and who will tell it no more in the future. Then it will fall back into everyday life and again be subject to the law of disintegration and dissolution.

VLADIMIR ZENZINOV (1880-1953), like Victor Chernov a prominent representative of the peasantophile wing of the Russian Revolution, was at once a political idealist and a selfless terrorist, a passionate participant in Russia's turmoil and an unusually objective observer. His path, that of many young Russians of the pre-revolutionary generations, led him at twenty from his studies at Berlin and Heidelberg into the underground Socialist Revolutionary Party, and through it into the thick of the revolutionary crisis of 1904-05. After twice escaping from prison, Zenzinov resumed his underground political activity once again, only to be exiled by the Okhrana to the extreme north. Elected to the Constituent Assembly in 1917, Zenzinov along with many other revolutionaries was again driven, this time by Cheka terrorism, into the underground—a far more hazardous way of life than it had been under the Tsars. Leaving Russia once more, in 1919, he took up the life of an exile politician and publicist, first in Paris, after 1940 in New York.

Among numerous articles and books from Zenzinov's pen, special mention should be made of "The Road to Oblivion" (1931) and "Memoirs" (1953). His writings, like his life as a revolutionary, were filled with compassion and with faith in man's capacity to shape a better future.

These same qualities led Zenzinov to the hopeful prognoses set forth in "The Bolsheviks and the Peasant" (October 1925). Once Lenin's New Economic Policy of 1921 had again permitted the peasants to till the soil and enjoy the fruits of their labor, Russian agriculture made a rapid recovery from post-revolutionary devastation and partial famine. Did this mean that the Soviet regime would henceforth be dependent on the peasantry for its survival and would evolve into an agrarian democracy, renouncing the Bolshevik claim to lead a world revolution? Many Communists and anti-Communists believed that since the revolutionary storm had blown itself out, the Soviet regime would now evolve into a more or less traditional member of the society of nations. Zenzinov's analysis reflected his hope that peasant Russia would now become the dominant force in the country he loved so deeply.

33

THE BOLSHEVIKS AND
THE PEASANT

By Vladimir Zenzinov

W HAT is there new in the peasant policy of the Soviet Government?
The history of the Soviet Government's method of dealing with the
peasants is a brilliant illustration of the truth of the Latin proverb,
"fata volentem ducunt, nolentem trahunt," that is, "fate—or better still
life—leads those who do not resist it, and forcibly drags along those who
try to oppose it."

Let us examine the facts. Until 1917 the attitude toward the peasant
adopted by the Bolshevik fraction of the Socialist party was definite,
and one befitting orthodox Marxists. The Bolshevik program embodied
the conceptions of a commonplace variety of Marxism, according to
which the peasantry were, first and last, a class of petty bourgeoisie,
alien and antagonistic not only to Socialist ideals but to all social progress. The proletariat were the sole organ of the Socialist ideal, that is
to say of the future. Accordingly the party was built up on exclusively
proletarian lines. Its program, so far as the peasant was concerned,
was restricted to political demands; for any economic improvement of
his condition was in their eyes not only without object but even objection-
able. Theoretically the peasants, being established on the land and possessing some means for its exploitation, would have to go through a
process of differentiation in the course of which the petty holders among
them would be absorbed by the larger ones. In conformity with this
theory of common Marxism, something analogous to the evolution of
industry was due to take place in the villages. Strengthening the petty
peasant would mean hampering the inevitable social progress. The only
thing the Socialist party could do for the peasant—said the Bolsheviks—
was to help organize the paid agricultural laborers. Such was the Marxist
doctrine professed by the Bolsheviks in its purest form.

For twenty years and more the Bolsheviks had been waging a tireless
theoretical battle against another Russian Socialist party, the Socialist-

Revolutionaries, whose chief distinction from the Bolsheviks and from the Marxists in general was this: The Socialist-Revolutionaries in their theoretical conceptions made no distinction between the proletariat and the peasantry; they considered both united in one laboring class, and argued that the socialist program and the socialist movement must be the common cause of these two armies of labor. This theoretical discussion between the Socialist-Revolutionaries and the Bolsheviks went on incessantly.

In 1905 the Bolsheviks were forced to make large concessions in this question. The peasantry, of whom they had thought up to this time as a purely reactionary class socially as well as politically, showed that they were a powerful revolutionary force. Indeed, the movement of 1905-6 which compelled the early concessions of the Government—"the first revolution," the manifesto of October 17th, the Duma—was largely a peasant movement. The Bolsheviks grasped this and made a change in their tactics in regard to the peasants, but only in their tactics, not in their program. To be sure, they officially proclaimed the slogan "nationalization of land," but they did not conceal that this slogan to them was only a tactical move, by which they wanted to lead the peasant to political revolution. As before, they deemed the paid laborers, the proletariat, to be the only class able to carry out a Socialist revolution. The peasant in revolt, demanding land, was to them at this historic moment only a traveling companion on the road to revolution.

A great gulf separated the Bolsheviks from the Socialist-Revolutionaries who proclaimed as their watchword "the socialization of the land." To the Socialist-Revolutionaries, "the socialization of the land" was a specific variety of nationalization. The difference consisted in this: while in "nationalization" the state becomes the legal owner of the land, in socialization the people acquire the supreme right to dispose of all the nationalized land, in accordance with a special legislative provision. Besides, the Socialist-Revolutionaries conceived of "the socialization of the land" as a far-reaching social reform creating favorable conditions for socialization and the introduction of the coöperative principle in all the other branches of industry, agriculture and city affairs.

Then came the year 1917. Contrary to the ordinary conception, the real revolution at that time was not made in the cities, but in the villages. The essential content of the Russian revolution was the tremendous, elemental process which took place among the peasants and resulted in

the disruption of the landed estates, the expulsion of the landed proprietors, most of them belonging to the nobility, from their villages, and
the forcible appropriation of all private and state lands by the peasants. The thing that many had foreseen as inevitable, namely the satisfaction of the peasant's age-long thirst for the land, took place in an
elemental way. The ideas of the Socialist-Revolutionaries on this point
were identical with those of the peasants—"the land must be excepted
from the exchange of goods," as they put it, and "the land is the Lord's
own, or nobody's, it's a sin to buy it and a sin to sell it," as the peasant
was wont to say. Consequently, they hoped to have this wholesale seizure
legalized in the Constituent Assembly by a fundamental law on the
socialization of the land. This was to be worked out by deputies from
all the people in the highest legislative and administrative organ of the
country, and the rules thus established would regulate the use of land
throughout the country, converting the peasant's primitive conviction of
his right into a law obligatory for all citizens.

History, however, disposed differently. Power was seized by the Bolshevist party and the Constituent Assembly was dissolved. But in 1917,
as in 1905, the Bolsheviks grasped correctly the significance of what
had happened. They saw that the only way for them to keep in power
and to strengthen themselves in it, was by staying on the crest of the
revolutionary wave. With the greatest haste—literally on the morrow
of their *coup d'état*—they promulgated a decree which contained a
project of socialization of the land previously prepared, but not yet definitely worked out, by the Socialist-Revolutionaries. This decree did not
regulate the agrarian question on a country-wide scale, but simply sanctioned and ratified the wholesale seizure and partition of land already
carried out by the peasants. By this means the Bolsheviks achieved their
purpose. They neutralized the peasant politically. He was satisfied in
the essential thing, his age-long craving for the land, and therefore he
remained indifferent to the dissolution of the Constituent Assembly to
which he had sent an overwhelming majority of deputies, indifferent also
to the seizure of power by the Bolsheviks, although it meant a power
entirely alien to him.

The Bolsheviks themselves never attempted to conceal the true character of the peasant policy they adopted in the first days after their *coup
d'état*. No less a person than Lenin himself several times publicly
acknowledged in speaking and writing that the Bolsheviks had taken
their decree on the socialization of land from the Socialist-Revolution-

aries. "Nine-tenths of the peasants," he wrote, "have gone over to our side within a few weeks because we adopted an agrarian program that was not our own but that of the Socialist-Revolutionaries, and put it into execution. Our victory consisted precisely in the carrying out of the Socialist-Revolutionary program. That is why it was so easy." "Indeed, why shouldn't we borrow from the Social-Revolutionists whatever was really good?" he used to say with a cunning smile. In doing so he never denied that to the Bolsheviks it was but a means of attracting the peasant or at least neutralizing him politically. As before, it was a matter of tactics, not of the program. As far as the theory was concerned, the proletariat still kept complete hegemony, the Bolsheviks kept assuring themselves and others that what they were bringing into being was "the dictatorship of the proletariat."

What was the further peasant policy of the Soviet Government?

At first, it bore a perfectly consistent and typical Marxist character. All the Bolsheviks wanted from the peasant was for him to help aggravate the class struggle. For this purpose the famous "Committees of the Destitute" were created all over the country, made up of needy peasants and farm-laborers. Usually these committees included as instructors typical city proletarians professing Bolshevism. The Committees of the Destitute had but one purpose, namely, to sequestrate for the benefit of the city population and city proletariat the grain produced by the more well-to-do peasants, whom they contemptuously called *kulaki* ("fists," the old name for the village usurer). Lenin called this process "prying bread out of the villages with bayonettes." The result could be easily foreseen—civil war on a vast scale throughout the country. The aim of Lenin's teaching was achieved. Trotsky, his faithful pupil, used to say at that time, "Bolshevism is organized civil war." It lasted for three whole years over the entire boundless expanse of Russia. It brought ruin, curtailment of areas under cultivation, the nightmare of the famine of 1920-21, and never-ceasing peasant uprisings which the Soviet Government drowned in rivers of blood by means of its well organized police forces. This could not continue indefinitely, for even the fanatics of civil war had their eyes opened, especially after such threatening events as the wholesale peasant revolt in the government of Tambov and the sailors' revolt in Kronstadt in the spring of 1921.

The peasant policy of the Bolsheviks had to be revised. This was done by Lenin who, with his characteristic crude frankness, explained the reasons for such a revision. In April, 1921, he made his famous speech on the product tax, thereby initiating the New Economic Policy. In this speech he pointed out directly—and others did it after him—that peasant unrest and the Kronstadt revolt made it imperative "to take immediate and decisive steps to better the condition of the peasant," and to abandon "the system of war-time Communism by which we practically took from the peasant all his surplus, and sometimes what was not his surplus but part of his necessary subsistence."

Then began the period of the so-called New Economic Policy, which so far as the peasant was concerned took the less onerous form of a product tax. The Soviet Government had at last divined that if you want to get eggs you must not kill the hen that lays them. The Committees of the Destitute were relegated to the background. The Government began to look toward the so-called middle peasant. There was talk about the union of the indigent and of the middle peasant. These two elements should combine together and with the city proletariat, of course under the guidance of the Communist Party, in order to combat the power of capital in town and village. The wealthier peasants, the *kulaki,* remained the enemy to be annihilated by the joint effort of all Communists.

The period of war-time Communism passed definitely away; the domestic life of Russia fortunately ceased to be disturbed by foolish foreign interventions; and attention was turned first and foremost to the economic reconstruction of the huge country that had been ruined first by the World War, then by a still more devastating civil war. Gradually one clear and simple thought came to dominate the consciousness of the country: the destinies of Russia depended entirely on the reconstruction of peasant industry.

After what the country has been through, the specific gravity of the peasantry has increased in proportion enormously. This fact penetrated the Bolshevik consciousness with difficulty, but it could not help penetrating at last.

And now we are witnessing a great object lesson. Apparently forgetting all of their Marxist dogma, the responsible Soviet leaders are beginning to reiterate the ABC of an economic policy which, from their lips, sounds as if it were a new gospel. Intensification of village production is the aim to which every effort of the Soviet reconstruction campaign must be bent. The Government must by all means help increase the welfare of the diligent, prosperous peasant. It is necessary to abandon the careless and demagogic persecution of the *kulaki.* The state can no longer commit itself to the village paupers as was done during the period of war-time Communism, because that would be a kind of "defeatism in production." Also, peasant agriculture cannot get along without hired labor. Such are the orations uttered nowadays by the most responsible Soviet statesmen, men like Smirnov, the Commissar for Agriculture (*Pravda,* April 5 and 7); Kamenev (*Izvestia,* April 14); Rykov, the President of the Council of People's Commissars (*Izvestia,* April 30), and many others.

These pronouncements are a complete refutation of the former Bolshevist peasant policy which was directed exclusively to the instigation of class war in the villages. Instead of staking on the pauper, the Government now stakes, if not on the *kulak,* at least on the well-to-do peasant. If the speeches that Kamenev, Rykov and Smirnov make nowadays had been made a few years ago, the culprits would have been brought before the revolutionary tribunal and dealt with as counter-revolutionists and enemies of the Soviet Government. Not long ago a well-to-do, prosperous peasantry, and the accumulation of capital in the villages, would have appeared as deadly sin in the eyes of the Marxist Bolsheviks. Today their leaders openly agitate in favor of these things in the press and at every conference and congress.

More than that, these appeals do not remain mere propaganda. They are being made the cornerstone of a practical peasant policy. On April 18 the Soviet of People's Commissars decreed "Provisional rules for the hire of auxiliary labor in agriculture." These new rules mean a break with the entire recent past of the Bolsheviks. They sanction officially hired labor in peasant agriculture, and at that, they set no limitations to the number of persons hired. Thereby they not only permit, they assist in the development of capitalistic relations in rural economy. It must be especially noted that the employer of this hired labor (the former *kulak* and "exploiter") does not in any degree forfeit his franchise at the Soviet elections, whereas originally, according to the Soviet Constitution, only laboring people enjoyed such franchise.

We hear very different talk today. The Bolsheviks now unanimously declare that they do not wish to aggravate the class struggle in the villages. In accordance with this new policy a very special theory is being evolved of harmony of interests between the peasants of all levels. *Pravda* (May 3) says squarely that "in view of the desirability of strengthening the productivity of the peasantry, we must

in every way facilitate the hiring of laborers in the interests of the
poor." The former apostles of class hatred now begin to preach one
of the commonplaces of classic political economy: the quicker capital
is developed the more profitable it will be for labor, for it will be so
much the easier for the labor that is for hire to find employment.

So it came about that life has made sport of the Bolshevik Communists. When at last they grasped that the foundation of Russia's
welfare lies in the development of the productivity of her peasantry,
and that there is no other way to the economic reconstruction of the
country except by raising the general standard of village life, they became *plus royalistes que le roi même*. In this connection a speech which
Bukharin made before the political workers of the Party in Moscow
on April 17 is very characteristic (*Pravda,* April 24). Naturally it
was not at all an accident that Bukharin was the man to speak on
this delicate question. He belongs to the left wing and heretofore
was known as the most extreme of Lenin's pupils, a passionate enemy
of capitalism, and apostle of world-wide Socialist revolution. And if
it was he who stepped forward to expound the Communist Party's
new peasant policy, it shows how definitely they have adopted this ·
stand, for nothing but party discipline could have forced him to
speak as he did.

Great, indeed, is the distance traversed by the Marxist Bolsheviks
from their original conceptions of the peasantry as a homogeneous reactionary mass, politically as well as socially; of the theory of fanning
the flames of class war in the villages; of a policy of deliberately ruining the peasant, relying on and organizing Committees of the Destitute! After eight years of government experience, they have learned
that all this policy was nothing but cheap demagogy, and that the
economic policy of a state demands something different. In a country
where the peasant population is in a huge majority, no policy can be
effectual that is not based on peasant interests. To be sure, the Bolsheviki understood this somewhat late, namely after their "dictatorship of the proletariat" (which, essentially, has never been anything
but a dictatorship of the Communist Party) had ruined the peasant.
But they have at last understood that their power will have no economic foundation unless they secure command of the national economy,
and that this can be only peasant economy. Hence all this recent
flirting with the peasant, all this swing of the pendulum in their
economic policy, with hymns of praise to the *kulak* and exhortations

to accumulate wealth. The hopes of obtaining foreign loans have collapsed; the reconstruction of industry under the existing general conditions is also not to be counted on. From one kind of demagogy the Bolsheviki have gone over to another.

It would be too cheap a satisfaction merely to point out that, in the eighth year of their control, the Bolsheviks have abandoned their old Marxist attitude toward the peasant, which had always been a cabinet theory, far from real life. Better late than never. While remaining politically opposed to Bolshevism, yet one may admit that the latest peasant policy of the Soviets is gradually becoming a healthy one, inasmuch as it pursues the practical purpose of developing the productive forces of the country, and primarily of the peasantry. But this is still very far from a practical settlement of that question, so vast and so fundamental for Russia's future. A German proverb says: Whoever has said A must say B. And of course, the Bolsheviks will never be able to say B as long as they remain Bolsheviks.

What do we understand by making the interest of the peasantry the foundation of policy? Certainly it is something more than mere cooperation in the enrichment of the peasant, for which Bukharin appealed. It means an appreciation of the fact that it is the Government's duty to meet half-way and satisfy the social and political demands of the peasant. In other words, more than purely economic measures are required. He must be granted the freedom of individual and personal initiative and the opportunity to intensify his productivity by hiring labor. He must have the right of free, unhampered coöperative association, with a voluntary—not as heretofore obligatory—membership, the right of free election to the administrative machinery—not appointment from above, as has been the practice all these years. But is this then enough? Freedom of economic determination is inseparably linked up with civic rights and with the possibility of influencing and determining the social and political life of the commonwealth. The peasant must feel that he is a full-fledged citizen with rights equal to those of the city dwellers. In his village he must feel that the central power is closely related to him, and he must trust it and be assured that it stands watch over his interests.

Can the peasant thus regard the Soviet Government? To formulate this question is to answer it in the negative. The Soviet press itself is full of facts which prove this. It harps upon the lack of connection between the peasant and the Soviet power, upon the distrust and even animosity of the village masses toward the Communists, upon the chasm existing between the villages and the cities, which latter, in the opinion of the peasant, are inhabited only by Bolsheviks. For some years now the Bolsheviks have been talking of the *"smychka,"* or close connection between town and village, yet the affair has not made a step of progress. The attempt at a so-called revival of the village Soviets, by which the Bolsheviks tried to give the village the possibility of somewhat greater self-administration, had very sad results: *Pravda,* of March 29, informs us of the election results in 406 *uiezdy* (districts), which means 94 percent of all the *uiezdy* of central Russia. 78,864 persons were elected to the village Soviets, of whom only 4,764 were Communists, that is six percent (at the previous elections they were 11.6 percent).

The Russian peasant as he is today and the Soviet Government as it now exists are two incompatible things. This is a matter of common knowledge to all who are familiar with the actual state of affairs in Russia—on which there can be no dispute.

It would be difficult to over-estimate the consequences of the events which have occurred in Russia during the last decade. The sum total includes the disappearance of the landed proprietor and the abolition of large estates, the seizure and distribution among the peasants of the private and state lands, the destruction of industry by the Bolsheviks who have tried by forcible measures to establish Socialism in an economically backward country, the gradual and growing consciousness on the part of the peasant of his own decisive rôle in its destinies. Russia has become even more a country of peasants and of agriculture than she was before 1917. In consequence of what Russia has been through—world war, revolution, civil war, foreign interventions—the outcome of which, as well as of the whole "White" movement were determined by the attitude of the peasant toward them—his specific gravity has increased enormously, both subjectively, in his own eyes, and objectively, in the life of the nation.

In spite of the danger of prophesying, one can foretell even now that Russia will be reborn—indeed is already being reborn—as a great peasant democracy. In eastern Europe an enormous new Denmark is evidently destined to arise. The Soviet Government, in whose hands are the keys of the life of the great country, is vaguely conscious of this. It is disturbed by the inevitable internal and external development of the peasant democracy, and is trying to establish its own ascendancy by flirting with the peasantry, with the hope that at the price of trifling concessions it may retain the whole power in its hands. Everything indicates that the attempt will not be successful. The only question of importance is how long the process of natural growth will take. The rock itself yields and crumbles under the living pressure of the roots of a growing tree.

"THE Foreign Policy of Soviet Russia" (July 1926) was written by Christian Rakovsky while serving as Soviet ambassador to France. Then and since, in a continuing effort to inform its readers of important and divergent points of view, *Foreign Affairs* has opened its pages to well-qualified spokesmen for Soviet policy. Rakovsky was unusually well equipped to state the Soviet view as an authentic revolutionary and a highly skilled diplomat.

Born in 1873 of Bulgarian parents, Rakovsky earned a medical degree in France and, under the pseudonym of "Insarov," collaborated with Lenin in *Iskra* ("The Spark") and later with Trotsky in *Pravda* ("The Truth") published in Vienna. Returning to Rumania, he organized and led the Rumanian Socialist Party until he was arrested in 1916, expelled to Bessarabia, and again arrested there. Set free by the February Revolution, Rakovsky joined the Bolshevik Party, took a leading part in the October Revolution and Civil War, and became premier of the Soviet Ukrainian Republic.

With the coming of the NEP, Rakovsky embarked on a new career, becoming, with Litvinov, Maisky and others, a diplomatic spokesman of the new Soviet state. In 1923-24 he conducted successful negotiations with the British Labor Government for the *de jure* recognition of the Soviet regime and the opening up of trade between Russia and Britain. After a similar but more complicated negotiation for recognition by France, he became Soviet ambassador in Paris.

Rakovsky's career as a diplomat was cut short in December 1927 by his expulsion from the Communist Party as a Trotskyite and by exile to Kazakhstan. Having retracted his oppositionist views in 1934 when Hitler's rise to power rallied most of the opposition around Stalin's leadership, Rakovsky was re-admitted to the Party. In March 1938 he was recalled from obscurity to stand in the floodlights of Moscow's Hall of Columns. Arrested and tried in Stalin's sweeping purge of past and potential rivals and critics, Rakovsky was pronounced guilty of high treason and sentenced to 20 years at hard labor.

"The Foreign Policy of Soviet Russia" was written at the height of Moscow's first major *rapprochement* with the West. In it Rakovsky expressed an official view of Soviet purposes in world affairs. In it he also demonstrated his own unusual abilities as a revolutionary turned diplomat.

THE FOREIGN POLICY
OF SOVIET RUSSIA

By Christian Rakovsky

IT is not my purpose to attempt a systematic and complete statement of the foreign policy of my government, but to lay down certain guiding lines which may aid an understanding of the relations between the Union of Soviets and other Powers and of the attitude that the Soviet Government has taken towards various international problems.

In order to comprehend the foreign policy of the Soviet Republic, it is essential first to consider another more general question. What is the aim of the foreign policy of every country? Foreign policy, it will readily be understood, is only a projection of domestic policy and, clearly, has a close relation to the form of political and social organization of the nation and to its institutions generally. Every government strives to establish with other countries the sort of relations most favorable to the strengthening and development of its own institutions.

This general rule obviously applies to the Soviet Government. Probably not many persons continue to hold the mistaken opinion that the régime created in Russia by the triumph of the revolution of October, 1917, was a transitory episode, the result of a sudden stroke organized by a handful of men who were strangers to the history of the country acting against the will of the people and against the interests and aspirations of the nation. The fact that the Soviet Government has endured for eight years and that no one questions its political solidity, proves that its appearance was not an accident but a necessity, for deep-lying reasons, both in the evolution of Russia and of the whole world.

Without going into a detailed analysis of Tsarist Russia, the following three characteristics of its political and social organization may be noted:

1. The existence of a class of feudal aristocracy possessing a great share of the land, and holding subject to its domination and exploitation the peasants who made up four-fifths of the population. A régime of

absolute power with a bureaucracy, which had all the vices of un-
regulated bureaucracies, was essential to maintain the power of the
feudal class.

2. A capitalist class, much weaker because the feudal agrarian system hampered the economic development of the country, but for this
reason the more rapacious in the exploitation of the workers.

3. Numerous national minorities, all together constituting a majority in comparison with those who could properly be called Great
Russians, but subordinated to the domination of Tsarism and deprived
not merely of political rights but of the most elementary rights of
development of their own cultural systems.

Opposed to the old régime, consequently, there were formidable
forces: peasants, workers and national minorities, waiting only a propitious moment to overthrow it. The war provided the occasion; it
completely disorganized the governmental and military apparatus and
opened the eyes of people who had been submitting apathetically to
the Tsarist régime, to its total incapacity and superannuation.

It may be regarded as an established fact that it was not the revolution which caused Russia to quit the war, but Tsarism which demanded
of its subjects an effort far in excess of their strength and which thereby
destroyed itself and prepared the way for the revolution. In the first
three months of the war, it is important to remember, the Tsarist
Government put in the field 4,000,000 soldiers, while France mobilized
3,000,000 and England 165,000. Further, the consideration that revenues per capita in Russia amounted to $43.10, while in Great Britain
they amounted to $260 and in France $182.50, reveals still further
how disproportionate to the economic resources of the country was the
effort Russia was called upon to make. During three years of war,
Russia mobilized 15,000,000 men, according to the statistics of the
Allied General Staff (18,000,000 according to the Russian General
Staff). The number killed was 2,500,000.

What assured the victory of the Bolshevik party was the fact that
it anticipated the desires of the workers and peasants and national
minorities—that is to say, of the great masses of the people—and put
an end to the war so far as Russia was concerned. Even before we
came into power, the Russian military front had ceased to exist in fact.
The disorganization of the army had been indicated even before the first
revolution of February, 1917, when the number of deserters had exceeded a million. The offensive organized by the Kerensky Govern-

ment in June, 1917, only hastened this disorganization and intensified the popular aversion for the war.

Such was the historical setting of the revolution of October, 1917. This review of the origins of the Soviet power is necessary to explain its foreign policy, the aim of which had to be the defense of the new state of affairs in Russia. The first manifestation of this foreign policy was peace with Germany.

The new government realized perfectly that a triumphant militarist Germany would be the most furious foe of the Soviet régime. That was why the tactics of the Soviet Government at first consisted in attempting to maintain the unity of Russia with the Allies for the purpose of concluding peace. If this proved impossible and the Allies desired to prosecute the war against Germany, the Soviet Government was under the necessity of concluding a separate peace, but in such a way as to leave no doubt in the minds of the Russian people that this was not a democratic peace but a peace imposed on the vanquished and consequently provisional.

Sooner or later such a peace would have to give way to a life-or-death struggle with German imperialism; but for Russia to have a chance of victory it was necessary that the peasants, workers and national minorities should experience the effects of the revolution. That alone would secure support and sacrifices from the masses of the people. The Soviet power required a truce to accomplish the nationalization of the land, reorganize industry on a new basis, and grant independence to oppressed national minorities. It had to create totally new governmental machinery, tap new economic resources, and organize a new army.

First proposing that negotiations with Germany for peace "without annexations or reparations" should be conducted not by Russia alone but by all the Allies, the Soviet Government requested of Germany an armistice of three months. The Allies rejected the proposal and Russia was forced to go alone to Brest-Litovsk, having secured an armistice of only one month.

The second part of the Soviet peace program was to unmask the hypocrisy of German militarism in consenting formally to peace "without annexations or reparations" but actually pursuing purposes of annexation and seeking considerable reparations. Our policy was of service not only to the Russian people but also to the subjects of the Central Powers, whose soldiers were deceived by successive assurances from their diplomats that Germany and Austria only desired to end the war as soon as possible. The Soviet delegation at first refused to subscribe to the German conditions and at the same time declared that Russia would not continue the war. Only when the Germans launched a new offensive did the Soviet Government sign the Treaty of Brest-Litovsk. But if the material victory rested with Germany and Austria, the Soviet delegation carried away the moral victory.

Despite the refusal of the Allies to negotiate peace at the same time with Russia, Soviet diplomacy sought to avoid a break with them and to keep the Germans within the limits of the treaty they had imposed. Since Germany compelled us to recognize and conclude peace with the "People's Republic of the Ukraine," which already had become a monarchist government with the aid of German bayonets, we attempted in the course of the negotiations with the Ukraine to fix a line of demarcation between the Russian army, then made up of a mixture of detachments of Red volunteers and the remainder of the old army, and the German armies.

The present writer, as head of a delegation which went in the month of April, 1918, first to Kursk and then to Kiev, was charged with the responsibility of conducting these discussions. But in spite of every effort, I was unable to get a line of demarcation fixed except on one part of the front. The Germans never were willing to establish a line in the Rostov sector, and also reserved to themselves freedom to advance whenever they wished towards the Kuban and Baku.

At the same time our Ambassador at Berlin, M. Joffe, as well as our Commissariat of Foreign Affairs at whose head was Chicherin, were trying to establish a *modus vivendi* on the basis of the Treaty of Brest-Litovsk.

Although Germany had very definite purposes with regard to the Soviet power, she did not enjoy a freedom of action sufficient to permit her fully to realize her plans. She was engaged in the struggle against the Allies; and while she was working for the collapse of the Soviet power, she also was attempting to profit, especially from an economic point of view, by the relations between the two countries. This explains why both at Berlin, where M. Joffe represented the Soviet, and at Kiev, where for five months I dealt with the Ukrainian Government (which was nothing but a screen for Germany) and with the German Ambassador Baron Mumm and the German generals, we were able to take advantage of the difficult strategic and political position of Germany in order to maintain a state of comparative peace. I strove to avoid any troublesome incident along the line of demarcation between our two armies and to foster economic relations with the Ukraine.

Actually, warfare with Germany continued. The workers and peasants of White Russia and the Ukraine, friendly toward the Soviet power, never ceased to struggle against German oppression. Labor strikes and peasant revolts followed each other in succession. The hope of the Germans to reprovision their armies and their country from the Ukraine, which they expected to find a rich granary, was disappointed.

During all this time we tried to maintain unbroken contact with the Allies. We felt no contradiction with our ideas in coöperation with powers having a different social structure. We recognized that the stage of economic development of our country did not favor socialistic organization of its productive system. Socialization could only be partial, since heavy industries were only slightly developed. At that time we had no idea of nationalizing all heavy industry; we accepted this necessity because the proprietors opposed a systematic resistance to our program of workers' control of industry. It was only in June, 1918, in order to conquer the resistance of the proprietors and prevent the large industrial enterprises belonging to Germans from being returned to them in accordance with the Treaty of Brest-Litovsk, that we promulgated the law nationalizing all industries with a capital of more than a half million rubles. This included only a small part of our economic system; there remained an enormous sphere for private enterprise, particularly for the peasants and also for foreign capital. The policy of concessions to foreigners for the purpose of attracting foreign capital to aid in the economic reconstruction of the country was formulated at that time by Lenin.

We communicated our concrete plan to the representative of the American Red Cross, Col. Raymond Robins, at the time of his departure for the United States in the spring of 1918. The Allied Ambassadors having left the capital for Vologda, we attempted to ascertain the attitude of the Allies through the American Consul, Mr. Poole, and through the secretary of the Norwegian Consulate, Mr. Christiansen, but we received no reply. We learned only one thing: the Allies had set themselves the aim of restoring the Russian front against Germany. This we could not do without imperiling the newly begun work of organizing the Soviet power and reconstructing the economic life of the nation.

What they could not accomplish by persuasion the Allies attempted to achieve by violence. The Czechoslovak Legionaries, who were permitted to leave Russia by way of Siberia, instead of Archangel as we wished, established the first internal front against the Soviet Government. On April 6, 1918, the Japanese occupied Vladivostok and began to advance into Siberia. On August 5 the English occupied Archangel. A series of revolts took place in the course of the summer of 1918 at the instigation, direct or indirect, of agents of the Allies.

One of the clauses of the armistice agreement between the Allies and Germany imposed on the Germans the obligation to keep their armies in the Russian provinces they were occupying until the arrival of Allied troops. Yet we did not give up our attempts to come to an understanding with the Allies. We accepted the first invitation extended to us in February, 1919, to attend a conference at Prinkipo. We made clear our plan for concessions, and even went so far as to declare our willingness to adjust the question of pre-war debts on condition that normal relations be reëstablished between Russia and the Allies.

In the years 1919 and 1920, the hardest years for the Soviet Government, we had to fight against Allied invasions, against the armies of Kolchak, Denikin and Wrangel supported by the Allies, and finally against Poland. The failure of the policy of intervention becoming evident to some of the Allies, the Conference of Ambassadors in Paris early in 1920 abolished the blockade against the Union of Soviets. During the war with Poland, there was an attempt on the part of England to bring about peace, made just at the time when our armies were drawing near Warsaw.

The first nations to conclude peace with us were the Baltic states, who hoped that recognition by the Soviet Government of these former parts of the Russian Empire would sanctify their political independence. In 1920 we signed treaties with Esthonia, Lithuania, Latvia and Finland, and the preliminary treaty of Riga with Poland; and the following year the final treaty with Poland and treaties with Persia, Afghanistan, Turkey and Mongolia, and commercial agreements with England, Norway and Italy. These developments indicated that gradually we were entering upon a period of peace.

Among the Allied Powers the first to begin the resumption of commercial relations with Russia was England, under the influence of her own economic difficulties. It was her initiative that was decisive in favor of sending Russia an invitation to the Genoa Conference. This permitted us for the first time to establish contact with official representatives of all the other important countries, except the United States who had no representation at Genoa. But the policy of the Powers was dominated by the idea that the Soviet power, having emerged victorious from its military trials, would be overthrown as a result of internal difficulties, and by the desire to secure from us the recognition of the debts and the reëstablishment of the right of private property. The credits we asked, without which acceptance of the obligation of the debts would have been only an empty phrase, were not granted. Similarly, we were invited to take part in the Lausanne Conference in the hope of our signing a convention for the neutralization of the Straits of the Bosphorus and the Dardanelles, which would have opened the Black Sea and made it a future theatre of war.

The year 1924 marked our achievement of recognition. The appointment of the Labor Cabinet in England brought about the renewal of diplomatic relations, and this was followed in the course of the year by renewal of relations in turn with Italy, Norway, Austria, Greece, Sweden, China, Denmark and France, and in 1925 with Japan.

We have succeeded in maintaining and consolidating our position in Russia because we have pursued a program comprising four points: solution of the agrarian problem, the labor problem, and the nationality problem, and finally a policy of peace in contrast to the policy of conquest of Russian Tsarism. We came into power partly as a result of the protest of the peoples of old Russia against the World War, of which the Tsarist imperialistic policy was one of the causes; and we are forced to seek peace as a primary necessity for the solution of the political and social problems on which depends the welfare of our working classes. This will require sacrifices for several generations, and automatically will exclude any aggressive or warlike spirit. The description of the Union of Soviets as an economic state expresses a truth, in that the problems facing the Soviet Government are all of an internal character, economic, intellectual and social. Its economic functions predominate over its administrative functions because it controls the means of transport, a large part of industry, foreign trade, credit and banking, and consequently is responsible for the conditions of agriculture. In a war, it is the Soviet Government itself which must suffer in its capacities as business promoter, manufacturer, banker and merchant.

Our immense task of reconstruction is only begun. We have a huge country, its territory comprising one-sixth of the land area of the globe, with unlimited potential wealth and a population which today numbers 140,000,000. But in economic organization it is one of the most backward in the world.

The national revenue per capita, which according to our statistics amounted before the war to about 101 rubles, had fallen to less than half that sum at the end of the civil war; and then rose again, but without reaching the pre-war level. Statistics for 1925 indicate that the revenue per capita was equivalent to about 72 rubles. The total national capital represented in industry, means of transport, agriculture, and buildings, within the present limits of the Union of Soviets, which was estimated at 54,500,000,000 rubles in 1913, now amounts after four years of reconstruction to about 36,800,000,000 rubles. That is to say, we have lost 32.7 percent.

Our system of public instruction, although well advanced in comparison to what it was under the Tsarist régime, is still far from meeting the most elementary needs of the people.

The best proof of the progress of our agriculture is the popularity of American tractors among the peasants, but it is still in a very backward stage. Our industries, railways, roads and canals need to be restored and developed. While in the United States there is said to be one automobile to every seven persons, in Russia there is one automobile to every 50,000. Our task is to bring Russia up to the level of a modern state, and to divert men or money from this to other ends would be criminal.

Although we have tremendously extensive frontiers to guard, we have reduced our army to 560,000 men, about one-half of the army maintained under the old régime; and we are prepared to make further reductions, for the 600,000,000 rubles that we spend on our army— more than one-sixth of our revenues—could be employed better in works immediately necessary to our people. So we regret that the intransigence of Switzerland has prevented us from taking part in the conference on disarmament.

The desire of the Soviet Government to avoid entanglements of all sorts should explain our refusal to enter the League of Nations and our antagonism to collective agreements lacking a definite purpose and to the system of alliances, to which we have opposed specific agreements such as we have concluded with Turkey and Germany and are concluding with other neighbors. If we were in the League of Nations, the necessity of taking positions on questions before it for settlement would compel us to choose between one or another political group, so that we should be continually involved in conflicts which we do not desire. Still less do we wish alliances which would involve our people in unknown issues. Even alliances formed for defense tend always to war. The example of the Triple Alliance and the Entente affords a lesson which we cannot forget.

What seems to us advisable, and what we have done, is to conclude with every possible nation accords carrying the obligations, first, to maintain neutrality in case one or the other party is attacked, and second, not to enter into political or financial or other combinations directed against either party. The advantage of these accords consists in their purely defensive nature and in the fact that nothing prevents their being concluded with all states without exception. The same obligations we have accepted towards Turkey and Germany we can accept toward all the other Powers.

I have said already that we are negotiating for similar agreements with our other neighbors. We have made proposals to all of them except Rumania, about which I shall speak further on. We believe that these proposals ultimately will be accepted. Our neighbors, including Poland, have an interest in according us reciprocal guarantees of peace, for economic as well as political reasons. Esthonia and Latvia cannot take advantage of their situation as maritime states except as the increasing exports of the Union of Soviets continue to pass by way of their railways and ports. The same may be said of Poland. Industry in Poland has been developed, thanks to the huge market of the former Russian Empire; and it is in Russia, rather than in the more developed countries to the west, that Poland will have to find an outlet for her production.

I have set apart the case of Rumania. There remains a cause of division between us and Rumania, which prevents the conclusion of the same sort of accord that we are discussing with our other neighbors. The circumstances in which Rumania annexed Bessarabia are well known. Russia, it also is well known, never was consulted regarding the fate of her former province. In March, 1918, the Premier of the Rumanian Government, General Averescu, who now is in power again, signed a treaty with the present writer, as representative of the Soviet Government, obligating Rumania to evacuate Bessarabia in two months. Taking advantage later of the fact that the Germans had occupied part of our territory, and of German support since at the time Gen. Mackensen was occupying Rumania, and also of the irresolution of the Allies in seeking to bolster up their coalition by conceding Bessarabia to Rumania, the Rumanians proclaimed themselves the masters of Bessarabia. We remember that the United States never recognized this act of violence.

The policy of the Soviet Government concerning the Bessarabian question is not to claim that Bessarabia should belong to the Union of Soviets, although this former Turkish province had only 200,000 inhabitants at the time when Russia conquered it and had 3,000,000 inhabitants at the time when it was annexed by Rumania, to whom it never had belonged. But we demanded at the Vienna Conference between Rumania and ourselves in 1924, and we are justified in demanding, that the population of Bessarabia itself be consulted. Rumania rejected a plebiscite. The people of Bessarabia, who were on the side of the Allies, are refused the rights which the Allies accorded to Germany in the question of Upper Silesia. Of course, a plebiscite should be conducted under conditions guaranteeing its genuineness. The Rumanian army and officials should leave Bessarabia.

Our policy in Asia finds its inspiration in the Constitution of the Union of Soviets, which we regard as a model of political equality between different races. It even goes so far as to admit the right of nations entering into the Union to leave it of their own free will without securing the consent of other members of the Union. And we do not apply our logic to ourselves alone; we act in the interest of conserving our institutions by applying in our policy in Asia this principle of "self-determination"—an American principle, by the way, transported to Europe by the Frenchmen who took part in the American War of Independence.

Relations between the United States and the Union of Soviets unfortunately have not been established. I do not believe that the question of the debts—granting the good will that our Government has evidenced to facilitate a solution within the limits of equity—could constitute a serious difficulty. I rather attribute the anomaly to the fact that the ocean separates the United States from us and that the United States has not yet fully realized the political and economic importance of the Union of Soviets. And I am not speaking solely from the point of view of direct commercial relations between our two countries, but also of the rôle that Russia may play in commercial relations with countries of Europe and Asia which enjoy financial and commercial contact with the United States.

I know that what is called "propaganda" often is cited as an argument against the reëstablishment of normal relations. But the Soviet Government should not be confused with the Third International. We cannot believe that America will maintain towards us a policy less liberal than the Russian Tsardom adopted during a long period towards the United States despite the fact that it was identified with the republican idea which Tsardom abhorred. Relations between peoples and states should be based, not on social theory, but on mutuality of political and economic interests.

In a wild lurch of the political dialectic, the relatively well-fed and relaxed Russia of NEP was pitched almost overnight, with inadequate preparation and in the midst of bitter struggles for control over the dictatorial party, into a headlong scramble to become a leading industrial power. By 1930 the slogan "overtake and surpass America" blared from every Soviet radio, as it does today. The most abundant resource Stalin had then was the ruling apparatus of the Party, buttressed by his personal supremacy and by a powerful secret police.

The Western world was slow to grasp the scope and thrust of Stalin's "great leap forward." People assumed generally that the Bolsheviks had already tried out their utopian theories in the period of War Communism, 1918-21, had found them unworkable, and had then settled down to make the best of a rather ramshackle compromise between doctrinaire statism and the "realities" of small-scale capitalist agriculture, trade and manufacturing. Widespread illusions of the "inevitability" of capitalism, even under the rule of a Communist Party, made it difficult to understand that Stalin was launching a second revolution, one that went far deeper than that of 1917.

The new revolution was designed to break up centuries-old customs and traditions of the peoples of the Soviet Union and press them into a new and untried mold. When the back-breaking victory was won, tens of millions of untrained peasants had been moved into factories and construction camps and the rest of the villagers had been regimented into collective farms. Other uncounted millions had been rounded up by the secret police to cut timber and build canals. Literature, science and cultural life had been painfully cramped to a new orthodoxy. With the struggle for Lenin's succession settled, the ruling Party was purged of the reluctant and recalcitrant, and its ranks replenished with new recruits attuned to the new era.

One of the most acute observers of the impending political and social earthquake was Paul Scheffer, Moscow correspondent of the *Berliner Tageblatt*. "The Crisis of the 'N.E.P.'" (January 1929) stands out as a penetrating analysis of the heavy-handed shifting of gears with which Stalin launched the Soviet Union on the first of a succession of Five-Year Plans. Mr. Scheffer presented a more detailed picture of the emerging Stalinist system, and the struggles from which it sprang, in his book "Seven Years in Soviet Russia" (1932; German original, 1930).

THE CRISIS OF THE "N. E. P." IN SOVIET RUSSIA

By Paul Scheffer

THE crossroads at which the economic policy of the Soviets stands today—and with it their general policy—was reached by wholly logical stages. When in 1921 Lenin abandoned "pure Communism," reversed his system of taxation, and decreed the "New Economic Policy" or "N. E. P."—that is, decided to support the socialization of the Soviet economic system by permitting individualistic and capitalistic business methods—his program assumed the correctness of a hypothesis that had never been tested. It assumed that two economic systems which in theory are hopelessly divided would in practice prove entirely compatible. Lenin's idea was that while wider and wider economic fields were methodically being brought under the sway of economic socialization, individual business should continue to fulfill such functions as socialization was not yet able to take over. This implied that socialization should extend its field of operations only when it felt itself capable of duplicating the accomplishments of private business. From the very beginning Lenin vigorously insisted on reserving for socialization the celebrated "controlling economic heights" of business, that is, industry and foreign trade. These, primarily, constituted the "socialized sector" of the economic structure. At the same time, in domestic trade Lenin created "starting points" of socialization, through state wholesale organizations; and in agriculture through the Soviet landed estates. He believed that in this way he had at the outset assured the dominance of the Bolshevik idea; and to that extent he was quite correct in advocating his N. E. P.

In 1921 private trading was permitted side by side with state retailing, and, in spite of the knowledge that the processes of distribution were sooner or later to be socialistically organized, private traders sprang up and even flourished under the wing of a bureaucracy which alternately blew hot and cold, fluctuating between grudging acquies-

cence to interfering regulation. Gradually the impediments were multiplied, and by the spring of 1924 more than 300,000 private firms
had been wiped out of existence either by taxes or by discrimination
in the credit furnished by the state banks or in the supplies obtainable
only from the state factories. Still it was found that these shackles
and limitations were not adequate enough to keep private enterprise
within bounds; harassed though it was at every turn, private enterprise continued to thrive, and so in 1927 the Soviets launched a policy
of wholesale and direct repression of both private trading and independent farming. By winter time the rigor of governmental action had
brought on a peasants' boycott, which the Government finally succeeded
in breaking by "extraordinary" measures of forcible seizure, since replaced by the present policy of systematically repressing the "kulaks"
—peasants who are relatively well off.

The Kremlin frankly saw in the success attendant on private trading
and independent farming a vital threat to the "socialistic sector" of
the Soviet economic system, both present and future. The Kremlin was
afraid of becoming hopelessly dependent upon these two forces if it
tolerated them any longer, even in their hitherto limited spheres. It
believed, and rightly, that through them not only its economic position,
but its political position as well, was threatened; and, considering its
peculiar situation, it had some justification for making no fundamental
distinction between these two interests.

In 1924 the state trading organization and the coöperatives dependent upon it were expanded into a single gigantic whole. This
process was begun at the same time that the harassing treatment of
private trading was intensified. In 1927 the collective rural agencies
of every kind were increased, at a rate corresponding to the rate at
which the unwanted independent rural organizations were annihilated.
Oppressive taxation and delivery delays worked toward the same end.
Both courses of action meant a bold advance in the policy of socialization.

Are not the most cherished hopes of Leninism being fulfilled, then,
much more rapidly than seemed possible a few years ago? Yet does it
not also seem as if the Soviet State's sheer struggle for existence were
compelling it to do the very thing which it originally proposed to do
solely of its own free will and from ideal motives? For the extension
of socialization is now being brought about much more rapidly than
Lenin foresaw, but in very different circumstances. He believed that as

the commercial methods of private business came into competition with the economic methods of socialism, they would die a natural death. The same hope has deluded his successors; the candidate for an early death turned out to be exceedingly lively. But though Moscow persistently hangs on to its ideals, it nevertheless handles uncomfortably practical realities energetically. No power on earth thinks in such large terms or with such reflection and deliberation as do the gentlemen in the Kremlin. Their position makes this necessary, for the present basis of their power is a dangerous provisional arrangement, a kind of twilight zone for which there are no historical precedents and, in the main, the only rules are those that they have learned through their own experience. At any rate, two things are perfectly clear to the Soviets today. First, the applicability of the N. E. P. is far more conditional, far more dangerous, than they conceived it to be. Secondly, the possibility of fostering socialism and private enterprise side by side in the Russian economic system was grossly overestimated. The vigor with which private trade and so-called "capitalistic" farming have been disrupted indicates what troubles and difficulties the N. E. P. has caused its authors in these last seven years, and shows what effort is required if the N. E. P. is to serve the end originally intended and not the opposite.

The natural result of the repression of private enterprise is that socialization must be speeded up and enlarged to just the extent that the rôle of private initiative is cut. Furthermore, from the beginning it has been suspected, and in 1923-24 the suspicion became almost a certainty among those acquainted with the facts, that any forced increase in the rate of socialization was impossible save at a very considerable sacrifice of the general prosperity. It has always been clear that these sacrifices would certainly be made, no matter how great they might be. Nor, after the critical experiences of the first few years, was there much doubt as to which was to make the sacrifices, the socialized section or the section left free for private initiative. The idea cherished outside Soviet Russia that the N. E. P. might provide an eventual means of departure from the socialistic principles of the revolution and a means of approach to our bourgeois individualistic economy, or that the Soviet State might possibly be regarded in the rôle of a prodigal son by the executives of Western banks—this idea, though still ineradicable from many minds, either represents astounding superficiality of thought or else is simply an *idée fixe* to which the Old World clings just because it is so used to it. The determination with which the Soviet State undertook a radical alteration in the structure of Russian economics through the introduction and development of a "socialized sector," might even in the first days of the N. E. P. have carried a significant moral to outside observers. Today we know in addition that the danger which the N. E. P. represents for the socialistic state organization forces the latter further along the path toward its communistic ideal.

So far we have said less about the picture which the Soviet economic system presents today than about the measures which brought the picture into being. From the beginning the Soviet Republic laid the principal stress upon "industrialization." In the last fiscal year alone (1927-28), no less than 1,800 million rubles has been spent on industry; as early as 1925-26 the sum of 800 millions was devoted to it. Obviously the whole energy of the country was required for this gigantic effort. Prices of crops were held at the 1914 level, though the prices of industrial products meantime increased many fold. The needs of "industrialization" have absorbed more and more of the relatively slight purchasing power of the Soviet State abroad, until today they require 80 percent of it. Result: a distressing lack of ordinary goods, especially those needed by the peasants. For ten years the peasant has been skimped both by domestic industry and foreign trade. In 1927-28 Soviet industry took for its own purposes, especially for expansion, 19 percent of the 23 percent increase of production, and left only 3 or 4 percent for the open market.

The advance in socialistic industrialization seems very imposing when viewed statistically, and from the Soviet standpoint it is the central factor in judging the whole economic situation, especially domestic policy. But its indisputably great success has also a number of negative aspects which we must not disregard in forming our opinions. First, let us consider the effects on agriculture. Before the war Russia was the leading flax-producing country of the world. Today Italy is far ahead. Russia used to be unquestionably the leading barley producer. Today that, too, is no longer true. Her cotton production is still far below pre-war figures. More serious still is the fact that within the last year the Soviet Union has ceased to be considered as a wheat-exporting country. In the coming year it will even be necessary to manage the domestic supply "with great care." This year, for the first time, even the official statistics show a falling off of 1.9 percent in grain production. Here, I think, as in other fields of rural production, the otherwise reliable Soviet statistics are merely trailing after disagreeable realities. The present disquieting condition of rural economics was prepared long ago by the increasingly repressive measures against the independents.

The business of the state coöperative has increased very significantly in scope since it set to work in earnest in 1924. In itself this is certainly an extraordinary achievement. But just what significance has it when we consider the business turn-over as a whole? The statistics reveal how sharply the share of private trade—retail and especially wholesale—has fallen off. Today we may estimate that the wholesale private trade comprises perhaps 15 percent of the entire turn-over, retail trade perhaps 20 or 30 percent—but with a strong trend downward. But in view of the increasing difficulties it constantly becomes more doubtful how far socialized trade will really be able to *replace* private management. During the harvest crisis of last year, the state set as its goal the collection of about ten million tons of produce for metropolitan food supply. The assumption was that private trade, in spite of persecutions, would cover the balance of the need. That was an error. The "de-individualizing" of private trade had already been more thorough than official calculations assumed. The realization that positive socialization was not advancing to a degree corresponding with the "de-individualizing" of industry had a disquieting effect not only on agricultural trade but also on all the relationships of private with socialized trade.

As a matter of fact, there is a crisis in Moscow today both in turn-over and in retail sales. People stand in line not only to buy many of the essentials of life, but even to get electric light bulbs! It is much the same throughout the whole Soviet realm. The situation has its origin either in under-production or in under-organization of retailing—or in both. This cannot be denied. It is difficult to imagine what would happen if the great variety of commodities which business might manipulate rose suddenly in price. For several years a lack of every sort of goods suitable for consumption has been felt, and it becomes more perceptible day by day. This shows how cautious one must be in assuming that the increase in the amount of commodities and distribution of all kinds shown statistically in the "socialistic sector" in itself constitutes proof that production as a whole is rising. We are thus compelled, at least provisionally, to assume that the repressive methods used by socialization against private initiative are having the same effects in trade as in agriculture.

Why and how does socialistic industrialization play so large and at the same time so dangerous a rôle in the Soviet economic policy? The idea of industrializing the Soviet Union without any adequate help from foreign capital (which financed and owned 80 percent of Tsarist industry) at first glance seems nothing less than heroic. We must admire the ambitious scale on which it was planned and the tenacity with which the Soviet Government—and especially the Party which today exercises dictatorship—still adheres to it, despite the critical situation. But we must not forget that an important and constant consideration is the necessity of providing support for the political-economic existence of the proletarian State. Without industrialization, without "proletarianization" of the land, the Soviet State some day or other will collapse in the sea of 139,000,000 peasants. It needs an island on which it can feel itself secure. It needs a gigantic labor supply. It has had success with its industrialization. But like everything else this, too, bears the mark of the forced methods which brought it about. The matter cannot be discussed thoroughly here. Suffice it to say that there exist today within Russian industry certain definitely retrograde tendencies—due to lack of raw materials, to increasing financial difficulties (although in a strictly socialist country money does not play precisely the same rôle as among us),[1] and to psychological and technical hindrances to bourgeois direction of the large-scale industrial and commercial affairs of the nation.

It is even admitted by the Soviets that, in addition to the unfavorable state of the whole economic structure, there is a lack of resources for the further industrial development of the country, especially building material and pig-iron. We must therefore conclude that even in this field, judging by technical and economic needs, there has been too much haste in dispensing with private initiative and the services of capital. Industrial production itself, then, has failed in the great task which it has undertaken. Not only does industry provide far too few goods for trade; it does not even provide enough for its own needs. The whole industrial position leads us to put the same query that we did in the case of commerce: Is not the increase of production in the "socialized

---

[1] In 1927-28 the State industries had 30 percent less money than in 1925, despite a marked increase in production, a marked increase in the number of businesses, and a marked decrease in the purchasing power of the ruble.

sector" merely a partial substitute for the destroyed achievements of private production? This is certainly true in some of the light industries, as for instance in leather manufacture, where during the last year thousands of tanneries have closed down.

But all these separate observations may be reduced to a single, all-embracing question, which day by day causes more and more worry to the responsible authorities in Moscow: Has not the expansion of the "socialized sector" inside the general economic structure (without concurrently satisfying the Russian economy) weakened the governmental organism more than it has strengthened it? If this question is answered in the affirmative, then another question arises. Will not the reaction of the unsatisfactory general situation upon the "socialized sector" as it is today, and on its further extension, constitute an immediate danger for the final success of socialization? These questions will inevitably occur to anyone who has given impartial attention to the course of events since 1924.

Perhaps it will be well to summarize the ideas that I have attempted to set forth in highly concentrated form. 1. The incompatibility between the socialistic and private forms of economics is greater than was anticipated when the N. E. P. was introduced. 2. Any adjustment of such friction as arises must be at the expense of private business. 3. The compulsion to socialization has thus overshadowed the will to socialization in practical politics. 4. Socialization has been unable adequately to replace private initiative as the latter has shrunk or disappeared. 5. The result is that the general economic condition becomes worse instead of improving. 6. Through the collapse of private business, socialization has continuously increased its importance in the Soviet economic system. 7. Nevertheless its rival's collapse has brought socialization to a crisis.

The American reader may perhaps suppose this to be abstract academic reasoning, culled from some economic textbook. But it is not just an ingeniously constructed theory. What I have described is a phenomenon involving the very real fate of very real Russians on Russian soil, 150,000,000 living beings—every living person in Russia, as far as Yakutsk, near the earth's cold pole—for the Soviet administration extends its drastic will with extraordinary unity over the whole of its immense empire. The terminology that one must employ in describing its activity, which is guided by ideas quite other than those which we have come to know in our Occidental life, sounds strange, abstruse.

But were this globe of ours completely occupied by socialistic states, then if some revolution suddenly injected among them a state devoted to private business, this phenomenon would not appear any more strange in their eyes. It is the fatal—and highly un-Socratic—method of many students of contemporary Russia either to recognize only such things as are already familiar or else to force into the scheme of the familiar a variety of things that do not belong there at all.

The fact that one must go to so much effort to comprehend what is going on in any phase of present-day life in Russia shows at least how deeply the socialism of the Bolsheviks has already penetrated into reality. It has of course entailed all sorts of tremendous sacrifices. These have not lessened, nor will they lessen. Indeed, as we have seen, socialism has been its own sacrifice. Today if it is to survive it *must* do what originally it wanted to do of its own free will. *"Beim ersten seid Ihr frei, beim zweiten seid Ihr Knechte."* The primal demands of self-preservation compel it, force it, to become a wholesaler, as well as to make a "rural proletarian" out of the peasant as fast as possible.

It would be a tremendous task to expand the foregoing observations and to show how it is primarily the logic of its own existence that is driving the socialistic State to achieve social goals by economic means and yet to try to win a political position by economic sacrifices. The same crisis that we have here tried to describe (while scrupulously omitting mention of all the other influences that affect the purely economic N. E. P.) exist also in the cultural, political, and even the diplomatic N. E. P. In each case one can see how Soviet socialism has been compelled by the inexorable force of circumstances to accentuate its position, or, to use a current word, to "radicalize." Only the rigidly theoretical training of the Bolsheviks makes it possible for them to keep their bearings amid the turmoil.

Part II

THE STALINIST REVOLUTION

1929-1945

PROBABLY no great and complex system has been shaped so intimately in its goals, its ideology and power, and its methods of rule as was the Soviet system by the personal decisions of Lenin and Stalin. Indeed, the denunciations of Stalin by his successor show how difficult it is to separate his achievements from his "crimes." They also make it clear that the dictator felt secure only when he was taking one rapid decision after another, with or without an adequate basis for them. *Shturmovshchina,* or administration by "storming" each new obstacle, seems to be an older Russian as well as a typically Soviet habit. Its good and bad effects have been greatly magnified by the pervading emphasis on militant slogans: "the revolutionary warrior," "the citadel of world revolution," "the final offensive," and so forth.

How far did Stalin use ideological dogmas to destroy his rivals and remove obstacles to achieving and consolidating his power? To what extent did he seek and exercise absolute power in order to achieve ideological purposes? This question plagued his contemporaries of the 1920s, and it puzzles historians of today. And the range of answers to it, then and now, has been a wide one. In his climb to power, indeed throughout his long years of absolute rule, Stalin had little direct or frequent contact with foreigners, except with a few foreign Communists. The "mystery" of Stalin became a fascinating theme of Soviet studies, and the search for the answer has made or broken many reputations. Who was Stalin? How had he become master of the Soviet regime? What did he intend to do with his vast power? These questions were, by 1930, both elusive and urgent.

One contemporary answer was given by Paul Scheffer, for seven years a correspondent in Moscow. An unusual sensitivity to the nuances of Soviet thinking and realities, a long immersion in the Soviet scene, personal friendships with many participants in the struggle for and against the new dictator, gave special weight to his interpretations of Soviet politics. "Stalin's Power" (July 1930) is, even in retrospect, a remarkably searching account of the nature of the new dictator, his rise to power, and the road over which he proposed to lead or drive his people.

66

STALIN'S POWER

By Paul Scheffer

THE official handbooks of the Soviets do not give Stalin's family name or the date of his birth. He was born in the year 1879, and is supposed to have come from a peasant family. Between 1892 and 1898 he attended a seminary for priests at Tiflis, whence, as the official "Communist's Calendar" states, he was expelled. Thereafter Stalin's life revolved within the monotonous triangle of secret revolutionary conspiracies, banishments and flights. This was the case with many other Russians, for Russia has always been a great producer of professional revolutionists.

But Stalin's ups and downs, or rather ins and outs, were more drastic than those of the average rebel. After he had reached his nineteenth year he was sent to Siberia four times. Thrice he escaped. He was sentenced to his fourth deportation in 1913, and this time stayed in Siberia till the February Revolution. Returning to Petrograd he was advanced to the organizing committee of the Bolshevik Party. The "Calendar" makes bare mention of the fact that he fought in the field in the Civil War between 1918 and 1921. He became People's Commissar for the Control by Workers and Peasants, then People's Commissar for Nationalities, and then secretary of the party. Since 1917, he has been a member of the Politbureau. The "Calendar" says nothing of his exploit as organizer and leader of the daylight robbery on a main street in Tiflis of a money transport of the Russian Bank (the party treasury was empty after the unlucky revolution of 1905!). It says nothing of a subsequent short trip abroad—Stalin's only contact with foreign countries. It says nothing of the activities whereby he put Lenin on the defensive during the latter's last year, closed Trotsky's mouth after Lenin's death, bested his partners, Kamenev and Zinoviev, in the all-powerful triumvirate which succeeded to Lenin's inheritance, and finally dethroned the new associates with whom he replaced them—Rykov, Bukharin, Tomsky. Stalin must have known that this insignificant *cur-*

67

riculum vitæ would fall under the eyes of a million or more Communists. He certainly saw it before it was published. He may even have revised it himself. Inconspicuousness is part of his policy. Stalin may be boundlessly ruthless; he is, nevertheless, shy and shrewd.

Stalin seems to have conceived his hatreds as a young man. They were strong enough to survive his many imprisonments under the Tsars. They endure to this day. One may say that they derive from an inferiority complex. Stalin is the homely, unattractive offspring of a handsome race: a bony, over-large nose; a deeply furrowed, uncommonly low but very broad forehead; small eyes under heavy lids and bushy brows; bristly upstanding hair; strongly marked cheek-bones; formidable jaws; a correspondingly strong chin; a puny, slender, apparently underfed figure, which, to judge by the way he carries himself, must in reality be wiry and muscular. Such things play their part in history. Stalin cannot derive his poise from his physical appearance. The latter, rather, must be counted among the deeper causes which make him one of those men whose whole life evolves around a struggle for self-assertion.

On one occasion, in 1928—it was a beautiful day in springtime—a parade of Communist athletic organizations was to be held in the Red Square at Moscow. The square easily accommodates fifty thousand people. The exercises had been scheduled for half-past eleven, but in accord with army customs everybody was on hand by eleven. The boys began killing time with one of the sports young people in Russia most enjoy—"girl-tossing" (a number of young men throw a girl high in the air and catch her as she comes down). All over the square one could see bright-colored shirts, skirts and bloomers sailing skyward and falling again. Stalin was to review the parade. As usual he came late. When he appeared, neither fanfares from the bands, nor a verse of the "International," nor the warnings of messengers sent hither and thither, could put an end to the "girl-tossing." In the pea-colored raincoat which he wears even on sunny days, and with his cap pulled as usual far down over his face, Stalin stood on the balustrade of Lenin's tomb. Nobody noticed. Nobody was interested in him. An hour later "retreat" was sounded. The crowd quietly dispersed.

Stalin is not a man who appeals to the sympathies of crowds or stirs their imaginations. He is not an electric person. Let us be more blunt: he is frankly unattractive, and all the more so since he knows he is, and shows by his demeanor that he does not care! Even his voice, a voice as hard and brittle as glass, lacks the undertones, the rhythm, that work so powerfully upon the music-loving populace of Russia. Zinoviev dazzles a crowd, but take him in his personal contacts, and the celebrated *tribunus populi* is surly, repellant. Without sharing Zinoviev's advantages in his public appearances, Stalin has his disadvantages in private contacts. He is a very impressive person, but works as man to man only by giving an impression of concentrated and unbending willfulness. You feel at once that he is "dangerous."

Shortly after the bloody conquest of Turkestan, a delegation from that country appeared in the Kremlin, and a number of Soviet notables assembled to receive the visitors. The hosts were seated around the table. Stalin came in, looked about, and began dragging up chairs, that the guests also might sit down. The trait did not exactly fit in with what people knew of him. Someone asked him why he did it. He answered: "What else, except our politeness, have we Asiatics to meet you Europeans with?" A significant remark! The seminary student from the Caucasus, the man who early in life had writhed under the contempt of European Russia, now speaks through his lips with an Asiatic's pride, with a sense of belonging to those vast regions of the Orient where conceptions of life are so much simpler and, in their forms, surer, colder, clearer than in sophisticated, spiritually distracted Europe, a Europe intellectually so pretentious, so arrogant, so sentimental, so full of fine phrases which, in most cases, deceive the people who use them.

Stalin never belonged to the brilliant group which gathered in Russia from all lands after the February Revolution and to which history has ascribed the triumph of the Revolution of October 1917. They were men who had drawn on all the resources of Western civilization as they lingered safe and snug (buried in many-sided troubles, perhaps, but also in newspapers) in the cafés of Munich, Geneva, Paris and London. That was the way they sharpened *their* weapons for the revolution! They had, to be sure, kept in close touch with the active fighters on Russian soil, and had even returned to the homeland at one time or another, such as during the Revolution of 1905. But they had not, or at least not entirely, led dangerously exposed lives as had Stalin. He saw himself as the one to whom the "dirty work" had been left. He liked to refer to himself as the "hall sweeper" of the Revolution. And now, in the hour of victory, he was being admitted to the inner councils of the leaders grudgingly if at all. The eyes of the aroused populace stubbornly looked past him to men who had the knack of holding the immense followings who came trooping to "the Cause" that year, men who knew how to make ringing speeches, mouth big ideas, rattle off fine theories—the Lenins and the Trotskys, the Zinovievs, the Radeks, and the Bukharins. For Stalin, all such were "Europeans," "émigrés." He had been the one, after the grievous failure of 1905, to keep the fires of revolution glimmering in Russia. In the first year of the new régime, he felt that they regarded him as necessary but did not take him at full value. In their eyes, he was still the "savage from the Caucasus," the man with more fist than brain, more nerve than intelligence—a fanatic. All the more keenly, therefore, did he feel the slight that was never uttered. (It is not difficult to understand that a man so inured to hardship should have very few personal needs, be indifferent to material advantages and dumb to æsthetic values.)

It is evident, now, that all along he felt that his hour would come. He had at his disposal, in a way no one else could have, an immense acquaintance with the 150 million inhabitants of Old Russia. In those swarming masses he knew just which individuals were the men to realize and sustain a proletarian revolution such as he conceived in that still barbaric country. The hypnosis of crowds and the frenzy of words of the first year, then the inspired and inspiring civil crusade against the remnants of Tsardom and its allies, must some day come to an end. It would then be a question of governing people no longer hypnotized, of using ways and means for forcing the masses together independently of such ephemeral throngs. No one knew Russia as Stalin did. No one realized as he realized what it meant to set up a single class of people, the proletariat—3 millions of human beings in a land far from being industrialized—as the only class entitled to live, the only class entitled to rule, and then to drag 135 millions of peasants along in the same direction. Stalin also knew, as no one else knew, where to find the people who could be used in such a project: people of his mind and of his hardness, who were willing to look at the world only from below up; people of his origins, with undying animosities against everything "bourgeois" and against the arrogance and pretentiousness of the "intellectuals" who now claimed they had "made the Revolution!" They were instinctively certain that such educated individuals would, knowingly or unknowingly, be bound by a thousand spiritual ties to bourgeois ideas and ways and would never quite grasp the realities of a Communist revolution in Russia.

During the Civil War no one surpassed Stalin in self-sacrifice. Watching a parade at Tsarskoe Selo during the winter of 1918, he noticed a soldier who seemed dissatisfied, and asked him what the matter was. The man pointed to a pair of worn-out straw shoes. Stalin ordered him to take them off, put them on himself, and wore them all that winter. Trotsky devotes a brilliant chapter in his "Memoirs" to the railroad train in which he hurried from one dangerous point to another along the front over a year's time. Stalin never attained any such position of command. He has never forgiven Trotsky for that train, nor has he forgiven him for the wild enthusiasms he aroused in the Russian throngs by his speeches in Petrograd in the summer of 1917, calling for revolutionary action. It is characteristic of Stalin that he spent most of the period of the Civil War in the provinces, establishing himself with a few friends on the lower Volga, where they did very much as they pleased and were finally coaxed out by the people in the Kremlin —but only with the greatest difficulty—Trotsky acting as intermediary.

Stalin's special significance, which the other leaders could never refuse to recognize, lay, even during the first years, in his close contacts with the second, third, fourth and lowest ranks in the Bolshevik Party. While momentous political issues were being talked out in Moscow, the cohesion of the party rested largely on its "power on the spot," as the phrase went; in other words, on autonomous domination by the party's local representatives in each of the cities, large or small, of the vast territory of Russia. (Such, for that matter, is the situation today.) On the filling of these different posts, as well as on the ideas and conduct of the men who held them, Stalin came to have an enormous influence, even in Lenin's lifetime, as secretary of the party. He was by no means the only one who gave orders; but he did manage to organize among the local party chiefs a "guard" of "tough customers" whose ruthlessness in the exercise of their power could be taken for granted. They were not the people whom Trotsky, Lenin and Zinoviev were inclined to favor. They were men like Stalin—"non-intellectuals," "non-Europeans."

Some four months before his death, Lenin broke with Stalin. It is established that thereafter Lenin refused to have any further personal contacts with him, and stuck to that decision to the end. The idol of the Revolution was lying sick in a luxurious manor-house near Moscow. The letters he wrote to Trotsky and to the Central Committee of the party in regard to Stalin's rôle in party politics betray the utmost irritation at what the Caucasian had been doing. Lenin's intermediary, in the fight he made from his deathbed, was Trotsky.

No one, of course, can claim to have fully uncovered the secrets of Lenin's relations to Stalin. That Lenin feared for the party, for the state, for his whole achievement, there is not the slightest doubt. Max Eastman has reported a few characteristic details of the struggle Lenin had to wage against the "Moscow clique" in the party in order, for example, that his article on the fusion of the Soviet Control by Workers and Peasants with the powerful Central Committee might be even published. At that time Lenin refers to the existence of a "bureaucracy within the party" and expresses a determination that it shall not become all-powerful; this was one of the causes of the proposal of fusion. He was unmistakably alluding to Stalin.

Undoubtedly this was the ignition point of all the later conflict with Trotsky. By the phrase "party bureaucracy" Lenin meant to convey, with caution as to possible effects on the public and on the party at large, that a "ring" of party officials was forming within the party, that it it had worked upward from deep down, that it was already making its influence felt in the Central Committee, in the Secretariat, in the Politbureau—and "on the spot" held the party agents and committees in the hollow of its hand. The ring in question seemed to Lenin and his intimates likely to eclipse the spontaneous coöperation of the whole party in the realization of Bolshevik ideals. And this, in the eyes of Lenin, was actually being done in an underhanded manner quite incompatible with Communist comradeship. It is an utterly unhistorical idea that Lenin ever ruled over his party with fatherly omnipotence. From the beginning to the very end he was called upon to fight vigorous battles on many subjects, battles in which blows were struck straight from the shoulder. Many a time Lenin knocked his opponents "cold"; but he seldom dropped them.

With Stalin he acted differently.

What worried Lenin in Stalin's case was the latter's secret, slinking, anonymous expansion of his personal power in the party and his preference for the backstairs to more conspicuous routes. The tactics which Stalin was later to use with such success against Trotsky, first to silence him and then to reduce him to complete helplessness, he used against Lenin, the moment the latter fell sick. This enraged Lenin. It is an interesting fact that Kubischev (the present chairman of the Supreme Economic Council), already Stalin's man at any decisive moment, was in a position to suggest that the article by Lenin which was in dispute should be laid before him in a single copy of the *Pravda* to be printed for his personal benefit! This sort of person from Stalin's following was already in evidence in the high councils of the party. It is an unanswerable, though far from idle question whether Stalin might not have succeeded in unseating Lenin, if Lenin had remained in the fullness of his powers. It must be recognized as at least possible. The tactics which enabled him to triumph over all rivals he was already turning against Lenin with success, in spite of the latter's immense popularity. Nobody, nothing, has so far been able to resist him— no prestige, no merit, no reputation.

When Lenin died, Trotsky's fate, as we may easily see after the fact, was already sealed. Trotsky was the most significant, the most influential, among the men whom the world at large regarded as masters at the Kremlin. Nothing better illustrates the antithesis between the two groups than the opposition which soon after Lenin's death (as Eastman relates) Trotsky set up to an order of Stalin's that all members of the party should be in duty bound to report all "intrigues directed against the party" which appeared in their groups or classifications. The order was in effect a death blow to the free play of opinion, indeed to any exchange of opinions, on the part of individuals within the party—a death blow to the spontaneous development of policies within party ranks. It was also a death blow to Trotsky's personal position, which, like Lenin's, had rested on his personal popularity and on the confidence which not only the party but widely scattered elements in the population, even a part of the bourgeoisie, reposed in him. Trotsky adopted Lenin's phrase "party bureaucracy" and balanced it with one of his own, "party democracy." The latter too, in Stalin's eyes, was just another "European" and "liberal" idea. It connoted belief in a free *consensus omnium* arising from a competition of opinions.

His answer was to consolidate the rigid system of party officials he had long been quietly perfecting, a system resting on the local agents who wielded power "on the spot," but with its peak entering the party secretariat. The latter was composed of five secretaries; one of them was Lenin (the leader until his death), another was Stalin. Stalin now made himself General Secretary (a title not existing until he brought it into use), with complete control over the routine of organization. Was he not the best-informed on all local questions, all questions of personnel? He spun his threads. The belief that the cohesion and strength of the party was guaranteed by common convictions lay very far from his mind. Everything he had ever done bespoke contempt for any such thing. He used men who had an active understanding of absolute power and possessed the means of using force with which alone, as he knew, absolute power may be sustained in a hostile and not very responsive environment. He used these means no less readily against followers of his own, bearing heavily upon any form of resistance, even verbal; but leaving officials far-reaching freedom of action in all matters (especially personal matters) which did not seem directly to concern the interests of the Bolshevik régime.

People on the outside long regarded the fight on Trotsky as the work of the "triumvirate": Kamenev, Zinoviev and Stalin. Kamenev was Trotsky's brother-in-law. He and Zinoviev had been close comrades of Lenin. That distracted attention from the fact that Stalin was pulling the wires. But how was it possible that the Central Committee of the party, which with the Council of People's Commissars had been in Lenin's time the decisive factor in guiding the party, could in any sense share or tolerate a baiting of Trotsky which—another impossibility—had been carried on for years within the very innermost circle of the party? Lenin's "Testament"—that great document in which carefully, judiciously, and with great self-control he reviews the capacities of his associates—contains two scathing words on Stalin: "Stalin is crude and narrow-minded." (Both words are there, not just "narrow-minded" as more often quoted.) Lenin said very positively that through these outstanding traits of character Stalin would ruin the party if ever he attained to leadership. In the past six years, by utilizing the very qualities for which Lenin coined his adjectives, Stalin has ascended to greater and greater power, and with him, if you like, the party. History has yet to judge whether Lenin was right.

In the Central Committee of the party Stalin found plenty of people available for the purposes of his tactics, people who had risen from the dark depths of revolutionary activity and whose intellectual horizons were as different from those of the "Europeans" as his own. He had worked tirelessly among them ever since 1917, while the "Europeans" held the spotlight. He worked with astounding shrewdness and foresight, with a keen instinct for the tempo at which his aims could mature. There was a group of "old Bolsheviks" (a discovery, it would seem, of Stalin himself), made up mostly of revolutionists who had passed their lives in agitation at home, and not in ease abroad. They were loyal to the Lenin group for the most part, but they were far removed, in the whole circle of their experience, from the sophisticated, cultivated intellectuals at the head of the government and were always full of honest anxiety lest the Revolution "go bourgeois." Their personal connections, like Stalin's, led toward the country, where Stalin had—and has—his "guard." The heirs of Lenin knew that they had to reckon with these gruff and bluff forces; but they thought they could easily do so, relying on the magic they had always used. But Stalin had come to the top precisely because he understood the organization of power from the bottom up better than anybody else.

"Old Bolsheviks," men of 1905 and earlier, had found their way into the Central Committee in great numbers. Stalin influenced them directly and indirectly. He played them against the lower orders of the active party membership, and the latter, to a much greater extent, against them. This net, woven strand by strand, artfully, with tireless energy, with brutal threats against the wavering and with well-calculated thrusts at Trotsky and Trotsky's followers, was the "party democracy" which Stalin aimed at. While he was quietly making these manœuvres, he was hacking in a thousand different ways at the tender roots of the "European." Fickle, jealous, and ambitious Kamenev and Zinoviev, whose nerves were not made of iron, he turned with great subtlety against Trotsky and toward himself. He reminded them that the European varnish on the party was very thin—that they had to look out for their own hides.

Meantime public opinion was worked as vigorously as possible. A short time after Lenin's letter became known (Stalin resisted its reading before the Central Committee as long as he could) there appeared in hundreds of thousands of copies, distributed all over Russia, a colored print which showed Lenin and Stalin sitting comfortable and smiling side by side on a bench in a garden. Stalin's dead enemy had become a friend! Lenin's apotheosis was launched the day of his death—just to keep Trotsky out of the public eye. No one worked for it more zealously than Stalin. No one sought more assiduously for the immediate falsifying of the version which the public, and even the party, would receive of Lenin's relationship to Trotsky and the latter's group.

When, next, he succeeded in preventing discussions and rectifications before the country and the rank and file of the party the battle was won. By that time Stalin had solidly established (in the minds of many people of good faith) his opinion that governing is the affair of those who govern, and of nobody else—a strictly "Asiatic" conception. He had already drawn all power from the circumference to the centre of the party. Observers of Soviet politics must have remarked with astonishment that Trotsky had to close his mouth. The Kremlin was with Stalin. That Trotsky was a poor politician, everybody, his friends and his enemies alike, are now agreed. When his newspaper articles began to be refused or censored he had the unlucky thought of exposing the Triumvirate in a history of October 1917. The book reached only an insignificant portion of the public when it appeared in the autumn of 1924. By its publication Trotsky, the would-be man of strenuous action, showed that he was at bottom a "literary fellow," full of superstitions as to the power of the word and of logic. Had not Stalin been right in his judgment of the "European"? Stalin had already so consolidated his position that neither anything Lenin may have said of him, nor any little episodes away back in 1917, could drag him from the saddle. He knew much better than Trotsky how the piles are driven to support a permanent edifice of power.

The history of the Bolshevik Party in Russia after Lenin's death (and, in many respects, even before) may be read today only with numerous lacunæ, which may never be filled. But looking back over these past years, one can remark only with astonishment how every one of Lenin's close associates, and later of Stalin's own associates, was shortly treated as a rival and a climber. Toward the end of 1925 he had driven Kamenev and Zinoviev from high position to secondary prominence; the competent and brilliant Sokolnikov had fallen even earlier. Kamenev and Zinoviev, with Trotsky, had been Lenin's closest comrades, and the former were Stalin's helpers against Trotsky after Lenin's death. Bukharin and Rykov came forward in 1926. Combining with these, Stalin drove the others, along with Trotsky and his followers (among them Radek, who had twice sacrificed himself for Stalin), first out of the party and then (in January 1928, four years after Lenin's death) definitely into exile. In the autumn of 1929, twenty-one months later, came the turn of Rykov and Bukharin and many other high dignitaries who had joined forces with Stalin against Trotsky. Toward the end of 1929 Stalin forced Bukharin and Rykov (who succeeded Lenin as President of the Council of People's Commissars) publicly to declare that they would no longer stray from "the general policies of the party" or lend their aid "to any further errors." There is something worse than banishment!

If anything shows the road which the spirit of the Bolshevik Party has traveled since Lenin's death, it is surely this declaration. Never for an instant would Lenin have thought of allowing such a degrading note-in-blank to be made in his name on the convictions of a political antagonist who was a comrade in his party. At that moment Stalin's strategy attained its highest triumph. From that point his star has been declining.

The foregoing survey would not reflect the facts, unless these were defined somewhat more precisely. Stalin got control of power in the state by withdrawing all important decisions and debates in the party from public view, and even from the view of the party at large. He shrouded the Kremlin in a thicker and thicker cloud of secrecy. Anyone who tried to work toward the outside or sought support in the majority sentiments of the party (to say nothing of publicity among the Soviets) was immediately and successfully dealt with as a traitor. Stalin had thoroughly convinced the Central Committee that the exclusion of the public from all controversies was the fundamental principle of self-preservation. By cutting off the danger of interference "from outside" Stalin was able to make use of the forces he held at his disposal inside his close and stuffy inner circle. Nobody had such a well-knit organization of henchmen to depend on. His opponents could rely on little more than the feelings and sympathies of people "outside." These for the most part they surely possessed; but by narrowing their contacts with such forces, Stalin progressively deprived them of their points of support.

Furthermore, it is important to observe that, in his war on Trotsky, Stalin did not proceed in such a way as to kill the man politically. He merely paralyzed him. Trotsky was already helpless in 1924. The end did not come till four years later. In the same way Kamenev and Zinoviev (an idol of the masses), all those individuals whose portraits were to be seen everywhere, who had had no end of buildings and institutions named after them, who received thunderous applause in public meetings even a day or two before their fall, were quietly paralyzed as a prelude to being eliminated. Only when sufficient poison had been administered in increasing doses in a thousand, ten thousand, party meetings, in pamphlets, and in resolutions from all over Russia, were they removed. Stalin never saw himself as replacing them with his own figure. He was all the more anxious, therefore, that they should disappear. He was resolved to be the darkest spot in the darkness at the

Kremlin! The imponderables of popular administration and party devotion he valued highly as political assets of his antagonists, however
much he may have despised affections which he could never hope to enjoy himself. But he was convinced that he could let mere popularities
gradually fade away, be slowly strangled, by his own methods. Then
would come the time to upset so many living corpses. He attacked his
opponents or rivals on the ebbing tide of their reputations and always
used the weaker against the stronger: first Trotsky, then Radek, and
then Zinoviev, Kamenev and the dashing Sokolnikov.

The finish was not altogether easy. When he had herded all the
people he thought dangerous together and saw that the opposition was
struggling desperately in its death agony, he drew back for his blow in
the open.

It was in July 1927 that for the first time he asked for their expulsion from the party. The blow missed. His motion was defeated.
However much Trotsky and former opponents of Trotsky's who had
joined him with gnashing of teeth may have lost prestige before the
Central Committee of the party, the Committee thought that to expel
them would be going a bit too far.

The story of how, unobserved by the world at large and by Soviet
Russia itself, this crisis was solved, is very instructive. Stalin's request
for the expulsion of Trotsky and Trotsky's friends for the first time
fully betrayed his power, his ruthlessness, his hatred for the men who
had stood godfather to the Revolution. For the first time all members of
the Central Committee could clearly see how far they had allowed
themselves to be carried and just where they had arrived. Even Stalin's
immediate henchmen must have wondered whether the shock would
not prove too great for the party, the country, the world.

Just before the meeting of the full Committee, Stalin had been in the
Caucasus. On his return he found keen opposition and determined faces.
Immediately he changed his tactics, as his method was. He got out of his
hole by introducing and forcing through an almost friendly resolution on
the sins of Trotsky and his friends, provided of course with a clause of
"probation." Then he drew off again, took another "vacation"; but he
was back within a fortnight. The opposition had been lead by Uglanov.
It came from Moscow—a typical trait, for Stalin's stronghold has always been in the provinces. Uglanov and the little Bukharin (always
enthusiastic, always hypnotized by someone) now had to betake themselves to Achilles in his tent. Since Stalin's defeat and "vacation," seri-

ous confusion and disorganization had arisen in the party. The effort to establish power on a broader basis, in the Politbureau and in the Central Committee, was not enjoying a very encouraging success. The incident showed what the party would be without Stalin. Not a few people had regarded Uglanov as the coming man. Those few days were the end of him. In December the expulsion of the Opposition of the Left ensued without any difficulties.

In this case too, at a time when Stalin had reached the summit of his power, he followed his old tactics. We see him avoid letting his conflict with the party come to a head, yield apparently, gather his forces, again lead them forward and—win!

In spite of all his successes, Stalin could not possibly have been cherishing any illusions as to the extent and intensity of his personal unpopularity, as to the general and growing doubt of his right to impose his will on everybody, and, above all, as to the soundness of his practical policy, a corollary to his fundamental conviction that the economic welfare of the country must be subordinated to the exigencies of power (which is shown most clearly by his agricultural policy). This man who strides restlessly back and forth in his office as he listens to his visitors (who usually come all-atremble into his presence), seldom looks at them, and then only to glare with fierce disdain—this man who derides anyone who incurs his displeasure with unprintable epithets—cannot count on sympathies. It is said that at the Politbureau of the party he always tries to speak last, avoids expressing any view of his own till he has fully grasped the tactical situation, and often gives the other fellow the impression that he agrees with him only to attack him from the rear later. Slow-moving, cautious, he more and more came to play against the men who were powerful at a given moment the men who felt they were being overshadowed by them. His choice of persons for such purposes was extraordinarily happy. It was not merely that he replaced the important Jews and Russians whom Lenin used with many Caucasians. He managed, by a process of systematic selection during these years, to develop all over the country petty bosses of a special type, individuals of his naturally quick intelligence and, like him, of ruthless self-assertion untempered by any influence of culture, men destined either to ruin Soviet Russia or else some day to give the capitalist world a real nightmare.

Let us push this characterization of his policy a little further. While progessively restricting the circle of individuals who participated in power at the top, he progressively transformed the whole public organization of the Soviet Union into the executive of the party and made the party itself the instrument of the few on top. The Politbureau, the highest executive body in the party, he made the supreme source of power as against the Council of People's Commissars and the Central Committee. The G. P. U. had already packed these bodies with their henchmen. He did the same. He brought now this, now that, Commissariat under his personal influence: in 1928, the Commissariat on Agriculture, whose personnel, partly taken over from the Tsar's régime, had hitherto been regarded as the most "conservative"; and, in 1929 the Foreign Commissariat, as shown by the incidents with Germany, the straining of relations with Great Britain, and the form of the reply to the American Government on intervention in Manchuria. Despite the fact that, since 1921, Stalin has not held any official post, he has been busy not only personally deciding, but during the last two years personally reviewing and supervising—in addition to many other things —the whole Five Year Plan; and he has had entire personal charge of the problem of collectivization. In these connections he has so managed that all important questions are considered concurrently by the party secretariat and the public departments. In 1930 he saw fit to propose that the Central Committee should be divided into sections corresponding to the various Soviet departments. He has a private code for communicating with his subordinates in the Soviet delegations. All nominations to posts of any importance pass through the Politbureau. These are all developments which Lenin sought to avoid.

Certainly Lenin would have objected strongly to the measures taken by Stalin against the trade unions in order to render them wholly dependent on the will of the party. The trade unions had been a serious rival to the party in influencing the general trend of the economic policy and they had procured special material privileges for their members. During the past two years they have been reduced to purely technical institutions, and by the same methods which Stalin used elsewhere. Their leader, uncontestably, was Tomsky. After a terrible scene in December 1928 (the explanation of which here would take us too far afield) Tomsky's fate was sealed. Nothing is more indicative of the balance of forces in Russia than the fact that his removal from office was not made public, that it took place illegally by the decision of a small group, and that many unions did not learn of it until several weeks after it had occurred.

And the party itself? As early as 1924, Trotsky tried to prevent Stalin from naming party secretaries. By the beginning of 1928 that had actually become an official arrangement. During the same year complicated proclamations were published. In connection with the question as to just how far, in view of the supremacy of the party, it was in point to speak of a "dictatorship of the proletariat," Stalin put forward the formula that the party dictated in the name of the proletariat. But there is a dictatorship over the party also—the dictatorship of the party secretaries, to whom Stalin in turn dictates. The formula of "party discipline" has proved useful again and again in this connection. Groupings and mass organizations are not tolerated. The union of the "old Bolsheviks," for example, has become meaningless. Stalin has driven its members, for the greater part, into Trotsky's camp.

All this has been taking place, it is true, under a zodiacal sign of self-hypnosis on the part of individual party members, under the sign of the "collective will" of the party, which speaks at all times, that no one else may have a chance to speak. But it has also been taking place under a sharp and uninterrupted "listening-in" on party and country, an accurate calculation of what is possible and not possible, and, further, with ever-present readiness to make detours if necessary. It has been taking place under constant warfare on the concept of party democracy. Was not Stalin obliged, in 1929, in order to deal with certain stirrings in the party, to put forward the ingenious formula of "central democracy"? Nevertheless, the concept of "party discipline" as the highest duty of a member had been playing an enormous rôle— practically, as regards the general trend of the policy, the decisive rôle.

I cannot describe in detail the last stages in the process of concentrating the power of the Politbureau in Stalin's hands, but I should like to touch upon the fate of such of his allies in the war on Trotsky as sat with him on the Politbureau—Stalin's treatment, in other words, of such prominent party members (and at the same time leaders in the Government) as Rykov, Bukharin, War Commissar Voroshilov, Tomsky, and the aged Kalinin, President of the Soviet Union.

At the moment when Trotsky's Opposition of the Left was expelled, the economic situation in Russia was the chief issue, especially the falling-off in agricultural production. Either there had to be a slowing-up in the tempo of industrialization and the available facilities supplied to the peasants; or else agriculture had to be brought to forced production by some method of socialization, so that its production could be assured independently of the willingness or unwillingness of the peasants, and the process of rapid industrialization continued as designed. Stalin chose the second course. The Five Year Plan became law during that same critical year, 1929. Its application had already begun in October 1928. The world may have observed the tremendous increase in inner worries and tensions in the economic sphere into which the Soviet Union was plunged by this decision. Looking backward now, one must say that in this phase of his policy also Stalin steered to his goal by keeping the latter as carefully concealed as possible from his collaborators. The destruction of the wealthy peasants, which had begun in earnest by July 1928, was protected from any interference on the part of the elements grouped about Rykov and Bukharin, which considered such a policy disastrous. Party resolutions had spoken against it as late as June. What was going on in the country was for months kept secret from party members in the great cities.

Nevertheless, directly after Trotsky's banishment serious personal friction arose in regard to agricultural policy among those who were then comrades in power. As early as March 1928, Kalinin said to a deserving civil employee who had been tossed into the gutter for differences of opinion in the domain of statistics, and had appealed to him for help: "My dear fellow, I am not sure I shall not be on the sidewalk myself tomorrow morning!" Rykov, Kalinin, Bukharin and even the insignificant Voroshilov felt growing around them the same creepy isolation which had spelled the finish of Trotsky and so many others. All through the year 1928, as one or another tried to assert themselves, there were bitter quarrels. In the secret meetings of the Central Committee Stalin was forced to allow his opponents to have their say. He even pretended to give in to them. In the Politbureau, however, he answered with short, sharp words, or with threats now veiled, now open; and in the meantime, making full use of his organization, he forced things to the point he wished to arrive at. It is characteristic of him that, later on, in October 1928, he admitted with undisguised cynicism that unfortunately, by some mistake, 12 percent instead of 3 percent of the rural population had been treated as "kulaks"— that is to say, more or less ruined. But Frumkin, who had courageously attacked him on this point, had to go. It was perfectly apparent now to everybody that Stalin had not only built up a state within a state, but also a party within a party.

In 1929, Bukharin, desperate, and in agreement with his comrades in misfortune, wrote a letter to Kamenev, who had succeeded in getting back to Moscow from the exile into which he had been sent with Trotsky. In this highly imprudent document, Bukharin stated that the Soviet Union would be ruined by Stalin's highhandedness and his disastrous policies. He urged that Kamenev take over the leadership against Stalin in the party, the majority of which, as well as the majority of the highest Soviet councils (as Bukharin very well knew) shared his opinion of Stalin and of the consequences of his policy. This letter was "stolen" from Kamenev. The Opposition of the Right was therefore obliged precipitately to come out into the open (always within the four walls of the Kremlin, I hardly need say). A majority vote in the Politbureau that Stalin should resign was supported by a similar resolution, based on four "whereases," which carried in the Soviet Executive Committee by 16 votes to 9. About the middle of March came an answer from Stalin: he would retire! But meanwhile he had been manœuvring. He was certain at that moment that no one would dare accept his resignation. He had again eluded the grasp of his antagonists; he was again playing the bottom against the top in the party, promising, threatening, browbeating, winning. During this period he cynically went so far as to telephone Bukharin in an effort to detach him from the enemy. He used the same argument he had put forward in the summer of 1928: "You and I, compared with others, are Schimborasso [Mount Everest]." Not a very courageous man as a rule, and standing with the stronger cohorts this time. Bukharin rang off. He had come to know his sometime partner too well!

In this proposal to Bukharin, Stalin clearly suggested the actual status of power in the Soviet Union. With or without allies, Stalin is Mount Everest. He is the dictator of dictators. Only, he prefers not to look the part. He is not Mussolini. Yet he has one trait in common with Mussolini—an extraordinary suppleness and pliancy—and he demonstrates it under a more difficult test. He has acted in full cognizance of the danger that lies in the usurpation of power by a small minority over a vast majority whose interests do not coincide with those of three million (or less) factory workers. He has not taken much stock in the myth of unity between workers and peasants, however much he may have supported the notion for propaganda purposes so long as it worked. He realized, with courageous insight, the futility of Lenin's conception of the NEP. He understood, without shirking any responsibilities, that active socialism and private initiative were incompatible in the same economic area, and he acted resolutely on the perception that the only salvation for the Soviet power lay in the ruthless socialization of the entire country, irrespective of the immediate consequences. These became very evident at once through the crisis in agriculture and through hunger in the towns. These consequences frightened his associates into desperate resistance (at the same time they evidently did not see fit to do without him). The fact that he reckoned with all these factors more accurately, more resolutely, with less disposition to compromise than his opponents and even than his sometime associates, has enabled him to achieve what he has achieved. His success is closely bound up with his perception of these factors. At the same time his success seems to be inseparably bound up with Lenin's characterization of him: "crude and narrow-minded."

The same factors which have operated in the past will, in the last resort, determine the future of Sovietism. Stalin's course is not yet run, nor is that of the Soviet State assured. The test will most probably come when Stalin disappears. It is not yet settled whether his policy of centralizing all decisions in a small group can be maintained. A year ago he was constrained, as I have said, to put forward the complicated formula of "centralized democracy" as exemplified in the Soviet Union. The fact is that the Union is ruled by a dictating minority which is dictated to by another minority to which a dictator dictates. These minorities are in constant change. Their only stable nucleus so far has been Stalin. The more exclusively he has become this, the greater the danger to the situation which his energy has created. For there has been a corresponding growth in the number of people whom Stalin has used and exalted, only to ostracize and deprive of their power at the first sign of independence or resistance. It may be that in the same proportion the number of people capable of assuming responsibility has decreased.

It may be that Stalin has gradually exhausted the reserves required by his tactics. Whereas formerly Stalin allowed his opponents to vanish, he no longer dares to do so. What does the top of the party look like today? Rykov and Tomsky, who have been threatened officially with expulsion from the party if they are caught in any further "deviations," have nevertheless been retained in the Politbureau, as have Kalinin and Voroshilov. The place of Bukharin has never been filled. This is the most astonishing manifestation of Stalin's tactics. Evidently he does not dare for the moment to give the party a spectacle calculated to prove that he discards everybody who has ever been anywhere near him in power. He is afraid of another and greater test of strength, of the danger which might reside in the appearance of new and not yet discredited people in the Politbureau, whose unworthiness he would soon be called upon to demonstrate to the Central Committee, the party, and the Soviets. He prefers to be surrounded by persons so weakened in their political prestige that he can hold them down without too great difficulty, even when inside the party distrust and suspicion of the wisdom of his policy grows apace. As a matter of fact, Stalin has created a vacuum between himself and the party at large. He has reduced the Politbureau very much to a farce. Of its eight members four are altogether in his hands. Three are dependent on him. He holds the Politbureau and the Central Committee of the party as in a pair of tongs, between himself and the rank and file of the "active" portion of the party—the party bureaucracy. The majority of the party as a whole is against him, or at least has become very critical. His precipitate retreat from forced socialization of the Russian peasants has added to the doubts which already existed. But there is no substitute for Stalin! Nobody would fit into the armor he has forged for himself during recent years.

But this personal security of Stalin's hides, implicitly, a very serious question as to the permanence of his system. The whole organism of the Soviet State and of the party that controls it has been adapted to Stalin's methods. In this sense it has ceased to be self-supporting. There seems to be nobody capable of taking over his inheritance and directing the state along new lines. The men who might have done so have been eliminated from political consideration. After Stalin men will come to the front who will try to be Stalin. They will eat each other in his name and in his manner. It is characteristic that his nearest helpers, at present Molotov and Saroslavsky, are regarded as third-rate men in every respect, even by the party. The artificiality of this whole structure of power is obvious. The danger for Soviet Russia comes first of all from the top of the party—a danger of partition and decomposition; and this may happen even in Stalin's lifetime. The event depends mostly on future economic developments. Or perhaps the younger generation of Communists may hasten the end. Stalin and his ring have educated young Russia along demagogical lines—certainly they have taught them to be "crude" and "narrow-minded." These young people may demand the fulfillment of the gigantic promises of power in the country—nay, of power in Europe and in the whole world—which have been held out to them. They have been taught to believe in imminent revolution. As young people, they are terribly young and terribly eager. They are by no means certain that they could not do what older people have not dared, replace Stalin.

DURING the course of the 1920s the new Soviet régime gradually developed and refined its techniques for pursuing two distinct but simultaneous lines of policy in more or less effective tandem. One line, operated through the Moscow headquarters of the Comintern and its "sections" in many countries, sought to prepare the way for an early expansion of Communism. It strove to rally the various forces of discontent to its standard and to organize and discipline cadres of local Bolsheviks as local detachments of a unitary army of world revolution. The other line, carried on through the Narkomindel first under Georgii Chicherin and later under Maxim Litvinov, sought diplomatic recognition, economic advantages, and political alliances with anti-status-quo powers. Weimar Germany and the emerging China of the Kuomintang were the principal arenas and targets of both Comintern and Narkomindel ambitions and actions.

In part as a reflection of its self-isolation from the traditional interplay of world politics, and in part because of its suspicion of Moscow's dual-line policies, the United States was the last of the major powers to extend recognition to the Soviet Union, which it did in 1933. The strong resistance to any change in the posture of nonrecognition was fed by a deep-seated repugnance to the aims and methods of the Bolshevik régime and by a moralistic assumption that diplomatic recognition implied some form of approval. The established attitude was gradually undermined by the growing importance of Soviet trade, which was especially welcome in the years of the post-1929 depression, and by the feeling that the absence of direct relations between Russia and America was encouraging the Japanese militarists in their ambition to conquer China.

In the early 1930s the debates over recognition were carried on with a vehemence and a slap-happy wielding of any and all arguments that are hard to understand today. "The Pros and Cons of Soviet Recognition" (January 1931), by Paul D. Cravath (1861-1940), presented an informed and influential analysis of the issues. A distinguished lawyer and civic leader, Mr. Cravath had also played a major role in organizing the American and Allied war effort in 1917-18. His appraisal of the problem reflected his experience as a scholar of international law and a man of public affairs.

THE PROS AND CONS OF
SOVIET RECOGNITION

By Paul D. Cravath

THE question of the recognition of the Soviet Government of Russia by the United States is one of the most vital international problems confronting the American people. The discussion of this problem should be based upon a sound appraisal of the principles involved and a clear understanding of the purposes and results of the recognition of one government by another. In the public discussion of this question there has been a great deal of loose thought and speech.

There seems to be a widespread impression that when the United States Government recognizes a new government in another country it is actuated primarily by motives of good will, and that the result of recognition is to fasten upon the new government the seal of approval of the United States. Nothing could be further from the truth. Usually the primary motive of a government in recognizing the government of another state is self-interest. It simply seeks to establish relations which will enable it to protect the life, liberty and property of its citizens and to promote their interests, and reciprocally to establish a basis for dealing with the other country and its citizens. The recognition of a newly established government by the United States Government does not remotely carry with it the implication that the aims and practices of the new government meet with our approval or inspire our admiration.

Our government was the first of the Great Powers to support the *de facto* theory of recognition as contrasted with the legitimacy theory. The American State Department has consistently adhered to the *de facto* theory for more than a century, except for occasional departures by Secretary Seward due to the exigencies of the Civil War and by other Secretaries of State in connection with the recognition of revolutionary governments in Latin America in the exercise of the somewhat paternal responsibilities imposed upon our government by the Monroe Doctrine.

The theory and practice of our State Department were admirably summarized in a memorandum of Mr. A. A. Adee, Assistant Secretary of State, on March 28, 1913, as follows:

It will, I think, simplify the matter to keep in mind the distinction between the recognition necessary to the conduct of international business between two countries and the recognition of the form of government professed by a foreign country.

In the former case, ever since the American Revolution, entrance upon diplomatic intercourse with foreign states has been *de facto,* dependent upon the existence of three conditions of fact: The control of the administrative machinery of the state; the general acquiescence of its people; and the ability and willingness of their government to discharge international and conventional obligations. The form of government has not been a conditional factor in such recognition; in other words, the *de jure* element of legitimacy of title has been left aside, probably because liable to involve dynastic or constitutional questions hardly within our competency to adjudicate, especially so when the organic form of government has been changed, as by revolution, from a monarchy to a commonwealth or vice versa. The general practice in such cases has been to satisfy ourselves that the change was effective and to enter into relation with the authority in *de facto* possession.[1]

Our government has frequently established cordial diplomatic relations with governments that were notoriously autocratic and vicious. Usually the sole test that our government seeks to apply is whether the new government is sufficiently entrenched in power effectively to govern within its own borders and to perform its international obligations. After that test has been met, our government in the recognition of governments in the eastern hemisphere does not usually concern itself with the morals or motives of the government seeking recognition.

If we bear these principles in mind, a brief review of the attitude of our government toward the recognition of the Soviet Government as compared with the policy pursued by other governments will go far to explain the present popular misapprehension in this country regarding the consequences of recognition of Soviet Russia.

The Soviet Revolution occurred in November 1917, a year before the armistice that ended the European War. During that year and for some time thereafter, certain of the Allied and Associated Powers acting in concert with White armies were engaged in hostilities against

[1] "Foreign Relations of the United States," 1913, p. 100.

Soviet Russia. Those hostilities did not end until early in 1920. At first the Allied Powers were disposed to boycott the Soviet Government. This was the natural result of the irritation caused by Russia's desertion of the cause of the Allies at a critical period of the war, of the aversion felt in capitalistic countries for the principles and practices of the Soviet Revolutionary Government and of the widespread doubt regarding its permanence.

As soon as it became apparent that the Soviet Government was the sole constituted authority in Russia and was likely to remain in power indefinitely, the principal European governments, recognizing the practical necessity of having dealings with Russia, began opening diplomatic relations. Estonia and Finland, having the greatest need of relations with their powerful neighbor, extended *de jure* recognition before the end of 1920. Poland followed in 1921 and Germany in 1922.

In the spring of 1922 occurred the Genoa Conference, instigated by Lloyd George, in the course of which the statesmen of Great Britain, France, Italy, Belgium and Germany met with Soviet statesmen in an effort to work out a formula under which Russia might be admitted to the European family of nations. This conference failed, but while it was in progress the representatives of Germany and Russia negotiated the Rapallo Agreement, which practically wiped the slate clean as between the two nations and confirmed the recognition of the Soviet Government by Germany which had already been granted by the Treaty of Brest-Litovsk.

Great Britain, France, Italy, Sweden, Denmark, Austria, Norway and Greece recognized the Soviet Republic in 1924, and by 1927 all the governments of Europe except Switzerland, Czechoslovakia, Jugoslavia, Rumania, Bulgaria, Spain, Hungary, Portugal, Holland and Belgium had extended *de jure* recognition. France expelled the Soviet representative in 1927, but his successor was appointed shortly thereafter. Great Britain withdrew its Ambassador to Russia the same year, but resumed diplomatic relations in 1929, upon the advent of the present Labor Government.

There can be no doubt that these European nations, in recognizing the Soviet Government, were actuated primarily by considerations of self-interest. It was natural that Estonia, Finland, Persia and Poland— all of which border on Russia—should be among the first to establish diplomatic relations. Germany, Great Britain, France, Italy and Japan established relations as soon as economic conditions in Russia showed signs of becoming sufficiently stable to justify the hope of commercial intercourse with the rest of the world on a substantial scale. It certainly did not occur to any of the European governments that in recognizing the Soviet Government they were placing the stamp of their approval on the methods used in establishing its power or on the policies it was pursuing in the exercise of that power.

Uninfluenced by the policy pursued by European governments, the United States Government has consistently pursued the policy of non-recognition. The first official statement of that policy was contained in a note which Secretary of State Colby addressed to the Italian Ambassador on October 10, 1920. Mr. Colby, while referring to the communistic doctrines and practices of the Soviet Government which were at variance with those of other civilized nations, emphasized as the principal ground of his policy of non-recognition what was clearly the soundest ground. It was that the Soviet Government by its own declarations could not be trusted to carry out its international obligations. He said:

The responsible leaders of the régime have frequently and openly boasted that they are willing to sign agreements and undertakings with foreign Powers while not having the slightest intention of observing such undertakings or carrying out such agreements. This attitude of disregard of obligations voluntarily entered into, they base upon the theory that no compact or agreement made with a non-Bolshevist government can have any moral force for them. They have not only avowed this as a doctrine, but they have amplified it in practice.

In a note transmitted to the American Consul at Reval on March 25, 1921, Secretary Hughes announced that relations would not be opened with Soviet Russia until convincing provision had been made for: 1, the safety of life; 2, the recognition of firm guarantees of private property; 3, the sanctity of contracts; and 4, the rights of free labor. In a letter to Samuel Gompers dated July 19, 1923, Secretary Hughes at greater length reiterated the same requisites of recognition, emphasizing the Soviet Government's "persistent attempts to subvert the institutions of democracy as maintained in this country."

In his message to Congress of December 6, 1923, President Coolidge somewhat liberalized the Government's attitude toward trade by American nationals with Russia; but he added:

Our government does not propose, however, to enter into relations with another régime which refuses to recognize the sanctity of international obligations. I do not propose to barter away for the privilege of trade any of the cherished rights of humanity. I do not propose to make merchandise of any American principles. These rights and principles must go wherever the sanctions of our government go.

But while the favor of America is not for sale, I am willing to make very large concessions for the purpose of rescuing the people of Russia. Already encouraging evidences of returning to the ancient ways of society can be detected. But more are needed. Whenever there appears any disposition to compensate our citizens who were despoiled, and to recognize that debt contracted with our government, not by the Czar, but by the newly formed Republic of Russia; whenever the active spirit of enmity to our institutions is abated; whenever there appear works meet for repentance, our country ought to be the first to go to the economic and moral rescue of Russia.

Mr. Chicherin, the Soviet Commissar for Foreign Affairs, thought, or professed to think, that he discovered an encouraging note in this pronouncement and promptly sent President Coolidge a despatch in which he expressed the Soviet Government's readiness to discuss with the United States Government all of the problems mentioned in the President's message, these negotiations to be based on "the principle of mutual non-intervention in internal affairs," and added that:

As to the questions of claims mentioned in your message, the Soviet Government is fully prepared to do all in its power, so far as the dignity and interests of its country permit, to bring about the desired end of renewal of friendship with the United States of America.

President Coolidge referred the Chicherin note to Secretary Hughes, who promptly made public the following statement:

There would seem to be at this time no reason for negotiations. The American Government, as the President said in his message to the Congress, is not proposing to barter away its principles. If the Soviet authorities are ready to restore the confiscated property of American citizens or make effective compensation, they can do so. If the Soviet authorities are ready to repeal their decrees repudiating Russia's obligations to this country and appropriately recognize them, they can do so. It requires no conference or negotiations to accomplish these results, which can and should be achieved at Moscow as evidence of good faith. The American Government has not incurred liabilities to Russia or repudiated obligations. Most serious is the continued propaganda to overthrow the institutions of this country. This Government can enter into no negotiations until these efforts directed from Moscow are abandoned.

In the light of subsequent events it is perhaps to be regretted that the Soviet offer of an attempt to negotiate a basis for recognition was not accepted, although it should be remembered that at that time none of the Great Powers except Germany had recognized the Soviet Government, and the failure of the Genoa Conference of the previous year was still fresh in the memory of statesmen.

The official utterances of the President and Secretary of State were sympathetically received by American public opinion, already aroused to distrust of the communistic régime in Russia and all its works. The note thus given to public discussion of American recognition of Soviet Russia goes far to account for the popular impression that recognition might involve a surrender of "cherished rights of humanity" or of "American principles."

Let us now turn the discussion to the sound utilitarian basis where it belongs. It must be recognized that the United States Government cannot be expected to enter into diplomatic relations with the Soviet Government except upon reasonable conditions. From the pronouncements of the State Department it is apparent that the "works meet for repentance" reasonably to be expected of the Soviet Government as a condition of recognition include satisfactory assurances upon the following questions: 1, recognition of the sanctity of international engagements; 2, the return of, or adequate compensation for, the property of American nationals confiscated by the Soviet Government after the revolution in 1917; 3, recognition of the debts contracted with our government and our nationals by the Kerensky Government; and 4, the cessation of subversive activities directed from Moscow against our institutions.

The soundness of the first of these conditions no one will question, for it is axiomatic that no government is entitled to recognition by other governments unless it is willing and able to perform its international obligations. It is probable that the Soviet Government would accept that condition without debate, for in spite of declarations to the contrary by Lenin and other Communist leaders, the Soviet Government has repeatedly professed a determination to perform its own obligations, even in its dealings with nations of the capitalistic world.

The second and third conditions present more serious difficulties. The abolition of private property and the transfer to the state of all property except purely personal belongings lies at the very foundation of the entire Soviet economic and political structure. The Soviet authorities profess to see no reason in principle why an exception in the application of that doctrine should be made in favor of foreigners. While the condition laid down by our State Department is confined to property owned by, and debts owing to, our government and our nationals, any concession made to Americans would doubtless have to be extended to other nations. Indeed, the Rapallo Agreement, which provides for the mutual cancellation of debts and claims as between Russia and Germany, expressly provides that in case the Soviet Government should at any time recognize claims held by nationals of other nations, the same recognition must be granted to German nationals. There is a similar agreement with Japan.

Another complication involved in the discussion of foreign claims against Russia is the insistence of the Soviet Government upon the simultaneous consideration of Russia's claims against certain of the Allied and Associated Powers, doubtless including the United States, for damages resulting from their support of the various campaigns waged against the Soviet Government by White armies during the three years following the outbreak of the Soviet Revolution. The contention of the Russian Government is that the support by foreign governments of counter-revolutionary warfare resulted in claims by Russia against those governments similar to the claims that were sustained by the Geneva award in favor of the United States against Great Britain for the depredations to American shipping caused by the *Alabama* and other privateers fitted out in British ports during our Civil War. This is no place for a discussion of the validity of the Russian counter-claims. It is enough to say that they are not so frivolous that they can be dismissed without consideration. Professor Schuman, of the University of Chicago, in his book "American Policy toward Russia since 1917," after a review of the facts and the law, reaches the conclusion that these counter-claims are valid in substantial amounts. However this may be, it is difficult to see how the United States can refuse at least to give its reasons for not recognizing them.

The aggregate amount of the American claims against Russia has never been ascertained. It is estimated that at their face value they may amount to as much as $750,000,000. Still more uncertain is the amount of Russia's claims against the United States. At the Genoa Conference, the Soviet representative submitted fantastic claims against the Allied Governments, far in excess of their aggregate claims against Russia. If they are ever admitted in principle, the Russian claims against the Allied and Associated Governments that supported the White armies will involve not only the determination of their aggregate amount but also their apportionment between the Allied nations and the United States, whose part in supporting the White armies in Russia was different from that of Great Britain and France. The United States might even escape liability entirely.

Enough has been said to show that it would be impossible to reach an agreement upon the reciprocal claims between the American and Soviet Governments without an extended inquiry. Even if there be ground for hope that an agreement might ultimately be reached, is it wise diplomacy to insist upon a definitive agreement as a condition of recognition? Would it not be wiser to pursue the course that was adopted by the United States Government in dealing with somewhat similar problems in its relations with the present revolutionary government in Mexico, which had assumed an attitude toward American property rights not dissimilar in principle to that of the Soviet Government? Instead of insisting upon a definitive settlement of the American claims as a condition of recognition, the United States Government sent a diplomatic mission to Mexico to ascertain by negotiation with the Mexican Government whether there could be found a promising basis for the ultimate recognition and determination of those claims. Upon receiving a satisfactory report from its mission, the American Government entered into diplomatic relations with the revolutionary government in Mexico and after prolonged negotiations the American Ambassador brought about a settlement of most of the questions at issue between the two nations. Would not a similar course in dealing with the Soviet Government be more likely to be effective than our continued insistence on unconditional recognition of the American claims as a prerequisite to recognition?

The fourth condition, that the Soviet Government shall give satisfactory assurance of the cessation of subversive activities against our institutions, may prove the most difficult of all. The Soviet Government insists that neither it nor any of its agents in this country has engaged in subversive activities within our borders directed against our institutions. This may be literally true. It seems highly improbable that the

Russian Government trading companies and their affiliated organizations have committed the fruitless folly of participating in subversive activities within our borders. On the other hand, there can be no doubt that the Russian Communist Party and the Third International have been and are likely to continue to be active in communistic propaganda all over the world. It is hard to accept the distinction that the Soviet spokesmen draw between the Soviet Government on the one hand and the Communist Party and the Third International on the other, inasmuch as in the last analysis the Soviet Government and the Third International are both creatures of the central organization of the Communist Party. Stalin, although holding no office in the Soviet Government, is the dominating figure in the Communist Party. One day he speaks for the Soviet Government as the exponent of the doctrines of his party, and the next he may openly support the plans of the Third International looking toward world revolution. He would doubtless say that the Soviet Government is no more responsible for the activities of the Third International and the Communist Party than our government is for the activities of the Republican Party or the Methodist Board of Foreign Missions. The obvious answer to this attempted parallel is that the Communist Party is the only recognized political party in Russia and the Soviet Government is its creature.

Considering that the Communist leaders are devoted to Communism with all the fervor of religious zealots, it is probably too much to expect, whatever may be their professions, that they will surrender the right of the Third International to continue communistic propaganda. In the face of the present open unfriendliness of our government and the American nation toward the Soviet Government, it would not be surprising if under existing conditions the leaders of the Communist Party felt justified in going the limit in their subversive propaganda in this country, provided the official Russian agents within our borders held aloof. On the other hand, in spite of the bad record of the Soviet Government in carrying out its promises to other governments to refrain from propaganda, it may well be that, when recognition has removed the principal cause of irritation in Russia against the United States, the Communist leaders will deem it to their interest to terminate their subversive activities in this country, which they must have found by experience to be futile in promoting the cause of Communism within our borders.

On the assumption that the question of our recognition of the Soviet

Government is to be dealt with primarily on the basis of our self-interest, it may be asked what advantage would recognition bring to us. The reverse of the question is more easily answered. How does the United States profit by the Government's policy of non-recognition? To many the obvious answer would be that we preserve our self-respect by not recognizing a government whose principles and practices are so abhorrent to us and so widely at variance with those on which our civilization is based. But as already pointed out, our self-respect is not involved, as recognition does not remotely involve approval of Soviet principles and methods. In the first years following the Soviet Revolution in 1917 the principal Allied nations of Europe and the United States by withholding recognition undoubtedly intended to discredit and weaken the Soviet Government in the hope that it would soon fall and be succeeded by some form of government based on principles more in harmony with those which actuate the other governments of the civilized world. That quite legitimate gesture failed. It certainly has ceased to be of value to the United States now that most other governments have adopted the policy of recognition. It may be said that it is against the interests of our government to encourage a government professing principles which, if they triumph, would be subversive of our social and political institutions. It is a question whether the attitude of our government in respect of recognition would have an appreciable influence on the ultimate fate of the Soviet Government. Our government is so fully committed to the policy of non-interference with the internal affairs of European nations that it would not be influenced by the factor which, for a time, undoubtedly influenced European governments, that by the policy of non-recognition they preserved their freedom to support counter-revolutionary movements in an attempt to overthrow the Soviet Government and bring about the substitution in its stead of one with which enlightened governments could more effectively coöperate.

The obvious advantages of a policy of recognition are those upon which the whole system of diplomatic relations between civilized nations is based. Our government would be in a position through its diplomatic representatives to protect the life, liberty and property of Americans visiting, or sojourning in, Russia, of whom there are already several thousand annually, who are now dependent upon the good offices of the diplomatic representatives of other governments. Our government would be able by the usual diplomatic methods to encourage

and protect American trade with Russia. There is much force in the
view that when in 1923 our government by presidential proclamation
encouraged American merchants and manufacturers to engage in trade
with Russia it owed our citizens the duty of protecting this trade by
the usual diplomatic machinery. Only by the establishment of diplomatic
relations can outstanding differences between the United States and
Russia, such as those in relation to dumping and convict labor, be dealt
with adequately. With an Ambassador at Moscow and consuls in the
principal trading centers of Russia our government would be able
to assemble reliable information for the guidance of our merchants,
manufacturers and bankers, who are now dependent upon the casual
and often prejudiced reports of unofficial observers.

Finally, it seems a great pity that the United States should be the
only one of the Great Powers which has deliberately excluded itself
from exercising any influence through the usual diplomatic channels in
the development of the institutions of the most populous nation in
Europe, whose return to economic, social and political stability is essential for the peace and prosperity of the civilized world.

An attempt by the United States to negotiate a satisfactory basis for
the recognition of the Soviet Government of Russia would be full of
difficulties, and diplomatic relations, if established, might prove hard
to maintain, for the Soviet statesmen have not shown an aptitude for
coöperation. But is not the stake sufficient to make the attempt worth
while?

KARL RADEK, who was Stalin's chief publicist on international affairs in the 1930s, wrote his article on "The Bases of Soviet Foreign Policy" (January 1934) at a time of change in Soviet foreign policy. The "hard" line of the Comintern, adopted at the 1928 Congress, had turned the main thrust of Communist activity toward overthrowing "bourgeois democracy" and destroying the "social fascists," as Moscow described the democratic Socialist Parties of Germany and France, and had thereby contributed to the rise of Hitler and the emergence of a new and genuine threat both to peace and to the Soviet Union. By mid-1934 Stalin was beginning to turn to a "broad" line, posing as defender of peace and democracy. He soon sought to check Hitler's rising military threat by promoting Popular Front alliances within France and Spain and by signing defensive military alliances with France and Czechoslovakia. Radek's article reflected elements of this transition and foreshadowed Moscow's forthcoming second major *rapprochement* with the West, now regarded, in comparison with Hitler, as "the lesser evil."

Karl Radek, born in Austrian Poland in 1885, took an active part in the pre-1914 Left wing of the Polish and German Socialist Parties. From his wartime refuge in Switzerland he accompanied Lenin to Russia in the famous "sealed train" of 1917. Having joined the Bolshevik Party, he was sent to Sweden in 1917 and Germany in 1918 to rally support for the new Soviet regime. Even while in a Berlin prison Radek gave political guidance to the Left Socialists and also negotiated actively with political and military leaders of the Right for a joint German-Soviet bloc against the victors of Versailles.

After returning to Moscow in 1921, Radek worked in the headquarters of the Communist International and also headed the Sun Yat-sen University, which trained numerous Chinese and other Asian Communists in the profession of revolutionaries. A first expulsion from the Party, in December 1927, was followed by banishment to the Urals, recantation and return to Stalin's grace. During the great purge, however, Radek was publicly arraigned in the second of the anti-Party trials, in 1937, and sentenced to 10-years' imprisonment, from which he did not return.

99

THE BASES OF SOVIET FOREIGN POLICY

By Karl Radek

I AM fully aware of the difficulties of the task which I undertake in attempting to give the readers of FOREIGN AFFAIRS an account of the main lines of Soviet foreign policy and the fundamental considerations which govern it. The first difficulty arises from the fact that the foreign policy of the Soviet Government differs as much from the foreign policy of the other Great Powers as the domestic policy of this first socialist state differs from the domestic policy of the states belonging to the capitalist system. Men and women who accept the capitalist point of view find it just as hard to understand the socialist state's foreign policy as its domestic policy. Moreover, this primary difficulty is increased by several propositions generally accepted in the capitalist world, although even there they are of questionable validity. I mean the theory of the priority of foreign over domestic policy and the theory of the continuity of foreign policy. In order to clear the way for an understanding of the foreign policy of the Soviet Union the reader must attempt to grasp our attitude toward these two propositions. We consider them erroneous because they are in contradiction with generally-known historical facts.

Foreign policy is a function of domestic policy. It solves problems which result from the development of a given society, a given state, under definite historical conditions.

The wars of the era when modern capitalism was born, the wars of Cromwell and Louis XIV, were the product of the struggle for the emancipation of the youthful capitalism, which gained strength under the mercantilist system, from the oppression of the domestic market, largely based on a peasant economy which met the requirements of the peasant and of his feudal exploiter. There was a need for colonies as sources of raw materials and as markets for the produce of young industries, and also for the plundering which provided the stimulus for the growth of manufactures, which became in turn the basis for the eventual development of machine industry. Industrial capitalism relegates the struggle for colonies to the background because industrial capitalism itself creates an immense domestic market as well as immense means of accumulation and has in cheap mass production a magnificent weapon for mobilizing raw materials from the colonies.

The wars of the industrial era served either as a means for breaking through the Chinese wall which separates the backward nations from the capitalist world (the Anglo-Chinese war, the Anglo-American threats to Japan), or as a way for achieving national unity, which means creating a large domestic market for infant industries (the unification of Germany, Italy, the United States).

Under monopolistic capitalism the mad struggle for colonies was again accentuated. In the war of 1914-1918 the attempt was made to re-distribute the world's surface in accordance with the strength of the imperialistic powers which took part in the struggle. The difference between the aims and methods of the imperialistic policy of the twentieth century and those of the foreign policy of the mercantilist era is made clear, despite their superficial similarity, by the consequences of that imperialistic policy. Whereas during the period of manufactures England did everything in her power to prevent the development of industry in the colonies, the policy of modern imperialism is a policy of exporting capital, that is, a policy of exporting the means of production. This policy, regardless of the intentions of its originators, leads to a certain degree of industrialization in the colonies—although the survivals of feudalism and the exploitation of the colonial countries hinder the process of industrialization and prevent emancipation. The revolutionary movement in the colonies, centering as it does around the young proletariat, shows how different are the policies of mercantilism and imperialism. The fate of India, the fate of China, furnish the proofs.

Where, in this process, is the priority of foreign policy and where is its continuity? Its aims are seen to be shaped by the economic and political structure of changing forms of society. Therefore they are not permanent but on the contrary variable.

The attempt to represent the foreign policy of the Soviet Union as a continuation of Tsarist policy is ridiculous. Bourgeois writers who do so have not grasped even the purely external manifestations of this policy. It used to be an axiom of Tsarist policy that it should strive by every available means to gain possession of the Dardanelles and of

an ice-free port on the Pacific. Not only have the Soviets not attempted
to seize the Dardanelles, but from the very beginning they have tried
to establish the most friendly relations with Turkey; nor has Soviet
policy ever had as one of its aims the conquest of Port Arthur or of
Dairen. Again, Tsarism, or any other bourgeois régime in Russia,
would necessarily resume the struggle for the conquest of Poland and
of the Baltic states, as is doubtless clear to any thoughtful bourgeois
politician in those countries. The Soviet Union, on the contrary, is
most anxious to establish friendly relations with these countries, considering their achievement of independence a positive and progressive
historical factor.

It is silly to say that geography plays the part of fate, that it determines the foreign policy of a state. Tsarist policy originated not in
geographical conditions, but in the privileges of the Russian nobility
and the demands of young Russian capitalism. The questions raised by
geography are dealt with by each social formation in its own way;
that way is determined by its peculiar economic and political aims.

II

We are thus led to the first fundamental question: What are the aims
which may and must be pursued by a society which is building up
socialism and which is based on socialism?

I shall not attempt to give here a historical survey of the foreign
policy of the Soviet Union. Suffice it to recall that when the Soviet Government came to power it set out promptly to rescue the country
from the conflagration of the World War, and that having achieved
this purpose at a heavy price it was forced for about three years to
defend its independence against the intervention of the leading imperialistic nations, an intervention due partly to the desire of these to
drag the Soviets back into the World War and partly to their desire
to destroy the first government of the workers, which the capitalist
world looked upon as a gross provocation to the capitalist system. This
fact compelled the Soviet Union to give a preliminary solution to the
problem of defense which had been forced upon it. But even in this
early period Soviet foreign policy displayed clearly its fundamental
lines, which are fully in harmony with the foreign policy of the socialist
system.

The main object for which Soviet diplomacy is fighting is *peace*.

Now this term "peace" is much abused. There is no diplomat whose official pronouncements do not use this term reverently over and over again, even though he is a representative of one of those imperialistic nations which are most active in preparing war. But those who are incapable of understanding the specific place occupied by the struggle for peace in Soviet foreign policy are altogether incapable of understanding that policy in whole or in part. Why is the struggle for peace the central object of Soviet policy? Primarily because the Soviet Union—to use the expression of Lenin—"has everything necessary for the building up of a socialist society."

As early as 1915 and 1916 Lenin, then preparing the struggle for the seizure of political power, maintained that it was possible to build up socialism in Russia. He saw the country's vast size, its immense natural resources, and that it possessed a degree of industrial development which would insure, on the one hand, the leadership of the working class and, on the other, provide the minimum of technical knowledge necessary for starting socialist construction.

In Lenin's lifetime the Soviet state, having victoriously ended the war against intervention, took up the work of reconstruction, re-building the industry that had been destroyed and establishing normal relations with the peasantry. These normal relations assured the proletariat the supply of raw materials and foodstuffs necessary for the expansion of industry, as well as the support of the peasant masses. Lenin's successor at the helm of the Soviet ship of state, Stalin, deciding the course of this ship, set as its object the building up of socialism within the borders of the former Empire of the Tsars. This object seemed utopian, not only to the capitalist world, but also to a group inside the Communist Party which followed Trotsky and rejected the fundamentals of Lenin's policy.

In this inner party struggle the policy of Stalin was victor; and his victory found its realization in the Five Year Plan. This plan has already been put into practice. Its achievement consists in the creation of an industry on such a large scale as to provide the solution of three problems. In the first place, it allows the Soviet Union to proceed independently with the further development of its industry, that is to say, in case of necessity, without importations from abroad, because under the Five Year Plan the Soviet Union has acquired a powerful heavy industry and machine-building equipment of all sorts.

Thanks to the solution of this first problem, the working class can now—and this is the solution of the second problem—provide the peasantry with a number of machines sufficient to prove to even the most backward groups of peasants the advantage of collectivization. On the basis of collectivization it became possible to liquidate those classes of the peasants which were pushing agriculture in the direction of capitalism. The economic annihilation of the kulaks and the creation of an agriculture which has for its chief driving power the products of large-scale machine industry—tractors, reapers and other agricultural machines—owned by the workers' state, has created a situation in which the peasantry can and must develop in the direction of socialism. The peasant today is still in an intermediate stage between the position of a small owner and that of a member of a society carrying on a collective enterprise with the help of means of production owned by the society. But it is already perfectly clear that as a result of the advantages of tractors, electricity and oil over horses, ploughs and scythes, the well-being of the peasantry will depend in increasing degree on the productive forces of the socialist society and not on labor arising from privately-owned means of production. Within the peasant ranks, too, differentiations in productive and economic standards will be abolished, and the peasantry will gradually be transformed into a uniform socialist mass. The economic lot of the peasants will continue to improve and year by year they will grow closer to the proletariat. This result is guaranteed not only by the increasing industrialization of the countryside, but also by the fact that industrialization is a means for raising the cultural level of the village to that of the urban proletariat. The solution of this second problem—the collectivization of farming—in conjunction with the solution of the first problem—industrialization—makes possible the accomplishment of the third object of the Five Year Plan, namely the creation of conditions which assure the national defense of the Soviet state.

This capacity for national defense is based on the creation of a heavy industry which provides the country with all the means of defense essential to success in modern war, and on the disappearance of all social classes hostile to the up-building of socialism. These classes have been defeated, even though remnants still survive and even though the psychology of the small owner, inimical to socialism, cannot disappear in all groups of the population at once. But if we ask the question, what is the general trend of development, it is clear that the fulfilment of the Five Year Plan and the development of the program of reconstruction in the Second Five Year Plan have proved that the Soviet Union, having laid down the foundations of socialism, is capable of proceeding to build up the complete structure of socialism, the integral socialist society, that is, a classless society which bases itself on all the discoveries of modern technique and that assures to the masses of the population social and cultural conditions of a type which capitalism cannot possibly achieve.

Does the Soviet Union need war in order to build up socialism? It does not. Certain capitalist circles have stubbornly asserted since the Soviet Union was founded that it would seek a solution of its difficulties in war; these assertions are repudiated by the history of the Soviet Union during its sixteen years of life. Even at the moment when we were particularly ill-equipped to undertake the building-up of socialism, immediately after we had assumed governmental responsibilities, we readily accepted the heaviest sacrifices in order to give peace to the country. We deeply believed—and this was of great importance—that we had in our hands everything necessary for building up a socialist society. Now we know that the problem of building socialism in the Soviet Union admits of a practical solution and that a considerable part of the problem has been already solved. The peace policy of the Soviet Union therefore rests on the granite foundation of triumphant socialist construction.

The enemies of the Soviet Union attempt to undermine the importance of this fact from two directions. Some of them accuse the Soviet Union of having given up its international aims. These aims, in their opinion, would demand military intervention by the Soviet Union to aid the emancipation of the international proletariat and of the colonial peoples. Others, on the contrary, maintain that, because the Bolshevik Party which controls the Soviet Union is inherently an international party, all the peace declarations of the Soviet Union are purely provisional and hence that having reached a certain economic level which enables it to wage an aggressive war the Soviet Union will repudiate its peace declarations and assume the initiative in a war. The best way of answering both these accusations is to quote the statement made by Stalin in December 1926:

This is what Lenin actually said: "From ten to twenty years of sound relations with the peasantry, and victory on the world scale is assured (even despite delays in the growing proletarian revolutions); otherwise from twenty to forty years of sufferings under the White terror." ("Leninski Sbornik," Vol. IV, p. 374.)

Does this proposition of Lenin give ground for the conclusion that "we are utterly incapable of building up socialism in twenty or thirty years?" No, it does not. From this proposition we can derive the following conclusions: (a) provided we have established sound relations with the peasantry, victory is assured to us (that is, the victory of socialism) within ten or twenty years; (b) this victory will be a victory not only within the U.S.S.R., but a victory on the world scale; (c) if we fail to gain victory within this period this will mean that we have been defeated, and that the régime of the dictatorship of the proletariat has given place to the régime of the White terror, which may last twenty to forty years.

And what is meant by "victory on the world scale"? Does it mean that such a victory is equivalent to the victory of socialism in a single country? No, it does not. Lenin in his writings carefully distinguished the victory of socialism in a single country from victory "on the world scale." What Lenin really means when he speaks of "victory on the world scale" is that *the success of socialism in our country, the victory of consolidating socialism in our country, has such an immense international significance that it (the victory) cannot be limited to our country alone but is bound to call forth a powerful movement toward socialism in all capitalist countries,* and even if it does not coincide with the victory of the proletarian revolution in other countries, it must in any event lead to a strong proletarian movement of other nations toward the victory of world revolution. Such is the revolutionary outlook according to Lenin, if we think in terms of the outlook for the victory of the revolution, which after all is the question in which we in the Party are interested.[1]

Such are the fundamentals of the Soviet peace policy.

III

The socialist society which is being built up in the Soviet Union has foundations already well established and its completion assured. It does not need war. This fact found expression in the Soviet proposal for a general disarmament by all the capitalistic Powers, first advanced at the Genoa Conference while Lenin was still alive. It has subsequently been the axis of the peace policy of the Soviet Union at the Disarmament Conference. This Conference required years of preparation and already has been engaged on its sterile deliberations for two years. Its

[1] J. Stalin: "Ob oppozitsii" ("On the Opposition"), articles and speeches, 1921-1927, State Publishing House, 1928, p. 465-466.

fate magnificently proves the truth of Lenin's thesis that "under capitalism, and especially in its imperialistic phase, war is inevitable."

Immediately after the capitalist world recovered from the post-war
commotion and achieved provisional economic stabilization, a new wave
of armaments came into being. All nations began developing feverishly
those methods of warfare which the war had proved important, such as
aviation, chemical warfare and tanks. The mechanization of armies
and the modernization of fleets have been taking place universally. The
attempt to keep these armaments at least within certain limits is frustrated by the action of the law which Lenin formulated as follows in
his work "Imperialism as the Highest Stage of Capitalism":

Financial capital and the trusts do not diminish but emphasize the difference in the tempo of growth between various parts of the world economy.
But if the balance of forces has been broken, what can be used under a
capitalistic system to bring about a settlement of the conflict except violence? [2]

And again:

Under capitalism no other basis is thinkable for the division of spheres
of influence, interests, colonies, etc., except an estimate of the strength
of the parties to the division, their general economic strength, their financial
and military strength, and so on. But the strength of the parties to division
changes unevenly, because an even development of separate enterprises,
trusts, branches of industries, countries, is impossible under capitalism.
Half a century ago Germany was a mere nonentity, if we compare her
capitalistic strength with that of contemporary England; the same was
true of Japan in comparison with Russia. Is it "thinkable" that one or two
decades hence the relationship between the imperialistic Powers should remain unaltered? Utterly unthinkable.

Under conditions actually prevailing in the capitalist world, therefore,
the "inter-imperialistic" or "ultra-imperialistic" alliances—irrespective of
the form these alliances might take, whether that of one imperialistic coalition against another imperialistic coalition, or that of a general alliance of
all the imperialistic Powers—will necessarily be merely "breathing spaces"
between wars. [3]

The opinions expressed by Lenin in 1916, in the midst of the World
War, have been fully corroborated by post-war history. They explain
why the capitalist world is incapable of obtaining any effective limitation

[2] Lenin: "Sobranie sochineni," Vol. XIX, p. 149.
[3] *Op. cit.,* Vol. XIX, p. 167-168.

in armaments and is therefore inescapably moving toward a new world war for a new re-distribution of the world.

Germany, having strengthened her industry with the help of American, English, Dutch and Swiss loans, and confronted with a shrinkage of the world market, cannot exist within the narrow limits assigned to her by the Treaty of Versailles. In seeking equality in armaments she is seeking the possibility for preparing a war for the revision of the Versailles peace.

Japan, who developed her industry first on the basis of an inhuman semi-feudal exploitation of the village population (which still continues), later with the help of billions of war profits, and who is half-strangled in the knot of surviving feudalism which, in an even stronger degree than the laws of imperialism, prevents the development of her domestic market—Japan, who understands that the United States is compelled by the entire course of its economic development to deepen and expand its struggle for economic influence in China—Japan, fearful that as a consequence of the industrialization of Siberia she will lose her monopolistic position as the only industrial country in the Far East—Japan tears up the Washington and the London agreements, occupies Manchuria, and gets ready to occupy China before the economic domination of the United States has been fully established there. She raises the question of her hegemony over Asia. This objective has been openly proclaimed by Japan's Minister of War, General Araki.

Italy, "offended at Versailles," seeks a re-distribution of colonial lands in her favor.

The relations between the United States and England have suffered a fundamental change since the United States has risen to the position of being the first industrial power in the world and has claimed equality in the control of the seas.

The uneven development of post-war capitalism has created a situation in which all the imperialistic Powers will seek to re-distribute the world in accordance with their own interests.

The Soviet Union is opposed to imperialism. It is opposed to an imperialistic war. It recognizes as equitable only one war, the war for the defense of socialism, the war of the enslaved peoples for their liberation. This point of view determines our attitude toward imperialism, as a system, and toward the consequences of its policy which find their expression in the preparation of a new war. It also dictates our attitude toward imperialistic alliances which evolve during the process of preparing a new war for the re-distribution of the world.

The Soviet Union takes no part in the struggle for the re-distribution of the world.

The words of Stalin at the Sixteenth Congress of the Communist Party of the Soviet Union—"We do not want a single bit of foreign land; but at the same time not an inch of our land shall ever be yielded to anyone else"—these words are the exact expression of the policy of the Soviet Union.

In the struggle for the new re-distribution of the world the Soviet Union does not share. Taking account of the solidarity of the workers of the whole world, it can take no part in the plundering of foreign lands. Moreover, it does not need foreign land to carry on the work of constructing socialism. This policy found expression in the Soviet attitude toward the struggle in Manchuria. Defending its economic interests in connection with the Chinese Eastern Railroad, the Soviet Union never accepted the partition of Manchuria into spheres of influence. It followed a similar policy in Persia, even though this rendered its relations with British imperialism somewhat more difficult. Non-participation in imperialistic alliances having for their purpose the plundering of foreign lands is the second leading principle of the foreign policy of the Soviet Union.

But the preparation of an imperialistic war is a fact, the existence of imperialistic alliances is a fact, and the Soviet Union can not limit itself to a mere expression of its negative attitude toward the objects of imperialism and toward imperialistic alliances. The Soviet Union must do everything to protect itself against the attack of the capitalist Powers who intend to conquer a portion of the Soviet territory or to overthrow the political framework of the socialist state.

The peace policy of the Soviet manifests itself not only in the struggle for disarmament, the struggle for the maximum reduction in armaments, but also in non-aggression pacts. In any given concrete case such a pact means a guarantee of Soviet neutrality in conflicts which may arise among the capitalist nations, conceded in exchange for the undertaking by the latter to refrain from attacking the Soviet Union or intervening in its domestic affairs. There is nothing surprising, therefore, in the fact that the first non-aggression pact concluded by the Soviet Union was with Turkey, for friendly relations between the two countries had developed from the early help offered by the Soviet Union to Turkey in her struggle for independence. Nor is it surprising that the next state with which the Soviet Union entered into a pact equivalent to a non-aggression pact was Germany (April 24,

1926). In its fight against the Treaty of Versailles, Germany tried to establish friendly relations with the Soviet Union as the only Great Power which opposed the enslavement of one nation by another. The non-aggression pacts with Afghanistan, in 1926, and with Persia, in 1929, were results of the policy of the Soviet Union which bases its relations with the Eastern peoples on the idea of equality and respect for their national independence.

It is not mere chance that for many years all attempts to conclude similar non-aggression pacts with the western neighbors of the Soviet Union remained fruitless. Those western neighbors for a long time participated openly or indirectly in the alignment of the victorious imperialistic Powers which had not given up the idea of intervention against the Soviets. Only experience—the experience which proved to these western neighbors of the Soviet Union that this policy not only does not protect their independence but might even weaken their position at the same time that they have to face the growing demand for the restoration of German imperialism—it was this experience only which developed their tendency toward peace with the Soviet Union and led to the conclusion of the non-aggression pacts between the Soviet Union, Poland, Latvia, Esthonia and Finland. A similar change in the general situation on the continent, Germany's growing desire to revise the conditions imposed upon her by the Treaty of Versailles—peacefully if possible, forcibly if necessary—proved to be one of the factors which induced France to enter into a non-aggression pact with the Soviet Union. Italy had been among the first to resume normal relations with the Soviet Union. It was her desire to strengthen her position with reference to France which influenced her to join the Soviet Union not only in a non-aggression pact but also in a pact of friendship. Soviet attempts to conclude a similar pact with Japan have up to the present time produced no positive results; this seems merely to indicate the existence in Japan of very strong tendencies to preserve complete freedom of action in case of conflict with the Soviet Union.

The Soviet Union is confronted both in Europe and the Far East with hostile camps which are preparing war against one another. It holds toward them a position of neutrality, and endeavors to guarantee its own peace by a policy of non-interference in their affairs and by entering into mutual obligations of non-aggression with all sides. These obligations have been stated concretely and precisely in the pact containing the definition of the aggressor. The Soviet Government has definitely undertaken not to move its armed forces by land, sea or air across the frontiers of states which have assumed similar obligations, and also not to intervene directly or indirectly in their domestic affairs. All this indicates to the world that the policy of peace and neutrality on which the Soviet Union has embarked is not a mere diplomatic gesture, but a concrete political obligation the earnestness of which should be beyond question.

The Soviet Union enters into pacts of non-aggression with any country which is willing to sign such a pact, that is to say it is ready to enter into non-aggression pacts with countries which may eventually be at war. It therefore must take into consideration that while its pledge of peace and neutrality strengthen one of the belligerent countries they may be disadvantageous to the other side, which in consequence may attempt to repudiate its non-aggression pact, violate its obligations, and attack the Soviet Union. Besides, of course, any action is possible on the part of the Powers which have refused to sign non-aggression pacts. It goes without saying that the Soviet Union's reply to any attack on it would be military action fully commensurate with the statement of Stalin that "not an inch of our land shall ever be yielded to anyone else." But then a situation might arise when the Soviet Union would carry on action parallel with the enemy of its own enemy, or would even coöperate with him in a joint action. The policy to follow in such an eventuality was foreseen by Lenin during the discussion of the Brest-Litovsk peace negotiations. Under quite different conditions, for then the Soviet Union was weak militarily, Lenin outlined the fundamental solution of the problem. This solution remains today one of the guiding principles of Soviet policy. "From the moment of the victory of socialist construction in one of the countries, the question must be settled not from the point of view of the desirability of this or that imperialism, but exclusively from the point of view of the best conditions for the development and strengthening of socialist revolution, which has already begun," wrote Lenin in his theses on the conclusion of a separate peace, on January 7, 1918.[4]

In his article "O chesotke" ("About the Rash"), of February 22 of the same year, Lenin, criticizing those who objected as a matter of principle to the conclusion of an agreement with the Allies against German imperialism, wrote as follows:

[4] *Op. cit.,* Vol. XXII, p. 195.

If Kerensky, representative of the dominating class of the bourgeoisie, that is of the exploiters, enters into an agreement with the Anglo-French exploiters under which he obtains arms and potatoes, but conceals from the people other agreements which promise (in case of success) to one robber Armenia, Galicia, Constantinople, to the other Baghdad, Syria, and so on—then is it difficult to understand that the transaction is a dishonest, disgusting and revolting one from the point of view of both Kerensky and his friends? No. It is not difficult to understand. Any peasant will understand it, even the most backward and illiterate one.

But what if the representative of the exploited class, of those who suffer, after that class has overthrown the exploiters and has published and annulled all secret and grasping agreements, is the object of a treacherous attack by the German imperialists? Is he to be condemned for dealing with the Anglo-French robbers, for accepting their arms and potatoes in exchange for timber and so on? Should such an agreement be called dishonest, shameful, unclean? [5]

By giving a positive answer to the question of the feasibility of an agreement between the Soviet Union and an imperialistic Power which, for the sake of its own imperialistic interests, was willing to help the Soviet Union in its struggle against other attacking imperialistic Powers, Lenin at the same time answered the question as to the possible expansion of the policy of the Soviet Union beyond the stage of neutrality in case of a struggle between the imperialistic Powers.

The Soviet Union does not close the door to the possibility of a deal, an agreement, with imperialistic Powers which are waging a struggle against other imperialistic Powers, if the latter attack the Soviet Union; but in entering into such an agreement the Soviet Union would not accept any responsibility for the specific purposes pursued by the imperialistic Powers parties to the agreement. Never and under no conditions would it participate in the plundering of other nations, because participation in such a plunder would be contrary to the international solidarity of the workers. But against attacking imperialism an agreement is permissible with any opponent in order to defeat an enemy invading Soviet territory.

I think I have named the fundamental principles of Soviet foreign policy and have explained their interdependence. They are all derived from the basic fact that imperialism is unable to solve the great problems which mankind has to face today. A new imperialistic war will

[5] *Op. cit.*, Vol. XXII, p. 273.

not solve them. It will lead to an immense destruction of productive forces, to unexampled sufferings among the masses of the people, and will achieve nothing except a new re-shuffling of the possessions of the capitalist world.

The Soviet Union is an enemy of imperialistic wars which arise from the fact that capitalism is no longer in a position to develop the productive forces of the human race, but that it is still capable of attempting to seize a piece of land which is being reserved for the exploitation of a given national bourgeoisie. That is how the world is pushed toward immense new upheavals. We are therefore certain that the masses, thrust into the turmoil of new wars, will seek a way out along the same road that was followed by the Soviet proletariat in 1917.

The object of the Soviet Government is to save the soil of the first proletariat state from the criminal folly of a new war. To this end the Soviet Union has struggled with the greatest determination and consistency for sixteen years. The defense of peace and of the neutrality of the Soviet Union against all attempts to drag it into the whirlwind of a world war is the central problem of Soviet foreign policy.

The Soviet Union follows the policy of peace because peace is the best condition for building up a socialist society. Fighting for the maintenance of peace, accepting obligations of neutrality toward the struggling camps of the imperialists, the Soviet Union has at the same time raised the military preparedness of the country to a level which answers the demands of national defense and the requirements of modern warfare. Its neutrality is a positive factor which the imperialistic Powers which have not yet lost the sense of realities will not fail to appreciate. Those of them which are unable to realize the importance of Soviet neutrality or are forced by the insoluble difficulties of their own position to risk an adventurous war against that huge country, with its dozens of millions of men united by a common desire for peace, a desire for peaceful creative work—to those Powers will be given the proofs that the generation which laid down the foundations of socialism is also capable of defending them with iron energy. And we are convinced that, irrespective of what might be the course of the war and who might be responsible for its origins, the only victor that would emerge from it would be the Soviet Union leading the workers of the whole world; for it alone has a banner which, in case of a war, can become the banner of the masses of the entire world.

LEON TROTSKY (1879-1940) had several lives, all equally dramatic. After taking up his first life, that of an active revolutionary, in 1898, he became one of the strongest and most vivid leaders of pre-1917 Russian Social Democracy. In 1905 he showed great talent as a popular leader and orator and was elected second chairman of the St. Petersburg Soviet during the general strike. His radical opposition to World War I brought his position closer to Lenin's, and after joining the Bolshevik Party in 1917, he became the principal organizer of the October Revolution.

His second life was that of one of the two principal leaders of the Soviet régime. As first Commissar of Foreign Affairs, Trotsky negotiated at length for a separate peace with Germany but refused to sign the Treaty of Brest Litovsk. Serving as Commissar of Military Affairs, he helped create the Red Army and defeat the White and Allied forces. In the struggle for Lenin's succession Trotsky had many initial advantages but was outmaneuvered by Stalin and other rivals and expelled from the Party in December 1927.

Exiled abroad, Trotsky took up his pre-1917 career again as a revolutionary publicist and organizer, and for a time his Fourth International was a factor of some importance on the revolutionary Left. Trotsky and Trotskyism were one of the main targets of Stalin's drastic purge of the Party after 1935. In 1940 Trotsky was assassinated in Mexico City.

A prolific journalist and polemicist, Trotsky is chiefly remembered by students of Russian history for "My Life" (1930), "The History of the Russian Revolution" (3 vols., 1933), and an unfinished study, "Stalin" (1941). His political views are probably best set forth in "The Permanent Revolution" (1931) and "The Revolution Betrayed" (1937).

Trotsky was vastly confident of the unique efficacy of Marxism-Leninism, as he understood it, as well as of his own powers of analysis and persuasion. Indeed, even his strongest opponents admired his penetrating mind and stormy rhetoric and feared his biting wit. How far his ideological commitment and his wide knowledge of world affairs in fact equipped Trotsky to assess realistically the increasingly ominous prospects of 1934 can be left to each reader of his article on "Nationalism and Economic Life" (April 1934) to judge for himself.

NATIONALISM AND ECONOMIC LIFE

By Leon Trotsky

ITALIAN fascism has proclaimed national "sacred egoism" as the sole creative factor. After reducing the history of humanity to national history, German fascism proceeded to reduce nation to race, and race to blood. Moreover, in those countries which politically have not risen— or rather, descended—to fascism, the problems of economy are more and more being forced into national frameworks. Not all of them have the courage to inscribe "autarchy" openly upon their banners. But everywhere policy is being directed toward as hermetic a segregation as possible of national life away from world economy. Only twenty years ago all the school books taught that the mightiest factor in producing wealth and culture is the world-wide division of labor, lodged in the natural and historic conditions of the development of mankind. Now it turns out that world exchange is the source of all misfortunes and all dangers. Homeward ho! Back to the national hearth! Not only must we correct the mistake of Admiral Perry, who blasted the breach in Japan's "autarchy," but a correction must also be made of the much bigger mistake of Christopher Columbus, which resulted in so immoderately extending the arena of human culture.

The enduring value of the nation, discovered by Mussolini and Hitler, is now set off against the false values of the nineteenth century: democracy and socialism. Here too we come into an irreconcilable contradiction with the old primers, and worse yet, with the irrefutable facts of history. Only vicious ignorance can draw a sharp contrast between the nation and liberal democracy. As a matter of fact, all the movements of liberation in modern history, beginning, say, with Holland's struggle for independence, had both a national and a democratic character. The awakening of the oppressed and dismembered nations, their struggle to unite their severed parts and to throw off the foreign yoke, would have been impossible without a struggle for political liberty.

The French nation was consolidated in the storms and tempests of democratic revolution at the close of the eighteenth century. The Italian and German nations emerged from a series of wars and revolutions in the nineteenth century. The powerful development of the American nation, which had received its baptism of freedom in its uprising in the eighteenth century, was finally guaranteed by the victory of the North over the South in the Civil War. Neither Mussolini nor Hitler is the discoverer of the nation. Patriotism in its modern sense—or more precisely its bourgeois sense—is the product of the nineteenth century. The national consciousness of the French people is perhaps the most conservative and the most stable of any; and to this very day it feeds from the springs of democratic traditions.

But the economic development of mankind which overthrew mediæval particularism did not stop within national boundaries. The growth of world exchange took place parallel with the formation of national economies. The tendency of this development—for advanced countries, at any rate—found its expression in the shift of the center of gravity from the domestic to the foreign market. The nineteenth century was marked by the fusion of the nation's fate with the fate of its economic life; but the basic tendency of our century is the growing contradiction between the nation and economic life. In Europe this contradiction has become intolerably acute.

The development of German capitalism was of the most dynamic character. In the middle of the nineteenth century the German people felt themselves stifled in the cages of several dozen feudal fatherlands. Less than four decades after the creation of the German Empire, German industry was suffocating within the framework of the national state. One of the main causes of the World War was the striving of German capital to break through into a wider arena. Hitler fought as a corporal in 1914-1918 not to unite the German nation but in the name of a supra-national imperialistic program that expressed itself in the famous formula "to organize Europe." Unified under the domination of German militarism Europe was to have become the drill-ground for a much bigger job—the organization of the entire planet.

But Germany was no exception. She only expressed in a more intense and aggressive form the tendency of every other national capitalist economy. The clash between these tendencies resulted in the war. The war, it is true, like all the grandiose upheavals of history, stirred up various historical questions and in passing gave the impulse to national revolutions in the more backward sections of Europe—Tsarist Russia and Austria-Hungary. But these were only the belated echoes of an epoch that had already passed away. Essentially the war was imperialist in character. With lethal and barbaric methods it attempted to solve a problem of progressive historic development—the problem of organizing economic life over the entire arena which had been prepared by the world-wide division of labor. Needless to say, the war did not find the solution to this problem. On the contrary, it atomized Europe even more. It deepened the interdependence of Europe and America at the same time that it deepened the antagonism between them. It gave the impetus to the independent development of colonial countries and simultaneously sharpened the dependence of the metropolitan centers upon colonial markets. As a consequence of the war, all the contradictions of the past were aggravated. One could half-shut one's eyes to this during the first years after the war, when Europe, aided by America, was busy repairing its devastated economy from top to bottom. But to restore productive forces inevitably implied the reinvigorating of all those evils that had led to the war. The present crisis, in which are synthesized all the capitalist crises of the past, signifies above all the crisis of *national* economic life.

The League of Nations attempted to translate from the language of militarism into the language of diplomatic pacts the task which the war left unsolved. After Ludendorff had failed to "organize Europe" by the sword, Briand attempted to create "the United States of Europe" by means of sugary diplomatic eloquence. But the interminable series of political, economic, financial, tariff, and monetary conferences only unfolded the panorama of the bankruptcy of the ruling classes in face of the unpostponable and burning task of our epoch.

Theoretically this task may be formulated as follows: How may the economic unity of Europe be guaranteed, while preserving complete freedom of cultural development to the peoples living there? How may unified Europe be included within a coördinated world economy? The solution to this question can be reached not by deifying the nation, but on the contrary by completely liberating productive forces from the fetters imposed upon them by the national state. But the ruling classes of Europe, demoralized by the bankruptcy of military and diplomatic methods, approach the task today from the opposite end, that is, they attempt by force to subordinate economy to the outdated national state.

The legend of the bed of Procrustes is being reproduced on a grand scale. Instead of clearing away a suitably large arena for the operations of modern technology, the rulers chop and slice the living organism of economy to pieces.

In a recent program speech Mussolini hailed the death of "economic liberalism," that is, of the reign of free competition. The idea itself is not new. The epoch of trusts, syndicates and cartels has long since relegated free competition to the back-yard. But trusts are even less reconcilable with restricted national markets than are the enterprises of liberal capitalism. Monopoly devoured competition in proportion as the world economy subordinated the national market. Economic liberalism and economic nationalism became outdated at the same time. Attempts to save economic life by inoculating it with virus from the corpse of nationalism result in blood poisoning which bears the name of fascism.

Mankind is impelled in its historic ascent by the urge to attain the greatest possible quantity of goods with the least expenditure of labor. This material foundation of cultural growth provides also the most profound criterion by which we may appraise social régimes and political programs. The law of the productivity of labor is of the same significance in the sphere of human society as the law of gravitation in the sphere of mechanics. The disappearance of outgrown social formations is but the manifestation of this cruel law that determined the victory of slavery over cannibalism, of serfdom over slavery, of hired labor over serfdom. The law of the productivity of labor finds its way not in a straight line but in a contradictory manner, by spurts and jerks, leaps and zigzags, surmounting on its way geographical, anthropological and social barriers. Whence so many "exceptions" in history, which are in reality only specific refractions of the "rule."

In the nineteenth century the struggle for the greatest productivity of labor took mainly the form of free competition, which maintained the dynamic equilibrium of capitalist economy through cyclical fluctuations. But precisely because of its progressive rôle competition has led to a monstrous concentration of trusts and syndicates, and this in turn has meant a concentration of economic and social contradictions. Free competition is like a chicken that hatched not a duckling but a crocodile. No wonder she cannot manage her offspring!

Economic liberalism has completely outlived its day. With less and less conviction its Mohegans appeal to the automatic interplay of forces.

New methods are needed to make skyscraper trusts correspond to human needs. There must be radical changes in the structure of society and economy. But new methods come into clash with old habits and, what is infinitely more important, with old interests. The law of the productivity of labor beats convulsively against barriers which it itself set up. This is what lies at the core of the grandiose crisis of the modern economic system.

Conservative politicians and theorists, taken unawares by the destructive tendencies of national and international economy, incline towards the conclusion that the overdevelopment of technology is the principal cause of present evils. It is difficult to imagine a more tragic paradox! A French politician and financier, Joseph Caillaux, sees salvation in artificial limitations on the process of mechanization. Thus the most enlightened representatives of the liberal doctrine suddenly draw inspiration from the sentiments of those ignorant workers of over a hundred years ago who smashed weaving looms. The progressive task of how to adapt the arena of economic and social relations to the new technology is turned upside down, and is made to seem a problem of how to restrain and cut down productive forces so as to fit them to the old national arena and to the old social relations. On both sides of the Atlantic no little mental energy is wasted on efforts to solve the fantastic problem of how to drive the crocodile back into the chicken egg. The ultra-modern economic nationalism is irrevocably doomed by its own reactionary character; it retards and lowers the productive forces of man.

The policies of a closed economy imply the artificial constriction of those branches of industry which are capable of fertilizing successfully the economy and culture of other countries. They also imply an artificial planting of those industries which lack favorable conditions for growth on national soil. The fiction of economic self-sufficiency thus causes tremendous overhead expenditures in two directions. Added to this is inflation. During the nineteenth century, gold as a universal measure of value became the foundation of all monetary systems worthy of the name. Departures from the gold standard tear world economy apart even more successfully than do tariff walls. Inflation, itself an expression of disordered internal relationships and of disordered economic ties between nations, intensifies the disorder and helps to turn it from a functional into an organic one. Thus the "national" monetary system crowns the sinister work of economic nationalism.

The most intrepid representatives of this school console themselves with the prospect that the nation, while becoming poorer under a closed economy will become more "unified" (Hitler), and that as the importance of the world market declines the causes for external conflicts will also diminish. Such hopes only demonstrate that the doctrine of autarchy is both reactionary and utterly utopian. The fact is that the breeding places of nationalism also are the laboratories of terrific conflicts in the future; like a hungry tiger, imperialism has withdrawn into its own national lair to gather itself for a new leap.

Actually, theories about economic nationalism which seem to base themselves on the "eternal" laws of race show only how desperate the world crisis really is—a classic example of making a virtue of bitter need. Shivering on bare benches in some God-forsaken little station, the passengers of a wrecked train may stoically assure each other that creature comforts are corrupting to body and soul. But all of them are dreaming of a locomotive that would get them to a place where they could stretch their tired bodies between two clean sheets. The immediate concern of the business world in all countries is to hold out, to survive somehow, even if in a coma, on the hard bed of the national market. But all these involuntary stoics are longing for the powerful engine of a new world "conjuncture," a new economic phase.

Will it come? Predictions are rendered difficult, if not altogether impossible, by the present structural disturbance of the whole economic system. Old industrial cycles, like the heartbeats of a healthy body, had a stable rhythm. Since the war we no longer observe the orderly sequence of economic phases; the old heart skips beats. In addition, there is the policy of so-called "state capitalism." Driven on by restless interests and by social dangers, governments burst into the economic realm with emergency measures, the effects of which in most cases it cannot itself foresee. But even leaving aside the possibility of a new war that would upset for a long time the elemental work of economic forces as well as conscious attempts at planned control, we nevertheless can confidently foresee the turning point from the crisis and depression to a revival, whether or not the favorable symptoms present in England and to some degree in the United States prove later on to have been first swallows that did not bring the spring. The destructive work of the crisis must reach the point—if it has not already reached it—where impoverished mankind will need a new mass of goods. Chimneys will smoke, wheels will turn. And when the revival is sufficiently advanced, the business world will shake off its stupor, will promptly forget yesterday's lessons, and will contemptuously cast aside self-denying theories along with their authors.

But it would be the greatest delusion to hope that the scope of the impending revival will correspond to the depth of the present crisis. In childhood, in maturity, and in old age the heart beats at a different tempo. During capitalism's ascent successive crises had a fleeting character and the temporary decline in production was more than compensated at the next stage. Not so now. We have entered an epoch when the periods of economic revival are short-lived, while the periods of depression become deeper and deeper. The lean cows devour the fat cows without a trace and still continue to bellow with hunger.

All the capitalist states will be more aggressively impatient, then, as soon as the economic barometer begins to rise. The struggle for foreign markets will become unprecedentedly sharp. Pious notions about the advantages of autarchy will at once be cast aside, and sage plans for national harmony will be thrown in the waste-paper basket. This applies not only to German capitalism, with its explosive dynamics, or to the belated and greedy capitalism of Japan, but also to the capitalism of America, which still is powerful despite its new contradictions.

The United States represented the most perfect type of capitalist development. The relative equilibrium of its internal and seemingly inexhaustible market assured the United States a decided technical and economic preponderance over Europe. But its intervention in the World War was really an expression of the fact that its internal equilibrium was already disrupted. The changes introduced by the war into the American structure have in turn made entry into the world arena a life and death question for American capitalism. There is ample evidence that this entry must assume extremely dramatic forms.

The law of the productivity of labor is of decisive significance in the interrelations of America and Europe, and in general in determining the future place of the United States in the world. That highest form which the Yankees gave to the law of the productivity of labor is called conveyor, standard, or mass production. It would seem that the spot from which the lever of Archimedes was to turn the world over had been found. But the old planet refuses to be turned over. Everyone defends himself against everybody else, protecting himself by a customs wall and a hedge of bayonets. Europe buys no goods, pays no debts, and in addition arms itself. With five miserable divisions starved Japan seizes a whole country. The most advanced technique in the world suddenly seems impotent before obstacles basing themselves on a much lower technique. The law of the productivity of labor seems to lose its force.

But it only seems so. The basic law of human history must inevitably take revenge on derivative and secondary phenomena. Sooner or later American capitalism must open up ways for itself throughout the length and breadth of our entire planet. By what methods? By *all* methods. A high coefficient of productivity denotes also a high coefficient of destructive force. Am I preaching war? Not in the least. I am not preaching anything. I am only attempting to analyze the world situation and to draw conclusions from the laws of economic mechanics. There is nothing worse than the sort of mental cowardice which turns its back on facts and tendencies when they contradict ideals or prejudices.

Only in the historic framework of world development can we assign fascism its proper place. It contains nothing creative, nothing independent. Its historic mission is to reduce to an absurdity the theory and practice of the economic impasse.

In its day democratic nationalism led mankind forward. Even now, it is still capable of playing a progressive rôle in the colonial countries of the East. But decadent fascist nationalism, preparing volcanic explosions and grandiose clashes in the world arena, bears nothing except ruin. All our experiences on this score during the last twenty-five or thirty years will seem only an idyllic overture compared to the music of hell that is impending. And this time it is not a temporary economic decline which is involved but complete economic devastation and the destruction of our entire culture, in the event that toiling and thinking humanity proves incapable of grasping in time the reins of its own productive forces and of organizing those forces correctly on a European and a world scale.

THE establishment by Stalin of his dominance over the Bolshevik Party was shortly followed by the launching of the first Five Year Plan of forced industrialization and rural collectivization. To the outside world, and to thousands of Western tourists who were escorted through the principal cities and resorts on prearranged tours, this much was clear: the Russian giant was thrashing about in the anguish of a drastic new revolution. However, even those expert observers—diplomats and journalists—who were stationed in Moscow found it extremely difficult to grasp the vast and unprecedented scope of the reshaping that was being imposed from the top. One instance of the gap between reality and knowledge was the great difficulty in securing reliable information about the widespread famine of 1932-33. Brought on in large part by Stalin's determination to break the peasants' resistance to the system of collective farms, the famine became known beyond Russia's borders only gradually and in fragmentary fashion.

One of the first, most authoritative, and vivid accounts of this period of profound misery was "The Ordeal of the Russian Peasantry" (April 1934), by William Henry Chamberlin. As Moscow correspondent of the *Christian Science Monitor* between 1922 and 1934, Mr. Chamberlin enjoyed and put to good use a remarkable opportunity to observe and reflect on the many dramatic struggles of those years, both within the power apparatus and between the increasingly ruthless dictatorship and the people. In this article he gave an eyewitness report of the post-famine conditions which he had observed in villages of the Ukraine and Southeast Russia. His account is an historic document in itself.

Among a large number of books and articles by Mr. Chamberlin, special mention must be made of "The Russian Revolution" (2 vols., 1935), a classic analysis, begun only five years after the events of 1917 and buttressed by innumerable discussions with eyewitnesses and participants in the events he described. "Russia's Iron Age" (1934) summed up his observations of the great and painful changes imposed under Stalin's dictatorship. Among Mr. Chamberlin's more recent books, to mention only two, are "America's Second Crusade" (1950), a vigorous critique of U.S. policy in World War II, and "Appeasement, Road to War" (1962).

THE ORDEAL OF THE RUSSIAN PEASANTRY

By *William Henry Chamberlain*

FOUR years have passed since the rulers of the Soviet Union decided to make an end of individual farming. These four years represent a period of what may be called agrarian revolution from the top, because no one with any realistic knowledge of the Russian village can believe that the majority of the peasants, left to their own volition, would have decided to sink their small holdings in the new *kolkhozi,* or collective farms. The best evidence on this question is the fact that only about two percent of the peasant households entered collective farms during the years of the New Economic Policy, up to 1929, when the choice was entirely free and before the overwhelming administrative and economic power of the highly centralized and dictatorial Soviet state had not been thrown on the side of the new organization of agriculture.

During these four years the Russian peasants have lived through a tremendous ordeal, second in degree of violent change and suffering only to the crowded years of social upheaval, civil war and famine which marked the period from 1917 until 1921. The very face of the countryside has been transformed. The traditional strips of land which signalized individual holdings have given way to the wide, compact fields of collective and state farms. The hum of the tractor is heard far more frequently. There are changes which are less favorable: if there are more tractors on the Soviet fields there are far fewer horses and cows, pigs and sheep; and the new harvesting combines which are supposed to symbolize the march of progress in agriculture sometimes find the going hard in the seas of weeds to be found on far too many state and collective farms.

In the human sphere the changes that one finds in the Russian country districts today are even more revolutionary. In a very literal sense, the first have often become last and the last have become first.

The former *batrak,* or farmhand, who used to be at the bottom of the village social hierarchy, may today be the manager of a collective farm, directing the work of hundreds of his fellow villagers. There has been a considerable influx of urban Communists, some of them ex-workers, into the villages as directors of state and collective farms or heads of the important political departments which were installed during the last year. There has been a gigantic "liquidation" of the more well-to-do and incorrigibly individualistic peasants, loosely and conveniently dubbed *kulaks.* They have been transported by hundreds of thousands, if not by millions, to forced labor in timber camps and on new construction enterprises and canals. And during the last winter and spring stark hunger, accompanied by a mortality rate that was three or four times the normal figure, stalked through the villages of wide areas of southern and southeastern Russia. This low point in the Soviet agrarian situation has been followed by an appreciable recovery, in connection with this year's good harvest; but much reconstruction remains to be done before Russian agricultural production can be regarded as normal and satisfactory.

The word experiment has been overworked in connection with the Soviet Union; but it is still applicable to the great upheaval in agricultural relations which set in during 1929. As it has directly affected the lives of more people than any other single Soviet policy, and as it has inaugurated completely novel methods of rural economy, the aims and the results of this experiment up to date seem worthy of careful study, especially as a certain degree of stabilization has now been reached in the organization of the Russian countryside.

The objective of Soviet agrarian policy may be summed up in the phrase: collectivization plus mechanization.[1] Under the new scheme, the collective farm, where hundreds or in exceptional cases thousands of peasant holdings would be thrown together, was to become the basic unit in agriculture. Side by side with the collective farms, of which there are now more than 230,000, were created a considerable number of new state farms. There are between 5,000 and 6,000 state farms at the present time. They differ from the collective farms in that they are

---

[1] The present organization of Soviet agriculture did not spring ready-made from the minds of the rulers in the Kremlin; important adjustments and modifications have been made from time to time; and some very significant innovations have been introduced during the last year. But the general trend of policy has been unbroken.

established on unused or confiscated land and equipped by the state, whereas the collective farms pool the resources of their members. The state farm is operated on the same principle as a state factory, with a manager appointed by the organization which has charge of the farm and hired labor paid at fixed rates. On the collective farm, on the other hand, no wages are paid. The earnings of the members, which are partly in money, partly in kind, depend on the outcome of each year's crops.

The cement that was to hold the collective farms together, and to increase their productivity, was to be supplied by tractors, harvesting combines, threshing-machines, and other large-scale agricultural implements. Three huge tractor plants (of which two are in full operation) were constructed during the Five Year Plan; the largest agricultural machinery works in Europe was erected at Rostov; and there has been an enlargement of old factories and a building of new ones for the manufacture of combines. It is noteworthy and significant for the new spirit of Soviet agriculture that tractors and similar large machines are not given or sold to the collective farms in direct ownership. They are concentrated in so-called machine-tractor stations, which may be considered the nerve-centers of Soviet agriculture. There are between 2,500 and 3,000 machine-tractor stations all over the Soviet Union; and they send out their machines to all collective farms within a convenient radius, exacting, in return for their services, a fee in kind that may run as high as twenty percent of the crop. There are now about 200,000 tractors working on Soviet fields.

The massing of equipment in the state-operated machine-tractor stations serves a double purpose, technical and political. Provided that the machine-tractor station is efficiently managed and keeps its machines in reasonable repair, this institution insures a more continuous use and a more even spread of mechanized power than would be possible if every collective farm had its own share, large or small, of machinery. Politically this system deprives the collective farmers of any direct ownership of their means of production. It is just one of a number of very powerful weapons which the state can use to bring a recalcitrant collective farm to submission in such matters as state grain deliveries.

Now the Soviet system of agricultural reconstruction has come up against two sets of obstacles, of somewhat different psychological origin. In the first place, it went sharply against the grain of long established habit for the peasant to give up the small individual holding, poor as might be the living which it afforded, and to take his place in the ranks of a large organization, the head of which might be a man whom he did not know and whose agricultural capacity might be open to doubt. The lack of a trained managerial class for the new large and medium-sized farms which were created so suddenly has been a big handicap, from the standpoint of productive efficiency; and managers of collective farms have not infrequently been selected for political zeal rather than for expert knowledge of agriculture. The wrench at parting with his own land, his own horse and his own working equipment was, of course, apt to be greater in proportion to the peasant's amount of material well-being. The poorest peasants naturally accepted the new order more acquiescently, if not more enthusiastically, than the well-to-do.

Secondly, the peasant, by virtue of the logic of development under the Five Year Plan, was compelled to fulfill his historic rôle as a heavily laden beast of burden for the state. It is a matter of historical record that Peter the Great, pursuing ambitious schemes of modernization and national aggrandizement, squeezed more out of the peasants than the sleepy Romanov Tsars who preceded him. And one cannot begin to count the cost of Magnitogorsk, Dnieprostroi and the other steel mills, electrical power plants, chemical factories and machine works of the Five Year Plan unless one travels in the villages and acquires first-hand knowledge of the additional levies which have been imposed on the peasants during recent years.

At a time when he was in sharp opposition to the Party leadership, embodied in Joseph Stalin, the well-known Communist theoretician, Nikolai Bukharin, let slip the phrase: "military feudal exploitation of the peasantry." Now he has repented and recanted it. And there is, of course, no official sanction for the view of Trotsky's former lieutenant, Eugene Preobrazhensky, that the peasantry in the Soviet Union represent a colony, from which fresh capital for industrial development must be extracted. But peasants who never heard of Bukharin and Preobrazhensky are keenly aware of the fact that their yoke has become steadily harder, at least up to the present year, in connection with the country's sweeping program of industrial construction; and this fact has had a disastrous effect on their morale and on their will to work. It was a distinguishing feature of the New Economic Policy that the peasant had entire freedom in disposing of his surplus produce. A tax in kind was imposed in 1921 and 1922, after which the peasant was liable to an income tax, payable in money. The necessity for meeting this tax and the desire to buy town products were the motives that induced the peasant to sell his grain and other foodstuffs.

The first breach in this system, the first violation of the peasant's right to dispose of his crop as he saw fit, occurred in 1928, when the Government, finding that grain was coming on the market slowly, employed threats of arrest and exile to compel the peasants to sell their grain at the fixed price. This system was greatly extended in succeeding years, and was applied to meat, milk, flax, cotton and most other staple agricultural products. Probably no words were so hated among the peasants in recent years as *khlebozagotovki* (grain collections) and *kontraktatsia* (contracting). The autumn period of grain collection was annually heralded by the publication of stern instructions to the rural Soviet authorities to buy up the maximum amount of grain from the peasants, on pain of being considered "right opportunists" and *"kulak* sympathizers," two very formidable terms of abuse in the Soviet Union. The method of carrying out these "purchases," which were much more suggestive of requisitions, was to set up a quota for deliveries of grain and other products which had to be filled out by every district, every collective farm, every individual peasant household. Failure to comply with the quota was often punished with fines, arrests and deportations. The agricultural produce was paid for at fixed prices, which became steadily smaller in relation to the soaring free market prices. While theoretically peasants who fulfilled their quotas were inclined to buy manufactured goods at correspondingly low prices, the supply of manufactured goods, as a general rule, never sufficed for more than a small fraction of the peasant demand.

This was one major objection of the peasants to this so-called "contracting" system (rather naïvely described by an enthusiastic visitor to the Soviet Union as a beneficent institution, from the peasants' standpoint, since it assured them a ready market and a fair price for their products). The other, even more serious, objection was that the demands of the state were apt to be given precedence over the food needs of the peasants. The peasants had no effective voice in determining the quotas which they were required to deliver up. And the state had several compelling reasons for extracting from the villages the maximum amount of foodstuffs. There was the growing army of workers and employees in the big new industrial plants and construction enterprises to be fed. There was the chronic need for foreign currency with which to pay for imported foreign equipment and machinery, a need which could be partially met by forcing the exportation of food products. After the autumn of 1931 a new element entered into the situation: the desire to create large reserves of staple provisions for the military forces which were concentrated in the Far East.

In view of these conditions it was quite natural that the peasants' needs should be given secondary consideration. And it was equally natural that the peasants, much less touched than the city population by Communist agitation and quite indisposed to make voluntary sacrifices on the altar of Soviet industrialization, should have resented a system under which much was taken from them and little was given to them. This feeling of resentment unquestionably played a large rôle in the poor functioning of the collective farms during the first years of their existence.

My travels in the country districts have not given me the impression that superstitious aversion to new ideas in general and to machinery in particular was in any sense an important factor in the passive resistance which certainly characterized the attitude of many of the peasants toward collective farming. A tractor or a harvesting combine might excite some such feeling in the forests of the north or in a Caucasian *aul,* or mountain village; but in the fertile grain belt of southern and southeastern Russia, whither most of the tractors were dispatched, the overwhelming majority of the peasants were sufficiently advanced to welcome labor-saving machinery. What they disliked about the new agricultural order was not the new power-driven machines, but the fact that neither these machines nor the crops which were produced belonged to them, and that the state claimed and exercised the right of making arbitrary and undetermined levies in kind on their produce.

I have been able to obtain some idea of the phases through which collective farming has passed in the course of three trips to agricultural regions of the Soviet Union. The first of these trips took me to the Lower Volga in the late summer of 1930; the second was to the Crimea and to the Odessa region of Ukraina a year later; the third was to the Kropotkin region of the North Caucasus and to the Kiev and Poltava regions of Ukraina in the latter part of September 1933.

The first trip was immediately after the vast upheaval which had followed the drive to introduce collectivization on a mass scale. The harvest of 1930 was excellent; and Soviet publicists somewhat incautiously and prematurely endeavored to interpret this bounty of nature as primarily attributable to the new system. On the other hand, one found everywhere a formidable diminution in the number of cows, sheep and pigs; the more well-to-do peasants had slaughtered their animals wholesale rather than give them up to the collective farms. There was at this time no acute distress, if one makes allowance for the traditionally low standard of living of the Russian peasants, except among the luckless *kulaki*, the four or five percent of the peasants who had been driven from their homes and expropriated as exploiters. Some of the *kulaki* had been shipped off to remote places of exile and hard labor in the forbidding north; others were living in great misery in dugouts and improvised huts outside the village limits, where they had been assigned stretches of poor land and told, more or less, to sink or swim. This was *Shrecklichkeit* on a large scale, for the total number of families which were liable to uprooting as *kulaki* all over Russia can scarcely have been much short of a million. Not all of them suffered the more extreme penalty of exile, because some fled in time and concealed themselves in the towns or in parts of the country where they were not known. At the same time this "liquidation" of the *kulaki* "as a class" was an important and probably an indispensable measure in breaking down the resistance of the peasants to the new system. The *kulak,* often better educated than his average neighbor and wielding influence simply because he was a successful farmer, was the natural leader of individualist resistance to the new system. With him disposed of in such summary fashion, the task of regimenting the other peasants became much simpler.

For the mass of the peasants the problem of goods exchange between city and village had become acute, and I recall a stormy general meeting of the members of one collective farm, where a representative of the regional Communist Party organization expounded a scheme under which the peasants were to be allowed to buy thirty-five kopecks worth of manufactured goods for every ruble's worth of grain which they sold to the state. The sentiment of the gathering was pretty faithfully voiced by the local blacksmith, who bellowed out: "Thirty-five kopecks on the ruble isn't enough. Couldn't they at least give us all one shirt?"

Although there was some extension of the planted area in 1931 nature turned unfavorable and the total harvest was lower than in the preceding year. There was a further grave decline in 1932; the food situation in the following winter and spring was strained in the towns and catastrophic in some country districts. On January 8, 1934, *Izvestia* published the following official statistics of harvest yields of the main grain crops for the past four years: 1930, 83,540,000 tons; 1931, 69,480,000; 1932, 69,870,000; 1933, 89,800,000. In 1913 the yield was 80,100,000 tons. The figures for 1932 and 1933 are considerably better than foreign unofficial estimates. Nevertheless, it is significant that in the two lean years, 1931 and 1932, the official estimate of the grain yield is lower by over ten million tons than the figure for 1913, when the population was much smaller. It is also interesting to note that both the yield per acre and the total yield in 1931 and 1932 were lower than was the case in any year between 1925 and 1929, when individual farming was the prevalent form of agriculture.

Weather alone could not be blamed for the poor harvest of 1932. Not only were climatic conditions unfavorable in two main grain-producing regions, Ukraina and the North Caucasus; but in many cases the peasants, discouraged by years of arbitrary requisitioning of their surplus, simply failed to work with normal efficiency. The results are reflected in the report of a correspondent of the Communist Party organ, *Pravda,* after returning from a tour of investigation in the North Caucasus: "The fields of the Kropotkin region are bearing a thick forest of man-size weeds. . . . In the upper Don corn, sunflower seeds and millet perished from late sowing. . . . The overgrowth of weeds creates extraordinary difficulties with the harvesting. Sheaves sometimes contain more weeds than grain. It is also difficult to stack the weedy grain."

During the first half of the present year the resident of Moscow was perplexed by two apparently contradictory sets of reports about conditions in the southern and southeastern provinces of Russia. Unofficial rumors of hunger on a scale unknown since 1921 and 1922, the years of the greatest famine in Russia's history, were offset by official claims of a successful spring planting and a favorable crop. In the course of visits to three widely separated regions of Ukraina and the North Caucasus I became convinced that both reports contained a considerable element of truth. Last winter and spring hunger wrote some of the darkest pages in the sombre history of the Russian peasantry. At the time of my trip, in the autumn, there had been a substantial seasonal improvement in food supply; the harvest yield was comfortably above the average, especially in Ukraina; and it did not seem probable that the widespread grim suffering of the early part of the year would be repeated.

Perhaps the Kuban Valley in the North Caucasus, in pre-war days a notably rich and prosperous farming region, offers the most vivid evidence of the havoc which class war has played with Russian agricultural production during the last years. The central point of my trip here was the Cossack village of Kazanskaya, which is some ten miles from the railroad station Kropotkin and is picturesquely located on a high bluff overlooking the Kuban River. I had visited the Kuban region many years ago; and my first reaction of surprise was excited by the complete absence of the fierce and vociferous dogs, of which every Cossack household had formerly possessed, as a rule, at least two or three. The dogs, as I was told by all the peasants whom I questioned, had been eaten or had perished during the hunger. The second unfavorable impresssion was the amazing growth of weeds, huge, tough and luxuriant, along the roads, in many of the gardens, and in some of the fields. Add to this the fact that almost everyone, from presidents of collective farms to boys and old women on the roads, was feverish as a result of a sweeping epidemic of malaria, and that every native of Kazanskaya and the surrounding villages had vivid tales of last winter's hunger, sometimes accompanied by stories of friends or relatives who had died either from the swelling which is the main sign of hunger or from the weakness and diseases which are associated with malnutrition, and one may well come to the conclusion that the triumph of collective farming in this part of the Soviet Union seemed to possess a good many elements of a Pyrrhic victory.

Even here, however, where the resistance of the population and the ruthless suppression of that resistance by the authorities had been intensified by the fact that a considerable part of the population consisted of Cossacks, the backbone of the White armies during the civil war, there was the negative consolation that the outlook was not so bad as it had been a year ago. The harvest, although not satisfactory, was better than in the previous year, and there was more certainty as to how much of it would remain at the disposal of the peasants. The head of the Kazanskaya Soviet, Mr. Nemov, estimated that about 850 of the village's population of 8,000 had perished during the last year. He furnished detailed figures for the first four months of the year, showing a steep rise in the mortality curve, accompanying the diminution of food reserves toward spring. According to his figures, 21 people died in January, 34 in February, 79 in March and 155 in April. Deaths from "exhaustion," of which there was one in January, increased to 98 in April.

One found much the same picture in wandering through villages around Poltava, site of Peter the Great's decisive victory over King Charles XII of Sweden, and Belaya Tserkov, a town in the former Jewish Pale of Settlement, southwest of Kiev. The Kazanskaya figure of approximately ten percent mortality was frequently found, although one found villages which had apparently fared better and one, named Cherkass, which had fared much worse, according to the figures of its Soviet. Except for one commune near Poltava, which had developed under relatively favorable auspices, I did not find a single place which did not report some casualties. The measure of the hunger from which the Soviet Union suffered during the past winter and spring may be gauged from the fact that the population of Ukraina is approximately 35,000,000, that of the North Caucasus about 10,000,000, and that of other regions which, according to general reports, did not escape the scourge of failure of food supply, such as the Middle and Lower Volga and Kazakstan, about 15,000,000.

The hunger was a direct result of the crisis, already mentioned, of collectivized agriculture in 1932. Although there had apparently been no violent resistance on a mass scale, many of the peasants unquestionably went on a passive strike and simply let a good deal of the crop go to waste on the fields. The government was unwilling to abate its grain demands in the face of what it regarded as deliberate sabotage. Consequently, although some state relief was furnished in the spring, especially to collective farms, there simply was not enough food to go around, and a heavy death toll followed. As might have been expected, the mortality was far greater in the villages than in the towns, where a regular if sometimes straitened bread ration was assured to workers and employees, and it was much heavier among *edinolichniki* (individual peasants) than among members of collective farms. For some less clearly explicable reason men apparently succumbed more readily than women.

That a generally good crop was harvested this year may seem amazing, in the light of what happened last winter and spring. One must remember, however, that there is a tenacious vitality in the semi-Asiatic Russian peasantry and that recovery comes more easily than might be the case in a softer country. Moreover, the very extremity to which the peasants were reduced was a very powerful incentive in driving them to work hard and to discard all thought of shirking. Other factors in the relative improvement which this year has witnessed in the Soviet agricultural situation may be listed.

In the first place, the weather, which plays a bigger part in harvest yields than Communist planners like to admit, was more favorable, Secondly, a very important change in the method of assessing the levies in kind on the peasants, adopted by the government last winter, yielded beneficial results. Up to 1933 there was no recognized limit to the amount of grain which an energetic local official might squeeze out of the peasants in his district. Now the peasant's obligation is clearly set down in the form of an acreage tax, which varies in different parts of the country according to the fertility of the soil (it amounts to about five bushels an acre in the rich black-earth regions of the south and southeast). Inasmuch as this tax cannot be either diminished or increased, it places a premium on efficient farming, since the peasant who raises more grain will retain more for his own use and for free sale on the market. Still another factor making for improvement is the institution throughout the countryside of so-called political departments, manned by picked Communists and entrusted with the function of supervising propaganda and developing leadership in the collective farms. The political departments are attached to machine-tractor stations and to the larger state farms. They give the central authorities a firmer grip on the rural areas and push ahead the necessarily slow process of creating in the collectivized peasant something of the psychology of the urban worker.

When the Soviet régime embarked on its policy of placing all agriculture on a state and collectivist basis it launched out on quite uncharted waters. No such organization of agriculture had been known since man began to plant. Friends and enemies alike were extravagant in their prophecies of triumph or disaster. Looking back over a perspective of four years, one clearly sees the mistaken character of many of these prophecies. There is perhaps no more striking illustration of the tremendously firm grip of the Soviet Government on the Russian population than its demonstrated ability to carry out a change which was certainly unwelcome to a great many peasants, which was accompanied by the dispossession of large numbers of well-to-do peasant households, which led during the last winter and spring to hunger on a scale unknown since 1921-1922, without exciting any serious mass resistance. The system now is irrevocably clamped down, barring some quite unpredictable general upheaval in Russian life; and dictatorships of any kind are not in the habit of reckoning very much with the amount of human suffering which the execution of their policies may imply.

So the predictions of complete collapse and forced reversion to individualist farming have been refuted by the course of events. There has been an equally signal refutation of the idea that, as a result of collectivization, Russian agriculture would leap forward to unprecedented productivity. It is significant in this connection that the official summary of the results of the fulfillment of the first Five Year Plan is silent about such important indices of agricultural prosperity as the size of grain crops and the number of livestock in the country. Presumably the discrepancies between plan and achievement (the Five Year Plan forecast a steady increase in the number of livestock and a grain crop of about a hundred million tons in its last year, 1932-1933) were too glaring to be deemed suitable for publication.

While no official figures for livestock in the entire Soviet Union have been published within recent years, I was able to obtain from the Ukrainian Commissariat for Agriculture comparative statistics as revealed by a livestock count of 1929 and by a census, covering 86 percent of the rural Soviets, carried out in the summer of 1933. According to these figures, the number of horses decreased from 5,543,000 to 2,772,000; the number of horned cattle from 7,611,000 to 3,832,600; the number of cows from 3,873,000 to 2,049,000; [2] the number of pigs from 3,472,000 to 1,390,000; the number of sheep from 6,652,000 to 1,543,300. There is no reason to suppose that Ukraina fared worse, as regards the destruction of its livestock, than other former main cattle regions, such as the North Caucasus and Kazakstan, where governmental policy was equally ruthless and deliberate destruction or neglect of livestock by the desperate peasants was probably equally great. It is obvious, therefore, that in such an important branch of agriculture as animal husbandry there has been disastrous retrogression during the last four years which can be fully made good, in all probability, only after the passing of a longer period.

The idea, often propounded by people with very scant practical knowledge of agriculture, that tractors and large farm units, apart

[2] The 1929 figures for horned cattle and cows were obtained not from the Ukrainian Commissariat for Agriculture, but from a publication of the Soviet central statistical bureau entitled "The USSR for Fifteen Years."

from other conditions, would mean increased productivity, has proved a fallacy. The general food rationing in the towns, the acute food shortage in the villages, which reached its formidable climax last spring, the relatively small exportation of foodstuffs from Russia—all these things offer convincing proof that the problem of increasing the output of foodstuffs has not been satisfactorily solved as yet.

What does the future hold for the Russian peasantry, after the stern ordeal of the last four years? Favorable elements in the situation are the increased supply of tractors which is insured by the steadier and larger output of the big factories at Stalingrad and Kharkov, and the weaning away from old individualist habits that may conceivably come with the passing of time. On the other hand, any attempt to depart from the definite limits of the food levy which have been laid down during the present year, any injudicious effort to socialize the remaining personal property of the peasants, might provoke a new crisis. During the last few years the peasant has been carrying a large share of the heavy load of the Five Year Plan on his shoulders. He has been definitely the "forgotten man" of a social order on fire with schemes of industrial expansion and military preparedness. The future will show whether the young generation now growing up under the new collectivized order will attain a standard of living that may seem, in retrospect, to compensate in some measure for what their parents have lived through.

NIKOLAI BUKHARIN (1887-1938) was still close to the seat of Soviet power when he wrote "Imperialism and Communism" for *Foreign Affairs* (July 1936). After a turbulent career as a revolutionary ideologist and leader, he seemed to have found a modest but secure niche within Stalin's dictatorship as editor of *Izvestia* and patron of a relatively tolerant and fruitful era in Soviet literature. Less than a year later he was expelled from the Party, and in March 1938, following the third of Stalin's public purge trials, he was declared guilty of high treason, condemned to death and executed.

Like many other young Russians, Bukharin had dropped his studies to plunge into the underground revolutionary struggle in 1906. After several arrests he fled abroad in 1912 to join Lenin at Cracow, where he helped edit the new Bolshevik newspaper *Pravda*. At this time he was also working on his major theoretical study, "Political Economy of the Leisure Class," while continuing his studies at the University of Vienna. After the February Revolution, Bukharin returned from his exile in New York to head up the Bolshevik organization in Moscow. From 1918 to 1929 he served again as editor of *Pravda,* and he also took a prominent role in the affairs of the Communist International. Attacked by Stalin as a Rightist because of his warnings against forcing the pace of industrialization and agricultural collectivization too hard, he was removed from all his posts; but later he made his peace with Stalin, who in 1934 appointed him editor of *Izvestia.*

In the 1920s, Bukharin achieved great influence through his popularized versions of Leninism: "ABC of Communism" (with Evgeny Preobrazhensky, 1920) and "Theory of Historical Materialism" (1921). Most of his important ideological and economic studies have never been brought together in English, but "The Soviet Industrialization Debate, 1924-28" (1960), by Alexander Erlich, provides a penetrating analysis of Bukharin's conception, highly relevant today, of the optimal path of economic development.

Bukharin's article of 1936, as an expression of orthodox Bolshevik thought, can be profitably compared with the articles by Rakovsky, Radek, Trotsky and Khrushchev. The reader will also see for himself how far Bukharin's analysis has stood the test of later events.

IMPERIALISM AND COMMUNISM

By N. Bukharin

IT is well known that people have sometimes talked prose without having the least idea what it is. This holds true not only of characters in French literature but also of professional politicians. Thus at the present time a regular epidemic of discussion is raging in certain sections of the capitalist press in the effort to find explanations for the acts of aggression which again threaten to rack the world with war. And they are being discovered in natural factors—territory, raw materials, growth of population. These are considered quite apart from the economic form of society and the political superstructure in which it finds expression. In this parlance, Germany, Italy, Japan are "nations without land." The natural growth of the population of these states necessarily leads to a hunt for new land and more raw materials. Here, according to this view, lie the roots of the future war. It is fate, historical destiny. And the only salvation lies in a redivision of territory.

A plan of this sort was proposed by the late Frank H. Simonds in an article entitled "The 'Haves' and 'Have-Nots' " in *The Fortnightly*.[1] *The Economist*[2] published detailed tables showing the distribution of land and raw materials among the various countries in order to prove Great Britain's right to the *status quo*. In France, the fascist proponents of a rapprochement with Germany at the expense of Soviet Ukraine are highly indignant over the vast territories of the Soviet Union and the comparative sparseness of its population. In Germany itself, imperialism is frankly proclaimed as the sacred right of "Aryans" suffocating for lack of "space" (*"Volk ohne Raum"*). Needless to say, the required "space" is sought in the Soviet Union, the government of which is moreover accused of continuing the foreign policy of the Tsars. In Italy and Japan analogous theories have become the creed of the ruling classes, which preach them *ex professo*. The basis of all these argu-

[1] London, June 1935.
[2] London, October 26, 1935.

ments—though most of their authors are unaware of the fact—is the so-called theory of "Geopolitik," now particularly fashionable in fascist Germany. It is with this geopolitical "prose" that we shall commence our analysis.

I. "GEOPOLITICS" IN THEORY AND PRACTICE

It need hardly be said that the forerunners of geopolitics, *e.g.* the English historian Buckle, were in their day on a far higher level scientifically than their contemporaries who adhered to theological conceptions of the historical process; they were able to explain much by material factors that could not be explained by heavenly illusions. In Germany this peculiar brand of geographic materialism, or rather geographical naturalism, was developed by the founders of so-called "political geography," especially by Richthofen and above all Ratzel. The latter declared that the explanation of the historical process and of all politics lay in the size, position and frontiers of a given territory; in the form of the earth's surface and the soil, with its vegetation, water resources, etc.; and, finally, in the relation of the territory in question to other parts of the earth's surface. He maintained "that the attributes of the state are composed of those of the people and of the land" ("dass sich die Eigenschaften des Staates aus denen des Volkes und des Bodens zusammensetzen"). Before him, Richthofen had also introduced the race factor, in addition to factors of a geophysical order. The present-day school of "geopoliticians" (a name invented by the Swedish imperialist and political theorist R. Kjellén), who are grouped around the German magazine *Zeitschrift für Geopolitik* and its editor, Professor Haushofer, reiterate substantially the same ideas.

But while the views of Buckle (in so far as we are discussing the influence of climate, etc.) were progressive in their day, now, after the historical materialism of Marx, the writings of contemporary geopoliticians seem so much childish prattle (that is, logically; politically they are far from that).

In effect, geopolitics flatly denies all history. Relatively constant factors such as territory, soil, climate (and racial attributes which biological sociologists also consider as constant) cannot serve to explain historical and social changes. "Politics" does not grow out of the "land" at all, but first and foremost out of economic relations. The "land" undoubtedly influences the historical process; but it does so primarily through the process of labor and through economics, and these in their turn exercise a decisive influence on politics. The territory and the racial attributes of the British Isles have changed very little since the nineties of the last century, and they cannot possibly be made to explain, let us say, Great Britain's rapid change from free trade to a high protective tariff. The existence of a foreign trade monopoly in the U.S.S.R. cannot be explained by the "Russian steppes" or by the so-called "Slavic soul." But Great Britain's change to a high protective tariff can very well be explained by the transition of her economic system to monopoly capitalism, with its trusts and syndicates; and the foreign trade monopoly in the U.S.S.R. can very easily be explained by the peculiarities of the socialist economic system, with its plan, and by the relationship of this system to the outside world. Arguments about space and territory *per se* remind one—if the adherents of these theories will excuse the remark—of people hunting for differential tariffs among crabs or for paper money on wheat fields.

But however ridiculous geopolitics is from the point of view of logic, it nevertheless plays a very active reactionary rôle *in practice*. It supplies an excuse for bellicose fascism, a justification for war and imperialism; it preaches new conquests and wars of intervention. The essence of the matter lies here, not in the quasimoralistic poetized sophistry with which imperialists often veil their prose.

II. "PERPETUUM MOBILE" IN WARS

In his article which I have already mentioned the late Mr. Simonds, after sharply (and to a great extent correctly) criticizing the League of Nations, draws the conclusion that foreign territory and raw materials are indispensable to Germany, Italy and Japan; that any attempt to persuade these countries to the contrary would be absurd; and that the League of Nations must adopt the rule of economic parity and make an equitable distribution of the world's resources of territory and raw materials. This will avert a world tragedy.

Indeed? But what will come of this plan objectively, that is, apart from the subjective intentions of its authors? Let us analyze this plan of the new "levellers."

First. Who are to be the *subjects* of this deal? Alas! These do not include such countries as Egypt or China or India. Nor do they include any of the small independent states like Czechoslovakia. The subjects of the deal are to be the biggest capitalist powers.

Second. Who are to be the *objects* of the deal? Apparently the U.S.S.R. and a number of small independent countries such as Lithuania (for the author of the scheme seeks to justify German fascist aspirations), China (for Japan's policy is similarly "justified") and the colonies (Italy's policy also finds "justification" in this scheme). Thus in effect it is proposed: (1) to cut up the U.S.S.R.; (2) to destroy the independence of small countries, such as Ethiopia; (3) to partition China; (4) to divide up the colonies again, like so much small coin thrown in to complete a bargain. In other words, the entire plan is aimed against: (a) the workers (the U.S.S.R.); (b) the masses in densely populated China (*i.e.,* the semi-colonies); (c) the colonial masses. *Cui prodest?* The biggest capitalist powers. Such is the scheme's "justice" and "morality."

Third. Let us assume that by some miracle or other the idea has been carried into effect. The great capitalist powers have divided up the spoils among themselves (the others, as we have seen, are *quantités négligeables*) on a "basic principle" of super-aristocratic world "parity." But what will happen the day after? That is the question.

It is not hard to answer. The mere fact that in different countries there are different levels of productive power, different quantities of skilled labor power, will lead to different results in the struggle for the world market. No amount of "autarchy" will save a country from having resort to this world market, the more so as the capitalist system will inevitably lead to overproduction. The search for new markets and spheres for capital investment will necessitate new re-divisions of land and resources. And since tariff barriers, trusts, armies and fleets will not disappear, the war song will break out afresh. Thus what is proposed is nothing more nor less than the continuing reproduction of wars, a *perpetuum mobile* of annihilating catastrophes. The picture is truly horrifying.

Fourth. Aside from all this, the plan recalls the verse about Roland's horse:

> *Wunderschön war diese Stute,*
> *Leider aber war sie tot.*

It is just another Utopia. The more powerful groups of capitalists wielding state power will not surrender their colonies for the benefit of their poorer relatives. If Germany, Japan and Italy cannot be persuaded to abandon their expansionist policy, then there is just as little expectation of philanthropy on the part of Great Britain, the United States or France. As regards the workers of the U.S.S.R., they can see absolutely no reason for surrendering their common property to their bitterest class antagonists.

Fifth. Capitalist states might ask themselves whether this levelling scheme does not have in it the germs of what Japanese diplomats would call "dangerous thoughts." For mankind is divided not only horizontally into states, but also vertically into classes. (By the way, this idea of a redivision, and of a blow at the maxim "Beati possidentes," calls to mind the whole class which is made up of the "possidentes." Here, however, it is not a question of re-dividing the factories and distributing the machines among the workers, but of common ownership of the means of production. And this is the course which history will take.)

III. WHAT IS IMPERIALISM?

So we may put the question as follows: Is the present tendency to violent expansion now being displayed so strikingly in Japan, Germany and Italy a purely natural function of land and race, or is it a function of the social-economic system?

The question can be most easily considered by taking the example of Japan. The density of population in Japan is great. There is little land per capita. Emigration has always been very considerable. The German professor, Paul Berkenkopf, in his recent work "Sibirien als Zukunftsland der Industrie," uses the very fact of overpopulation ("Druck der japanischen Übervölkerung") to explain Japanese imperialist expansion, assuming, however, that this expansion will proceed primarily in the direction of Australia and the Philippines. And thus it would seem that here as nowhere else the bare laws of geopolitics are the determining factor. But in that case how can we explain the crisis of overproduction? And how can we explain the paradox that this strange profusion of products is constantly impelling Japan's ruling classes to more intensive expansion? What becomes, then, of all the primitive argumentation that where there is little land, nothing to eat, and too many people, *ergo,* new territory is needed? It simply goes to pieces. Obviously the matter is not at all so simple. In reality, it is a bastard form of *fin de siècle* monopoly capitalism coupled with considerable survivals of feudal barbarism: savage exploitation of the workers and peasants, land-hunger on the part of the latter, exorbitantly high rents, poverty, and consequently low purchasing power of the masses—all leading to the paradox of plenty and poverty, overproduction and the quest for new territories. And are not these things peculiar to capitalism as a whole? Is not the hunt for markets, coupled with overproduction and underconsumption, a characteristic feature of the special capitalist "mode of production"?

Or take Germany. We hear the chorus that it is absolutely essential for her to steal new territory from the U.S.S.R., since she, Germany, is starved for raw materials. We shall not speak here about the German war industry, which has swelled to gigantic proportions, which swallows up vast quantities of raw materials, and which does not in any way "grow" out of the properties of the German "soil." Nor shall we talk about the stocks of raw materials for war at the expense of consumption, nor about the sabotage on the part of the peasants. We only put the following elementary question: Why should not Germany *buy* raw materials from the U.S.S.R.? Does the latter want a high price? No, on the contrary. Many persons have shouted at the top of their voices that the U.S.S.R. is practising dumping—so favorable to the purchaser are the prices at which the U.S.S.R. has sold raw material. But German monopoly capital wants to have monopoly ownership of Ukrainian raw materials for military-economic autarchy, which in its turn is a weapon for further world struggle. "Territory," "space" (fascist philosophers have raised the category of "space" five heads higher than that of "time") do not produce any policy *by themselves*. It is definite social-historical conditions that lead to wars.

Mr. Simonds quoted Signor Mussolini's dictum: "For us Italians the choice is between foreign expansion and domestic explosion." And he added: "And that is why Italy and Germany, like Japan, are preparing for war." About Germany he spoke still more clearly: either a war of conquest, or Communism.

Let us assume that this is so. But what does it signify? It simply signifies that Communism can live without wars, whereas the other social form, capitalism, through the mouths of its own politicians and ideologists, declares: Better a war of conquest than Communism. This only serves to corroborate the proposition that a war of conquest is a function of the social order, that it is not a non-historical category connected directly with geophysical and biological factors.

The structure of modern capitalism must be analyzed scientifically, soberly and without prejudice. The Italian fascists claim that there is no capitalism in Italy, but a special kind of order which is neither capitalism nor socialism. Herr Hitler's followers declare that in their country they have national socialism. Mr. Araki and the other ideologists of Japanese aggression speak about the "imperial path," about Japan's peculiar traditions and her celestial mission: God himself points out definite strategic and tactical plans to Mr. Araki. Camouflage and juggling with words constitute one of the distinguishing features of profound social decadence. But fact remains fact. In none of the above-mentioned countries has one hair fallen from the head of the finance-capital oligarchy. Herr Fried in his book, "Das Ende des Kapitalismus," painted a very graphic picture of this oligarchy. But Hitler's régime has left it in complete immunity; these oligarchs have only been converted (in words) into "leaders of industry" on the basis of "public service." If we recall that fascism's most outstanding philosopher, Spengler, considered the Hohenzollern Officers' Corps and the Prussian Government officials as the epitome of "socialism" there is really no need for surprise. Has it not been said that "man was given a tongue to hide his thoughts"?

The same kind of camouflage is observable in another form even in capitalistic countries with democratic régimes. Not so long ago, for example, Mr. Thomas Nixon Carver, an indiscreet Pindar of "prosperity," proclaimed *urbi et orbi* that in the United States every worker is a capitalist. The subsequent spread of the crisis and of so-called "technical unemployment" have given a tragic refutation of this capitalist optimism.

What is in fact the real state of affairs? And why does this real state of affairs give rise to imperialist wars?

Since the eighties of the last century, as a result of the triumph of large-scale production and the centralization of capital, the form of capitalism has changed. From the previous stage of industrial capitalism, with its freedom of competition, its individualism, its principle of *laissez faire, laissez passer,* it entered the stage of monopoly capitalism (trusts, intergrowth of banking capital and industrial capital, monopoly prices). The partition of the world led to accentuated competition; to the policy of dumping (the losses incurred were compensated for by high monopoly prices in the home market) ; and to the system of a high protective tariff. In its turn, protectionism intensified the export of capital (in place of commodity exports, now hampered by tariff barriers). The monopolistic possession of markets, raw materials and spheres of capital investment, together with the whole system of monopoly exploitation, tariffs, etc., based on the already accomplished partition of the so-called "free lands" (which meant putting an end to the principle of the Open Door), led capitalist competition on the world market to acquire more and more clearly the character of forcible pressure (*Machtpolitik*). The diminished possibilities of "peaceful penetration" were remedied by the brutal policy of armed force.

Accordingly, the state power of capital, its "interference" in economic life, acquires increased significance. We witness the militarization of the economic system and an extreme intensification of the tendency to economic autarchy, which is also important militarily and politically in determining the *Machtposition* in the arena of world struggle. Here the inner motive is represented by the interests of profit, which on the one hand maintain the purchasing power of the working masses at an extremely low level (even in Ricardo's day it was a well-known fact that profit stands in inverse proportion to wages), and which on the other hand continually force commodities and capital beyond the bounds of the given state, compelling a constant search for fresh markets, fresh sources of raw materials and fresh spheres for capital investment. The greater the contradiction between the productive forces of capitalism and the mass impoverishment which is immanent in this system, the more intensive grows world competition, the more acute becomes the problem of war.

Imperialist war is an expression of the expansionist policy of monopoly capitalism. Such is the specific, historically limited, significance of imperialist wars. On the one hand, monopoly capitalism acts as a check on the development of the productive forces (the decay of capitalism) ; on the other, it leads to catastrophes of the most devastating kind.

Thus not every sort of war, not even every predatory war, is an imperialist war. Slave-owning forms of society waged wars for slaves; feudal lords fought for land; merchants and traders fought for markets and for exploitation through trade and plunder ("Handel und Piraterie," as Goethe called it) ; and so forth. Imperialism wages wars to extend the domination of one country's finance capital, for the monopoly profits of trusts and banks. Its wars are universal (for the whole world is already divided up) ; its wars confront all mankind with the dilemma: either death or socialism. *Hic Rhodus! Hic salta!*

IV. IMPERIALISM AND THE U.S.S.R.

From the above it will be clear how senseless it is to talk about the "imperialism" of the U.S.S.R., as is done *con amore* by fascist theoreticians and by "researchers" of the type of Herr von Kleinow. A phrase like "the imperialism of the U.S.S.R." is a contradiction in terms, like "dry water" or "square circles."

But it may be asked: Will not the U.S.S.R. pursue an aggressive policy, not in favor of finance capital, but against it? Will it not fight for the expansion of socialism? Here again let us begin with an example.

As is well known, the Empire of the Tsars formerly occupied present territory of the Soviet Union, plus Poland, plus Finland, etc. It possessed even more territory and more "natural wealth" than does the U.S.S.R. But it was continually engaged in wars of conquest. On the eve of 1914 it dreamed of seizing Constantinople and the Dardanelles and of subjugating all Turkey, of seizing the whole of Galicia from Austria-Hungary, of dealing Germany a blow and of concluding a trade agreement with her on onerous terms; and so on. What, under Tsarism, drove not only the landlords but also the bourgeoisie (even before they had a share in the government) to these adventures? First and foremost, the weakness of the home market. The peasant was fleeced to the skin by the landlord, the worker's wages were meagre. Hence the policy which the Tsar's minister Vyshnegradsky characterized in the words: "We'll go hungry but we'll export." Hence the Far Eastern adventure—and the "Russo-Japanese War," during which, by the way, all sections of Russian society except the landlord aristocracy desired the Tsarist Government's defeat. Hence, too, Russia's participation in the World War, with a frenzied imperialist program (here the grain exporters played the biggest part).

Now let us take the U.S.S.R. One does not need to be a genius to observe that in the U.S.S.R. *the demand is not less but greater than the supply*. In our country we have a tremendously strong home market. Despite the enormous scale of production there is a shortage of commodities, there are still too few goods on sale.

The socialist system contains within itself much greater possibilities for productive forces to develop, for labor to increase its productivity and for technique to progress. But in the Soviet Union, be it noted, this cannot result either in unemployment or in overproduction. Our national economy is conducted not with a view to profits for a capitalist class, but to satisfy the requirements of the masses. This means that when production of necessary articles is increased their consumption is proportionately raised, and not lowered into the sea like Brazilian coffee. If completely superfluous articles are produced—a highly improbable contingency—corrections can be made in the production process itself. Under planned economy it is easy to redistribute the productive forces; they can be transferred to new sectors, engendering new requirements and supplying the masses with new lines of production. There will never be any threat of unemployment, and a universal rise in labor productivity will only lead to a growth of plenty, shorten the working day, and leave more scope for cultural development.

Thus the motive inherent in the very nature of the capitalist system, which begets surplus value and prevents its realization—the motive which is most glaringly manifested in the era of imperialism and impels the ruling classes to war—is reduced in a socialist society to absolute nonsense.

This was why beggarly Tsarist Russia, where the "upper ten thousand" of landlords and bourgeois lived in splendor while the masses starved, pursued a policy of wars of conquest. And that is why the U.S.S.R., which is rapidly growing rich in the sense that well-being is spreading throughout the entire mass of the people while social wealth is concentrated in the hands of the socialist state, pursues an exactly opposite policy, the policy of peace. The U.S.S.R. is not interested in conquests in any direction whatever. But it is interested, very deeply and lastingly interested, in peace. What, then, remains of the celebrated argument that the U.S.S.R. "is continuing the policy of the Tsars?"

There is another piece of geopolitical sophistry in circulation which goes more or less as follows. Fact remains fact: in 1914 Russia was in conflict with Japan in the Far East; in 1914-18 she was in conflict with Germany; the same thing is happening again, *mutatis mutandis,* and the fundamental geophysical laws are again breaking their way through all obstacles.

What is the reply to this piece of sophistry?

First, even the facts themselves are distorted. For example, in 1914 and the years following Japan was in league with Russia against Germany; now Japan is in league with Germany against the U.S.S.R. The

Japanese Samurai have even been proclaimed oriental Prussians of Aryan extraction.

Second, the question must be stated more clearly. What, in effect, is under discussion? What we are discussing is not the mere fact of a conflict (for a conflict presupposes at least two parties—our object in this case not being to analyze the inner struggles of a Hamlet), but the policy of one party and the policy of another. After this logical dissection the question becomes perfectly clear. In Japan power is in the hands of approximately the same classes as before, and Japan is continuing its policy of imperialist aggression, heading for war. The U.S.S.R. is not Tsarist Russia and the radical change of the country's economic system demands an exactly opposite policy, the policy of peace. Nevertheless war *may* break out, for the situation is not determined by the one-sided will to peace of the Soviets. War may be forced upon us. Contiguity of frontiers and territory certainly have an influence here, but not directly, and the war guilt will lie not with "the land" but with Japanese imperialism.

Finally, there is one other argument with which the opponents of the U.S.S.R. try to discredit Soviet foreign policy. It is trotted out regularly by Herr Hitler and his ideological agents. It runs, roughly speaking, as follows: National Socialism is based on "nationality" ("Volkstum," "Volksgemeinschaft"); its business is with the domestic, internal affairs of Germany; National Socialism is *national* socialism, and is not super- or supra-national. Accordingly it never meddles in "other folks' affairs," but speaks exclusively *pro domo sua*. Conversely, Sovietism—Bolshevism, Communism—has a super- and supra-national orientation; it is an international force, dreaming of world domination; it is the *spiritus rector* of all sedition and unrest.

Clearly this argument is intimately connected with our theme.

First of all, a few words about the Germany of Herr Hitler. The German fascists, it is true, are idolaters of the fetish of so-called "race purity"; they even castrate those who are not pure Aryans and imprison people for the "crime" of sexual intercourse with non-Aryan men and women. They propagate economico-national autarchy, as a vessel containing the holy and precious body and blood of the "Nordic Aryan race." But it would be a childish absurdity to suppose that this leads to a policy of "noninterference." Quite the contrary. Fascist action is most energetic in all foreign countries. And this is easy to understand, for their very "national narrowness" is nothing more nor less than the clenching of the military-economic and ideological fist. Their orientation is towards world hegemony, entailing the crushing and enslavement of all other nations. No, to be sure, they are not internationalists. But they are potential nationalistic oppressors of all other nations (those of "low degree"). It is precisely from this point of view that the Nazis meddle in the internal affairs of all other states. It is worth knowing, for instance, that even in the case of the United States the Nazis count on the millions of citizens of German blood to act against the Anglo-Saxon and other elements. In fact, it is to fear of a German revolt that Herr Colin Ross ascribes the unfavorable attitude of Americans towards National Socialism.[3] Setting out from the premise that "present-day America is tired and old, amazingly old" (*"das heutige Amerika ist müde und alt, erstaunlich alt"*) the author threatens a national upheaval of millions of "self-knowing" Germans. Approximately the same arguments ("salvation" of the Ukraine or of the Volga Germans) are employed by Herr Rosenberg in his appeals for war against the U.S.S.R. It is thus quite futile for the Nazis to pose as offended children, occupied in the washing of purely domestic linen. That argument is mendacious.

However, *revenons à nos moutons.* Do we believe in the world-wide triumph of socialism? Of course we do. Moreover, we know for sure that this will undoubtedly come, as a result of the inner contradictions of capitalism, through the victory of the historically progressive forces within it. We know that our diagnosis and prognosis are scientific and exact. But does this mean that the U.S.S.R. should interfere in the affairs of other states or pursue a policy of conquest? Of course not. For the best "propaganda" of all is the very fact of the existence and uninterrupted development of the new economic relations and the new culture. It would be sheer stupidity to interrupt this process.

Hence it follows that not only from the economic but also from the purely political standpoint—not only from the standpoint of the U.S.S.R. proper but also from that of the ultimate world-wide victory of socialism—it is utterly senseless to think of a policy of war being adopted by the proletarian state. And as regards the "last days" and the "world rule of communism," history will settle this question. *"Que les destinées s'accomplissent!"*

[3] *Zeitschrift für Geopolitik,* XII Jahrg., 3 Heft. p. 135: "Idee und Zukunfts-gestaltung der Vereinigten Staaten von Amerika."

However, in the interests of full scientific clarity we cannot leave un-
answered one further argument against the Marxist presentation of the
question concerning the destinies of society. It is set forth in an article
in *The Round Table* (No. 99) entitled "Economics and War." The
author asserts that Marxism is wrong, because:

> If, as its disciples hold, the existing economic system leads inherently to
> the class war, which of its nature cuts across national boundaries, then
> surely it cannot also lead inherently to the war between nations, in which
> all classes are ranged side by side against their fellows of another country.
> . . . For experience amply proves that war is the great opportunity of
> the forces of the Left to overthrow the established régime. The calculating
> communist, far more than the calculating capitalist, ought to foment war.

I regret to say that the author errs on every point. War "between
nations" (or rather between capitalist states) formally unites classes,
but only to aggravate class antagonisms still further later on and speed
up the revolutionary process. So it was in Germany and Austria, so it
was in Russia, where the revolutionary party was able to carry things
through to the end. It is precisely for this reason that war enables "the
forces of the Left" to "overthrow the established régime." But they
are able to do so for the further reason that they rally the masses against
war. It is as the force of peace, the only consistent force of peace, that
they are victorious—not as the fictitious and silly-clever "calculating
Communist" imagined by *The Round Table*. As regards the capitalists,
they are driven on by the blind, supra-rational, elemental forces of an
unorganized society. One of the characteristic features of this society is
that people get results quite different from those intended: thus none
of the capitalists wanted the crisis, but the crisis is the result of their
actions. This is the so-called law of the heterogeneity of aims, characteristic of irrational (capitalist) society and non-existent in rational, organized (socialist) society. Thus, the peace policy of the socialist state is
not just a passing "juncture" for it, not a temporary zigzag in policy,
not an opportunist compromise. It expresses the very essence of the
socialist system.

We are not obliged to think for the capitalists. But, contrary to
The Round Table's advice, we stand and will continue to stand for
peace, peace and yet again peace. And precisely for this reason we shall
conquer in a war if the imperialists force one on us.

V. THE SYSTEM OF PROLETARIAN STATES: COMMUNISM AND WAR

Now it will be easy to answer the question as to whether wars between proletarian states will be possible—wars for markets, for raw materials, for spheres of capital investment—and whether wars will be possible under Communism, *i.e.*, in the subsequent stage of mankind's evolution, after it has already taken to socialism.

Basic actuating motives are represented by definite interests. The world economic system of the capitalist régime is broken up into "national" economic units with conflicting interests (we put the word "national" in quotation marks, for the term includes bourgeois states composing many nationalities). The most acute form of conflict in which this clash of interests finds expression is war between these states. War is a special form of capitalist competition, peculiar to the capitalist world as such. The question of relations between proletarian states is altogether different.

Logically: there is no clash of real interests between proletarian states whatsoever; on the contrary, their real interest is in maximum coöperation. From the very start this real interest is realized as the actuating motive of all activity, for it is commensurate with the whole system of rationally organized labor with the ideology of the revolutionary proletariat.

Genetically: the very process of the struggle waged by the proletarian states for their existence will knit them together in a still closer bond. There can be no doubt that after a certain stage of development tremendously powerful centripetal tendencies will be revealed—tendencies toward a state union of proletarian republics.

Empirically: the experience of the U.S.S.R. fully confirms these considerations. Tsarist Russia collapsed as an integral whole, and in those parts where the bourgeoisie remained in power (Finland, Estonia, Lithuania, Poland) it has split apart and now forms mutually antagonistic elements (*cf.* Poland versus Lithuania). On the other hand, in those places where the workers were victorious they have joined the Union of proletarian republics, united by a single economic plan and a centralized government, but organized in a federation. The constituent nations have full rights, and their various cultures, national in form and socialist in content, are flourishing now as never before. This, of course, is far from being an accident; it is a manifestation of the most profound historical law, linked with a new social structure.

With the further flowering of proletarian states throughout the entire world war will become unnecessary. War will be impossible in a system of unified Communist society, where there are no classes and even—*horribile dictu*—no coercive state power nor armies. This society will really "turn swords into ploughshares" and release gigantic masses of energy for national creative work for the benefit of all mankind. If even the first historical phases of socialist development in our country have already produced such brilliant creative results as the Stakhanov movement, and the heroic feats accomplished by our youth in all fields of culture, then what abundant sources of social wealth will pour forth in the splendid fraternal society of Communism!

This, it will be said, is utopian. But we know very well that Aristotle was no fool, that he was one of the greatest men of all times. Yet he held that society was inconceivable without slaves. Not so long ago the planters of the southern states held that Negroes are innate slaves. So today the bourgeois and their little "Aristotles" hold that society would be as inconceivable without war as without wage slavery, and that the U.S.S.R. is a *lapsus historiæ*. Let them think so. *Qui vivra verra.*

THE "reversal of alliances" wrought by the Nazi-Soviet Pact of August 1939 effected a profound revolution in the constellation of power in Europe, especially by giving Hitler the one-front war he sought. In Asia its repercussions, if less direct and immediate, threatened to be no less far-reaching. The cabinet that had allied Japan with Hitler was dismissed overnight, and the Japanese army in Manchuria ceased its harassments of the Soviet border. Was this to be a prelude to a second reversal of alliances? Would Moscow drop the cautious but indispensable military support it had been giving Chiang Kai-shek's government since 1937? And would the Chinese Communists take advantage of the threatened isolation of Nationalist China to drop the unpopular truce and resume their offensive against the central government? These questions, and the answers to them, were vastly important to the future of China, Japan and America.

In "Will Stalin Sell Out China?" (April 1940), Edgar P. Snow gave an acute analysis of this crucial question. His answers were based on a long background of interpreting Asian developments and particularly on his numerous and recent discussions with several of the Chinese Communist leaders in Yenan. His appraisal showed a realistic appreciation of the ideological and power-politics factors that were, in fact, to shape Stalin's policy toward China and its warring forces right down to the defeat of Japan and its expulsion from the Asian mainland. Mr. Snow's account is also, in a real sense of the term, an historic document.

Edgar P. Snow has been a foreign correspondent and analyst since 1929, when he became assistant editor of the *China Weekly Review* in Shanghai. He was the first Western correspondent to visit the Yenan stronghold of the Chinese Communists, and "Red Star Over China" (1937) was his report on this extensive sojourn in Soviet China. In numerous later books of reportage he described the struggle for Asia, as well as giving his estimates of Soviet and Chinese Communist policies. His appraisals, which have varied a good deal over the years, have always been expressed with vigor and with the authority of first-hand observation. Mr. Snow has been a correspondent for American newspapers and press associations and for *Look* magazine, and an associate editor of *The Saturday Evening Post*.

WILL STALIN SELL OUT CHINA?

By Edgar Snow

THE formation of the Moscow-Berlin Axis, followed by the conquest of Poland and the attack on Finland, has changed the balance of land power in Asia and of sea power in the Pacific. China's struggle for independence is now more than ever tied up with the fate of Europe, while at the same time the field in which she can manœuvre diplomatically has become even more restricted than hitherto. Though the Nazi-Soviet Pact has deprived Japan of a fickle friend in Hitler, it has at least immobilized two hated rivals, France and Britain. On the United States, too, the "diplomatic revolution" of August 1939 has imposed new hazards and heavy responsibilities.

But with the Chinese the question overshadowing all others is whether Stalin will sell them out. They are in deadly fear that Japan and Russia may yet get together to concoct a pact against them. From the consequences of such a pact the United States could not remain immune: a real Russo-Japanese alliance might well have the United States as its chief victim.

How far will Stalin go? Is there a limit to the new Commu-Nippon courtship, and if so, where? I have asked—and been asked—for the answers, from Sian to Hong Kong. Some hasty observers were gleeful when Japanese generals, the cuckolds of Nazi betrayal, ignominiously liquidated their anti-Comintern cabinet, and in temporary confusion restored to the civilian parties a faint voice in Japanese politics. But the generals, or rather Admiral Yonai, may have the last laugh.

The European war has definitely eliminated the remote chance of independent action by Britain and France, two of the three land and sea Powers capable of challenging Japan in Eastern Asia. Today the United States remains the only maritime Power that acting alone can menace Japan; and only Russia can offer a major threat on land. Perhaps only the United States and the Soviets, together with China, could now bring about a speedy humiliation of Japan. Considering such

154

an arrangement highly improbable, the Tokyo diplomats have decided that business isn't so bad after all.

In an article I wrote last summer I explained why Britain was impotent to take naval action against Japan in Eastern waters. Subsequently Mr. Chamberlain admitted in Parliament, rather naïvely, that such indeed is the case. Since then Britain's position in the Orient, along with that of France and the Netherlands, has worsened. Despite the comical collapse of the anti-Comintern basis of German-Japanese cooperation, nothing can prevent Japan from exploiting the physical fact of German attacks on the Allies. Conceivably, Britain and France might even now take reprisals against Japan if the United States led the move. Otherwise, wide appeasement of Tokyo becomes imperative for the Allies.

By her recent invasion of Kwangsi, Japan closed the last seaport on the southern coast, and acquired for the first time land bases within easy operating range of France's richest colony. From Kwangsi the Japanese control China's main highway and dominate her only railway connection with Indo-China. The French recently put still further restrictions on the use of this railway, but the Japanese demand its absolute closure to many vital supplies. In February they began a heavy bombardment of the line to emphasize their threats. The French Ambassador in Tokyo would like to reach a permanent accord with Japan by persuading Chiang Kai-shek to end the war with a compromise.

Should the British make a similar capitulation by limiting traffic over the Burma road to Yunnan, China would be almost cut off from all aid, other than financial, of the nations beyond the seas. Already the southern routes have lost much of their value. Shipments of European war materials have been reduced since last July by over 60 percent. There are Chinese who consider it possible that by next spring they may be left with only one way open from Chungking to Europe: the 2500-mile road across the mountains and grasslands and deserts of the Northwest through Chinese Turkistan into Russian Central Asia.

Those facts, as well as Russia's new security deriving from the pact with Germany, greatly strengthen the Soviet strategic position in Eastern Asia. Here, as in Europe, Stalin holds the balance of power. Today the Kremlin can, without much difficulty, give increased help to China, reject any real collaboration with Japan, and encourage Chungking to continue resistance. Or it can seek an alliance with Japan, attempt to arrange a Sino-Japanese compromise, and unite the two warring Orientals in a joint campaign against far greater game, the Western Powers. Or it can sign a simple non-aggression pact with Japan, in which each recognizes the other's sphere of territorial or strategic interest but is left free to make its own policies toward China and the Pacific nations. Or it can merely draw close enough to Japan to make any one of those moves seem possible, using "war-of-nerves" tactics to keep the Orient in a continuous state of suspense.

After the Russo-German Pact was signed Chinese Communists conceded that Soviet-Japanese rapprochement was not impossible. The Nomonhan Truce, which ended the heavy Russo-Japanese border fighting in Mongolia, confirmed their opinion. By lucky coincidence I happened to be in Yenan during the European events climaxed by the invasion of Poland. This bomb-shattered citadel, far up behind the guerrilla front near the Great Wall, is today still the capital, after 33 months of war, of a regional Communist government in China. To Yenan hundreds of thousands of armed Communists in China, Manchuria and Mongolia, look for guidance from their leader, Mao Tse-tung.

I spent many hours talking to Mao. There is no question that he completely approved of current Soviet policy in Europe. "Hitler," he chuckled, "is now in Stalin's pocket." He did not say so, but it must have occurred to him that there might be another Stalinite pocket for Japan —perhaps a vest pocket. For he agreed that a Russo-Japanese reconciliation had become a possibility "within the logic of Leninism." This apparent complacency is explained farther on.

So it was no surprise to the Chinese Reds when, in October, Molotov made his conciliatory remarks concerning Japan, and Stalin sent a new Soviet Ambassador, Smetanin, to restore a friendly atmosphere in Tokyo. He and Mme. Smetanin drank tea with the Mikado and the Empress. Shortly afterward an agreement was signed arranging for the opening of formal talks. These settled disputed questions of fishery rights and payment for the Chinese Eastern Railways. Meanwhile, in Hong Kong a high and worried British official exclaimed: "America's uncompromising attitude is throwing Japan into the arms of Stalin. British interests are at stake. America must either act out here, or hush up and let us reach our own agreement with Tokyo."

The question now is: What next?

Before we give an answer, we must try to comprehend the bases of Soviet political strategy. To do that we must get along without devils or saints, without the muddleheaded sentimentality of either Left or Right. We are required to pass a judgment, not voice a prejudice. And we should endeavor to make it as nearly scientific as possible. Otherwise we will find it difficult to understand the Comintern mind and why it continues to be a powerful factor in the Orient. The penalty of making a decision on erroneous preconceptions might be war. I do not propose here to offer any easy lessons in Stalinism. I only wish to set forth a few principles relevant to an estimate of Soviet strategy in the East. I have been studying this subject on the spot for a decade, not simply as historical data, but as it affects living men.

Soviet strategy is based, in the reasoning of those Communists whom I understand, on somewhat the following credo. First, a joint "imperialist war" against the Soviet Union is almost inevitable. During and after the Allied intervention against the Reds, Lenin's tactics were strongly influenced by that belief. He was then dealing with reality; we should not forget that even the United States joined (with Japan!) in the invasion of Siberia. Only after the end of foreign intervention and the painful abandonment of the early theory in which Marx, Engels and Lenin himself had assumed that proletarian dictatorship would occur more or less simultaneously in all countries or in none, did the Bolsheviks begin to see that they might win a period of peace permitting them to "construct Socialism in one country." Nevertheless, the fear of a second invasion was politically useful and was carefully nurtured to help consolidate Communist power. Russia remained, therefore, the "threatened base of the world revolution." Everything else was made relative to the pivotal fact of "capitalist encirclement." The Comintern repeated *ad nauseam* what Lenin said in an early period: "All the events of world politics are inevitably concentrating around one central point, namely, the struggle of the world bourgeoisie against the Soviet Russian Republic."

Under Stalin this belief came to have in practice a more particular meaning. All interests of revolutionary parties in other countries had to be subordinated, or sacrificed if necessary, to the needs of Moscow's foreign policy. Such interests were "partial" or "local" in character. The universal interests of the working-class parties were identical with the task of preserving the "base" in the U.S.S.R. Any step which strengthened the strategic security of the Soviet state, therefore, was in the long-view interests of all Comintern parties, even though it might mean their virtual extinction—as it did in the case of the Communist organizations in France and England after the Soviet-German Non-Aggression Pact. Moscow was quite sincere, after 1927, in advocating international peace. While peace lasted, the contradiction between the capitalist and socialist worlds could be expressed by internal class conflicts. Intensification of class antagonisms within the various national states, as well as between them, meant prolongation of the "breathing spell" in which to make the Soviet Union impregnable.

The Communists believe that bourgeois states may assume a variety of forms—military dictatorship, parliamentary democracy, Fascism, Nazism, etc.—but that there are no fundamental differences between them. Nevertheless, the Comintern makes distinctions between actively hostile and temporarily friendly states, so that Moscow may combine with one or the other in order to "utilize the contradictions between them" and to "divert the imperialist war" to other countries. Stalin has no objection to a quarrel confined to capitalist states; for, as he remarked last March, "the second imperialist war may lead to the victory of the revolution in one or several countries." Hence it is the Comintern's duty to "convert imperialist war into civil war" and to "defend the Soviet Union by both constitutional and unconstitutional means," including "working for the defeat of one's own [imperialist] country."

Lastly, the promise of "ultimate victory of the world revolution" is predicated upon the belief that the capitalist Powers will proceed to dissipate their resources and man power in inter-imperialist war, undermine their own security, cancel out the greatest achievements of capitalist civilization, bring about the complete moral and material bankruptcy of "bourgeois society," and lay themselves open to internal disintegration, revolution and final destruction if they clash with Russia.

Against that framework of logic, which is simply a special terminology of power politics to anyone but a devout Stalinist, every manœuvre of Soviet policy is consistent. The Hitler-Stalin Pact is just as logical a part of the general strategy as was the "democratic front against imperialist war and Fascism." If left-wing liberals, idealists, and even some Communist intellectuals—in whom Stalin's interest is purely utilitarian—were shocked by the former it was because they never understood the strategic purpose of the latter. Nor does it seem likely that Trotsky, had he kept power, would have followed a greatly different strategy; for that strategy is not simply the result of Stalin's will, but the synthesis of a vast complex of historical conditions plus the special limitations of Russia.

No, it is not the Red Dictator, but the disillusioned liberals who are inconsistent. For, logically speaking, a mere shift in the *tactics* of Soviet foreign policy should not shake a faith based on the internal physical facts of the Stalinist Utopia, which are exactly as before. All that has happened is that Stalin, taking advantage of a favorable world situation, is grabbing territories wherever possible without (he imagines) risking a "serious" war.

Now, it is an observable fact that a political folklore, if persistently fostered by a ruling bureaucracy, and believed and acted upon by masses of men, in time becomes in itself a dynamic social force which helps to set up its own dialectical reaction. Presently, for instance, the "joint imperialist attack" may cease to be the hypothesis that to a large extent it was even as late as last July. Before the invasion of Poland and Finland, the "little people" who fight the world's battles could not have been induced to become cannon fodder against non-aggressive Russia. Today, now that the "little people" everywhere have lost sympathy for the Soviet Union, such a war becomes a living possibility. Finland provided the anti-Communist standard-bearers with a necessary moral slogan. It is at least thinkable that Britain and France will eventually find a *modus vivendi* with Germany and mobilize Europe against the Soviets.

The point is that the same danger now confronts Russia in the Orient. More than ever, therefore, the strategic principles mentioned above become a guide to Soviet action. Keeping those credos in mind, what would an alliance with Japan offer to Moscow? Viewed from a materialist viewpoint—and no Communist has ever claimed Stalin is an idealist— the possible advantages are about as follows:

A Russo-Japanese alliance would remove the danger of an anti-Soviet combination in the Pacific, now feared by Moscow. It would give Stalin a free hand in Europe. It might encourage the Japanese, as well as some elements among the Chinese, to launch an attack on Britain. It might embolden Japan to risk war with the United States— long devoutly wished in Moscow. In case Russia became directly involved in war with the British, the fact that the border between Manchukuo and Siberia was peaceful would enable the Soviets to concentrate their military strength along the Indian frontier. Japan's naval predominance in the Western Pacific would also be of value to Stalin.

In exchange for Russia's promise of help against Britain and France (or the United States), and for her friendly mediation in the Sino-Japanese war, Japan might agree to abandon her anti-Comintern slogans and tolerate the existence of Chinese Reds as neighbors. Should the Japanese blunder into war with the United States and Britain, the long-run outcome would be of advantage to Russia. For such a war would leave the Bolsheviks in a dominant position *vis-à-vis* an exhausted

Japan, a revolutionary China, and a United States and Britain lacking decisive land power in Asia.

Japan might also find that a Russo-Japanese alliance offered superficial attractions. With Russia as an ally she would have less fear of the effects of an American embargo. Presumably Japan would be given access to Siberian resources, including petroleum, steel, iron and coal. Russia could please both Japan and Germany by giving their trade facilities over the Siberian railways. If Japan could really feel free of all menace of invasion from Siberia, she would release her reserve forces for a quick cleanup and consolidation in areas mutually agreed upon. The elusive conclusion to the China Incident might be found, and the navy freed to pursue its "southward expansion" program.

But how could such Japanese gains be reconciled with the advantages expected by Russia? The political basis of Japan's aggression in China is weak enough now. After her anti-Comintern slogan had been scuttled would not her bid for Asiatic political hegemony collapse entirely? Sections of the army might not fall into line. The effects in Manchuria and Korea might also be explosive. As a well-informed Japanese newspaper editor explained it to me: "The trouble is that nobody could get to the Emperor with such a proposal. Not because the Emperor would not listen, but because it would almost be necessary to seize the Palace in a *coup* in order to overcome the army's opposition to its presentation."

A Russian alliance, moreover, would probably bring about Anglo-American naval coördination. This is the one thing Japan wants to avoid, since it would at last give her two most hated rivals an effective point of unity. At the very least Japan would lose her markets, her sources of raw materials, and her credit in Britain and in the United States. If it came to war, she could not rely on Russia to see her through to victory, except on Bolshevist terms. Japan, too, suspects that Hitler is in Stalin's pocket, and does not envy him his position.

And for Moscow, too, there are disagreeable possibilities to pose against hypothetical temptations. Stalin could no more trust the Japanese as a permanent ally than they could trust him. In practice he could no more reduce his border defences in Siberia than he can today reduce them in the Ukraine, despite his pact with Hitler. Instead of forestalling an Anglo-Japanese entente, a Russo-Japanese alliance might provoke a real Anglo-American anti-Red front, to which Japan might readily desert.

Finally, in fighting for herself, China is necessarily fighting also for the strategic security of the Soviet Union. It would seem unrealistic for Moscow to immobilize China's war machine in exchange for a dozen alliances with a nation that breaks treaties as easily as most people break a soft-boiled egg. Obliged to deploy an army of nearly a million men below the Great Wall and forced constantly to replenish it, Japan cannot seriously think of invading Siberia. Even British officers along the China coast have now stopped drinking toasts to the "second Russo-Japanese war."

The fact is that a "Fighting China" is an indispensable decoy, just now, in Soviet strategy. It diverts war from Russia, keeps Japanese ambitions in China irreconcilable with American policy, deepens estrangements, increases the range of "inter-imperialist collision," and brings internal revolt nearer in Japan. As long as Anglo-Japanese-American dilemmas are unresolved because of the war in China, the "capitalist encirclement" in the East, as in the West, is incomplete. Continued Chinese resistance in the hinterland also means greater Soviet economic and political entrenchment in western China. Russia loses nothing by Japanese activities on the eastern coast, where she has nothing at stake. She can mirthfully watch Japan's "strip tease" acts at the expense of John Bull. And all the time millions of Chinese, growingly dependent on Soviet friendship, are being conditioned as useful allies for the future. To sell out China would be to sacrifice Russia's best guarantee of maximum security with minimum risks.

Another factor must interest us. China is the only non-Soviet country where Stalin may, in a sense, be said to have a reliable armed ally. I refer to the Chinese Red Army, which now operates under various divisional insignia in common cause with the Nationalist Government. But it remains, nevertheless, an army under the absolute disciplinary command of the Chinese Communist Party, which loyally adheres to the Comintern and may be counted upon usually to support it. It differs from Communist parties in Europe and America; for they represent no fire-power factor whatever, and therefore do not enter into Stalin's military calculations.

Yet Stalin cannot be absolutely sure that the Chinese Communists would always and everywhere follow any Comintern directive. Mao Tse-tung emphasized to me that a Russo-Japanese rapprochement was a "Leninist possibility" *on condition* that it "does not interfere with Soviet support for China." This is not so contradictory as it sounds, as I shall show farther on. The significant thing is that it exhibits a certain amount of independence of judgment not always characteristic of Communist parties elsewhere. The reasons are obvious. Here is a party with many years of unique experience in armed struggle for power, during which, with but little encouragement from Stalin, it built up a considerable military organization, acquired wide practical political and military experience, wrote some minor epics of history, and developed a degree of morale, fortitude, courage and self-reliance unequaled in China. It has a tradition and resources all its own, independent of Russia. It has something else, which no group of mere Marxist theoreticians possesses: the daily sobering responsibility to a nation for the defense and administration of big areas which it actually controls. Mao Tse-tung and the other leaders won their following with little or no physical help from Moscow. Long contact with the unusual responsibilities of insurgent power has engendered in them a considerable degree of nationalist feeling. Stalin is very likely aware of this, and would not expect their approval for a policy inimical to the interests of China, or one which might destroy their prestige and strategic value.

In any case, there is as yet no indication that the Russians will withdraw their support—which has been far greater and more consistent than that of the United States, whose "help" remains largely rhetorical. Travelling over the new Northwest Highway to Sinkiang (I have just returned from a long trip over part of it) one discovers, for the first time in history, signs in Russian. These guide the crews of hundreds of trucks (Soviet-made, but of American models) which are now bringing in supplies across the desert from Turkistan—mostly bombs, torpedoes and shells to service Russian planes and artillery. The construction of this highway was not a caprice, but involved careful planning, immense labor and long-view strategy. Dozens of repair shops, storage depots, rest houses, and munitions dumps had to be built over hundreds of miles of wasteland. An army of road workers, engineers, cooks, interpreters, mechanics and officials was mobilized to service the new system. And there is an air of permanence about these establishments.

Near Chengtu, close to the Tibetan border, Russians are helping in the construction of a center for aërial activity in China. About 150 Soviet Russians were billeted near the place when I was there in October, and the Chinese told me they were preparing accommodations for 600. At Lanchow, in the Northwest, there were about 50 Russian trainers, pursuit ships and bombers, and 50 more were expected. Preparations suggested that Russia intended to maintain a force of perhaps 250 planes of all types in the western provinces.

In addition to her air force personnel, Russia has in China a number of military instructors, advisers and technicians. Exactly how many it is difficult to say: Moscow insists upon secrecy and probably with good reason. But there are more Russians than there ever were Germans —and the German mission at one time numbered over a hundred. Several dozen Russians are quartered in a commodious apartment house at Chungking, where they teach in various military schools and occasionally advise the Generalissimo. There are also Soviet advisers with nearly every army at the front, most of them young officers trained entirely in the Red Army.

Even Chang Ch'un, until recently anti-Red Vice-Premier at Chungking, told me that Russian military credits—the figure is said to be 750 million rubles—were "very generous and entirely adequate." China's main problem is not so much to find means for purchasing armament goods as for transporting them to her bases. In payment for the enormous credit, Moscow reportedly agreed to accept the Chinese dollar at its prewar value, which helped save the Chinese currency. More significant, perhaps, is the fact that final arrangements for the credit were not completed until August, shortly before Moscow's pact with Berlin.

All this is not being done for Chiang Kai-shek, over whom Stalin (remembering 1927) probably wastes less love than does Tokyo. But Chiang is the pivot, just now, of a United Front between Nationalists and Communists, which is still the Communists' basic condition for resistance to Japan. Until recently Moscow required no other assurances from the Generalissimo. Not a single truckload of Russian military supplies, not a Soviet plane or gun, not even an adviser, was permitted to go to the Chinese Communist troops. All Soviet equipment was delivered direct to the central command.

After September, however, when Chiang's dependence on Moscow increased enormously, it became evident that he would have to concede a measure of political and military equality to the Chinese Reds. The latter began a campaign of vociferous criticism of the Government, undoubtedly with the support of Moscow. It was this new sense of internal power (which I felt reflected in Mao Tse-tung's conversation with me) that I think made Chinese Communists feel satisfied with Stalin's manœuvres in Europe. Mao demanded an end to the one-party dictatorship of the Kuomintang, and the establishment of a representative democracy in which Communists could have a voice. He also demanded the elimination of all "wavering" (pro-peace) and anti-Soviet elements from the Governement, an end to sporadic armed attacks against Communist troops, and an end to other forms of sabotage and discrimination.

Chiang's efforts to conciliate his Communist supporters, both indigenous and otherwise, are evident in his surprising *volte face* on "democracy." In the last interview I had with him he declined to be quoted to the effect that even local democracy was advisable in China. Yet in November the Kuomintang met in plenary session and, at Chiang's behest, passed a resolution promising to convene a constitutional convention in 1940, to liquidate the "one-party dictatorship" over the central government, and to inaugurate the long-deferred representative democracy. Meanwhile Soviet Russians in China say frankly that the main barrier to increased aid from Moscow is the extremely slow rate of political progress since the war began.

Russia already has a strong political voice in the Turkistan régime, which is beginning to resemble that in Outer Mongolia and which may be considered a strategic bulwark of the Red empire. There is at present no necessity for arbitrarily seizing so friendly an area at the expense of antagonizing Chiang Kai-shek and stampeding Chungking into an anti-Soviet peace compromise with Japan, arranged by Britain and France. At enormous cost, Japan has created a "New Disorder in East Asia" that beggars all former concepts of chaos. Stalin, by patience and practical political sagacity, has the possibility of creating an order in West China of real strategic value.

So the prospect in China is not unattractive for Moscow. Until an alliance with Japan can offer a future of more specific promise than is now clearly immanent in continued Soviet coöperation with the Chinese, there will be no sudden changes in Stalinist strategy. But future change is by no means to be ruled out entirely. It may occur, though by no means "inevitably," under any one of at least four conditions: (1) an Anglo-Soviet war; (2) an anti-Communist split in Chungking, possibly backed by Britain with some American connivance, and with the object of capitulating to Japan; (3) the imminence of an Anglo-Japanese alliance, or even a basic reconciliation, which Moscow holds can only be anti-Soviet in nature; and (4) an Anglo-Japanese or a Japanese-American war.

Barring those conditions, there remains the possibility suggested in an earlier paragraph: a simple non-aggression pact, providing for closer trade relations with Japan, to keep Tokyo on Moscow's diplomatic hook, but excluding the question of either nation's policy toward the Chinese Government. Though such a possibility may on its face seem to be fantastic and incompatible with the Soviet position in western China, it nevertheless represents the most probable *limit* of Russo-Japanese rapprochement just now. But even this, unless the situation becomes urgent, will be pursued in a leisurely war-of-nerves manner in order to produce the most exquisite jitters in all the capitals concerned, and perhaps provoke them into some action of ill-considered haste.

The policy of the United States in the Western Pacific is no longer static but dynamic. Whatever the American public may think, we are no longer neutral in Japanese eyes. We are no longer passive objectors to Japanese aggression; we are taking active steps to check it. The consequence of a judgment is its execution. Such directed movement of a great nation's policy, once begun, must be maintained by anticipating all the obstacles in its path, and planning to manœuvre among them. The weeks and months ahead require piloting of the most consummate skill.

Which is another way of saying that the United States is now deep in the power game in the East, and willy-nilly must adopt the methods of *Realpolitik* to play it. What will those methods be? Obviously, a first necessity would seem to be to seek more positive understanding with other Powers affected by our move against Japan. Specifically, Washington may try to prevent the realization of those conditions under which Japan would get that indispensable help from Russia, without which she could not contemplate a fight with the United States.

First. The United States has already asserted the validity of its treaties with and concerning China. This action is based upon a secondary assumption that the unity and aims of the Chungking Government, and its friendship for the United States, are dependable constants and will endure against all pressure. But it would be naïve not to take all measures insuring that such a faith will not be betrayed. To risk war by penalizing Japan, without identifying that stand with direct help to China on concrete terms of lasting coöperation, would be to prepare for battle by leaving the decisive flank open.

Second. Present undercover work by certain British factions in the Far East, which are actively seeking to "make a bargain with Japan" on the basis of recognition of Japan's conquests and coöperation with her puppets, will probably be closely watched. London committed itself, through the Craigie-Arita Agreement last summer, not to embarrass in any way Japanese military operations in China. We must not forget that the Chamberlain-Craigie appeasement program, interrupted in Tokyo last July only by the dramatic abrogation of our commercial treaty with Japan, is in abeyance but not abandoned. If hard-pressed in Europe, and offered reconciliation at not too high a price, Chamberlain might think it best to heed the "bargain makers" advice.

Third. Washington will probably be compelled to adopt positive measures in order to nullify the effects of a possible Russo-Japanese rapprochement on our position in the Western Pacific. Unlike Britain, which has India to defend, America has no physical point of conflict with Russia. At the moment both are backing the same government in China. Nor does either one covet any Chinese or Russian territory. All this might usefully be reaffirmed in a special agreement.

The strategic problem involved is how to narrow the hazards of a positive policy. Nominally, that should have nothing to do with the widespread American dislike of Stalin, his credos, and his methods of work. A Russo-American pact of amity, restricted to the Pacific, would probably have a stabilizing effect in the Orient. Indubitably it would be of no more permanent value than any other pact with Russia—or with any other Power—but its usefulness in diplomatic manœuvre might be astonishing. Mere conversations of such a nature might end Japan's bellicosity overnight, and send her envoys flying to Washington, ready to talk terms.

Such a move would probably offend many Americans in their present state of excitement. In practice the Administration may prefer popularity to sagacity. American sentimentality and indignation over the stupid and clumsy invasion of Finland, for example, may continue to express itself in an attitude facilitating Russo-Japanese combination against us. But a policy based on this popular feeling might prove very costly. The world is moving with streamlined speed toward a cataclysm of which the current wars in Europe and Asia are but the preliminaries. The United States cannot will an end to it; the wisest living man cannot even foresee what that end will be. At present nobody is listening to Washington's political moralizing, for other nations do not understand its language or the folklore from which it springs. Combinations and recombinations may be made which will cause recent liaisons to pale into insignificance. To survive in this furiously dynamic world requires the maintenance of a high degree of diplomatic mobility, and no road should be closed until all its possibilities are fully explored and exhausted.

Part III

STALIN'S BID FOR WORLD POWER

1945-1953

By early 1947 thoughtful Americans were deeply engaged in one of the periodic re-appraisals of the basic purposes and directions of U.S. national policy. Wartime hopes for a tolerably friendly and coöperative relationship with postwar Russia had turned to ashes. The paralysis inflicted on the United Nations by its dependence on "great-power unanimity" had disillusioned many Americans. Eastern Europe was being pressed by Moscow into the Stalinist mold, and after much soul-searching the U.S. government, through the Truman Doctrine, had given the Soviet government a clear warning against pursuing its efforts to take over Greece and Turkey. The Marshall Plan for the restoration of Europe's strength was in full gestation.

In this bleak situation many asked whether Soviet antagonism to the West was inevitable and unmovable. Could Stalin's hostility still be assuaged within reasonable limits? Was a new war unavoidable? What were the sources of Soviet hostility? Would the hostility persist unchanged into the indefinite future? In this debate one of the best informed and most potent voices was that of X, author of "The Sources of Soviet Conduct" (July 1947). Soon thereafter, X was identified as George F. Kennan, a highly experienced diplomat and soon-to-be an equally distinguished historian.

Trained in the Russian language and Soviet affairs in the 1920s, Mr. Kennan had had two long periods of service in Moscow before becoming, in 1947, Chief of the newly established Policy Planning Staff in the State Department. After a period of fruitful historical work at the Institute of Advanced Study, Mr. Kennan served briefly as U.S. ambassador to the Soviet Union in 1952; after a longer scholarly interval he became ambassador to Jugoslavia in 1961. He is the author of two volumes, so far, on American-Soviet relations: "Russia Leaves The War" (1956) and "Decision to Intervene" (1958). Among Mr. Kennan's analyses of American and Soviet policies special attention should be drawn to "Realities of American Foreign Policy" (1954), "Russia, the Atom and the West" (1958), and "Russia and the West Under Lenin and Stalin" (1961). Many things have changed in Soviet life since 1947, and Mr. Kennan's views have also evolved considerably over the years, especially since Stalin's death in 1953. In this article the reader will find a vigorous analysis of the East-West problem, one which exerted a powerful influence in a period of challenge to American hopes and purposes.

THE SOURCES OF SOVIET CONDUCT

By George F. Kennan

THE political personality of Soviet power as we know it today is the product of ideology and circumstances: ideology inherited by the present Soviet leaders from the movement in which they had their political origin, and circumstances of the power which they now have exercised for nearly three decades in Russia. There can be few tasks of psychological analysis more difficult than to try to trace the interaction of these two forces and the relative rôle of each in the determination of official Soviet conduct. Yet the attempt must be made if that conduct is to be understood and effectively countered.

It is difficult to summarize the set of ideological concepts with which the Soviet leaders came into power. Marxian ideology, in its Russian-Communist projection, has always been in process of subtle evolution. The materials on which it bases itself are extensive and complex. But the outstanding features of Communist thought as it existed in 1916 may perhaps be summarized as follows: (a) that the central factor in the life of man, the factor which determines the character of public life and the "physiognomy of society," is the system by which material goods are produced and exchanged; (b) that the capitalist system of production is a nefarious one which inevitably leads to the exploitation of the working class by the capital-owning class and is incapable of developing adequately the economic resources of society or of distributing fairly the material goods produced by human labor; (c) that capitalism contains the seeds of its own destruction and must, in view of the inability of the capital-owning class to adjust itself to economic change, result eventually and inescapably in a revolutionary transfer of power to the working class; and (d) that imperialism, the final phase of capitalism, leads directly to war and revolution.

The rest may be outlined in Lenin's own words: "Unevenness of economic and political development is the inflexible law of capitalism.

It follows from this that the victory of Socialism may come originally in a few capitalist countries or even in a single capitalist country. The victorious proletariat of that country, having expropriated the capitalists and having organized Socialist production at home, would rise against the remaining capitalist world, drawing to itself in the process the oppressed classes of other countries." [1] It must be noted that there was no assumption that capitalism would perish without proletarian revolution. A final push was needed from a revolutionary proletariat movement in order to tip over the tottering structure. But it was regarded as inevitable that sooner or later that push be given.

For 50 years prior to the outbreak of the Revolution, this pattern of thought had exercised great fascination for the members of the Russian revolutionary movement. Frustrated, discontented, hopeless of finding self-expression—or too impatient to seek it—in the confining limits of the Tsarist political system, yet lacking wide popular support for their choice of bloody revolution as a means of social betterment, these revolutionists found in Marxist theory a highly convenient rationalization for their own instinctive desires. It afforded pseudo-scientific justification for their impatience, for their categoric denial of all value in the Tsarist system, for their yearning for power and revenge and for their inclination to cut corners in the pursuit of it. It is therefore no wonder that they had come to believe implicitly in the truth and soundness of the Marxian-Leninist teachings, so congenial to their own impulses and emotions. Their sincerity need not be impugned. This is a phenomenon as old as human nature itself. It has never been more aptly described than by Edward Gibbon, who wrote in "The Decline and Fall of the Roman Empire": "From enthusiasm to imposture the step is perilous and slippery; the demon of Socrates affords a memorable instance how a wise man may deceive himself, how a good man may deceive others, how the conscience may slumber in a mixed and middle state between self-illusion and voluntary fraud." And it was with this set of conceptions that the members of the Bolshevik Party entered into power.

Now it must be noted that through all the years of preparation for revolution, the attention of these men, as indeed of Marx himself, had been centered less on the future form which Socialism [2] would take

[1] "Concerning the Slogans of the United States of Europe," August 1915. Official Soviet edition of Lenin's works.

[2] Here and elsewhere in this paper "Socialism" refers to Marxist or Leninist Communism, not to liberal Socialism of the Second International variety.

than on the necessary overthrow of rival power which, in their view, had to precede the introduction of Socialism. Their views, therefore, on the positive program to be put into effect, once power was attained, were for the most part nebulous, visionary and impractical. Beyond the nationalization of industry and the expropriation of large private capital holdings there was no agreed program. The treatment of the peasantry, which according to the Marxist formulation was not of the proletariat, had always been a vague spot in the pattern of Communist thought; and it remained an object of controversy and vacillation for the first ten years of Communist power.

The circumstances of the immediate post-revolution period—the existence in Russia of civil war and foreign intervention, together with the obvious fact that the Communists represented only a tiny minority of the Russian people—made the establishment of dictatorial power a necessity. The experiment with "war Communism" and the abrupt attempt to eliminate private production and trade had unfortunate economic consequences and caused further bitterness against the new revolutionary régime. While the temporary relaxation of the effort to communize Russia, represented by the New Economic Policy, alleviated some of this economic distress and thereby served its purpose, it also made it evident that the "capitalistic sector of society" was still prepared to profit at once from any relaxation of governmental pressure, and would, if permitted to continue to exist, always constitute a powerful opposing element to the Soviet régime and a serious rival for influence in the country. Somewhat the same situation prevailed with respect to the individual peasant who, in his own small way, was also a private producer.

Lenin, had he lived, might have proved a great enough man to reconcile these conflicting forces to the ultimate benefit of Russian society, though this is questionable. But be that as it may, Stalin, and those whom he led in the struggle for succession to Lenin's position of leadership, were not the men to tolerate rival political forces in the sphere of power which they coveted. Their sense of insecurity was too great. Their particular brand of fanaticism, unmodified by any of the Anglo-Saxon traditions of compromise, was too fierce and too jealous to envisage any permanent sharing of power. From the Russian-Asiatic world out of which they had emerged they carried with them a skepticism as to the possibilities of permanent and peaceful coexistence of rival forces. Easily persuaded of their own doctrinaire "rightness," they insisted on the submission or destruction of all competing power. Outside of the Communist Party, Russian society was to have no rigidity. There were to be no forms of collective human activity or association which would not be dominated by the Party. No other force in Russian society was to be permitted to achieve vitality or integrity. Only the Party was to have structure. All else was to be an amorphous mass.

And within the Party the same principle was to apply. The mass of Party members might go through the motions of election, deliberation, decision and action; but in these motions they were to be animated not by their own individual wills but by the awesome breath of the Party leadership and the overbrooding presence of "the word."

Let it be stressed again that subjectively these men probably did not seek absolutism for its own sake. They doubtless believed—and found it easy to believe—that they alone knew what was good for society and that they would accomplish that good once their power was secure and unchallengeable. But in seeking that security of their own rule they were prepared to recognize no restrictions, either of God or man, on the character of their methods. And until such time as that security might be achieved, they placed far down on their scale of operational priorities the comforts and happiness of the peoples entrusted to their care.

Now the outstanding circumstance concerning the Soviet régime is that down to the present day this process of political consolidation has never been completed and the men in the Kremlin have continued to be predominantly absorbed with the struggle to secure and make absolute the power which they seized in November 1917. They have endeavored to secure it primarily against forces at home, within Soviet society itself. But they have also endeavored to secure it against the outside world. For ideology, as we have seen, taught them that the outside world was hostile and that it was their duty eventually to overthrow the political forces beyond their borders. The powerful hands of Russian history and tradition reached up to sustain them in this feeling. Finally, their own aggressive intransigence with respect to the outside world began to find its own reaction; and they were soon forced, to use another Gibbonesque phrase, "to chastise the contumacy" which they themselves had provoked. It is an undeniable privilege of every man to prove himself right in the thesis that the world is his enemy; for if he reiterates it frequently enough and makes it the background of his conduct he is bound eventually to be right.

Now it lies in the nature of the mental world of the Soviet leaders, as well as in the character of their ideology, that no opposition to them can be officially recognized as having any merit or justification whatsoever. Such opposition can flow, in theory, only from the hostile and incorrigible forces of dying capitalism. As long as remnants of capitalism were officially recognized as existing in Russia, it was possible to place on them, as an internal element, part of the blame for the maintenance of a dictatorial form of society. But as these remnants were liquidated, little by little, this justification fell away; and when it was indicated officially that they had been finally destroyed, it disappeared altogether. And this fact created one of the most basic of the compulsions which came to act upon the Soviet régime: since capitalism no longer existed in Russia and since it could not be admitted that there could be serious or widespread opposition to the Kremlin springing spontaneously from the liberated masses under its authority, it became necessary to justify the retention of the dictatorship by stressing the menace of capitalism abroad.

This began at an early date. In 1924 Stalin specifically defended the retention of the "organs of suppression," meaning, among others, the army and the secret police, on the ground that "as long as there is a capitalist encirclement there will be danger of intervention with all the consequences that flow from that danger." In accordance with that theory, and from that time on, all internal opposition forces in Russia have consistently been portrayed as the agents of foreign forces of reaction antagonistic to Soviet power.

By the same token, tremendous emphasis has been placed on the original Communist thesis of a basic antagonism between the capitalist and Socialist worlds. It is clear, from many indications, that this emphasis is not founded in reality. The real facts concerning it have been confused by the existence abroad of genuine resentment provoked by Soviet philosophy and tactics and occasionally by the existence of great centers of military power, notably the Nazi régime in Germany and the Japanese Government of the late 1930's, which did indeed have aggressive designs against the Soviet Union. But there is ample evidence that the stress laid in Moscow on the menace confronting Soviet society from the world outside its borders is founded not in the realities of foreign antagonism but in the necessity of explaining away the maintenance of dictatorial authority at home.

Now the maintenance of this pattern of Soviet power, namely, the

pursuit of unlimited authority domestically, accompanied by the cultivation of the semi-myth of implacable foreign hostility, has gone far
to shape the actual machinery of Soviet power as we know it today.
Internal organs of administration which did not serve this purpose
withered on the vine. Organs which did serve this purpose became
vastly swollen. The security of Soviet power came to rest on the
iron discipline of the Party, on the severity and ubiquity of the secret
police, and on the uncompromising economic monopolism of the state.
The "organs of suppression," in which the Soviet leaders had sought
security from rival forces, became in large measure the masters of
those whom they were designed to serve. Today the major part of the
structure of Soviet power is committed to the perfection of the dictatorship and to the maintenance of the concept of Russia as in a state
of siege, with the enemy lowering beyond the walls. And the millions of
human beings who form that part of the structure of power must
defend at all costs this concept of Russia's position, for without it
they are themselves superfluous.

As things stand today, the rulers can no longer dream of parting
with these organs of suppression. The quest for absolute power, pursued now for nearly three decades with a ruthlessness unparalleled
(in scope at least) in modern times, has again produced internally, as
it did externally, its own reaction. The excesses of the police apparatus
have fanned the potential opposition to the régime into something far
greater and more dangerous than it could have been before those
excesses began.

But least of all can the rulers dispense with the fiction by which
the maintenance of dictatorial power has been defended. For this fiction
has been canonized in Soviet philosophy by the excesses already committed in its name; and it is now anchored in the Soviet structure of
thought by bonds far greater than those of mere ideology.

II

So much for the historical background. What does it spell in terms
of the political personality of Soviet power as we know it today?

Of the original ideology, nothing has been officially junked. Belief
is maintained in the basic badness of capitalism, in the inevitability
of its destruction, in the obligation of the proletariat to assist in that
destruction and to take power into its own hands. But stress has come

to be laid primarily on those concepts which relate most specifically to the Soviet régime itself: to its position as the sole truly Socialist régime in a dark and misguided world, and to the relationships of power within it.

The first of these concepts is that of the innate antagonism between capitalism and Socialism. We have seen how deeply that concept has become imbedded in foundations of Soviet power. It has profound implications for Russia's conduct as a member of international society. It means that there can never be on Moscow's side any sincere assumption of a community of aims between the Soviet Union and powers which are regarded as capitalist. It must invariably be assumed in Moscow that the aims of the capitalist world are antagonistic to the Soviet régime, and therefore to the interests of the peoples it controls. If the Soviet Government occasionally sets its signature to documents which would indicate the contrary, this is to be regarded as a tactical manœuvre permissible in dealing with the enemy (who is without honor) and should be taken in the spirit of *caveat emptor*. Basically, the antagonism remains. It is postulated. And from it flow many of the phenomena which we find disturbing in the Kremlin's conduct of foreign policy: the secretiveness, the lack of frankness, the duplicity, the wary suspiciousness, and the basic unfriendliness of purpose. These phenomena are there to stay, for the foreseeable future. There can be variations of degree and of emphasis. When there is something the Russians want from us, one or the other of these features of their policy may be thrust temporarily into the background; and when that happens there will always be Americans who will leap forward with gleeful announcements that "the Russians have changed," and some who will even try to take credit for having brought about such "changes." But we should not be misled by tactical manœuvres. These characteristics of Soviet policy, like the postulate from which they flow, are basic to the internal nature of Soviet power, and will be with us, whether in the foreground or the background, until the internal nature of Soviet power is changed.

This means that we are going to continue for a long time to find the Russians difficult to deal with. It does not mean that they should be considered as embarked upon a do-or-die program to overthrow our society by a given date. The theory of the inevitability of the eventual fall of capitalism has the fortunate connotation that there is no hurry about it. The forces of progress can take their time in preparing the final *coup de grâce*. Meanwhile, what is vital is that the "Socialist fatherland"—that oasis of power which has been already won for Socialism in the person of the Soviet Union—should be cherished and defended by all good Communists at home and abroad, its fortunes promoted, its enemies badgered and confounded. The promotion of premature, "adventuristic" revolutionary projects abroad which might embarrass Soviet power in any way would be an inexcusable, even a counter-revolutionary act. The cause of Socialism is the support and promotion of Soviet power, as defined in Moscow.

This brings us to the second of the concepts important to contemporary Soviet outlook. That is the infallibility of the Kremlin. The Soviet concept of power, which permits no focal points of organization outside the Party itself, requires that the Party leadership remain in theory the sole repository of truth. For if truth were to be found elsewhere, there would be justification for its expression in organized activity. But it is precisely that which the Kremlin cannot and will not permit.

The leadership of the Communist Party is therefore always right, and has been always right ever since in 1929 Stalin formalized his personal power by announcing that decisions of the Politburo were being taken unanimously.

On the principle of infallibility there rests the iron discipline of the Communist Party. In fact, the two concepts are mutually self-supporting. Perfect discipline requires recognition of infallibility. Infallibility requires the observance of discipline. And the two together go far to determine the behaviorism of the entire Soviet apparatus of power. But their effect cannot be understood unless a third factor be taken into account: namely, the fact that the leadership is at liberty to put forward for tactical purposes any particular thesis which it finds useful to the cause at any particular moment and to require the faithful and unquestioning acceptance of that thesis by the members of the movement as a whole. This means that truth is not a constant but is actually created, for all intents and purposes, by the Soviet leaders themselves. It may vary from week to week, from month to month. It is nothing absolute and immutable—nothing which flows from objective reality. It is only the most recent manifestation of the wisdom of those in whom the ultimate wisdom is supposed to reside, because they represent the logic of history. The accumulative effect of these factors is to give to the whole subordinate apparatus of Soviet power an unshakeable stubbornness and steadfastness in its orientation. This orientation can be changed at will by the Kremlin but by no other power. Once a given party line has been laid down on a given issue of current policy, the whole Soviet governmental machine, including the mechanism of diplomacy, moves inexorably along the prescribed path, like a persistent toy automobile wound up and headed in a given direction, stopping only when it meets with some unanswerable force. The individuals who are the components of this machine are unamenable to argument or reason which comes to them from outside sources. Their whole training has taught them to mistrust and discount the glib persuasiveness of the outside world. Like the white dog before the phonograph, they hear only the "master's voice." And if they are to be called off from the purposes last dictated to them, it is the master who must call them off. Thus the foreign representative cannot hope that his words will make any impression on them. The most that he can hope is that they will be transmitted to those at the top, who are capable of changing the party line. But even those are not likely to be swayed by any normal logic in the words of the bourgeois representative. Since there can be no appeal to common purposes, there can be no appeal to common mental approaches. For this reason, facts speak louder than words to the ears of the Kremlin; and words carry the greatest weight when they have the ring of reflecting, or being backed up by, facts of unchallengeable validity.

But we have seen that the Kremlin is under no ideological compulsion to accomplish its purposes in a hurry. Like the Church, it is dealing in ideological concepts which are of long-term validity, and it can afford to be patient. It has no right to risk the existing achievements of the revolution for the sake of vain baubles of the future. The very teachings of Lenin himself require great caution and flexibility in the pursuit of Communist purposes. Again, these precepts are fortified by the lessons of Russian history: of centuries of obscure battles between nomadic forces over the stretches of a vast unfortified plain. Here caution, circumspection, flexibility and deception are the valuable qualities; and their value finds natural appreciation in the Russian or the oriental mind. Thus the Kremlin has no compunction about retreating in the face of superior force. And being under the compulsion of no timetable, it does not get panicky under the necessity for such retreat. Its political action is a fluid stream which moves constantly, wherever it is permitted to move, toward a given goal. Its main concern is to make sure that it has filled every nook and cranny available to it in the basin of world power. But if it finds unassailable barriers in its path, it accepts these philosophically and accommodates itself to them. The main thing is that there should always be pressure, unceasing constant pressure, toward the desired goal. There is no trace of any feeling in Soviet psychology that that goal must be reached at any given time.

These considerations make Soviet diplomacy at once easier and more difficult to deal with than the diplomacy of individual aggressive leaders like Napoleon and Hitler. On the one hand it is more sensitive to contrary force, more ready to yield on individual sectors of the diplomatic front when that force is felt to be too strong, and thus more rational in the logic and rhetoric of power. On the other hand it cannot be easily defeated or discouraged by a single victory on the part of its opponents. And the patient persistence by which it is animated means that it can be effectively countered not by sporadic acts which represent the momentary whims of democratic opinion but only by intelligent long-range policies on the part of Russia's adversaries— policies no less steady in their purpose, and no less variegated and resourceful in their application, than those of the Soviet Union itself.

In these circumstances it is clear that the main element of any United States policy toward the Soviet Union must be that of a long-term, patient but firm and vigilant containment of Russian expansive tendencies. It is important to note, however, that such a policy has nothing to do with outward histrionics: with threats or blustering or superfluous gestures of outward "toughness." While the Kremlin is basically flexible in its reaction to political realities, it is by no means unamenable to considerations of prestige. Like almost any other government, it can be placed by tactless and threatening gestures in a position where it cannot afford to yield even though this might be dictated by its sense of realism. The Russian leaders are keen judges of human psychology, and as such they are highly conscious that loss of temper and of self-control is never a source of strength in political affairs. They are quick to exploit such evidences of weakness. For these reasons, it is a *sine qua non* of successful dealing with Russia that the foreign government in question should remain at all times cool and collected and that its demands on Russian policy should be put forward in such a manner as to leave the way open for a compliance not too detrimental to Russian prestige.

III

In the light of the above, it will be clearly seen that the Soviet pressure against the free institutions of the western world is something that can be contained by the adroit and vigilant application of counter-force at a series of constantly shifting geographical and political points, corresponding to the shifts and manœuvres of Soviet policy, but which cannot be charmed or talked out of existence. The Russians look forward to a duel of infinite duration, and they see that already they have scored great successes. It must be borne in mind that there was a time when the Communist Party represented far more of a minority in the sphere of Russian national life than Soviet power today represents in the world community.

But if ideology convinces the rulers of Russia that truth is on their side and that they can therefore afford to wait, those of us on whom that ideology has no claim are free to examine objectively the validity of that premise. The Soviet thesis not only implies complete lack of control by the west over its own economic destiny, it likewise assumes Russian unity, discipline and patience over an infinite period. Let us bring this apocalyptic vision down to earth, and suppose that the western world finds the strength and resourcefulness to contain Soviet power over a period of ten to fifteen years. What does that spell for Russia itself?

The Soviet leaders, taking advantage of the contributions of modern technique to the arts of despotism, have solved the question of obedience within the confines of their power. Few challenge their authority; and even those who do are unable to make that challenge valid as against the organs of suppression of the state.

The Kremlin has also proved able to accomplish its purpose of building up in Russia, regardless of the interests of the inhabitants, an industrial foundation of heavy metallurgy, which is, to be sure, not yet complete but which is nevertheless continuing to grow and is approaching those of the other major industrial countries. All of this, however, both the maintenance of internal political security and the building of heavy industry, has been carried out at a terrible cost in human life and in human hopes and energies. It has necessitated the use of forced labor on a scale unprecedented in modern times under conditions of peace. It has involved the neglect or abuse of other phases of Soviet economic life, particularly agriculture, consumers' goods production, housing and transportation.

To all that, the war has added its tremendous toll of destruction, death and human exhaustion. In consequence of this, we have in Russia today a population which is physically and spiritually tired. The mass of the people are disillusioned, skeptical and no longer as accessible as they once were to the magical attraction which Soviet power still radiates to its followers abroad. The avidity with which people seized upon the slight respite accorded to the Church for tactical reasons during the war was eloquent testimony to the fact that their capacity for faith and devotion found little expression in the purposes of the régime.

In these circumstances, there are limits to the physical and nervous strength of people themselves. These limits are absolute ones, and are binding even for the cruelest dictatorship, because beyond them people cannot be driven. The forced labor camps and the other agencies of constraint provide temporary means of compelling people to work longer hours than their own volition or mere economic pressure would dictate; but if people survive them at all they become old before their time and must be considered as human casualties to the demands of dictatorship. In either case their best powers are no longer available to society and can no longer be enlisted in the service of the state.

Here only the younger generation can help. The younger generation, despite all vicissitudes and sufferings, is numerous and vigorous; and the Russians are a talented people. But it still remains to be seen what will be the effects on mature performance of the abnormal emotional strains of childhood which Soviet dictatorship created and which were enormously increased by the war. Such things as normal security and placidity of home environment have practically ceased to exist in the Soviet Union outside of the most remote farms and villages. And observers are not yet sure whether that is not going to leave its mark on the over-all capacity of the generation now coming into maturity.

In addition to this, we have the fact that Soviet economic development, while it can list certain formidable achievements, has been precariously spotty and uneven. Russian Communists who speak of the "uneven development of capitalism" should blush at the contemplation of their own national economy. Here certain branches of economic life, such as the metallurgical and machine industries, have been pushed out of all proportion to other sectors of economy. Here is a nation striving to become in a short period one of the great industrial nations of the world while it still has no highway network worthy of the name and only a relatively primitive network of railways. Much has been done to increase efficiency of labor and to teach primitive peasants something about the operation of machines. But maintenance is still a crying deficiency of all Soviet economy. Construction is hasty and poor in quality. Depreciation must be enormous. And in vast sectors of economic life it has not yet been possible to instill into labor anything like that general culture of production and technical self-respect which characterizes the skilled worker of the west.

It is difficult to see how these deficiencies can be corrected at an early date by a tired and dispirited population working largely under the shadow of fear and compulsion. And as long as they are not overcome, Russia will remain economically a vulnerable, and in a certain sense an impotent, nation, capable of exporting its enthusiasms and of radiating the strange charm of its primitive political vitality but unable to back up those articles of export by the real evidences of material power and prosperity.

Meanwhile, a great uncertainty hangs over the political life of the Soviet Union. That is the uncertainty involved in the transfer of power from one individual or group of individuals to others.

This is, of course, outstandingly the problem of the personal position of Stalin. We must remember that his succession to Lenin's pinnacle of preëminence in the Communist movement was the only such transfer of individual authority which the Soviet Union has experienced. That transfer took 12 years to consolidate. It cost the lives of millions of people and shook the state to its foundations. The attendant tremors were felt all through the international revolutionary movement, to the disadvantage of the Kremlin itself.

It is always possible that another transfer of preëminent power may take place quietly and inconspicuously, with no repercussions anywhere. But again, it is possible that the questions involved may unleash, to use some of Lenin's words, one of those "incredibly swift transitions" from "delicate deceit" to "wild violence" which characterize Russian history, and may shake Soviet power to its foundations.

But this is not only a question of Stalin himself. There has been, since 1938, a dangerous congealment of political life in the higher circles of Soviet power. The All-Union Congress of Soviets, in theory the supreme body of the Party, is supposed to meet not less often than once in three years. It will soon be eight full years since its last meeting. During this period membership in the Party has numerically doubled. Party mortality during the war was enormous; and today well over half of the Party members are persons who have entered since the last Party congress was held. Meanwhile, the same small group of men has carried on at the top through an amazing series of national vicissitudes. Surely there is some reason why the experiences of the war brought basic political changes to every one of the great governments of the west. Surely the causes of that phenomenon are basic enough to be present somewhere in the obscurity of Soviet political life, as well. And yet no recognition has been given to these causes in Russia.

It must be surmised from this that even within so highly disciplined an organization as the Communist Party there must be a growing divergence in age, outlook and interest between the great mass of Party members, only so recently recruited into the movement, and the little self-perpetuating clique of men at the top, whom most of these Party members have never met, with whom they have never conversed, and with whom they can have no political intimacy.

Who can say whether, in these circumstances, the eventual rejuvenation of the higher spheres of authority (which can only be a matter of time) can take place smoothly and peacefully, or whether rivals in the quest for higher power will not eventually reach down into these politically immature and inexperienced masses in order to find support for their respective claims? If this were ever to happen, strange consequences could flow for the Communist Party: for the membership at large has been exercised only in the practices of iron discipline and obedience and not in the arts of compromise and accommodation. And if disunity were ever to seize and paralyze the Party, the chaos and weakness of Russian society would be revealed in forms beyond description. For we have seen that Soviet power is only a crust concealing an amorphous mass of human beings among whom no independent organizational structure is tolerated. In Russia there is not even such a thing as local government. The present generation of Russians have never known spontaneity of collective action. If, consequently, anything were ever to occur to disrupt the unity and efficacy of the Party as a political instrument, Soviet Russia might be changed overnight from one of the strongest to one of the weakest and most pitiable of national societies.

Thus the future of Soviet power may not be by any means as secure as Russian capacity for self-delusion would make it appear to the men in the Kremlin. That they can keep power themselves, they have demonstrated. That they can quietly and easily turn it over to others remains to be proved. Meanwhile, the hardships of their rule and the vicissitudes of international life have taken a heavy toll of the strength and hopes of the great people on whom their power rests. It is curious to note that the ideological power of Soviet authority is strongest today in areas beyond the frontiers of Russia, beyond the reach of its police power. This phenomenon brings to mind a comparison used by Thomas Mann in his great novel "Buddenbrooks." Observing that human institutions often show the greatest outward brilliance at a moment when inner decay is in reality farthest advanced, he compared the Buddenbrook family, in the days of its greatest glamour, to one of those stars whose light shines most brightly on this world when in reality it has long since ceased to exist. And who can say with assurance that the strong light still cast by the Kremlin on the dissatisfied peoples of the western world is not the powerful afterglow of a constellation which is in actuality on the wane? This cannot be proved. And it cannot be disproved. But the possibility remains (and in the opinion of this writer it is a strong one) that Soviet power, like the capitalist world of its conception, bears within it the seeds of its own decay, and that the sprouting of these seeds is well advanced.

IV

It is clear that the United States cannot expect in the foreseeable future to enjoy political intimacy with the Soviet régime. It must continue to regard the Soviet Union as a rival, not a partner, in the political arena. It must continue to expect that Soviet policies will reflect no abstract love of peace and stability, no real faith in the possibility of a permanent happy coexistence of the Socialist and capitalist worlds, but rather a cautious, persistent pressure toward the disruption and weakening of all rival influence and rival power.

Balanced against this are the facts that Russia, as opposed to the western world in general, is still by far the weaker party, that Soviet policy is highly flexible, and that Soviet society may well contain deficiencies which will eventually weaken its own total potential. This would of itself warrant the United States entering with reasonable confidence upon a policy of firm containment, designed to confront the Russians with unalterable counter-force at every point where they show signs of encroaching upon the interests of a peaceful and stable world.

But in actuality the possibilities for American policy are by no means limited to holding the line and hoping for the best. It is entirely possible for the United States to influence by its actions the internal developments, both within Russia and throughout the international Communist movement, by which Russian policy is largely determined. This is not only a question of the modest measure of informational activity which this government can conduct in the Soviet Union and elsewhere, although that, too, is important. It is rather a question of the degree to which the United States can create among the peoples of the world generally the impression of a country which knows what it wants, which is coping successfully with the problems of its internal life and with the responsibilities of a World Power, and which has a spiritual vitality capable of holding its own among the major ideological currents of the time. To the extent that such an impression can be created and maintained, the aims of Russian Communism must appear sterile and quixotic, the hopes and enthusiasm of Moscow's supporters must wane, and added strain must be imposed on the Kremlin's foreign policies. For the palsied decrepitude of the capitalist world is the keystone of Communist philosophy. Even the failure of the United States to experience the early economic depression which the ravens of the Red Square have been predicting with such complacent confidence since hostilities ceased would have deep and important repercussions throughout the Communist world.

By the same token, exhibitions of indecision, disunity and internal disintegration within this country have an exhilarating effect on the whole Communist movement. At each evidence of these tendencies, a thrill of hope and excitement goes through the Communist world; a new jauntiness can be noted in the Moscow tread; new groups of foreign supporters climb on to what they can only view as the band wagon of international politics; and Russian pressure increases all along the line in international affairs.

It would be an exaggeration to say that American behavior unassisted and alone could exercise a power of life and death over the Communist movement and bring about the early fall of Soviet power in Russia. But the United States has it in its power to increase enormously the strains under which Soviet policy must operate, to force upon the Kremlin a far greater degree of moderation and circumspection than it has had to observe in recent years, and in this way to promote tendencies which must eventually find their outlet in either the break-up or the gradual mellowing of Soviet power. For no mystical, Messianic movement—and particularly not that of the Kremlin—can face frustration indefinitely without eventually adjusting itself in one way or another to the logic of that state of affairs.

Thus the decision will really fall in large measure in this country itself. The issue of Soviet-American relations is in essence a test of the over-all worth of the United States as a nation among nations. To avoid destruction the United States need only measure up to its own best traditions and prove itself worthy of preservation as a great nation.

Surely, there was never a fairer test of national quality than this. In the light of these circumstances, the thoughtful observer of Russian-American relations will find no cause for complaint in the Kremlin's challenge to American society. He will rather experience a certain gratitude to a Providence which, by providing the American people with this implacable challenge, has made their entire security as a nation dependent on their pulling themselves together and accepting the responsibilities of moral and political leadership that history plainly intended them to bear.

THE expectation, cherished by so many in the years of the second great war, that the affairs of the world would, after a period of reconstruction, settle into some new kind of "normalcy," was a natural and tenacious one. The generous vision of the great allies continuing their coöperation into the peace was slow to fade even in the harsh light of Soviet words and actions. After all, the allies had managed to arrange a modicum of collaboration in occupied Germany and "liberated" Austria. They had, after many months of haggling and jostling, negotiated peace treaties for Italy, Hungary, Rumania, Bulgaria and Finland. The United Nations had ridden through two serious crises and seemed to be gaining strength.

The undercurrent, however, was moving strongly toward new and sharper clashes. In divided Germany the Soviet leadership was evading any genuine fulfillment of the Potsdam and other agreements on treating Germany as a unit. It was probing actively in Greece, and challenging Turkey's independence. In East Central Europe it was tightening its grip on each of the satellites. Its vituperative denunciations of any and all U.S. policies had been rising in a crescendo, from Stalin's election speech of February 1946 to the public declaration of all-out political warfare by the Cominform in October 1947.

The founding conference of the Cominform had not yet assembled in secret conclave when Henry L. Stimson wrote "The Challenge to Americans" (October 1947). After retiring for the third time from public service, Mr. Stimson could look back on several great national crises that his country had surmounted in his lifetime. Having worked hard in wartime to establish closer coöperation with the Soviet leadership, he was doubly anxious to interpret correctly the new challenge that Stalin's aims and methods were presenting to the West. His words, carefully weighed as always, had a wide resonance at home and abroad.

A distinguished lawyer, Henry L. Stimson (1867-1950) was called again and again to help define and execute his country's foreign policies. He was Secretary of War in the Taft Administration, Secretary of State under President Hoover, and again Secretary of War under Presidents Roosevelt and Truman. Among his principal writings are: "American Policy in Nicaragua" (1927), "The Far Eastern Crisis" (1936, for the Council on Foreign Relations), and, with McGeorge Bundy, "On Active Service in War and Peace" (1948).

186

THE CHALLENGE TO AMERICANS

By Henry L. Stimson

WE Americans today face a challenging opportunity, perhaps the greatest ever offered to a single nation. It is nothing less than a chance to use our full strength for the peace and freedom of the world. This opportunity comes when many of us are confused and unready. Only two years ago we triumphantly ended the greatest war in history. Most of us then looked forward eagerly to the relative relaxation of peace. Reluctantly we have now come to understand that victory and peace are not synonymous. Over large areas of the world we have nothing better than armed truce; in some places there is open fighting; everywhere men know that there is yet no stable settlement. Close on the heels of victory has loomed a new world crisis.

Particularly to Americans the appearance of disquieting facts and possibilities has been upsetting. We are having our first experience of constant, full-scale activity in world politics. Other nations have lived for years as principals in the give-and-take of diplomacy. Until now we have been, except in wartime, on the fringe. It is no wonder that, when suddenly placed in the center of the alarms and excursions of international affairs, we are abnormally sensitive. And, of course, it does not help to find ourselves selected as chief target for the abuse and opposition of a very bad-mannered group of men who take their orders from the Kremlin. It is not surprising, then, that many of us are confused and unhappy about our foreign relations, and that some are tempted to seek refuge from their confusion either in retreat to isolationism or in suggested solutions whose simplicity is only matched by their folly. In the main, our difficulties arise from unwillingness to face reality.

It must be admitted that the elements of the new unrest appear to be unusually complex and trying. The war-shattered world must be rebuilt; the problem of atomic energy insistently demands solution; the present policy of Russia must be frustrated. But it is my belief that the American people have it well within their power to meet and resolve all of these problems. The essential test is one of will and understanding. We require a skillful foreign policy, of course, but we may have confidence that the farsighted and experienced men now in charge of our State Department know how to frame a policy. In outline the President and the Secretary of State have already set their course. They can develop their policy with success, however, only if they have the understanding support, on basic principles, of the American people.

II

First, and most important, Americans must now understand that the United States has become, for better or worse, a wholly committed member of the world community. This has not happened by conscious choice; but it is a plain fact, and our only choice is whether or not to face it. For more than a generation the increasing interrelation of American life with the life of the world has out-paced our thinking and our policy; our refusal to catch up with reality during these years was the major source of our considerable share of the responsibility for the catastrophe of World War II.

It is the first condition of effective foreign policy that this nation put away forever any thought that America can again be an island to herself. No private program and no public policy, in any sector of our national life, can now escape from the compelling fact that if it is not framed with reference to the world, it is framed with perfect futility. This would be true if there were no such thing as nuclear fission, and if all the land eastward from Poland to the Pacific were under water. Atomic energy and Soviet Russia are merely the two most conspicuous present demonstrations of what we have at stake in world affairs. The attitude of isolationism—political or economic— must die; in all its many forms the vain hope that we can live alone must be abandoned.

As a corollary to this first great principle, it follows that we shall be wholly wrong if we attempt to set a maximum or margin to our activity as members of the world. The only question we can safely ask today is whether in any of our actions on the world stage we are doing enough. In American policy toward the world there is no place for grudging or limited participation, and any attempt to cut our losses by setting bounds to our policy can only turn us backward onto the deadly road toward self-defeating isolation.

Our stake in the peace and freedom of the world is not a limited liability. Time after time in other years we have tried to solve our foreign problems with halfway measures, acting under the illusion that we could be partly in the world and partly irresponsible. Time after time our Presidents and Secretaries of State have been restrained, by their own fears or by public opinion, from effective action. It should by now be wholly clear that only failure, and its follower, war, can result from such efforts at a cheap solution.

We have fresh before us the contrary example of our magnificent success in wartime, when we have not stopped to count the cost. I have served as Secretary of State in a time of frightened isolationism, and as Secretary of War in a time of brave and generous action. I know the withering effect of limited commitments, and I know the regenerative power of full action. I know, too, that America can afford it—as who does not know it, in the face of our record in the last seven years?

It is altogether fitting and proper, of course, that we should not waste our substance in activity without result. It is also evident that we cannot do everything we would like to do. But it would be shriveling timidity for America to refuse to play to the full her present necessary part in the world. And the certain penalty for such timidity would be failure.

The troubles of Europe and Asia are not "other people's troubles"; they are ours. The world is full of friends and enemies; it is full of warring ideas; but there are no mere "foreigners," no merely "foreign" ideologies, no merely "foreign" dangers, any more. Foreign affairs are now our most intimate domestic concern. All men, good or bad, are now our neighbors. All ideas dwell among us.

III

A second principle, and one which requires emphasis as a necessary complement to any policy of full participation, is that we are forced to act in the world as it is, and not in the world as we wish it were, or as we would like it to become. It is a world in which we are only one of many peoples and in which our basic principles of life are not shared by all our neighbors. It has been one of the more dangerous aspects of our internationalism in past years that too often it was accompanied by the curious assumption that the world would overnight become good and clean and peaceful everywhere if only America would lead the way. The most elementary experience of human affairs should show us all how naïve and dangerous a view that is.

The most conspicuous present examples of this sort of thinking are to be found among those who refuse to recognize the strong probability that one of our great and powerful neighbor nations is at present controlled by men who are convinced that the very course of history is set against democracy and freedom, as we understand those words. A very large part of what I believe to be the mistaken thinking done by my friend Henry Wallace about Soviet Russia results simply from a goodhearted insistence that nobody can dislike us if we try to like them.

We have been very patient with the Soviet Government, and very hopeful of its good intentions. I have been among those who shared in these hopes and counseled this patience. The magnificent and loyal war effort of the Russian people, and the great successful efforts at friendliness made during the war by President Roosevelt, gave us good reason for hope. I have believed—and I still believe—that we must show good faith in all our dealings with the Russians, and that only by so doing can we leave the door open for Russian good faith toward us. I cannot too strongly express my regret that since the early spring of 1945—even before the death of Mr. Roosevelt—the Soviet Government has steadily pursued an obstructive and unfriendly course. It has been our hope that the Russians would choose to be our friends; it was and is our conviction that such a choice would be to their advantage. But, for the time being, at least, those who determine Russian policy have chosen otherwise, and their choice has been slavishly followed by Communists everywhere.

No sensible American can now ignore this fact, and those who now choose to travel in company with American Communists are very clearly either knaves or fools. This is a judgment which I make reluctantly, but there is no help for it. I have often said that the surest way to make a man trustworthy is to trust him. But I must add that this does not always apply to a man who is determined to make you his dupe. Before we can make friends with the Russians, their leaders will have to be convinced that they have nothing to gain, and everything to lose, by acting on the assumption that our society is dying and that our principles are outworn. Americans who think they can make common cause with present-day Communism are living in a world that does not exist.

They are not alone. An equal and opposite error is made by those who argue that Americans by strong-arm methods, perhaps even by a "preventive war," can and should rid the world of the Communist menace. I cannot believe that this view is widely held. For it is worse than nonsense; it results from a hopeless misunderstanding of the geographical and military situation, and a cynical incomprehension of what the people of the world will tolerate from *any* nation. Worst of all, this theory indicates a totally wrong assessment of the basic attitudes and motives of the American people. Even if it were true that the United States now had the opportunity to establish forceful hegemony throughout the world, we could not possibly take that opportunity without deserting our true inheritance. Americans as conquerors would be tragically miscast.

The world's affairs cannot be simplified by eager words. We cannot take refuge from reality in the folly of black-and-white solutions.

IV

In dealing with the Russians, both uncritical trust and unmitigated belligerence are impossible. There is a middle course. We do not yet know surely in what proportion unreasonable fears and twisted hopes are at the root of the perverted policy now followed by the Kremlin. Assuming both to be involved, we must disarm the fears and disappoint the hopes. We must no longer let the tide of Soviet expansion cheaply roll into the empty places left by war, and yet we must make it perfectly clear that we are not ourselves expansionist. Our task is to help threatened peoples to help themselves.

This is not easy. It is quite possible, indeed, that the blind reaction of some anti-Communist governments may succeed to some extent in nullifying our labors. We must make every effort to prevent such a result. Success in this task depends so much on men and circumstances that I do not venture to prescribe a theoretical solution. It is an undertaking that demands a bold and active policy, combined with skillful and understanding execution. In such an undertaking, it is only the exceptionally well-informed who may properly give advice from the sidelines.

But our main answer to the Russians is not negative, nor is it in any sense anti-Russian. Our central task in dealing with the Kremlin is to demonstrate beyond the possibility of misunderstanding that freedom and prosperity, hand in hand, can be stably sustained in the western democratic world. This would be our greatest task even if no Soviet problem existed, and to the Soviet threat it is our best response.

Soviet intransigence is based in very large part on the hope and belief that all non-Communist systems are doomed. Soviet policy aims to help them die. We must hope that time and the success of freedom and democracy in the western world will convince both the Soviet leaders and the Russian people now behind them that our system is here to stay. This may not be possible; dictators do not easily change their hearts, and the modern armaments they possess may make it hard for their people to force such a change. Rather than be persuaded of their error, the Soviet leaders might in desperation resort to war, and against that possibility we have to guard by maintaining our present military advantages. We must never forget that while peace is a joint responsibility, the decision for war can be made by a single Power; our military strength must be maintained as a standing discouragement to aggression.

I do not, however, expect the Russians to make war. I do not share the gloomy fear of some that we are now engaged in the preliminaries of an inevitable conflict. Even the most repressive dictatorship is not perfectly unassailable from within, and the most frenzied fanaticism is never unopposed. Whatever the ideological bases of Soviet policy, it seems clear that some at least of the leaders of Russia are men who have a marked respect for facts. We must make it wholly evident that a nonaggressive Russia will have nothing to fear from us. We must make it clear, too, that the western non-Communist world is going to survive in growing economic and political stability. If we can do this, then slowly—but perhaps less slowly than we now believe—the Russian leaders may either change their minds or lose their jobs.

V

The problem of Russia is thus reduced to a question of our own fitness to survive. I do not mean to belittle the Communist challenge. I only mean that the essential question is one which we should have to answer if there were not a Communist alive. Can we make freedom and prosperity real in the present world? If we can, Communism is no threat. If not, with or without Communism, our own civilization would ultimately fail.

The immediate and pressing challenge to our belief in freedom and prosperity is in western Europe. Here are people who have traditionally shared our faith in human dignity. These are the nations by whose citizens our land was settled and in whose tradition our civilization is rooted. They are threatened by Communism—but only because of the dark shadows cast by the hopelessness, hunger and fear that have been the aftermath of the Nazi war. Communism or no Communism, menace or no menace, it is our simple duty as neighbors to take a generous part in helping these great peoples to help themselves.

The reconstruction of western Europe is a task from which Americans can decide to stand apart only if they wish to desert every principle by which they claim to live. And, as a decision of policy, it would be the most tragic mistake in our history. We must take part in this work; we must take our full part; we must be sure that we do enough.

I must add that I believe we should act quickly. The penalty of delay in reconstruction is to increase the size of the job and to multiply difficulties. We require a prompt and large-scale program. The government must lead the way, but we who are private citizens must support that leadership as men in all parties supported help to our Allies in 1941. The sooner we act, the surer our success—and the less it will cost us.

The need of Europe is a challenge partly to our generosity and partly to our good sense. We have ample justification for action on either ground. It is an opportunity for the best that is in America, a chance for us to show the practical idealism on which we have with reason learned to pride ourselves.

This is the way to disappoint the Russians. But it is not anti-Russian. This is a course which must be followed not because we fear the Russians, but simply because we have confidence in ourselves.

As we take part in the rebuilding of Europe, we must remember that we are building world peace, not an American peace. Freedom demands tolerance, and many Americans have much to learn about the variety of forms which free societies may take. There are Europeans, just as there are Americans, who do not believe in freedom, but they are in a minority, and—as the Editor of this review so clearly explained in its last issue—we shall not be able to separate the sheep from the goats merely by asking whether they believe in our particular economic and political system. Our coöperation with the free men of Europe must be founded on the basic principles of human dignity, and not on any theory that their way to freedom must be exactly the same as ours. We cannot ask that Europe be rebuilt in the American image. If we join in the task of reconstruction with courage, confidence and goodwill, we shall learn—and teach—a lot. But we must start with a willingness to understand.

The reconstruction of western Europe is the immediate task. With it we have, of course, a job at home. We must maintain freedom and prosperity here. This is a demanding task in itself, and its success or failure will largely determine all our other efforts. If it is true that our prosperity depends on that of the world, it is true also that the whole world's economic future hangs on our success at home. We must go forward to new levels of peacetime production, and to do this we must all of us avoid the pitfalls of laziness, fear and irresponsibility. Neither real profits nor real wages can be permanently sustained—and still less increased—by anything but rising production.

But I see no reason for any man to face the American future with any other feeling than one of confident hope. However grave our problems, and however difficult their solution, I do not believe that this country is ready to acknowledge that failure is foreordained. It is our task to disprove and render laughable that utterly insulting theory. Our future does not depend on the tattered forecasts of Karl Marx. It depends on us.

VI

In counseling against policies which ignore the facts of the world as it is, I do not, of course, mean to argue that we can for a moment forget the nature of our final goal.

Lasting peace and freedom cannot be achieved until the world finds a way toward the necessary government of the whole. It is important that this should be widely understood, and efforts to spread such understanding are commendable. The riven atom, uncontrolled, can be only a growing menace to us all, and there can be no final safety short of full control throughout the world. Nor can we hope to realize the vast potential wealth of atomic energy until it is disarmed and rendered harmless. Upon us, as the people who first harnessed and made use of this force, there rests a grave and continuing responsibility for leadership in turning it toward life, not death.

But we cannot have world government or atomic control by wishing for them, and we cannot have them, in any meaningful sense, without Russia. If in response to our best effort there comes no answer but an everlasting "NO," then we must go to work in other fields to change the frame of mind that caused that answer. We cannot ignore it.

It is a part of any practical policy that it must keep our principles out in the open. In the imperfect, veto-ridden United Nations there is now incarnate the hope of people everywhere that this world may become one in spirit as it is in fact. No misconceived idea of "realism" should induce us to ignore this living hope or abate in its pursuit. We should be foremost among those who seek to make the United Nations stronger; if the Russians will not help us, let them be forced to make their opposition clear. As a starting-point, we might simply ask for a clear ruling that there shall be no veto on the right of investigation and report.

Because the United Nations can at present be hamstrung by the obstruction of a single major Power, we will probably find ourselves sometimes forced to act outside its system. So far as possible, we should avoid this course, and we should so conduct our operations as to make it wholly clear to all the world that it is not we who choose to make the United Nations weak, and that when we act outside it we are still acting in harmony with its declared objectives. It must be our constant endeavor to conduct our policy with full and deep respect for our signed and ratified adherence to this new league which we have done so much to build. Our insistence upon world coöperation must be unremitting; only so can we deserve and win the confidence of those who, caring nothing for the politics of power, now see only the overriding need for peace. Both policy and principle bind us to the support of the United Nations.

VII

It is clear, then, that in this country we are still free to maintain our freedom. We are called to an unprecedented effort of coöperation with our friends in every country. Immediately, we are called to act in the rebuilding of civilization in that part of the world which is closest to us in history, politics and economics. We are required to think of our prosperity, our policy and our first principles as indivisibly connected with the facts of life everywhere. We must put away forever the childishness of parochial hopes and un-American fears.

We need not suppose that the task we face is easy, or that all our undertakings will be quickly successful. The construction of a stable peace is a longer, more complex and greater task than the relatively simple work of war-making. But the nature of the challenge is the same. The issue before us today is at least as significant as the one which we finally faced in 1941. By a long series of mistakes and failures, dating back over a span of more than 20 years, we had in 1941 let it become too late to save ourselves by peaceful methods; in the end we had to fight. This is not true today. If we act now, with vigor and understanding, with steadiness and without fear, we can peacefully safeguard our freedom. It is only if we turn our backs, in mistaken complacence or mistrusting timidity, that war may again become inevitable.

How soon this nation will fully understand the size and nature of its present mission, I do not dare to say. But I venture to assert that in very large degree the future of mankind depends on the answer to this question. And I am confident that if the issues are clearly presented, the American people will give the right answer. Surely there is here a fair and tempting challenge to all Americans, and especially to the nation's leaders, in and out of office.

By mid-1948 the situation of the free nations was in ever worsening jeopardy. The Communist take-over in Prague in February of that year had destroyed the best hope for some kind of ideological coexistence and accommodation in the areas of Europe that had come under Soviet domination. In Asia the Chinese Communists had already made decisive advances toward their complete victory. Under Marshall Plan stimulus, Western Europe was just beginning its march toward economic recovery. Unlike the West, Russia had retained a powerful military establishment, and the need for collective efforts to resist a new wave of conquest was a matter of deep concern to many perceptive and worried observers of the ominous imbalance of power.

"Coalition for Peace" (October 1948) was an important contribution to this debate. Going beyond generalities, its author sketched in some detail the structure and purposes of a coalition of free nations, to achieve for its partners the guarantee of survival and prosperity that the United Nations could not give. Should the free nations build their strength around the emerging common will on the two shores of the North Atlantic? Or should they press for a much wider coalition? The question has been revived today by proposals to form a new organization entirely separate from the United Nations, for the free countries have not yet found a solution to the question of how they can best organize their great material and human resources to safeguard their freedom and prosperity. Mr. Armstrong's proposal of 1948 still offers a valid alternative.

Hamilton Fish Armstrong served as Managing Editor of *Foreign Affairs* in its first years and has been its Editor since 1928. After military service in World War I, he served as acting military attaché at Belgrade. In World War II he was a member of the President's Advisory Committee on Postwar Problems, was briefly attached to the U.S. Embassy in London with the rank of Minister, and served with distinction in the U.S. Delegation to the San Francisco Conference in 1945. Among his principal books are "Hitler's Reich—The First Phase" (1933), "Europe Between Wars?" (1934), "Can We Be Neutral?" (1936, with Allen W. Dulles), "We or They" (1937), and "Chronology of Failure" (1947). His "Tito and Goliath" (1951) was the first major analysis of the causes and consequences of the break between Jugoslavia and the Soviet Union.

COALITION FOR PEACE

By Hamilton Fish Armstrong

FROM the time of the Dumbarton Oaks Conference, overenthusiastic advocates of the United Nations emphasized its function as a guarantee of peace and failed to explain that if the guarantee were ever to be reliable the organization would have to develop the opposite and much less palatable function—it would have to fit itself to make war. Actually, of course, the Charter not only specifically authorized wars against aggression but pledged members to take part in them. Its authors did not expect that the long shadow in which mankind has always lived could be obliterated at one stroke, but hoped that it might be reduced. They therefore did not "outlaw" war as such, but tried to arrange that any future aggressive force which might appear would be inferior in strength to forces already assembled to deal with it. Thus a potential aggressor might be induced to stay his hand, or if he did not, might be defeated—in the one case at the risk of war, in the other by war.

The present risk of war, however, comes not so much from the possibility that the Charter must be enforced as from the lack of means to enforce it. The obligation of United Nations members to support the purposes and principles set forth in Articles 1 and 2 of the Charter still exists; but all efforts at Lake Success and Flushing Meadows to match this obligation with preparations for action have been thwarted. The work of the Security Council, which must make decisions involving enforcement, has been stalemated by the Soviet Union's abuse of the veto. So has the work of its two all-important committees. The Military Staff Committee, which was to have forearmed the Council by arranging the military contingents to be supplied to it by members, has been prevented from making any significant progress in that direction; and the Atomic Energy Commission, on which the world's eyes were fixed in desperation and hope, has suspended deliberations, having failed to find a way to regulate the production of fissionable materials which would satisfy the western requirement for airtight international controls and the Soviet requirement that controls must not violate the secrecy veiling all the operations of a police state. To intensify the risk, the members of the United Nations left in this anomalous and exposed position have not concerted any substitute measures of their own to tide over the organization's present inadequacy.

In other words, a prescription for warding off aggression and a plan of the surgical steps which would be required to remedy it have been written out on paper; but the prescription has not been filled and the instruments for an emergency operation have not been assembled. Furthermore, the friends of a possible victim have not agreed what to do if the bacilli of the old, old plague suddenly become active while the doctors are talking. All of which means that if a showdown comes under present conditions, loyal members of the United Nations will find themselves no better able to carry out their agreement to meet force with force than members of the League of Nations were able to deal with Japan's aggression in Manchuria, Mussolini's aggression in Ethiopia or Hitler's aggression in Poland.

At San Francisco one heard it said often that the United Nations could not survive defiance by one of the Great Powers; the machinery of the organization would grind to a stop and the whole fabric would crumble to pieces. Americans who helped draft a Charter which gave the veto to nations bearing the main responsibility for enforcement did not ignore this possibility; but they also knew the hazards of going too far in curtailing sovereignty, given the need of getting the measure both accepted (here Wilson's 1919 failure counted heavily) and lived up to. They may also have felt incompetent to legislate for a certain type of future emergency. As Gladstone said of a similar decision by other men who framed a Constitution without inserting in it a formula for dealing with secession, "such a question could only arise for any practical purpose at a time when the foundations of the great social deep are broken up, and when the forces brought into unrestrained play are by far too gigantic to be controlled by paper conventions." [1]

Nevertheless, when the Roosevelt Administration began studying international organization problems intensively in 1942, it assumed that the veto should apply only to decisions involving the use of force or leading directly to the use of force. This attitude was modified somewhat

[1] William E. Gladstone, August 26, 1891; quoted in John Morley's biography, v. 1, p. 707 (London: Macmillan, 1905).

at Dumbarton Oaks and again at Yalta, but not to the extent that
Generalissimo Stalin thought, or later pretended that he thought. Indeed, a major crisis arose at San Francisco over the radical change in
the Yalta formula (already a compromise) demanded by Mr. Gromyko
on June 1, 1945. Secretary Stettinius, with President Truman's approval, staked the continuance of the Conference and the whole future
of the United Nations on a demand, carried to Marshal Stalin personally, that the veto must not apply to the initial steps designated in
Chapter VI for the settlement of disputes by peaceful means. Although
that fight was won, the American delegation still were apprehensive
over the Soviet attitude, and succeeded in getting all the "Big Five"
(Soviet Russia of course included) to undertake not to use the veto
"willfully to obstruct the operation of the Council."

Since then, world relationships have steadily deteriorated. Efforts
to solve the major postwar problems by a process of negotiation and
compromise have failed. In view of this, American officials and Congressional leaders like Senator Vandenberg have modified their ideas
about the effect on national interests and national safety of some of
the most rigid shibboleths of national sovereignty. Today the United
States is on record as wishing to free the whole procedure of Chapter
VI from the veto and as seeking some practicable way to mitigate the
absolute right of veto even in connection with decisions involving force.
For example, the American delegation at Lake Success has favored a
program of forceful sanctions, free from possibility of veto, against
violators of atomic warfare controls. And in the Pan American treaties
signed recently at Rio de Janeiro and Bogotá we agreed on a series of
steps against an aggressor in this hemisphere, running from severance
of diplomatic relations to war, to be invoked by vote of two-thirds
of the signatories (a commitment modified only by the proviso that
no signatory may be called on to take the final step of providing armed
forces without its own consent).

Yet even at San Francisco there was an answer to the criticism of
the smaller nations (and of many individuals) that the Great Power
veto condemned the United Nations to futility in precisely the most
dangerous crises. For even if a Great Power did wreck the United
Nations as a formal organization by committing or protecting aggression
and then taking cover behind the veto, there would remain a group
of members who presumably would not forget their obligations simply
because the prescribed method of carrying them out had been blocked.

In looking about for an alternative method, too, they would find themselves substantially better off than members of the old League of Nations had been in the life-and-death crises at Geneva. For they would have not only a political coördinating organ, the Secretariat; they would also possess what the League did not, a military planning organ—the Military Staff Committee—and it would have assembled in advance the elements of a powerful international police force. This force would be ready for use, though minus, of course, the contingent promised by the aggressor. No one would expect it to be able to deal conclusively, by itself, with the full forces of the aggressor. But it would be prepared for the first phase of hostilities, which the new weapons have made crucial; and it would commit the nations represented to the use of their full forces as the struggle progressed.

The group thus committed would almost surely include the United States. This would be vital for all nations who remembered the American attitude in 1914 and 1939. Both times the United States had been plainly menaced, at only one remove, by the war of aggression just beginning; yet each time it had failed to throw itself into winning that war at the start, but instead had waited until its natural allies had been all but defeated.

One reason why the present situation is so dangerous is that although in theory the faithful U.N. members might form a coalition in a crisis of the sort described, they do not have the encouragement of possessing ready instruments for action and the potential aggressor does not have the discouragement of knowing that they possess them. Our sad conclusion must be that the ability of the United Nations to deal with a Great Power aggressor has diminished somewhat since the Charter was signed three years ago. For in these three years the capacities of the Security Council and its committees under existing rules have been fully explored; and what really determined aggressor would be deterred by what has been revealed?

Unless they are reconciled to the prospect of meeting aggression piecemeal, and to the penalties that such improvidence enacts, loyal U.N. members must find a legal method to make the Charter work beyond the roadblock of the veto. Needless to add, they should choose whatever adequate method is least provocative to members differently disposed. They cannot remove the roadblock. The conditions under which the veto may be used cannot be changed while the present Charter exists;

and the present Charter cannot be changed while the veto exists and the Soviets stand ready to use it.

There are two exits from this impasse. Members who are determined not to let the attitude of certain other members block them from carrying out the purposes of the United Nations can change the Charter even at the cost of changing the organization's universal character. That is, those who desire to modify the use of the veto in specific circumstances can insist on calling a general conference to revise the Charter and form a "world government," driving out in the process members who will not agree to the changes. This is a counsel of despair and should certainly be avoided.

A more constructive and less provocative course, it seems to me, would be for members who are unhappy over the deficiencies of the present U.N. procedure to undertake that they themselves will carry out the obligation to resist aggression even beyond the point when a veto prevents the Security Council from telling them that they must. Thus they will bring into being, formally and at once, the coalition of loyal members which has always existed in embryo, and which some of us at San Francisco thought of as a virtue of the United Nations that would more than outweigh the handicap of the veto through the period of the organization's growing pains. This "coalition for peace" will be open to all members; but only those who are willing to prepare seriously for collective action against aggression will join.

II

Those who wish to form the coalition for peace find all the encouragement and authority they need in Article 51 of the Charter, which states that members retain their inherent right to act in self-defense, either individually or in groups, "if an armed attack occurs against a Member of the United Nations, until the Security Council has taken the measures necessary to maintain international peace and security." The way thus stands open for them to agree, voluntarily and in advance, to act together if the foreseen circumstances should arise.[2]

They might make the commitment in one of two ways. A general

[2] Cf. the author's article in The New York Times Magazine, Sunday, September 14, 1947; later expanded in "The Calculated Risk" (New York: Macmillan, 1947).

protocol might be adopted, as suggested above, open to all United Nations members. Signatories would register their willingness to participate in joint defensive action when, say, 7 of the 11 members of the Security Council, including 4 of the 5 permanent members, vote that aggression has occurred; and they would specify some simple procedure to supplement the Security Council procedure beyond that point. Alternatively, groups of members could work toward the same result by stages, in a series of regional treaties after the example of the Inter-American Treaty of Reciprocal Assistance signed at Rio de Janeiro on September 2, 1947, and the West European security pact signed at Brussels on March 17, 1948.

Either method of supplementing the Charter machinery would be legal under Article 51 and within the spirit of the Charter as a whole. Significantly, however, Article 51 does not form part of Chapter VIII of the Charter, dealing with regional arrangements, but stands as the last article in Chapter VI, dealing with threats to the peace and acts of aggression. Its position there emphasizes its character as a sort of optional reinsurance clause for the protection of all members in case the enforcement measures set out in the preceding articles (including the preparation of military forces and of plans for using them) should fail.

The protocol would have much the same aim as the Geneva Protocol which was drawn up in 1924 to make the Covenant of the League of Nations "work." The specific problem then was to integrate steps for the compulsory settlement of disputes and plans for joint action against aggression with the League's disarmament program, which obviously could not be even discussed intelligibly until nations had reason to feel more secure. The Geneva Protocol failed of ratification; and that, as some saw then and many see in retrospect, was a turning point in the fortunes of the League (and of the world). The present problem is simpler because the Charter is more precise than was the Covenant. What is needed is for members of the United Nations to reaffirm their willingness to do in a specified case what they have said they should do in all cases, and to make ready for doing it by preparing an emergency procedure paralleling the last stages of the projected United Nations procedure.

The supplementary procedure could and should be extremely simple. The protocol would itself define the point at which it was to be considered applicable and fix the method by which its provisions would be brought into operation. The first could properly be done in the words of Article 51, quoted above, describing the emergency which would arise if the Security Council failed to act in face of armed attack on a member; the second could be done by providing that the protocol would become automatically operative when the specified Security Council majority had voted to act but had been thwarted by the veto. Or there might be agreement that when the stated conditions arise the signatories of the protocol shall at once be canvassed by one of the Great Powers, and as soon as a stipulated majority (say two-thirds) has been found ready to act, all shall be bound to act. If a more deliberate method seemed advisable, the General Assembly or the Little Assembly (if it is continued) might be given the responsibility of deciding, when the Security Council reaches the roadblock, whether or not resort should be had to the protocol, and could be authorized to declare it in effect by a two-thirds vote. This would maintain the principle of collectivity—an undeniable advantage, even though Article 51 foresees the need to abandon it for certain crises.

The protocol would of course make clear that it in no respect impairs the signatories' rights and obligations under the Charter. It should state that the governments concerned look upon the United Nations as a living organism and are confident that in time it will develop capacities of its own to enforce its principles and purposes. In any event, the Charter laid down minimum not maximum obligations of membership; nations which are willing to increase the efficacy of their undertakings on behalf of peace and security are free to do so.

There remains the mechanism of enforcement. The phrase usual in mutual assistance pacts is that each signatory shall go to the aid of a member state which is the victim of armed aggression, "with all the assistance within its power." In the present case, however, the signatories of the protocol would need to begin discussions at once regarding its implementation. They should allocate to a military staff composed of representatives of the principal military Powers concerned the same forces and facilities which they would have allocated to the Military Staff Committee of the United Nations if that body had been permitted to function.

III

Many will feel that since there now exists a West European defense organization as a result of the Brussels Pact of March 17, we shall naturally make it the basis for whatever supplementary security arrangements are called for by the deadlock in the United Nations and the growing tension with Russia. The Brussels Pact has indeed created a cohesive group with which to negotiate conveniently; it includes the two Great Powers which must form the basis for any defense scheme in Western Europe; and it must have been in the minds of the 64 Senators who by voting for the Vandenberg Resolution on June 11, 1948, empowered the Administration to favor the "progressive development of regional and other collective arrangements for individual and collective self-defense in accordance with the purposes, principles and provisions of the Charter," and our association with such of them "as are based on continuous and effective self-help and mutual aid" and affect our national security. Under authority of the Vandenberg Resolution, moreover, the United States Government is already collaborating *de facto* with the Brussels Pact group, having sent Major-General Lemnitzer and other American officers to sit as observers with the military committee which is one of its organs.

Despite these apparent advantages, we should not decide as a matter of course that the Brussels Pact is the best starting point for accomplishing the long journey which lies ahead.

The Brussels Pact covers a number of fields in which the United States and many other nations will not wish to assume responsibility. Thus Article I provides that the signatories "will so organize and coördinate their economic activities as to produce the best possible results by the elimination of conflict in their economic policies, the coördination of production and the development of commercial exchanges." Article II provides that they will make efforts "to promote the attainment of a higher standard of living by their peoples and to develop on corresponding lines the social and other related services of their countries"; also that they will "conclude as soon as possible conventions with each other in the sphere of social security." Article III provides for the promotion of cultural exchanges.

Further, the Brussels Pact omits many democratic European nations which are menaced by aggression, among them some for whose safety the United States feels particular concern. Several of these—Eire, Portugal, Austria and Finland—are not members of the United Nations because Soviet Russia vetoed their applications; another, Switzerland, did not apply for membership, more because she did not wish to court a Soviet veto than because she is unwilling to reconsider her traditional neutrality. There seems no legal reason, however, why states which are still outside the United Nations should not undertake voluntarily to live up to certain of the standards of membership. The question is whether they would be more likely to want to do this in a regional agreement based on the Brussels Pact, which contains varied economic, commercial and social obligations, or in a general underwriting of the Charter's mutual assistance obligations. My guess would be that in view of the prevailing desire not to offend Soviet Russia unduly they would choose the latter. This would certainly be true of Sweden, who joined the United Nations in November 1946 and whose real aim is to remain neutral between the Soviet Union and the west in all circumstances. Apparently she does not think that the obligations of U.N. membership jeopardize this aim; but she would be most unlikely to increase them by a pact which did not stand open to all members of the organization, the Soviet Union included. Though Norway and Denmark consider Sweden's trust in neutrality quite unrealistic, they have a strong sense of Scandinavian solidarity; if they are to be persuaded to ignore Swedish protests and enter a defensive union, it will not be one which could have hardly any other *raison d'être* than resistance to Russia.

Italy, bound by the Peace Treaty and not yet a member of the United Nations, is a special case. She must be careful not to give any excuse for the Soviets to allege that she is breaking the letter of the Treaty (as we must be careful also), remembering that the *casus belli* in the treaties between Soviet Russia and her satellites is any illegal action by a former member of the Axis. Whatever guarantee against aggression Italy receives, and whatever reciprocal obligation she assumes, must be worked out with special care for that fact. However, Moscow would be hard put to it to prove that Italy's assumption of certain United Nations responsibilities conflicted with her duty as an ex-enemy state; for the Soviet Union tried to get other ex-enemies such as Hungary and Bulgaria admitted to United Nations membership, and what would not have been a violation for them would certainly not be a violation for Italy.

Nations on the periphery of the Continent like Greece and Turkey, where we are spending great sums of money in an effort to increase their capacity for self-defense, would come into a broad arrangement more naturally than into a group centering on the Atlantic. The psychological effect of our course of action on East Europe must also be considered. Nations under Soviet domination cannot at present be expected to join; but it would be an error for us to exclude them even by implication.

In this connection Britain has a special interest which interests us as well. Some Britishers have criticized the League of Nations and the United Nations for their alleged tendency to break up the British Commonwealth. Mr. L. S. Amery, who has served both as Minister for the Colonies and Minister for Dominion Affairs, is one of those critics. As he puts it, Geneva gave Dominion statesmen a chance to utter "appropriate platitudes" without forcing them to substitute real international obligations for the Commonwealth bonds which simultaneously were being loosened.[3] Without arguing this debatable point, I might note that in any event Commonwealth solidarity might be better protected if Britain, having decided that she must enter into a special defensive pact, assumed her new obligations on a general rather than a regional basis. For a pact supplementing the Charter and open to all United Nations members might gain the adherence not only of Canada, whose External Affairs Secretary, Mr. St. Laurent, strongly supports some such course in any event, but also of other Dominions, who might feel it natural enough to reiterate their Charter obligations but would hardly be minded to give a special guarantee to specific distant states. Whatever the new arrangement, Britain should come into it with enthusiasm, bringing with her as much of the weight of the Commonwealth as possible. To facilitate this we ought to favor a general rather than a geographical engagement.

The Brussels Pact is a valuable achievement in itself, and signalizes a rapprochement among certain states which are a necessary part of a wider defense agreement. But from the American viewpoint, and in the eyes of various other states, including some that belong to it as well as some that do not, it does not provide a satisfactory basis for the additional security measures that the present world crisis seems to demand.

[3] "Thoughts on the Constitution." London: Oxford, 1947, p. 126.

IV

And what of Soviet Russia? One can imagine circumstances in which even against her will she would choose to sign a protocol against aggression rather than face a period of lasting isolation. The chances of this happening under present conditions seem next to nil. All the more reason for us to do nothing which unnecessarily affronts her. And certainly we do not want to do anything which adds unnecessarily to the present disabilities of the United Nations. By stressing "unnecessarily" I do not mean that we should appease Soviet Russia by allowing the present condition of international unpreparedness to continue, or that we should maintain the roster of United Nations members at any price. But in deciding our action we should choose the course least open to proper Soviet objection and least likely to make her quit the United Nations entirely. She might, of course, do that in any event, whether or not we take any initiative. But if she resigned from the United Nations because we tried to make the Charter itself work, she would not only be placing herself on the losing side of a great moral debate but she would be repudiating her own attitude toward similar efforts to make the Covenant of the League of Nations work on the eve of the last war—efforts which her propagandists often recall in order to glorify Soviet consistency and heap scorn on British and French weaklings.

A fair critic reads with conflicting emotions today the speeches made by Maxim Litvinov while he was Commissar for Foreign Affairs and especially in the period from Hitler's arrival in power through the British and French capitulation at Munich. We admire Litvinov's intellectual virtuosity, the liveliness of his argument and the correctness of his diagnosis of the strangulation of will which was ruining the League. But when we recall the Soviet-Nazi pact of August 23, 1939, and how Moscow ignored its own nonaggression pact with Poland when a few days later that country became the victim of Hitler's flagrant aggression, we are entitled to speculate what the Soviet action would have been if the two chief western Powers had been directed through preceding years not by Baldwin and Chamberlain, Laval and Daladier, but by strong-willed men like Winston Churchill and Charles de Gaulle. The sphinx who knows the answers to the ifs of history gives no reply. Litvinov's outraged sarcasm may have been meant to sting and shame the western nations into wars from which Russia would at the last moment hold aloof. But we certainly have no right to assume that this would have happened.

On March 17, 1936, Litvinov made one of his most impassioned addresses to the Assembly of the League of Nations on behalf of effective collective security.[4] In the preceding 18 months Germany had violated the military clauses of the Versailles Treaty and Italy had invaded Ethiopia. Now Germany was violating the Locarno Pact. The Soviet Foreign Commissar said: "One cannot fight for the collective organization of security without taking collective measures against the violation of international obligations." And he concluded: "We believe that the true adherents of peace are entitled to submit their scheme for the organization of European peace no less than those who violate treaties. We are in favor of establishing the security of all peoples of Europe as against the half-peace which is not peace, but war." Later, in Geneva on July 1, Litvinov ridiculed the League's inadequacies to deal with aggression and argued strongly against those who favored weakening it further by emasculating Article 10 of the Covenant, or throwing it out entirely, in a desperate effort to win the adherence of additional states. Of that project he said bitterly: "In other words, let us make the League safe for aggressors. I say we do not want a League that is safe for aggressors." Such a League would become a "philanthropic institution," a "debating society." The Covenant must be made "explicit and stronger." It must define aggression. Obligatory economic sanctions against aggressors must be continued. And obligatory military sanctions should be added. If that were not attainable, he said, "all continents and, for a start, at least all Europe [should] be covered with a system of regional pacts, on the strength of which groups of states would undertake to protect particular sectors from aggression; and the performance of these regional obligations should be deemed equivalent to the performance of the covenanted obligations and should enjoy the full support of all members of the League of Nations. These regional pacts should not supersede the League Covenant, but supplement it, otherwise they would be nothing but prewar groups of alliances."

At the time, Germany's repudiation of the Locarno Pact being the latest in the series of aggressive moves which had been horrifying Europe

---

[4] "Against Aggression. Speeches by Maxim Litvinov." New York: International Publisher Co., 1939.

and ruining the League's prestige, the Soviet Foreign Commissar stressed his approval of regional pacts. Today Soviet Russia would probably find less to resent in a general pact against aggression than in a pact of West European nations supported by the United States. The general pact would be open to all, herself included, and would apply to situations in all parts of the world, not just to an area where she is suspected of aggressive designs. The West European pact, though purely and only defensive, could operate against nobody but herself, the only Great Power in a position to menace the independence of that area.

If those who find the Soviet arguments of 1936 decisive today begin to put the Soviet remedies of 1936 into effect, will the Soviet Union resign from the United Nations, taking her satellite group with her? Perhaps. The Russians have shown by their insistence on the absolute veto that they no longer want (if they ever did) an effective international enforcement agency. We must weigh the risks and consequences of a new effort to make the United Nations such an agency against the risks and consequences of allowing it to continue in a position at least as unsatisfactory as that to which the League of Nations had degenerated when Litvinov spoke—only three years, significantly, before history justified his words and the Second World War began. As I have written elsewhere, the present risk of war seems to me to come chiefly from allowing the world to continue in a twilight zone where one side assumes that collective security exists and the other counts on taking advantage of the fact that it does not. The danger that Soviet Russia will deliberately choose to make war on the west does not at the moment seem so strong as the danger that the credulity and arrogance to which all dictatorships are prey will mislead her as to the limits of our tolerance and that in her ignorance she will commit an act so little different from aggression that we shall inevitably adopt countermeasures, with unpredictable results. A prudent course, then, all other considerations aside, would be to put Stalin on notice that we and others are determined and able to meet force with force.

What if, meanwhile, the Soviet Union offers guile rather than force? How, for example, should we respond if the Soviet delegates at the General Assembly in Paris this autumn try to forestall western moves to strengthen the Charter by bringing forward a disarmament scheme of their own or some version of the Litvinov nonaggression pacts? We should test their sincerity, I should think, by welcoming their initiative and asking very simple questions. Would disarmament on paper be implemented by inspection and control machinery on the spot, as proposed for atomic weapons in the Atomic Energy Commission's report? Would nonaggression pacts include provisions for more effective enforcement machinery than provided now by the United Nations, without which they would be meaningless?

V

Even broader considerations than those so far mentioned speak for a move to strengthen the United Nations as a whole rather than to underwrite a group of its members. In the first place, the commitments of the United States under the Charter are general, not regional. Secondly, we should take advantage of the fact that we have a good cause— the best cause of all, peace—and that many nations everywhere may be expected to rally to it. Thirdly, the difficulty of defining a "region" in a way which will be satisfactory under varying world conditions is very great.

In the minds of some observers regions tend to form or divide with amoebic dexterity as the desirability of including this or that nation varies with changes in the political climate. Thus one version of the so-called "Atlantic Community" which has been discussed takes in Italy on the Mediterranean but not Greece on the Mediterranean, Sweden on the Baltic but not Finland on the Baltic, Switzerland in the Alps but not Austria in the Alps, and, if I recall rightly, Australia and New Zealand in the South Pacific. This tortures the term "region" out of all meaning.

It seems to me preferable to set standards of conduct rather than standards of geography. The United States is a World Power, with world-wide interests. One of them is peace, which in the most primary terms of international organization means protection of the peaceful against aggression by the warlike. We should welcome as a partner any peace-loving state which is willing to assume and able to fulfill defense obligations on a reciprocal basis. Under the Charter we already have a responsibility for helping to protect states with such qualifications, wherever they may be situated. The only novelty would be that under the proposed underwriting agreement the obligation to execute this responsibility would come into operation when something less than all the members of the Security Council voted that it should.

The American people still have great hopes for the United Nations and want to do anything reasonable to make it a success. They might accept a plan to make the Charter fulfill its purposes even more willingly than they would agree to guarantee certain individual nations. The latter course is entirely legal under Article 51, and it would be much better for the United States to take it than to do nothing. But the general protocol would benefit the United Nations as a whole at the same time that it met the particular requirements of the situation in Europe. Even though certain nations held aloof, it still would protect the universal character of the United Nations; whereas a series of regional pacts might in time overshadow the organization's universal character and aims. The Vandenberg Resolution left the choice of methods open. It recalled the world-wide interests of the United States by reaffirming its unreserved devotion to the purposes, principles and provisions of the Charter. And in informing the President of the sense of the Senate that the United States should associate itself with groups of nations in support of the Charter, it not only referred to "regional" arrangements but "other collective arrangements" as well.

In England, recently, Mr. L. S. Amery, already mentioned, has been criticizing the United Nations as inimical to the British Commonwealth and suggesting that it be replaced by several limited special groups. Now the terms "regional organization" and "world organization" certainly are not mutually exclusive; but the thesis that they are is one which American isolationists have argued in the past. Their method was to try to defeat the conception of an international organization with the wholly inadequate conception of hemispheric defense. The recent attempt in Congress to hamstring E.R.P. by withholding agreed appropriations revealed that our isolationists are not so powerless as they supposedly were after our experience in two world wars. We may take a cue from Mr. Amery not to encourage American isolationism by favoring any basic security arrangement which aims to be less than universal.

The United States has of course long been a member of the important organization of 21 republics in the Western Hemisphere. A year ago at the Conference at Rio de Janeiro, and later at Bogotá, the American republics assumed a more specific collective obligation than ever before to oppose aggression and agreed to act by a two-thirds vote, that is, free of the possibility of veto by any one state (a significant step, despite the proviso that a signatory would not be called on to use its armed forces without its own consent). The Brussels Pact created another nucleus of comparative stability in a very uneasy world; and an underwriting now of its five member nations by the United States and Canada would add immeasurably to its importance and strength. The procedure could be extended by the formation of other special groups, with many interlocking memberships.

The ideal goal seems to me to be different from this, and no harder to attain. A general pact open to all United Nations members willing to accept its specific obligations, and entered into from the start by the most powerful members of the Brussels Pact and the Organization of American States, would achieve all that a limited security pact could achieve, and much more besides. It would be evidence that among some of the strongest members of the United Nations there was a new determination to make the Charter come alive in its full integrity. It would not merely underwrite the safety of those brave enough to risk something in order to gain more for themselves; the same act would underwrite the United Nations itself.

If as a matter of practical politics we find we can do no more, let us by all means help to form a series of special groupings for peace. And in that event let the first of these groups to receive our guarantee of help be composed of the democratic nations of Western Europe which stand today in the shadow of a new aggression. But before we conclude that this must be our maximum effort let us see whether we cannot lay the basis for a coalition for peace that is potentially as wide as the membership of the United Nations. Let us not presume that only ill is concealed in "the giant mass of things to come." Our action today can be evidence of a hope that the full goal can be achieved ultimately, and perhaps the very reiteration of that hope can itself bring the day a little nearer. Here is a challenge worthy of the men who will write the next chapter in American foreign policy.

DID Stalin mean what he said? Did he say what he meant? If the reader's answer to both questions is "No," he need not read Stalin—or Khrushchev—any more, and he will rescue a large slice of his time, so long as he is free to enjoy it, for pleasanter avocations. If, however, his answer to either question is "Yes," he will find much to reflect on in "Stalin on Revolution" (January 1949).

Of course, no one body of statements can serve the man of action as an infallible guide in day-to-day decisions. Any corpus of writings contains numerous contradictions and inconsistencies. And then there are the unruly subliminal contradictions of the human psyche, even when it is encased in a totalitarian armor. In systems where written dogma is held aloft as a standard of revolutionary action the leader, as the ultimate custodian of truth, must retain and make use of his power to select, emphasize or suppress this or that part of the body of sacred writings. Since Khrushchev made his attacks on Stalin as a very fallible leader, he has had published an entire volume containing certain of Lenin's writings that had been suppressed by Stalin's censorship. What further additions may still be made to Lenin's collected works remains unknown for the time being.

In a totalitarian system the statement of dogma ex cathedra has great importance, even though it is only one among several stimuli to action. It defines, for an "epoch of history," the goals of the ruling party and thus shapes the uses to which the available human and material resources are devoted. By setting forth an analysis endowed with a unique claim to authority, party dogma often inhibits the ability to perceive or the courage to report any facts that diverge from its rigid assumptions. It sets, so far as it can, the categories into which its adherents are trained to classify people, facts and events. By attaching the aura of "scientific" infallibility to its predictions, it helps and hopes to bring them to fulfillment. Ideology is a serious matter in a Communist system, and ideological self-discipline a strenuous exercise of mind and will.

George Allen Morgan, who wrote "Stalin on Revolution" under the pen name Historicus, is a philosopher by training, a historian by choice, and a diplomat by profession. Mr. Morgan has held many responsible posts abroad and in Washington.

214

STALIN ON REVOLUTION

By George Allen Morgan

THE stress laid by Stalin on the importance of theory is so foreign to American habits of mind that we are prone to underestimate the influence which theory plays in determining his action. Any such tendency would lead us into especially grave error when we come to estimating the importance of his theoretical conception of the nature of revolution; for on this he has been amazingly consistent.

In a preface to the first volume of his collected works, Stalin takes the trouble to point out deficiencies in certain views expressed in his youthful writings, years before the October Revolution.[1] Since then eight volumes of the collected works have appeared, but they contain no more prefaces by Stalin; the inference is that he considers the rest doctrinally correct. Stalin exhibits the same meticulous care about doctrine in a letter to members of the Politburo in which he opposes the republication of an obscure article of Engels' in *Bol'shevik* unless the errors in its conception of imperialism are pointed out. Publication of an article in "our fighting magazine," he holds, means that it is to be taken "as directive or at least deeply informative for our party workers."[2] Back of such pains about detail on the part of so busy a man lies a conviction that correctness of theory is vitally important. Stalin

Note: Where the period of republication of particular items for mass consumption is relevant to the discussion, this information is supplied in parentheses in the footnotes. Thus (1925-1939) means "originally published in 1925, republished until 1939," and (1925 to present) means "originally published in 1925, republished up to the present time."

[1] "Sochineniia," Vol. I, 1946, p. xi. The author of the present study found only one other instance in which Stalin in his mature years modified an earlier statement. "K voprosam Leninizma" (1926) quotes the original version of one paragraph in "Ob osnovakh Leninizma" (1924), relating to the victory of Socialism in one country, and points out its inadequacy; and subsequent versions of "Ob osnovakh Leninizma" contain a revised wording of the passage. ("Voprosy Leninizma," 11th ed., 1945, p. 25, 137.)

[2] *Bol'shevik*, May 1941, p. 1.

denies that "Leninism is the primacy of practice over theory." On the contrary, "the tendency of practical workers to brush theory aside contradicts the whole spirit of Leninism and is pregnant with great dangers for the cause." And again: "None other than Lenin said and repeated tens of times the well-known thesis that: *'Without revolutionary theory there can be no revolutionary movement.'* " [3]

The present study summarizes the body of ideas on revolution which has presumably played a part in Stalin's thought and action, as revealed in his published writings and statements. Except for two reports of interviews with Stalin published in the United States but apparently not in the Soviet Union, it makes use of Russian sources only. The author believes that he has discovered and examined for relevant material nearly everything by Stalin originally published between January 1, 1929, and March 28, 1948; and, in addition, he has read all of Stalin's writings likely to be of central importance as far back as February 1919. Much of the material was republished on a large scale during the periods investigated. The general character of Communist thought makes it extremely unlikely that this would have happened if the statements were considered out of date or in any way inconsistent with current ideology, and, above all, if the outmoded features were not at the same time pointed out clearly. The sacredness in which the faithful hold every word of Stalin's makes it doubly improbable that anything of his which was obsolete would be republished without proper correction. "Voprosy Leninizma" ("Problems of Leninism," the basic collection of Stalin's writings, hereafter referred to in this study as "Voprosy") has gone through 11 editions to date and has been reprinted in many millions of copies; the 1947 printing of the eleventh edition (first published in 1939) states, on the last page, that it amounts to 4,000,000 copies. Stalin's "Istoriia vsesoiuznoi kommunisticheskoi partii" ("History of the All-Union Communist Party," hereafter referred to in this study as "Istoriia"), first published in 1938, is still being reprinted; in 1946, *Pravda* stated that the total number of copies exceeded 31,000,000.[4] The fundamental rôle played by these two volumes in the indoctrination of party workers and in the compulsory courses in Marxism-Leninism justifies us in attributing high value to their testimony on matters of current orthodoxy according to Stalin.

The few instances where passages in republished works are (or at first

[3] "Ob osnovakh Leninizma" (1924 to present), "Voprosy," 11th ed., 1945, p. 14.
[4] *Pravda,* Oct. 2, 1946, p. 2.

sight appear to be) inconsistent with passages in new publications will be discussed on their merits when occasion arises. In view of the acknowledged Communist practice of pursuing long-range strategy by means of highly variable tactical lines, the presumption is by no means necessarily in favor of the new statements. The burden of proof must rather fall on whoever maintains that the new statement represents a permanent change in doctrine and not a mere temporary shift in the "line."

The cornerstones of "Voprosy" are found in two works by Stalin published in 1924, "Ob osnovakh Leninizma" and "Oktiabr'skaia revoliutsiia i taktika russkikh kommunistov." They contain the essence of his revolutionary theory, which he attributes to Lenin. This theory has been clarified or supplemented from time to time with respect to particular points. Thus it received more explicit Marxist-Leninist philosophical setting in the "Istoriia." But it has never been abandoned or altered in fundamentals.

Americans, though of course admitting the rôle of science in engineering, industry and similar fields, will be surprised by Stalin's conviction that in Leninist-Marxism he has a science of human society and its development in history which makes possible the prediction— and, within limits, the engineering—of the course of history. Thus he writes in his history of the Party: "Marxist-Leninist theory is science of the development of society, science of the workers' movement, science of proletarian revolution, science of the construction of Communist society." And again: "The strength of Marxist-Leninist theory consists in the fact that it enables the Party to orient itself in a situation, to grasp the internal connection of surrounding events, to foresee the course of events and to discern not only how and when events are developing in the present but also how and when they must develop in the future." [5]

Only such a view could explain the strong language Stalin uses on the ideological training of party cadres:

One can say with confidence that if we could prepare our cadres in all branches of work ideologically and temper them politically to such a degree that they can easily orient themselves in the domestic and international situation, if we could make them fully mature Marxist-Leninists, able to solve the problems of running the country without serious errors—then we

[5] "Istoriia" (1938 to present), p. 339; "Voprosy," 11th ed., 1945, p. 598.

would have reason to consider nine-tenths of all our problems already solved. And we are absolutely able to accomplish this task.[6]

II. THE SCIENCE OF REVOLUTION

In outlining Stalin's revolutionary theory, we shall first consider his views on those determinants of revolution which he calls "objective," *i.e.,* those historical forces which, though modified by the action of conscious human wills, determine the basic pattern of history regardless of human will.

Stalin calls the philosophical framework of his theory "dialectical and historical materialism." It is, in effect, revolution writ large into the cosmos; its basic postulates are so many reasons why "the bourgeoisie" are on the way down and "the proletariat" on the way up, why "capitalism" must inevitably give way to "Socialism" everywhere, and why this must occur by violent revolution. It is sufficient for our present purposes to state briefly those postulates which are most important for Stalin's theory of revolution.

Relativity. Nature is a "connected, single whole" in which "phenomena are organically related to each other, depend on each other and condition each other." Applied to human society, this means "that every social system and every social movement in history must be evaluated not from the point of view of 'eternal justice' . . . but from the point of view of the conditions which gave birth to that system and that social movement with which they are connected." Thus a slave-owning economy, which would be absurd for modern conditions, was once a "step forward" in comparison with the primitive communal system; and "a bourgeois-democratic republic," though it would have represented a "step forward" for Russia in 1905, would be a "step backward" for the U.S.S.R. today.

Change. Nature is constantly changing; "there is always something arising and evolving, something declining and living out its time." This means that "the dying off of what is old and the growth of something new is the law of evolution," hence that there are no " 'stable' social orders" or " 'eternal principles' of private property." It means further that "only that which is rising and developing is invincible," *i.e.,* that a rising class, though yet relatively weak, is a better bet politically than

6 "Otchetnyi doklad t. Stalina na XVIII s"ezde partii o rabote TsK VKP (b)" (1939 to present), "XVIII s"ezd. Stenograficheskii otchet," Moscow, 1939, p. 31.

one which has had its rise and, though still relatively powerful, is beginning to decline. Hence, according to Stalin, the Marxists were right in basing their policy on the proletariat even in Russia in the 1880's, because it was evolving as a class, while the peasantry, though in the enormous majority, was declining as a class.

Sudden Qualitative Change. The process of evolution is not simply one of quantitative growth; "insignificant and hidden quantitative changes" repeatedly accumulate to a point at which radical and "open" "qualitative changes" suddenly occur. For human society this means that "revolutionary overturns, produced by oppressed classes, are a perfectly natural and inevitable phenomenon." In contemporary terms, "it means that the transition from capitalism to Socialism . . . can be accomplished not by means of slow change, not by means of reform, but only by means of qualitative change of the capitalist system, by means of revolution."

Progress. The previous postulate, according to Stalin, implies that evolution is progress, *i.e.,* that nature moves not in a circle but in an upward direction, from "the simple to the complex, from the lower to the higher." [7] We state this here as a separate postulate, because on it depends the claim that revolution is not merely inevitable but right, since it leads to a "qualitative change for the better." Stalin does not go into this, preferring, as Marxists generally do, to stress the "scientific" rather than the ethical aspects of his theory. But that he has deep convictions on the matter is evident from the general tone of his writings. When in an interview with Stalin, Emil Ludwig compares him to Peter the Great, Stalin replies: "The task to which I am dedicating my life consists in elevating . . . the working class. That task is not the strengthening of any national state but the strengthening of a Socialist, and that means international, state. . . ." [8]

Contradiction and Struggle. ". . . the process of evolution from the lower to the higher takes place not as a harmonious unfolding of phenomena but as a disclosure of the contradictions inherent in things and phenomena, as a 'struggle' of opposite tendencies which operate on the basis of these contradictions . . . in order to overcome these contradictions." This means that "the class struggle of the proletariat is a per-

---

[7] This quotation and the quotations used in the preceding three paragraphs are from "Istoriia" (1938 to present), p. 101, 102, 104, 105.

[8] "I. Stalin, Beseda c nemetskim pisatelem Emilem Liudvigom," *Bol'shevik,* April 30, 1932, p. 33.

fectly natural and inevitable phenomenon," that "we must not cover up the contradictions of the capitalist system but uncover and draw them out, not extinguish the class struggle but carry it to its conclusion." Here, and in the theory of sudden qualitative change, is Stalin's philosophical ground for his position that a basic policy (as distinguished from temporary tactics) of compromise and reform is a mistake.

Materialism. Objective reality is material; consciousness is a "reflection" of matter and a product of it. From this Stalin infers that "the material life of society . . . is primary, and its spiritual life secondary, derivative," *i.e.,* that "one must look for the source of social ideas, social theories, political views and political institutions . . . in the conditions of the material life of society," of which the ideas and institutions are a "reflection."

The Means of Production. Of the various factors composing "the material life of society," the one which determines "the character of the social system and the evolution of society from one system to another" is "the means of production of material goods." This in turn consists of "productive forces"—the instruments of production and the people who operate them—and "productive relations," *i.e.,* the relations between people in the productive process, such as master-slave, capitalist-laborer. "Changes in the means of production inevitably evoke change of the whole social system," including political institutions.

The Primary Contradiction of Capitalism. The prime mover of social progress is change in the productive forces, especially tools: as new types of tools develop they enter into "contradiction" or "nonconformity" with the increasingly outmoded productive relations, until the latter are demolished and new ones created to correspond with the requirements of the productive forces. With this "sudden, qualitative" change comes a change in the whole social system. Such is the inmost dynamic of revolution. Capitalism, for example, develops large-scale industrial plants as productive forces; but "by gathering millions of workers together in enormous factories and plants, capitalism gives a social character to the process of production and thereby undermines its own basis," namely, the productive relations that center around private ownership of industry. Thus the primary contradiction that develops inside capitalism as it evolves is that between actual private ownership and the new productive forces which require social ownership for their full expansion. This maladjustment expresses itself in the periodic crises of overproduction familiar to capitalism, and finally in revolution which resolves the contradiction by socializing the means of production.[9]

The foregoing is not a complete summary of Stalin's dialectical and historical materialism, but it gives the basis of his claim to know with "scientific" certainty that Socialist revolution must come sooner or later in capitalist countries. It should be stressed that for Stalin the decisive issue is the substitution of Socialist ownership and operation for private ownership and operation of the means of production: all other differences in modern social systems are of subordinate importance. This is the basis of his insistence to H. G. Wells, in 1934, that the New Deal reforms in the United States cannot affect the ultimate necessity for revolution, and to Harold E. Stassen, in 1947, that the United States and Nazi Germany had the same kind of economic systems.[10]

The next step in our inquiry is to analyze in greater detail Stalin's conception of the social forces, apart from conscious leadership, which contribute to the build-up and final achievement of revolution. These forces are formed around four secondary contradictions, which are aggravated by the primary contradiction between productive forces and productive relations.

The Class Struggle. Antagonism between classes is not peculiar to capitalism, in Stalin's view. It is inherent in slave-owning and feudal social systems as well—in short, wherever one class monopolizes ownership of the means of production and thereby "exploits" the rest. Under capitalism the chief protagonists of class struggle are the "capitalists" and those who must sell their labor to the capitalists in order to live—the "proletariat." The rest of society—petty bourgeois, peasants, intelligentsia—form a comparatively amorphous and fluctuating mass, gravitating now to one side, now to the other.[11]

Hence the proletariat is the inevitable vehicle for the Socialist revolution. In contrast to the peasantry, it is connected with the most advanced form of economy and therefore has "more future." Further, "the proletariat as a class is growing year by year, is developing politi-

[9] The quotations in this paragraph and the preceding three paragraphs are from "Istoriia" (1938 to present), p. 103, 105, 106, 110, 114, 117.

[10] "Beseda t. Stalina s angliiskim pisatelem G. D. Uellsom" (1934-1939), *Bol'shevik,* Sept. 15, 1934, p. 8; "Zapis' besedy tov. I. V. Stalina s deiatelem respublikanskoi partii SShA Garol'dom Stassenom," *Pravda,* May 8, 1947, p. 1.

[11] "Istoriia" (1938 to present), p. 120, 15; "Ob osnovakh Leninizma" (1924 to present), "Voprosy," 11th ed., 1945, p. 54, 60, 74.

cally, is easily accessible to organization by reason of its work in large-scale production, and is most revolutionary because of its proletarian position, as it has nothing to lose by revolution except its chains." [12] In contrast to the intelligentsia, on the other hand, the proletariat has the mass necessary for revolutionary power: "for that, a large class is needed, which would replace the class of capitalists and become just as sovereign a master as it is. . . ." [13] Thus arises the central Leninist doctrine that Socialist revolution can occur only through substitution of the dictatorship of the proletariat for the dictatorship of the bourgeoisie (which, in Stalin's view, is the essence of all capitalist states). [14]

It is ultimately from the growing contradiction between social productive forces and private property productive relations that the class struggle receives the dynamism, the increasing tension, which impels it toward revolution. [15] Just how this occurs is not fully clear from Stalin's writings. The earlier Marxist doctrine of "increasing misery" of the proletariat was modified by Lenin and others in view of the observable fact that workers were not getting poorer. Stalin does not discuss this topic; but possibly, he, too, as a disciple of Lenin, does not hold the earlier view. What certainly does increase, according to Stalin, is tension between the two classes—the bourgeoisie put more and more "pressure" on the proletariat, which the proletariat meets with growing resistance and resentment. The "pressure" or "oppression" by the bourgeoisie takes various forms. One is the effort to reduce wages or hold them down, which becomes ever more powerful as capitalism enters its monopoly stage. Another is the actual misery caused by falling wages and unemployment in times of economic crisis—the recurrent crises being due to the fact that the capitalists do not allow wages to rise in proportion to production, thus curtailing purchasing power and resulting in "overproduction." Another form of pressure by the bourgeoisie is Fascism, which deprives workers of important means of resistance—labor unions, parliaments, the freedom to form labor or Communist parties. [16]

[12] *Ibid.*, p. 14.
[13] To Wells, *loc. cit.*, p. 13.
[14] "Ob osnovakh Leninizma" (1924 to present), "Voprosy," 11th ed., 1945, p. 26; "Istoriia" (1938 to present), p. 11.
[15] "Istoriia" (1938 to present), p. 117, 121.
[16] "Ob osnovakh Leninizma" (1924 to present), "Voprosy," 11th ed., 1945, p. 3, 17; "XVI s"ezd" (1930-1939), *Pravda*, June 29, 1930, p. 1; "XVII s"ezd" (1934 to present), *Pravda*, Jan. 28, 1934, p. 1; "Istoriia" (1938 to present), p. 117, 121, 288.

As will be explained later, the tension between bourgeoisie and proletariat does not increase uniformly but in a wave-like ebb and flow.
While tension mounts, the social system nears the flash-point of revolution: there is "aggravation of the revolutionary crisis inside the capitalist countries, accumulation of explosive elements on the internal,
proletarian front." [17]

The Imperialist Stage of Capitalism. Stalin, following Lenin, holds
that capitalism in its last stage, when it becomes ripe for revolution,
turns monopolist and imperialist. The scene is dominated by giant trusts
and combinations of international finance which rival each other for
control of world markets, raw materials and opportunities for investment of surplus capital. This means that there is no longer an as-
sortment of capitalist systems, one for each country, but one world
capitalist system. Revolution accordingly occurs in particular countries
as a result of the total interplay of forces within the world system and
not, as earlier Marxists expected, simply as the result of local conditions. "Formerly it was usual to speak of the presence or absence of
objective conditions for proletarian revolution . . . in one or another
well developed country. . . . Now we must speak of the presence of
objective conditions of revolution in the entire system of world imperialist economy as an integral whole; the existence within this system
of some countries that are not sufficiently developed industrially cannot
serve as an insurmountable obstacle to revolution . . . *because* the system as a whole is already ripe for revolution." [18]

From this it follows that revolution need not occur first in the countries that are most advanced industrially, as Marx's historical materialism seemed once to imply. Revolution occurs rather as a break in the
world "front" of the capitalist system, and therefore at the point where
the chain has its weakest link. So in 1917 it came first in Russia, an ad-
mittedly backward country, and in 1924 Stalin said it might occur next
in Germany or in India—in any case, again at the weakest point in the
world system. In a later comment Stalin points out that the weakest
point in the world system of capitalism is not the point where industry
is *least* developed, else revolution would have begun somewhere in
central Africa. A "certain minimum" of industrial development and
of culture is prerequisite for revolution.[19]

[17] "Ob osnovakh Leninizma" (1924 to present), "Voprosy," 11th ed., 1945,
p. 17, 55.
[18] *Ibid.*, p. 18.
[19] *Pravda*, Dec. 18, 1929, p. 3.

The direct effect of the rise of monopoly capitalism on the contradiction between bourgeoisie and proletariat has been mentioned. In addition, two further contradictions are now generated within the capitalist system.

One of these is the international counterpart of the class struggle: the great monopolies seek to exploit the foreign as well as the domestic field, which leads to a few powerful capitalist countries dividing up the world as colonial possessions and spheres of influence. Thus arises a contradiction within the capitalist world economy between the exploiting imperialists and the exploited colonies. As tension rises, a revolutionary crisis develops in the exploited countries, taking the form primarily of movements for national liberation from imperialism.[20]

The other contradiction develops between rival capitalist countries. Since some evolve more rapidly than others, they come to demand a larger share of colonies and spheres of influence than the one allotted on the basis of their former power. Since no country will voluntarily hand over part of its present share, tension mounts until imperialist war—for example, the First and Second World Wars—inevitably breaks out as the sole means of redividing the world and restoring equilibrium.[21] In Stalin's thinking, the importance of war as a midwife of revolution can scarcely be exaggerated.

The Contradiction Between Capitalists and Socialist Systems. According to Stalin, the contraditions above described created the "objective" basis for the October Revolution of 1917, but in so doing they helped to generate yet another contradiction, that between the capitalist and Socialist systems. For henceforth the system of world capitalism has lost its monopoly of the world and its claim to be the latest work in progress. Beside it grows a Socialist system which "by the very fact of its existence demonstrates the rottenness of capitalism and shakes loose its foundations."[22] This predicament, together with the loss both of economic equilibrium and of authority in colonial areas occasioned by the war of 1914, constitutes what Stalin calls the "general crisis of capitalism," a condition of permanently impaired health. The capitalist system will never recover its pre-1914 stability and self-assurance.

---

[20] "Ob osnovakh Leninizma" (1924 to present), "Voprosy," 11th ed., 1945, p. 3, 17.

[21] *Ibid.*, p. 3, 17; *Pravda*, Feb. 10, 1946, p. 1.

[22] "XVI s"ezd" (1930-1939), *Pravda*, June 29, 1930, p. 1.

Increasing tension grows from both sides of this contradiction between the social systems. It is an axiom with Stalin that capitalists are filled with envy and hatred, and that whenever they can and dare they will seek to intervene in the Socialist country and restore capitalism. This danger he dramatizes as "capitalist encirclement," declaring that Socialism cannot be considered finally achieved as long as this danger of intervention and restoration persists.[23] From the other side of the contradiction, every triumph of the Soviet Socialist system is considered by Stalin to have a profoundly revolutionizing effect on capitalist countries. In 1933 he states: "The successes of the Five Year Plan are mobilizing the revolutionary forces of the working class of all countries against capitalism. . . ."[24] In addition, there are various kinds of deliberate aid on the part of the Socialist system for revolutionary movements inside the capitalist system. These are, properly speaking, not part of the "objective" determinants of revolution.

The primary and secondary contradictions of capitalist society, which we have just described, interact upon one another to produce revolution. There are three chief types of interaction.

Productive Forces vs. Productive Relations: Economic Crises. The effects which the fundamental capitalist contradiction and economic crises have on the class struggle were briefly discussed above. The most striking feature of Stalin's treatment of the contradiction between productive forces and productive relations under capitalism is how little he has to say about it. He does not formulate it expressly until 1938, in his exposition of historical materialism. We have found only one brief earlier allusion to it, as the cause of economic crises.[25]

It would nevertheless be unsafe, as in other cases, to infer from Stalin's comparative silence on this subject that he considers it of minor importance or that he only half believes in it. On the contrary, this doctrine is an integral part of the bedrock of Marxist "scientific" certainty about the future course of history on which Stalin evidently

[23] "Ob osnovakh Leninizma" (1924 to present), "Voprosy," 11th ed., 1945, p. 25, 32; "K voprosam Leninizma" (1926 to present), *ibid.*, p. 140; "O nedostatkakh partiinoi raboty i merakh likvidatsii trotskistskikh i inykh dvurushnikov," *Pravda*, March 29, 1938, p. 2; "Otvet t-shchu IVANOVU Ivanu Filippovichu," *Pravda*, Feb. 14, 1938, p. 3; "Otchetnyi doklad" (1939 to present), "XVIII s"ezd. Sten. otchet," p. 32; "Istoriia" (1938 to present), p. 261.
[24] "Itogi pervoi piatiletki" (1933 to present), *Pravda*, Jan. 10, 1933, p. 1. The example of the Stalin Constitution is likewise expected to exert such a revolutionizing force. *Pravda*, Nov. 26, 1936, p. 3.
[25] "XVI s"ezd" (1930-1939), *Pravda*, June 29, 1930, p. 1.

bases his entire life work. It is his cardinal reason for holding that, no matter what happens, in the long run all the contradictions of capitalism will get worse and worse until revolution cures the source of trouble by substituting Socialism. Indeed, the chief function which this central contradiction of capitalism performs in Stalin's thinking may be to impart certainty to the doctrinal framework. If so, that would explain the brevity of its rôle in his published writings.

If, however, the idea also operates directly in Stalin's concrete estimates of the pattern of forces in the capitalist world system, this should find expression as some definite relationship between the increasing disparity between productive forces and productive relations—the ultimate mainspring of the trend to revolution—and resultant increases of tension in the derivative contradictions of capitalism. The sole clue of this kind discovered during the present investigation is Stalin's explanation of economic crises. Noting that they have occurred in capitalist countries every eight to twelve years for a century, he claims that they are "an example of the non-correspondence of productive relations to productive forces," in other words, of the contradiction between "the social character of production and the capitalist form of appropriating the results of production." As capitalism evolves, productive forces (*i.e.,* productive capacity) are dynamically expanded but wages are kept as low as possible in order to make more profits. The result is a "relative curtailment of purchasing power"; goods accumulate for which there is no market and a crisis of overproduction is precipitated; finished goods and even productive forces are destroyed, factories are closed and millions suffer unemployment and hunger not because goods are scarce but because they are plentiful. Stalin stresses the destruction of productive forces as conspicuous evidence of the way in which their development is hampered by capitalist productive relations. His account in 1930 concludes: "If capitalism could adapt production not to getting maximum profit but to the systematic improvement of the material conditions of the masses of the people . . . then there would not be any crises. But then also capitalism would not be capitalism." [26]

The rôle of economic crises in Stalin's writings must be stated carefully. He pays almost no attention to them until after 1929 and, as his writings show, probably did not expect the world depression. The em-

[26] *Ibid.,* p. 1; "Istoriia" (1938 to present), p. 117, 121; to Wells (1934-1939), *Bol'shevik,* Sept. 15, 1934, p. 9.

phasis given to economic crises after 1929—notably in the reports to the Party Congress in 1930, 1934 and 1939—suggests that the lesson of 1929 actually produced an important change in Stalin's thinking about the capitalist world. However, that change appears to have been a modification not in fundamental theory but on an intermediate level between it and concrete data. The doctrine of the contradictions of capitalism remains the basic framework. Within it, after 1929, economic crises play a very prominent rôle as *symptoms* of the progressive decay of capitalism at its roots—namely, of the increasing contradiction between productive forces and relations—and as added *causes* of greater tension in the four secondary contradictions. In 1930 Stalin sums up his first analysis of the world economic crisis by saying: "The most important results of the world economic crisis are to uncover and aggravate the contradictions inherent in world capitalism." [27]

The fact that Stalin depicts the crisis of 1929 as the worst so far in capitalist history, and that of 1937 as worse still,[28] together with his general picture of capitalism as now in its decadent phase, suggests that such crises do in fact play an important diagnostic rôle in Stalin's estimates of the degree of deterioration reached at a given time by the capitalist system, and also that he would expect each future crisis— at the customary interval of eight to twelve years—to be worse than the last. The principle indices used in his discussions of particular crises are statistics of production and of unemployment. These are further possible clues to his method of diagnosis.[29]

The "Objective" Conditions for Revolution: War. We have seen that, for Stalin, capitalism in its imperialist stage has become a single world system in which the total interplay of forces determines the ripeness of conditions for revolution in particular countries, revolutions actually occurring where the world front of capitalism is weakest in relation to

[27] "XVI s"ezd" (1930-1939), *Pravda*, June 29, 1930, p. 1. See also "XVII s"ezd" (1934 to present), *Pravda*, Jan. 28, 1934, p. 1; "Otchetnyi doklad" (1939 to present), "XVIII s"ezd. Sten. otchet," p. 11.
[28] "XVI s"ezd" (1930-1939), *Pravda*, June 29, 1930, p. 1; "Otchetnyi doklad" (1939 to present), "XVIII s"ezd. Sten. otchet," p. 9.
[29] Stalin mentions, but does not give statistics on, bankruptcies, ruin of peasants, falling prices, maintenance of monopoly prices at the expense of restricting production, bank failures, trade wars, dumping, currency wars. In 1939 he gives statistics on gold reserves as evidence that the avoidance of economic crisis in Fascist countries is only temporary. See "XVI s"ezd" (1930-1939), *Pravda*, June 29, 1930, p. 1; "XVII s"ezd" (1934 to present), *Pravda*, Jan. 28, 1934, p. 1; "Otchetnyi doklad" (1939 to present), "XVIII s"ezd. Sten. otchet," p. 10.

the forces of revolution. The foregoing discussion of capitalist contradictions has provided a ground-plan of the lines along which the revolutionary forces are organized. The next step is to consider the criteria for judging the ripeness of the revolutionary situation. Stalin writes that "the proletarian revolution must be regarded primarily as the result of the development of the contradictions within the world system of imperialism, as the result of the snapping of the chain of the imperialist world front in one country or another." [30] How does Stalin estimate when and where the chain is ready to break?

Pointing out that there are "several absolutely necessary conditions, in the absence of which seizure of power by the proletariat is not to be thought of," Stalin quotes Lenin's formulation of them:

The fundamental law of revolution . . . consists in this: for revolution it is not enough that the exploited and oppressed masses should feel the impossibility of living in the old way and demand change; for revolution it is necessary that the exploiters should not be able to live and rule in the old way. Only when the *"lower classes" do not want* the old way and when the "upper classes" *cannot carry on in the old way*—only then can revolution conquer. This truth may be expressed otherwise in the words: *revolution is impossible without a nation-wide crisis (affecting both the exploited and the exploiters).*[31]

"Revolutionary crisis" is accordingly Stalin's usual name for the total complex of forces constituting the "objective" conditions necessary for revolution.[32]

Two features stand out in the above quotation: the power of the bourgeoisie is shaken; the proletariat is aroused. More detail is supplied by a sketch written in 1921 but first published in 1947:

[30] "Ob osnovakh Leninizma" (1924 to present), "Voprosy," 11th ed., 1945, p. 19.

[31] *Ibid.,* p. 25.

[32] Stalin uses the term "crisis" in so many ways that we must not jump to conclusions from a particular statement. Besides "revolutionary crisis" he speaks of "economic crises," "general crisis of capitalism," "crisis of world capitalism," etc. So "crisis" does not necessarily mean "revolutionary crisis." Moreover, "revolutionary crisis" does not necessarily mean revolution, for leadership may fail to take advantage of the situation. Again, "revolutionary crisis" sometimes means the full ripeness of the objective conditions for revolution, sometimes the long period of rising tensions which in some cases culminates in ripeness, for which Stalin sometimes employs a special term, "the immediate revolutionary situation." On the latter see *Pravda,* Feb. 10, 1930, p. 2.

How define the arrival of the moment for revolutionary outbreaks? . . .
When the revolutionary mood of the masses . . . brims over and our slogans for action and directives lag behind the movement of the masses . . .
When uncertainty and confusion, disintegration and dissolution in the adversary's camp have reached the highest point . . . when the so-called
neutral elements, all that mass of many millions of city and village petty
bourgeoisie, begin definitely to turn away from the adversary . . . and
seeks alliance with the proletariat.[33]

This introduces a third feature of the "objective" conditions for
revolution: the masses (other than the proletariat) swing away from
the bourgeoisie and toward the proletariat, thus isolating the former
and becoming allies or "reserves," as Stalin's military phraseology often
puts it, of the proletariat. The above quotation mentions petty bourgeoisie, but in other passages Stalin stresses even more the rôle of the
peasantry as ally of the proletariat.[34] In the present context only the
general point is important: the bourgeoisie proper must be bereft of
mass popular support and the proletariat must have it.

Support is not confined to the boundaries of one country: the local
bourgeoisie must to a considerable degree be isolated internationally,
while the proletariat receives direct or indirect support from the proletariat of other capitalist countries and from the proletarian state already in existence—the U.S.S.R. Hence a further condition for successful revolution is that the balance of potential outside aid for revolution as against potential outside aid for counterrevolution must be
sufficiently favorable.[35]

To sum up, Stalin's necessary "objective" conditions for revolution
are: bourgeoisie isolated and disorganized, proletariat aroused to revolt
and supported by the masses, and a favorable balance of proletarian as
against bourgeois aid from outside the country. With these as a frame

[33] "Sochineniia," Vol. V, p. 73.
[34] "Ob osnovakh Leninizma" (1924 to present), "Voprosy," 11th ed., 1945, p.
23, 56, 60; "Istoriia" (1938 to present), p. 65.
[35] Stalin does not formulate this condition definitely, but it is a clear implication of: 1, his thesis that capitalism is now a world system and revolution the
product of forces throughout the system; 2, his emphasis on the international
ties of the bourgeoisie and the constant threat of intervention from that quarter
(e.g. "Ob osnovakh Leninizma," "Voprosy," 11th ed., 1945, p. 26); 3, his statement that the proletariats of capitalist states, and the state in which Socialism
has already won, will assist the proletariats in other countries to achieve revolution. See "Oktiabr'skaia revoliutsiia i taktika russkikh kommunistov" (1924 to
present), ibid., p. 104. The topic of outside aid for revolution includes conscious leadership and will be dealt with later in this study.

of reference, we are now able to indicate how, according to Stalin, the contradictions of capitalism interact to produce revolutionary crises. Only certain main lines of influence will be described; details vary endlessly with the concrete configuration of forces.

The primary contradiction, both chronically and in its acute manifestation as economic crisis, impels the bourgeoisie to increase pressure against the proletariat, against colonial peoples, against each other (in rivalry for spheres of influence) and against the Soviet Union. The culmination of these trends is war of one kind or another: the colonies fight for liberation, the capitalist nations who demand greater spheres of influence fight to get them or capitalist countries attack the Soviet Union as the major threat to their whole system and also as another big area to be exploited. Preparation for war on the part of the bourgeoisie further arouses the proletariat and the other masses who desire peace and resent having to die for their masters, and who also resent the added economic and political pressures—including Fascism, in some cases—which are imposed in order to prepare for war. When the war is to be directed against the Socialist Fatherland, this fact of course greatly adds to the resentment of the proletariat, whose deeper sympathies are on the side of the Soviet Union. Bourgeois preparation for war likewise leads to increased pressure on colonies, with a correspondingly greater tendency of colonies to rebel.[36]

Actual war, however, is the crux of the matter. Stalin writes of the relation of the First World War to the contradictions of capitalism that "the imperialist war . . . gathered all these contradictions into one bundle and threw them onto the scales, thereby accelerating and facilitating the revolutionary battles of the proletariat." [37] War between capitalist countries further intensifies the resentment of the masses and at the same time both exhausts the strength of the bourgeoisie at home and makes it difficult for them to intervene against revolution abroad. Again writing in 1924 of the First World War, Stalin speaks of "the enormous significance of the fact of mortal war between the chief groups of imperialists in the period of the October Revolution, when the imperialists, occupied with war among themselves, lacked the ability to

[36] "Politicheskii otchet TsK" (1927), "XV s"ezd. Sten. otchet," p. 44; "Ob itogakh iiul'skogo plenum TsK VKP (b)" (1928), "Voprosy," 9th ed., 1932, p. 336; "XVI s"ezd" (1930-1939), Pravda, June 29, 1930, p. 1; "XVII s"ezd" (1934 to present), Pravda, Jan. 28, 1934, p. 1.

[37] "Ob osnovakh Leninizma" (1924 to present), "Voprosy," 11th ed., 1945, p. 4.

concentrate forces against the young Soviet power, and the proletariat just for that reason was able to get down to the work of . . . consolidating its power. . . . It must be presumed that now, when the contradictions among the imperialist groups are becoming more and more profound, and when a new war among them is becoming inevitable, reserves of this description will assume even greater importance for the proletariat." [38]

Thus for the past quarter century, according to the overwhelming testimony of his writings, Stalin has expected the next crop of revolutions to come during, or in the immediate aftermath of, the Second World War. To the Seventeenth Party Congress in 1934 he stated that a new imperialist war "will surely turn loose revolution and place in jeopardy the very existence of capitalism in a number of countries, as happened in the course of the first imperialist war." [39] His history of the Party makes explicit the connection between war and the development of a "weak link" in the chain of world imperialism: "Lenin showed that precisely in consequence of this unevenness in the development of capitalism imperialist wars occur, which weaken the forces of imperialism and make possible a break-through in the front of imperialism at the point where it proves to be weakest." [40]

Imperialism, he maintains, is the fundamental antagonist of the Soviet Union, and Fascism only its worst reactionary form. "Hitler, Goebbels, Ribbentrop, Himmler and the other administrators of present-day Germany are the chained dogs of the German bankers." [41] The capitalist, not the Nazi, is the ultimate enemy. The theoretical framework is made fully explicit in Stalin's election speech of February 1946: "It would be incorrect to think that the Second World War arose accidentally or as a result of the mistakes of some statesmen or other. . . . The war in fact arose as the inevitable result of the development of world economic and political forces on the basis of contemporary monopolistic capitalism." [42]

---

[38] *Ibid.*, p. 56. Stalin here used the term "reserves" to include all favorable factors, not merely men.

[39] "XVII s"ezd" (1934 to present), *Pravda*, Jan. 28, 1934, p. 1. The inevitability of war is the central theme of the foreign affairs section of each of Stalin's reports to the Party Congresses from 1925 to the last one in 1939; the direct connection with revolution is obvious in each case, and made explicit in most.

[40] "Istoriia" (1938 to present), p. 162.

[41] *Pravda*, May 1, 1942.

[42] *Pravda*, Feb. 10, 1946, p. 1.

The case of a war against the Soviet Union, according to Stalin, presents an additional factor favorable to revolution. To the Seventeenth Party Congress in 1934 he declares: "It can hardly be doubted that this war will be the most dangerous for the bourgeoisie. . . . The numerous friends in Europe and Asia of the working class of the U.S.S.R. will endeavor to strike from the rear their oppressors who have started criminal war against the Fatherland of the working class of all countries." [43] Though Stalin hopes for proletarian revolutions in certain colonial areas, he values all local movements for national liberation, whether proletarian or not: in any case, each step they take toward emancipation is "a steam-hammer blow against imperialism" and thus has "objective" revolutionary significance, *i.e.,* weakens the bourgeoisie of imperialist countries by depriving them of markets and raw materials. [44] Hence a colonial war would become an added factor promoting a revolutionary crisis in the metropolitan country.

The Law of Ebb and Flow. According to Stalin, the October Revolution of 1917 ushered in "a new era in the history of humanity—the era of proletarian revolutions," in fact, "the epoch of world revolution." [45] This means, in terms of his theory, that the contradictions in the world system of capitalism have evolved to the point where revolutions are generally in order. Actual revolution, however, occurred first in only one country, and Stalin expects further revolutions usually to occur in one country at a time, as state after state breaks away from the capitalist system and joins the Socialist one. [46]

But the course of the revolutionary movement is not expected to be uniform. Stalin notes that it has always moved in a wavelike rhythm of ebb and flow, rise and fall. For example, one wave reached its crest in the 1905 Revolution and subsided in the Stolypin reaction. Another rise occurred in the years 1912-1914. Under the stress of the First World War a major crest came with the two revolutions of 1917— though in the short interval between them there were also rapid changes

[43] "XVII s"ezd" (1934 to present), *Pravda,* Jan. 28, 1934, p. 1.
[44] "Ob osnovakh Leninizma" (1924 to present), "Voprosy," 11th ed., 1945, p. 48, 3, 17, 54; "XIV s"ezd. Sten. otchet," p. 12; "XV s"ezd. Sten. otchet," p. 44; "Sochineniia," Vol. IV, p. 166, 238, 378.
[45] "Istoriia" (1938 to present), p. 214, 338; "Ob osnovakh Leninizma" (1924 to present), "Voprosy," 11th ed., 1945, p. 54.
[46] "Oktiabr'skaia revoliutsiia i taktika russkikh kommunistov" (1924 to present), "Voprosy," 11th ed., 1945, p. 102.

of ebb and flow—and the wave spread out to Europe in the years immediately following. In 1925 Stalin announces that another decline has set in, corresponding to a "partial and temporary stabilization of capitalism," but he now generalizes the alternation of ebb and flow in a prediction of the future: "The epoch of world revolution . . . is a whole strategic period, embracing a whole series of years and, I dare say, even a number of decades. In the course of this period there can and must be ebbings and flowings."

Though an ebb tide has set in, Stalin goes on to say, the contradictions of capitalism will inevitably bring on a new flood tide in due time. With the flood tide new victories may be won for the revolution; if they do not complete world revolution, there will follow another ebb, and so on until revolution has spanned the globe.[47] In 1927 Stalin announces that the "stabilization of capitalism" is drawing to a close, a new "crisis of world capitalism" is gathering, and with it is beginning another revolutionary rise. In 1930 and 1934, successive reports to Party Congresses continue the same line of thought: the contradictions of capitalism, accentuated by the world economic crisis of 1929, are converging inevitably on another imperialist war. Therefore "a revolutionary crisis is ripening and will continue to ripen." [48] In his report to the Party Congress in 1939 he announces that the imperialist war has already begun and is gradually becoming a world war.[49]

Up to March 1948, Stalin has published nothing to indicate that the revolutionary wave—so long expected in connection with World War II—has passed its crest, though his doctrine of ebb and flow suggests that he must expect another ebb within a few years unless capitalism collapses completely in the meantime. Thus the entire period from 1929 to March 1948 moves before Stalin's eyes on a rising tide of revolutionary opportunities.

[47] "K itogam rabot XIV konferentsii RKP(b)" (1925-1934), "Voprosy," 9th ed., 1932, p. 109, 111; "Ob osnovakh Leninizma" (1924 to present), "Voprosy," 11th ed., 1945, p. 55; "Beseda s inostrannymi rabochimi delegatsiiami," "Voprosy," 9th ed., 1932, p. 301; "XV s"ezd. Sten. otchet," p. 44; "Istoriia" (1938 to present), p. 27, 80, 84, 127, 138, 140, 221, 258.
[48] "XVII s"ezd" (1934 to present), *Pravda,* Jan. 28, 1934, p. 1; "Politicheskii otchet TsK" (1927), "XV s"ezd. Sten. otchet," p. 38, 44; "XVI s"ezd" (1930-1939), *Pravda,* June 29, 1930, p. 1.
[49] "Otchetnyi doklad" (1939 to present), "XVIII s"ezd," p. 11.

III. THE ART OF REVOLUTION

Having outlined Stalin's conception of the "objective" determinants of revolution, our inquiry now turns to the "subjective" side: the rôle of conscious organization.

Communist Leadership. Notwithstanding the remorseless and unavoidable evolution of the contradictions of capitalism, making Socialist revolution sooner or later inevitable, Stalin holds that actual revolution can occur only through conscious human efforts. In this he is a disciple of Lenin, and his history of the Party records with sympathy Lenin's battles against "reformist" Marxists, compromisers, opportunists, gradualists—any and all who held that the "objective" factors would automatically bring about the change to Socialism, or that anything short of the most resolute and uncompromising revolutionary policy should be adopted.[50]

Stalin's ultimate reason for this position lies in his dialectical and historical materialism. As has been noted, one postulate of this theory is that objective reality is material, and consciousness only a "reflection" of it. This view now requires further elaboration. Stalin does not mean that consciousness plays no causal rôle, but only that its rôle is secondary. The direction of history, its movement from one mode of production to another, with consequent changes in class structure, social institution and ideas, is indeed determined by the evolution of the means of production, and no conscious human effort can change this direction. But consciousness does have a positive and important function: it affects, not the pattern of history, but its pace. It can accelerate or retard the coming of the inevitable. Social theories which accelerate historical evolution do so because they "reflect the needs of the development of the material life of society" and by mobilizing the masses lead them in the direction of revolutionary change. Social theories arise "because they are necessary for society, because without their organizing, mobilizing and transforming work the solution of the problems which have come to a head in the evolution of society is *impossible.*"

This is Stalin's ground for holding that conscious leadership is necessary for revolution. The primary contradiction in capitalism gets worse and worse, and increasing strain works out from it through the

[50] For references in this and the following two paragraphs, see "Istoriia" (1938 to present), especially p. 11, 36, 105, 337, 343, 110, 111, 16, 45, 339.

secondary contradictions, causing suffering, war and destruction: but conscious effort, following correct theory, is necessary to help these blind forces produce the readjustment which alone can bring relief. Hence arises the necessity for the Communist Party. Stalin writes that "Socialist ideology arises not from the spontaneous [working class] movement but from science." The Party is that vanguard of the working class which, because it is guided by "scientific" insight into the ills of capitalism and the sole means of cure, can and must organize the proletariat and lead it to revolutionary victory: "The Marxist Party is a part of the working class. . . . The Party differs from other detachments of the working class primarily in that it is . . . the *leading* detachment, the *class-conscious* detachment . . . armed with knowledge of social life, knowledge of the laws of the class struggle, and for this reason able to lead the working class and to direct its struggle."

Stalin's conception of Marxist theory is likewise his justification for the character and organization of the Bolshevik Party as opposed to Marxist parties of the western type. Because the Party is the embodiment of "scientific" truth, and because that truth is uncompromisingly revolutionary—teaching that class war must be fought to a finish—the Party must be "monolithic," a centrally controlled army under strict military discipline, tolerating no other parties except for temporary reasons of expediency, hunting down and destroying compromisers— all who are disposed to take the edge off the revolutionary drive, to let things move more gradually—both in society at large and within its own ranks. The same claim to infallible "science" lies at the base of Stalin's theory of the Party purge, so strange to western modes of thought: "The Party strengthens itself by purging itself of opportunist elements. . . ." A procedure that to western minds is a sign and a further cause of weakness is for Stalin a means to strength because strength derives ultimately, not from numbers, but from "knowledge" which harnesses revolution to the laws of history: the purge eliminates those whose allegiance to this "knowledge," and the program based on it, is dubious.[51]

From Stalin's point of view "democratic liberties" have always been compatible with strict Communist Party control. In his report on the Draft Constitution, he claims that the Soviet system is more democratic than any other. And in reply to foreign critics who object that the

---

[51] "Istoriia" (1938 to present), p. 40, 45, 135, 337, 343; see also "Ob osnovakh Leninizma" (1924 to present), "Voprosy," 11th ed., 1945, p. 64-75.

one-party system is undemocratic, he praises the constitution because it leaves in force the dictatorship of the working class and "the present directing position of the Communist Party." [52] Further, Stalin is on record as holding that proletarian revolution may legitimately be carried out when the proletariat is only a minority of the population—the Party, of course, being only a minority of the proletariat.

Stalin expresses the contrast between Bolshevism and western Socialism most vividly in his 1934 interview with H. G. Wells, already mentioned. Wells approaches Stalin from the point of view of a western Socialist; he states that conceptions of violent class war are obsolete; leading businessmen are not ruled wholly (or even primarily in many cases) by the profit motive and there is therefore no radical conflict of interest between capital and labor; modern technology makes Socialism inevitable through gradual extension of government controls; hence the need is for intelligent direction, not violent revolution; eastern and western Socialists should develop a common language and work together rather than emphasize their historic antagonisms. Stalin replies with denial on all points and puts the crux of the matter as he sees it thus: ". . . the replacement of one social system by another social system is a complicated and protracted revolutionary process. It is not a merely spontaneous process. . . . No—revolution . . . has always been struggle, an excruciating and cruel struggle, struggle for life and death."

Communists, he continues, do not idealize force and violence: they would gladly dispense with them if the bourgeoisie would consent to turn things over peaceably to the proletariat. But abundant historical experience teaches (as he said to Wells) that "classes which have had their day do not leave the stage of history voluntarily." His history of the Party picks up this theme in describing (p. 125) how the revolutionary period comes after social forces have evolved spontaneously to a certain point:

After the new productive forces have matured, the existing productive relations and their bearers, the ruling classes, turn into that "insurmountable" obstacle which can be removed only by means of the conscious action of the new classes, by the forcible acts of these classes, by revolution. . . . The masses are welded into a new political army, create a new revolutionary authority and use it to abolish by force the old system of productive relations and establish the new system. The spontaneous process

[52] "O proekte konstitusii Soiuza S.S.R." (1936 to present), *Pravda,* Nov. 26, 1926, p. 3.

of development gives place to the conscious action of men, peaceful development to violent upheaval, evolution to revolution.

The "combat staff" of the new political army is the Communist Party.[53] Effective Communist Party action is Stalin's "subjective" condition for revolution which, when timed with the "objective" conditions previously described, actually brings revolution to pass. As he puts it to the Seventeenth Party Congress: "Some comrades think that as soon as there is a revolutionary crisis the bourgeoisie must be in a situation from which there is no way out. . . . that the victory of revolution is thus secure. . . . This is a profound mistake. The victory of the revolution never comes of itself. It must be prepared for and won. And only a strong proletarian revolutionary party can prepare for and win it. Moments occur when the situation is revolutionary, the power of the bourgeoisie is shaken to its very foundations, and yet the victory of the revolution does not come, because there is no revolutionary party of the proletariat sufficiently strong and authoritative to lead the masses and take power in its own hands." [54]

World Strategy: The Soviet Union as Base. Before we proceed to examine Stalin's views on how revolution is "prepared for and won" by the Communist Party, a word of caution is in order. As generals are not accustomed to publish their operational directives, so it is unreasonable to expect Stalin to publish his. From his writings it is possible to reconstruct certain main lines of strategy and tactics, but the writings also contain definite acknowledgment that "illegal" or underground activities play a major rôle in Communist operations. Speaking of the revolutionary uses of compromise and reform, he states: ". . . in revolutionary tactics under a bourgeois régime, reform naturally becomes an instrument for disintegrating this régime, an instrument for strengthening revolution. . . . The revolutionary accepts reform in order to use it as a means of meshing the legal work with the illegal work, in order to use it as a cover for the strengthening of the illegal work which aims at revolutionary preparation of the masses for the overthrow of the bourgeoisie." [55] Therefore it must remain a question to what ex-

[53] "Ob osnovakh Leninizma" (1924 to present), "Voprosy," 11th ed., 1945, p. 66.
[54] "XVII s"ezd" (1934 to present), *Pravda,* Jan. 28, 1934, p. 1; see also "Beseda s pervoi amerikanskoi rabochei delegatsiei" (1927-1939), "Voprosy," 9th ed., 1932, p. 266; "Istoriia" (1938 to present), p. 337.
[55] "Ob osnovakh Leninizma" (1924 to present), "Voprosy," 11th ed., 1945, p. 63. See also "Istoriia" (1938 to present), p. 127, 133, 136, 151.

tent Stalin's published views on Communist strategy and tactics are supplemented or modified by doctrine reserved for the Communist high command.

In any case, Stalin's approach is characteristically military, and it is hardly by accident that his writings are strewn with military figures of speech—tactics and strategy; staff, cadres, vanguards, reserves; strong points, forward positions; advances, assaults, retreats, manœuvres; encirclement, flanking movement, regrouping of forces, etc.[56] An early sketch not published until 1947 shows most succinctly the connection between theory and strategy: "The *theory* of Marxism, studying primarily the objective processes . . . defines the tendency of evolution, points out the class or classes which are inevitably rising to power or which are inevitably falling, must fall. . . . The *program* of Marxism, basing itself on the conclusions of the theory, defines the goal for the movement of the rising class, in this case of the proletariat. . . . *Strategy,* guiding itself by the directives of the program and resting on a calculation of the contending forces, internal . . . and international, defines that . . . general direction along which the revolutionary movement of the proletariat should be directed with a view to achieving the biggest results with the . . . developing correlation of forces. . . ." [57]

The program thus defines the objectives at which strategy aims. Stalin distinguishes the "maximum program"—"Socialist revolution, overthrow of the capitalists' rule, establishment of the dictatorship of the proletariat"—from the "minimum program" formulated for a particular phase of the total process.[58] Stalin writes in "Voprosy" that "Strategy has to do with the main forces of revolution and their reserves. It changes with the passage of revolution from one stage to another, remaining essentially without change for the whole period of a given stage." The first stage was 1903 to February 1917, the second March to October 1917. The third stage began after the October Revolution: "*The goal is to consolidate the dictatorship of the proletariat in one country, using it as a base for the overthrow of im-*

---

[56] Stalin remarks that he and other younger members of the Central Committee were required by Lenin to study the fundamentals of warfare. ("Otvet tov. Stalina na pis'mo Razina," *Bol'shevik,* Feb. 1947, p. 6.)

[57] "Sochineniia," Vol. V, p. 62; see also p. 162.

[58] "Istoriia" (1938 to present), p. 40, 38; "Sochineniia," Vol. V (1947), p. 63, 162.

perialism in all countries. Revolution spreads beyond the limits of one country; the epoch of world revolution has begun." [59]

The fundamental, not merely incidental, intention to use the Soviet Union as the base for world revolution has thus been on the record in Stalin's most important doctrinal work, repeatedly republished for mass circulation from 1924 to the present time. In another passage which has had similar authoritative distribution from 1924 to the present Stalin elaborates his view:

. . . the very development of world revolution . . . will be more rapid and more thorough, the more thoroughly Socialism fortifies itself in the first victorious country, the faster this country is transformed into a base for the further unfolding of world revolution, into a lever for the further disintegration of imperialism.

While it is true that the *final* victory of Socialism in the first country to emancipate itself is impossible without the combined efforts of the proletarians of several countries, it is equally true that the development of world revolution will be the more rapid and thorough, the more effective the aid rendered by the first Socialist country to the workers . . . of all other countries.

In what should this aid be expressed?

It should be expressed, first, in the victorious country "carrying out the maximum realizable in one country *for* the development, support, awakening of revolution in all countries" . . .

It should be expressed, second, in that the "victorious proletariat" of the one country . . . "after organizing its own Socialist production, should stand up . . . *against* the remaining, capitalist world, attracting to itself the oppressed classes of other countries, raising revolts in those countries against the capitalists, in the event of necessity coming out even with armed force against the exploiting classes and their governments" . . .[60]

This passage deserves detailed comment. The supreme aim of world revolution is the logical outcome of Stalin's entire theoretical position

[59] "Ob osnovakh Leninizma" (1924 to present), "Voprosy," 11th ed., 1945, p. 54 (italics added); see also "Sochineniia," Vol. V, p. 173-180; "K itogam rabot XIV konferentsii RKP(b)" (1925-1934), "Voprosy," 9th ed., 1932, p. 110.

[60] "Oktiabr'skaia revoliutsiia i taktika russkikh kommunistov" (1924 to present), "Voprosy," 11th ed., 1945, p. 104. The latter part of this passage, including the reference to using armed force, is a quotation from Lenin which Stalin employs also in "K voprosam Leninizma" (1926 to present), *ibid.,* p. 142, and in "K itogam rabot XIV konferentsii RKP(b)" (1925-1934), "Voprosy," 9th ed., 1932, p. 122. This repetition in widely circulated works is added evidence that Stalin means every word.

as outlined in the present study—notably the thesis that capitalism is a single *world-system* fatally torn by contradictions which can be cured only by a consciously directed Socialist revolution. Granted these assumptions, the determination to use the foothold won in the Soviet Union as a base for world revolution is elementary common sense. This outlook is confirmed by many other passages in widely published statements by Stalin.[61] The sole contradictory passages—unless cunningly interpreted—are remarks made by Stalin to two foreigners, under circumstances where it is obviously to his advantage to convey another impression. For example, he tells Roy Howard in 1936 that the Soviet Union has never had plans for fostering revolution in other countries because exporting revolution is nonsense.[62] The other statement, made to Mr. King, of Reuters, in May 1943, will be described in a moment. These two statements are not republished in "Voprosy" or otherwise for wide and lasting distribution in the Soviet Union. When they are weighed against the mass of contrary evidence on Stalin's views presented above, the only conclusion is that they are misleading.

In 1938 the Party history appears with the revolutionary motto on its title page: "Workers of all countries, unite!" And the introduction declares: "Studying the history of the CPSU(b) strengthens confidence in the final victory of the great cause of the party of Lenin and Stalin, the victory of Communism in the whole world." The history also repeats the fundamental quotation from Lenin on the country of Socialism "rising against" the capitalist world after organizing its own production; states that "the victory of proletarian revolutions in capitalist countries is a vital interest of the toilers of the U.S.S.R."; and quotes Stalin's "great vow" of "fidelity to the principles of the Communist International." All these points, it should be remembered, are made in a work used for mass indoctrination down to the present time.

In 1936, Howard asks Stalin if he has not to some extent abandoned his plans for world revolution. Stalin replies, "We never had such plans

<hr/>

[61] See the statement to Ludwig above, and the vow of fidelity to the principles of the Comintern quoted below; also "Mezhdunarodnyi kharakter oktiabr'skoi revoliutsii" (1927, 1934 to present), "Voprosy" 11th ed., 1945, p. 179; "Sochineniia," Vol. IV, p. 166, 238 and Vol. V, p. 85, 169, 179; "K itogam rabot XIV konferentsii RKP (b)" (1925-1934), "Voprosy," 9th ed., 1932, p. 132. This list of corroborating passages is by no means exhaustive.

[62] "Beseda tovarishcha Stalina s predsedatelem amerikanskogo gazetnogo ob"edineniia 'Skripps-Govard N'iuspeipers' g-nom Roi Govardom," *Pravda*, March 5, 1936, p. 2.

and intentions," thus excluding the interpretation that what he is saying to Howard represents in any way a change of mind.[63] He then declares that "we Marxists hold that revolution will occur in other countries too. But it will occur only when the revolutionaries of these countries find it possible or necessary. The export of revolution—that is nonsense." But this statement says nothing about ways in which local revolutionaries may be used, directed, and aided by outside agencies; the only "export" of revolution which it denies would be the very crudest kind, which dispensed with forming even a minimum of local Communist leadership. Carefully analyzed, then, Stalin's remarks turn out to be a sort of legalistic quibble used to convey a general impression which is in fact false.

It has at times been thought that some of Stalin's statements during the current period indicated a change of mind on his part with regard to long-term relations with the "capitalist" democracies. A careful search through all his published statements from July 1941 to March 1948 yields only one case which appears to warrant such a belief—a letter in May 1943 to King, Reuters correspondent (mentioned above), about the dissolution of the Comintern. The interview with Stassen merely says that the important point is not whether coexistence is possible but whether both sides desire it. If "one side" does not want coöperation, "the result will be conflict, war." [64] In other words, if "one side" does not like the terms of the Soviet Union, it is lacking in desire to coöperate. Also, when Stassen asks if wartime experience has changed things, Stalin denies that he ever said the two systems could not coöperate; he thus implies that his views remain unchanged and makes it impossible to attribute to his current statements on coöperation a more generous meaning than to his earlier ones. Stalin's remark that the postwar international security organization "will be effective if the Great Powers . . . continue to act in a spirit of unanimity" [65] is another expression of this same conception of "coöperation"; when queried by

---

[63] The denial that the U.S.S.R. ever had "such plans and intentions" amounts to denying that it had ever given aid to revolutions abroad, *e.g.* to China. The import of the statement for the future can be no greater than its application to the past.

[64] *Loc. cit.,* p. 1.

[65] "XVII godovshchina velikoi oktiabr'skoi sotsialisticheskoi revoliutsii," *Pravda,* Nov. 7, 1944, p. 2.

Hugh Baillie about the veto, Stalin denies that the Soviet Union has abused it in the United Nations or the Council of Foreign Ministers.[66]

But the letter to the Reuters correspondent on the dissolution of the Comintern is an explicit contradiction of Stalin's earlier statements of revolutionary methods and aims. Here he says that the dissolution of the Comintern is right because, among other reasons: "(a) it exposes the lie of the Hitlerites that 'Moscow' intends to intervene in the life of other states and 'bolshevize' them. Henceforth an end is put to that lie. (b) It exposes the slander of the enemies of Communism in the workers' movement to the effect that the Communist Parties of the various countries act not in the interests of their own nation but according to orders from outside. Henceforth an end is put to that slander too." [67]

These propositions, reminiscent of the 1936 Howard interview, can be reconciled with Stalin's established revolutionary doctrine only by very special pleading. Since they are made to a foreign correspondent and contain no express disavowal of pertinent basic writings currently republished in quantity in the Soviet Union, the balance of evidence is that they are merely part of the current tactical and propaganda line and do not reflect a fundamental change. The most decisive evidence to this effect is the republication of Stalin's vows of fidelity to Lenin and his cause originally made before the Second Congress of Soviets on January 26, 1924. Toward the close Stalin says that "Lenin was the leader not only of the Russian proletariat, not only of the workers of Europe, not only of the colonial East, but also of the earth's entire toiling world." Then he makes his last vow, set off in boldfaced capitals from the rest of the text: "In departing from us, Comrade Lenin bequeathed to us fidelity to the principles of the Communist International. We swear to thee, Comrade Lenin, that we will not spare our life in order to strengthen and expand the union of toilers of the whole world—the Communist International." [68] In the light of this vow, repeatedly republished, Stalin's real view evidently is that the Comintern was dissolved only in form, not in spirit. Stalin's charge

[66] "Otvety tov. Stalina I. V. na voprosy prezidenta amerikanskogo agentstva Iunaited Press g-na Kh'iu Beili," *Pravda,* Oct. 3, 1946, p. 1.

[67] "Otvet tov. I. V. Stalina na vopros glavnogo korrespondenta angliiskogo agentstva Reiter," *Pravda,* May 30, 1943, p. 1.

[68] "Po povodu smerti Lenina," in V. I. Lenin, "Izbrannye proizvedeniia v dvukh tomakh," 4th ed., Moscow, printing of 1946, Vol. I, p. 8, which in turn refers to Stalin's "O Lenine," 1942, p. 17-22. The vow is also quoted in "Istoriia" (1938 to present), p. 257. Thus it has been widely circulating in at least three authoritative versions during the current period.

that the United States and Great Britain are not interested in agreement and coöperation with the U.S.S.R., made in the interview by a *Pravda* correspondent, are also to be read against this background.[69] The passages in Stalin's various interviews in which he indicates the possibility or desirability of coexistence and coöperation between capitalist and Socialist systems do not really contradict the strategic aim of world revolution because they refer to a temporary tactic.

The second paragraph in the long passage quoted above places the problem of the "final" victory of Socialism in one country within the wider context of world revolution, thus excluding the hypothesis that the more limited objective—involving merely enough additional revolutions to end "capitalist encirclement" and provide security for the Soviet Union—marks the outer limit of Stalin's program for Communist expansion. Further, the passage quoted indicates that the Soviet Union will first be prepared as a base, and only then, *"after* organizing its own Socialist production," will be used more aggressively to aid revolution abroad. This tallies with the predominant absorption of the Soviets with internal affairs during the earlier five-year plans. Further, the phrase does not define the stage at which production is to be considered adequately organized. Hence the prospect of three or more additional five-year plans, as announced in 1938 and again in 1946, may indicate that the base is still not ready for contemplated operations.

Finally, the passage definitely states that armed force will be used against capitalist governments if necessary. There thus is nothing except expediency to limit the aid which Stalin contemplates giving to revolutions abroad. However, the phrase "if necessary" indicates that armed force is not to be used by preference; ahead of it come propaganda and Communist Party control, by which is meant that the Soviet Union should attract to itself "the oppressed classes of other countries, raising revolts in these countries against the capitalists." [70]

The ultimate resort to armed force is a logical development of the

---

[69] *Pravda,* Oct. 29, 1948.

[70] Stalin's belief in the necessity for strict Party discipline on an international and not merely a national scale is illustrated in his speeches in the Comintern in May 1929, in which he castigates members of the American delegation for refusing to accept a decision of the Presidium disciplining American Party leaders: debate and criticism are permissible in advance of decision, he concludes, but once a decision is made all must accept it, else there can be no "collective direction." ("O pravykh fraktsionerakh v amerikanskoi kompartii," *Bol'shevik,* Jan. 15, 1930, p. 8-26).

Leninist thesis that only consciously-led revolution can drive the capitalists from the stage of history, as explained in the preceding section. The assumption that the world has been fundamentally divided into two camps since the October Revolution runs through Stalin's writings from his early days and is grounded in his Marxist philosophy.[71] Stalin pictures the long-range evolution of the two camps as follows:

Most probably, in the course of development of the world revolution, side by side with the centers of imperialism in individual capitalist countries and the system of these countries throughout the world, centers of Socialism will be created in individual Soviet countries and a system of these centers throughout the world, and the struggle between these two systems will fill up the history of the development of the world revolution.[72]

The systems are expected to be organized around two centers:

Thus in the course of further development of international revolution two centers will form on a world scale: a Socialist center, binding to itself the countries that gravitate to Socialism, and a capitalist center, binding to itself the countries that gravitate to capitalism. The struggle between these two centers for the possession of the world economy will decide the fate of capitalism and Communism in the whole world.[73]

The plan to make the Soviet Union the base for world revolution implies that it will be one of the two centers. Evidence will be presented later that the United States is expected to be the other. The ultimate inevitability of war to the finish between the two camps is made clear in one of Stalin's favorite quotations from Lenin: "We live . . . not only in a state but in a system of states, and the existence of the Soviet Republic side by side with the imperialist states for

[71] "Sochineniia," Vol. IV, p. 232, 380; "Ob osnovakh Leninizma" (1924 to present), "Voprosy," 11th ed., 1945, p. 26, 54; "K voprosam Leninizma" (1926 to present), *ibid.*, p. 113, 140; "Itogi pervoi piatiletki" (1933 to present), *Pravda*, Jan. 10, 1933, p. 1; "Privetstvie tov. I. V. Stalina," *Pravda*, Sept. 7, 1947, p. 1. These are only a few of the many passages which reflect a two-world conception.

[72] "Oktiabr'skaia revoliutsiia i taktika russkikh kommunistov" (1924 to present), "Voprosy," 11th ed., 1945, p. 105.

[73] "Beseda s pervoi amerikanskoi rabochei delegatsiei" (1927-1939), "Voprosy," 9th ed., 1932, p. 287; also reproduced in the introductory section of a popular edition of Lenin's works, "Izbrannye proizvedeniia v dvukh tomakh," 4th ed., Moscow, printing of 1946, Vol. I, p. 28. See also "K itogam rabot XIV konferentsii RKP (b)" (1925-1934), "Voprosy," 9th ed., 1932, p. 111; "Politicheskii otchet TsK" (1925), "XIV s"ezd. Sten. otchet," p. 19; "Ob itogakh iiul'skogo plenuma TsK VKP (b)" (1928-1934), "Voprosy," 9th ed., 1932, p. 338.

a long time is unthinkable. In the end either one or the other will conquer. And until that end comes, a series of the most terrible collisions between the Soviet Republic and the bourgeois states is inevitable." [74] Stalin appended to this forecast of inexorable wars a succinct, "Clear, one would think." Thus Stalin expects not merely one but several world wars before the end of capitalism.

At the very close of the struggle the forces of Socialism will be so superior that Stalin foresees an exception to the general rule that revolutionary violence is necessary to overthrow capitalism: "Of course, in the distant future, if the proletariat wins in the most important capitalist countries and if the present capitalist encirclement is replaced by a Socialist encirclement, a 'peaceful' path of development is fully possible for some capitalist countries, whose capitalists, in view of the 'unfavorable' international situation, will consider it expedient to make serious concessions to the proletariat 'voluntarily.' " [75] The technique of "cold revolution," as it has been called, illustrated recently in Eastern Europe, may be interpreted as a variety of "Socialist encirclement" in that it also dispenses with the need for overt violence. In any case, the passage quoted excepts "the most important capitalist countries," and so does not apply to the United States.

Flexibility of Strategy and Tactics. We are now in a position to link Stalin's strategy and tactics with his conception of the "objective" conditions making for revolution. It is the business of strategy and tactics, he holds, to prepare the "subjective" conditions of revolution— *i.e.,* the mobilization of the proletariat and its allies—and bring them into action at the most favorable times and places as determined by the development of the "objective" conditions.[76] More than this, preparation of the "subjective" conditions really involves gaining leadership of social forces which often in the first place develop spontaneously. Describing the skill shown by the Communist Party in Russia in 1917 in uniting "in one common revolutionary stream such different revolu-

---

[74] "K voprosam Leninizma" (1926 to present), "Voprosy," 11th ed., 1945, p. 140; see also p. 113. Quoted again in "Otvet t-shchu IVANOVU Ivanu Filippovichu," *Pravda,* Feb. 14, 1938, p. 3.

[75] "Ob osnovakh Leninizma" (1924 to present), "Voprosy," 11th ed., 1945, p. 32. On Socialist encirclement see also "XVIII s"ezd. Sten. otchet" (1939 to present), p. 33, 36.

[76] "Sochineniia," Vol. V, p. 62, 74, 161; "O pravykh fraktsionerakh v amerikanskoi kompartii," *Bol'shevik,* Jan. 15, 1930, p. 13, 23; "Voprosy sverdlovtsev i otvet t. Stalina," *Pravda,* Feb. 10, 1930, p. 2.

tionary movements as the general democratic movement for peace, the peasant democratic movement for seizure of the landed estates, the movement of the oppressed nationalities for national liberation and national equality, and the Socialist movement of the proletariat for the overthrow of the bourgeoisie and the establishment of the dictatorship of the proletariat," Stalin declares that "undoubtedly, the merging of these diverse revolutionary streams in one common, powerful revolutionary stream decided the fate of capitalism in Russia." [77]

In general, despite his comparatively rigid doctrinal framework, Stalin's conception of Communist strategy and tactics is highly flexible. It rests on a continual assessment of the status of forces in both the capitalist and the Socialist systems. Thus he writes: *"Tactics,* guiding itself by the directives of strategy and by experience of the revolutionary movement . . . calculating at every given moment the state of forces inside the proletariat and its allies (greater or less cultivation, greater or less degree of organization and class-consciousness, presence of particular traditions, presence of particular forms of movement, forms of organization, *basic* and *secondary*), as well as in the camp of the adversary, profiting by discord and every kind of confusion in the camp of the adversary—marks out those *concrete courses* for winning the wide masses to the proletarian side and leading them to battle stations on the social front . . . which most surely pave the way for strategic successes." [78]

In view of this flexibility, and of the way in which Stalin expects Communist leadership to win control of many movements which originate spontaneously, it must be concluded that the "objective" conditions of revolution are not fixed quantities in Stalin's thinking, but rather interdependent variables which are to be manipulated to satisfy just one equation: revolution occurs where the Communist command concentrates superiority of forces at a point on the capitalist front where the bourgeoisie can be isolated and overwhelmed. In other words, "revolutionary crises" do not have to be waited for; they can to some extent be organized; and an extremely favorable balance of outside aid can compensate to a considerable degree for a deficiency in favorable internal conditions.

For the period of world revolution, Stalin's grand strategy is to use

[77] "Istoriia" (1938 to present), p. 204.
[78] "O politicheskoi strategii i taktike russkikh kommunistov" (written 1921, first published 1947), "Sochineniia," Vol. V, p. 63.

the Soviet Union as a base linking the proletariat of the west with the movements for national liberation from imperialism in the east into "a single world front against the world front of imperialism." In this way he harnesses two of the major contradictions of capitalism to his chariot—contradictions between proletariat and bourgeoisie, and contradictions between capitalist and colonial countries. The front thus formed is to be used to exploit the third contradiction of capitalism— that between capitalist countries, whose rivalry for spheres of influence must lead periodically to war, the event most propitious for revolution.[79]

One of the chief conditions to which tactics must be adjusted, according to Stalin, is the ebb and flow of the forces favoring revolution. Aggressive tactics should be timed with a rising tide; tactics of defense, the assemblage of forces, and even retreat go with an ebbing tide.[80] The importance of gauging the direction of the tide is illustrated by Stalin's remarks in 1929 concerning a controversy with Bukharin, who apparently held that the "stabilization of capitalism" was persisting unchanged: "This question, comrades, is of decisive importance for the sections of the Comintern. Is the capitalist stabilization going to pieces or is it becoming more secure? On this the whole line of the Communist Parties in their day-to-day political work depends. Are we in a period of decline of the revolutionary movement . . . or are we in a period when the conditions are maturing for a new revolutionary rise, a period of preparing the working class for coming class battles— on this depends the tactical position of the Communist Parties." Stalin holds that it is a period of revolutionary upswing.[81]

Stalin's insistence on flexibility of tactics is ground for a very important maxim in the interpretation of his public statements; one must avoid, if possible, mistaking a change in tactics for a change in fundamental doctrine and strategic objectives. The example of a change in tactics often thus mistaken is Stalin's remarks about peaceful coexistence of and coöperation between the Socialist and capitalist systems. The whole body of mutually reinforcing propositions in Stalin's philosophy adds up to a veritable religion of conflict and contradiction. This is

---

[79] "Ob osnovakh Leninizma" (1924 to present), "Voprosy," 11th ed., 1945, p. 17, 54; "Sochineniia," Vol. IV, p. 166, 238, 378.

[80] "Ob osnovakh Leninizma" (1924 to present), "Voprosy," 11th ed., 1945, p. 55; "Sochineniia," Vol. V, p. 64.

[81] "O pravom uklone v VKP (b)" (1929 to present), Bol'shevik, Dec. 1929, p. 20.

described as not only inevitable but desirable, until revolution is achieved. Here we find further strong evidence that Stalin's statements on coöperation represent nothing deeper than a tactic.

Stalin first announced a period of "peaceful coexistence" for proletarian and bourgeois worlds in 1925, saying that the revolutionary movement was ebbing and capitalism achieving a temporary stabilization. But the context of his statement makes plain that he expected peaceful coexistence to be as temporary as the stabilization.[82] In 1927 he stated that capitalist stabilization was coming to an end and that the period of "peaceful coexistence" was likewise giving way to one of imperialist attacks. But he added that the Soviet Union must continue to pursue a policy of maintaining peace for the following reason:

We cannot forget the saying of Lenin to the effect that a great deal in the matter of our construction depends on whether we succeed in delaying war with the capitalist countries, which is inevitable but which may be delayed either until proletarian revolution ripens in Europe, or until the colonial revolutions come fully to a head, or, finally, until the capitalists fight among themselves over division of the colonies. Therefore the maintenance of peaceful relations with capitalist countries is an obligatory task for us.

The basis of our relations with capitalist countries consists in admitting the coexistence of two opposed systems.[83]

This concern for peaceful relations in order to build the Socialist economy at home should be read in the context of the previous discussion in this paper of the Soviet Union as a base for world revolution; in that light, a peace policy is an intelligible tactic. Stalin continues to advocate it in the years after 1927, while at the same time urging the Communist Parties to adopt aggressive tactics in keeping with the end of capitalist stabilization.[84] Thus appears an important variation of tactics on different levels of activity: peaceful coexistence for the Soviet Government, preparation for attack by Communist Parties.

The peace policy has another tactical function in Stalin's strategy of revolution. He notes how successfully the Communists capitalized on

---

[82] "XIV s"ezd. Sten. otchet," p. 8, 10, 17; "K itogam rabot XIV Konferentsii," "Voprosy," 9th ed., 1932, p. 110.

[83] "XV s"ezd. Sten. otchet," p. 47.

[84] On aggressive tactics, see "O pravom uklone v VKP(b)" (1929 to present), Bol'shevik, Dec. 1929, p. 15-49 (including passage quoted immediately above in text); "O pravykh fraktsionerakh v amerikanskoi kompartii," Bol'shevik, Jan. 15, 1930, p. 8-26.

the general popular craving for peace during the October Revolution; accordingly he manœuvres the Soviet Union and the Communist Parties into position as apostles of peace, unmasking the imperialist "warmongers" in order to profit by popular sentiments for peace in the future. Particularly interesting in this connection is the way Stalin combines his peace stand with verbal onslaughts on Social Democratic pacifism as a mere mask of the warmongers.[85]

Apart from their bearing on peace, the tasks of developing trade and obtaining technological assistance from capitalist countries have a direct relationship to building the industrial base of the Soviet Union, especially during the early stage of the five-year plans. Stalin makes several unsentimental and businesslike proposals for improved relations along these lines, particularly with the United States.[86] His fullest and frankest statement on coöperation between Soviet and capitalist worlds is made in 1927, shortly before his announcement that the capitalist stabilization is coming to an end. To the American Workers' Delegation, who asked to what extent such coöperation is possible and whether it has definite limits, Stalin replies:

The matter concerns, obviously, temporary agreements with capitalist states in the field of industry, in the field of trade, and, perhaps, in the field of diplomatic relations. I think that the presence of two opposed systems . . . does not exclude the possibility of such agreements. I think that such agreements are possible and expedient under conditions of peaceful development. . . .

The limits of these agreements? The limits are set by the opposition of the two systems, between which rivalry and struggle go on. Within the limits permitted by these two systems, but only within these limits, agreements are fully possible. . . .

Are these agreements merely an experiment or can they have more or less lasting character? That depends not only on us; that depends also on those who contract with us. That depends on the general situation. War can upset any agreement whatever. . . .[87]

[85] "Ob itogakh iiul'skogo plenuma TsK VKP(b)," "Voprosy," 9th ed., 1932, p. 336; "Otchetnyi doklad" (1939 to present), "XVIII s"ezd. Sten. otchet," p. 15; "Oktiabr'skaia Revoliutsiia" (1924 to present), "Voprosy," 11th ed., 1945, p. 78.

[86] "Gospodin Kempbell priviraet," Bol'shevik, Nov. 30, 1932, p. 12; interview reported by Eugene Lyons, New York Herald Tribune, Nov. 24, 1930, p. 1, 2.

[87] "Beseda s pervoi amerikanskoi rabochei delegatsiei" (1927-1939), "Voprosy," 9th ed., 1932, p. 280, 287.

A few pages later the same interview reads: "Thus in the course of further development of international revolution two centers will form on a world scale: a Socialist center . . . and a capitalist center. . . . The struggle between these two centers for the possession of the world economy will decide the fate of capitalism and Communism in the whole world." This passage places coöperation clearly as a temporary tactic on the way to world revolution. When read against the foregoing as background, Stalin's statements to Howard, Duranty, Lyons, Werth, Elliott Roosevelt and Stassen, to the effect that the two systems can coexist and compete peacefully, appear not so much inconsistent with his basic principles as merely elliptical: he neglects to specify how long and on what terms. To that extent the effect is misleading, as we have seen, and properly comes under the heading of propaganda.

IV. REVOLUTION IN THE UNITED STATES

In a speech in the Comintern in May 1929, Stalin rebukes representatives of the American Communist Party for exaggerating the "specific traits" of American capitalism. The basis for the activities of all Communist Parties, he states, is the "common traits" of capitalism, which are fundamentally the same for all countries—the specific traits of capitalism in a particular country merely supplement the general traits. This implies that Stalin makes no major exceptions on behalf of the United States in regard to the application of his theory of capitalism and his objective of world revolution. In April 1947, Stalin presents an unchanged view in his talk with Stassen: he even says that the economic systems of the United States and of Nazi Germany are identical—namely, monopoly capitalism. When Stassen argues that the American system is really very different, he is politely but firmly parried.

As we have noted, Stalin's portrait of the capitalists paints them as utterly unprincipled and ruthless men, dominated by the lust for profits, to which they are willing to sacrifice all else. In his interview with Lyons (intended for publication in America and appealing for better business relations) he remarks, apropos of the alleged sanctity of the old war debts, which were a stumbling block: "Since when has the bourgeoisie placed principle above money?" In his report to the Eighteenth Congress in 1939, he complains of the policies of the United States and other countries toward Germany and Japan, and declares: "Far be it from me to moralize on the policy of nonintervention, to talk of treason, of treachery, etc. It is naïve to read a moral to people who do not recognize human morality." [88] To Wells in 1934, he says that American or other capitalists will never permit abolition of unemployment because they need a "reserve army of unemployed" to ensure cheap labor; capitalists are "riveted to profit" and "see nothing except their own interest." The government is merely their tool: if Roosevelt seriously threatens private property and the profit system, they will put in another president.

How does Stalin regard Americans in general? His admiration for American technological prowess and business efficiency are well known. To Ludwig in 1931 he also mentions the democratic simplicity of American manners; but he denies "worship of everything American." As far as Soviet sympathies with the majority of any other nation are concerned, those with the Germans are beyond comparison with "our feelings toward Americans." [89] On no occasion does Stalin appeal to lasting ties of sentiment or culture as a basis for coöperation with the United States. Even to Howard in 1936 he specifies that neither of the rival systems will evolve into the other. "The Soviet system will not grow into American democracy, and vice versa." The utterly unsentimental basis of Stalin's approach to coöperation despite ideological differences is made particularly clear by his statement to Stassen in 1947 that the Soviet Union would have coöperated with Germany as much as with any other capitalist country if Germany had desired. Stalin bids for coöperation on the basis of interest, such as maintaining peace and securing profitable trade.

Stalin has long evinced a belief that proletarian forces are backward in the United States. To the American Labor Delegation in 1927 he comments that American labor leaders are "reactionary" and "reformist," and points to the small fraction of workers who are unionized. He also observes that both political parties are bourgeois, and asks: "Don't you Comrades consider that the absence of your own mass workers' party, if only one like the English [Labor Party], weakens the strength of the working class in its political struggle with capitalism?" In 1947 he remarks to Stassen that he sees little difference between Democrats and Republicans. Likewise in speaking to American Communist Party representatives in 1929 he attacks them for "rightist factionalism," saying: "It cannot be denied that American life offers an environment which favors the Communist Party's falling into error

---

[88] "Otchetnyi doklad" (1939 to present), "XVIII s″ezd. Sten. otchet," p. 14.
[89] To Emil Ludwig, *Bol'shevik*, April 30, 1932, p. 38.

and exaggerating the strength and stability of American capitalism." [90]
He has said nothing since to indicate a change of opinion. Thus such
evidence as his writings afford points to an expectation that the United
States will be one of the last countries to go Communist.

This conclusion is reinforced by Stalin's views on the American
economy. He notes that the United States—"the chief country of capitalism, its stronghold"—is hardest hit by the economic crisis of 1929,
and that the crisis of 1937 originates here. But he also observes that
the country leads world recovery in 1925 and 1933, and in 1939 he
implies that it will pull out of the later crisis.[91] Thus the United
States is the center of the capitalist world system, its "stronghold," and,
though affected by the general decadence of capitalism, shows some
remnants of health in its powers of recovery. As early as 1925 Stalin
observes that the center of capitalist financial power is moving across
the Atlantic, and he describes how the United States, with England
as partner, is becoming the hub of the capitalist system; ". . . two chief,
but opposed, centers of attraction are being formed," he writes, "and,
in conformity with this, two directions of pull toward these centers throughout the world: Anglo-America . . . and the Soviet Union . . ." [92] In the years immediately following, Stalin sees the United
States and England becoming rivals rather than partners, but at no
time up to the present has he implied that the United States has ceased
to be the center of world capitalism. To Stassen in 1947 he comments on
the unique opportunities for rapid economic development enjoyed by
this country from the beginning, and also points out that with the
elimination of Germany and Japan as competitors it has access to
world markets as never before, and thus has opportunity for further
development.

Thus Stalin's conception of the United States as the "stronghold of
capitalism" dovetails with his picture of the future course of world
revolution. The United States is expected to be the center of the rival
world system which finally must clash with the Soviet system until
capitalism goes down and Socialism conquers the world. This means

[90] "O pravykh fraktsionerakh v amerikanskoi kompartii," *Bol'shevik,* Jan. 15,
1930, p. 8.
[91] "XVI s"ezd" (1930-1939), *Pravda,* June 29, 1930, p. 1; "Politicheskii
otchet" (1925), "XIV s"ezd. Sten. otchet," p. 11; "Politicheskii otchet" (1927),
p. 38; "XVII-omu s"ezdu" (1934 to present), *Pravda,* Jan. 28, 1934, p. 1;
"Otchetnyi doklad" (1939 to present), "XVIII s"ezd. Sten. otchet," p. 9.
[92] "XIV s"ezd. Sten. otchet," p. 10, 19.

that Stalin expects revolution in the United States only near the end of the "epoch of world revolution." [93] As he declares to the American Commission of the Comintern in 1929, "when a revolutionary crisis has developed in America, that will be the beginning of the end of all world capitalism."

V. THE NEXT PHASE

Thus it is probable that Stalin hardly expected revolution to occur in the United States during World War II or its aftermath. But the evidence presented in the present article makes it likely that his perspective on this period was (and is) as follows:

(1) The time for the next harvest of revolution is at hand. The world war, predicted since 1927, has come to pass, and the upheaval it has created will bring to a climax the contradictions of capitalism in a way that will make revolution possible in "a number of countries in Europe and Asia." [94] Precisely such revolution is required to guarantee once and for all that the forces of capitalism will not obliterate Socialism (even in the U.S.S.R. itself) and compel the whole process to begin again from scratch. Therefore the minimum revolutionary objective for World War II and its aftermath is to bring enough countries into the Soviet camp to effect such a guarantee.

(2) The "law of ebb and flow" implies that unless the whole of capitalism collapses under the present revolutionary wave, the surviving remnant will temporarily stabilize itself a few years after the end of the war and an ebb in the tide of revolution will set in: the revolutionary objective for World War II must therefore be consolidated before the tide begins to ebb. This imparts a certain urgency to revolutionary tactics in the immediate postwar period.

(3) Though the Soviet Union has not yet equaled the United States in industrial production per capita, its industrial and military strength has increased greatly since 1928, and with the defeat of Germany

[93] The factor of geographical position obviously supports such a view also. Stalin recognizes that proximity is an important factor in assisting revolution in another country from the Soviet base. Among the unfavorable circumstances of the October Revolution in Russia he mentions "the absence, next to it or in its neighborhood, of a Soviet country which it could lean upon. Undoubtedly, a future revolution, in Germany for example would be in a more favorable situation in this respect, for it has nearby so powerful a Soviet country as our Soviet Union." "Voprosy" (1924 to present), 11th ed., 1945, p. 79.

[94] "XVII s"ezd" (1934 to present), p. 1.

and Japan its relative strength among the Powers of Europe and Asia will be enormous. Therefore the Soviet Union will be in position to serve as base for much more active fostering of revolutionary movements in other countries, though not ready to establish Communism throughout the world. This indicates a much more aggressive tactic toward other countries, but not so aggressive as deliberately to bring on war for world hegemony in the immediate future.

The success of this tactic would depend in part, according to Stalin's theory of revolution, on the extent to which the critical areas were isolated from foreign influences hostile to revolution. This gives a major clue to Stalin's war and postwar policies toward Britain and the United States. Many of them can be regarded as a delaying action: by retarding realization on the part of these countries of what is really going on, then minimizing efforts to intervene as realization gradually dawns, they, in effect, tend to isolate the "bourgeoisie" in the countries singled out for revolution until Communist control is established. Stalin's profession of nonaggressive war aims served to lull suspicion. So did the dissolution of the Comintern and his comments thereon. So did his statements on the possibility of coexistence and coöperation and the necessity for unanimity among the big Powers after the war. These and similar moves imposed a serious reluctance on the part of the Allies to do or say anything that could be construed as a breach in the spirit of wartime collaboration. When at last Allied public opinion began to denounce Soviet or Communist actions, the same statements served as a basis for propaganda counterattack. Stalin launched this attack with his comments on Churchill's speech at Fulton, declaring it a "dangerous act," sowing discord among the Allies, harming the cause of peace and security, in short, warmongering.[95] Thereafter those who like Churchill object to Soviet policies in Eastern Europe and elsewhere are denounced as "warmongers," and an attempt is made to mobilize against them the popular craving for peace.

Even the United Nations has to some extent been exploited by Stalin's tactics. The possibility of using the veto to cripple Allied action in revolutionary areas is obvious. But if, as some think, Stalin might prefer a deal based on spheres of influence to the United Nations pattern, such an arrangement could be depended on to further, not to limit, revolutionary operations. Within his sphere Stalin would have

---

[95] "Interv'iu tov. I. V. Stalina s korrespondentom 'Pravdy' otnositel'no rechi g. Cherchillia," *Pravda*, March 14, 1946, p. 1.

a free hand, and Communist action would also continue across the demarcation line into the other sphere.

When Stalin looks to the more distant future, the United States, which has emerged from the last war more truly than ever the "stronghold of capitalism," probably continues to figure in his thinking as it has done in his basic writings since the mid-1920's—as the center around which the capitalist system will form for the final war to the death between the two systems. Meanwhile, Stalin (*Pravda*, February 10, 1946) projects further industrial expansion in the Soviet Union on a scale which suggests, other factors aside, that the climactic struggle will not be risked before 15 or 20 years have elapsed. Stalin's theory of "ebb and flow" would lead him to expect a new stabilization of capitalism within a few years, followed some years later by another wave of crisis and revolution generated by capitalism's inexorable contradictions. He apparently is timing completion of the Soviet base of operations for the crest of this next wave. Tactics of the moment may swing this way or that, but the Marxist doctrine to which he is committed is uncompromisingly revolutionary. In that doctrine, world Communism is the supreme aim, Soviet power the major instrument by which it will be achieved.

WHEREVER its power reached into postwar Europe, the Soviet leadership was especially alert to contain or destroy the competing forces of democratic socialism. Where Communist parties were weak, they sought "working-class unity" with the Socialists, hoping thereby to bring the rank-and-file under their own control. "Fusion" of trade unions, youth, women's and veterans' organizations was likewise to be, they hoped, a prelude to the destruction of rivals with claims to speak for the working class. In this way the Communists could even hope to gain power in some countries by legal and peaceful means.

On the other hand, where popular support was weak and Soviet intrusion deeply resented, the Communists followed a different road to fusion, primarily by destroying the Socialist organizations and by imprisoning the recalcitrant. Perhaps Moscow's first great blunder in occupied Germany was the haste with which, in January 1946, it forced the Social Democrats of the Soviet Zone into a shotgun wedding with the small Communist Party. Was this a sign of Stalin's contempt for the West's capacity to understand what he was up to, or was it due to Ulbricht's bad advice? In any event, the effect was to dig an ever wider chasm between the Communists and their hopes for influence over the working class of West Germany.

In "liberated" Poland the Polish Socialist Party played an even more crucial role. This party, older than any Russian party, had a long tradition of national pride and of sacrifice for Poland's independence. It had played a major part in the government-in-exile and in the armed resistance in the homeland. The Kremlin's determination to fit Poland neatly into the Communist bloc called for the destruction of this proud and ably led party.

The uprooting of rival organizations could not reach into all the crannies of men's minds. Some traces of the democratic socialist view of politics clung even to those who tried to destroy it. In the Polish "October" of 1956 many non-Moscovite Communists recalled Socialist Party traditions and appealed to the national pride of the Polish workers to rally behind a policy of partial independence from Soviet dictation.

The Communist technique of "fraternal embrace" is presented clearly and soberly in "The Fate of Polish Socialism" (October 1949). Richard T. Davies, then a beginning diplomat at his first post abroad, was an alert, first-hand witness to the events he describes.

256

THE FATE OF POLISH SOCIALISM

By Richard T. Davies

IN Soviet eyes, Poland is the most important of the satellites. Even after her enormous losses in the war years, she has by far the largest population of any member of the group. She is the largest in area; she is the greatest producer of food and coal; and she has in the Dabrowan-Silesian basin an industrial area potentially capable of playing the part of an Eastern European Ruhr.

Of even greater importance, however, Poland is the bridge to Germany. Having served alternately as the channel through which Lenin hoped to reach the German working class in order to touch off the world revolution, and the obstacle which prevented the realization of that aim, today Poland offers an open road over which men, materials and ideas roll westward into Germany from the Soviet Union.

Thus what Lenin attempted, Stalin has been able to achieve: Poland today is on the way to sovietization. She has been won for Communism methodically and relatively quietly. There have been no "February days," there has been as yet no Mindszenty trial, and incipient Polish "Titoism" has been effectively knocked on the head.[1]

The end of effective and open political opposition to the process of sovietization was signalized by the defeat of Stanislaw Mikolajczyk's Polish Peasant Party in the rigged elections of January 19, 1947. Mikolajczyk had not been alone, of course, in his attempt to ward off absolute Communist control. A majority of the prewar membership of the Polish Socialist Party stood with him on this issue, and so did many of its post-1944 leaders. The relative ease of the success of the Communists in Poland was the result of their ability to keep Mikolajczyk and the Socialists from forming a common front against them. The destruction of the Socialist Party followed soon after Mikolajczyk's disappear-

[1] The Red Army had withdrawn by the time the Provisional Government of National Unity was established in June 1945. However, "line-of-communications" troops with the Soviet occupation troops in Eastern Germany remained; and Soviet troops are still stationed in the ex-German territories.

ance from the scene. This ended all hope that Poland might manage her own affairs in a fashion divergent in even the slightest measure from that ordained by her "big brother" to the east.

At the time the Polish Committee of National Liberation was constituted in July 1944, it contained a small group of Polish Communists and a large group of ephemeral opportunists and confused exponents of the belief that "we can do business with Stalin and still maintain our domestic freedom of action." The Communists, who formed its continuing core, were faced with three principal tasks: 1, to gain immediately the support of the mass of the peasantry, or at least to render the peasants passive; 2, then to destroy the representative institutions of the peasantry, the most important of which was the party of Wincenty Witos and Mikolajczyk; and 3, thereafter to destroy or transform into Communist instruments the institutions of the next largest segment of the population, the working class, the most important of which were the Socialist Party, the trade unions and the coöperative movement. In accomplishing these ends, they isolated each victim in turn and then prevented the formation of a Populist-Socialist anti-Communist front.

The story of the Polish Peasant Party's fight against the attempt to sovietize Poland has been told in part by Mikolajczyk and the former American Ambassador to Poland, Arthur Bliss Lane.[2] The story of the confused and foredoomed struggle of Polish Socialism has received much less attention, despite the fact that it possibly is even more significant. At all events, it carries a moral which although it has become almost banal through reiteration still apparently has not sunk into the consciousness of Socialist leaders of Western Europe.

II

The Polish Communists used four main tactics in their campaign against the Socialists.

In the period when they were destroying the Peasant Party, led by Mikolajczyk, the Communists sedulously fostered the belief among the Socialist Party leaders that the only alternatives before them were acceptance of a dictatorial working-class party régime, complete with secret police and political prisons, or the "return of reaction." The Socialist leaders, who had experienced a long period of repression under

---

[2] Stanislaw Mikolajczyk, "The Rape of Poland." New York: Whittlesey, 1948. Arthur Bliss Lane, "I Saw Poland Betrayed." Indianapolis: Bobbs-Merrill, 1948.

Pilsudski and the subsequent "régimes of the colonels" (1926-1939), were thoroughly frightened by this prospect. And when they saw National Democrats and other elements even farther to the right entering the Peasant Party they were the more willing to believe that the Party as a whole and its leaders were, either wittingly or unwittingly, bearing the seeds of a reviving Polish counter-revolution. The Communists also were quick to point out that should a "reactionary" government be elected, the Soviet Union might well occupy the country. The only way for Poland to be free to work out her own destiny, they argued, was by preventing, through any and all means, a Mikolajczyk victory.

This was the first Communist tactic. It provided the basis for combining the strength of the Socialists with that of the Polish Workers' Party (Communist) against Mikolajczyk and his associates.

An even more important instrument used by the Polish Communists was the Kremlin. When differences between them and the Socialists arose, representatives of the two parties journeyed to Moscow to submit them to arbitration. Naturally the influence of the Soviet leaders was always exerted to further the aims of the Communist-dominated Workers' Party and to reconcile the Socialists to those very policies which were designed eventually to destroy them.

The third tactic of the Communists was to capture or neutralize the important mass organizations which had traditionally linked the Socialist Party and the working class—the coöperatives and the trade unions. The Communists manipulated the leadership of these organs so that all democracy in them was stifled. The effectiveness of the coöperatives was undermined by transference of their functions to state organizations; when they had been sufficiently weakened and infiltrated on the local levels, the Workers' Party moved in on the national level, captured the leadership and turned the coöperative system into a mere organ of the state. The trade unions were subverted by variations of the same technique.

The final Communist instrument was the political police. At the height of Socialist resistance to the Workers' Party, in the summer of 1947, there began a series of trials of "rightist" Socialists. The charges, usually of espionage and anti-state activities, were made in such a way as to serve warning on the post-1944 leaders of the Socialist Party that their failure to continue coöperating with the Communists would be tantamount to treason. The warning had the desired effect. The police also were used to destroy the democratic bases of the trade-union movement by breaking strikes and proceeding against local leaders who clung to prewar conceptions.

III

The original link between the Socialist Party and the Workers' Party was forged during the period of "liberation," when the Red Army invaded Poland and the German occupation came to an end. In the chaos and obscurity of those days, when any sort of normal political activity was restricted, the Communists applied to political parties the technique which they had used in their efforts to secure control of states such as Finland and Greece. In those cases they had set up a "shadow government" on the fringe of a state. Now in a similar way they arranged for the Socialist Party to be taken over by a Communist-sponsored splinter-group, the Workers' Party of Polish Socialists, which had been formed in 1942 in Krakow under the leadership of Edward Osobka-Morawski and Stanislaw Szwalbe. This group of left Socialists opposed what they looked upon as the futile policy of the majority of the "London Socialists" who, through the Socialist underground organization "Freedom-Equality-Independence" (known from its Polish initials as "WRN"), were already going over from combatting the German occupation forces to fighting the small Polish Communist underground groups.

When the Red Army entered Poland, these left-wing Socialists hastened to join the Communists in forming the Polish Committee of National Liberation, already mentioned above. Soviet intentions towards the old Socialist Party and the WRN were quickly made obvious when several of the "London Socialists," among them Kazimierz Puzak and Aleksy Bien, were included among the 16 arrested underground leaders who stood trial in Moscow on June 18-21, 1945. The left-wing Socialists, meanwhile, proclaimed themselves *the* Socialist Party; and, as the Red Army moved through Poland, they took over the prewar properties of the Party and summoned all Party members to register with their agencies.

During this period, Zygmunt Zulawski, who had been the Socialist trade-union leader before 1939, endeavored, together with Bien (who had returned from the Soviet Union), Dorota Kluszynska, Antoni Zdanowski, Stanislaw Garlicki, Stefan Zbrozyna and others, to form a Social-Democratic Party. The provisional government refused to permit the formation of new parties, and Zdanowski, Garlicki and Zbrozyna were arrested. Shortly thereafter, Zulawski, Kluszynska and some other members of the group joined the "concessioned" Socialist Party.

The entry of most of the prewar Socialist leaders into the "new" Socialist Party induced two mutually supporting developments. On the one hand, the Party lost its puppet character. The rank-and-file were not satisfied to play second fiddle to the Communists of the Workers' Party. They disdained the latter as johnny-come-latelies and opportunists and feared them as perverters of the ideals of true Socialism. They demanded that the Socialist Party be at least an equal partner in any combination with the Workers' Party. On the other hand, the Socialist leadership itself, emboldened by the discovery that it now had a living political organism behind it, began to act more and more independently of the Communists.

The new spirit found expression in two ways. In the first place, the Polish Socialists began to resume their contacts with the international Socialist movement. The Party sent representatives to the International Socialist Conference at Clacton-on-Sea in May 1946, and joined the Committee for the International Socialist Conference (COMISCO). This development had, of course, partial Communist approval, since the Communists hoped that the Polish Socialists might help to persuade left-wing Socialists in other countries of the desirability and necessity of forming Communist-Socialist united fronts throughout Europe. Primarily, however, it represented an effort by the Polish Socialist Party to strengthen its domestic position by reëstablishing itself as a significant factor in European politics.

At home, simultaneously, the Party set to work to reconstruct its influence in the trade unions and coöperatives and to strengthen the rôles of these organizations in the national economy. Success in this field was reflected in the fact that candidates of the Party beat those of the Workers' Party so decisively in elections to the Works Councils that the Communists finally ceased competing openly with the Socialists and demanded the establishment of joint election lists. At the first postwar Trade Union Congress in November 1945, the Socialist Party controlled about 60 percent of the delegates and a Socialist, Kazimierz Rusinek, became Secretary-General of the new Central Committee of Trade Unions.

IV

The feeling of growing strength among the Socialist leadership led them, in the middle of 1946, to the first severe friction with the Workers' Party. They saw that the Workers' Party intended to relegate the Socialist Party to the status of junior partner, and this was particularly galling because quite clearly a very large majority of the working class supported the Socialist viewpoint on most political questions and not that of the Communists.

The Socialists accordingly brought up the fact that they had smaller representation than the Communists in the Provisional Government of National Unity, established by the "Moscow Agreement" of June 1945. Although each Party had six ministers in that Government in its latter days, the Communists held the decisive posts: Public Security, Recovered Territories, Industry, Food Supply and Trade. In addition, they controlled the Ministry of National Defense through the "non-party" Minister, General Zymierski, and Communist vice-ministers. The Socialists held less significant positions, such as Treasury, Justice and Labor.

The action of the Communists in their spheres of power, moreover, was very arbitrary. Their use of police methods in implementing ministerial policy, and the clear indication they gave that political considerations constituted their rationale for action in distributing UNRRA supplies, hiring and firing executives in nationalized industry and repopulating the "Recovered Territories" made the Socialists realize that they ran the risk of being seriously weakened in the elections, which had finally been scheduled to take place early in 1947.

The Socialists decided, therefore, on a counterattack. Osobka-Morawski, then Premier and Chairman of the Central Executive Committee of the Socialist Party, wrote in the Party's central organ, *Robotnik* (*The Worker*), on August 6, 1946: "It seems to me that the greatest difficulties [in the maintenance of a united front] arise from the fact that one partner operates too much under the slogan of 'the leading party.' . . . A united front may not be based on the principle that the one rules, while the other subordinates himself, that the one lays down the conditions while the other submissively nods his head. . . ." The Workers' Party organ, *Glos Ludu* (*The Voice of the People*), countered two days later by implying that the "difficulties" to which

Osobka referred were, in part at least, due to "elements inimical to democracy" within the Socialist Party.

The climax of this friction was the resignation of Henryk Wachowicz, the leader of the Socialist Party in Lodz, from the post of Vice-Minister of Public Security. The Workers' Party demanded that he resign because he had released from prison certain minor officials of the Peasant Party who had been arrested at the time of the referendum on June 30. Wachowicz believed that the Communists were abusing the police power for their own political ends; and his resignation was forced because he gave evidence of that belief.

Leaders of the Socialist right wing thereupon entered into negotiations with the Peasant Party, offering it 25 percent of the seats in the proto-parliamentary National Council of the Homeland (*Krajowa Rada Narodowa*—or "KRN"), if it would enter the government bloc. The Peasant Party leaders, believing they could win a much larger number of mandates than this in the coming "free" election, refused the offer. But the two Parties maintained contact.

It was at this juncture (August 29, 1946) that Socialist and Communist leaders made the first of their significant joint trips to Moscow. In an attempt to reconcile the differences of the two Parties, a conference was arranged there between Soviet leaders and Osobka-Morawski, Jozef Cyrankiewicz and Stanislaw Szwalbe for the Socialists and Wladyslaw Gomulka, Jakob Berman and Roman Zambrowski for the Communists. The main disputes seem to have been over the methods of coöperation to be pursued during the electoral campaign and over the representation which each party would have in the government to be formed in January. Apparently the results were inconclusive.

Convinced that the efforts of the Socialist Party to maintain an independent line were proving futile, Zulawski left the Party in November 1946 and concluded an agreement with the Peasant Party under which he was to run as an independent Socialist on its electoral ticket. Local Socialist leaders who were known to favor ending the "united front" were meanwhile being harassed by the secret police and arrested on one charge and another. Among them was Boleslaw Galaj, Chairman of the Warsaw Committee of the Party.

The approach of the elections and the danger that the Socialist half of the bloc might be seriously fragmented necessitated a second visit to Moscow in November by the six Socialist and Communist veterans of the August journey. This meeting proved more fruitful than the first, as shown by the signature of a United-Front Agreement (published November 29) providing methods for combatting the "elements" of the Peasant Party and the WRN within the Socialist Party and for close coöperation in the coming electoral struggle. The Agreement declared that the Socialist Party and the Workers' Party were "separate, independent and equal political organisms," which would "mutually respect the organizational structure of each." [3] Simultaneously, it was announced that the Secretary-General of the Socialist Party, Cyrankiewicz, was appointed Minister without Portfolio, and Dr. Stanislaw Leszczycki, a minor Party leader, was appointed Vice-Minister of Foreign Affairs. These obviously were Communist concessions to the Socialist complaint about inferior representation in the Government.

During the electoral campaign, the Communists intensified their tactic of playing upon the Socialist fear of a "return to reaction." In a speech delivered at Lodz,[4] the Secretary-General of the Workers' Party Central Committee, Gomulka, painted a vivid picture of the probable result if Mikolajczyk met with success. He concluded by hinting plainly that the Soviet Union would not tolerate any government in which the Workers' Party was not a leading element and that the consequences of the election of such a government would be the occupation of Poland by the Red Army.

The results of the Moscow conversations about the new Government became apparent when its composition was announced following the "free" elections of January 19, 1947. The Socialist Party gained in number of cabinet posts, retaining the premiership (which Osobka-Morawski yielded to Cyrankiewicz) and obtaining six ministries. The Workers' Party received only five cabinet posts, but among them was included that of Education in addition to the other key positions it had occupied in the Provisional Government of National Unity. Moreover, it succeeded in placing strong vice-ministers in most of the other ministries; some of these, in effect, preëmpted the authority of weak ministers appointed from smaller parties. In all, it had 17 vice-ministries in the new Government to 12 for the Socialists.

[3] *Robotnik*, Warsaw, November 29, 1946.
[4] *Glos Ludu*, Warsaw, January 5-6, 1947.

V

By removing Mikolajczyk from participation in the Government the elections of January 1947 returned the situation to something like that which had prevailed under the "Lublin coalition" before June 1945. The difference was that the Socialists, who in the Lublin days had had no popular support behind them, now led a mass working-class party with such influence in the trade-union and coöperative movements that they were even stronger, in terms of representation of that class, than the Communists.

The new Constituent Sejm (diet) passed an act on February 19 amending certain articles of the 1921 Constitution, as the new Government had been pledged to do. Thus amended, the old Constitution was to serve as the organic law of the state until the Sejm should elaborate a new one. The act represented a defeat for the Socialist Party, which had expressed its desire, in editorial comment following the election, for a "strong government and a strong Sejm." It favored separation of legislative and executive functions and a diet which would play a meaningful rôle. The Workers' Party, taking its cue from a statement of President Boleslaw Bierut shortly after the election, had espoused the necessity of "a new superior organ which would act under the direction of the President of the Republic" and would, in effect, be a continuation of the Presidium of the KRN, which had legislated largely by decree. The "new superior organ" instituted by the amended Constitution was the Council of State, a body corresponding to the Presidium of the Supreme Soviet of the U.S.S.R. The Sejm was reduced to little more than a rubber-stamp, with the function of approving decrees issued by the Council or passing into law bills submitted to it by that body.

The Socialists supported the "Little Constitution," as it was called, despite their desire for returning to real parliamentarism and ending the extraordinary powers of the secret police and the army. They had tied themselves too closely to the Communists to be able to break away on so fundamental an issue.

The friction between the two parties, which had subsided during the election campaign, now revived, and in February it became necessary to establish a system of "mediation commissions" between them.[5]

[5] *Glos Ludu,* February 13, 1947.

On May Day, the Communists issued a clear call for the merger of the two parties. Gomulka declared that the parties were "on the road to complete unity of the Polish working class." The Socialists were greatly disturbed. They felt that Gomulka's statement flouted the recognition given by the Communists, in the United-Front Agreement, of the "separateness and independence" of the Socialist Party. Szwalbe, in *Robotnik* for May 10, asked whether the Workers' Party contemplated turning Poland into a one-party state, and averred that organic unity of the two parties could not occur during the period of people's democracy but only when Poland was ready to enter the stage of Socialism. Answering him in *Glos Ludu* the next day, Roman Werfel, one of the chief Communist ideologists, said that his party had no desire to create a one-party state; that as long as different classes existed in Poland, they must each be represented by separate parties. He asked what class interests the Socialists represented in contradistinction to the Workers' Party, and vice versa. The answer, he said, was none. He pointed out that the two parties were separated, rather, by traditions, history and ideology. The task of the moment, he said, was to attain ideological unity, to which organic unity would be the logical consequence.

In this atmosphere the Socialists felt free to enter upon some substantive criticism of the Workers' Party's activities. Adam Kurylowicz, a prewar trade-union leader, protested against the action of "the clan of personnel managers" in ousting non-Communist executives and employees of nationalized industries on political grounds.[6] The Ministry of Industry, a Communist stronghold presided over by the Politburo member, Hilary Minc, issued a denial of the charge.

More fundamental matters came under fire in a polemic later in the month between Minc and the Socialists. On May 14, Minc attacked the Socialist views on how to combat inflation. In general, the Communists held that there was plenty of grain available domestically to supply the country's needs, but that strong measures, possibly even involving the use of the army, were needed to collect it. Specifically, they complained that the rural coöperative structure, operated by the Socialist-dominated *Spolem* system, was incompetent as a collecting agent; they proposed that a governmental organization be constructed alongside *Spolem,* and that most of *Spolem's* responsibilities be turned over to it. The Socialists, believing that the reason for the inflation was the understandable failure of war-ravaged Polish agriculture to produce enough

[6] *Robotnik,* May 7, 1947.

grain, objected strongly to this proposal; they saw in it a manifestation of the Communist desire to vitiate one of the two important Socialist links with the people.[7]

The upshot of the argument was that the Sejm passed the Workers' Party plan for combatting inflation, substantially as proposed. The Socialists, yielding to entreaties not to rupture the "united working-class front," supported the proposal and contented themselves with expressing reservations. It was at this point that Julian Hochfeld emerged as the chief Socialist leader opposed to the idea of merging the two parties. He voiced a strong warning in *Robotnik* that continued Communist criticism of the Socialist Party might result in the dissolution of the united front.

Socialist opposition to the Communist offensive crystallized at a meeting of local organizational delegates (the Chief Council) on June 30. Osobka-Morawski attempted to resign as Chairman of the Central Executive Committee and Hochfeld as President of its Sejm Deputies' Club, in protest against what they regarded as the weak position taken by the other Socialist leaders towards the Workers' Party. They were persuaded to retain their offices by the usual appeal to refrain from breaking the united front in the face of the danger of reaction.

VI

Acrimony had by this time reached such a point that the Communists felt the need of a new weapon to break the deadlock, and turned to the coercive tactic of the political trial. Their aim was twofold: to raise again their bogey of the "reversion to reaction" by showing the Socialist Party that its own ranks contained germs of a counter-revolution in those of its members who had formerly belonged to the WRN; and to intimidate the Socialist leaders by implying that they too might be stigmatized as "reactionary" if they resisted the demands for a merger— and, indeed, if they proved too obstinate, might be tried for "anti-state activity."

The first of the political trials was that of members of the WRN and of members of a nationalist underground organization called *Wolnosc i Niepodleglosc* ("Freedom and Independence"). The chief de-

---

[7] Time proved the Socialists to be right. Poland had to borrow 300,000 tons of grain from the U.S.S.R. at the end of the year, despite an all-out collection effort along the lines of the Communist proposal.

fendant was Galaj, who voiced a warning which played into the Communists' hands: "If the Socialist Party does not carry out a purge in good time, it will have unnecessary trouble." At another trial in Krakow the defendants were questioned in a way designed to elicit admissions that the underground had hoped to use rightist members of the Socialist Party as a base of political action against the Workers' Party. The climax of these tactics was reached in December. One of the defendants, Obarski, who had been secretary of the Socialist cell in the Ministry of Reconstruction, stated that after Zulawski's failure to obtain permission to organize a Social-Democratic Party the WRN had disbanded and its members had been instructed to join the "concessioned" Socialist Party. Obarski said, "There were no actual differences between the WRN and the Socialist Party." The threat to the Socialist Party implied by the introduction of such testimony was plain.

This sort of pressure soon produced tangible results in the political arena. At a joint meeting of the Socialist and Workers' Parties, held in Warsaw on July 26, Socialist leaders echoed the call of the Communist representatives for joint meetings throughout the country to organize mutual assistance in uncovering "reactionary and alien elements" in both parties and for "liquidating" all differences between the two parties through the mediation commissions. The watchword was, "The enemy is only on the right; the ally and friend is on the left." In the sequel, Socialist leaders toured the country, speaking at the joint meetings and exhorting their followers to maintain the united front and to coöperate more closely with the Communists. Many of the meetings were stormy; local Socialist members often rose to assert that such coöperation was a one-way street. But the leaders persevered in their campaign, and simultaneously they undertook a purge of ex-members of WRN and other "rightists."

In the final months of the year, the identification of the two parties seemed to be almost complete. Following the formation of the Cominform, the Central Executive Committee of the Socialist Party passed a resolution echoing the Communist line; and on the anniversary of the United-Front Agreement, Roman Zambrowski, Secretary of the Workers' Party Central Committee, again openly voiced the call for merger: "We know that the Central Executive Committee of the Socialist Party and the Central Committee of the Workers' Party, tracing the perspectives of organic unity in the Agreement, are proceeding with the deep faith that the valuable united-front experience and ideological rapproche-

ment are creating an ever more realistic perspective of the day when the
*Workers' Party and the Socialist Party, as separate and independent
Marxist parties, will multiply the strength of the working class a
hundredfold by creating one party of the working class of Poland."*
(Emphasis as in the original.) Cyrankiewicz, however, gave no indication that he considered any such unity to be in the offing. He rather
guardedly declared: "The year which has passed has not been wasted.
We shall shortly discuss the experiences of that period, all its lights
and shadows, and the problems of the next stage, at the Wroclaw
Congress. That Congress will decide upon the next step on the united-
front road of the reborn Socialist Party." [8]

After all the emphasis laid during the autumn on "ideological rapprochement" and "deepening coöperation" between the parties, the Socialist Party Congress which opened in Wroclaw on December 14
proved surprisingly unreceptive to the Communist demand for a merger.
This demand was voiced unequivocally by Gomulka, the Workers' Party
leader, on the opening day. "Our Party," he said, "represents the viewpoint that . . . a united front must lead to . . . establishment of one
working-class party. . . . We stand on the ground of accelerating this
process." Cyrankiewicz answered Gomulka by stating that the Socialists
had an international task to fulfill: to create a united front on an
international scale. The Polish Socialist Party, an old and respected
Socialist group, would serve as a link between the left-Socialism of
Western Europe and Communism. "By this method," he said, "we will
prove that the Socialist Party is, and will continue to be, necessary to
the Polish people." [9]

The central event of the Congress, however, came at the final session
when Julian Hochfeld presented a "Plan of Platform Principles." It
consisted of 1, a carefully worked-out analysis, along orthodox Marxist
lines, of the "present phase of imperialism"; and 2, a definition of the
part which the Socialist Party should play in this situation, at home
and abroad. The Plan applied the "third-force" theory to Polish politics and was one of the few creative Socialist theoretical formulations
to appear since the end of the war.

Hochfeld put forward certain conclusions. The masses had seized
power in Poland. While their power was being consolidated, and
while the framework of bourgeois liberalism was being smashed, a cer-

[8] *Glos Ludu,* November 29, 1947.
[9] *Glos Ludu,* December 15 and 16, 1947.

tain amount of dictatorship was inevitable. He implied that this transitional period would shortly end in Poland. Once it was over, the people's government must effect certain reforms. It would have to:

"Guarantee . . . the control and influence of the social factor . . . upon political and economic management;

"Guarantee . . . the possibility of liquidating dictatorial ways and means of wielding power;

"Ensure to citizens the right . . . to vote and run for central and local political representative bodies; ensure freedom of conscience, of convictions, of press and assembly and coalition;

"Create particularly favorable conditions for the development of self-governing organizations of the labor world (trade unions, coöperatives, etc.)."

Hochfeld postulated a justification for continuing a multi-party system throughout the period of people's democracy, and possibly (he was not clear on this) into the period of Socialism. For the traditional party function of representing classes he substituted that of exercising "mutual control" and being "guarantors of the free exchange of thought and opinion." He said: "Even in the course of the period of hard strife against the counter-revolution and external intervention, it is necessary . . . to widen and deepen . . . civil rights and liberties. . . . The scope of civil rights and liberties is of a distinctly functional character with relation to the prosperity and living standard of a nation."

The Congress referred Hochfeld's libertarian Marxist platform to a committee, which did not act upon it before adjournment. Thus the program evidently was put up by the leadership of the Party as a trial balloon. The Party as a whole was not committed.

The balloon was immediately riddled with Leninist-Stalinist slugs. Roman Werfel, editor of the Workers' Party ideological organ, *Nowe Drogi,* published a devastating analysis of it in the January issue. He dismissed Hochfeld's demand for civil liberties with a question—"Civil liberties in general, or freedom for the people's masses?" And he concluded by saying that he saw no reason why the merger of the two parties should be contingent upon victories of Communist-Socialist united fronts in the west, as Cyrankiewicz put it.

VII

The refusal of the Communists to accept the Hochfeld plan as a proper Socialist platform precipitated a crisis in the Socialist Party.

The Socialists had hoped to find an ideological ground for their contention that "the Socialist Party is necessary to the Polish people," and they had utterly failed; for a program unacceptable to the Workers' Party was presumed to be, *ipso facto,* unacceptable to the U.S.S.R.

On January 15, 1948, a governmental delegation, headed by Cyrankiewicz and including Gomulka and Minc, went to Moscow to negotiate a trade agreement with the Soviet Government. What Cyrankiewicz was told there is not known, but his action was decisive. At a meeting of the Warsaw Committee of the Socialist Party on March 17, he declared, in effect, that the Party was ready to merge with the Workers' Party. Once the decision had been taken, there was no longer any need for the Socialists to maintain their claim to need a separate existence because of their potential international influence. The Party withdrew from COMISCO on March 23.

The reaction of the Communists to the offer to merge was disappointing. Gomulka accepted Cyrankiewicz's offer in principle, but stipulated that the Socialist Party must first undertake an extensive cleansing of its ranks. There had developed, in fact, an anomalous situation. After having pressed so hard and so long for merger, the leaders of the Workers' Party now felt unable to accept the Socialist Party into full partnership until it had been radically purged and, consequently, weakened. The Communists were aware, moreover, that the leaders of the Socialist right-wing were just as anxious for merger as they themselves had been, and that they wanted it immediately. The reason was plain. The Socialist right hoped that if the merger could take place without delay they would be able to move into the united party "with all of their old ideological baggage," and that they could exert an influence on it even beyond what their relative numerical strength justified, by virtue of the fact that they commanded a larger number of trained and experienced political activists than the Workers' Party could muster. The Communists, of course, knew of this hope; and it precluded them from accepting Cyrankiewicz's offer until the right wing had been driven out of the Socialist Party from top to bottom. Thus an impasse was reached.

Both parties started purges, however, and combined to give "joint schooling courses" to their members. As a result, it was believed in June that the merger would take place at the end of September. But just at this point the blast of the Cominform resolution against the Jugoslav Communist Party, and the implications it carried for Communists in Poland blew this hope out the window. Gomulka, Secretary-General of the Workers' Party, held nationalist views similar to Tito's. Indeed, he had defended these views in the Cominform, and he continued to defend them in the Workers' Party. The Resolution of the Central Committee of the Party, which condemned Gomulka's deviationism and dismissed him from office, revealed incidentally that he had not been as averse to rapid merger as he had sounded in his answer to Cyrankiewicz. On the contrary, Gomulka had hoped to see the Socialists bring a sizable number of rightists and moderates into the united party. When his own position had been endangered by his "nationalist deviationism," he had resorted to "Bonapartism." He believed that if a mass party could be formed, in which the Socialists—traditionally "Polish first and Socialist second"—would amalgamate with the opportunists, band-wagon-hoppers and pseudo-Marxists of the Workers' Party, the nationalistic Polish Communism in which he believed would acquire such a strong base that it could not be overturned except by direct intervention by the Soviet Union.

Following the session of the Central Committee at which Gomulka was dismissed as Secretary-General, the Chief Council of the Socialist Party held a "purge session" (September 18-23). Here, further action was taken against rightists still holding seats in the Party's organs, and critiques of the "false course" of these party members were delivered by Cyrankiewicz and Matuszewski. The latter was a crypto-Communist who had been expelled from the Socialist Party in 1946 for advocating merger; he had been allowed to reënter the Party and had been elected to the Central Executive Committee in the summer of 1948. The Council adopted an ideological declaration which characterized many leaders, including Hochfeld and Szwalbe, as "revisionists." As *Robotnik* said, this meeting "did not take place in the traditional atmosphere of a love feast." As a result, Hochfeld recanted his heresy, the "theory of the golden mean," explaining that he did so not only because he "now recognized it as erroneous" but also because he was greatly afraid of one thing: "personal separation from the labor movement."

The Merger Congress met in Warsaw December 15-21. After the successive crises which had agitated the two parties during the year, it proved an anticlimax. The Socialist Party had lost its independent leadership, both national and local, in the purges. Those who had not been expelled were cowed. The Workers' Party, on the other hand, had not expelled any of its rightists and nationalists but had simply put them in cold storage, against a day when Moscow's orders might veer again to the right.

So as to take no chances, the Workers' Party had brought various Socialist leaders to trial just before the Merger Congress. Among them were the prewar Secretary-General of the Party, Kazimierz Puzak, and some of his fellow leaders in the WRN—Szturm de Sztrem, Dziegielewski, Krawczyk and others. The case against them was blatantly political. Krawczyk, for example, was questioned on his membership in a military detachment which had fought the Red Guards in the Dabrowan Basin in 1919-1920. The warning which the trial was meant to carry was not lost on the remaining Socialist leaders.

The new party was named the United Polish Workers' Party. Of course it is completely Communist-dominated. Of the Politburo's 11 members, for example, eight are Communists. The government was entirely reorganized and every significant office, with the exception of the premiership, was taken over by a Communist. On January 1, 1949, before the reorganization began, the Communists occupied 33 out of 60 governmental posts of the rank of vice-minister and higher; they now hold 53 out of 74.

VIII

The Socialist Party always stood for an essentially western solution of the "Polish problem." Its participation in the battle for Polish independence during the First World War in the Pilsudski Legions, and its subsequent rejection of the Bolshevism imported in the van of Tukhachevsky's Red Army, had long ago made it anathema to the Kremlin.

In the period between the two wars the Socialist Party expressed the conviction that German Nazism and Soviet Communism were equally enemies of Poland, and equally fatal to democratic Socialism.

In the Second World War, many of its members turned to fighting the Soviet occupying forces as soon as the German occupying forces were on the run. After the war, the rank and file kept their old convictions to a large extent, but the Party's leaders vacillated. Some of them were weak or naïve; others were opportunistic. The attempts of those who were sincere to create a Polish Socialism based on real democracy were confused and blundering. Their complete and final failure affirms once again that compromise with Stalinism is the end of freedom.

AMERICANS are accustomed to think that "war" is war and "peace" is peace; and even now, after years of cold and hot wars, it is difficult for them to conceive of the world as existing indefinitely in a state that is neither war nor peace. In the first half of the twentieth century Americans saw Europe plunged twice into great wars without believing at first that either of them would eventually involve Americans or that their outcome would be determined in large part by America's own contribution of blood and treasure. To many, World War I seemed a mere aberration. In any case, war was an unpleasant duty to be met manfully. And, once it had been won, it was something to be forgotten as quickly as possible; that is, as soon as a reasonable and durable settlement had been arranged so that people could return to "peace."

The European experience was not altogether dissimilar. Although wars had occurred and would probably occur in the future, Europe's peoples did not feel that they were living in a perpetual state of latent war. They assumed that wars were fought for limited purposes—for border territories, or for a higher rating in the scale of power—and that both the major states and a loose society of European nations would continue to exist after a war. True, World War I had taken on some of the characteristics of a total war, and by its conclusion several old states had disappeared and national or social revolutions had drastically reshaped the eastern half of the continent. It was Lenin and Hitler, however, who provided the neo-Hobbesian rationale for a type of war whose goal is total victory for some systems and total defeat for others.

The philosophy of Lenin and Stalin, and now of Khrushchev, rests primarily on Lenin's re-interpretation of Marxism, which explains all history, past and future (until the triumph of Communism), as a relentless struggle in which the complete victory of Communism is to be the preordained and righteous outcome. However, not only Marx but the very un-Marxian General Carl von Clausewitz had a profound impact on Lenin's thinking and, through him, on Soviet ideology and strategy. This essential but neglected strand in Leninism has been explored in "Clausewitz and Soviet Strategy" (October 1950), by Byron Dexter, a historian and essayist, who served for many years as Managing Editor of *Foreign Affairs*.

CLAUSEWITZ AND SOVIET STRATEGY

By Byron Dexter

THERE is in train today a development without parallel in history—a war which has as its frank objective the overthrow of all the parliamentary governments of the world and their replacement by Communist dictatorships centrally controlled in Moscow. The distinguishing characteristic of the campaign is the interchangeability of political and military weapons. A "peace offensive" in Moscow, a cultural conference in Warsaw, a strike in France, an armed insurrection in Czechoslovakia, the invasion of Greece and Korea by fully equipped troops—all are instruments of one war, turned on and turned off from a central tap as a gardener plays a hose up and down a piece of land on which he is nurturing a crop, watering some plants lightly, some heavily.

The theory of a "unified" war directed by a supreme central intelligence, in which political and military instruments are used indifferently to suit a particular object in the pursuit of a gigantic plan, was first and most comprehensively advanced by the German general, Carl von Clausewitz in his book, "On War," in the early nineteenth century. It is not surprising that in an effort to understand the current Soviet campaign and to find a means of thwarting it, Americans have turned to Clausewitz for such illumination as he may offer, and that references to his aphorisms on the relation of war and politics are everywhere heard.

The concept that underlies the whole of Clausewitz' discussion of the nature of war is, quite simply, that "war is an act of social life"—that is to say, that it is not an act performed by military men only, but is an expression of the conflict of ideas, objectives and way of life of an entire society with those of some other society. Conflict by high explosives is thus merely one aspect of a war, and is resorted to when and if it helps achieve some particular objective which cannot be achieved in any other way.

Clausewitz elaborated this idea at length, and expressed it in various

275

ways. In his best known passage he put it thus: "We see, therefore, in the first place, that under all circumstances War is to be regarded not as an independent thing, but as a political instrument; and it is only by taking this point of view that we can avoid finding ourselves in opposition to all military history. This is the only means of unlocking the great book and making it intelligible. Secondly, this view shows us how Wars must differ in character according to the nature of the motives and circumstances from which they proceed."

From this Clausewitz reasoned that, generally speaking, there are two kinds of wars—those in which the object is the overthrow of the enemy, and those in which the object is merely to make some conquests on the frontier of his country or to win booty of some kind and gain advantages in negotiations.

Obviously, this is a point of view, not a set of answers to concrete political and military questions, and there is room for much misunderstanding in these generalizations. "On War" is unfinished, an elaborate treatise on strategy and tactics written before the day of railroads or even of the rifled gun barrel, and largely out of date in its strictly military aspects. Though the work is full of sharp insight into the nature of war, expressed in many striking phrases, long stretches of the eight books which comprise it are dull reading today. It has never been published in full in the United States.[1] The upshot is that Clausewitz' ideas tend to be discussed in terms of famous quotations, all too often with little regard for the meaning he intended to convey. Thus one historian recently cited Clausewitz to prove that final decisions in war must be made on military grounds, though Clausewitz wrote the eight books of "On War" in order to prove the opposite. And, in what is surely one of the most remarkable feats of interpretation on record, Ellsworth L. Raymond quoted a passage from the work of the Soviet strategist Marshal Shaposhnikov, author of the book, "The Brain of the Army," which has exerted much influence upon the rulers of Russia, in order to show that "a revolutionary change" in military philosophy had turned the Soviet Union away from Clausewitz. The quoted passage was in fact a tissue of phrases from Clausewitz, including his premise that war is an act of social life. Rear Admiral Zacharias

---

[1] An excellent abridged edition was published in the Modern Library in 1943, now out of print. The work was first published in English in a translation by Colonel J. J. Graham in 1873 (London: Kegan Paul). Quotations in this paper are from the 1940 edition.

apparently took over Mr. Raymond's interpretation in his book, "Behind Closed Doors." The costly popular assumption that Soviet doctrine had separated "political" from "military" instruments of war and was depending solely on the political was a result of failure to estimate correctly Clausewitz' place in Soviet strategy.

Furthermore, since Clausewitz makes no attempt to distinguish between "right" and "wrong" in his study of war, his amoral tone, with its connotations of aggressive militarism, has understandably enough caused a great many people to dismiss his ideas out of hand, as the very embodiment of evil in modern times. And for the group of writers represented by the British military critic, Captain B. H. Liddell Hart, Clausewitz has come to typify the major obstacle to a program of "limiting" and humanizing war—a question which bears very importantly on aspects of United States policy.

Before attempting to pass judgment on Clausewitz, then, let us try to understand as clearly as possible what it was he really said, or intended to say; but let us also try to get our minds around it as it might seem from the angle of the Kremlin—that is to say, as it would seem today to a group of implacable men prosecuting a world-wide insurrection.

II

To say that Clausewitz' body of ideas provides the best description there is of the Soviet Russian method of making war is not to imply that the Soviet leaders adopted this objective, and developed the instrument of "unified" war for achieving it, because they had at some time read the book written by this German Major General. Nonetheless, we do know that the Russian Marxists have studied Clausewitz with care, and have appropriated his ideas, and even his actual words, very freely. Engels, Karl Marx's great collaborator—called "the general" by his associates—was a devoted student of Clausewitz. Lenin seems to have come upon Clausewitz' work about the time the First World War was beginning, and the notebook which he kept is evidence of the zest with which he devoured it. Long excerpts, stabbed with marginal notations and interlineations, are included alongside the extracts from Marx and Engels. The Soviet Government published Lenin's notebook on Clausewitz in 1933. It is interesting to see that though Lenin paid little or no attention to the military detail—the chapters on "Camps,"

"Marches," "Cantonments," etc., he paused at and copied the passages dealing with the need of boldness in war. Of the axiom about war as a continuation of policy he said: "The Marxists have always considered this axiom as the theoretical foundation for the meaning of every war."

But the most interesting and recent evidence of the significance which the Soviet strategists attach to Clausewitz today is the letter which Stalin wrote to the Soviet military historian, Colonel Razin, in 1946, in order to define the Communist line toward Clausewitz with unimpeachable authority. The letter was published in February 1947 in the magazine *Bolshevik*. Because of Stalin's peculiar talent for making plain things seem contradictory and confusing, while at the same time bringing to bear upon them a good deal of horse sense, it must be read in some detail to be understood:

Respected Comrade Razin!

I have received your letter of January 30th on Clausewitz and your brief theses on war and military art.

1. You are inquiring whether Lenin's propositions evaluating Clausewitz are obsolete?

In my opinion, the question is incorrectly formulated.

Under such a formulation of the question it is possible to think that Lenin analyzed Clausewitz' military doctrine and military works, gave them a military appraisal and left us a heritage of a set of guiding propositions on military problems, which we have to accept. Such a formulation of the question is incorrect for, in fact, there do not exist any such "propositions" by Lenin on Clausewitz' military doctrine and his works.

In distinction to Engels, Lenin did not consider himself an expert in military matters. . . . During the civil war, Lenin had obliged us, then young comrades in the Central Committee, "to thoroughly master the knowledge of military art." As for himself, he frankly declared to us that it was too late for him to study military art. In this lies the proper explanation of the fact that in his references to Clausewitz and remarks on Clausewitz' books, Lenin did not touch upon the strictly military problems, such as the problem of military strategy and tactics, and of the inter-relationship between advance and retreat, defense and counteroffensive, etc., etc.

What did interest Lenin in Clausewitz, then, and what did he praise him for?

He praised Clausewitz first of all, because, as a non-Marxist, Clausewitz, who enjoyed the reputation of an expert on military art in his time, had confirmed in his works the familiar Marxist thesis that there is a direct connection between war and politics, that politics gives birth to war, that war is the continuation of politics by violent means. The reference to Clausewitz was necessary for Lenin in this connection in order once more to convict Plekhanov, Kautsky and others of social-chauvinism, of social-imperialism.

Further, he praised Clausewitz for confirming in his works the thesis, which is correct from the Marxist viewpoint, that under certain unfavorable circumstances the retreat is as appropriate a form of strife as the advance. Lenin needed the reference to Clausewitz here in order once more to refute the "left" Communists, who did not recognize retreat as a legitimate form of struggle.

Consequently, Lenin approached Clausewitz' works not as a military man, but as a politician, and was interested in those problems in Clausewitz' works which demonstrated the connection between war and politics.

Thus, in the question of criticism of Clausewitz' military doctrine, we, Lenin's heirs, are not bound by instructions from Lenin limiting our freedom of criticism. . . .

2. Should we criticize Clausewitz' military doctrine in accordance with its substance? Yes, we should. From the viewpoint of our interests and of those of military science of our time, we are obliged to criticize not only Clausewitz, but also Moltke, Schlieffen, Ludendorff, Keitel and other bearers of military ideology in Germany. . . .

What must be noted in particular about Clausewitz is that he is, of course, obsolete as a military authority. Strictly speaking, Clausewitz was the representative of the hand-tool period of warfare. But we are now in the *machine* age of warfare. The machine age undoubtedly demands new military ideologists. It is ridiculous to take lessons from Clausewitz now. . . .

In our criticism we must be guided not by separate propositions and utterances of the classics, but by the famous instruction which Lenin gave us in his time:

"We do not regard Marx's theory as something completed and untouchable; we are convinced, on the contrary, that it has merely laid the cornerstone of that science, which Socialists *must* move further in all directions, unless they want to be left behind by life. . . ."

This approach is even more obligatory for us with respect to the military authorities.

3. Because of the schematic character of your brief theses on war and military art, I am able to offer only some general remarks. The theses contain too much philosophy and too many abstract propositions. Clausewitz' terminology for the grammar and logic of war grates on the ear. The problem of the party aspects of military science is put too primitively. Dithyrambs in Stalin's honor grate on the ear—it is simply awkward to read them. Consideration of the *counteroffensive* (not to be confused with the

counterattack) is absent. I am speaking of the counteroffensive after a successful enemy advance which, however, failed to yield decisive results, during which the party on the defensive collects forces, launches a counteradvance and inflicts upon the antagonist a decisive defeat. I think that a well-organized counteroffensive is one of the most interesting forms of offensive. As an historian, you should take an interest in this. . . .

J. Stalin

February 23, 1946.

Obviously there is a good deal of counterpoint in this composition, but the major theme is sounded at the beginning. Stalin carefully reformulates the question that has been put to him—whether Lenin's propositions evaluating Clausewitz are obsolete—in order to distinguish between Clausewitz' "strictly military" doctrines and his view of the relation of war and policy. The latter is thus saved from attack. Though Stalin probably underestimates Lenin's knowledge of military problems, he is quite right in saying that, as we have noted, Lenin paid no attention to the chapters of "On War" dealing with strictly military matters. Stalin's references to the " 'left' Communists who did not recognize retreat as a legitimate form of struggle" is, apparently, a shot at Trotsky, and an unjust one; and Stalin's blunderbuss attack on German military science, which brings down Moltke, Schlieffen, Ludendorff and Keitel in one bag, is also rather unreal. (Schlieffen is distinguished among these generals precisely for his disregard of Clausewitz' doctrine; and Keitel's relationship with Hitler is still another story.) But we need not follow those involutions of Stalin's thought. It is plain that Stalin has chosen to emphasize three things about von Clausewitz: 1, that his strictly military precepts are out of date; 2, that his theory of the relation of war and policy is relevant and important; and 3, that his views on the counteroffensive are worth special attention. No better estimate of the timeliness of "On War" could be made. Let us, therefore, examine these particular aspects of Clausewitz' work which Stalin recommends to our attention.

III

To see Clausewitz as he was, it is necessary to see him against the background of his own time. Despite the associations that cluster about his name, he is not an unattractive figure. Carl von Clausewitz was of Polish descent, from a family in East Silesia. His father was a doctor, and an officer in the army of Frederick the Great. His patent of nobility, by which he was enabled to hold a commission in the Prussian Army, was of doubtful validity; Clausewitz never felt that he was one of the Prussian Junkers, nor did they. His portrait, drawn in his thirties apparently, shows a man with a sensitive, open face and a mass of curly hair—with features rather resembling the poet Shelley. He is far from being Shelley—but he is also quite unlike the conventional figure of the bullet-headed German general.

He was born in 1780, and entered the Prussian Army as a cadet at the age of 12. He fought in the wars of the monarchical coalition against France, and then the Napoleonic Wars, and was wounded and captured. His quickness and intelligence caught the attention of General Scharnhorst, and after 1807 he was closely associated with Scharnhorst and Field Marshal Gneisenau in the effort of reform of the Prussian Army which followed the cataclysmic defeat of Prussia at Napoleon's hands on the battlefield of Jena.

Gneisenau and Scharnhorst (neither of them Prussians, incidentally) were men of vision, and they perceived that a revitalized Prussian Army could be created only on the basis of a revitalized nation. With the collaboration of the statesman, Baron Stein, they sought to bring the Prussian peasant out of his feudal condition and to introduce some degree of self-government in the Prussian state. They succeeded partially, but their effort at reform was overtaken by the reaction which followed the downfall of Napoleon. General von Clausewitz, their protégé, fell under the suspicion and, in fact, the open enmity which the Prussian nobility entertained for these reformers. When he was appointed director of the Prussian War School in Berlin in 1818, through the interposition of Gneisenau, the hostility of the nobility was too strong to permit him to carry out the changes in curriculum which he envisaged. He was not permitted even to lecture. Like not a few famous writers, he took to the pen because all other activity was closed to him. It was at this period that he wrote "On War." He died suddenly, of cholera, in 1831 and the book, much of which he considered only an outline of the volume he intended to write, was prepared for publication by his wife.

"On War" is a work of genius. The wonder is not that it has infusions of dialectic, but that, considering the scope of the subject which it undertakes to treat, it is so unpedantic and sensible. Some of the detail that seems wearisome today was, indeed, inserted reluctantly by von

Clausewitz in order to dispose of the intricate ratiocinations of the
eighteenth century military writers, who had reduced warfare to a
geometrical science—so they thought—and developed a marvelous jargon for elucidating its mysteries. (In pursuit of the concept of the "key
position" of Europe, for example, supposedly the highest source of its
waters, one strategist had found himself ensconced triumphantly on
the tallest peak of the Swiss Alps with his troops—fortunately creatures
of paper and ink only. "In general," said Clausewitz dryly, "the best
key to the country lies in the enemy's Army.") And he apologized for
the unspectacular nature of his own demonstration: "The reader expects
to hear of angles and lines, and finds instead of these citizens of the
scientific world, only people out of common life, such as he meets with
every day in the streets."

That is the measure of the originality of his book. "On War" deals
with human beings. It is the first study of modern war in which the factor
which we know by the term "morale" is held to be almost everywhere
decisive.

Clausewitz addresses himself to those who are, or who intend to be,
the commanders; and he will permit them to set for themselves nothing
but the highest standards. He is dealing with war, and he does not
paint a pleasant picture. "It is the whole feeling of the dissolution of all
physical and moral power, it is the heart-rending sight of the bloody
sacrifice which the Commander has to contend with in himself, and then
in all others who directly or indirectly transfer to him their impressions,
feelings, anxieties and desires," he says. But what makes this self-command possible, he continues, is, simply—intelligence: "This counterpoise
[to the "excited passions"] is nothing but a sense of the dignity of man,
that noblest pride, that deeply-seated desire of the soul always to act
as a being endowed with understanding and reason." This is not
rhetoric; Clausewitz develops the theme with insight into the strengths
and weaknesses of men. "Men who have little intelligence can never be
resolute," he repeats. "There is nothing more common than to hear of
men losing their energy on being raised to a higher position, to which
they do not feel themselves equal; but we must also remind ourselves
that we are speaking of preeminent services." He was looking for greatness.

It is for this reason that he emphasizes the importance of theory. He
puts it thus: "In real action, most men are guided merely by the tact
of judgment which hits the object more or less accurately, according as

they possess more or less genius. This is the way in which all great Generals have acted, and therein partly lay their greatness and their genius, that they always hit upon what was right by this tact. Thus also it will always be in action, and so far this tact is amply sufficient. But when it is a question, not of acting oneself, but of convincing others in a consultation, then all depends on clear conceptions and demonstrations of inherent relations." In short, if you want other men to take over your ideas, you have to have an intelligible theory.

Many misunderstandings of Clausewitz stem from a failure to note the method by which he develops his argument. His procedure is, first, to trace the lines of the "absolute"—by which he means the abstract— concept of whatever aspect of strategy he is considering; then to show how, in practice, things are likely to be different from this abstract picture of them; and then to return to the theoretical perfection to see what lessons it offers for improving practice. Thus *in theory,* says Clausewitz in Book VIII—"Plan of War," which is the heart of his doctrine—war is an unceasing act of "utmost violence," which starts in full fury, rages without pause in a series of increasingly desperate combats, until it comes to the climax, which is the annihilation of the enemy. But, *in fact,* once the "probabilities of real life" take the place of abstractions, the act of war is different. There is in actual warfare little direct movement to the goal, and there is usually a vast confusion of purposes. "The normal act of war is doing nothing"; and, moreover, there are wars of all degree of importance and energy, from "wars of extermination" down to the use of an army merely for intimidation.

Obviously, something intervenes to alter the "absolute" picture of war. Clausewitz points out that in practice two factors thus intervene. On the battlefield there is "friction"—the word he gives to rain, snow, mud, fatigue, timidity, false reports—everything that goes wrong. But, more importantly, there is politics. Clausewitz never uses the term "politics" in the sense in which it is common in Anglo-Saxon countries, with the invidious connotations of patronage, pull, "ward politics." The political element for him is the purposive element—human reason as contrasted with blind, brute rage. Politics thus is responsible for the cross purposes, the clash of plans, the inefficiency, the uncertainty of aim. It is likewise responsible for whatever intelligence there is in war.

Clausewitz points out that except among complete savages, war can never be an act of utter senselessness. The object of war remains combat: "the bloody solution of the crisis, the effort for the destruction of the enemy's force, is the firstborn son of War." But it is also true that: "If we speak of the destruction of the enemy's armed force, we must expressly point out that nothing obliges us to confine this idea to the mere physical force; on the contrary, the moral is necessarily implied as well, because both in fact are interwoven with each other, even in the most minute details, and cannot be separated." In short, the distinguishing characteristic of a "perfect" war would be that both political and military means were used harmoniously for the accomplishment of one, great, clear plan. In order that they may be so used, the political must predominate. Policy uses war. That is Clausewitz' principal contention. He concludes thus:

If War belongs to policy, it will naturally take its character from thence. If policy is great and powerful so also will be the War, and this may be carried to the point at which War attains to its absolute form.

It is only through this kind of view that War recovers unity; only by it can we see all Wars as things of one kind and only thus can we attain the true and perfect basis and point of view from which great plans may be traced out and determined upon.

There is upon the whole nothing more important in life than to find out the right point of view from which things should be looked at and judged of and then to keep to that point, for we can only apprehend the mass of events in the unity from *one* standpoint, and it is only the keeping to one point of view that guards us from inconsistency.

These are passages copied and underscored by Lenin, to whose mind they were congenial.

Lenin underscored, too, the passage in which Clausewitz summed up his argument: "War is to be regarded as an organic whole, from which the single branches are not to be separated and in which therefore every individual activity flows into the whole." Or, as we might say— hot or cold, it is still one war.

IV

What shall we say of this doctrine? How shall we criticize it?

It is apparent that the search for the perfect war is a dangerous ideal. Clausewitz was not seeking to glorify war, and long before Tolstoy or Shaw had debunked war he derided the popular notion that the symbol of the battlefield is a hussar at full gallop brandishing a sword over his head. "Usually before we have learnt what danger really is, we form an idea of it which is rather attractive than repulsive," he remarked caustically. But for all his good sense, he was, at the end, carried away by the enchantment of his own investigation—the possibility of finding the man who could make war in fact as perfect an instrument for the realization of state purposes as it can be shown to be in theory. Book VIII—"Plan of War"—is the clearest directive ever written for the waging of aggressive war. It is not surprising that, for Clausewitz, only one man had succeeded in laying hands on this shining instrument—Napoleon, "the very god of war," as he called him. Nor is it surprising that in the nineteenth century Clausewitz' greatest disciple became Bismarck, and in the twentieth, the leaders of the three Great Power dictatorships which have destroyed the peace of the world—the Imperial Japanese, the Nazi German and the Communist Russian. What is perhaps astonishing is the candor with which the Soviet weekly journal *New Times* for December 21, 1949, celebrating the 70th birthday of Marshal Stalin with an article "Stalin's Military Genius," by Major General F. Isayev, uses as the yardstick for measuring Stalin's military achievements the very criteria which Clausewitz in "Plan of War" employed to exalt the genius of Napoleon.

General Isayev's remarkable encomium repays examination in more detail; but first, let us note that the distinction between the two kinds of war, on which Clausewitz laid so much emphasis—"absolute" war which seeks the overthrow of the enemy, and "limited" war, which seeks to use an army to win booty or concessions of some kind—has tended to disappear in our time. But it has done so precisely because, as Clausewitz insists, war *is* an act of social life—and because, as a result of the technological developments of the past 50 years or so, society has now come to be world-wide. Clausewitz never foresaw the industrialization of society, or guessed the degree of bitterness and horror with which this would endow the act of war. There are, indeed, "small" wars even now which do not become world-wide, as we have seen and no doubt always shall see; but no one dares draw an easy breath until they have been terminated. Unpalatable though the idea may be, Clausewitz' premise remains irrefutable. For 1950 even more plainly than for 1812, the recognition that war is a social act is the key that unlocks the great book and makes it intelligible. The scope of the political objective is the measure of the scope of a war. "If policy is great and powerful, so also will be the War."

In the shadow of the Soviet world insurrection, some who are very sincere, and some who are not, suggest that the nations of the world can at least mitigate these dangers by an agreement to return to "limited" warfare, following the precedents of the eighteenth century. No one will deny that of all the wars in history, the "languid and parsimonious" wars of the eighteenth century are the least repellent. But the problem for democratic nations is not merely how to obtain from the Politburo an agreement that will be kept; the problem of reverting to an eighteenth century kind of war is the problem of reverting to an eighteenth century kind of society.

We may note in this connection that Clausewitz' patron, Field Marshal Gneisenau, served as a young officer with the German mercenaries in the American War for Independence, and was deeply impressed by the contrast between the "open order" combat of the Americans and the "line" of the German and British troops. The seed of Clausewitz' concept of war as a social act lies in the contrast. The Americans fought from behind trees and stone walls, not because they held a particular political theory, but because that was the most effective tactic for untrained soldiers and skilled marksmen in such country; but the use of such tactics nonetheless was a direct expression of their own social order. They were able to adopt them because they were fighting of their own volition, for their own farms and their own country—in their eyes one and the same thing. The Hessians could not adopt such tactics for the simple reason that if the soldiers were once permitted to disperse they would never come together again.

At this time, European armies were still organized on the principles of Frederick the Great, whose armies were composed of mercenaries, serfs or vagabonds. Frederick was capable of inspiring devotion and great feats of endurance from his men, yet the primary fact of the army organization was that the soldiers would instantly desert if they got the chance; forage parties could never be allowed, for example, and night encampments were never made near a wood. Discipline was ruthless and terrible (Frederick's officers were instructed to make the troops fear the "corporal's cane" more than the guns of the enemy) and when these troops lined up, elbow to elbow, for volley firing, an officer or non-commissioned officer stood one pace behind them, instructed to plunge his sword or bayonet into the back of any man who stepped from line. Eighteenth century war "by code" was an expression of an hierarchial, pastoral society, plus an exact but momentary balance of power in Europe which prevented any one nation from pushing its conquests beyond a certain point. To talk of limiting war in this way in 1950 is to play with abstractions. The concept of limited war has meaning only for the aggressor, who of course would prefer to destroy his victims one by one. The present threat to civilization does not lie in the nature of the atom, but in the nature of Communist policy.

In a passage of Book VI, "Strategic Defense," Clausewitz discussed the paradoxical fact that fighting between armies does not begin until the country which is attacked resists the invader. He wrote acidly: "A conqueror is always a lover of peace (as Bonaparte always asserted of himself); he would like to make his entry into our state unopposed." Lenin had copied this in his notebook, and beside it put the delighted notation: "Ah! Ah! Witty!" It is significant to note that in his interview with H. G. Wells in 1934, Stalin remarked that "Communists do not in the least idealize methods of violence. . . . They would be very pleased to drop violent methods if the ruling class agreed to give way to the working class." Like many another humorist, Marshal Stalin was borrowing his joke. Clausewitz, however, was less cynical than the instigator of the Korean invasion and the Stockholm "peace petition." Is it not precisely because of this final irony by which, under the law of the jungle, the victim will be punished for resisting, that civilized society has no choice but to insist that the use of aggressive war as an instrument of policy is a crime?

V

The second aspect of Clausewitz' thought that Marshal Stalin recommended to our attention is his study of the counteroffensive. In the concrete illustrations for the argument of "On War," Clausewitz ranges widely, but his major sources of examples are two—the wars of Frederick the Great and the wars of Napoleon; and of them all, the Russian campaign of 1812 (in which Clausewitz fought as one of the "free German" corps on the Russian side) is the most often and most importantly cited. "On War" is the great, doctrinal expression of that triumph of Russian arms.

Marshal Stalin is not unaware that his own strategy in the defense of Russia against German attack, at Moscow and at Stalingrad, has already become a classic instance of the validity of Clausewitz' principles of the counteroffensive—in brief, to trade space for time, to raise new armies, to enlist the people against the invader in guerrilla warfare, to recognize the culminating point of the enemy's advance, and then to advance against him. Clausewitz thought of the defensive not as a passive method of resisting the enemy but as an active strategy for destroying him, and so the Soviet command employed it.

In Major General Isayev's article on the occasion of Stalin's 70th birthday last December, Clausewitz' name nowhere appears; nor does Shaposhnikov's. The Russian leaders are not in a mood for passing credit around (one reason, among others, for Stalin's circumlocutions in the letter to Colonel Razin). But we may note that in the chapter of Book VIII which he called "Interdependence of the Parts in War," Clausewitz spelled out his prescription for the waging of an "absolute" war (*i.e.,* one that is theoretically perfect) in the following particulars:

1. At the commencement of every war its character and main outline shall be defined according to what the political conditions and relations lead us to anticipate as probable.

2. The whole series of combats must follow one another in rapid and mounting succession.

3. The Commander should have clearly in view "the object to which every line must converge."

4. The Commander must possess the art of selecting from among an infinite multitude of objects and relations the "center of gravity" of the enemy's strength, *i.e.,* whether it be the enemy's army, his capital, "the unity of interests" (as in a confederacy), public opinion (in an insurrection), etc. The genius of the Commander lies in his ability to locate this center of gravity and direct his blows against it.

5. "If the enemy loses his balance, no time must be allowed for him to recover it. There must be a continued and irresistible following up of victory."

For Clausewitz, only Napoleon possessed the genius for carrying on war in this way: "We might doubt whether our notion of its [*i.e.,* war's] absolute character or nature was founded in reality, if we had not seen real warfare make its appearance in this absolute completeness just in our own times," he says. "After a short introduction performed by the French Revolution, the impetuous Bonaparte quickly brought it to this point. Under him it was carried on without slackening for a moment until the enemy was prostrated, and the counter stroke followed almost with as little remission."

In his article, "Stalin's Military Genius," General Isayev takes as his premise the interdependence of political and military (in accordance, of course, with Marxist dialectics no less than with Clausewitz): "Unity of political and military strategy is one of the most characteristic features of J. V. Stalin, both as a great statesman and a great leader of armies. In Comrade Stalin alone does modern history see for the first time a great leader who combines the genius of a statesman and military leader of the new type." More concretely, in his view, Stalin's leadership is marked by the following characteristics:

1. His farsightedness and breadth of vision in planning the war as a whole. ("How far into the future peered the eagle gaze of our great leader.")

2. His ability to deal the enemy blows of *"mounting force."*

3. His elaboration of a "new type of strategy, which supplanted the old and obsolete linear strategy."

4. The use of surprise against the enemy.

5. The use of the method of active defense in depth, while at the same time mobilizing the main forces, thus enabling Russian armies to pass to the counteroffensive.

6. Above all, the ability to choose the right direction for the main blow. "The unsurpassed faculty displayed by Comrade Stalin both in the Civil War and the Great Patriotic War of properly selecting the direction for the main strategic blow is the basic characteristic of the Stalin school of military leadership."

Whether General Isayev had actually looked up Clausewitz' "Plan of War," in his desire to place Comrade Stalin's military accomplishments in as magnificent a frame as possible, and deliberately modeled his composition upon it, or whether he drew on Shaposhnikov or on some other Soviet writer who had borrowed from Clausewitz, we need not try to guess. The evidence of Soviet enchantment with the Napoleonic lineaments in the 33rd year of the Bolshevik Revolution is all the more revealing if unwittingly offered.

It seems evident that Soviet strategic thought has hardened into a pattern. In the official view, the Soviet Union is the one nation in the world, led by the unique military genius of modern times, which has succeeded in turning what it professes to believe is an invasion-proof defensive position into an irresistible weapon of attack. It alone possesses a strategy of a new type, in which the entire economic, moral and military potential of the nation is enlisted for the attainment of a clear and overriding goal. "The Anglo-American warmongers are plotting a new world war with the aim of establishing their supremacy over the whole world," concludes General Isayev. "But their strategy is as defective as was the strategy of the German-Fascist invaders. The time has long passed when the leaders of the bourgeois armies could contribute anything new and progressive in the sphere of strategy. They cannot, because their aims in war run counter to the development of human society."

If there is no hope of persuading the rulers of the Soviet Union to change their minds, then at least there is stimulus for our own thinking in knowing the outline of the early nineteenth century doctrine which governs their strategy.

ONE of the basic instruments of totalitarian power is the centralized control and direction of information, science, art and literature. In depicting an ideal state to be ruled by philosophers, Plato emphasized the importance of images and myths as a means of molding the emotional and rational natures of its subjects into a harmonious and stable whole. Modern totalitarianism, in its emphasis upon relentless struggle in the present toward a conflictless Utopia to be attained in the future, claims and exercises, so far as it can, a monopoly in the market place of ideas. The writing and rewriting of history to justify their monopoly of power and to promote the achievement of their goals has, logically enough, been a constant preoccupation of modern totalitarian rulers. It is "not accidental," as Soviet Russian jargon puts it, that Stalin eventually claimed authorship of the "History of the Communist Party of the Soviet Union (Bolsheviks)," thus establishing himself as the sole authorized historian of the Party and its régime. All historians were required to bring their factual findings and conclusions into harmony with those of "the great teacher." Since Stalin's death the Party's history has been revamped in many respects, again primarily to serve the interests of the new dictator in establishing his own legitimate succession to Lenin's heritage.

"Operation Rewrite: The Agony of Soviet Historians" (October 1952) examines with erudition and irony some of the contortions that have been inflicted on Soviet writers of history by the changing demands of the leader. Bertram D. Wolfe is a talented historian and publicist. "Three Who Made a Revolution" (1948) is an exacting and exciting account of Lenin, Trotsky and Stalin in the two decades that preceded the revolutions of 1917. The author's earlier experiences in the Communist Party of the U.S.A. and at Comintern headquarters in Moscow have given him an authentic appreciation of the factors that shaped the revolutionary forces and the leaders of the Soviet régime; deep political and intellectual convictions, arrived at over the years, have added to his work the indispensable element of historical perspective. The author of many books and articles on Soviet affairs and on Latin America, Mr. Wolfe has also been a Guggenheim Fellow and a Senior Fellow of the Hoover Institution at Stanford and of the Russian Institute at Columbia.

OPERATION REWRITE
THE AGONY OF SOVIET HISTORIANS

By Bertram D. Wolfe

FOR over two decades, Soviet historiography has been in steadily deepening crisis. Histories succeed each other as if they were being consumed by a giant chain smoker who lights the first volume of the new work with the last of the old. Historians appear, disappear and re-appear; others vanish without a trace.

Originally, only Party history was subject to rigid prescription. Then Soviet history was added. Latterly, the area of command performance and commanded conclusions has spread outward to America and Asia and the wastes of Antarctica, backward to the Middle Ages, to Byzantium, to the shadowy origins of the Slavs and the pre-dawn of the Kievan state, to China's earliest culture. One day a given statement of events or interpretation is obligatory. The next it is condemned in words which seem to portend the doom of the historian who faithfully carried out his instructions. If it is a pronouncement of Stalin which he is following, all the more severely must he condemn himself—of course, without involving the Leader in his "self-criticism."

Often the central personages of an event become *unpersons,* as if they had never existed. The Civil War must now be rewritten as if there never had been a War Commissar named Leon Trotsky. The Soviet theatre, once the subject of so many histories, is historyless once more, until somebody contrives to write a new version without a trace of the great innovator-director, Vsevolod Meierhold. On February 15, 1951, *Pravda* accomplished the feat of "commemorating" the tenth anniversary of the Eighteenth Party Conference, in which Voznesensky delivered the main report, without so much as mentioning the name of the reporter!

Today the Balkarians are missing from Volume "B" of the new edition of the "Great Encyclopedia"; the Volga Germans have become an *unpeople;* and the Crimean Tartars, having been expelled from their centuries-old home to a region under the Arctic Circle, have had the place names of their former habitations extirpated, and are now being subjected to the shrinking of their historical rôle in the Crimea to the point where they are gradually becoming an *unpeople,* too.[1]

During the past spring even objects began to become *unobjects,* as *Pravda* and the regional press from February to May reported a grim and thoroughgoing purge of scores of local and national museums all the way from Lithuania to Kazakhstan. The Lithuanian museums were rebuked for failing to show the influence of Great Russian culture and the struggles and longings of their peoples for the extinction of their independence, while the Kazakh museums were condemned for the nostalgic splendor of their daggers, guns, harnesses, bridal costumes, and for failing to display any objects showing Great Russia's civilizing influence and the "progressive" character of her annexation of Kazakhstan.

It would require many volumes to give an account of this continual retroactive rewriting of history. The present article aims to give some notion of the scope of this vast *operation palimpsest,* to seek the "line," or rather some of the fragmentary and frequently contradictory lines, discernible in the revisions; to seek the reasons, or a rationale, for what seems to contain an element of the personal and irrational as well; and to ask what these tamperings with the historical record portend concerning the present and immediate future intentions of the régime. History has become a "weapon," an arm of propaganda, the essential function of which is the justification of the changing policies of the Soviet Government through reference to the "facts" and "documents" of the past. The penchant for making every change in foreign relations or domestic policy historically retroactive serves as a vast though distorting glass through which the observer may see these policy changes magnified. It is that which makes *Voprosy istorii* (*Questions of History*) undoubtedly the most interesting and revealing of all present-day Soviet publications.

Macaulay once said that his idea of hell would be to have to listen to fiends endlessly misquoting history and be unable to correct them. But in the Soviet Union, the historian himself must do the misquoting. His own point of view is neither consulted, nor, except by the accident of coincidence with the line of the moment, ever likely to find expression. The textbook writers and lecturers under the limited absolutism of the

[1] *Cf. Pravda* and *Izvestia,* June 4, 1952.

last Tsars could easily be identified as liberal and democratic, as in the
case of a Platonov, or as conservative and monarchical, as in the case of
an Ilovaisky, or as Marxist, as in the case of a Pokrovsky. But under
total state absolutism, history, as all of culture, has been "nationalized"
and there are no individual viewpoints or private judgments or pluralis-
tic approaches. Tarlé, specialist on Napoleon, is ordered to rewrite
his principal work in such fashion as to "prove" that Napoleon himself
burned Moscow (no doubt to make it untenable as his winter quarters!).
The liberal-democratic Vipper, who first wrote on Ivan the Terrible
in the early years of the century, is charged with bringing his book of
1922 "up-to-date" and glorifying the protagonist.

From my experience as a student at Moscow University in 1939-41
[writes S. V. Utechin] I know that the late Professors K. V. Bazilevich
and S. V. Bakhrushkin held a negative attitude towards the present régime.
Yet in their volumes we find no traces of views different from those professed by Stalin. Thus the personal political opinions of the authors do not
necessarily coincide with, and may even be contrary to, the views expressed in their books. These reflect not their political biases . . . but their
understanding of the party line.[2]

As the great editing process embraces more and more of the remote
corners of the earth and earliest past, there are no longer safe and
neutral topics. Nor does the historian enjoy the right to pick his period
and theme, nor the right of silence where he cannot in good conscience
speak. As in music the politician-critic or the Supreme Critic in the
Politburo tells the composers what and how and in what style to compose, so in history. *Voprosy istorii* bristles with menacing strictures
upon historians for picking remote, neutral, sharply delimited or apoliti-
cal subjects; for neglecting fields which have been given priority in
Party directives and the Historical Plan, for drawing their own conclusions or failing to find in the materials the conclusions predeter-
mined for them.

It is suggestive both of the hazards in the field and the real feelings
of the historians that, despite urgings, dangled prizes and repeated
threats, no one has yet been found to complete a single volume or a
single serious article in the field of the history of the Party and the
régime, though Stalin himself first suggested it in 1931, has ordered
it at regular intervals since, and forced it into the place of top priority

[2] S. V. Utechin, "Textbooks on History. Soviet Studies," Vol. iv, No. 1.

in the Five-Year Plan for Soviet Historians adopted in 1946. Fifteen years after the task was first assigned by the Dictator, the lead editorial in *Voprosy istorii* (No. 8, 1949) warned that the failure to produce the ordered works creates a "completely impermissible situation" which "it would be completely wrong to look for objective circumstances to explain." This stubborn silence, continuing up to the moment in which I write, constitutes the most eloquent page in present-day Soviet historiography.

II

In the twenties, not a politician but a professional Marxist historian, M. N. Pokrovsky, was the virtual dictator in Soviet historiography. He represented a consistent general line ("history is politics projected into the past") and made life difficult for fellow historians who did not accept it. But he held to professional standards, had regard for documents and evidence, though at times he wrestled mightily with them to compel them to yield what he sought. And as a historian he had enormous prestige, which was further enhanced by Lenin's preface to his "Short History of Russia," praising it warmly and insisting that it become a textbook and be translated into other European languages.

But in 1931 his excessive respect for the facts of Party history came under Stalin's personal scrutiny. In 1934 he was posthumously purged— he had the luck to die in time—along with all his works and disciples. At about the same time, Ryazanov, Russia's outstanding Marxicologist, whose headstrong, self-directed devotion to Marxist documentary scholarship closely resembled Pokrovsky's attitude toward history, suffered a similar posthumous fate.

Pokrovsky was accused of being anti-national and anti-patriotic (he shared Lenin's internationalism and disliked Tsarist wars); of neglecting actual events, dates, facts, periods and personages in favor of generalized sociological schemata (until then considered a hallmark of Marxist historical interpretation); of being "anti-scientific" and "anti-Marxist"; of "underestimating" Lenin (he wrote: "Whenever Lenin differs from me I blindly accept his view; he can see ten feet deeper into the earth than any of the rest of us"); and of underestimating Stalin (which was undoubtedly true and the immediate though not the only explanation of his downfall).

At first it seemed to historians that a new line might emerge which would put pluses where he had minuses, and offer them considerably more freedom for examination of sources without regard to Marxist interpretive schemata. But alas, life was not to be that simple. Though Pokrovsky had been condemned for neglect of concrete historical facts, ere long *Voprosy istorii* (No. 12, 1948) was to give warning that "the proper historian" must be free from "objectivism" and from "an exaggerated attachment to facts," and at home in the citation and application of the "theoretical generalizations" and dictates of the Party line. Now it was not a single, simplicist, recognizable line like Pokrovsky's, but a continuous bombardment by *ad hoc* fragments of lines, changing with each political shift or change in mood, frequently internally contradictory, constantly being altered and even suddenly reversed.

Apparently these fragments issue from Stalin's latest pronouncement or some earlier one exhumed from context after four decades, or from the quotations from Lenin or Marx or Engels which adorn their promulgation. But study of such texts will not help the historian, nor is there any real defense in an umbrella of quotations, for in any vast and historically evolved sacred scripture you can find quotations for any side of anything. To quote yesterday's Stalin may today be "talmudism and scholasticism." The historian must divine the Dictator's coming pronouncement, for his latest word is always the last word in history even though Marx, Engels, Lenin and yesterday's Stalin all be united against it. A sudden reversal in Stalin's relations with Germany or England or America is pushed backward retroactively so that the present enemy is absolute evil, and though yesterday an ally, must always have been an enemy. All books, articles and documents that testify to the contrary must be consigned to the Orwellian "memory hole" to be consumed in flames, or must be "rectified" and brought up to date without any mention of the fact that there was ever an earlier version.

Not only changes in relationships, strategy and tactics, even changes in the Dictator's awareness of the nature of his own régime, or his subjective identification with some deed of a figure of the past, say an Ivan IV or a Marshal Kutuzov, can require a complete retroactive revision of the figure thus honored. Such revaluations cannot be deduced by the historian from a study of sources, but only by sensing the reactions of the Dictator whose attitude toward history has been summed up by Orwell in the formula: "Who controls the present, controls the past."

III

Stalin first entered historiography through the field of personal and Party history. In January 1924, one week after the death of Lenin, he chose the occasion of a Memorial Address to predate by some four years the beginning of their personal acquaintance.[3] At the time it might have seemed merely a faintly ghoulish example of the natural human inclination to reshape the past nearer to the heart's desire. But when one remembers that Lenin had just called for the removal of Stalin as General Secretary, and when one contemplates the subsequent revisions that carried Stalin from "loyal disciple" to "best disciple" and then "only loyal disciple," and on to "faithful companion-in-arms" (*soratnik*) and "wise guide and counsellor" and more than equal partner, one cannot but be struck by the meticulous attention to detail and long-range planning implied in this first little retouching of history.

A Napoleon, a Trotsky, a Thucydides, a Xenophon or a Josephus may wait to turn his energies into the writing of history until defeat has deprived him of the opportunity of making it. But Stalin engaged in writing history as one of the means by which he climbed to power. That explains the ruthless political utilitarianism, the pugnacious factionalism or *partiinost* which he has impressed upon it. That is why first "rotten liberalism" and then "objectivism" were to become the gravest of historiographical crimes. History was one of the "weapons" with which he fought his way to power, and he enlarged the scope of his revisions with every increase in the actual power drawn into his hands.

There was much to revise. First there was that personal symbol of the Revolution and the régime: the duality-unity, *Lenin-Trotsky*. Mountains of books, newspapers, pamphlets, decrees and documents had to be consigned to the "memory hole," mashed to pulp, or brought out in "corrected" editions, in order to substitute for *Lenin-Trotsky* a new duality-unity, *Lenin-Stalin*.

Then there were the other close associates of Lenin, glorified as "Old Bolshevism" in the struggle with Trotsky, and then themselves destroyed. To obscure all traces of their actual deeds and substitute nameless and monstrous evils that would justify their murder is another task that Stalinist historiography has never ceased to concern itself with.

[3] For the evidence, see the writer's "Three Who Made a Revolution." New York: The Dial Press, 1948, p. 424-7.

With notable impartiality Stalin has barred foreign and domestic accounts, pre-Stalinist Bolshevik histories, Stalinist histories written to order by Knorin, Popov and Yaroslavsky, the footnotes to the Second and Third Editions of Lenin's "Works," the "Great Encyclopedia," and all the telltale passages in the letters, writings and speeches of Lenin, and of Stalin himself. There is a mass of Lenin-Trotsky correspondence at Harvard that can never be published in the Soviet Union. There is Lenin's "Testament." Typical of Stalin's self-censorship is his omission from his "Collected Works" of his tribute to Trotsky published in *Pravda* of November 6, 1918, on the occasion of the first anniversary of the Bolshevik Revolution.

For the foreign observer, the most important document that Stalin has omitted from the corresponding volume of his "Works" is a letter he wrote Lenin in 1920, criticizing the latter's "Theses on the National and Colonial Question" because they failed to provide an intermediate or transitional form for the annexation of new Soviet states, like a "Soviet Germany, Hungary, Poland, Rumania," which have never formed part of the old Tsarist Empire and therefore may object to immediate incorporation in the Soviet Union. This early foreshadowing of the future "People's Democracies" can be found, however, as a footnote to Lenin's "Theses" in the Second and Third Russian Editions of his "Works," Vol. XXV, p. 624.

The present writer was in Moscow during the first six months of 1929, when on central command every periodical and paper in the Soviet Union broke out with a picture of Stalin on the front page. This was the beginning of the Stalin cult. At first it seemed to me wholly "rational." Having just eliminated Bukharin, the last of the close comrades of Lenin, Stalin had now to become "Old Bolshevism." But a number of circumstances have since caused me to conclude that there is an irrational element also.

First, there was the fury of the purges, with the arrest, execution or reduction to unskilled slave labor of millions: the neutral, the indifferent, the innocent, the loyal, including entire technical, bureaucratic and military layers desperately needed for the enhancement of the very power of the state. It may be urged that such random terror was "needed" on the principle: "If you want to make your enemies afraid, begin by cutting off the heads of your friends." And that total state power in a populous state can spend a few million lives on the process of completely atomizing society so that every particularized atom depends absolutely on the state and no man can depend upon any other. Still, it is hard to believe that so many millions were required, or that the state had so greatly to weaken itself technically in the process.

Second, there is the insatiable and unappeasable appetite of the dictator for the enlargement of the incense, the trembling obedience, the worship, to the point where he is now the "Coryphaeus" of all the arts and sciences (history of course among them), and is increasingly being endowed with the attributes of a living god.

Third, there was the unexpected discovery while going through the pages of *Zhizn natsionalnostei* (*Life of the Nationalities*—Stalin's personal organ when he was Commissar of Nationalities) that Stalin had retroactively inserted two minor "prophecies" into one of his articles when he included it in his "Collected Works." And more startling still, the discovery of an item headed, "Greetings to Comrade Stalin," with the following (slightly abbreviated) text:

The Conference of National Sections . . . sends you its greetings and declares its conviction that by following firmly along the path pointed out by you for the solution of the national question . . . we will create throughout the world a united, brotherly Communist family which we will teach to appreciate those great merits which belong to you—the leader of the oppressed peoples.

Here is the beginning of that *potok privetstvii* (flood of greetings) which has filled the columns of all the Soviet papers and journals for these many years. But the date was December 24, 1920! Lenin was still alive and in leadership, and, by general consent, it was Lenin who had pointed out the solution of the national question and who was the leader of the oppressed peoples of the world. Stalin was still outranked by five or six of Lenin's associates and had neither expropriated their deeds, nor executed them. Thus the craving for flattery and the need that "the world appreciate his great merits" preceded by almost a decade the "rational" motivation of the Stalin cult.

In 1931 Stalin issued his first public directive on the spirit of the new historiography, in the form of an angry open letter to the editors of *Proletarskaya Revolyutsia* (*Proletarian Revolution*) charging them with "rotten liberalism" for having printed a "discussion article" on the problem of why Lenin had continued to admire Kautsky and the Orthodox-Marxist majority of the German Social Democracy until he was shocked by their stand on the war of 1914. *Bolshevik* (No. 22, 1931) published Stalin's Open Letter with its own appropriate editorial gloss, headed: "Give the Study of the History of Our Party a Scientific Bolshevik Footing!" All the earlier histories, from Shlyapnikov's to Yaroslavsky's and Popov's, were attacked. "There must be a thorough housecleaning in all book, textbook and journalistic literature dealing with the history of the Party. . . . The ruthless struggle against every manifestation of rotten liberalism must be intensified. . . . The significance of Stalin's letter far transcends the gateposts of history. . . ."

The Dictator next turned his attention to a close supervision of a new history of the Civil War which was to eliminate all trace of Trotsky—except as a secret agent of the other side. Then he began to dictate all the details of the now renowned "History of the Communist Party: Short Course." On January 20, 1946, *Pravda* reported that Stalin was himself the author of this strange work of historical falsification, endless self-quotation and self-glorification, and that it would appear as Volume XV of his "Collected Works."

But even Stalin's mighty name has not protected the "Short Course" from the ravages of retroactive obsolescence. Thus the first edition had substituted for a number of *unpersons* the new chief purger, Yezhov, as the "preparer of an uprising of the soldiers on the Western Front in Byelorussia." [4] It soon developed that Yezhov was only 16 at the time, and, moreover, that the chief purger must himself be purged. Stalin's "Short Course" keeps appearing in revised editions as the greatest, dullest and most mendacious best seller in the history of literature. But he himself has streamlined the Great October Revolution further and further, until the latest version to appear, in the Chronology in the back of the corresponding volume of his own "Collected Works," actually reads:

Oct. 24 (Nov. 6, New Style)—Lenin arrives at Smolny in the evening. Stalin briefs him on the course of political events.
Oct. 24-25—Lenin and Stalin lead the October uprising.

Whether it be wholly "rational" in terms of the rationale of the total state and the absolute ruler, or whether there be also an irrational element, it should be clear that we are dealing with the most striking example in all history of a man who has succeeded in inventing himself. It takes total organization and total power—not propaganda skill, but the union of pen and sword in a single hand—to do so complete a job.

[4] New York: International Publishers, 1939, p. 206.

Once the total state has concentrated in its control not only all the means of production of material but no less of spiritual goods—all the modes of expression, communication, criticism, thought, feeling, all cheers and boos, all love and hate, all paper, ink, type, loudspeakers, microphones, cameras, cinemas, montage and cutting rooms, theatres, walls, schools, churches, streetcorners, all books, magazines, newspapers, leaflets, caricatures, pulpits, chairs, lecterns, meeting halls, all import and export of and traffic in ideas—it becomes possible to reshape the public past nearer to the heart's desire. Having worked so efficiently in personal and Party history, this spirit and method were now applied to general historiography.

IV

Since the beginning of the thirties, Stalin's policies have determined with steadily increasing rigor and detail the character of Soviet historiography. His letter of 1931 on "rotten liberalism," his brief dogmatic remarks of 1934 on what a Soviet history text and a modern history text should be; the successive liquidations of the two professional journals that preceded *Voprosy istorii;* the spiritual trauma of the purges—all serve as urgent reminders to the historian that "Stalin is the Creator of Soviet Historical Science" (title of article in No. 2, 1949). Yet, if we except his "History of the Communist Party," all his historical writings, directives and overworked *obiter dicta* which are supposed to serve as guides to historiography would not together make a single chapter. How, then, does the Soviet historian divine what is expected of him? And how shall the observer deduce from the twists and turns of the historiographical line what the real policies and intentions of the Kremlin are?

An especially revealing moment for the examining of these questions is the end of World War II. Dictatorship thrives on war, and total dictatorship thrives on total war on two fronts: against its own people and against the outside world. Hitherto it had offered three justifications for the cruelty, ubiquity and perpetual strain: 1, it was necessary to crush the enemy within; 2, to protect the land of Socialism from a completely hostile world; 3, and it was justified by the fact that it was already producing an incomparably more glorious life than that beyond its borders. Now all three justifications were suddenly called in question, and the régime was faced with an acute, all-embracing crisis:

(1) The internal enemy had been officially liquidated some time ago, in the late thirties, when it was proclaimed that classes had been abolished, that Socialism had been achieved, that every one loved the Government and the Leader. The "Stalinist Constitution" was supposed to have institutionalized this new state of affairs.

(2) The theory that the Soviet Union was surrounded by a completely hostile world in which it could find neither friends nor allies but only enemies collapsed the day Hitler attacked and—perhaps contrary to Hitler's expectation and Stalin's—Churchill and Roosevelt called upon their peoples to give unstinting support to the Soviet Union. The Soviet people noted with warmth that they had friends and allies. They heard Stalin himself, on the anniversary of the October Revolution in 1941, proclaim that "England and the United States of America possess elementary democratic liberties . . . trade unions . . . parties . . . parliaments." They saw that the Kremlin was summoning them not to defend the dictatorship but the Fatherland and democratic freedoms. Confidently they looked forward to the dawn of a new day in return for their unstinting sacrifices.

(3) As in 1813, once more the many-peopled Russian armies entered the outside world, and felt its impact. The whole fictional world of evil and misery without, and of superiority and perfection within, fell to pieces. Either the dictatorship had to relax, or new enemies and new superiorities had to be synthetically created.

Out of this crisis came Stalin's address to his electors on the inseparability of war and capitalism and the need to continue the strain-and-storm tempo to prepare for future wars; Zhdanov's attacks on the permeation of the "world's most advanced" music, painting, literature and philosophy by "servility to everything foreign," "rootless cosmopolitanism," "kowtowing to the West," lack of *partiinost* and *ideinost* (party spirit and high level of ideas, literally *party-ness* and *idea-ness*) ; the "revival" of the Comintern; the rejection of Marshall Plan aid by Molotov who, while his régime hesitated, took 89 advisers to Paris, in the end only to advise him on how to say *niet*.

In June 1945, exactly one month after V.E. Day, *Istoricheskii zhurnal* (meaning, simply enough, *Historical Journal*), which had naturally been edited in the spirit of the Grand Alliance, was informed that it had been unequal to its tasks, had lowered the level of historical scholarship, and was forthwith liquidated in favor of a new journal to be called *Voprosy istorii,* or *Questions of History.* The "questions"

or "problems" it has had to handle were those of this spiritual recon-
version and rearmament.

V

The first problem was to make the Soviet people forget their most
recent and greatest experience. They must forget, or press down into
the unverbalized, unthought, unfelt unconscious, the memory of the
fact that their Leader had joined in a pact with Hitler, which touched
off the war. Since the *Vozhd* had made one of the greatest mistakes
in history, the extravagant cult of his infallibility and wisdom must now
reach new and unheard-of heights. The memory of lend-lease, the memory of the titanic joint effort and the embrace on the Elbe, of England's
valiant holding out alone during the period of the Stalin-Hitler pact—
so many memories had to be forgotten, or rather, transformed into their
opposites.

A sample will serve. The collective history text on the "History of
the U.S.S.R.," edited by Pankratova, in its 1945 edition quotes Joseph
Stalin on the Normandy landing:

A brilliant achievement. . . . The history of war knows no other enterprise like it for breadth of purpose, grandiose skill, and masterful execution.

One year later the book had been replaced by a new edition in which
the passage reads: "On June 6, 1944, Allied forces accomplished a landing in Northern France."

And the latest approved history text, that of textbook prize-winner,
Shestakov, describes the Normandy landing in these terms:

England and the United States, in the course of three years of war,
dragged out in every way the opening of a second front. . . . But when,
after the gigantic victories of the Soviet Army, it became clear that the
Soviet Union might alone defeat the enemy, occupy the territory of Germany and liberate all Western Europe, including France . . . in June
1944, the English and American armies left England and landed on the
coast of Northern France.[5]

Every such revision of history has its *resonance effect,* spilling over
into a score of unexpected places, reverberating backward into the past,
so that the enemy of the moment must always have been the enemy. Espe-

[5] Moscow: 1951, p. 277-8.

cially must the high points of alliance and friendship be turned into sinister and hateful acts. And every such revision is the product of *multiple determination*. Thus the Russia-won-the-war-alone-against-a-Hitler-Anglo-American-Imperialist-conspiracy version of World War II inevitably reverberated into the hate-America campaign. But the latter campaign had many additional causes and implications.

It was the United States that had contributed the greatest help and evoked the greatest warmth. It represented the greatest power. Its productivity was the envy and admiration of the materialistic, technocratic official culture. Its conduct in the Philippines and Latin America, above all in war-ruined Europe (like that of Great Britain in India) was the startling refutation of the Lenin-Stalin dogmas of "monopoly capitalist imperialism" and of "capitalist encirclement." And the living refutation, no less, of the dogma that total statism was the most productive system. America represented the possibility of social reform without revolution ("reformism"), a land of plenty and freedom, visibly achieving an expanding economy and an ever greater measure of social justice and labor-farmer welfare, without the liquidation of entire classes.

The war ended with the Soviet Union as the only Great Power astride the Eurasian land mass, with a power vacuum to the west, and a power vacuum to the east of it. The United States represented the only possible obstacle to the rapid expansion of the Soviet Empire into both vacuums. America sought to restore a balance of power by restoring Europe, and —a little more hesitantly and uncertainly—by reconstructing and restoring a free Asia. Not only was its postwar use of its unprecedented power a reproach and a refutation. Increasingly, it was the main obstacle to the march of Soviet power to world conquest, as America moved from the blind illusions of the Grand Alliance to the sadder and wiser policy of "containment"; from containment to "defense of the free world from positions of strength"; and then to collective defense of Korea as a victim of aggression. The Truman Doctrine stood between the Soviet Union and the Dardanelles; the Marshall Plan and the North Atlantic Pact blocked the road to Western Europe; American troops formed the backbone of the United Nations armies holding the narrow waist of Korea.

The slow development of America's postwar policies began to inspire hope in all those who dreamed of ultimate liberation. It offered refuge (a little too niggardly) to escaping fighters for freedom. And when it

decided that it would not be a party to the forced repatriation of those
who had escaped or been taken prisoner, it adopted—almost unwittingly—a policy which makes the Soviet armies and all auxiliary armies
potentially unreliable. In this writer's judgment, the decision not to return the Chinese and North Korean prisoners by force will prove to
be the turning point in the great conflict between slavery and freedom.

All of these elements, and others like them, enter into the calculations of the Stalin régime, but none of them can be so much as mentioned in overt expression. The vocabulary of *newspeak* and the "re-
searches" and "documentation" of Soviet historians must be employed
to make each of these look like its opposite, and to envelop the whole
concept of America in hatred. It is sufficient to look at the list of books
that are praised and awarded Stalin prizes, to see the volume and the
titles of the articles in *Voprosy istorii,* or to note that the articles vilify-
ing the United States are criticized only because they do not go far
enough.

If it were an individual instead of the head of a great state and its
passive members that were making these statements, ranging from assertions regarding bacteriological warfare to those about castration
of colored peoples, we would regard it as pure pathology: loss of
memory of recent events, loss of the reality principle, persecutory de-
lusions. But there is "method in his madness," as proved by the fact
that while Stalin's Ministry of Hate is filling all the earth with its
roars, his Ministry of Love is cooing in a tiny whisper in the Moscow
News . . . in English.

VI

No field of historiography is now exempt from this inexorable process
of retroactive reëditing. The early Middle Ages must be revised to
predate by three or four centuries the origins of a high Great Russian
culture and of a centralized state. The Varangian theory has to be rejected, not on the basis of the evidence, but because it implies that the
Great Russians did not know how to set up a powerful centralized state
of their own, except by conquest from without. The new total state is
very sensitive about this matter of a "centralized, powerful state." That
which the democratic and earlier Marxist historians regarded as oppressive has now become "progressive." It is no longer permitted to
suggest that this great state arose in the course of the defense of the

Eurasian plain against outside invasion, nor that bondage in its wide and sparsely settled lands arose through political imposition, so that the recruiting sergeant and tax collector might know where to find the peasant. Ivan the Terrible must become a progressive and heroic tsar because he enlarged the Russian lands, strove to take the Baltic, set up the *Oprichnina* which Stalin recognizes as an analogue of the G.P.U., purged his opponents and even faithful servitors and son in ways which in his heart Stalin also recognizes, and because he completed the centralization of the state and the absolute power of its ruler.

Soviet Byzantine scholarship has to break with Western, in order to refute the idea that the declining Empire was "rigid, static and obscurantist," in order to show that the countries of southeast Europe, "which have embarked on the path of the People's Democracies," had an early, "progressive and original culture." Soviet historians must discover "the influence of the Slavs on the history of Byzantium." They must "expose" the Ottoman conquest of Byzantium in 1453 and show that "the Turkish assimilators are the most brutal of all assimilators who tortured and maimed the Balkan nations for hundreds of years." Indeed, "the very fact that the 1953 Congress of Byzantine scholars (on the 500th anniversary of 1453) is being held in the capital of Marshallized Turkey" is evidence enough that it will serve "American imperialist and Pan-Turkish aims." After all, Istanbul is but another name for Constantinople, and that for Byzantium, always the Tsargrad of imperial dreams, and the gateway, to boot, to the Mediterranean and the Near East for the Stalinist Empire.

If Turkey or Iran is slated as victim of the next forward move in the Near East, then Lenin's friendship with the new Turkey and denunciation of Tsarist aspirations in Iran must be buried seven fathoms under the ground. The influence of the high Iranian civilization upon the Tadjiks must be denied, or, as has actually been done, reversed. So must the influence of the Turks upon the Turkic peoples of the Soviet Union. Only Great Russian influence remains, even if it has to be invented. Adding to the multiple determination of the process, there is the restlessness of these Soviet Iranian and Turkic Mohammedan peoples, the growth of their national feelings, the specter of Pan-Turanianism and Pan-Iranianism as possible counterfoils to Pan-Slavism.

The history of the Balkans and other "People's Democracies" is also being rewritten in the Soviet Historical Section of the Academy of Sciences, and particularly in the Slavic Studies Section. Bulgaria is getting a new look. Non-Slavic Albania has "longed for centuries for liberation from the Turkish yoke and has long sought the friendship which now binds it to the Soviet peoples." Rumania's animus toward old Russia is being retroactively transformed, and her language being considered for honorary Slavic citizenship. Tito has become the eternal traitor, and in 1941 was simultaneously serving Hitler and the Anglo-American imperialists.

Two successive editings of Czechoslovak history have been scrapped, and the third, only a year old, is already under fire. The Polish historians are in continuous torment. Poland's culture must of course be decisively influenced by the Great Russian, but not by Rome or the West, while all trace of Polish influence upon Great Russian culture is being deleted or equipped with a minus sign. "The task of scientific history is to relate events truthfully," the Poles are admonished by *Voprosy istorii* (Nov. 4, 1949) "and to show that the responsibility for the policy of hostility toward Russia in the past rests not with the Polish people but with the governing classes." In all the partitions, the Russian share of Poland was justified.

To the "memory hole" have been consigned all the works of Marx and Engels on the menace of Russian absolutism, imperial expansion, Pan-Slavism, in favor of the restoration of Poland "with the boundaries of 1772," in favor of Shamil and Georgian independence. After 15 years of suppression, Stalin published his secret attack of 1934 on Engels' article "On Russian Foreign Policy." But Marxism is still needed as an ostensibly invariant philosophy to refer to in vindicating changing policies, so for the most part this censorship proceeds in absolute silence. With the retroactive purging of Ryazanov, no Marxist scholar dares continue the publication of these articles in the *Gesamtausgabe*.[6]

In 1934 Stalin could still rebuke a textbook for failing to brand "the annexationist-colonializing rôle of Tsarism . . . the Prison-House of Peoples"; its "counter-revolutionary rôle in foreign policy . . . as the international gendarme"; and for failing to show the influence of Western thought upon the democratic and Socialist revolutionary movements in Russia. To quote the 1934 Stalin in Russia in 1952 would be to take one's life into one's hands.

---

[6] This autumn these suppressed writings will furnish material for a book, edited by Blackstock and Hoselitz, entitled "The Russian Menace to Europe: A Collection of Articles, Speeches, Letters and News Dispatches by Karl Marx and Friedrich Engels."

Now Great Russian nationalism is inextricably blended with "Soviet patriotism." Internationalism is for use abroad, and is defined by Stalin as "unconditional loyalty to the Soviet Union." At home it is "cosmopolitanism" and "servility to all things foreign." Nationalism of any other variety than Great Russian is "bourgeois nationalism" and is fatal. A Sosyura may not "love the Ukraine" except he remember to love above all its yearning for annexation and the Great Russian imprint upon its culture. With each revision, the Balkan states move longingly another step toward incorporation.

Each of the "autonomous republics" is rewriting its history, revising its poetry, remaking its memories. Heroes become anti-heroes (Shamil, Kennessary); insurrections against tsarism until yesterday celebrated are today execrated; epics become anti-epics ("Dede Korkut") or the versions that have lived so long in oral tradition and are the very national memory of illiterate peoples are purged and reissued in "new authentic texts."

The expurgation of the epic ["Manas"] should be strictly scientific and principled. It should take into account all the historical circumstances in the life of the people. This demands a suitable selection of variants, songs and episodes, a selection of which the fundamental principle must be the preservation in the epic of all the best elements inherent in the past of the Kirgiz people.[7]

Even so did Orwell picture a functionary in his Ministry of Truth whose task was to "produce garbled versions—definitive texts they were called—of poems which had become ideologically offensive but which, for one reason or another, were to be retained in the anthologies."

Thus the great operation rewrite which began with Stalin's obliteration of his contemporary political and personal history and the invention of a new past for himself has spread outward through the boundaries of the Old Russian and the New Soviet Empires, and backward to the beginning of recorded time. The process is vast and all-embracing, even as the total state is total. But the immediate aims are simple enough:

To strengthen the power of the state over the minds of men and make it ever more complete and absolute.

To enlarge the power of the Leader and the cult of his infallibility and grandeur by identifying him with every mighty tsar and military leader, with every hero of thought and deed, with the deepest historical

[7] *Literaturnaya Gazeta,* May 27, 1952, p. 2.

memories of the people over whom he rules, for his omniscience, omnipotence, omnicompetence and infallibility are the very fulcrum of all the levers of totalitarian organization and power.

To destroy the critical sense, the historical perspective, the possibility of objective check or comparison from outside the system.

To "justify" the global ambitions and "demonstrate" the inevitable global triumph of the total state régime as well as its inexorably intensifying total organization within its own borders and its empire.

To strengthen its centralization by the increasing Russification and Stalinization of the "autonomous" units of the "federation" and the "sovereign People's Democracies" of the empire.

To root out all memories of comradeship with recent allies and as far as possible all friendliness and all common human fellow-feeling for the peoples who have been selected as the next victims and for those selected as the long-range enemy.

To counteract the war-weariness and the weariness with the unending internal war on the part of a people who have been kept unremittingly on the stretch for over a third of a century.

To provide, in the form of a synthetic national glory and glory of the state and system, *ersatz* satisfactions as a substitute for any real fulfillment of the revolution's promises.

To close the eyes of Soviet citizens and conquered subject peoples to the shabby and cruel realities that the régime inflicts upon them and to close their ears to the peaceful, friendly and attractive message of the outside, non-totalitarian world.

To prepare the next steps in the long-range aim: the total conquest of the world.

By an examination of each sudden historical revision or reversal one can deduce what the next tactical objectives of the Kremlin are, even though not the tempo of its moves—for into the actual moves themselves enter other calculations of power and of relations of forces that reside in the non-totalitarian world.

We can, however, deduce from the spirit and sweep of the new Soviet historiography that there will be no relaxation in the cold and not-so-cold war of the total state on its own people, on its neighbors, and on all the peoples of the earth. The unending war of nerves of which the rewriting of all history is a significant segment grows sharper not gentler, more reckless not more cautious, more inclusive not less.

As long as all the more spacious cities of the world have not been reduced to slums and rubble, Stalin's 1947 address proclaiming the 800-year-old Moscow the only city of the world free of slums is in danger of objective refutation. As long as anywhere in the world there is more freedom, more happiness, more comradeship and love, or simply a higher standard of living and higher productive power, Stalin cannot make good his boast that the Soviet system and way of life are superior.

Indeed, as long as anywhere in the world there is a lone surviving copy of any document which he has consigned to the "memory hole," or a single historian writing and pursuing research in freedom from the "guidance and control" of the total state, there is always the danger that world history, Russian history, Soviet history, Party history and the personal history of Joseph Stalin may once more be reconstructed, and that History itself, embodiment of the human memory and consciousness of self, may revive out of the ashes of its works.

Part IV

KHRUSHCHEV'S RUSSIA:
OLD GOALS, NEW METHODS

Since 1953

"THE Progress of Soviet Science" (April 1954), by John Turkevich, appeared in *Foreign Affairs* at a time when few Americans, including few American scientists, were paying much if any attention to the colossal efforts that Soviet scientists and the Soviet government had long been making to establish their country as a leading scientific power in the world. Indeed, since launching their first sputniks in 1957 the Soviet leaders have made vast propaganda gains in many countries by their loud trumpeting of Russia's impressive achievements in the fields of nuclear physics and space technology.

Before 1957 most Americans complacently assumed that there was a complete incompatibility between dictatorship and scientific progress that would keep Soviet science limping in perpetuity behind the advances of the West. Since then an exaggerated tribute has been paid to the alleged superiority of Soviet science and Soviet education. Often Soviet educators are far more critical of their own system of identifying, training and advancing young talents than are some of the commentators in the West. "The Progress of Soviet Science" stands out even today as a deeply informed and judicious appraisal of the strengths and weaknesses of science in the Soviet Union.

John Turkevich, who has taught and done research in chemistry at Princeton since 1936, is also deeply grounded in mathematics, physics and biology and has received numerous scientific distinctions. In World War II he served in the Manhattan Project, and he has been a frequent consultant to the Atomic Energy Commission, the Brookhaven National Laboratory and the National Science Foundation. He was a member of the U.S. Delegation to the Geneva Conference on Peaceful Uses of Atomic Energy in 1955, and he served as Minister Counsellor for Scientific Affairs in the U.S. Embassy at Moscow in 1961. Long before there was any sustained public or university support for the comprehensive appraisal of Soviet scientific research, Professor Turkevich, with the assistance of Mrs. Turkevich, had been conducting on his own a systematic survey and abstracting service in order to overcome the great lag in American efforts to keep abreast in this crucial area of knowledge and power.

THE PROGRESS OF SOVIET SCIENCE

By John Turkevich

SINCE the beginning of the nineteenth century science and technology have been playing a greater and greater rôle in shaping the lives of individuals, communities and nations. This has been true particularly in the West, where economic, social and political institutions and customs have been largely transformed by technological advances based on scientific accomplishments. Economic, social, political and spiritual values all still play their independent parts in creating the pattern of modern civilization. Nevertheless, running through nearly all of the complex mechanism of modern living are strands of technological advance which run back to the knot of some major scientific discovery. It is only reasonable to assume that this process will continue. If so, our ways of living and the direction of world affairs 10 to 20 years from now will be materially affected by what is being done or not done in the industrial development and engineering laboratories at the present time. Similarly the shapes of things a half-century hence will depend a great deal on what is going on in the pure science research laboratories now.

All these truisms about science and technology in the West apply to the Soviet Union. Perhaps they have not applied for quite so long a time, but there can be no doubt that the powerful Soviet state confronting the world today is based on substantial accomplishments by Soviet scientists and educators as well as on effective performance by Soviet engineers and technologists. Beyond this, it is clear that the future balance of world power will depend to a considerable extent on Soviet success or lack of success in the international race for scientific knowledge and technological achievement. Knowledge of the main features of Soviet science—its traditions, ideology, organization and personnel— may therefore enable us to assess some of the accomplishments of Soviet science and its hopes for the future.

Science was introduced into Russia by Peter the Great. Impressed by scientific demonstrations on his Western travels, he brought back

313

to St. Petersburg a number of scientific curios and sketched a plan for the organization of science. In 1725, a year after his death, his successor, Catherine I, founded the Imperial Academy of Sciences. It consisted of a group of scholars, a scientific museum and a secondary school. The scientists themselves had to be imported from the West, since Russia at that time had none. They were well chosen; among them were the Swiss, Leonhardt Euler, one of the greatest mathematicians of all time, and several of the Bernoulli family, internationally known scientists, along with others of less illustrious name. When a sufficient group of native scholars had been trained, a reaction against their foreign teachers developed under the leadership of the genius of eighteenth century Russian culture, Michael Lomonosov.

The development of science in the latter half of the eighteenth century and in the nineteenth century did not produce a large number of outstanding Russian scholars. Yet the names of Mendeleev (the discoverer of the periodic system of chemical elements), Lobachevski (the founder of the non-Euclidean geometry), and Pavlov (the formulator of the concept of the conditioned reflex) are now part of the world's cultural heritage. There were others, such as the physicists Jacobi, Lenz and Lebedev; the mathematicians Kovalevski, Chebyshev, Liapunov, Markov; the chemists, Markovnikov, Butlerov, Menshutkin, Beilstein, Chugaev, Reformatski; the biologists Kovalevski, Vinogradski, Pavlovski, Mechnikov, and Bekhterev, whose discoveries helped in the development of some aspect of science and whose work is valued by specialists in their fields.

The many Russian inventories of that period whose "discoveries" recently have been publicized by the Soviet Government were mostly so localized that they not only did not affect the development of Russian technology but were not heard of in the West. The language barrier, ever present in the relationship of Russia with the West, helped to keep the latter ignorant of the work of these Russians. The Soviet régime, however, while doing its best to keep the cultural barrier between East and West, is very sensitive about the reputations of these "inventors" and points with exaggerated national pride to such discoveries as that of the steam engine by Palzunov, the electric arc for illumination by Yablochkov, the incandescent lamp by Lodigin and the radio by Popov.

Although these men had little influence on Russian scientific development, the twentieth century opened with a good deal of promise. There was a respectable though small Imperial Academy of Sciences, and several active universities (St. Petersburg, Moscow, Kiev and Kazan) where scientific teaching and research were going on in a manner not inferior to that of comparable Western institutions. A small group of highly trained scientists and engineers had supplemented their excellent Russian education with studies at Western centers. Finally, Russian science was being strengthened by the availability of an unusual source of personnel—the Russian intelligentsia, that group of people socially uprooted by the economic changes taking place in nineteenth-century Russia whose general education and culture was as advanced as any in the West.

World War I, the Revolution and the havoc of the Civil War that followed dealt a telling blow to the intelligentsia. Persecuted by the rising proletariat, many lost their lives in the cataclysm of 1917-1923, and others left Russia to enrich the culture of many other lands. Science, which had been tolerated though not encouraged by the Imperial Government in its later days, gradually assumed an important rôle in the development of the Soviet state. The small, staid Imperial Academy of Sciences became the active, expanded U.S.S.R. Academy of Sciences. The four or five prominent universities spawned 33 new ones scattered across the expanse of the Soviet Union. It was decided to give a large number of people a scientific and technical education, and the small group of the intelligentsia that had survived persecution and avoided exile served as leaven for the creation of a new class of scientists.

Science comes into the Marxist scheme of things in a number of ways. In the Marxist thinking, the control of the state cannot be separated from the control of economic production. Technological advances change the economic balance and introduce new methods of production. Since scientists and engineers are responsible for technological advances, their activities must also be controlled. Several methods were tried by the Communist Party. The victorious "proletarian" régime tried immediately after the Revolution to make the scientist its slave, hoping in this way to guarantee its control of production and consequently continue to control the state. The attempt to make slaves out of the scientist and the engineer failed, in the Marxist view, because of the unreliable bourgeois background and Western leanings of the people in these professions. It was accordingly attempted to create a group of scientists from the proletariat. Although this was not entirely successful, Soviet scientists and engineers, together with other members of the Soviet intelligentsia, had by the time of the Second World War attained a position of prestige and economic advantage in Soviet society reflected in the common Soviet claim that the three pillars of the Soviet state are the workers, the peasants and the intelligentsia.

Marxism also affects science in a more subtle way through its philosophy of science. To its adherents, Marxism is a total philosophy and as such includes a philosophy of science. Marx, Engels and Lenin thought that they themselves were scientists and laid down rules to govern scientific thought which were embodied in the philosophy of dialectic materialism. The philosophy of dialectic materialism was not only formulated by people who did not know modern science, but is also full of contradictions. It is a materialistic philosophy emphasizing the overriding importance of the material aspect of nature. On the other hand, in its dialectic approach (through what the Marxists call "the three subsidiary laws of change," "negation of the negative" and the "transition of the quantitative to the qualitative change") it emphasizes idealism. For more than a decade after the Revolution Soviet philosophers argued as to the proper balance between these two components of their philosophy. Their conclusions were often decisively influenced by the dictates of party leaders, and as a result the chair of Marxist philosophy at the universities became a perilous one to hold. Eventually, in the Stalinist society, the Marxist dialectic materialism was replaced by a Stalinist philosophy of science whose main tenets were: do not be an idealist; make your research useful for building up the new Soviet state; criticize others and yourself; do not be subservient to the West; and honor your Russian scientific forebears.

Through its party functionaries, its Marxist professors of philosophy and its security officers, the state keeps a close watch at all educational and scientific institutions for possible "deviations" among staff members. Scientists who have had close personal ties with Western scientists are particularly suspected. Those whose work has been translated into English are invariably scrutinized for idealism, subservience to the West and neglect of Russian scientific forebears. This activity culminated in the famous genetics controversy and in the "reëxamination" of the various branches of science which followed.

Science in the Soviet Union is highly organized and well financed by the government. The main administrative agency is the U.S.S.R. Academy of Sciences, which occupies the key position in the organization, development, planning, execution and financing of science in Russia.

This self-perpetuating organization is composed of 150 full members and 250 associate members, drawn not only from all fields of natural sciences but also from other fields such as philosophy, history, economics and law. The Academy is divided into the following sections: physics-mathematics, chemistry, geology, biology, engineering (technical sciences), literature, language, economics and law, history and philosophy. Election to membership is preceded by wide publicity. At the election last October, the first in seven years, 199 new academicians and associate members were inducted. This marked a significant stage in the life of the Soviet science, indicating that a new generation of Russian scientists has become available to establish firm control over the Academy, which for some time contained a relatively high percentage of scholars trained under the Imperial régime.

The president of the Academy is a man of high prestige in the Soviet Union, elected by the Academy for a five-year term and holding a rank equivalent to that of a major cabinet minister. His portrait often appears in newspapers and magazines: and his prominence is attested by his inclusion in the group of the 25 Soviet leaders who gather on Lenin's tomb for the celebration of the October Revolution. The present president of the Academy is Alexander Nikolaevich Nesmeyanov, a member of the Communist Party, born in 1899, who studied organic chemistry under the dean of Russian organic chemists, Zelinski, at the Moscow State University. His scientific work has been in the field of organo-metallic compounds, of which tetraethyl lead used in gasoline is a good example. He was elected president of the Academy in 1951 on the death of Sergei Ivanovich Vavilov. Since 1947 Nesmeyanov has been chairman of the Stalin Prize Committee, Chancellor of the Moscow State University, Vice-President of the Supreme Soviet of the R.S.F.R., member of the Moscow City Soviet and of the World Peace Committee.

The Academy carries on its research work in a number of institutes, most of them centered in Moscow and Leningrad. The institutes, whose number has been relatively stabilized in recent years at about 60, employed about 6,000 scientific workers in 1949, and about 14,000 workers in administrative and service functions. A representative list of the names of the institutes gives an indication of their activities: The Institute of Physical Problems, the Institute of Physical Chemistry, the Geophysical Institute, the Radium Institute, the Institute of Genetics. These institutes are the élite guard of Soviet science, well equipped with apparatus, both imported and of Soviet manufacture, and attracting the best-trained Soviet scientists. The findings of a large amount of creditable scientific work are published by them, and these results are available outside the Iron Curtain. Research is also carried on at the major universities of Moscow, Leningrad, Kiev, etc., and there is close liaison between the universities and the institutes. There is also a very determined effort to organize scientific research in the outlying sections of the Soviet Union through branches of the Academy of Sciences and academies maintained by the various Soviet republics. The number of sophisticated scientific articles coming from centers far removed from Moscow testifies to the widespread distribution of highly-trained scientific personnel. In addition to these research institutes and the laboratories of the universities, research organizations are set up and controlled by the Ministries of Defense, Heavy Industries, etc. The Academy of Sciences exerts a powerful influence over the whole administration of Soviet science: it poses the key problems to institutes, approves their programs, appropriates the financial support, reviews each year the accomplishments of the various projects, and publicly reprimands institutes and individual academicians for failures in assigned work.

The Soviet scientist enjoys marked economic advantage over his fellow citizen. Judged by Soviet standards he is very well paid. If he is elected to membership in the Academy, he receives a monthly bonus, a good flat in Moscow, a fine country home in the Academy village, an automobile and other privileges. Scientists doing research at the universities and the institutes receive a higher financial compensation than those in industry. Every attempt is made to attract the best young men and women into scientific and technological work.

Exchange of scientific information has long been recognized as a necessary mechanism for the rapid development of scientific knowledge. This is admitted, at least to a limited degree, by the Soviet Government. The Academy publishes about 30 journals. Their top scientific journal is the *Dokladi* (Reports) of the U.S.S.R. Academy of Sciences and its four-page articles reporting original investigations indicate the broad scope of Soviet scientific work: in 1952 it contained 250 articles on physics alone. The other journals report in more detail the completed investigations as well as the proceedings of the numerous scientific conferences held in the Soviet Union. Most of these journals are regularly received in the United States. In September 1947, the Soviet Union discontinued the practice of publishing scientific work in other languages than Russian. Few Western scientists know the Russian language, and attempts to make results of Russian scientific work available to them have not been too successful.

The Soviet scientists are, on the other hand, very well informed about what is happening outside the Iron Curtain. Almost all important scientific books are translated into Russian and are given a wide distribution at low cost. At least four journals are devoted to the presentation of new developments in the various branches of science and these report fully and promptly on Western scientific results; anyone who reads them gets a very good picture of the status of Western science.

The Soviet Government lays great stress on education, especially technical and scientific education. Compulsory, free education in the so-called seven-year school is given to all children from the ages of seven to 14. In all the larger population centers there are ten-year schools that complete the secondary education at age 17. There is a slight fee for the three additional years of secondary education. An entrance examination in several school subjects, Russian, and a foreign language must be passed for admission to a university, of which there are 33, in addition to the 880 institutes of higher education. In 1951 there were about 6,000 professors in the Soviet Union, 25,000 assistant professors and about 1,200,000 students. The students in the universities are subsidized by the government on a merit basis. There has been considerable excitement in the Soviet press during the last several years about the construction of the new Moscow University in the Lenin hills just outside Moscow—a mammoth skyscraper, 850 feet high and more than a mile and a half in circumference. The central section, 37 stories high, will house the departments of geology, geography and mathematics, and a library of more than 1,000,000 volumes. Four 19-story wings will contain apartments for the staff and student dormitories, and other buildings outside the central block will be devoted to chemistry, physics, biology and administration. The departments of the humanities and social sciences will continue to be housed in the old University building near the Kremlin. With these new facilities, the Moscow University will be able to admit 5,000 students a year. The new university skyscraper which dominates the Moscow landscape is a symbol of pride of Moscovites in the Communist régime. We may take it as an indication of the importance that the Soviet state pays to scientific research and education.

There is strong competition for the university graduates, and it is reported that heads of industrial and research organizations attend the final oral examination of the university students to assess the merits of the candidates and offer positions. The best students are encouraged to continue their scientific work for advanced degrees at the universities and research institutes. It is an established fact, though not widely recognized, that the Russians use women far more extensively than other countries in their industry, agriculture and professions; the number of women scientists in the U.S.S.R. is many times that in the United States, and the Soviet state has recognized that women seem to have aptitudes which fit them better than men for certain types of scientific research.

A clear picture emerges from these facts about Soviet scientific and technological education. A larger and larger group of Soviet citizens is being given a scientific and technical education. Moreover, to the best of our knowledge, the education is sound in most fields. A new Soviet intelligentsia is being groomed to discharge the many technological tasks necessary for the advancement of a modern state. Scientific instruments can be bought and delivered overnight, but several years are required to build a scientific laboratory or an industrial plant; scientific and technological manpower is a product of decades. There is ample evidence that the Communist Party and the Soviet Government are aware of this factor of time, and they are doing their utmost to build up a large pool of highly trained scientific and technical personnel.

Soviet science has its weaknesses also, as the fantastic story of the genetics controversy reveals. This is one of the greatest mistakes made by the Communist Party, and one that stems naturally from Communist ideology. Genetics, a science that has been developing rapidly during the last 40 years, deals with the way inherited characteristics of plants and animals are transmitted from one generation to another and also with the way the organisms change their inherited characteristics. We have learned in the last 30 years that inherited characteristics are transmitted through genes arranged in a definite order in chromosomes, which are thread-like materials often visible in the light microscope and particularly apparent in the electron microscope. A knowledge of heredity is important not only as a clue to the basic life processes but also has immediate practical applications, for example in the development of better livestock and crops of higher yield and viability. These are major considerations for a state like Russia, where food has never been plentiful.

In the years following the Revolution, the Soviet Union had one of the best schools of genetics in the world. Its dynamic leader was Nicholas Ivanovich Vavilov, a scientist who had studied in his youth in England, had travelled widely on plant-collecting expeditions and had many friends in Western scientific circles. Nicholas Vavilov was placed by Lenin at the head of the Institute of Genetics and of the Lenin Academy of Agricultural Sciences. Vavilov proceeded to organize genetics research on a sound scientific basis and to develop new strains for Soviet agriculture: his scientific reputation is attested by his inclusion among the 50 foreign scientists honored with a Foreign Membership by the Royal Society of London. For some unknown reason, Vavilov's relation with the government deteriorated. A new prophet of genetics, Trofim Lysenko, appeared on the Soviet scene and promised Russian agriculture fast results. His Marxist ideological verbiage and his highly questionable scientific methods and findings received the blessing of the Central Committee of the Communist Party. The full story of the struggle between the genetics science of Nicholas Vavilov and the pseudo-science of Trofim Lysenko is too long to present here, but we may note that in the end Nicholas Vavilov was displaced from his scientific posts and disappeared to an unknown death. Sergei Ivanovich Vavilov, the physicist, was a bystander in his brother's dramatic exit and, as the President of the U.S.S.R. Academy of Sciences, had the rather uncomfortable task of proscribing the friends and the disciples of his brother. In the Grand Soviet Encyclopedia of which Sergei Vavilov was the chief editor there is no mention of Nicholas Vavilov. But though Lysenko triumphed, genetics died as a science in the Soviet Union. Michurinism, a pseudo-science derived from Lysenko's theories, dominates Soviet agriculture. Time alone will tell how much the present woes of Soviet farming can be ascribed to the fatal decision of the Central Committeee of the Communist Party in imposing its ideology on the genetics branch of science.

The Lysenko affair did not affect scientific and technological work that was obviously closely associated with the external security of the Soviet state. In the persons of Alexandrov, Kolmogorov, Khinchin and Pontriagin, Soviet mathematics has scholars of the highest caliber. Soviet physics is outstanding in the three main branches of nuclear work, low temperature investigations, and in studies of the solid state. Wechsler proposed a novel method of accelerating nuclear particles almost at the same time that McMillan did in this country. Cherenkov discovered a luminous effect of rapidly moving nuclear particles that bears his name and is studied extensively all over the world. Zavoiski, using modern radar methods, discovered electron paramagnetism in solids. The Soviet school of the chemistry of radioactive substances is of long standing. The Soviet physical chemist Semenov laid the theoretical foundations for the theory of explosions and nuclear processes. Soviet chemists seem to be concentrating their activity in the more technological fields of plastics, metal manufacture, insecticides, dyes and medicinals. Basic studies in the various branches of engineering are extensively reported in the Russian scientific journals. The geologists appear to be concentrating on exploration of the natural resources of the Soviet Union. Recently the various branches of the Academy and its institutes were called on to build canals, dams and irrigation systems as part of "the grand plan to transform nature" more recently whittled down in order to permit greater emphasis on consumer goods.

In short, we must not underrate the competence of Soviet scientists, nor ignore the fact that the Communist Party and the Soviet Government are spending large sums of money in building up laboratory facilities, encouraging scientific research and technical development and training personnel. This is a long-range program, successful completion of which will enhance the economic and military strength of the Soviet Union. The new leaders of Soviet science and engineering receive the best material comforts that the Soviet Union can offer. They will have increasing facilities for research and a large number of trained assistants. On the other hand, they will be wedded to an unsound philosophy of science which already has to its credit the death of the science of genetics in the Soviet Union; and the ideology of the Party may strike again. But in the meantime a strong and highly-organized system of science and technology is doing effective work.

"AMERICAN Policy and the Soviet Economic Offensive" (January 1957), by Willard L. Thorp, raised two issues of policy that continue to have great urgency today. One is the question of the purposes and effectiveness of U.S.-sponsored controls over trade with the Communist bloc. The other concerns the nature and extent of Soviet aid programs for developing countries and the problem of whether, and how, to combat them head-on or to accommodate U.S. policies to this new form of East-West rivalry. In his article Mr. Thorp stated these issues with concise clarity and also recommended definite changes in the posture of U.S. policy.

Since 1952 Mr. Thorp has been Merrill Professor of Economics at Amherst College and Director of the Merrill Center for Economics. In a varied career he has been a staff member of the National Bureau of Economic Research, 1923-34, and director of economic research for Dun & Bradstreet, Inc., 1935-45. Among many services to the U.S. government he was, in 1933-34, Director of the U.S. Bureau of Foreign and Domestic Commerce, chairman of the Advisory Council of the National Recovery Administration, 1934-35, and economic adviser to the Secretary of Commerce, 1939-40. He was Assistant Secretary of State for Economic Affairs, 1946-52; during that time he served on the U.S. delegations to the Council of Foreign Ministers, the Paris Peace Conference, and the General Assembly of the United Nations, and also represented the United States on the U.N. Economic and Social Council, 1947-50. Mr. Thorp has written or edited numerous authoritative analyses of domestic and international economic problems. Thus, when he writes on the economic issues in the cold war, it is from the perspective of long experience in economic research and in public policy.

Some of the policy recommendations that Mr. Thorp advanced in his article, as well as being proposed and discussed by other analysts, have been reflected in U.S. policy decisions since then; others have not. The publication of these forceful views illustrates the constant effort that *Foreign Affairs* has made during 40 years to inform the public of new and important issues and views of national policy.

323

AMERICAN POLICY AND THE SOVIET ECONOMIC OFFENSIVE

By Willard L. Thorp

IN the early years after the war, the Russians expanded their ideological exports while pursuing a policy of economic isolationism whenever more tangible goods were involved. Wherever they could make themselves heard, they challenged United States concepts of trade and aid as exploitation and imperialism, but they did not compete in substance. Within its own self-imposed limitations, American foreign economic policy was relatively free to engage in trade and aid with the countries not in the Soviet bloc.

The partial oxidation of the Iron Curtain by Bulganin and Khrushchev has not only made possible some degree of controlled artistic, athletic and scientific interchange, but it appears also to have important economic implications. Soviet bloc economic negotiators are busy in both the industrial and the underdeveloped countries. Arrangements are being made for the expanded bartering of commodities, the extension of credit and the provision of technical assistance. At the same time, American policy in this area has become even more hesitant and vacillating, awaiting the results of half a dozen new Administrative reappraisals and Congressional investigations.

The background of the Soviet economic offensive is relatively simple. In 1937, the Soviet Union carried on 96 percent of its limited foreign trade with countries now in the free world.[1] Taking all the Eastern European countries as a group, their prewar trade with the present free world was more than 85 percent of their total trade.

The postwar period witnessed not only a political convergence of the

---

[1] The chief sources of material for this article were the *Seventh* and *Eighth Report to Congress* by the International Coöperation Administration on operations under the Mutual Defense Assistance Control Act of 1951; the United Nations, *World Economic Survey 1955;* and the United Nations, *Economic Bulletin for Europe,* August 1956.

Soviet Union and her new satellites but also an economic integration. By the end of the postwar decade, the trade pattern was completely altered. After eliminating the effect of changes in price level, the volume of their trade with each other has expanded more than 2.5 times while their trade with the rest of the world was less than half its prewar level. Thus in 1954 only 20 to 30 percent of the trade of most Eastern European countries (21 percent for the U.S.S.R.) was with the rest of the world. Within the Eastern European group, the Soviet Union had emerged as the most important trading partner. Even by 1948, its exports to the other countries in the bloc had multiplied by 25 times and imports by 10 times, compared to the very low prewar levels.

The basis of this new trade pattern was primarily the effort to develop the Soviet bloc as a self-contained economic unit. There were four reasons for this. First was the concentration on military strength and development, an objective which obviously involves reducing economic dependence upon unreliable (foreign) sources of strategic raw materials and finished goods. Second was the Iron Curtain policy, with its effort to reduce contacts with the Western world to a minimum in order to insure discipline and acceptance of the régime. Third was the reliance upon economic planning and the consequent effort to eliminate those uncertainties which are introduced by dependence upon transactions with buyers and sellers beyond the control of the planners. Finally, many of the arguments were applied to the bloc as a whole which are now being advanced for a "common market" in Europe. At first the plans were essentially nationalist, but more recently special emphasis has been given to the desirability of organizing to permit large-scale production and specialization, thereby increasing productivity for the group as a whole.

Even had there not been internal reasons for developing this Soviet-bloc autarky, other forces would have contributed to reducing their trade with the free world. Their industrial expansion and lagging agriculture ran counter to the reconstruction of the prewar trade pattern when they exported food and feedstuffs in return for manufactured goods, largely consumer items. Furthermore, the imposition of strategic trade restrictions by Western countries put obstacles in the way of trade in those very items for which presumably these countries had the greatest demand.

For all these reasons, in spite of economic expansion within the Soviet bloc and rapid recovery and growth in the free world, the trade between the two declined from a not very high postwar peak in 1948 to a low point in the first half of 1953. Since then, trade between the bloc and the rest of the world has more than doubled and is still expanding rapidly, although it is not large in volume. Trade with the bloc countries, which was 7.4 percent of the free world's trade in 1938, was only 2.3 percent in 1954 and 2.6 percent in 1955. And it is still true that the countries within the bloc do about 75 percent of their trade with each other.

The increases in trade with the free world since 1953 are not merely random economic variables. They represent a definite shift in policy and emphasis. There has been an even greater increase in the volume of talk by Soviet leaders, broadcasting their desire for increased trade with the free world. This recent development is clearly a part of the new post-Stalin picture. It is consistent with the so-called peace offensive and the call for reduced international tensions. But it seems to be more than an adaptation to the new mood. It looks as though the past occasional and insignificant use of economic means to achieve foreign objectives (*i.e.*, a shipload of wheat to Italy at a critical time) is being replaced by a positive utilization of foreign economic policy as a major instrument in the struggle to win friends and influence people.

On the more strictly economic side, the new structure of trade is suggestive. There is a definite tendency to expand exports of manufacturers in exchange for imports of food and raw materials, and this would seem to correspond to the productivity record in the Communist countries. There may therefore be some economic logic behind the expansion of trade as well as its use to further the continuing political objectives of Soviet Communism.

So far as Western Europe and the United States are concerned, the main expression of trade policy toward the bloc in recent years has been the operation of the so-called strategic controls. While American economic foreign policy in general has sought to lower trade barriers and encourage trade expansion, trade with the bloc countries has been restricted with respect to items which might contribute to Communist military strength. Furthermore, so far as the United States is concerned, the reductions in tariffs negotiated under the Trade Agreements Act, usually generalized to other countries in accordance with most-favored-nation commitments, have not been extended to countries in the Soviet bloc. Nevertheless, there is a considerable area for trade in so-called "peaceful trade" items not covered in the restrictive trade program.

However, although a wide network of trade agreements has been negotiated, the volume of trade actually achieved has been relatively small.

Strategic controls originated at the time when it became apparent that we were engaged in an arms race with a dangerous adversary. We had demobilized while the Russians had not, and our immediate defense lay in the atomic bomb, obviously a temporary advantage. Military strength is relative, and it was important to gain time by delaying Russian progress. Thus the policy was adopted of restricting trade in goods which might contribute to Soviet military strength. In general, the other industrial countries joined in the program, although its specific application was a constant source of friction. That it was incorporated as a condition for the receipt of United States assistance made it an even greater irritant. Nevertheless, it undoubtedly created some delays in the Russian military program and helped hold the line until the NATO defenses could be developed.

Assuming that there will continue to be an embargo on actual military items, additional restrictions no longer can be said to have much importance for our security. Whatever bottlenecks were created by the original policy have undoubtedly been broken by this time. In fact, it was clear at the beginning that one of the results of the restrictive policy would be to force the Soviet bloc to develop its own production of the prohibited items. With such a primary position in planning given to the military, it is hard to conceive that the Soviet bloc has left itself in any way dependent upon foreign trade to meet its military requirements.

If the significance of the strategic controls in terms of military requirements is reduced to a minimum, there still remains the possibility of using controls to hamper the general economic progress of the countries in the bloc. However, this cuts both ways. From the economic point of view, it is impossible to conclude that trade in one direction is more valuable than trade in the other. How can one say that fuel and raw materials flowing out of Eastern Europe are more or less valuable than wheat and tobacco flowing in, or than small ships, or even than electric motors?

The changing pattern of trade is clearly relevant to this argument for continuing controls. In 1954, the increase in bloc imports was largely in consumer goods—food, tobacco, textiles and paper. In 1955, imports of consumer goods held level and the chief increases were in ships, iron and steel, and nonferrous metals. The imports of machinery, which had been declining in earlier years, did not increase in 1955 even though there was some relaxation of the strategic controls by the Western countries in August 1954.

The largest export items from the bloc were coal (although in 1955 United States shipments of coal to Western Europe were larger than those from Eastern Europe by two and a half times), petroleum and petroleum products, and timber, but iron and steel products and machinery exports are increasing rapidly. In 1955, for the first time, Eastern European exports of manufactured products to Western Europe exceeded food exports. However, the two categories together were less than fuel and raw material exports. The new pattern which is developing, particularly in relation to overseas trade, is the export by the bloc of manufactured goods and the import of foodstuffs and raw materials.

In the light of the present situation, it seems more appropriate that efforts should be made by Western Europe and the United States to increase their trade with the bloc, particularly with the satellite countries. This can have much more than economic importance. When Jugoslavia pulled out from under Soviet domination, its most difficult problem was created by the trade embargo immediately placed upon it by the Soviet bloc. In 1948, 50.7 percent of its exports and 45.6 percent of its imports came from Eastern Europe. From then until 1954, its trade with the bloc was zero. The success of its effort to throw off the Moscow yoke depended in large part upon how quickly its trade could be reoriented toward the free world. This was no easy matter, and it was only because the United States, the United Kingdom and France gave special assistance that "Titoism" was possible. Similar assistance may be used again to encourage satellite independence, but this can be only a temporary substitute for the development of trade channels.

The Soviet Union clearly recognizes the importance of binding the satellites to itself and to each other by strong economic ties. Drew Middleton reported in *The New York Times,* shortly after the political developments in Poland, that the Soviet Union had offered to buy the Polish coal now going to the West. Clearly, this is an effort to strengthen the economic interdependence of Poland and the U.S.S.R. Furthermore, in the Soviet Union's policy statement of October 30, 1956, on relations with other Communist nations, the subject is raised but not resolved, by the statement that "the Soviet Government is ready to discuss, together with the governments of other Socialist states, measures insuring the further development of economic ties between Socialist countries."

It will not be an easy matter to make any substantial break in the volume of intra-bloc trade. The more recent East-West trade agreements, negotiated, to be sure, before the unrest broke out in the satellites, all provide for increases in trade, and the early months of 1956 show both imports and exports up by about 15 percent above early 1955. While there have been talks of very large increases (the Russian tourist-team talked in London of a fivefold increase in five years), it is difficult to envisage what the bloc might supply in such a case. Since this trade is such a small proportion of free Europe's trade, it probably could easily be supplied on the Western side, but the necessary reverse flow is more difficult to envisage. Foodstuffs are out of the picture, but increases in petroleum and coal may be possible, as well as the kind of diversified trade with which countries such as Czechoslovakia are familiar. In short, there seems to be little possibility for any spectacular developments in trade between Western and Eastern Europe, but such increases as are possible should now be encouraged as at least one step in the process of liberation.

Two fears which have often been expressed are that the Soviet bloc might use any significant trade position to disturb and disrupt markets, and that expanded trade might create dependence upon it by countries that are now free. So far as market disturbance is concerned, such leverage is largely on the selling side of the market and is a matter of magnitudes and alternatives. When Soviet manganese was withdrawn from the world market, it did create a shortage and there was a delay before other sources such as India were able to fill the gap. On the other hand, the Western purchasers of Polish coal have always known that American coal was readily available if the bargaining became too difficult. Russian and Rumanian petroleum are also easily replaceable, assuming normal channels are open. To be sure, sudden dumping on a market can cause short-run confusion, but this might raise a serious problem only if it took the form of dumping large quantities of precious metals. A large gold flow, not a likely development, might conceivably lead to inflation in countries with weak monetary controls.

There are a few countries for whose products the Soviet bloc provides an important market, notably Iceland and Finland. These are both special cases and the free world has perhaps been somewhat negligent in permitting them to slip so far into the Soviet economic orbit. In 1953, after desperate efforts to find other markets, Iceland began to sell its fish products in quantity to the Soviet bloc, and the volume and percentage of its exports to the bloc have increased each year since then. Finland's trade was directed to the Soviet bloc in large part by its reparations commitments. Although its exports to the bloc were larger in 1955 than ever before, the proportion of its trade which this volume represented has declined somewhat since the peak in 1953.

There are two other countries in the free world where one can expect that trade with Eastern Europe may soon reach the 20 percent mark, Austria and Jugoslavia. The signing of the Austrian State Treaty in May 1955 was followed by a payments agreement relating to former German assets and by a series of trade agreements. As a matter of fact, it may well be that most of any apparent statistical increase in Austrian exports to the bloc will be merely the explicit recognition of unrecorded exports during the Soviet occupation. However, of all the Western European countries, Austria had the greatest Eastern European trade before the war and is still far below those earlier percentages.

In the case of Jugoslavia, after a period of orientation toward the Soviet bloc, trade relations were completely severed in late 1948. Trade was resumed in 1954 and increased rapidly in 1955. Larger quotas plus substantial Soviet credits augur a further substantial increase in 1956. Some of Jugoslavia's traditional exports, such as fruit, vegetables and tobacco, were never easily marketed in Western European markets and her trade with the West has had to be supported by grants and credits.

For Western Europe as a whole, trade with Eastern Europe (excluding trade between West and East Germany) is still exceedingly small— 3.4 percent of its imports and 3.2 percent of its exports, less than half the prewar figures.

In the special cases described above, the problem for the free world is one of providing alternatives—not necessarily alternatives which need to be used but options which are there as a protection against increasing dependence and the threat of coercion. And the same considerations, directed at the satellites, would argue for the effort to increase their trade with the free world.

II

The new economic policy has been much more spectacular in relation to the underdeveloped countries. Although the expansion of trade with countries supplying food and raw material is explained by some analysts in terms of economic advantage, the fact that this new interest in trade is not solely an economic matter was made clear by Mr. Khrushchev in speaking to a group of visiting United States Senators: "We value trade least for economic reasons and most for political purposes as a means of promoting better relations between our countries." Although he was talking about United States-Soviet relations, this pronouncement takes on even greater significance when related to the underdeveloped countries, where the Communists have their greatest hope for further accessions to their ranks. With this in mind, a whole series of new policies has been put into practice by the Soviet bloc.

One technique has been to provide a market for goods which are proving difficult to sell in the free world. The purchase of fish from Iceland, rice from Burma and cotton from Egypt are all illustrations of this approach. In 1955, the Sino-Soviet bloc purchased more than 10 percent of the exports of nine countries: Iceland (27.8 percent), Egypt (26.7), Finland (25.8), Turkey (21.8), Iran (15.2), Jugoslavia (13.8), Burma (12.0), Austria (10.2) and Afghanistan (estimated at 50 percent). Only five countries purchased as much as 10 percent from the bloc: Finland (27.0), Hong Kong (24.2), Iceland (22.2), Turkey (18.3) and Afghanistan (exact percent not known). These are important percentages, many of which are still rising, but they still do not indicate that dominance over any considerable area is being achieved through trade.

The Soviet effort to expand economic relations with the underdeveloped countries has involved not only trade but also credits, technical assistance, trade fairs, technical exchange, trade missions and propaganda. The most common trade pattern is the exchange of primary products for manufactured goods on an intergovernmental basis. In addition, credits have been extended on an expanding scale. Credit agreements concluded during 1955 amounted to nearly $600 millions, most of which went to Jugoslavia, Egypt, Afghanistan and India. These credits involved low interest rates, long periods of repayment and sometimes arrangements for compensation in kind, as in the case of

Egyptian cotton. In addition to credit, substantial technical assistance has been made available, ranging from aid in oil exploration (India) to the setting up of a technical institute in Rangoon and a 100-bed hospital in Kabul.

These new programs are not to be regarded lightly. To be sure, the members of the Soviet bloc would probably be embarrassed if all their offers were accepted but they do have the capacity to carry out substantial programs. In fact, they could probably equal our present levels of non-defense-support aid to the underdeveloped countries if they should determine to do so. Of course, the extension of substantial credits in any one year cannot be compared with an actual flow of trade, since the credit usually relates to shipments to be made over a period of several years. The Soviet bloc is starting from a very low level of trade with most underdeveloped countries. However, its emphasis is on support of economic development and this is undoubtedly the area of greatest political impact.

The political values are clearly uppermost. The economic effects are decidedly marginal. By expanding trade, they may even improve the position of their own consumers by obtaining rice for a product such as cement. By exporting capital, they may slow down their own rate of expansion a little or even delay the rate at which their growth is reflected in the standard of living, but neither of these will clearly appear to their citizens as a calculated and explicit burden. For various reasons, they can easily send more technicians abroad than can we under our present procedures. Furthermore, their programs often have more appeal than ours, even if they may be less sensible in terms of the allocation of resources. They may do the more conspicuous or symbolic project, such as paving the streets in Kabul, or the more impressive, such as building a steel mill in India. And always there is the steady beat of propaganda asserting that Soviet programs are disinterested without strings, while Western programs are militaristic, imperialistic and set about with conditions.

What is the basis for this new Soviet activity? One can of course find many self-serving declarations by the Russian leaders. Marx originally predicted the revolution as the result of the explosion of misery and clearly the present-day Communists are not acting on that basis, for assistance interferes with Marx's economic determinism. Nor can they be operating upon the American thesis that improvement will deter the embrace of Communism. There is very little evidence that the

Slavic temperament or the Soviet rulers have ever relied on gratitude as an important source of motivation. But they always have placed great weight on economic factors. Perhaps this new policy is simply a combination of a desire to demonstrate the economic strength of the Communist bloc and an effort to establish closer economic ties as a basis for political rapprochement. From our point of view, it would appear to imply a recognition that the American programs, which took their shape in the first five years after the War, were sufficiently effective and successful to require some counteraction.

The problems already mentioned with respect to Iceland and Finland appear also among the underdeveloped countries. In several instances, the Soviet bloc has been able to inject itself by purchasing commodities not easily marketed in the free world. In the cases of cotton, rubber and rice, American developments contributed to the marketing difficulties of the underdeveloped countries, and Egypt, Ceylon and Burma found outlets in the Soviet bloc. All these arrangements were more or less barter deals and they obtained manufactured goods which they wanted in exchange for their own surpluses. In strictly economic terms, such arrangements cannot be automatically censured. The bartering of commodities for which there is no market in the free world can be a definite economic gain provided useful commodities are obtained in exchange. Furthermore, assistance presently available to the underdeveloped countries is not at the limit of their absorptive capacity. Such aid and assistance as can come from the Soviet bloc (and it is likely to prove disappointing over time) will add to the resources available for economic development.

This having been said, there appears to be no justification for adopting a nonchalant view of the new Soviet offensive. The great danger, of course, is that some countries may get into the position where economic pressure can be applied as a method of obtaining political concessions. As in the case of countries in Western Europe, the amount of leverage which can be obtained from economic ties is related in large part to the degree to which alternatives are readily available. If economic opportunities and assistance are readily available from the West, then the danger is less one of coercion and is reduced to the level of contact and persuasion.

This new situation has a real bearing upon our own policy of economic assistance. We may well find ourselves in the difficult position of competing against a fairly secretive competitor, and be dependent upon the beneficiary for our information or misinformation about the score (as in the case of Egypt and the Aswan Dam). We can of course withdraw from the scene or make it an all-or-none issue, but neither course is likely to improve our international relations. In the last analysis, the consequence of the new Soviet offensive should be to improve the performance of the competitors. So long as we were the main source of economic aid, we could function with a kind of positive and magisterial assurance. But now, even more than before, we must review our methods and procedures to see whether or not we can do a better job of it.

We still have substantial assets in our hands. We can outbid the Soviet bloc with economic goods and services whenever we wish to do so. In one area, that of foodstuffs, we have surpluses where they are hard pressed. In fact, our recent programs for agricultural disposal have indicated one promising way of contributing to economic development. Unfortunately, the fact that our internal political discussion of this problem has been in terms of getting rid of surpluses rather than contributing to economic development has created the notion in the beneficiary countries that they are performing a service for us rather than receiving assistance. And the fact that the citizens in the recipient country pay for the products in their local currency conceals the fact that our action is creating a fund for economic development which would otherwise not be available to the government. Perhaps this is merely a matter of public education, both at home and abroad. Since our own reports are in terms of how much surplus we have managed to dispose of, how can we expect the program to be put in its proper perspective? The agricultural disposal program suggests that the weakness in our assistance programs is less in what they are than in how they are done and what they are believed to be.

The centralized character of Soviet operation gives it certain advantages in developing the assistance aspect of foreign policy. There is no public debate involving the antecedents, present performance and future prospects of the prospective beneficiary. There is no framework fixed by legislation within which each operating act must fit. There is no limitation with respect to the period of time to be covered by a commitment. And people and goods can be coöpted without due process of law. To be sure, we are convinced that the development of individualism, the review of public policy by the people and their representatives, and the operation of government within a process of checks and balances are all essential to democracy. That this may lead to delays, unfortunate publicity and inflexibility is a price we have always been willing to pay in dealing with domestic problems. But it does raise difficulties for the detailed operation of foreign policy, and we should be ingenious enough to find ways and means of reducing the obstacles which we continually place in our own way.

It does not now appear that the new programs will place the Soviet Union in a position within the next few years to take over political control through economic domination, except possibly in the case of Afghanistan. Yet it is still quite likely that the new policies may strengthen its political position and possibly weaken that of the Western countries. However, this is clearly the objective of the new total policy and not merely of the new "aid through trade" programs.

In the ideological competition, Soviet policy now looks toward a great expansion in contacts. Trade and technical assistance will contribute added opportunities for Communist enthusiasts to spread their ideas. That more Communist propaganda will be loose in the world adds to the danger. However, the important impact of the new economic programs may be less in terms of the personnel which goes along with them than in the encouragement that these programs will give to those already in the country with a tendency to lean toward the left.

If our basic concern is to make it possible for the underdeveloped countries to maintain their independence, giving them freedom to design their own future in so far as any nation is ever able to do so, we must be concerned not only about political ties but also about economic independence. This involves two considerations—enough economic progress so that internal pressures do not force them to turn to a dictatorship of the extreme right or left, and sufficient economic alternatives so that they do not become exposed to economic coercion. These are not negative goals, but essential bases for the development of free nations. Perhaps the most important objective for American policy must be to convince the underdeveloped countries that our interest is not in using them as pawns in the cold war, but rather in supporting their freedom and assisting in their own development.

To the West, one of the most puzzling features of Soviet development has been the recurrent ebb and flow of tension and partial relaxation throughout the life of the Soviet body politic. One reflection of this process is the complex and variable blending of attraction and hatred in the Soviet attitude to the West.

In the totalitarian system for which Lenin laid the groundwork, and which Stalin then elaborated into an all-directing structure of power, the activating force is the dictatorial party or its leader. This force denies to any real or potential competitor the right to act, or even to think contrary thoughts. Using the "engineers" of philosophy, science, literature and the arts as mere instruments of its will, the custodian of "Truth"—the self-appointed leadership of the monopolistic Party—reserves to itself the sole right to define both the purposes and the direction of its acts.

Stalin's death in March 1953 was followed by a partial but marked release of the over-taut spring. Within a few weeks and months his successors had made several significant shifts. The arbitrary power of the secret police was curbed. Plans to improve the supply of consumer goods, food and housing were proclaimed with loud fanfare. The demand for "sincerity," i.e., for some limited right of individual judgment, was raised by some writers and artists. Though checked after some time, the first "thaw" of 1953-54 and its reversal have been followed by two or perhaps three later periods of relaxation.

Does this mean that Russia will henceforth move inevitably and more or less continuously toward a condition of genuine personal and intellectual freedom? Or are these convulsive movements a prolongation of the previous Soviet pattern of the purposeful alternation of tensions and relaxations? From a long study of Russian life and thought, Sir Isaiah Berlin has traced in "The Silence in Russian Culture" (October 1957) the historical roots of Soviet totalitarian Messianism.

A Fellow of All Souls, Oxford, and Chichele Professor of Social and Political Theory since 1957, Sir Isaiah has also been deeply involved in affairs of state. In World War II he rendered important services as a member of the British embassies in Washington and Moscow. Among his principal studies are "Karl Marx" (1939), "The Hedgehog and the Fox" (1953), and "Two Concepts of Liberty" (1959).

THE SILENCE IN RUSSIAN CULTURE

By Isaiah Berlin

ONE of the most arresting characteristics of modern Russian culture is its acute self-consciousness. There has surely never been a society more deeply and exclusively preoccupied with itself, its own nature and destiny. From the eighteen-thirties until our own day the subject of almost all critical and imaginative writing in Russia is Russia. The great novelists, and a good many minor novelists too, as well as the vast majority of the characters in Russian novels, are continuously concerned not merely with their purposes as human beings or members of families or classes or professions, but with their condition or mission or future as Russians, members of a unique society with unique problems. This national self-absorption is to be found among novelists and playwrights of otherwise very different outlooks. An obsessed religious teacher like Dostoevsky, a didactic moralist like Tolstoy, an artist regarded in the West as being dedicated to timeless and universal psychological and aesthetic patterns like Turgenev, a "pure" unpolitical writer, careful not to preach, like Chekhov, are all, and throughout their lives, crucially concerned with the "Russian problem." Russian publicists, historians, political theorists, writers on social topics, literary critics, philosophers, theologians, poets, first and last, all without exception and at enormous length, discuss such issues as what it is to be a Russian; the virtues, vices and destiny of the Russian individual and society; but above all the historic rôle of Russia among the nations; or, in particular, whether its social structure—say, the relation of intellectuals to the masses, or of industry to agriculture—is *sui generis,* or whether, on the contrary, it is similar to that of other countries, or, perhaps, an anomalous, or stunted, or an abortive example of some superior Western model.

From the eighties onwards a vast, now unreadably tedious, mass of books, articles, pamphlets began to flood upon the Russian intelligentsia, mostly concerned to prove either that Russia is destined to obey unique laws of its own—so that the experience of other countries has little

337

or nothing to teach it—or, on the contrary, that its failures are entirely
due to an unhappy dissimilarity to the life of other nations, a blindness
to this or that universal law which governs all societies, and which
Russians ignore at their peril. The writers of Western countries, as
often as not, produce their works of art or learning or even day-to-day
comment (even in America where there exists similar self-consciousness,
though not on so vast a scale) without necessarily tormenting themselves with the question whether their subject matter has been treated
in its right historical or moral or metaphysical context. In Russia, at
any rate since the second half of the nineteenth century, the reverse
obtained. There no serious writer could think of taking a step without
concerning himself with the question whether his work was appropriately
related to the great ultimate problems, the purposes of men on earth.
The duty of all those who claimed to have the insight to understand,
and the moral courage to face, their personal or social or national
condition was always the same: in the first place to relate the relevant
problems to the path which the given society (*i.e.*, Russian; and only
after that, human) was inexorably pursuing (if one was a determinist),
or should be pursuing (if one thought one had freedom of choice), at
the particular historical (or moral or metaphysical) stage of its development.

No doubt the Romantic doctrines, particularly in Germany, with
their emphasis on the unique historical missions of different groups of
men—Germans, or industrialists, or poets—which dominated European
literature and journalism in the eighteen-thirties and forties, are partly
responsible for this pervasive Russian attitude. But it went further in
Russia than elsewhere. This was partly due to the fact that the effective
advance of Russia to the center of the European scene (after the Napoleonic wars) coincided with the impact of the Romantic Movement; it
derived partly from a sense of their own cultural inferiority which
made many educated Russians painfully anxious to find a worthy part
of their own to play—worthy, above all, of their growing material
power in a world that was apt to look down upon them, and cause
them to look down upon themselves, as a dark mass of benighted bar-
barians ruled by brutal despots and good only for crushing other freer,
more civilized peoples. Again there may be, as some writers maintain,
a strong craving for teleological and indeed eschatological systems in all
societies influenced by Byzantium or by the Orthodox Church—a craving that the Russian priesthood, lacking as it conspicuously did the

intellectual resources and tradition of the Western churches, could not
satisfy, at any rate in the case of the better educated and critically inclined young men.

Whatever the truth about its origins, the state of mind of virtually
all Russian intellectuals in the nineteenth and early twentieth centuries (there were some exceptions) was dominated by the belief that all
problems are interconnected, and that there is some single system in
terms of which they are all in principle soluble; moreover, that the
discovery of this system is the beginning and end of morality, social
life, education; and that to abandon the search for it in order to concentrate upon isolated or personal ends, say, the pursuit of knowledge,
or artistic creation, or happiness, or individual freedom for their own
sakes, is willful, subjective, irrational, egoistic, an immoral evasion of
human responsibility. This attitude is characteristic not merely of the
left-wing Russian intelligentsia, but of the outlook of civilized Russians
of all shades of political opinion, spread widely both in religious and in
secular, in literary and in scientific circles. Almost any philosophical
system that affected to give a comprehensive answer to the great
questions found a marvelously, indeed excessively, enthusiastic welcome
among these eager, over-responsive, idealistic, impeccably consistent,
sometimes only too rigorously logical thinkers.

And the systems were not slow in arriving. First came German his-
toricism, particularly in its Hegelian form, which conceived of history
as the essential, indeed the only genuine science. True, Hegel looked
on the Slavs with contempt as "unhistorical," and declared that (like
the "extinct" Chinese civilization) they had no part to play in the
march of the human spirit. This part of Hegel was quietly ignored,
and adequate room made in the universal schema for the Slavs in
general, and (on the authority of Hegel's formidable rival, Schelling)
for the Russians in particular. After the infatuation with Schiller, Fichte,
Hegel and other German Idealists came a similar faith in French
social prophets—Saint-Simon, Fourier and their many disciples and
interpreters, who offered cut-and-dried "scientific" plans of reform
or revolution for which some among their Russian disciples, with their
will to believe in literal inspiration, were ready to lay down their lives.
This was followed by many another *Lebensphilosophie*—inspired by
Rousseau, by Comtian Positivism, Darwinism, neo-mediævalism, An-
archism, which in Russia went far beyond their Western prototypes.
Unlike the West where such systems often languished and declined

amid cynical indifference, in the Russian Empire they became fighting faiths, thriving on the opposition to them of contrary ideologies—mystical monarchism, Slavophil nostalgia, clericalism, and the like; and under absolutism, where ideas and daydreams are liable to become substitutes for action, ballooned out into fantastic shapes, dominating the lives of their devotees to a degree scarcely known elsewhere. To turn history or logic or one of the natural sciences—biology or sociology—into a theodicy; to seek, and affect to find, within them solutions to agonizing moral or religious doubts and perplexities; to transform them into secular theologies—all that is nothing new in human history. But the Russians indulged in this process on a heroic and desperate scale, and in the course of it brought forth what today is called the attitude of total commitment, at least of its modern form.

Over a century ago Russian critics denounced European civilization for its lack of understanding. It seemed to them characteristic of the morally desiccated, limited thinkers of the West to maintain that human activities were not all necessarily interconnected with each other— that what a man did as a writer was one thing and what he did as a citizen was another; that a man might be a good chemist and yet maltreat his family or cheat at cards; that a man might compose profound music and yet hold stupid or immoral political views that were no business of the critics or of the public. This notion of life, according to Russians of almost all shades of opinion, was artificial and shallow and flew to pieces before the deeper insight of the all-embracing view, according to which the life of individuals and the life of their institutions was one and indivisible. Every faculty and element in the individual were in a state of constant interplay; a man could not be one thing as a painter and another as a citizen, honest as a mathematician and false as a husband; it was impossible to draw frontiers between any aspects of human activity, above all between public and private life. Any attempt to insulate this or that area from the invasion of outside forces was held to be founded upon the radical fallacy of thinking that the true function and purpose of a human being does not penetrate every one of his acts and relationships—or worse still, that men had, as men, no specific function or purpose at all. It followed that whatever most fully embodies this ultimate total human purpose—the State, according to the Hegelians; an élite of scientists, artists and managers, according to the followers of Saint-Simon or Comte; the Church, according to those who leaned towards ecclesiastical authority; an elected body of persons embodying the popular or national will, according to democrats or nationalists; the class designated by "history" to free itself and all mankind, according to Socialists and Communists—this central body had a right to invade everything. The very notion of the inviolability of persons, or of areas of life, as an ultimate principle was nothing but an effort to limit, to narrow, to conceal, to shut out the light, to preserve privilege, to protect some portion of ourselves from the universal truth—and therefore the central source of error, weakness and vice.

The doctrine that there is one truth and one only, which the whole of one's life should be made to serve, one method, and one only, of arriving at it, and one body of experts alone qualified to discover and interpret it—this ancient and familiar doctrine can take many shapes. But even in its most idealistic and unworldly forms, it is, in essence, totalitarian. Even those critical versions of it which permit doubts about the nature of the central truth, or about the best method of its discovery, or the title of its preachers, allow none about the right and the duty, once it is established, to make everyone and everything obey it; they allow no intrinsic virtue to variety of opinion or conduct as such; indeed, the opposite. For there can be no more than one truth, one right way of life. Only vice and error are many. Consequently, when Marxism finally came to Russia in the seventies and eighties it found an almost ideal soil for its seeds.

II

Marxism contained all the elements which the young *révoltés* in Russia were looking for. It claimed to be able to demonstrate the proper goals of human existence in terms of a pattern of history of which there was "scientific" proof. The moral and political values which it preached could, so it claimed, be determined "objectively," that is to say, not in terms of the subjective and relative and unpredictable attitudes of different individuals or classes or cultures, but in terms of principles which, being "founded" on the "objective behavior of things," were absolute and alone led to the salvation and liberation of all men to the degree to which they were rational. It preached the indissoluble oneness of men and institutions. It claimed, just as the eighteenth century French philosophers had in effect claimed, that all real, that is to say soluble, problems were fundamentally technological; that the ends of man—what human beings could be, and, if they knew their true interests, would necessarily want to be—were given by the new scientific picture of the universe. The only problem was how to realize these ends. This was not a moral or political problem but a technical task: that of finding and using the right means for the "demonstrably" valid, universal goal; a problem of engineering.

Stalin's famous and most revealing phrase about intellectuals as "engineers of human souls" was faithfully derived from Marxist premises. The duty of intellectuals was to elucidate the correct social goals on the basis of a "scientific" analysis of society and history; and then, by means of education, or "conditioning," so to attune the minds of their fellow citizens that they grasped demonstrated truths and responded accordingly, like the harmonious constituents of a properly regulated and efficiently functioning mechanism. The simile which Lenin used in one of his most famous statements of political doctrine—*State and Revolution*—according to which the new free society, liberated from the coercion of one class by another, would resemble a factory or workshop in which the workers did their jobs almost out of mechanical habit, was a piece of imagery drawn from this technocratic view of human life. The watchwords were efficiency, tidiness, security, freedom for the good to do what they wanted; this last being necessarily one and the same goal for all those who were rational and knew the truth, not freedom to do anything whatever, but only what is right— the only thing which any rational being can wish to do—that which alone will make for true, everlasting universal happiness. This is an old Jacobin doctrine, and indeed much older—in its essentials as old as Plato. But no one, perhaps, had believed it quite so naïvely or fanatically in any previous age.

During the decade that followed the October Revolution these principles—the moral and metaphysical foundations of totalitarianism— were genuinely accepted, at any rate by some among the Communist leaders. Whatever the personal shortcomings of Trotsky or Zinoviev or Bukharin or Molotov or the heads of the secret police, and perhaps even of Stalin at this stage, there is no reason for doubting the sincerity or depth of their convictions or principles. A great many disagreements arose, of course, but they were concerned not with ends but with means; when they went sufficiently far they were stigmatized as deviations. Thus Trotsky thought that there was a danger of a too-well-entrenched bureaucracy which would function as a brake—like all vested interests—upon the progress of the Revolution which needed agents who

were more imaginative, more bloody, bold and resolute—men not
tempted to stop halfway on the path of the world revolution. The so-
called Workers' Opposition objected to the concentration of authority
in the hands of the Central Committee of the Communist Party, and
wanted more equality, and more democratic control exercised by workers' organizations. The Right-Wing Deviationists thought that over-
rapid collectivization of agriculture would produce a degree of economic
dislocation, pauperization and ruin likely to be more damaging to the
Soviet economy than the adoption of a slower pace in the harsh process
of liquidating peasant property and its defenders together with other
so-called survivals of the capitalist régime; and advocated a less urgent
tempo and milder measures. There were disagreements as to how far
the army might be used in the regimentation of industry. There were
memorable disagreements about foreign policy and the policy towards
Communists abroad.

The acutest of all disagreements occurred, perhaps, on the cultural
front: there were those who thought that any "slap in the face" (as
it used to be called) to the bourgeois culture of the West, in whatever
form—aggressive futurism and modernism in the arts, for example, or
any violent revolt against tradition—was *eo ipso* an expression of Bolshevism, in so far as it was a blow at the Western establishment, lowered
its morale and undermined its moral and aesthetic foundations. A good
deal of experiment, sometimes bold and interesting, at other times
merely eccentric and worthless, occurred at this time in the Soviet Union
in the guise of cultural warfare against the encircling capitalist world.
This was the "Cultural Bolshevism," particularly popular in Germany,
against which Communist policy later so sternly set its face. For one
thing the audacities of the cultural Bolsheviks were, as might be
expected, the personal acts of individual artists and therefore found
little favor in the eyes of those members of the Party for whom Communism meant belief in the task of creating a specifically proletarian culture
by means of collective action, and for whom the aberrations of the *avant
garde* poets, painters and producers were merely so much individualist
eccentricity—an *outré* and decadent perversion of the very bourgeois
civilization which the Revolution was out to destroy. Lenin, be it
noted, disliked all forms of modernism intensely: his attitude to radical
artistic experiment was bourgeois in the extreme. But he made no
attempt to enforce his aesthetic views, and, under the benevolent patronage of the Commissar of Education, Lunacharsky, a failed critical play-

wright but a sincere opponent of open barbarism, the controversies continued unabated. There were splits within factions: the champions of "proletarian" culture could not agree on whether it was to be produced by
individual men of gifts who distilled within themselves the aspirations
of the proletarian masses, actual and potential, acting, as it were, as
their mouthpieces or rather megaphones; or whether, as the extremer
ideologists proclaimed, individuals as such had no part at all to play
in the new order, for the art of the new collectivist society must itself be
collective. These latter in effect believed that works of art must be
written collectively by groups, and criticism—reviews, essays, directives
—by squads of critics, bearing collective responsibility for their work,
each member being an anonymous component of a social whole. Again,
some maintained that the business of proletarian art was to present the
new reality in an intenser form, to heighten it if necessary by the inventions of the socialism-impregnated imagination; others thought that
the business of artists was strictly utilitarian: to help with the making
of Communist society by documentary reportage of the new life—the
building of factories, collective farms, power stations, the destruction
of the old installations, the production of the essentials of the socialist
economy—tractors, combines, uniform food, identical clothing, mass-
produced houses, books, above all good, happy, uncomplicated, standard
human beings.

One could go on to multiply examples; the point I wish to make is
that these "programmatic" controversies were, in the first place, genuine; that is to say, the contending parties, on the whole, believed what
they were saying, and the disagreements between them could justly be
described as real differences in the interpretation of an accepted Marxist
doctrine. Moreover they were, to some degree, carried on in public; and,
most important of all, they were differences not about ends but about
means. The ends had become universally accepted since the opponents
and doubters had been eliminated or silenced. The intransigence of the
Comintern in dealing with foreign Communist and still more Socialist
parties, and the merciless heresy hunts, probably derived, for the most
part, from the honest belief that these parties might compromise on the
central truth—on the dogma of what constituted the desired society—or
else that they had chosen, or might choose, paths that could lead away,
however imperceptibly at first, from these sacred and undisputed goals.

It was its own conception of itself that divided Bolshevism so sharply
from its parent, Western Marxism—a conception which made it not

merely a set of political or social or economic beliefs or policies, but a way of life, all-penetrating and compulsory, controlled absolutely by the Party or the Central Committee of the Party in a way for which little authority can be found even in the most extreme pronouncements of Marx or Engels. This was the "Tsarism in reverse," which Herzen in the early fifties had gloomily and accurately predicted that Communism in Russia would become, and which it owes primarily to the personality of Lenin himself. No doubt the conditions of Russian life, which molded both him and it, in part created the need for religious certainty and messianic doctrine which Marxism provided. But the authoritarian element is among Lenin's specific contributions—the conception of the Party as a sect ruled ruthlessly by its elders and demanding from its members the total sacrifice upon its altar of all that they most cherished (material goods, moral principles, personal relationships), the more defiant and horrifying to tender-minded morality the better. It was this streak of stony fanaticism enlivened by a sardonic humor and vindictive trampling upon the liberal past that unnerved some of Lenin's socialist colleagues and attracted such disciples as Stalin and Zinoviev.

It was part and parcel of this vision of the millennium, disguised as a rational doctrine, to ignore the fact that as a scientific theory, claiming to be able to explain and predict social and economic change, Marxism had, by the beginning of the twentieth century, been decisively refuted by events in ways which have been described too often and too fully to be worth recapitulation. In the West, efforts to save the theory from intellectual bankruptcy, some orthodox, some heretical, were from time to time made by conscientious socialists and others. In Russia this was, by and large, not required. In Russia, especially after the October Revolution, Marxism had become a metaphysics, professedly resting on an analysis of history but stubbornly ignoring all awkward facts, designed by force or persuasion to secure conformity to a set of dogmatic propositions with its own esoteric, half-intelligible terminology, its own "dialectical" techniques of argument, its own clear and rigid *a priori* notions of what men and society must, at whatever cost, be made to be.

One of the most striking differences between the Soviet Union and the West was (and is) that in Russia those who were defeated in these internal Soviet controversies were liable from the very beginning of the régime—even before the official beginning of the terror—to be at best silenced, at worst punished or executed. Yet even these Draconian measures did not make the controversies less real. Indeed they had the opposite effect—the fact that the fruit of victory was power, and of defeat elimination, added an element of violent excitement to the duels in which the antagonists had so much to lose or win. I do not mean to assert that all or even the majority of those engaged in these febrile and perilous controversies were persons of integrity or moved by disinterested motives; a great deal of ruthless or desperate fighting for position or survival, with little regard for the professed principles of Marxism, was evident enough in Russia in the twenties. But at least some sort of wage was paid by vice to virtue; the protagonists in these struggles still felt traditionally obliged to advance some kind of theoretical justification for their conduct, and since some of them seemed to believe deeply in what they said, the issues were at times matters of genuine principle. This was most obviously the case on the "cultural front," which has at all times yielded the most reliable symptoms of what was going on in other spheres of Soviet life. Moreover, among the controversialists, men of remarkable gifts and temperament were to be found, and their attitudes, whether honest or opportunist, were those of exceptional human beings. Lunacharsky, Vorovsky, Averbakh were not, by any possible standard, critics of the first water, but they possessed a genuine revolutionary eloquence; Bukharin, Trotsky, Radek were as thinkers negligible, but one of them was a man of genius, and the others were at the very least gifted agitators. And among the creative writers and artists there still were some figures of the first rank who had not emigrated, or had returned. This alone made the twenties memorable, not only in Russian history but in Russian culture.

To all this Stalin put an abrupt end, and a new phase began.

III

The ideological policy of Stalin's régime is a fascinating topic, deserving separate study to itself, which no one has yet attempted seriously, and towards which I should like only to make one or two suggestions.

Once it had become clear to Stalin and his henchmen that an early world revolution was not be expected, and that the doubtless inevitable fulfillment of Marxist prophecies in the capitalist world might take place at a time and in ways very different from those which the earlier, more optimistic founding fathers had prophesied, he concentrated upon three interconnected purposes. Firstly, the perpetuation of the Bolshevik régime, and in particular of those of its leaders who were prepared to accept his own authority. Secondly, the maintenance and increase of Soviet power, political, economic and military, in a hostile world, by every possible means short of those entailing a radical change in the Soviet system itself. And thirdly, the elimination of all factors, whether at home or abroad, likely to jeopardize either of these two central purposes, whether or not such elimination was consistent with Marxism, Socialism or any other ideological attitude.

Stalin has at times been compared to Napoleon. It is, on the whole, a fanciful and misleading comparison. Stalin did not suppress or pervert the Bolshevik Revolution as Napoleon "liquidated" the Jacobins. There never was a Thermidor (still less a Brumaire) in the Russian Revolution: neither in the mid-twenties (where Trotsky naturally placed it), nor after the assassination of Kirov, nor after the death of Stalin. But there is something also in this analogy that is illuminating. To ask whether Stalin was a faithful Marxist or even a faithful Leninist is like asking whether Napoleon believed in the ideals or ideas of the French Revolution. Napoleon was sufficiently a child of the Revolution to be instinctively opposed to everything connected with the pre-revolutionary régime, and to wish to come to terms with some of its survivals solely for limited periods and for reasons of expediency. Just as Napoleon took it for granted that the relics of feudalism in Europe were doomed beyond recall, that the dynastic principle was not worth respecting, that nationalism was a force that must be used, that centralization and uniformity were policies favorable to his rule and the like, so it may be assumed that Stalin was Marxist and Leninist enough to believe that capitalism was inescapably doomed to be destroyed by its own "internal contradictions," although it might here and there engage in a desperate struggle for survival, whether it realized this or not and however useless such a struggle might be. Similarly Stalin probably accepted the tactical corollary that wherever such "contradictions" reached an acute stage, those who wished to survive and inherit the earth must seek to exacerbate these critical situations and not to palliate them; whereas in situations where these contradictions had not yet reached a critical point the path of prudence on the part of the members of the new society, *i.e.,* the Communists, was not to promote premature risings but to bore from within and concentrate on Popular Fronts and Trojan horses of various kinds. It is clear that he genuinely believed that the future of human society was inevitably collectivist and not individualist; that the power of religion and the churches was collapsing;

that control of economic power was more important (*i.e.,* capable of effecting greater changes or stopping them) than, say, nationalist sentiment or political power; and in all these respects he was, of course, a true, if exceedingly crude follower of Marx. But if it be asked whether he was a Marxist in the sense in which Lenin undoubtedly was one— *i.e.,* of believing that as the result of the dreadful birth pangs a new world would be born in which men would in some sense be freer than before, capable of developing their faculties on a vastly more productive scale, living in a world without wars, starvation and oppression, it seems doubtful whether he troubled himself with such questions any more than the Emperor Napoleon reflected about the ultimate validity of any of the ideals of the French Revolution. And, to his intellectual credit be it said, Stalin paid little enough regard—even by way of lip service—to the many utopian elements in Lenin's outlook.

It is, perhaps, a second point of similarity with Napoleon that Stalin firmly grasped a truth which perhaps Napoleon was the first among secular rulers fully to realize and act upon, namely that discussion of ideas—disputes about issues apparently remote from politics, such as metaphysics or logic or aesthetics—was, by promoting the critical spirit, in principle more dangerous to despotic régimes engaged in a struggle for power than belief in any form of authoritarianism. Napoleon's open hostility to the *Idéologues*—the empiricists and positivists of his day—is well known. He openly preferred the implacable legitimist and ultramontane Bonald, who abused him and would have no truck with him, to the politically mild and conformist liberal, Destutt de Tracy. Similarly Stalin, when he felt himself securely in power, decided to put an end to all ideological controversy as such in the Soviet Union. He did this by proclaiming one school to be victorious over all others (it does not historically matter which). The new directive was that the business of the intelligentsia—writers, artists, academics and so forth— was not to interpret, argue about, analyze, still less develop or apply in new spheres, the principles of Marxism, but to simplify them, adopt an agreed interpretation of their meaning and then repeat and ingeminate and hammer home in every available medium and on all possible occasions the selfsame set of approved truths. The new Stalinist values were similar to those proclaimed by Mussolini: loyalty, energy, obedience, discipline. Too much time had been wasted in controversy, time which could have been spent in promoting enforced industrialization or educating the new Soviet man. The very notion that there was an

area of permissible disagreement about the interpretation of even un-
questioned dogma created the possibility of insubordination; this, beginning indeed in spheres remote from the centers of power—say musical
criticism or linguistics—might spread to more politically sensitive areas
and so weaken the drive for economic and military power for which no
sacrifice was too great or too immoral. The celebrated Marxist formula
—the unity of theory and practice—was simplified to mean a set of
quotations to justify officially enunciated policies. The methods taken
to suppress the least symptom of independence on the part of even
the most faithful Stalinist intellectuals (let alone so-called deviationists or unreconstructed relics of older dispensations)—and, let it be
added, the success of these methods—are a phenomenon without parallel
in the recorded history of human oppression.

The result has been a long blank page in the history of Russian culture. Between 1932 and, say, 1945 or indeed 1955, it would not be too
much to say that—outside natural science—scarcely any idea or piece
of critical writing of high intrinsic value was published in Russia, and
hardly any work of art—scarcely anything genuinely interesting or important in itself and not merely as a symptom of the régime or of the
methods practised by it, that is to say, as a piece of historical evidence.

This policy was, perhaps, chiefly due to Stalin's personal character.
He was a half-literate member of an oppressed minority, filled with
resentment against superior persons and intellectuals of all kinds, but
particularly against those articulate and argumentative socialists whose
dialectical skill in the realm of theory must have humiliated him often
both before the Revolution and after it, and of whom Trotsky was
only the most arrogant and brilliant representative. Stalin's attitude towards ideas, intellectuals and intellectual freedom was a mixture of
fear, cynical contempt and sadistic humor that took the form (a touch of
Caligula) of discovering to what grotesque and degrading postures he
could reduce both the Soviet and foreign members of his cowering
congregation. After his death this policy has on occasion been defended
by his heirs on the ground that when an old world is being destroyed
and a new world brought into being, the makers and breakers cannot
be expected to have time for the arts and letters, or even ideas, which
must, at any rate for the moment, suffer what befalls them without
protest.

It is interesting to ask how such absolute subservience, and for so
long a period, could have been secured on the part of an intelligentsia

which had after all not merely contributed the very term to the languages of Europe, but had itself played so prominent and decisive a rôle in bringing about victory of the Revolution. Here was a body of persons the blood of whose martyrs had been the seed of the entire revolutionary movement, a body to which Lenin, far more than Marx, had assigned a leading rôle in the task of subverting the old order and of keeping the new one going; and yet, when it was crushed, not a mouse stirred: a few indignant voices abroad, but inside the Soviet Union silence and total submission. Mere intimidation, torture and murder should not have proved sufficient in a country which, we are always told, was not unused to just such methods and had nevertheless preserved a revolutionary underground alive for the better part of a century. It is here that one must acknowledge that Stalin achieved this by his own original contributions to the art of government—inventions that deserve the attention of every student of the history and practice of government.

IV

The first invention has been called by Mr. Utis "the artificial dialectic." [1] It is well known that according to the systems of Hegel and of Marx events do not proceed in direct causal sequence but by means of a conflict of forces—of thesis and antithesis—ending in a collision between them, and a Pyrrhic victory, in the course of which they eliminate each other, and history takes "a leap" to a new level, where the process, called dialectical, begins once again. Whatever may be the validity of this theory in any other sphere, it has a very specific applicability to revolutionary situations.

As every student of the subject must know, the principal practical problem before those who have successfully brought off a large-scale revolution is how to prevent the resultant situation from collapsing into one of two opposed extremes. The first—let us, following Mr. Utis, call it Scylla—is reached when the zealots of the revolution, observing that the new world which the revolution was meant to create has somehow not yet come to pass, seek for explanations, culprits, scapegoats, blame it on criminal weakness or treachery on the part of this or that group of their agents or allies, declare the revolution in mortal

---

[1] See "Stalin and the Art of Government," by O. Utis, *Foreign Affairs*, January 1952.

peril and start a witch hunt which presently develops into a terror, in the course of which various groups of revolutionaries tend to eliminate each other successively, and social existence is in danger of losing the minimum degree of cohesion without which no society can continue to be. This process tends to be checked by some form of counter-revolution, which is brought on by a desperate effort on the part of the majority, whose security is threatened, to preserve itself and achieve stability, an instinctive social recoil from some imminent-looking collapse. This is what occurred during the great French Revolution, to some extent during the Commune of 1871, in some parts of Eastern Europe in 1918, and might have occurred in 1848 had the extreme left-wing parties begun to win. The mounting spiral of terror was, in fact, what Trotsky was suspected of wishing to promote.

The opposite extreme—Charybdis—is subsidence into a weary indifference. When the original impetus of the revolution begins after a time to ebb, and people seek a respite from the terrible tension of the unnatural life to which they have been exposed, they seek relief, comfort, normal forms of life; and the revolution slides by degrees into the ease, *Schlamperei,* moral squalor, financial chicanery and general corruption of the kind which marked, for example, the French Directoire; or else subsides into some conventional dictatorship or oligarchy, as has happened so often in Latin America and elsewhere. The problem for the makers of the revolution, therefore, is how to keep the revolution going without falling foul of either the Scylla of utopian fanaticism or the Charybdis of cynical opportunism.

Stalin should be credited with having discovered and applied a method which did, in fact, solve this particular problem in a certain sense. Theoretically, history or nature (as interpreted by Hegel or Marx) should, by pursuing its own dialectical process, cause these opposites to collide at the crucial stage, forcing reality to ascend a creative spiral instead of collapsing into one-sided forms of bankruptcy. But since history and nature evidently tend to nod, man must from time to time come to the aid of these impersonal agencies. The government, as soon as it sees signs of the fatal hankering after the fleshpots of the older life, must tighten the reins, intensify its propaganda, exhort, frighten, terrorize, if need be make examples of as many conspicuous backsliders as may be required to stop the rout. Malingerers, comfort-lovers, doubters, heretics, other "negative elements" are eliminated. This is the "thesis." The rest of the population, duly chastened, dominated by terror rather than hope or desire for gain or faith, throw themselves into the required labors, and the economy bounds forward for a while. But then the élite of the revolutionary purists, the fanatical terrorists, the simon-pure heart of the Party, who must be genuinely convinced of the sacred duty of cutting off the rotten branches of the body politic, inevitably go too far. If they did not, if they could stop in time, they would not have been the kind of people to perform the task of inquisition with the desperate zeal and ruthlessness required; hypocrites, half-believers, moderates, opportunists, men of cautious judgment or human feeling are of no use for this purpose, for they will, as Bakunin had warned long ago, compromise halfway. Then the moment arrives when the population, too terrorized to advance, or too starved, becomes listless, downs tools, and efficiency and productivity begin to drop off; this is the moment for clemency. The zealots are accused of having gone too far, they are accused of oppressing the people, and—always a popular move— they are in their turn publicly disciplined, that is, in Stalin's heyday, purged and executed. Some small increase of freedom is allowed in remote fields—say, that of literary criticism or poetry or archæology, nothing so near the center of things as economics or politics. This is the "antithesis." The people breathe again, there is optimism, gratitude, talk of the wisdom of their rulers now that their eyes have been opened to the "excesses" of their unfaithful servants, hope of further liberties, a thaw; production leaps up, the government is praised for returning to some earlier, more tolerant ideal, and a relatively happier period ensues.

This once more leads to the inevitable relaxation of tension, slackening of discipline, lowering of productive effort. Once more there is (the new thesis) a call for a return to ideological purity, for the reëstablishment of fundamental principles and loyalties, for the elimination of the parasitical saboteurs, self-seekers, drones, foreign agents, enemies of the people who have in some way managed to creep into the fold. There is a new purge, a new spurt of ideological fanaticism, a new crusade, and the heads of the counter-revolutionary hydra (the new antithesis) have to be cut off once again.

In this way the population is, as it were, kept perpetually on the run, its development proceeds by a zigzag path, and individual self-preservation depends on a gift for perceiving at which precise moment the central authority is about to order a retreat or an advance, and a knack for swiftly adjusting oneself to the new direction. Here timing is all. A miscalculation, due to inertia or political insensitiveness or, worse still,

political or moral conviction, causing one to linger too long on a road
that has been condemned, must almost always, particularly if persisted
in, mean disgrace or death.

It cannot be denied that by this deliberate policy of carefully timed
purges and counter-purges of various intensities, of contraction and
expansion, Stalin did manage to preserve in being a system that cannot
be actively approved or felt to be natural by most of those concerned,
and indeed to keep it going for a longer period than that for which any
other revolution has, thus far, managed to survive. There is a full discussion of the method in the article by Mr. Utis already cited. Although,
as the author there maintains, the method, to be successful, requires the
master hand of its inventor, it appears to have survived him. Despite
the grave shocks to the system caused by the struggle for power among
Stalin's successors, the emergence into the open of conflicts and factions,
the risings of oppressed peoples in the West totally unforeseen in Moscow, what Mr. Utis calls the "artificial dialectic" appears to be functioning still. The succession, in strict sequence, during the last five
years, of "liberal" and repressive moves by the Soviet rulers, both at
home and abroad, although no longer conducted with the virtuosity (or
the deep personal sadism) of Stalin, has too much regularity of pattern
to be unintended. The hypothesis advanced by the author to explain only
Stalin's own methods of government seems to fit his successors.

The method is an original political invention, and Stalin deserves
full credit for it. One of its deliberate by-products has been the total
demoralization of what is still in the U.S.S.R. called the intelligentsia—
persons interested in art or in ideas. Under the worst moments of
Tsarist oppression there did, after all, exist some areas of wholly free
expression; moreover, one could always be silent. This was altered by
Stalin. No areas were excluded from the Party's directives; and to refuse to say what had been ordered was insubordination and led to punishment. "Inner emigration" requires the possibility of the use of one's
mind and means of expression at least in neutral ways. But if one's
chances of sheer survival have been made dependent on continuous
active support of principles or policies which may seem absurd or
morally abhorrent; and if, moreover, the whole of one's mental capacity is taxed by the perpetual need to chart one's course in fatally
dangerous waters, to manœuvre from position to position, while one's
moral fiber is tested by the need to bow one's head low not to one but
to many capricious, unpredictably changing divinities, so that the least

inattention, slackness or error costs one dear—then there is less and less possibility of thinking one's own thoughts, or of escaping into an inner citadel in which one can remain secretly heterodox and independent and know what one believes. Stalin went further. He forbade more than a minimum degree of official intercommunication between one academic faculty and another, between laboratory and institute, and successfully prevented the growth of any center of intellectual authority, however humble and obedient, however fraudulent and obscurantist. No priest-hood of dialectical materialism had been allowed to arise, because no discussion of theoretical issues was permitted; the business of the Academy of Sciences or the Institute of Red Professors or the Marx-Engels Institute was to quote Marx in supporting Stalin's *acts:* the *doctrine* he, or some other member of the Politbureau (certainly not a professor), would supply for himself.

Where there is an official church or college of augurs, with its own privileges and mysteries, there is a relatively fenced-off area, with walls within which both orthodoxy and heresy can flourish. Stalin set himself to repress ideas as such—at a very high cost, be it added, not merely in terms of the basic education of Soviet citizens (not to speak of disinterested intellectual activity, "pure" research and so on), but even in the useful and applied sciences which were gravely handicapped by the lack of freedom of discussion and suffered an abnormally high admixture of adventurers, charlatans and professional informers. All this was effective in stifling every form of intellectual life to a far greater degree than was realized by even the most hostile and pessimistic observers in the West, or, for that matter, by Communist Parties outside the Soviet orbit. To have created such a system is a very striking achievement on Stalin's part, whose importance should not be underrated. For it has crushed the life out of what once was one of the most gifted and productive societies in the world. At any rate for the time being.

V

There is yet a second consequence of this system which is worthy of remark, namely that most of the standard vices so monotonously attributed by Marxists to capitalism are to be found in their purest form only in the Soviet Union itself. Most readers of this journal will be familiar with such stock Marxist categories as capitalist exploitation, the iron law of wages, the transformation of human beings into mere

commodities, the skimming off of surplus value by those who control
the means of production, the dependence of the ideological superstructure on the economic base, and other Communist phrases. But where
do these concepts best apply?

Economic exploitation is a phenomenon familiar enough in the West;
but there is no society in which one body of men is more firmly, systematically and openly "exploited" by another than the workers of the
Soviet Union by their overseers. True, the benefits of this process do not
go to private employers or capitalists. The exploiter is the state itself,
or rather those who effectively control its apparatus of coercion and
authority. These controllers—whether they act as Party officials or state
bureaucrats or both—act far more like the capitalist of Marxist mythol-
ogy than any living capitalist in the West today. The Soviet rulers really
do see to it that the workers are supplied with that precise minimum
of food, shelter, clothing, entertainment, education and so forth that
they are thought to require in order to produce the maximum quantity
of the goods and services at which the state planners are aiming. The
rest is skimmed off as surplus value far more conveniently and neatly
than it can ever have been detached in the unplanned West. Wages
are regulated in the most "iron" way possible—by the needs of production.
Economic exploitation here is conducted under laboratory conditions
not conceivable in Western Europe or America.[2] It is again in the Soviet
Union that official professions of "ideology"—principles, slogans, ideals
—correspond least to actual practice. It is there, too, that some intellectuals can most truly be described as lackeys (some sluggish and
reluctant, others filled with a kind of cynical delight and pride in their
own virtuosity) of the ruling group. It is there, far more obviously than
in the West, that ideas, literature, works of art act as "rationalizations"
or smoke screens for ruthless deeds, or means of escape from the contemplation of crimes or follies, or as an opium for the masses. It is
there that the state religion—for that is what the dead and fossilized
"dialectical materialism" of the official Soviet philosophers has, in effect,
more or less avowedly become—is nothing but a consciously used weapon
in the war against the enemy, within and without; and lays no claim
to "objective" truth.

[2] Mr. Milovan Djilas corroborates this forcibly in his book, "The New Class"
(New York: Praeger, 1957). Whether the system is to be called state capitalism
(the state being anything but a democracy) or a "degenerate workers' state"
or a naked autocracy is a question of the most appropriate label. The facts
themselves are not in doubt.

The materialist theory of history teaches us that the primary factors that determine the lives of individuals and societies are economic, namely the relationships of human beings in the productive system; while such cultural phenomena as their religious, ethical, political ideas, their judicial and political institutions, their literature, arts, scientific beliefs and so forth belong to various tiers of the "superstructure," that is, are determined by—are a function of—the "base." This celebrated and justly influential doctrine, embodying as it does a great deal that is new, important, illuminating and by now very widely accepted, has, nevertheless, never been easy to fit in detail to any given society or period of history in the past. Every attempt to apply it narrowly [3] always encountered too many exceptions: if these were to be explained away, they usually had to be stretched till the theory became too vague or encrusted with too many qualifications to retain any utility. But it holds only too faithfully of Soviet society. There it is absolutely clear to everyone what is part of the base and what is part of the superstructure. Writers and architects can have no illusions about which level of the pyramid they constitute. Economic, military and other "material" needs really do wholly determine—because they are deliberately made to determine—ideological phenomena, and not vice versa. It is not nature nor history that has produced this situation, but a piece of highly artificial engineering, by which Stalin and his officials have transformed the Russian Empire.

It is an extraordinary irony of history that categories and concepts invented to describe Western capitalism should turn out to fit most closely its mortal enemy. But this is scarcely an accident, a *lusus historiae*. Every student of the Russian Revolution knows that the issue that divided the Bolsheviks most deeply from the orthodox Marxists— the Mensheviks—was the practicability of an immediate transition to socialism. The Mensheviks maintained that according to any interpretation of Marx, genuine socialism could be established only in a society which had reached a high degree of industrialization—were the organized proletariat formed the majority of the population, and was, through the working of the "inexorable" and mounting "contradictions" of economic development, in a position to "expropriate the expropriators"

---

[3] Say, to demonstrate that the writings of Thomas Love Peacock could not possibly have arisen save in the economic conditions of early nineteenth century England; and that these in their turn made some such writings as those of, let us say, Aldous Huxley (or others like him) quite inevitable a century later.

and initiate socialism. No one could maintain that this stage had yet been reached in the Russian Empire. But the Bolsheviks, mainly under Trotsky's inspiration, claimed that instead of semi-passively waiting for capitalism (a bourgeois republic) to do the job, leaving the workers insufficiently protected from the free play of "history," "nature," etc.— this process could be controlled by a proletarian dictatorship; Russia could be made to go through the stages demanded by the "dialectic of history" under hothouse conditions regulated by the Communist Party. This was to be the famous "transitional" period of the dictatorship of the proletariat—the artificial or controlled equivalent of "natural" capitalist development in the West: two roads leading equally to full-blown Communism, but the Russian corridor less painful because not left to the vagaries of "nature," but planned by men in control of their own fate owing to their possession of the "scientific" weapon of Marxist theory and able, therefore, to "shorten the birth pangs" by a well exe-cuted revolution. If, like Lenin, one begins with fanatical faith in the truth of the Marxist analysis of history, the fact that it does not too well fit even the capitalist West, which it was designed to describe, will make little difference. If the pattern does not correspond to the facts, the facts must be made to tally with the pattern. There was rela-tively little capitalism, and a feeble proletariat, in Russia in 1917. But the dialectic of history cannot be cheated. Unless Marxism rested on a gigantic fallacy there *could* be no salvation without the equivalent of the capitalist phase. Hence the corresponding phenomena had to be synthetically produced—made to emerge by artificial means.

This can sometimes be done with success, as in Japan, for example. But the Japanese followed the light of reason and experience. They modernized themselves by the methods that seemed to work best, with-out being chained to a dogmatic theory. They achieved their purpose not without brutalities, but rapidly and with spectacular success. This course was not open to Lenin and his followers. They were compelled by their fidelity to the Marxist classics to subordinate their practical judgment to the demands of theory: the social and economic develop-ment of Russia had to proceed by fixed steps whose order was laid down by the Marxist manuals. This created fantastic handicaps that were over-come at a terrible human cost. Russia *had* to go through phases which, according to Marx, Western capitalism passed during and after its industrial revolution. Russian reality had to be altered to resemble a model constructed, not too competently, to account for the progress of a society very unlike itself. A society was vivisected, as it were, to fit a theory which began life as no more than the explanation of its evolution. Something which began as descriptive became normative: a theory intended to account for the development and behavior of Western Europe in the nineteenth century had been turned into a blueprint for Eastern Europe in the twentieth.

Actions founded upon errors of social observation do not necessarily end badly. There is, for all to see, that part of American constitutional development which was inspired by Montesquieu's mistaken interpretation of British political theory and practice. Lenin's error proved more costly. Russia was precipitated into unheard-of horrors of industrialization largely because Marx had drawn a dark picture of Western capitalism and said that no society could escape something analogous. The imposition of the Bolshevik system upon an economically retarded country is a unique and monstrous monument to the power of a few men's wills and their sovereign contempt for history and empirical evidence; and a bloodcurdling interpretation of the Unity of Theory and Practice.

VI

Faced with crises and the possibility of collapse, Lenin executed a partial retreat. And his successors, under the pressure of events, substituted various practical makeshifts and realistic devices and policies in place of the extravagant utopian design which dominates Lenin's thinking. Nevertheless the violent break with reality that is at the heart of the Bolshevik Revolution can evidently not be eliminated without causing the régime to collapse; at any rate no serious attempt to do so has ever been made. For this reason Soviet society is not, in the normal sense, a civil society at all.

The purpose of normal human societies is in the first place to survive; and, after that, to satisfy what Mill called "the deepest interests of mankind," that is to say, to satisfy at any rate a minimum number of men's normal desires after their basic needs are satisfied—say, for self-expression, happiness, freedom, justice. Any government which realizes these values to a reasonable degree is held to fulfill its function. These are not the principal ends of Soviet society, or of its government. Conditioned by its revolutionary origins, it is organized to achieve objectives, to respond to challenges, win victories. Like a school, a team of players,

still more like an army on the march, it is a specialized institution designed for specific purposes that must be made explicit to its members
by the leaders. Soviet life is constructed to strive for goals. It makes
little difference what the particular goals may be—military or civil, the
defeat of the enemy within or without, or the attainment of industrial
objectives—announced goals there must be, if Soviet society is to continue to be. The leaders understand this well, and whether or not they
are to be regarded as prisoners of their own system, they know that
they must continue to exhort their subjects to greater and greater endeavors if they are to avoid the disintegration of the régime. They
are in the position of army commanders in a war, who realize that
unless their troops see a minimum amount of active service, the discipline, the esprit de corps, the continued existence of the armies as
fighting units cannot be guaranteed.

The leaders of the Soviet Union, for all we know, may by now be
secretly hankering after the peaceful existence, to abandon the exiguous
splendors and unending cruelties and miseries of the régime and subside
into "normal" existence. If they harbor any such desires, they know
that in the short run, at least, this is not practicable. For Soviet society
is organized not for happiness, comfort, liberty, justice, personal relationships, but for combat. Whether they wish it or not the drivers and
controllers of this immense train cannot now halt it or leap from it in
mid-course without risk of destruction. If they are to survive and above
all remain in power, they must go on. Whether they can replace parts
of it while it is moving, and so transform it (themselves) into something
less savage, less dangerous to themselves and mankind, remains to be
seen. At any rate that must be the hope of those who do not think war
inevitable.

In the meanwhile this caricature of *dirigisme* has discredited the tradition of social idealism and liquidated the intelligentsia connected with
it, perhaps more decisively than unaided persecution could have done.
Nothing destroys a minority movement more effectively than the official
adoption and inevitable betrayal and perversion of its ends by the
state itself. There are cases where nothing succeeds less well than success.

THE use of nuclear threats to back its foreign policy demands was first applied by the Soviet leadership during the Suez crisis of 1956, and the practice became notably frequent in the next three years. True, the careful timing of each successive threat to fit into the declining curve of the Suez, Lebanese and Formosa Straits crises suggested that on those occasions the Kremlin was seeking a propaganda and prestige bonus rather than a nuclear showdown. Still, the repetition of those threats, even without a specific ultimatum in hand, made it urgent to re-examine, so far as Soviet secrecy permitted, the drastically changed bases of Soviet strategic planning. "The Revolution in Soviet Strategic Thinking" (January 1958), by Herbert S. Dinerstein, is one of a substantial number of pioneering analyses of strategic problems that have been presented in the pages of *Foreign Affairs*.

Under Stalin's guidance published Soviet writings had continuously stressed the central role of large mass armies, to which naval and air power were to be auxiliary. They had discounted vigorously the value of surprise and, by implication, that of preventive nuclear war. Obviously, since 1945 the Soviet Government and many talented scientists and engineers had been pressing forward the development of nuclear power and rockets of great range and thrust, even while official dogma denied any decisive value to the new weapons. American and NATO counterstrategy, meanwhile, were based on the assumption that superior Soviet land armies could be held in check for many years to come by an American monopoly or clear-cut superiority in nuclear weapons and the means of their delivery. Now that this had been placed in question, it was important to divine how Soviet strategists appraised the role of the new strategic power. Mr. Dinerstein's article, based on many years of meticulous research, supplied an important piece of evidence, one that is still relevant to a proper understanding of the problem.

Trained as a historian, Herbert S. Dinerstein has been a member for many years of the social science division of the RAND Corporation. Among his published studies are "Communism and the Russian Peasant" (1955) and "War and the Soviet Union; Nuclear Weapons and the Revolution in Soviet Military and Political Thinking" (1959).

THE REVOLUTION IN
SOVIET STRATEGIC THINKING

By Herbert S. Dinerstein

NO one is likely to deny that since August 1945, when the first atomic bomb was used, the nature of warfare has changed. In the United States the great importance of the change was quickly appreciated, and as nuclear weapons have developed the doctrine for their employment has been continuously revised. In the Soviet Union, by contrast, the first years following the American acquisition of nuclear weapons were marked by the ostensible rejection of any belief in their exceptional importance. Since 1953, however, the Soviet Union has come to grips with the problems posed by the existence of these weapons. In this article we shall examine how Soviet military thinkers have radically altered some of their hoary ideas about warfare and how differences on military policies played an important rôle in the political crises terminated by Malenkov's demotion in February 1955. By contrast, Zhukov's dismissal in October 1957 probably arose from differences on political rather than military policy.

Soon after Stalin died in March 1953, Russian military leaders began to incorporate the problems logically raised by the existence of nuclear weapons into more or less public discussions of military matters. Until that time Soviet ideas on warfare had been formed by combining the lessons of World War II with Marxian theories. The Soviet concept, in essence, was that modern war was necessarily a war of attrition in which political factors played a major rôle. Stripped of excess verbiage, "the teachings of Marxism on war" said that the morale of the fighting front and the home front had grown in importance since the time when mercenary armies fought with forces in being without appreciable accretions in strength through mobilization. Although the validity of this idea was widely recognized, the Marxists pretended to a monopoly of the concept.

In Stalin's version of this view of war, surprise was minimized; the factors emphasized were those that would be of greatest importance in a war of attrition. In 1942 Stalin listed certain "permanently operating factors," as they were called, which he said determined victory or defeat in war. These factors were the stability of the rear, the morale of the army, the quantity and quality of divisions, the army's weapons, and the organizing ability of the commanding officers. Nothing but these permanently operating factors counted in the final result. Transitory factors, such as the use of military surprise, could not in themselves determine the outcome of the war. Under such a theory, surprise attack with nuclear weapons could not be decisive.

While Stalin lived, this theory was imposed as dogma on all Soviet military thinking. It fostered complacency and a false confidence in Soviet strength and hampered an open-minded examination no less of the country's military opportunities than of her difficulties. It was more the tone than the content of Stalin's formulation that was harmful. What Stalin said was so truistic that it had little practical utility. Who could deny that a country with a larger, better-equipped, better-led force, a country which enjoyed superior morale and had a superior industrial base, would win a war with a country notably inferior in all these respects? But, since such a discrepancy between the capability of warring nations is rarely found, Stalin's dogma is of limited use as a guide for achieving the proper military posture.

Stalin's dogma was not merely too general to be useful; it was positively harmful, because it was interpreted to mean that the Soviet Union was and always would be superior to other nations in the permanently operating factors, and would therefore automatically win any war in which it became involved. When the Soviet authorities stated that the Soviet Union would always be superior in the permanently operating factors, they meant that the political advantages inherent in a socialist society more than compensated for its inferior economic strength.

Thus, Soviet morale had to be superior, for Soviet citizens love the state in a way impossible for the victims of capitalism, and they fight and toil more valiantly in the knowledge that theirs is the just cause. Socialist leadership was better because it rested on Marxism; Soviet military science was better because it was Marxist. The Soviet Union also had important material advantages because it was a Marxist state. It could mobilize for war more rapidly and thoroughly than the capitalist countries because its economic organization was better planned and more efficient.

All this was not so much a theory of war as an elaborate ritual of reassurance. Complacency this was, but not the kind of complacency that breeds apathy. Convinced that History helps those who help themselves, the Soviet leaders imposed great sacrifices upon their people in order to create a formidable military establishment. But was it formidable in the age of nuclear weapons?

The Soviet military establishment had been designed in accordance with Stalin's theory that the Soviet Union could win a war of attrition against capitalism, and that only a war of attrition was possible. It was not admitted that the employment of nuclear weapons might compress the effects of years of normal attrition into a few days. Under Stalin the Russian military leaders could neither analyze the situations where defeat was probable nor devise measures to reduce its likelihood. To establish an adequate military posture in spite of the dogma that your side will inevitably win is to do it the hard way—if indeed it can be done at all.

After Stalin's death some of his successors still felt that the old way was the only way; others wanted to break the fetters of the past. The innovators won the argument after a hard fight. Its course can be followed in the pages of *Voennaia mysl'* (*Military Thought*), the organ of the general staff, which has only a limited circulation within the Soviet Union.[1] At first the controversy was confined to its pages, but when the issue was finally resolved, in early 1955, in favor of a revision of Stalinist military thinking, the whole military press reflected the change in the official line.

The first public indication of a conflict behind the scenes was an article written for *Military Thought* in November 1953, by its editor, Major General Talenskii, a general staff expert on military history who had formerly been editor of *Red Star,* the daily organ of the Ministry of Defense. When he opened what was obviously the most far-reaching discussion of military theory in the Soviet Union in a quarter century, it was clear to Soviet readers that he was speaking for others beside himself.

[1] With the exception of a partial account by Mr. N. Galai in the June 1956 issue of the *Bulletin of the Institute for the Study of the U.S.S.R.,* no comprehensive account of the debate appears to have been published outside the Soviet Union.

Talenskii's arguments were couched in the language of Marxian philosophical generalization, but the conclusions were down to earth. His main point was that the battle was what counted. Attention had to be focused on the armed conflict itself, which the Soviet Union might win or lose, depending on the situation. Talenskii made three main points. First, the military planner had to abandon his slavish adherence to the permanently operating factors as the only possible basis for all military planning. Second, he had to restrict the discussion to military factors and avoid all the political considerations which automatically led to the conclusion that the Soviet Union would win. Third, he had to insist on the essential identity of the principles of warfare for both sides.

Talenskii dealt with Stalin's dogma concerning the permanently operating factors by flatly stating that it did not constitute a law of war. Talenskii and his supporters rejected not the importance of making the Soviet Union superior in these factors, but the unquestioning assumption that the Soviet Union, by virtue of being a socialist state, must always be superior in them. No longer was the phrase "permanently operating factors" to be regarded as an abbreviated article of faith, and by early 1956 it disappeared from the Soviet military press.

Talenskii's second argument was a corollary of the first: military people and military science ought to stick to military matters and leave political considerations to the Party. Marxist-Leninist teachings, he said, are not within the purview of military science. In the past, reference to Marxist-Leninist teachings automatically led military theorists to the conclusion that a socialist state had the advantage in war because, by definition, a socialist state was superior in political strength to its capitalist enemies. Talenskii's abandonment of the assumption of inevitable Soviet victory was a most important step toward realism.

Talenskii's third point was the essential identity of the principles of warfare for both sides. The Stalinist view was that a socialist society was governed by basic social laws different from those governing a capitalist society. It followed that the war activity of these two kinds of society was also governed by different laws. Talenskii firmly insisted that, in armed conflict, the same laws governed both sides. The consequence of this position was again to focus attention on the battle and to push aside the social and political differences between capitalism and Communism.

In rejecting the rigid dogmatism of the Stalinist approach, what was

Talenskii putting in its place? Victory, he said, is to be accomplished by successive blows of cumulative force delivered by a Power superior in the basic economic, political and military potentialities. Although Talenskii's preferred war is the extended war of attrition, he makes it unequivocally clear that in certain conditions the issue might be decided in a short time. But he does not substitute one dogma for another. In harmony with the new realism, he does not insist that the war of the future *must* be won or lost in the first phase: given the proper measures in air defense and intelligence, a surprise attack need not decide the outcome during the initial stage of the war.

In his article of November 1953, Talenskii made no explicit connection between the possibility of a short war and the employment of nuclear weapons. During the ensuing year, this connection was made in passing by others in the many pages of *Military Thought*. But it was only after the clear-cut victory of the new view early in 1955 that the connection between surprise attack, nuclear weapons and the possibility of a short war was made sharply and prominently in the general press.

The proponents of the new view did not win easily. Talenskii's views were described as anti-scientific and anti-Marxist. For espousing "naked" strategy he was compared to Douhet and Fuller. The majors and colonels who discharged these damning epithets in Talenskii's direction could hardly have done so if Talenskii's views had already represented official thinking about war. Any doubts on this score would have been dispelled by Marshal Vasilevskii's statement in an article in *Red Star* for February 22, 1954, that Soviet military science was based on the permanently operating factors which determined the fate of war. Vasilevskii reiterated his rejection of the new trend in *Red Star* for May 7, 1954, where he quoted Stalin as having demonstrated "that the outcome of war is determined not by the collateral factors but by the permanently operating factors." Vasilevskii's stand on the tried and true Stalinist formula was echoed in the pages of *Military Thought,* in *Red Star,* and in books on military doctrine. In fact, in mid-1954 Talenskii was relieved as editor of *Military Thought.*

The turning point came after Malenkov was demoted. In February 1955, after Marshal Zhukov had become Minister of Defense, the new editorial board finally agreed to print an article by Marshal Rotmistrov, "On the Rôle of Surprise in Contemporary War," which spelled out the full implications of Talenskii's cautious statements of November 1953. Talenskii had said that his formulation of the basic law of war did not "exclude the possibility of a decisive defeat in a limited time of one or the other opponent, given the existence of certain conditions." Rotmistrov's formula was positive: "It must be plainly said that, in the situation of the employment of atomic and hydrogen weapons, surprise is one of the decisive conditions for the attainment of success not only in battles and operations but also in the war as a whole."

When, in April of 1955, the editors of *Military Thought* officially endorsed the major points of Talenskii's position and rejected the criticisms of his opponents, it was something of an anticlimax, for the belated publication of Rotmistrov's article in February 1955 had already spelled the end of the orthodox Stalinist view of military doctrine.

II

One is immediately struck by the timing of the Rotmistrov article. Its appearance, signifying that the bitter and extended controversy had been decided in favor of the innovators, was practically simultaneous with the demotion of Malenkov, the elevation of Khrushchev, and Marshal Zhukov's assumption of the post of Minister of Defense in February 1955. Zhukov's dismissal from that post last fall is probably not a sign that the strategy then adopted will now be dropped in its turn. The strategy officially adopted in 1955 was based on Khrushchev's conviction that the Soviet Union must be ready for a nuclear war even though the likelihood of such a war was small. Both Malenkov and Khrushchev apparently agreed that Soviet policies, including military ones, had to be changed to meet the requirements of the nuclear age.

But they differed as to what these changes should be. Malenkov thought that Soviet policies should be based on the assumption that the United States was effectively deterred from initiating war on Russia. Five months after Stalin's death, Malenkov, in a major speech, pointed to the basis for the Soviet policy of deterrence and, at the same time, proposed a radical redirection of Soviet economic policies. He announced that the Soviet Union had developed an H-bomb (though it had not yet exploded one); and he said that the time had now come to force the development of light industry. Malenkov was suggesting, but not quite saying, that the new Soviet strength had changed the situation so radically that one could revise the traditional Soviet formulation that war was inevitable as long as capitalism existed. If existing Soviet strength was enough to keep the peace, greater attention to Soviet consumer needs was justified. If the United States was deterred from making war because of Soviet strength, Malenkov's often-repeated statement that all international problems could be settled by negotiation was a reasonable hope.

An obscure writer, M. Gus, in the November 1953 issue of *Zvezda* made explicit what was implicit in Malenkov's position. He wrote that it was possible "to paralyze the law of the inevitability of war," and he advocated a foreign policy for the Soviet Union which would involve "wise compromise" and "expedient and necessary concessions." This revision of doctrine was immediately rejected in the following issue of the magazine, and in other places prominent Party and military writers reiterated the standard position that war would cease to be inevitable only when capitalism was destroyed.

Although no one after Gus has ever flatly said that war is no longer inevitable, many prominent Soviet leaders made speeches whose tone was consistent with this assumption. On Lenin's anniversary in January 1954, Pospelov made a speech in which there was not a single word about the danger of war or the warlike plans of the capitalists. In March of 1954, Mikoyan said in Erevan that the danger of war had receded largely because the Soviet Union possessed the atomic and hydrogen bombs. The United States now had to face the possibility of the destruction of American cities, and was therefore more inclined to negotiate with the Soviet Union. These paragraphs in Mikoyan's speech were excised from the accounts carried by the Moscow press. In the same month, Malenkov made his famous plea for an end of the cold war.

Malenkov and his group were proceeding from the assumption that the destructiveness of nuclear weapons had created a real opportunity for reliance on a policy of deterring the United States. But they went beyond the mere statement of a theoretical position; they came into open collision with others on the subject of the military budget. In March 1954, Malenkov, Pospelov, Pervukhin and Saburov made speeches in which they said that the armed forces of the Soviet Union possessed everything necessary to carry out their functions. Khrushchev, Bulganin, Molotov, Kaganovich and Voroshilov were clearly ranged on the other side of the argument. Using the old formula about capitalist encirclement of the Soviet Union, they insisted again and again that the armed forces had to be further strengthened.

Any doubts as to the existence of fundamental differences between Malenkov and his opponents were dispelled in April 1954 when

Malenkov, probably under duress, suddenly abandoned the line that peace might be preserved through fear of the "destruction of world civilization," and substituted for it an orthodox prediction that, if war came, only capitalism would collapse. In the same statement, he also reversed his position on the armed forces and called for an increase in military strength. From that time forward, Malenkov's opponents were unchallenged in their general assertions that the capitalists wanted war, and their more specific warnings against surprise attack with nuclear weapons. Khrushchev and Bulganin having warned in a general way that the Soviet Union should be prepared for any surprises, their supporters spoke explicitly of the danger to the Soviet Union if the capitalist enemy succeeded in a surprise nuclear attack. Clearly, if it was at all possible for such a surprise attack to win a war, it would be reckless to rely on American fear of the "destruction of world civilization" to protect the Soviet Union. Soviet prospects for deterring the United States had improved, but possession of nuclear weapons did not guarantee immunity from attack.

It is unlikely that Malenkov believed war was ruled out by the existence of nuclear weapons and that, as long as the Soviet Union had some sort of nuclear striking force, her interests were securely guarded. It is equally improbable that Khrushchev and his supporters believed a nuclear attack by the United States to be imminent. More likely, Malenkov expected that a combination of Soviet nuclear strength and conciliatory policies could assure peace for a long time with no necessity for important changes in the Soviet military posture. Khrushchev, in turn, probably reasoned that, although a United States attack upon the Soviet Union was unlikely, the Soviet Union had to be prepared to meet such an attack, and that the better prepared the Soviet Union, the smaller the likelihood of such an attack. This he expressed at the Twentieth Party Congress, in February of 1956, when he revised the formula of "inevitable war" to read that war was not "fatalistically inevitable."

Khrushchev's position was the more traditional and more cautious of the two. It took into account the worst that might happen. Military planners like to be prepared to deal with a presumptive enemy's capabilities irrespective of his good intentions or self-restraint. During the spring of 1954, Khrushchev frequently pointed to the irrationality of American behavior and warned that the Soviet Union must depend on its own strength, without relying on the enemy's desire for peace. The military posture required to deter a *potential* enemy from nuclear attack is not identical with that required to fight an *actual* enemy in nuclear war. The bare minimum required to deter the United States would be the capacity to inflict great damage on the United States. For deterrence alone, the survival of the Soviet retaliatory force was sufficient; it would not be essential to protect Soviet cities. But Khrushchev's position necessitated a more elaborate and more expensive military establishment. If one granted that deterrence might fail and the Soviet Union be compelled to wage a nuclear war, then a major objective must be to minimize destruction in Soviet Russia. This would require elaborate warning systems and extensive defense measures, both active and passive. The only real limit on expenditure for such a posture is the extent of available resources.

The most recent Soviet developments in weapons are the fruits of the decision taken some years ago to have not only a deterrent capability, but also a war-making capability. The requirements the Soviet leaders have placed on the ballistic missile demonstrate that the missile is not viewed primarily as a blunderbuss with which to threaten the United States, but as a weapon intended to destroy military targets. As early as 1956, Major General Pokrovsky characterized the missile as an excellent weapon because (1) it could be developed to high accuracy, (2) launching platforms could be readily built and easily concealed, and (3) the missile, once it had been launched, was difficult to detect and intercept. After the official announcement of a successful test of a long-range ballistic missile, the chief of the Soviet Air Force, Marshal Vershinin, repeated these points, emphasizing the reliability and accuracy of ballistic missiles. Other Soviet military writers have also stressed that accuracy is an essential requirement for the ballistic missile.

All these reflections on the military value of the ballistic missile as the most perfect weapon of surprise reinforced the conviction that surprise could make a vital difference. It was precisely this need to prepare for more than deterrence and to prepare against surprise nuclear attack that was spelled out for the first time in Marhsal Rotmistrov's article, published in February 1955, immediately after Malenkov had lost out to Khrushchev. Rotmistrov stated that the Soviet Union must be ready to strike a preëmptive or forestalling blow, in case the United States was about to attack. In the public media, only General Shatilov, in his speech of May 1955, preserved this emphasis on beating the opponent to the punch, when he referred to surprise as a "double-edged weapon."

Several other Soviet generals, including air force generals, restated Rotmistrov's position more guardedly when they said that the Soviet Union must be able to deprive the enemy of the fruits of surprise and be prepared to do more than trade blow for blow. Quite obviously, whatever the formulation of the problem, the emphasis was on the conduct of nuclear war, and not only on the deterrence of it.

More was to be gained from strengthening the Soviet armed forces than a better military capability to meet a possible, but unlikely, threat from the United States. In 1954 the United States had a clear preponderance in air nuclear strength and warned that it was prepared to employ that strength, not only in the event of a direct attack upon the United States, but also in the event of Soviet aggression anywhere in the free world. Since that time the Soviet Union has increased its nuclear air strength, thereby increasing the damage the United States might suffer in responding to Russian aggression by an attack upon the Soviet Union. Thus, Khrushchev and his colleagues may reason, American retaliation against Soviet aggression becomes less certain and perhaps uncertain. Consequently, new opportunities open up for Soviet expansion. Whether the Soviet Union will assume the terrible risk of exploiting such opportunities by making war for limited objectives no one can say. But without a military establishment roughly equivalent to that of the United States in nuclear strength, the Soviet leaders would never be in a position to even consider running such a risk. Greater military strength increases the policy alternatives among which Soviet leaders can choose. That, by itself, could be a sufficient argument in the Soviet Union. Coupled with the other considerations described above, it won the day against Malenkov.

The allocation of resources to the armed forces, to heavy industry and to light industry was a function of the military posture adopted. A posture directed primarily to deterrence would obviously leave more resources available for light industry. Shepilov, however, in a *Pravda* article of January 24, 1955, pointed directly to the consequence of Malenkov's policy for weapons procurement. If the Soviet Union had adopted the policy of the "pseudo-economists," said Shepilov, the result would have been to "surrender the privilege of the forced development of heavy industry, machine construction, energy, chemical industry, electronics, jet technology, guidance systems, etc. to the imperialists. . . ." The progression of items from the general category of "heavy industry" to "guidance systems" made it clear that Malenkov was being charged, among other things, with failure to push the development of guidance systems which are an essential component of satellites, long-range missiles systems and active air-defense systems.

Since Malenkov's deposition in February 1955, the Soviet armed forces have greatly improved their capability both to deter and to wage nuclear war. The ground forces have received large quantities of improved equipment; the strategic air force has been expanded; active and passive air-defense measures of impressive proportions have been taken; the possession of a long-range ballistic missile has been announced, and this claim is supported by the successful launching of two heavy satellites which testify to Soviet advances in power plant and guidance systems.

It was between the launching of the first and second satellites that the Soviet war hero, Minister of Defense and member of the Presidium of the Central Committee of the Communist Party, was dismissed from all his high offices. This dramatic event seems to have been connected with the problem of army-Party relations rather than with questions of military policy. The armed forces have participated in high-level Soviet politics since Stalin's death. They played a rôle in the elimination of Beria and in reducing the influence of the secret police. The air force excepted, they evidently sided with Khrushchev during 1954 in the struggle against Malenkov's conceptions. Significantly, Marshal Zhukov was immediately promoted to the Ministry of Defense and to alternate membership on the Party Presidium—both offices never before held by a field general. As the army forces increased in strength, Party control declined. In fact, Zhukov publicly charged the political officers with interference in proper military training. The political lectures which had been separate and under the control of the political officers were now combined with regular military training; the whole of the soldier's education, political and military, became the direct responsibility of the regular officer, who could call upon the political officer for assistance.

In June 1957, when Khrushchev evicted Malenkov, Kaganovich and Molotov from the Party Presidium, the generals publicly endorsed the change; indeed both Zhukov and the military press were more extreme in their charges than anybody else. Zhukov now was elevated to full membership in the Presidium. The best clue to the reason for his dismissal five months later is the absence of any successor to Zhukov in the Party post of Presidium member. The Party's ascendancy is demonstrated.

Zhukov's removal from power does not portend major changes in Soviet strategic thinking. Since 1955, billions have been spent on making the Soviet armed forces fit both to deter and to wage a nuclear war. The military parade on November 7 emphasized tactical weapons designed for both purposes. The very magnitude of the investment in the present military posture makes it doubtful that the Soviets will turn back to what Malenkov advocated—primary reliance on deterrence.

Yet the strategy imposed by present conditions cannot be completely satisfactory to the Soviet leaders. The strategy of fighting a preëmptive war—getting in the first blow against an opponent poised to strike—as advocated by General Rotmistrov and officially adopted in 1955, is essentially a strategy of the second-best. For under these conditions, it is the opponent who chooses war; the Soviet Union simply makes the best of it in seeking by earlier action to blunt the opponent's first blow. As long as the Soviet Union has no hope, in its first strike, of hitting the opponent's striking forces effectively enough to preclude retaliation, the initiation of war is an act of extreme desperation. If the Soviet Union could create a weapons system permitting the elimination of our striking force without fear of effective retaliation, the Soviet leaders could attack if and when they pleased.

If the Soviet Union should continue to gain technologically while the NATO alliance made little progress, the Soviet Union would be able to make war without fear of the consequences. It will be difficult to attain the ability to eliminate the opponent's nuclear striking forces in a single blow. But that is the goal which the Soviet leaders must strain to reach. If they should acquire such preponderant military strength, they would have policy alternatives even more attractive than the initiation of nuclear war. By flaunting presumably invincible strength, the Soviet Union could compel piecemeal capitulation of the democracies. This prospect must indeed seem glittering to the Soviet leaders.

"THE Delicate Balance of Terror" (January 1959), by Albert Wohlstetter, raised in an urgent and authoritative way the basic questions of strategic power and national survival in a world that has been moving inexorably toward a precarious parity of nuclear-missile might. If parity was or would soon be inevitable, would its coming open the way to a new if dangerous stability, or would it re-enforce the already hardly manageable factors of instability? These complex questions, and the half-veiled, half-guessed scientific and technological developments that underlie them, seem to many to make man a prisoner of his own technical achievements.

In his article Mr. Wohlstetter made a notable contribution to clarifying these issues for a deeply concerned people. Its immediate impact was to call into question some of the basic assumptions of U.S. and NATO strategy. Its further effect was to stimulate several intensive reviews of the present and prospective strategic posture of the United States. If some of the doubts it raised about the adequacy and direction of U.S. defense efforts became a political issue, these repercussions, though not desired or provoked by the author, were unavoidable and, indeed, desirable in a democracy. The debate was, of course, sustained by many clashing voices, and on this, as on many other issues, *Foreign Affairs* has always provided a forum for a wide variety of well-informed views, often, as in this case, giving them their first public hearing.

Trained originally in the rigors of economic and statistical analysis, Albert Wohlstetter has been a pioneer in the blending of scientific with strategic thinking. For many years he has played a prominent part in the strategic analysis work of the RAND Corporation, and has also served as a consultant to various agencies of the U.S. government on defense matters. Mr. Wohlstetter is a scientist of independent mind and he speaks it firmly; therefore, the views presented in this article are not to be regarded as those of the RAND Corporation, or of any other body, legal or physical, except Albert Wohlstetter.

THE DELICATE BALANCE
OF TERROR

By Albert Wohlstetter

THE first shock administered by the Soviet launching of sputnik has almost dissipated. The flurry of statements and investigations and improvised responses has died down, leaving a small residue: a slight increase in the schedule of bomber and ballistic missile production, with a resulting small increment in our defense expenditures for the current fiscal year; a considerable enthusiasm for space travel; and some stirrings of interest in the teaching of mathematics and physics in the secondary schools. Western defense policy has almost returned to the level of activity and the emphasis suited to the basic assumptions which were controlling before sputnik.

One of the most important of these assumptions—that a general thermonuclear war is extremely unlikely—is held in common by most of the critics of our defense policy as well as by its proponents. Because of its crucial rôle in the Western strategy of defense, I should like to examine the stability of the thermonuclear balance which, it is generally supposed, would make aggression irrational or even insane. The balance, I believe, is in fact precarious, and this fact has critical implications for policy. Deterrence in the 1960s is neither assured nor impossible but will be the product of sustained intelligent effort and hard choices, responsibly made. As a major illustration important both for defense and foreign policy, I shall treat the particularly stringent conditions for deterrence which affect forces based close to the enemy, whether they are U.S. forces or those of our allies, under single or joint control. I shall comment also on the inadequacy as well as the necessity of deterrence, on the problem of accidental outbreak of war, and on disarmament.[1]

[1] I want to thank C. J. Hitch, M. W. Hoag, W. W. Kaufmann, A. W. Marshall, H. S. Rowen and W. W. Taylor for suggestions in preparation of this article.

II. THE PRESUMED AUTOMATIC BALANCE

I emphasize that requirements for deterrence are stringent. We have heard so much about the atomic stalemate and the receding probability of war which it has produced that this may strike the reader as something of an exaggeration. Is deterrence a necessary consequence of both sides having a nuclear delivery capability, and is all-out war nearly obsolete? Is mutual extinction the only outcome of a general war? This belief, frequently expressed by references to Mr. Oppenheimer's simile of the two scorpions in a bottle, is perhaps the prevalent one. It is held by a very eminent and diverse group of people—in England by Sir Winston Churchill, P. M. S. Blackett, Sir John Slessor, Admiral Buzzard and many others; in France by such figures as Raymond Aron, General Gallois and General Gazin; in this country by the titular heads of both parties as well as almost all writers on military and foreign affairs, by both Henry Kissinger and his critic, James E. King, Jr., and by George Kennan as well as Dean Acheson. Mr. Kennan refers to American concern about surprise attack as simply obsessive; [2] and many people have drawn the consequence of the stalemate as has Blackett, who states: "If it is in fact true, as most current opinion holds, that strategic air power has abolished global war, then an urgent problem for the West is to assess how little effort must be put into it to keep global war abolished." [3] If peace were founded firmly on mutual terror, and mutual terror on symmetrical nuclear capabilities, this would be, as Churchill has said, "a melancholy paradox"; none the less a most comforting one.

Deterrence, however, is not automatic. While feasible, it will be much harder to achieve in the 1960s than is generally believed. One of the most disturbing features of current opinion is the underestimation of this difficulty. This is due partly to a misconstruction of the technological race as a problem in matching striking forces, partly to a wishful analysis of the Soviet ability to strike first.

Since sputnik, the United States has made several moves to assure the world (that is, the enemy, but more especially our allies and ourselves) that we will match or overmatch Soviet technology and, spe-

[2] George F. Kennan, "A Chance to Withdraw Our Troops in Europe," *Harper's Magazine,* February 1958, p. 41.

[3] P. M. S. Blackett, "Atomic Weapons and East-West Relations." New York: Cambridge University Press, 1956, p. 32.

cifically, Soviet offense technology. We have, for example, accelerated the bomber and ballistic missile programs, in particular the intermediate-range ballistic missiles. The problem has been conceived as more or better bombers—or rockets; or sputniks; or engineers. This has meant confusing deterrence with matching or exceeding the enemy's ability to strike first. Matching weapons, however, misconstrues the nature of the technological race. Not, as is frequently said, because only a few bombs owned by the defender can make aggression fruitless, but because even many might not. One outmoded A-bomb dropped from an obsolete bomber might destroy a great many supersonic jets and ballistic missiles. To deter an attack means being able to strike back in spite of it. It means, in other words, a capability to strike second. In the last year or two there has been a growing awareness of the importance of the distinction between a "strike-first" and a "strike-second" capability, but little, if any, recognition of the implications of this distinction for the balance of terror theory.

Where the published writings have not simply underestimated Soviet capabilities and the advantages of a first strike, they have in general placed artificial constraints on the Soviet use of the capabilities attributed to them. They assume, for example, that the enemy will attack in mass over the Arctic through our Distant Early Warning Line, with bombers refueled over Canada—all resulting in plenty of warning. Most hopefully, it is sometimes assumed that such attacks will be preceded by days of visible preparations for moving ground troops. Such assumptions suggest that the Soviet leaders will be rather bumbling or, better, coöperative. However attractive it may be for us to narrow Soviet alternatives to these, they would be low in the order of preference of any reasonable Russians planning war.

III. THE QUANTITATIVE NATURE OF THE PROBLEM AND THE UNCERTAINTIES

In treating Soviet strategies it is important to consider Soviet rather than Western advantage and to consider the strategy of both sides quantitatively. The effectiveness of our own choices will depend on a most complex numerical interaction of Soviet and Western plans. Unfortunately, both the privileged and unprivileged information on these matters is precarious. As a result, competent people have been led into critical error in evaluating the prospects for deterrence. Western journalists have greatly overestimated the difficulties of a Soviet surprise attack with thermonuclear weapons and vastly underestimated the complexity of the Western problem of retaliation.

One intelligent commentator, Richard Rovere, recently expressed the common view: "If the Russians had ten thousand warheads and a missile for each, and we had ten hydrogen bombs and ten obsolete bombers, . . . aggression would still be a folly that would appeal only to an insane adventurer." Mr. Rovere's example is plausible because it assumes implicitly that the defender's hydrogen bombs will with certainty be visited on the aggressor; then the damage done by the ten bombs seems terrible enough for deterrence, and any more would be simply redundant. This is the basis for the common view. The example raises questions, even assuming the delivery of the ten weapons. For instance, the targets aimed at in retaliation might be sheltered and a quite modest civil defense could hold within tolerable limits the damage done to such city targets by ten delivered bombs. But the essential point is that the weapons would not be very likely to reach their targets. Even if the bombers were dispersed at ten different points, and protected by shelters so blast resistant as to stand up anywhere outside the lip of the bomb crater—even inside the fire ball itself—the chances of one of these bombers surviving the huge attack directed at it would be on the order of one in a million. (This calculation takes account of the unreliability and inaccuracy of the missile.) And the damage done by the small minority of these ten planes that might be in the air at the time of the attack, armed and ready to run the gauntlet of an alert air defense system, if not zero, would be very small indeed compared to damage that Russia has suffered in the past. For Mr. Rovere, like many other writers on this subject, numerical superiority is not important at all.

For Joseph Alsop, on the other hand, it is important, but the superiority is on our side. Mr. Alsop recently enunciated as one of the four rules of nuclear war: "The aggressor's problem is astronomically difficult; and the aggressor requires an overwhelming superiority of force." [4] There are, he believes, no fewer than 400 SAC bases in the NATO nations alone and many more elsewhere, all of which would have to be attacked in a very short space of time. The "thousands of coördinated air sorties and/or missile firings," he concludes, are not feasi-

[4] Joseph Alsop, "The New Balance of Power," *Encounter,* May 1958, p. 4. It should be added that, since these lines were written, Mr. Alsop's views have altered.

ble. Mr. Alsop's argument is numerical and has the virtue of demonstrating that at least the relative numbers are important. But the numbers he uses are very wide of the mark. He overestimates the number of such bases by a factor of more than ten,[5] and in any case, missile firings on the scale of a thousand or more involve costs that are by no means out of proportion, given the strategic budgets of the great powers. Whether or not thousands are needed depends on the yield and the accuracy of the enemy missiles, something about which it would be a great mistake for us to display confidence.

Perhaps the first step in dispelling the nearly universal optimism about the stability of deterrence would be to recognize the difficulties in analyzing the uncertainties and interactions between our own wide range of choices and the moves open to the Soviets. On our side we must consider an enormous variety of strategic weapons which might compose our force, and for each of these several alternative methods of basing and operation. These are the choices that determine whether a weapons system will have any genuine capability in the realistic circumstances of a war. Besides the B-47E and the B-52 bombers which are in the United States strategic force now, alternatives will include the B-52G (a longer-range version of the B-52); the Mach 2 B-58A bomber and a "growth" version of it; the Mach 3 B-70 bomber; a nuclear-powered bomber possibly carrying long-range air-to-surface missiles; the Dynasoar, a manned glide-rocket; the Thor and the Jupiter, liquid-fueled intermediate-range ballistic missiles; the Snark intercontinental cruise missile; the Atlas and the Titan intercontinental ballistic missiles; the submarine-launched Polaris and Atlantis rockets; and Minuteman, one potential solid-fueled successor to the Thor and Titan; possibly unmanned bombardment satellites; and many others which are not yet gleams in anyone's eye and some that are just that.

The difficulty of describing in a brief article the best mixture of weapons for the long-term future beginning in 1960, their base requirements, their potentiality for stabilizing or upsetting the balance among the great powers, and their implications for the alliance, is not just a matter of space or the constraint of security. The difficulty in fact stems from some rather basic insecurities. These matters are wildly uncertain; we are talking about weapons and vehicles that are some time off and, even if the precise performances currently hoped for and

[5] *The New York Times,* September 6, 1958, p. 2.

claimed by contractors were in the public domain, it would be a good idea to doubt them.

Recently some of my colleagues picked their way through the graveyard of early claims about various missiles and aircraft: their dates of availability, costs and performance. These claims are seldom revisited or talked about: *de mortuis nil nisi bonum*. The errors were large and almost always in one direction. And the less we knew, the more hopeful we were. Accordingly the missiles benefited in particular. For example, the estimated cost of one missile increased by a factor of over 50—from about $35,000 in 1949 to some $2 million in 1957. This uncertainty is critical. Some but not all of the systems listed can be chosen and the problem of choice is essentially quantitative. The complexities of the problem, if they were more widely understood, would discourage the oracular confidence of writers on the subject of deterrence.

Some of the complexities can be suggested by referring to the successive obstacles to be hurdled by any system providing a capability to strike second, that is, to strike back. Such deterrent systems must have (a) a stable, "steady-state" peacetime operation within feasible budgets (besides the logistic and operational costs there are, for example, problems of false alarms and accidents). They must have also the ability (b) to survive enemy attacks, (c) to make and communicate the decision to retaliate, (d) to reach enemy territory with fuel enough to complete their mission, (e) to penetrate enemy active defenses, that is, fighters and surface-to-air missiles, and (f) to destroy the target in spite of any "passive" civil defense in the form of dispersal or protective construction or evacuation of the target itself.

Within limits the enemy is free to use his offensive and defensive forces so as to exploit the weaknesses of each of our systems. He will also be free, within limits, in the 1960s to choose that composition of forces which will make life as difficult as possible for the various systems we might select. It would be quite wrong to assume that we have the same degree of flexibility or that the uncertainties I have described affect a totalitarian aggressor and the party attacked equally. A totalitarian country can preserve secrecy about the capabilities and disposition of his forces very much better than a Western democracy. And the aggressor has, among other enormous advantages of the first strike, the ability to weigh continually our performance at each of the six barriers and to choose that precise time and circumstance for attack which will reduce uncertainty. It is important not to confuse our uncertainty with his. Strangely enough, some military commentators have not made this distinction and have founded their certainty of deterrence on the fact simply that there are uncertainties.

Unwarranted optimism is displayed not only in the writings of journalists but in the more analytic writings of professionals. The recent writings of General Gallois [6] parallel rather closely Mr. Alsop's faulty numerical proof that surprise attack is astronomically difficult—except that Gallois' "simple arithmetic," to borrow his own phrase, turns essentially on some assumptions which are at once inexplicit and extremely optimistic with respect to the blast resistance of dispersed missiles sites subjected to attack from relatively close range. [7] Mr. Blackett's recent book, "Atomic Weapons and East-West Relations," illustrates the hazards confronting a most able analyst in dealing with the piecemeal information available to the general public. Mr. Blackett, a Nobel prize-winning physicist with wartime experience in military operations research, lucidly summarized the public information available when he was writing in 1956 on weapons for all-out war. But much of his analysis was based on the assumption that H-bombs could not be made small enough to be carried in an intercontinental missile. It is now widely known that intercontinental ballistic missiles will have hydrogen warheads, and this fact, a secret at the time, invalidates Mr. Blackett's calculations and, I might say, much of his optimism on the stability of the balance of terror. In sum, one of the serious obstacles to any widespread rational judgment on these matters of high policy is that critical elements of the problem *have* to be protected by secrecy. However, some of the principal conclusions about deterrence in the early 1960s can be fairly firmly based, and based on public information.

IV. THE DELICACY OF THE BALANCE OF TERROR

The most important conclusion is that we must expect a vast increase in the weight of attack which the Soviets can deliver with little warning, and the growth of a significant Russian capability for an essentially warningless attack. As a result, strategic deterrence, while feasible, will be extremely difficult to achieve, and at critical junctures in the

[6] General Pierre M. Gallois, "A French General Analyzes Nuclear-Age Strategy," *Réalités*, Nov. 1958, p. 19; "Nuclear Aggression and National Suicide," *The Reporter*, Sept. 18, 1958, p. 23.

[7] See footnote, p. 391-392.

1960s, we may not have the power to deter attack. Whether we have it or not will depend on some difficult strategic choices as to the future composition of the deterrent forces as well as hard choices on its basing, operations and defense.

Manned bombers will continue to make up the predominant part of our striking force in the early 1960s. None of the popular remedies for their defense will suffice—not, for example, mere increase of alertness (which will be offset by the Soviet's increasing capability for attack without significant warning), nor simple dispersal or sheltering alone or mobility taken by itself, nor a mere piling up of interceptors and defense missiles around SAC bases. Especially extravagant expectations have been placed on the airborne alert—an extreme form of defense by mobility. The impression is rather widespread that one-third of the SAC bombers are in the air and ready for combat at all times.[8] This belief is belied by the public record. According to the Symington Committee Hearings in 1956, our bombers averaged 31 hours of flying per month, which is about 4 percent of the average 732-hour month. An Air Force representative expressed the hope that within a couple of years, with an increase in the ratio of crews to aircraft, the bombers would reach 45 hours of flight per month—which is 6 percent. This 4 to 6 percent of the force includes bombers partially fueled and without bombs. It is, moreover, only an average, admitting variance down as well as up. Some increase in the number of armed bombers aloft is to be expected. However, for the current generation of bombers, which have been designed for speed and range rather than endurance, a continuous air patrol for one-third of the force would be extremely expensive.

On the other hand, it would be unwise to look for miracles in the new weapons systems, which by the mid-1960s may constitute a considerable portion of the United States force. After the Thor, Atlas and Titan there are a number of promising developments. The solid-fueled rockets, Minuteman and Polaris, promise in particular to be extremely significant components of the deterrent force. Today they are being touted as making the problem of deterrence easy to solve and, in fact, guaranteeing its solution. But none of the new developments in vehicles is likely to do that. For the complex job of deterrence, they all

---

[8] See, for example, "NATO, A Critical Appraisal," by Gardner Patterson and Edgar S. Furniss, Jr., Princeton University Conference on NATO, Princeton, June 1957, p. 32: "Although no one pretended to know, the hypothesis that one-third of the striking force of the United States Strategic Air Command was in the air at all times was regarded by most as reasonable."

have limitations. The unvaryingly immoderate claims for each new weapons system should make us wary of the latest "technological breakthroughs." Only a very short time ago the ballistic missile itself was supposed to be intrinsically invulnerable on the ground. It is now more generally understood that its survival is likely to depend on a variety of choices in its defense.

It is hard to talk with confidence about the mid and late 1960s. A systematic study of an optimal or a good deterrent force which considered all the major factors affecting choice and dealt adequately with the uncertainties would be a formidable task. In lieu of this, I shall mention briefly why none of the many systems available or projected dominates the others in any obvious way. My comments will take the form of a swift run-through of the characteristic advantages and disadvantages of various strategic systems at each of the six successive hurdles mentioned earlier.

The first hurdle to be surmounted is the attainment of a stable, steady-state peacetime operation. Systems which depend for their survival on extreme decentralization of controls, as may be the case with large-scale dispersal and some of the mobile weapons, raise problems of accidents and over a long period of peacetime operation this leads in turn to serious political problems. Systems relying on extensive movement by land, perhaps by truck caravan, are an obvious example; the introduction of these on European roads, as is sometimes suggested, would raise grave questions for the governments of some of our allies. Any extensive increase in the armed air alert will increase the hazard of accident and intensify the concern already expressed among our allies. Some of the proposals for bombardment satellites may involve such hazards of unintended bomb release as to make them out of the question.

The cost to buy and operate various weapons systems must be seriously considered. Some systems buy their ability to negotiate a given hurdle—say, surviving the enemy attack—only at prohibitive cost. Then the number that can be bought out of a given budget will be small and this will affect the relative performance of competing systems at various other hurdles, for example penetrating enemy defenses. Some of the relevant cost comparisons, then, are between competing systems; others concern the extra costs to the enemy of canceling an additional expenditure of our own. For example, some dispersal is essential, though usually it is expensive; if the dispersed bases are within a warning net, dispersal can help to provide warning against some sorts of attack, since it forces the attacker to increase the size of his raid and so makes it more liable to detection as well as somewhat harder to coördinate. But as the sole or principal defense of our offensive force, dispersal has only a brief useful life and can be justified financially only up to a point. For against our costs of construction, maintenance and operation of an additional base must be set the enemy's much lower costs of delivering one extra weapon. And, in general, any feasible degree of dispersal leaves a considerable concentration of value at a single target point. For example, a squadron of heavy bombers costing, with their associated tankers and penetration aids, perhaps $500,000,000 over five years, might be eliminated, if it were otherwise unprotected, by an enemy intercontinental ballistic missile costing perhaps $16,000,000. After making allowance for the unreliability and inaccuracy of the missile, this means a ratio of some ten for one or better. To achieve safety by *brute* numbers in so unfavorable a competition is not likely to be viable economically or politically. However, a viable peacetime operation is only the first hurdle to be surmounted.

At the second hurdle—surviving the enemy offense—ground alert systems placed deep within a warning net look good against a manned bomber attack, much less good against intercontinental ballistic missiles, and not good at all against ballistic missiles launched from the sea. In the last case, systems such as the Minuteman, which may be sheltered and dispersed as well as alert, would do well. Systems involving launching platforms which are mobile and concealed, such as Polaris submarines, have particular advantage for surviving an enemy offense.

However, there is a third hurdle to be surmounted—namely that of making the decision to retaliate and communicating it. Here, Polaris, the combat air patrol of B-52s, and in fact all of the mobile platforms—under water, on the surface, in the air and above the air—have severe problems. Long distance communication may be jammed and, most important, communication centers may be destroyed.

At the fourth hurdle—ability to reach enemy territory with fuel enough to complete the mission—several of our short-legged systems have operational problems such as coördination with tankers and using bases close to the enemy. For a good many years to come, up to the mid-1960s in fact, this will be a formidable hurdle for the greater part of our deterrent force. The next section of this article deals with this problem at some length.

The fifth hurdle is the aggressor's long-range interceptors and close-in missile defenses. To get past these might require large numbers of planes and missiles. (If the high cost of overcoming an earlier obstacle—using extreme dispersal or airborne alert or the like—limits the number of planes or missiles bought, our capability is likely to be penalized disproportionately here.) Or getting through may involve carrying heavy loads of radar decoys, electronic jammers and other aids to defense penetration. For example, vehicles like Minuteman and Polaris, which were made small to facilitate dispersal or mobility, may suffer here because they can carry fewer penetration aids.

At the final hurdle—destroying the target in spite of the passive defenses that may protect it—low-payload and low-accuracy systems, such as Minuteman and Polaris, may be frustrated by blast-resistant shelters. For example, five half-megaton weapons with an average inaccuracy of two miles might be expected to destroy half the population of a city of 900,000, spread over 40 square miles, provided the inhabitants are without shelters. But if they are provided with shelters capable of resisting over-pressures of 100 pounds per square inch, approximately 60 such weapons would be required; and deep rock shelters might force the total up to over a thousand.

Prizes for a retaliatory capability are not distributed for getting over one of these jumps. A system must get over all six. I hope these illustrations will suggest that assuring ourselves the power to strike back after a massive thermonuclear surprise attack is by no means as automatic as is widely believed. In counteracting the general optimism as to the ease and, in fact, the inevitability of deterrence, I should like to avoid creating the extreme opposite impression. Deterrence demands hard, continuing, intelligent work, but it can be achieved. The job of deterring rational attack by guaranteeing great damage to an aggressor is, for example, very much less difficult than erecting a nearly airtight defense of cities in the face of full-scale thermonuclear surprise attack. Protecting manned bombers and missiles is much easier because they may be dispersed, sheltered or kept mobile, and they can respond to warning with greater speed. Mixtures of these and other defenses with complementary strengths can preserve a powerful remainder after attack. Obviously not all our bombers and missiles need to survive in order to fulfill their mission. To preserve the majority of our cities intact in the face of surprise attack is immensely more difficult, if not impossible. (This does not mean that the aggressor has the same problem in preserving his cities from retaliation by a poorly-protected, badly-

damaged force. And it does not mean that *we* should not do more
to limit the extent of the catastrophe to our cities in case deterrence
fails. I believe we should.) Deterrence, however, provided we work
at it, is feasible, and, what is more, it is a crucial objective of national
policy.

What can be said, then, as to whether general war is unlikely? Would
not a general thermonuclear war mean "extinction" for the aggressor
as well as the defender? "Extinction" is a state that badly needs analysis. Russian casualties in World War II were more than 20,000,000.
Yet Russia recovered extremely well from this catastrophe. There are
several quite plausible circumstances in the future when the Russians
might be quite confident of being able to limit damage to considerably
less than this number—if they make sensible strategic choices and we do
not. On the other hand, the risks of not striking might at some juncture
appear very great to the Soviets, involving, for example, disastrous
defeat in peripheral war, loss of key satellites with danger of revolt
spreading—possibly to Russia itself—or fear of an attack by ourselves.
Then, striking first, by surprise, would be the sensible choice for them,
and from their point of view the smaller risk.

It should be clear that it is not fruitful to talk about the likelihood
of general war without specifying the range of alternatives that are
pressing on the aggressor and the strategic postures of both the Soviet
bloc and the West. Deterrence is a matter of comparative risks. The
balance is not automatic. First, since thermonuclear weapons give an
enormous advantage to the aggressor, it takes great ingenuity and
realism at any given level of nuclear technology to devise a stable
equilibrium. And second, this technology itself is changing with fantastic
speed. Deterrence will require an urgent and continuing effort.

V. THE USES AND RISKS OF BASES
CLOSE TO THE SOVIETS

It may now be useful to focus attention on the special problems of
deterrent forces close to the Soviet Union. First, overseas areas have
played an important rôle in the past and have a continuing though less
certain rôle today. Second, the recent acceleration of production of intermediate-range ballistic missiles and the negotiation of agreements with
various NATO powers for their basing and operation have given our
overseas bases a renewed importance in deterring attack on the United

States—or so it would appear at first blush. Third, an analysis can throw some light on the problems faced by our allies in developing an independent ability to deter all-out attack on themselves, and in this way it can clarify the much agitated question of nuclear sharing. Finally, overseas bases affect in many critical ways, political and economic as well as military, the status of the alliance.

At the end of the last decade, overseas bases appeared to be an advantageous means of achieving the radius extension needed by our short-legged bombers, or permitting them to use several axes of attack, and of increasing the number of sorties possible in the course of an extended campaign. With the growth of our own thermonuclear stockpile, it became apparent that a long campaign involving many re-uses of a large proportion of our bombers was not likely to be necessary. With the growth of a Russian nuclear-delivery capability, it became clear that this was most unlikely to be feasible.

Our overseas bases now have the disadvantage of high vulnerability. Because they are closer than the United States to the Soviet Union, they are subject to a vastly greater attack by a larger variety as well as number of vehicles. With given resources, the Soviets might deliver on nearby bases a freight of bombs with something like 50 to 100 times the yield that they could muster at intercontinental range. Missile accuracy would more than double. Because there is not much space for obtaining warning—in any case, there are no deep-warning radar nets—and, since most of our overseas bases are close to deep water from which submarines might launch missiles, the warning problem is very much more severe than for bases in the interior of the United States.

As a result, early in the 1950s the U.S. Air Force decided to recall many of our bombers to the continental United States and to use the overseas bases chiefly for refueling, particularly post-strike ground re-fueling. This reduced drastically the vulnerability of U.S. bombers and at the same time retained many of the advantages of overseas operation. For some years now SAC has been reducing the number of aircraft usually deployed overseas. The purpose is to reduce vulnerability and has little to do with any increasing radius of SAC aircraft. The early B-52 radius is roughly that of the B-36; the B-47, roughly that of the B-50 or B-29. In fact the radius limitation and therefore the basing requirements we have discussed will not change substantially for some time to come. We can talk with comparative confidence here, because the U.S. strategic force is itself largely determined for this period. Such a force changes more slowly than is generally realized. The vast majority of the force will consist of manned bombers, and most of these will be of medium range. *Some* U.S. bombers will be able to reach *some* targets from *some* U.S. bases within the 48 states without landing on the way back. On the other hand, some bomber-target combinations are not feasible without pre-target landing (and are therefore doubtful). The Atlas, Titan and Polaris rockets, when available, can of course do without overseas bases (though the proportion of Polaris submarines kept at sea can be made larger by the use of submarine tenders based overseas). But even with the projected force of aerial tankers, the greater part of our force, which will be manned bombers, cannot be used at all in attacks on the Soviet Union without at least some use of overseas areas.

What of the bases for Thor and Jupiter, our first intermediate-range ballistic missiles? These have to be close to the enemy, and they must of course be operating bases, not merely refueling stations. The Thors and Jupiters will be continuously in range of an enormous Soviet potential for surprise attack. These installations therefore re-open, in a most acute form, some of the serious questions of ground vulnerability that were raised about six years ago in connection with our overseas bomber bases. The decision to station the Thor and Jupiter missiles overseas has been our principal public response to the Russian advances in rocketry, and perhaps our most plausible response. Because it involves our ballistic missiles it appears directly to answer the Russian rockets. Because it involves using European bases, it appears to make up for the range superiority of the Russian intercontinental missile. And most important, it directly involves the NATO powers and gives them an element of control.

There is no question that it was genuinely urgent not only to meet the Russian threat but to do so visibly, in order to save the loosening NATO alliance. Our allies were fearful that the Soviet ballistic missiles might mean that we were no longer able or willing to retaliate against the Soviet Union in case of an attack on them. We hastened to make public a reaction which would restore their confidence. This move surely appears to increase our own power to strike back, and also to give our allies a deterrent of their own, independent of our decision. It has also been argued that in this respect it merely advances the inevitable date at which our allies will acquire "modern" weapons of their own, and that it widens the range of Soviet challenges which Europe can meet. But we must face seriously the question whether this move will in fact assure either the ability to retaliate or the decision to attempt it, on the part of our allies or ourselves. And we should ask at the very least whether further expansion of this policy will buy as much retaliatory power as other ways of spending the considerable sums involved. Finally, it is important to be clear whether the Thor and Jupiter actually increase the flexibility or range of response available to our allies.

One justification for this move is that it disperses retaliatory weapons and that this is the most effective sanction against the thermonuclear aggressor. The limitations of dispersal have already been discussed, but it remains to examine the argument that overseas bases provide *widespread* dispersal, which imposes on the aggressor insoluble problems of coördination.

There is of course something in the notion that forcing the enemy to attack many political entities increases the seriousness of his decision, but there is very little in the notion that dispersal in several countries makes the problem of destruction more difficult in the military sense. Dispersal does not require separation by the distance of oceans—just by the lethal diameters of enemy bombs. And the task of coördinating bomber attacks on Europe and the eastern coast of the United States, say, is not appreciably more difficult than coördinating attacks on our east and west coasts. In the case of ballistic missiles, the elapsed time from firing to impact on the target can be calculated with high accuracy. Although there will be some failures and delays, times of firing can be arranged so that impact on many dispersed points is almost simultaneous—on Okinawa and the United Kingdom, for instance, as well as on California and Ohio. Moreover, it is important to keep in mind that these far-flung bases, while distant from each other and from the United States, are on the whole close to the enemy. To eliminate them, therefore, requires a smaller expenditure of resources on his part than targets at intercontinental range. For close-in targets he can use a wider variety of weapons carrying larger payloads and with higher accuracy.

The seeming appositeness of an overseas-based Thor and Jupiter as an answer to a Russian intercontinental ballistic missile stems not so much from any careful analysis of their retaliatory power under attack as from the directness of the comparison they suggest: a rocket equals a rocket, an intercontinental missile equals an intermediate-range missile based at closer range to the target. But this again mistakes the nature of the technological race. It conceives the problem of deterrence as that of simply matching or exceeding the aggressor's capability to strike first. A surprising proportion of the debate on defense policy has betrayed this confusion. Matching technological developments are useful for prestige, and such demonstrations have a vital function in preserving the alliance and in reassuring the neutral powers. But propaganda is not enough. The only reasonably certain way of maintaining a reputation for strength is to display an actual power to our friends as well as our enemies. We should ask, then, whether further expansion of the current programs for basing Thor and Jupiter is an efficient way to increase American retaliatory power. If overseas bases are considered too vulnerable for manned bombers, will not the same be true for missiles?

The basis for the hopeful impression that they will not is rather vague, including a mixture of hypothetical properties of ballistic missiles in which perhaps the dominant element is their supposedly much more rapid, "push-button" response. What needs to be considered here are the response time of such missiles (including decision, preparation and launch times), and how they are to be defended.

The decision to fire a missile with a thermonuclear warhead is much harder to make than a decision simply to start a manned aircraft on its way, with orders to return to base unless instructed to continue to its assigned target. This is the "fail-safe" procedure practised by the U.S. Air Force. In contrast, once a missile is launced, there is no method of recall or deflection which is not subject to risks of electronic or mechanical failure. Therefore such a decision must wait for much more unambiguous evidence of enemy intentions. It must and will take a longer time to make and is less likely to be made at all. Where more than one country is involved, the joint decision is harder still, since there is opportunity to disagree about the ambiguity of the evidence, as well as to reach quite different interpretations of national interest. On much less momentous matters the process of making decisions in NATO is complicated, and it should be recognized that such complexity has much to do with the genuine concern of the various NATO powers about the danger of accidentally starting World War III. Such fears will not be diminished with the advent of I.R.B.M.s. In fact, widespread dispersion of nuclear armed missiles raises measurably the possibility of accidental war.

Second, it is quite erroneous to suppose that by contrast with manned bombers the first I.R.B.M.s can be launched almost as simply as pressing a button. Count-down procedures for early missiles are liable to interruption, and the characteristics of the liquid oxygen fuel limits the readiness of their response. Unlike JP-4, the fuel used in jet bombers, liquid oxygen cannot be held for long periods of time in these vehicles. In this respect such missiles will be *less* ready than alert bombers. Third, the smaller warning time available overseas makes more difficult any response. This includes, in particular, any active defense, not only against ballistic missile attacks but, for example, against low altitude or various circuitous attacks by manned aircraft.

Finally, passive defense by means of shelter is more difficult, given the larger bomb yields, better accuracies and larger forces available to the Russians at such close range. And if the press reports are correct, the plans for I.R.B.M. installations do not call for bomb-resistant shelters. If this is so, it should be taken into account in measuring the actual contribution of these installations to the West's retaliatory power. Viewed as a contribution to deterring all-out attack on the United States, the Thor and Jupiter bases seem unlikely to compare favorably with other alternatives. If newspaper references to hard bargaining by some of our future hosts are to be believed, it would seem that such negotiations have been conducted under misapprehensions on both sides as to the benefits to the United States.

But many proponents of the distribution of Thor and Jupiter—and possibly some of our allies—have in mind not an increase in U.S. deterrence but the development of an independent capability in several of the NATO countries to deter all-out attack against themselves. This would be a useful thing if it can be managed at supportable cost and if it does not entail the sacrifice of even more critical measures of protection. But aside from the special problems of joint control, which would affect the certainty of response adversely, precisely who their legal owner is will not affect the retaliatory power of the Thors and Jupiters one way or the other. They would not be able to deter an attack which they could not survive. It is curious that many who question the utility of American overseas bases (for example, our bomber bases in the United Kingdom) simply assume that, for our allies, possession of strategic nuclear weapons is one with deterrence.

There remains the view that the provision of these weapons will broaden the range of response open to our allies. In so far as this view rests on the belief that the intermediate-range ballistic missile is adapted to limited war, it is wide of the mark. The inaccuracy of an I.R.B.M. requires high-yield warheads, and such a combination of inaccuracy and high yield, while quite appropriate and adequate against unprotected targets in a general war, would scarcely come within even the most lax, in fact reckless, definition of limited war. Such a weapon is inappropriate for even the nuclear variety of limited war, and it is totally useless for meeting the wide variety of provocation that is well below the threshold of nuclear response. In so far as these missiles will be costly for our allies to install, operate and support, they are likely to displace a conventional capability that might be genuinely useful in limited engagements. More important, they are likely to be used as an excuse for budget cutting. In this way they will accelerate the general trend toward dependence on all-out response and so will have the opposite effect to the one claimed.

Nevertheless, if the Thor and Jupiter have these defects, might not some future weapon be free of them? Some of these defects, of course, will be overcome in time. Solid fuels or storable liquids will eventually replace liquid oxygen, reliabilities will increase, various forms of mobility or portability will become feasible, accuracies may even be so improved that such weapons can be used in limited wars. But these developments are all years away. In consequence, the discussion will be advanced if a little more precision is given such terms as "missiles" or "modern" or "advanced weapons." We are not distributing a generic "modern" weapon with all the virtues of flexibility in varying circumstances and of invulnerability in all-out war. But even with advances in the state of the art on our side, it will remain difficult to maintain a deterrent, especially close in under the enemy's guns.

It follows that, though a wider distribution of nuclear weapons may be inevitable, or at any rate likely, and though some countries in addition to the Soviet Union and the United States may even develop an independent deterrent, it is by no means inevitable or even very likely that the power to deter all-out thermonuclear attack will be widespread. This is true even though a minor power would not need to guarantee as large a retaliation as we in order to deter attack on itself. Unfortunately, the minor powers have smaller resources as well as poorer strategic locations.[9] Mere membership in the nuclear club might carry

---

[9] General Gallois argues that, while alliances will offer no guarantee, "a small number of bombs and a small number of carriers suffice for a threatened power to protect itself against atomic destruction." (*Réalités, op. cit.*, p. 71.)

with it prestige, as the applicants and nominees expect, but it will be rather expensive, and in time it will be clear that it does not necessarily confer any of the expected privileges enjoyed by the two charter members. The burden of deterring a general war as distinct from limited wars is still likely to be on the United States and therefore, so far as our allies are concerned, on the military alliance.

There is one final consideration. Missiles placed near the enemy, even if they could not retaliate, would have a potent capability for striking first by surprise. And it might not be easy for the enemy to discern their purpose. The existence of such a force might be a considerable provocation and in fact a dangerous one in the sense that it would place a great burden on our deterrent force which more than ever would have to guarantee extreme risks to the attacker—worse than the risks of waiting in the face of this danger. When not coupled with the ability to strike

---

His numerical illustrations give the defender some 400 underground launching sites (*ibid.*, p. 22, and *The Reporter, op. cit.*, p. 25) and suggest that their elimination would require between 5,000 and 25,000 missiles—which is "more or less impossible"—and that in any case the aggressor would not survive the fall-out from his own weapons. Whether these are large numbers of targets from the standpoint of the aggressor will depend on the accuracy, yield and reliability of offense weapons as well as the resistance of the defender's shelters and a number of other matters not specified in the argument. General Gallois is aware that the expectation of survival depends on distance even in the ballistic missile age and that our allies are not so fortunate in this respect. Close-in missiles have better bomb yields and accuracies. Moreover, manned aircraft—with still better yields and accuracies—can be used by an aggressor here since warning of their approach is very short. Suffice it to say that the numerical advantage General Gallois cites is greatly exaggerated. Furthermore, he exaggerates the destructiveness of the retaliatory blow against the aggressor's cities by the remnants of the defender's missile force—even assuming the aggressor would take no special measures to protect his cities. But particularly for the aggressor—who does not lack warning—a civil defense program can moderate the damage done by a poorly organized attack. Finally, the suggestion that the aggressor would not survive the fall-out from his own weapons is simply in error. The rapid-decay fission products which are the major lethal problem in the locality of a surface burst are not a serious difficulty for the aggressor. The amount of the slow-decay products, strontium-90 and cesium-137, in the atmosphere would rise considerably. If nothing were done to counter it, this might, for example, increase by many times the incidence of such relatively rare diseases as bone cancer and leukemia. However, such a calamity, implying an increase of, say, 20,000 deaths per year for a nation of 200,000,000, is of an entirely different order from the catastrophe involving tens of millions of deaths, which General Gallois contemplates elsewhere. And there are measures that might reduce even this effect drastically. (See the RAND Corporation Report R-322-RC, *Report on a Study of Non-Military Defense,* July 1, 1958.)

in retaliation, such a capability might suggest—erroneously, to be sure, in the case of the democracies—an intention to strike first. If so, it would tend to provoke rather than to deter general war.

I have dealt here with only one of the functions of overseas bases: their use as a support for the strategic deterrent force. They have a variety of important military, political and economic rôles which are beyond the scope of this paper. Expenditures in connection with the construction or operation of our bases, for example, are a form of economic aid and, moreover, a form that is rather palatable to the Congress. There are other functions in a central war where their importance may be very considerable and their usefulness in a limited war might be substantial.

Indeed nothing said here should suggest that deterrence is in itself an adequate strategy. The complementary requirements of a sufficient military policy cannot be discussed in detail here. Certainly they include a more serious development of power to meet limited aggression, especially with more advanced conventional weapons than those now available. They also include more energetic provision for active and passive defenses to limit the dimensions of the catastrophe in case deterrence should fail. For example, an economically feasible shelter program might make the difference between 50,000,000 survivors and 120,-000,000 survivors.

But it would be a fatal mistake to suppose that because strategic deterrence is inadequate by itself it can be dispensed with. Deterrence is not dispensable. If the picture of the world I have drawn is rather bleak, it could none the less be cataclysmically worse. Suppose both the United States and the Soviet Union had the power to destroy each other's retaliatory forces and society, given the opportunity to administer the opening blow. The situation would then be something like the old-fashioned Western gun duel. It would be extraordinarily risky for one side *not* to attempt to destroy the other, or to delay doing so, since it not only can emerge unscathed by striking first but this is the sole way it can reasonably hope to emerge at all. Evidently such a situation is extremely unstable. On the other hand, if it is clear that the aggressor too will suffer catastrophic damage in the event of his aggression, he then has strong reason not to attack, even though he can administer great damage. A protected retaliatory capability has a stabilizing influence not only in deterring rational attack, but also in offering every inducement to both powers to reduce the chance of accidental war.

The critics who feel that deterrence is "bankrupt" sometimes say that we stress deterrence too much. I believe this is quite wrong if it means that we are devoting too much effort to protect our power to retaliate; but I think it is quite right if it means that we have talked too much of a strategic threat as a substitute for many things it cannot replace.

VI. DETERRENCE, ACCIDENTS AND DISARMAMENT

Up to now I have talked mainly about the problem of deterring general war, of making it improbable that an act of war will be undertaken deliberately, with a clear understanding of the consequences, that is, rationally. That such deterrence will not be easy to maintain in the 1960s simply expresses the proposition that a surprise thermonuclear attack might *not* be an irrational or insane act on the part of the aggressor. A deterrent strategy is aimed at a rational enemy. Without a deterrent, general war is likely. With it, however, war might still occur.

In order to reduce the risk of a rational act of aggression, we are being forced to undertake measures (increased alertness, dispersal, mobility) which, to a significant extent, increase the risk of an irrational or unintentional act of war. The accident problem is serious, and it would be a great mistake to dismiss the recent Soviet charges on this subject as simply part of the war of nerves. In a clear sense the great multiplication and spread of nuclear arms throughout the world, the drastic increase in the degree of readiness of these weapons, and the decrease in the time available for the decision on their use must inevitably raise the risk of accident. The B-47 accidents this year at Sidi Slimane and at Florence, S. C., and the recent Nike explosion are just a beginning. Though incidents of this sort are not themselves likely to trigger misunderstanding, they suggest the nature of the problem.

There are many sorts of accidents that could happen. There can be electronic or mechanical failures of the sort illustrated by the B-47 and Nike mishaps; there can be aberrations of individuals, perhaps quite low in the echelon of command; there can be miscalculations on the part of governments as to enemy intent and the meaning of ambiguous signals. Not all deterrent strategies will involve the risk of accident equally. One of the principles of selecting a strategy should be to reduce the chance of accident, wherever we can, without a corresponding increase in vulnerability to a rational surprise attack. This is the purpose of the "fail-safe" procedures for launching SAC.

These problems are also relevant to the disarmament question. The Russians, exploiting an inaccurate United Press report which suggested that SAC started en masse toward Russia in response to frequent radar "ghosts," cried out against these supposed Arctic flights. The United States response, and its sequels, stated correctly that such flights had never been undertaken except in planned exercises and would not be undertaken in response to such unreliable warning. We pointed out the importance of quick response and a high degree of readiness in the protection of the deterrent force. The nature of the fail-safe precaution was also described.

We added, however, to cap the argument, that if the Russians were really worried about surprise attack they would accept the President's "open skies" proposal. This addition, however, conceals an absurdity. Aerial photography would have its uses in a disarmament plan—for example, to check an exchange of information on the location of ground bases. However, so far as surprise is concerned, an "open skies" plan would have direct use only to discover attacks requiring much more lengthy, visible and unambiguous preparations than are likely today.[10] The very readiness of our own strategic force suggests a state of technology which outmodes the "open skies" plan as a counter to surprise attack. Not even the most advanced reconnaissance equipment can disclose an intention from 40,000 feet. Who can say what the men in the blockhouse of an I.C.B.M. base have in mind? Or, for that matter, what is the final destination of training flights or fail-safe flights starting over the Pacific or North Atlantic from staging areas?

The actions that need to be taken on our own to deter attack might usefully be complemented by bilateral agreements for inspection and reporting and, possibly, limitation of arms and of methods of operating strategic and naval air forces. But the protection of our retaliatory power remains essential; and the better the protection, the smaller the burden placed on the agreement to limit arms and modes of operation and to make them subject to inspection. Reliance on "open skies" alone to prevent surprise would invite catastrophe and the loss of power to retaliate. Such a plan is worthless for discovering a well prepared

---

[10] Aerial reconnaissance, of course, could have an *indirect* utility here for surveying large areas to determine the number and location of observation posts needed to provide more timely warning.

attack with I.C.B.M.s or submarine-launched missiles or a routine mass training flight whose destination could be kept ambiguous. A tremendous weight of weapons could be delivered in spite of it.

Although it is quite hopeless to look for an inspection scheme which would permit abandonment of the deterrent, this does not mean that some partial agreement on inspection and limitation might not help to reduce the chance of any sizable surprise attack. We should explore the possibilities of agreements involving limitation and inspection. But how we go about this will be conditioned by our appreciation of the problem of deterrence itself.

The critics of current policy who perceive the inadequacy of the strategy of deterrence are prominent among those urging disarmament negotiations, an end to the arms race and a reduction of tension. This is a paramount interest of some of our allies. The balance of terror theory is the basis for some of the more light-hearted suggestions: if deterrence is automatic, strategic weapons on one side cancel those of the other, and it should be easy for both sides to give them up. So James E. King, Jr., one of the most sensible writers on the subject of limited war, suggests that weapons needed for "unlimited" war are those which both sides can most easily agree to abolish, simply because "neither side can anticipate anything but disaster" from their use. "Isn't there enough stability in the 'balance of terror,' " he asks, "to justify our believing that the Russians can be trusted—within acceptable limits—to abandon the weapons whose 'utility is confined to the threat or conduct of a war of annihilation'?" [11]

Indeed, if there were no real danger of a rational attack, then accidents and the "nth" country problem would be the only problems. As I have indicated, they are serious problems and some sorts of limitation and inspection agreement might diminish them. But if there is to be any prospect of realistic and useful agreement, we must reject the theory of automatic deterrence. And we must bear in mind that the more extensive a disarmament agreement is, the smaller the force that a violator would have to hide in order to achieve complete domination. Most obviously, *"the abolition* of the weapons necessary in a general or 'unlimited' war" would offer the most insuperable obstacles to an inspection plan, since the violator could gain an overwhelming ad-

[11] James E. King, Jr., "Arms and Man in the Nuclear-Rocket Era," *The New Republic,* September 1, 1958.

vantage from the concealment of even a few weapons. The need for a deterrent, in this connection, is ineradicable.

VII. SUMMARY

Almost everyone seems concerned with the need to relax tension. However, relaxation of tension, which everyone thinks is good, is not easily distinguished from relaxing one's guard, which almost everyone thinks is bad. Relaxation, like Miltown, is not an end in itself. Not all danger comes from tension. To be tense where there is danger is only rational.

What can we say then, in sum, on the balance of terror theory of automatic deterrence? It is a contribution to the rhetoric rather than the logic of war in the thermonuclear age. The notion that a carefully planned surprise attack can be checkmated almost effortlessly, that, in short, we may resume our deep pre-sputnik sleep, is wrong and its nearly universal acceptance is terribly dangerous. Though deterrence is not enough in itself, it is vital. There are two principal points.

First, deterring general war in both the early and late 1960s will be hard at best, and hardest both for ourselves and our allies wherever we use forces based near the enemy.

Second, even if we can deter general war by a strenuous and continuing effort, this will by no means be the whole of a military, much less a foreign, policy. Such a policy would not of itself remove the danger of accidental outbreak or limit the damage in case deterrence failed; nor would it be at all adequate for crises on the peripherey.

A generally useful way of concluding a grim argument of this kind would be to affirm that we have the resources, intelligence and courage to make the correct decisions. That is, of course, the case. And there is a good chance that we will do so. But perhaps, as a small aid toward making such decisions more likely, we should contemplate the possibility that they may *not* be made. They *are* hard, *do* involve sacrifice, *are* affected by great uncertainties and concern matters in which much is altogether unknown and much else must be hedged by secrecy; and, above all, they entail a new image of ourselves in a world of persistent danger. It is by no means *certain* that we shall meet the test.

Nikita Sergeyevich Khrushchev has emerged since Stalin's death in March 1953 as the dominant figure in the Soviet dictatorship. After holding posts of great responsibility during Stalin's rule and serving as a full member of Stalin's Politbureau from 1939 on, he was appointed First Secretary of the Moscow Oblast Committee of the Party in 1949 and simultaneously a Secretary of the Central Committee. In September 1953 he was advanced to First Secretary of the Central Committee; in February 1956 to Chairman of the Party's newly formed Russian Republic Bureau; and in 1958 to Chairman of the Council of Ministers.

While there has been a continuing debate, reflected in the pages of *Foreign Affairs,* over whether Khrushchev's power is as absolute as Stalin's or whether he exercises this vast power under certain limitations imposed either by Party institutions or by a continuing rivalry for leadership, there is no doubt that Chairman Khrushchev constantly lays down the line in matters of domestic, foreign and strategic policy. He has, of course, made a determined break with many features of Stalin's methods of domination, and he has struck out on many new and more imaginative lines of policy. In foreign affairs his innovations have been striking, and he has greatly enlarged the spectrum of both threats and blandishments that are now in common use by the Soviet Government. Unlike Stalin, he has sought to present his views directly to many foreign leaders and has visited many foreign lands.

The political philosophy and the purposes of such a powerful world leader are of great importance to people everywhere. For this reason the Editor of *Foreign Affairs* invited Chairman Khrushchev, even before the announcement of his forthcoming first visit to America, to present his views in its columns. "On Peaceful Coexistence" (October 1959) was actually published in September of that year, just a few days before Khrushchev was welcomed to Washington by President Dwight D. Eisenhower. Each reader will want to judge for himself whether and how far Khrushchev's recommendations on how to achieve or safeguard "peaceful coexistence" promise to lead the nations of the world to a stable balance of power and permanent relaxation of tensions.

ON PEACEFUL COEXISTENCE

By Nikita S. Khrushchev

I have been told that the question of peaceful coexistence of states with different social systems is uppermost today in the minds of many Americans—and not only Americans. The question of coexistence, particularly in our day, interests literally every man and woman on the globe.

We all of us well know that tremendous changes have taken place in the world. Gone, indeed, are the days when it took weeks to cross the ocean from one continent to the other or when a trip from Europe to America, or from Asia to Africa, seemed a very complicated undertaking. The progress of modern technology has reduced our planet to a rather small place; it has even become, in this sense, quite congested. And if in our daily life it is a matter of considerable importance to establish normal relations with our neighbors in a densely inhabited settlement, this is so much the more necessary in the relations between states, in particular states belonging to different social systems.

You may like your neighbor or dislike him. You are not obliged to be friends with him or visit him. But you live side by side, and what can you do if neither you nor he has any desire to quit the old home and move to another town? All the more so in relations between states. It would be unreasonable to assume that you can make it so hot for your undesirable neighbor that he will decide to move to Mars or Venus. And vice versa, of course.

What, then, remains to be done? There may be two ways out: either war—and war in the rocket and H-bomb age is fraught with the most dire consequences for all nations—or peaceful coexistence. Whether you like your neighbor or not, nothing can be done about it, you have to find some way of getting on with him, for you both live on one and the same planet.

But the very concept of peaceful coexistence, it is said, by its alleged complexity frightens certain people who have become unaccustomed to trusting their neighbors and who see a double bottom in each suitcase.

People of this kind, on hearing the word "coexistence," begin to play around with it in one way and another, sizing it up and applying various yardsticks to it. Isn't it a fraud? Isn't it a trap? Does not coexistence signify the division of the world into areas separated by high fences, which do not communicate with each other? And what is going to happen behind those fences?

The more such questions are piled up artificially by the cold-war mongers, the more difficult it is for the ordinary man to make head or tail of them. It would therefore be timely to rid the essence of this question of all superfluous elements and to attempt to look soberly at the most pressing problem of our day—the problem of peaceful competition.

II

One does not need to delve deeply into history to appreciate how important it is for mankind to ensure peaceful coexistence. And here it may be said parenthetically that the Europeans might have benefited a great deal in their day if, instead of organizing senseless crusades which invariably ended in failure, they had established peaceful relations with the differently-minded peoples of the Moslem East.

But let us turn to facts concerning the relatively recent past when the watershed between states no longer consisted of different religious creeds and customs, but of much deeper differences of principle relating to the choice of social systems. This new situation arose on the threshold of the 1920s when, to the booming of the guns of the Russian cruiser *Aurora* which had joined the rebellious workers and peasants, a new and unprecedented social system, a state of workers and peasants, came into the world.

Its appearance was met with the disgruntled outcries of those who naïvely believed the capitalist system to be eternal and immutable. Some people even made an attempt to strangle the unwanted infant in the cradle. Everybody knows how this ended: our people voted with their arms for Soviet power, and it came to stay. And even then, in 1920, V. I. Lenin, replying to the question of an American correspondent as to what basis there could be for peace between Soviet Russia and America, said: "Let the American imperialists not touch us. We won't touch them."

From its very inception the Soviet state proclaimed peaceful coexistence as the basic principle of its foreign policy. It was no accident that the very first state act of the Soviet power was the decree on peace, the decree on the cessation of the bloody war.

What, then, is the policy of peaceful coexistence?

In its simplest expression it signifies the repudiation of war as a means of solving controversial issues. However, this does not cover the entire concept of peaceful coexistence. Apart from the commitment to non-aggression, it also presupposes an obligation on the part of all states to desist from violating each other's territorial integrity and sovereignty in any form and under any pretext whatsoever. The principle of peaceful coexistence signifies a renunciation of interference in the internal affairs of other countries with the object of altering their system of government or mode of life or for any other motives. The doctrine of peaceful coexistence also presupposes that political and economic relations between countries are to be based upon complete equality of the parties concerned, and on mutual benefit.

It is often said in the West that peaceful coexistence is nothing else than a tactical method of the socialist states. There is not a grain of truth in such allegations. Our desire for peace and peaceful coexistence is not conditioned by any time-serving or tactical considerations. It springs from the very nature of socialist society in which there are no classes or social groups interested in profiting by war or seizing and enslaving other people's territories. The Soviet Union and the other socialist countries, thanks to their socialist system, have an unlimited home market and for this reason they have no need to pursue an expansionist policy of conquest and an effort to subordinate other countries to their influence.

It is the people who determine the destinies of the socialist states. The socialist states are ruled by the working people themselves, the workers and peasants, the people who themselves create all the material and spiritual values of society. And people of labor cannot want war. For to them war spells grief and tears, death, devastation and misery. Ordinary people have no need for war.

Contrary to what certain propagandists hostile to us say, the coexistence of states with different social systems does not mean that they will only fence themselves off from one another by a high wall and undertake the mutual obligation not to throw stones over the wall or pour dirt upon each other. No! Peaceful coexistence does not mean merely living side by side in the absence of war but with the constantly remaining threat of its breaking out in the future. *Peaceful coexistence*

*can and should develop into peaceful competition for the purpose of
satisfying man's needs in the best possible way.*

We say to the leaders of the capitalist states: Let us try out in
practice whose system is better, let us compete without war. This is
much better than competing in who will produce more arms and who
will smash whom. We stand and always will stand for such competition
as will help to raise the well-being of the people to a higher level.

The principle of peaceful competition does not at all demand that
one or another state abandon the system and ideology adopted by it.
It goes without saying that the acceptance of this principle cannot lead
to the immediate end of disputes and contradictions which are inevitable
between countries adhering to different social systems. But the main thing
is ensured: the states which decided to adopt the path of peaceful
coexistence repudiate the use of force in any form and agree on a
peaceful settlement of possible disputes and conflicts, bearing in mind
the mutual interests of the parties concerned. In our age of the H-bomb
and atomic techniques this is the main thing of interest to every man.

Displaying skepticism about the idea of peaceful competition, Vice
President Nixon, in his speech over the Soviet radio and television in
August 1959, attempted to find a contradiction between the Soviet
people's professions of their readiness to coexist peacefully with the capitalist states and the slogans posted in the shops of our factories calling
for higher labor productivity in order to ensure the speediest victory
of Communism.

This was not the first time we heard representatives of the bourgeois
countries reason in this manner. They say: The Soviet leaders argue
that they are for peaceful coexistence. At the same time they declare
that they are fighting for Communism and they even say that Communism
will be victorious in all countries. How can there be peaceful coexistence with the Soviet Union if it fights for Communism?

People who treat the question in this way confuse matters, willfully
or not, by confusing the problems of ideological struggle with the question of relations between states. Those indulging in this sort of confusion
are most probably guided by a desire to cast aspersions upon the Communists of the Soviet Union and to represent them as the advocates of
aggressive actions. This, however, is very unwise.

The Communist Party of the Soviet Union at its Twentieth Congress
made it perfectly clear and obvious that the allegations that the Soviet
Union intends to overthrow capitalism in other countries by means of

"exporting" revolution are absolutely unfounded. I cannot refrain from reminding you of my words at the Twentieth Congress: "It goes without saying that among us Communists there are no adherents of capitalism. But this does not mean that we have interfered or plan to interfere in the internal affairs of countries where capitalism still exists. Romain Rolland was right when he said that 'freedom is not brought in from abroad in baggage trains like Bourbons.' It is ridiculous to think that revolutions are made to order."

We Communists believe that the idea of Communism will ultimately be victorious throughout the world, just as it has been victorious in our country, in China and in many other states. Many readers of FOREIGN AFFAIRS will probably disagree with us. Perhaps they think that the idea of capitalism will ultimately triumph. It is their right to think so. We may argue, we may disagree with one another. *The main thing is to keep to the positions of ideological struggle, without resorting to arms in order to prove that one is right.* The point is that with military techniques what they are today, there are no inaccessible places in the world. Should a world war break out, no country will be able to shut itself off from a crushing blow.

We believe that ultimately that system will be victorious on the globe which will offer the nations greater opportunities for improving their material and spiritual life. It is precisely socialism that creates unprecedentedly great prospects for the inexhaustible creative enthusiasm of the masses, for a genuine flourishing of science and culture, for the realization of man's dream of a happy life, a life without destitute and unemployed people, of a happy childhood and tranquil old age, of the realization of the most audacious and ambitious human projects, of man's right to create in a truly free manner in the interests of the people.

But when we say that in the competition between the two systems, the capitalist and the socialist, our system will win, this does not mean, of course, that we shall achieve victory by interfering in the internal affairs of the capitalist countries. Our confidence in the victory of Communism is of a different kind. It is based on a knowledge of the laws governing the development of society. Just as in its time capitalism, as the more progressive system, took the place of feudalism, so will capitalism be inevitably superseded by Communism—the more progressive and more equitable social system. We are confident of the victory of the socialist system because it is a more progressive system than the capitalist system. Soviet power has been in existence for only a little more than 40 years, and during these years we have gone through two of the worst wars, repulsing the attacks of enemies who attempted to strangle us. Capitalism in the United States has been in existence for more than a century and a half, and the history of the United States has developed in such a way that never once have enemies landed on American territory.

Yet the dynamics of the development of the U.S.S.R. and the U.S.A. are such that the 42-year-old land of the Soviets is already able to challenge the 150-year-old capitalist state to economic competition; and the most farsighted American leaders are admitting that the Soviet Union is fast catching up with the United States and will ultimately outstrip it. Watching the progress of this competition, anyone can judge which is the better system, and we believe that in the long run all the peoples will embark on the path of struggle for the building of socialist societies.

You disagree with us? Prove by facts that your system is superior and more efficacious, that it is capable of ensuring a higher degree of prosperity for the people than the socialist system, that under capitalism man can be happier than under socialism. It is impossible to prove this. I have no other explanation for the fact that talk of violently "rolling back" Communism never ceases in the West. Not long ago the U.S. Senate and House of Representatives deemed it proper to pass a resolution calling for the "liberation" of the socialist countries allegedly enslaved by Communism and, moreover, of a number of union republics constituting part of the Soviet Union. The authors of the resolution call for the "liberation" of the Ukraine, Byelorussia, Lithuania, Latvia, Estonia, Armenia, Azerbaijan, Georgia, Kazakhstan, Turkmenistan and even a certain "Ural Area."

I would not be telling the full truth if I did not say that the adoption of this ill-starred resolution was regarded by the Soviet people as an act of provocation. Personally I agree with this appraisal.

It would be interesting to see, incidentally, how the authors of this resolution would have reacted if the parliament of Mexico, for instance, had passed a resolution demanding that Texas, Arizona and California be "liberated from American slavery." Apparently they have never pondered such a question, which is very regrettable. Sometimes comparisons help to understand the essence of a matter.

Traveling through the Soviet Union, leading American statesmen and public figures have had full opportunity to convince themselves that there is no hope of sowing strife between the Soviet people and the

Communist Party and the Soviet Government, and of influencing them to rebel against Communism. How, then, are we to explain the unceasing attempts to revive the policy of "rolling back" Communism? What do they have in mind? Armed intervention in the internal affairs of the socialist countries? But in the West as well as in the East people are fully aware that under the conditions of modern military technique such actions are fraught with immediate and relentless retaliation.

So we come back to what we started with. In our day there are only two ways: peaceful coexistence or the most destructive war in history. There is no third choice.

III

The problem of peaceful coexistence between states with different social systems has become particularly pressing in view of the fact that since the Second World War the development of relations between states has entered a new stage, that now we have approached a period in the life of mankind when there is a real chance of excluding war once and for all from the life of society. The new alignment of international forces which has developed since the Second World War offers ground for the assertion that a new world war is no longer a fatal inevitability, that it can be averted.

First, today not only all the socialist states, but many countries in Asia and Africa which have embarked upon the road of independent national statehood, and many other states outside the aggressive military groupings, are actively fighting for peace.

Secondly, the peace policy enjoys the powerful support of the broad masses of the people all over the world.

Thirdly, the peaceful socialist states are in possession of very potent material means, which cannot but have a deterring effect upon the aggressors.

Prior to the Second World War the U.S.S.R. was the only socialist country, with not more than 17 percent of the territory, 3 percent of the population, and about 10 percent of the output of the world. At present, the socialist countries cover about one-fourth of the territory of the globe, have one-third of its population, and their industrial output accounts for about one-third of the total world output.

This is precisely the explanation of the indisputable fact that throughout the past years, hotbeds of war breaking out now in one and now in another part of the globe—in the Near East and in Europe, in the Far East and in Southeast Asia—have been extinguished at the very outset.

What does the future hold in store for us?

As a result of the fulfillment and overfulfillment of the present Seven Year Plan of economic development of the U.S.S.R., as well as of the plans of the other socialist countries of Europe and Asia, the countries of the socialist system will then account for a little more than half of the world output. Their economic power will grow immeasurably, and this will help to an even greater extent to consolidate world peace: the material might and moral influence of the peace-loving states will be so great that any bellicose militarist will have to think ten times before risking going to war. It is the good fortune of mankind that a community of socialist states which are not interested in new war has been set up, because to build socialism and Communism the socialist countries need peace. Today the community of socialist countries which has sprung up on the basis of complete equality holds such a position in the development of all branches of economy, science and culture as to be able to exert an influence towards preventing the outbreak of new world wars.

Hence we are already in a practical sense near to that stage in the life of humanity when nothing will prevent people from devoting themselves wholly to peaceful labor, when war will be wholly excluded from the life of society.

But if we say that there is no fatal inevitability of war at present, this by no means signifies that we can rest on our laurels, fold our arms and bask in the sun in the hope that an end has been put to wars once and for all. Those in the West who believe that war is to their benefit have not yet abandoned their schemes. They control considerable material forces, as well as military and political levers, and there is no guarantee that some tragic day they will not attempt to set them in motion. That is why it is so much the more necessary to continue an active struggle in order that the policy of peaceful coexistence may triumph throughout the world not in words but in deeds.

Of much importance, of course, is the fact that this policy has in our day merited not only the widest moral approval but also international legal recognition. The countries of the socialist camp in their relations with the capitalist states are guided precisely by this policy. The principles of peaceful coexistence are reflected in the decisions of the Bandung Conference of Asian and African countries. Furthermore, many countries of Europe, Asia and Africa have solemnly proclaimed this principle as the basis of their foreign policy. Finally, the idea of peaceful coexistence has found unanimous support in the decisions of the twelfth and thirteenth sessions of the United Nations General Assembly.

In our view, peaceful coexistence can become lasting only if the good declarations in favor of peace are supported by active measures on the part of the governments and peoples of all countries. As far as the Soviet Union is concerned, it has already done a good deal in this respect, and I am able to share some experiences with you.

As far back as March 12, 1951, the Supreme Soviet of the U.S.S.R. adopted a "Law on the Defense of Peace," stating:

(1) Propaganda for war, in whatever form it may be conducted, undermines the cause of peace, creates the menace of a new war and therefore constitutes the gravest crime against humanity.

(2) Persons guilty of war propaganda should be brought to court and tried as heinous criminals.

Further, the Soviet Union has in recent years unilaterally reduced its armed forces by more than 2,000,000 men. The funds released as a result have been used to develop the economy and further raise the material and cultural living standards of the Soviet people.

The Soviet Union has liquidated its bases on the territories of other states.

The Soviet Union unilaterally discontinued the tests of atomic weapons and refrained from conducting them further until it became finally clear that the Western powers refused to follow our example and were continuing the explosions.

The Soviet Union has repeatedly submitted detailed and perfectly realistic proposals for disarmament, meeting the positions of the Western powers halfway. But to solve the disarmament problem it is necessary for our Western partners to agree and desire to meet us halfway too. This is just what is lacking.

When it became clear that it was very difficult under these conditions to solve the complex disarmament problem immediately, we proposed another concrete idea to our partners: Let us concentrate our attention on those problems which lend themselves most easily to a solution. Let us undertake initial partial steps on matters concerning which the views of the different parties have been brought closer together.

It is perfectly clear that one of these questions today is the question of discontinuing atomic and hydrogen weapon tests. The progress achieved in this matter justifies the hope that an agreement on the discontinuation of nuclear weapon tests will shortly be reached. Implementation of this measure will, of course, be an important step on the way to the solution of the disarmament problem and the banning of nuclear weapons in general.

Attributing much importance to contacts and intercourse between statesmen of all countries, the Soviet Government a few years ago proposed that an East-West heads of government conference be convened in order to come to terms—taking into account present-day realities and guided by the spirit of mutual understanding—on concrete measures, the realization of which would help to relax international tension.

We also proposed that this conference consider those international questions for the settlement of which realistic prerequisites already existed. As a first step toward such a settlement, we proposed to the powers concerned that a peace treaty be concluded with Germany and that West Berlin be granted the status of a demilitarized free city. I want to emphasize particularly that we were guided primarily by the desire to put a final end to the aftermath of the Second World War. We regard the liquidation of the consequences of the Second World War and the conclusion of a peace treaty with the two German states—the German Democratic Republic and the German Federal Republic—as the question of questions.

Indeed, 14 years have already passed since the war ended, but the German people are still without a peace treaty. The delay has afforded wide scope for renewed activities of the West German militarists and revanchists. They have already proclaimed their aggressive plans, laying claim, for instance, to lands in Poland and Czechoslovakia. Of course, the German revanchists are thinking not only of a march to the East; they also know the way to the West. In the Second World War the Hitlerites occupied Western Europe before advancing against the Soviet Union.

Will the direction chosen by the modern German revanchists for their aggression be any consolation to the peoples of Europe if a global war breaks out on that continent? The lessons of history should not be ignored. To do so often ends in tragedy.

Some say: The Soviet people are unduly sensitive. Can one assume that Western Germany is now in a position to precipitate another world war? Those who put the question thus forget that Western Germany is at present acting in the world arena not alone but within the military North Atlantic bloc. She plays a paramount rôle in this bloc. And more than that, life has shown that the North Atlantic Alliance is being gradually converted into an instrument of the German militarists, which makes it easier for them to carry out aggressive plans. It is not at all impossible, therefore, that Western Germany, taking advantage of her position in the North Atlantic Alliance, might provoke hostilities in order to draw her allies into it and plunge the whole world into the chasm of a devastating war.

All this indicates how timely and realistic are the proposals of the Soviet Government for the conclusion of a peace treaty with Germany and for bringing the situation in West Berlin back to normal.

And yet, some of the Western opponents of the Soviet proposals say that if the Soviet Union really stands for peaceful coexistence it should even be asked to commit itself to the preservation of the existing status quo. Others argue that if the Western powers agree to the conclusion of a peace treaty with the two German states that would amount to a retreat on their part, and the Soviet Union should make some compensation for this "retreat."

There are no grounds whatever for these assertions, in our opinion. The task before us is to do away with the aftermath of the Second World War and to conclude a peace treaty. And any possibility of someone gaining and others losing, of someone acquiring and others making concessions, is out of the question here. All the parties concerned acquire a stronger foundation for the maintenance of peace in Europe and throughout the world in the shape of a peace treaty. Does this not accord with the interests of all the peoples?

At times, and of late especially, some spokesmen in the West have gone so far as to say that the abolition of the aftermath of the Second World War is a step which would allegedly intensify rather than ease international tension. It is hard to believe that there are no secret designs behind allegations of this kind, especially when attempts are made to present in a distorted light the policy of the U.S.S.R., which is intended to secure a lasting and stable peace, by alleging that it all but leads to war. It seems to us, on the contrary, that the Soviet position on the German question corresponds most of all to the present-day reality.

It now seems that no sober-minded leader in the West is inclined any longer to advance the unrealistic demand for the so-called reunion of

Germany before the conclusion of a peace treaty, in as much as more and more political leaders are becoming aware of the fact that reunion in the conditions now obtaining is a process which depends upon the Germans themselves and not upon any outside interference. We should start from the obvious fact that two German states exist, and that the Germans themselves must decide how they want to live. In as much as these two states, the German Democratic Republic and the German Federal Republic, do exist, the peace treaty should be concluded with them, because any further delay and postponement of this exceptionally important act tends not only to sustain the abnormal situation in Europe but also to aggravate it still further.

As for Germany's unity, I am convinced that Germany will be united sooner or later. However, before this moment comes—and no one can foretell when it will come—no attempts should be made to interfere from outside in this internal process, to sustain the state of war which is fraught with many grave dangers and surprises for peace in Europe and throughout the world. The desire to preserve the peace and to prevent another war should outweigh all other considerations of statesmen, irrespective of their mode of thinking. The Gordian knot must be cut: the peace treaty must be achieved if we do not want to play with fire—with the destinies of millions upon millions of people.

IV

In this connection it is impossible to ignore also the question of West Berlin. It is commonly known that the German revanchists have made West Berlin the base for their constant undermining and subversive activity directed towards the provoking of war. We resolutely reject any attempts to ascribe to the Soviet Union the intention of seizing West Berlin and infringing upon the right of the population in this part of the city to preserve its present way of life. On the contrary, in demanding the normalization of the situation in West Berlin, we have proposed to convert it into a free city and to guarantee, jointly with the Western states, the preservation there of the way of life and of the social order which suits the West Berlin inhabitants best of all. This shows that the positions of the Government of the Soviet Union and the Governments of the Western states, judging by their statements, coincide on this question. We, and so do they, stand for the independence of West Berlin and for the preservation of the existing way of life there.

It is, therefore, only necessary to overcome the difficulties born of the cold war in order to find the way to an agreement on West Berlin and on the wider question of the conclusion of a peace treaty with the two German states. This is the way to ease international tensions and to promote peaceful coexistence. It would strengthen confidence between states and assist in the gradual abolition of unfriendliness and suspicion in international relations.

Implementation of the Soviet proposals would not injure the interests of the Western powers and would not give any one-sided advantages to anybody. At the same time, the settlement of the German question would prevent a dangerous development of events in Europe, remove one of the main causes of international tension and create favorable prospects for a settlement of other international issues.

The proposals of the Soviet Union were discussed at the Foreign Ministers' Conference in Geneva. The Ministers did not succeed in reaching an agreement, but the Geneva Conference did accomplish a great deal of useful work. The positions of the two sides were positively brought closer together and the possibility of an agreement on some questions has become apparent.

At the same time, we still have substantial differences on a number of questions. I am deeply convinced that they are not fundamental differences on which agreement is impossible. And if we still have differences and have not reached agreement on certain important questions, it is, as we believe, with adequate grounds—a result of the concessions made by the Western powers to Chancellor Adenauer, who is pursuing a military policy, the policy of the German revanchists. This is a case of the United States, Britain and France dangerously abetting Chancellor Adenauer. It would have been far better if the NATO allies of Western Germany would persuade Chancellor Adenauer, in the interest of the maintenance of peace, that his policy imperils the cause of peace and that it may ultimately end in irreparable disaster for Western Germany. All this emphasizes again that the representatives of the states concerned must do some more work in order to find mutually acceptable decisions.

I believe that my trip to the United States and the subsequent visit of President Eisenhower to the Soviet Union will afford the possibility for a useful exchange of opinions, for finding a common tongue and a common understanding of the questions that should be settled.

V

We are prepared now as before to do everything we possibly can in order that the relations between the Soviet Union and other countries, and, in particular, the relations between the U.S.S.R. and the U.S.A., should be built upon the foundation of friendship and that they should fully correspond to the principles of peaceful coexistence.

I should like to repeat what I said at my recent press conference in Moscow: "Should Soviet-American relations become brighter, that will not fail to bring about an improvement in the relations with other states and will help to scatter the gloomy clouds in other parts of the globe also. Naturally, we want friendship not only with the U.S.A., but also with the friends of the U.S.A. At the same time we want to see the U.S.A. maintain good relations not only with us, but with our friends as well."

What, then, is preventing us from making the principles of peaceful coexistence an unshakable international standard and daily practice in the relations between the West and East?

Of course, different answers may be given to this question. But in order to be frank to the end, we should also say the following: *It is necessary that everybody should understand the irrevocable fact that the historic process is irreversible.* It is impossible to bring back yesterday. It is high time to understand that the world of the twentieth century is not the world of the nineteenth century, that two diametrically opposed social and economic systems exist in the world today side by side, and that the socialist system, in spite of all the attacks upon it, has grown so strong, has developed into such a force, as to make any return to the past impossible.

Real facts of life in the last ten years have shown convincingly that the policy of "rolling back" Communism can only poison the international atmosphere, heighten the tension between states and work in favor of the cold war. Neither its inspirers nor those who conduct it can turn back the course of history and restore capitalism in the socialist countries.

We have always considered the Americans realistic people. All the more are we astonished to find that leading representatives of the United States still number in their midst individuals who insist on their own way in the face of the obvious failure of the policy of "rolling back"

Communism. But is it not high time to take a sober view of things and to draw conclusions from the lessons of the last 15 years? Is it not yet clear to everybody that consistent adherence to the policy of peaceful coexistence would make it possible to improve the international situation, to bring about a drastic cut in military expenditures and to release vast material resources for wiser purposes?

The well known British scientist, J. Bernal, recently cited figures to show that average annual expenditures for military purposes throughout the world between 1950 and the end of 1957 were expressed in the huge sum of about 90 billion dollars. How many factories, apartment houses, schools, hospitals and libraries could have been built everywhere with the funds now spent on the preparation of another war! And how fast could economic progress have been advanced in the underdeveloped countries if we had converted to these purposes at least some of the means which are now being spent on war purposes!

VI

It is readily seen that the policy of peaceful coexistence receives a firm foundation only with increase in extensive and absolutely unrestricted international trade. It can be said without fear of exaggeration that there is no good basis for improvement of relations between our countries other than development of international trade.

If the principle of peaceful coexistence of states is to be adhered to, not in words, but in deeds, it is perfectly obvious that no ideological differences should be an obstacle to the development and extension of mutually advantageous economic contacts, to the exchange of everything produced by human genius in the sphere of peaceful branches of material production.

In this connection it may be recalled that soon after the birth of the Soviet state, back in the early 1920s, the Western countries, proceeding from considerations of economic interest, agreed to establish trade relations with our country despite the acutest ideological differences. Since then, discounting comparatively short periods, trade between the Soviet Union and capitalist states has been developing steadily. No ideological differences prevented, for instance, a considerable extension of trade relations between the Soviet Union and Britain and other Western states in recent years. We make no secret of our desire to establish normal commercial and business contacts with the United States as well, without any restrictions, without any discriminations.

In June of last year the Soviet Government addressed itself to the Government of the United States with the proposal to develop economic and trade contacts between our two countries. We proposed an extensive and concrete program of developing Soviet-American trade on a mutually advantageous basis. The adoption of our proposals would undoubtedly accord with the interests of both states and peoples. However, these proposals have not been developed so far.

Striving for the restoration of normal trade relations with the United States, the Soviet Union does not pursue any special interests. In our economic development we rely wholly on the internal forces of our country, on our own resources and possibilities. All our plans for further economic development are drawn up taking into consideration the possibilities available here. As in the past, when we outline these plans we proceed only from the basis of our own possibilities and forces. Irrespective of whether or not we shall trade with Western countries, the United States included, the implementation of our economic plans of peaceful construction will not in the least be impeded.

However, if both sides want to improve relations, all barriers in international trade must be removed. Those who want peaceful coexistence cannot but favor the development of trade, economic and business contacts. Only on this basis can international life develop normally.

VII

Peaceful coexistence is the only way which is in keeping with the interests of all nations. To reject it would mean under existing conditions to doom the whole world to a terrible and destructive war at a time when it is fully possible to avoid it.

Is it possible that when mankind has advanced to a plane where it has proved capable of the greatest discoveries and of making its first steps into outer space, it should not be able to use the colossal achievements of its genius for the establishment of a stable peace, for the good of man, rather than for the preparation of another war and for the destruction of all that has been created by its labor over many millenniums? Reason refuses to believe this. It protests.

The Soviet people have stated and declare again that they do not want war. If the Soviet Union and the countries friendly to it are not attacked, we shall never use any weapons either against the United States or against any other countries. We do not want any horrors of war, destruction, suffering and death for ourselves or for any other peoples. We say this not because we fear anyone. Together with our friends, we are united and stronger than ever. But precisely because of that do we say that war can and should be prevented. Precisely because we want to rid mankind of war, we urge the Western powers to peaceful and lofty competition. We say to all: Let us prove to each other the advantages of one's own system not with fists, not by war, but by peaceful economic competition in conditions of peaceful coexistence.

As for the social system in some state or other, that is the domestic affair of the people of each country. We always have stood and we stand today for non-interference in the internal affairs of other countries. We have always abided, and we shall abide, by these positions. The question, for example, what system will exist in the United States or in other capitalist countries cannot be decided by other peoples or states. This question can and will be decided only by the American people themselves, only by the people of each country.

The existence of the Soviet Union and of the other socialist countries is a real fact. It is also a real fact that the United States of America and the other capitalist countries live in different social conditions, in the conditions of capitalism. Then let us recognize this real situation and proceed from it in order not to go against reality, against life itself. Let us not try to change this situation by interferences from without, by means of war on the part of some states against other states.

I repeat, there is only one way to peace, one way out of the existing tension: peaceful coexistence.

ONCE China had emerged by 1949 as the second major Communist state, there emerged with it a new set of problems: What would henceforth be the relations between the two great centers of Communist power? Would their leaders always see eye-to-eye in questions of ideological orthodoxy and political action? Would Mao's China make good its claim to be the model, and perhaps the mentor and patron, in the program for installing Communist régimes throughout Asia? Analysts, observers and statesmen alike are racking their brains over these and other varieties of the Sino-Soviet conundrum.

Will the Soviet leadership pursue an ever more active forward policy in Southeast Asia, following the Communist success in Laos? Is it taking advantage of China's economic weaknesses to build up a client federation centered around the energetic Communist Party of North Viet-Nam? These and other implications of the Moscow-Peking rivalry may, indeed, have far-reaching consequences.

"Russia and China: The Dilemmas of Power" (October 1960), by G. F. Hudson, was one of the earliest and best efforts to identify the visible clues and extrapolate the hidden links between them. Writing just after the Bucharest conference of June 1960 had lifted the veil ever so briefly on the behind-the-scenes dissonances within the Communist bloc, Mr. Hudson drew on a long and intimate knowledge of modern China and a detailed study of the continuities and changes in Communist ideology to make a shrewd appraisal of the probable scope and thrust of the emerging conflict of outlook and purposes. Since then new contours have emerged and new and perhaps more dangerous implications have become visible, but the basic analysis presented by Mr. Hudson is well worth pondering today.

G. F. Hudson, a Fellow of St. Antony's College, Oxford, in charge of the Center of Far Eastern Studies, was formerly on the editorial staff of *The Economist*. He is the author of "The Far East in World Politics" (1937), co-author of "An Atlas of Far Eastern Politics" (1942), editor of collected sources on the Chinese communes and on Sino-Soviet relations, and author of numerous articles of contemporary analysis.

416

RUSSIA AND CHINA:
THE DILEMMAS OF POWER

By G. F. Hudson

INTENSE anti-American propaganda has been a permanent feature of the Chinese Communist scene for the last decade, and it might have been supposed that a point of saturation would by now have been reached in the endeavor to incite the Chinese people to the emotional state desired by their rulers. But the month of June 1960 saw the launching of a campaign of unprecedented vehemence, described as "a new storm of struggle against United States imperialism," culminating in a special "Anti-American Week" organized throughout China from June 21 to 27.

With the Chinese people as a whole being overworked, underfed and ruthlessly coerced, and nature adding its quota of misery through last year's floods and this year's drought, it is no time for the Chinese leaders to encourage a basking in the sunshine of peaceful coexistence and relaxation of international tension. On the contrary, the masses must be persuaded that outside their borders the devilish American imperialists are waiting for the opportunity to invade and subdue their country, that their salvation depends on the speedy transformation of China into a vigilant armed camp, and that every wheelbarrow of earth moved in the struggle for "socialist construction" is a blow in defense of the motherland. But how could such emotions be evoked if there were any doubt about the malevolence of the imperialists or their will to war? Fear and hatred of "the enemy" would lose their force if it came to be believed that the imperialists could resign themselves to perpetual peace and that "different social systems" could live side by side indefinitely without war. The "new storm" in China is designed precisely to persuade the Chinese people that this cannot happen.

So far, indeed, the bark has been worse than the bite, and the absence of actual crises recently in relations with Communist China has led

417

Western opinion largely to ignore the intensity of the anti-Western indoctrination to which the Chinese people are daily being subjected. To the time of writing there has been no renewal of serious Communist attack in the Formosa Straits since 1957; the symbolic bombardment of Quemoy to mark President Eisenhower's visit to Taipeh was a relatively feeble affair. The armistice line in Korea remains unbroken; Hong Kong carries on as usual; even on the Indian border the Chinese have for some time been quiescent.

Such discrepancy between violence of speech and practical inaction was also characteristic of Communist Russia at the beginning of the thirties; this was the so-called "third period" of the Comintern when the democratic Socialist and Labor parties of Europe were denounced as "social fascists," and it was also the time of the Ramzin and Menshevik show trials in Moscow, when the amalgam of internal disaffection and foreign imperialist instigation was first presented to the Soviet public through carefully prepared confessions in court. It was not, however, a period of actual Soviet aggression abroad, for the reason that the short-term effect of Russia's "great leap forward"—as distinct from the long-term effect—was to weaken her as a military power. Far from being in a position to undertake foreign conquests during this time, she had to accept the humiliation of complete passivity while the Japanese army overran her long-established sphere of influence in northern Manchuria; the food shortages and economic confusion rendered it out of the question to risk a major war.

II

Today, Soviet reasons for not wanting to risk a major war are quite different, but no less compelling. Moreover, with the relaxation of internal tensions, policies of national self-isolation, cultivated xenophobia and predictions of inevitable war no longer appear so expedient as they once did.

In the new Russian mood of incipient prosperity and *embourgeoisé* self-satisfaction these tactics merely served to cast a chill over the hopefulness which the Party was trying to turn to its advantage, while in the West they created a wall of suspicion and opposition which Soviet diplomacy and publicity could not penetrate. Moreover, they were averse to success in the international movement which showed the greatest promise of aid to the Communist cause—the campaign for "peace" with its various front organizations throughout the world. The theme of universal disarmament made a profound appeal to the peoples of the Western democracies. But how could Communism exploit these powerful emotions in the Western world if it continued to assert that the very existence of the capitalist system made war inevitable? For those whom the Communist "peace" propaganda was designed to persuade—or at least for the more intelligent of them—this doctrine made nonsense of Moscow's appeals. It was therefore of great assistance to all those concerned with the public relations of the Soviet Union, whether as diplomats or as propagandists, when Khrushchev announced at the Twentieth Party Congress that war with the imperialist powers need not be regarded as inevitable.

There was of course a further reason which made such a declaration desirable from the point of view of the Soviet leadership. Soviet publicity for internal consumption and for Communists everywhere was by habit excessively boastful, and it had made the most of Russia's invincible military might as manifested by the victory of Russian arms in the Second World War. It was indeed important to give the utmost credit to the régime for Russia's new power and also to show that Moscow was not afraid of "massive retaliation" or of anything else the West might threaten to do. But privately, no doubt, anyone in the top leadership with knowledge of the facts about the potency of the new weapons and the Western capacity for delivery could hardly fail to take the view that, even if Russia were to emerge victorious from a major war, the damage to her own territory and population would be so great as to threaten the survival of the régime. War therefore was something to be avoided.

On the other hand, such wisdom, in so far as it did affect the top leadership, did not easily penetrate to the middle and lower levels of the Soviet Communist Party. These consisted of men and women who had been brought up to believe that the world-wide victory of Communism was historically inevitable—and the extension of Communism from Russia to Eastern Europe and China after the Second World War appeared to support this idea. They further had been taught that wars imposed by imperialists on the Communist states were historically inevitable—and Hitler's invasion seemed to prove it; and that now Soviet science and technology had provided armaments superior to those of the West in addition to the political and moral superiority which had won the victory over Germany and Japan virtually single-handed. To these minds,

therefore, there was no longer any need for caution or restraint in dealings with the capitalist world; the Soviet Government should enforce
its will on every disputed issue. The Party expected from its leaders
new victories and glorious affirmations of the greatness and power of
Russia. But this was very embarrassing for the leaders, whose continual
boasting and grandiloquence were all the time building up the state of
mind which produced the expectation. They found themselves under
pressure to carry on an expansionist foreign policy involving a risk of
the war they now had good reason to fear, or else appear to their
followers as weak and cowardly—to the prospective intra-party advantage of advocates of bolder policies.

It was at least partly in order to emerge from this dilemma that
Khrushchev and his associates from 1956 onwards sought to propagate
the view that war with the imperialist states was not inevitable and
that Soviet foreign policy could be based on the idea of permanent
"peaceful coexistence." Attempts have been made to claim the authority
of Lenin for this new outlook, but it has been so obvious that it was
not Lenin's view that Khrushchev has had to fall back—even at some
danger to the authority of Marxism-Leninism as a sacrosanct doctrine—
on the argument that Lenin was out of date in this respect because he
lived before the era of nuclear weapons. The propaganda of "peaceful
coexistence" has been primarily directed against those within the Soviet
Union who, even if they do not desire war, advocate policies which must
lead to war. But it not only serves to curb the arrogance and vainglory
of the Soviet chauvinist; it also, in so far as it is taken seriously, reduces
fear and suspicion of Russia in the Western democracies and increases
the scope for diplomatic initiatives by the Kremlin.

By the time of Stalin's death Soviet foreign policy had reached an
impasse; it had been successful in consolidating Communist rule in
Eastern Europe, but it had dissipated all the assets of good will for
Russia which had existed in the West after the joint victory over Hitler,
and it had produced the NATO coalition as a counter to Soviet expansion. Stalin's successors deemed it expedient to allay the universal
alarm which Soviet postwar policy had aroused. The West, which had
not willed the cold war, was looking for signs that the new rulers of
the Soviet Union genuinely wished to end it, and despite lingering sus-
picions in official quarters and the revival of anti-Soviet popular feeling
due to the suppression of the revolt in Hungary, was gradually won
over to the idea of a negotiated settlement of outstanding issues, by a

conference at "summit" level if ordinary diplomatic channels proved inadequate. Khrushchev himself promoted the trend by his personal expeditions abroad culminating in his visit to the United States. He saw a prospect of obtaining by means of peaceful diplomacy, and by allaying the fears that had caused so many nations to combine against him, the three main objectives of his foreign policy: the subjugation of West Berlin, the dissolution of NATO and large-scale disarmament without effective measures of control.

Unfortunately for Khrushchev there was a basic contradiction in his whole approach to world affairs. Churchill once remarked that the rulers of Russia "do not want war, but they want the fruits of war." What he meant was that the fundamental idea of Communist diplomacy is always to get something for nothing, to gain without paying a price the kind of advantage which is normally only to be obtained at the point of a gun. This attitude is in fact inherent in the Communist outlook. In a system of ordinary international relations among states which, however sharp may be the conflicts between them, regard other governments as having the same right to existence as themselves, there is a tacit assumption that negotiations which are not directly subject to duress can produce results only through a process of mutual give and take. The ideal diplomatic agreement is a trade between a willing buyer and a willing seller, to the advantage of both sides. But the fundamental Communist attitude is that all non-Communist governments are only interim authorities; they are representatives of the class enemy, historically doomed to destruction sooner or later. They cannot in any circumstances be right in a dispute with a Communist state and they cannot have points of view for which a true believer should feel any sympathy. Communist diplomacy, to accord with the processes of history, should always be on the offensive against them; the task of the Communist statesman is to make them yield to his demands, and if he cannot do that, to manifest a proper hostility towards them. Only under pressure of dire need should he ever make concessions to them; if he is in a position of strength there can be no justification for compromises with the enemy. Talk about peaceful coexistence does not alter this attitude; as Khrushchev has himself explained, it means only that military conflict is ruled out, while ideological, political and economic struggle continues.

What Khrushchev, however, seems not to have understood at the outset and what has brought him disappointment in his foreign policy is the fact that it is not possible to attain peacefully and without paying a price political objectives which deeply encroach on the interests and security of other nations. Peaceful coexistence requires the aims of policy to be brought into harmony with it, or at least a willingness to pay an adequate price for their attainment. Paradoxically, the more the West has come to believe that Khrushchev means what he says when he claims that all-out war would be suicidal for all concerned, the more remote has become the prospect of his getting what he wants. Confidence in Khrushchev's intention to keep the peace has indeed reduced the tension caused by the overshadowing fear of war and has to that extent made it easier for Moscow to negotiate on friendly terms with the West, but at the same time it has made the West less ready to yield to Soviet demands without concessions in return. In the Western view, peaceful coexistence should mean a diplomacy of normal negotiations on a give and take basis. But an examination of the record of the last two years shows that this is just what Khrushchev has never been prepared to contemplate. At no point has he had anything to offer in return for acceptance of his demands about Berlin and Germany except reduction of the danger of war—a danger which Soviet policy had created but which the preaching of the impossibility of a major war rendered less and less convincing.

In fact, the whole of Khrushchev's diplomatic offensive from the autumn of 1958 onwards was based on a threat of war. His demand for an alteration of the status of West Berlin, contrary to existing agreements and originally in the form of a six months' ultimatum, followed the Soviet sputnik successes and the consequent alarm in the West at the discovery of the "missile gap." Each subsequent major occasion of Soviet political action—the arrival of Khrushchev in America and the summit conference—was marked by a spectacular new manifestation of Soviet rocketry in outer space, and the intention was clearly not only to impress the world with Soviet zeal and skill in the pursuit of astronomical science, but also to scare everybody with the Soviet capacity to hit distant targets with nuclear warheads. Unfortunately, from Khrushchev's point of view, the effect he thus produced by frightening people was cancelled by the effect he produced by preaching the doctrine that war had become too terrible to resort to it.

During the months before the summit conference the West came round more and more to the conviction that Khrushchev was not going to risk war over Berlin, and as the fear of war receded, so grew the West's determination to resist Soviet demands. After all, the Russians had no legal or moral right to change the status of West Berlin unilaterally and they had nothing to offer which might serve as the basis for an agreed settlement. What reason was there then to submit to their dictation? It is clear that the Western attitude on Berlin hardened in the period between the Camp David talks and the summit conference. Khrushchev thus found himself frustrated; it was probably only after his visit to President de Gaulle, who is said to have done some plain speaking, that he realized he was not going to get his way on Berlin at the conference. Since he could not come back from such a conference without a great diplomatic success and since he had lost his earlier expectation of achieving one, there was nothing for him to do except to wreck the conference at the outset on an extraneous issue—for which the U-2 episode provided a stratosphere-sent opportunity. If he could not get Berlin, at least as a good Communist, he could show he was tough. He showed himself tough again at the disarmament conference; it had become evident that the West was not going to give him what he wanted without sufficient guarantees of inspection and control, so here too a walkout was the solution most conducive to the prestige of Khrushchev as a Communist leader.

There has been much speculation in the West about the possible domestic pressures on Khrushchev and some observers have claimed to detect an organized faction compelling him to change the previous direction of his policy. But there is no need to attribute the pressure to a particular group of persons; Khrushchev appears still to have a firm grip on the Party apparatus and to be able to prevent the emergence of a dangerous rival for leadership. He is nevertheless the prisoner of the Party in the sense that he must act in the way that all right-thinking Communists expect him to act; if he fails to do so, he will lose the prestige essential to his position as leader. The kind of diplomatic agreement which would be regarded as a success for a Western foreign minister is of no use to a Soviet First Secretary in 1960; if he cannot get what he wants in his foreign policy on his own terms, he can save face only by smashing up the shop—which at the stage short of military violence means wrecking conferences. But the comrades may expect him to go further than wrecking conferences. Have they not been informed that Russia has the best rocketry in the world? So after the breakdown of his summit diplomacy Khrushchev more than ever had to try to persuade his followers that war must be ruled out. One can abuse the imperialists and make faces at them, but one must try to avoid a shooting war with them because hydrogen bombs are not things to be taken lightly.

Khrushchev has not, therefore, succeeded by his doctrine of peaceful coexistence in escaping from the dilemma between a bellicosity which involves the risk of a real war and a really peaceful diplomacy which falls short of what is expected of a Communist leader. He must intimidate nations and aggravate tension in order to acquire the fruits of an aggressive foreign policy, but at the same time he must explain to everybody—to reassure the West and to restrain his own supporters— that war is out of the question, with the result that his threats lose their force and the tension becomes a cause of annoyance rather than fear. When the intimidation thus fails and his demands are not conceded, he flies into a rage, tells the world's assembled journalists how he used to treat cats when he was a boy, and talks about protecting Cuba with Soviet rockets. But at the same time he lashes out at those in the Communist world who suggest that war with the imperialists is after all inevitable and says he will "not retreat an inch" from the policy of peaceful coexistence. In practice, he simply keeps on jumping from one horn of the dilemma to the other. The only way to get clear from it would be for him to accept the principle that in a system of sovereign states from which war is excluded the only alternative is to seek agreements on a basis of mutual benefit and compromise. But this is what his position as leader of the Communist Party of the Soviet Union and his own background as a militant Communist make it impossible for him to do.

III

In such a situation the part played by China becomes an increasingly important one. It should not be exaggerated or described in terms of Russian versus Chinese, because it is the Russian Party itself that is the main source of the pressure on Khrushchev to pursue objectives that are unattainable without victorious war. But just because the assumptions and sentiments implied in this pressure are so much more explicit and uninhibited in contemporary China, the Chinese influence has an important effect in reinforcing and strengthening the trends in Russia towards international intransigence. Conditions in China and in Russia are not indeed the same, for the strain of the industrialization drive in China provides a reason for cultivating fear of imminent foreign aggression such as no longer exists in Russia. But since Russia is unwilling to make a settlement with the West on any terms but those of complete diplomatic victory, Western-Soviet tension continues and the posture of Russia in relation to the West, in spite of all Khrushchev's speeches and state visits abroad, tends to be indistinguishable from that of China. It is the Chinese who can say "I told you so!" when the highly publicized diplomacy of Camp David ends in diatribes against President Eisenhower as a false friend and a tool of imperialism. The Chinese Communists kept on warning that it would end in failure. In this the wish indeed was father to the thought, for there can be no doubt that there is nothing they feared so much as a real Soviet-American rapprochement leading to a fulfillment of Soviet ambitions in Europe, but with no pickings for China in the Far East. They had not sufficient confidence in Khrushchev to believe that if he saw a prospect of achieving Soviet aims in agreement with Washington on condition of dropping support for the claims of Peking he would hesitate for a moment in accepting the bargain. A Soviet-American deal, if it could have been attained on Khrushchev's terms, would necessarily have been at the expense of Western Europe, but it would also have been at the expense of Communist China. The Chinese, therefore, hoped that the Soviet-American negotiations would fail, and long before Khrushchev's buoyant self-confidence was deflated they became convinced that the event would be as their interests required. They explained in their press that the nature of American imperialism was unchanged and that it was useless to try to come to an agreement with it. When therefore the summit conference collapsed, they were able to claim that it was just what they expected to happen.

With regard to nuclear weapons, the Chinese Communist leaders do not have to make excuses to the Party for not using them, since they do not as yet possess them. They can preach the inevitability of war and launch a "new storm of appeal" against American imperialism without anyone asking why they do not launch against American cities the missiles that they have not got. At the same time, so that their own people may not be intimidated by awareness that the enemy does possess the weapons which China still lacks, their domestic propaganda minimizes the effectiveness of nuclear weapons, and this can be extended to reproach "revisionists" for overestimating them. To be "afraid of war" and to "dream of begging peace from the imperialists" are now high among the mortal sins of the Chinese Communist code, and it is broadly hinted that persons more important than Tito have been guilty of such cowardly defection from their Communist duty; hence the vigor of the official Soviet counter-attack, which claims that "it is not sufficient to repeat the old truth that imperialism is aggressive" and that the task today is "to make full use of the factors making for peace in order to save humanity from the catastrophe of another war."

It may well be that Mao Tse-tung really is less daunted by the prospect of a nuclear war because of the vast numbers of the Chinese population and the dispersal of the Chinese economy. As an old guerrilla fighter he is no doubt inclined to be unimpressed by massive armaments. But at any rate he has no need to make any decisions about launching an atomic war since he has not the power to do it. He can be as warlike as he pleases inside China and stage "anti-American weeks" as often as he will, but it does not cause a world crisis because the ultimate weapons are not his. But since Khrushchev *does* possess them, *he* can only make warlike gestures by threatening to use them; and since a general belief that he was going to use them would rapidly raise international tension to the point at which they might be launched, he must continually counter his own threats by reaffirming his resolve to avoid war. As a consequence of this situation the contemporary Soviet attitude is far less consistent than the Chinese. Communist China is coherently truculent. But Khrushchev keeps on rattling the nuclear equivalent of a sabre in support of an aggressive diplomacy while assuring everyone that he will never draw it except in self-defense. The danger for the world is that confusion about his intentions may exist not only among foreign observers who try to interpret his policy but also in the mind of Khrushchev himself.

MANY changes have been made in the operating methods of the Soviet system since Stalin's death opened the way to a more rational adjustment of means to ends, and for important segments of Soviet society this has made their lives considerably easier, more varied and more satisfying. The provision of daily necessities has been substantially improved, thus furnishing more incentives to better work. Large-scale building programs have cut deeply into the decades-long backlog of urban housing needs. Access by average citizens to ordinary (i.e., nonpolitical) justice has been strengthened by several reforms, and the arbitrary power of the secret police has been restricted to some extent. The various measures adopted since 1953 to overcome the great lag in collectivized agriculture have fallen far short of their goals, but at least the régime has convinced its people that it is seeking more workable solutions to some of the recognized deficiencies.

This gradual easing of strains has had many repercussions in the intellectual, literary and artistic fields to which educated Russians are particularly responsive by tradition and earnest devotion to cultural values. Nowadays various literary journals, all controlled ultimately by the Party, conduct polemics over how to picture "real people" and how to present "genuine human conflicts" in literature and on the stage. In an interesting "collective interview" with leading Soviet intellectuals Khrushchev has suggested that the "party people in literature" ought to decide what supports or hinders the Party's purposes, instead of expecting him to decide what is or is not within the pale of its ideology.

Ever since 1953 these and other changes have raised two basic questions for people in the West, and to them very different answers are being given. One is whether recent and future changes represent an irreversible current of renovation and self-assertion which will one day enable the Soviet people to impose on its rulers its own aspirations for individual security and cultural freedom. The other and closely related problem is whether the many improvements in Soviet life have weakened or reënforced the ability of the Soviet leaders to use the human and material resources of the Soviet people to achieve the proclaimed goal of the worldwide victory of Communism. One answer to these questions is set forth in "Soviet Myths and Realities" (April 1961), by Philip E. Mosely.

SOVIET MYTHS AND REALITIES

By Philip E. Mosely

IT may be useful, on the eighth anniversary of Stalin's death, to review some of the misconceptions and mirages that have plagued Western efforts to interpret the changing Soviet scene under his successors. A stock-taking, even though brief and incomplete, may help Americans to understand better the international environment in which a new Administration will have to cope with old and new challenges to its hopes and purposes.

One persistent theme of Western analysis has been the concept of a debilitating and perhaps fatal struggle for supremacy within the Soviet apparatus of dictatorship. One widespread view runs somewhat as follows. A totalitarian system, by its very nature, cannot be legitimate. It cannot provide for the orderly transmission of absolute power. It is bound to be caught in a dog-eat-dog struggle for supreme control. On this premise, the top Soviet leadership is inevitably riven by a continuing and desperate rivalry among competing leaders and cliques. Hence, it is assumed, Khrushchev is constantly engaged in a struggle against multiple challengers within his own apparatus, and the function of "Kremlinology" is to identify his rivals for power by reading the obscure portents of personnel changes and turgid ideological hints.

One extreme interpretation of this alleged instability was current in May and June 1960. Supposedly, Khrushchev's vehement behavior at the abortive summit conference was dictated to him by unseen forces within the top Soviet hierarchy, perhaps by a ganging up of military leaders and Stalinist ideologues. Supposedly, Khrushchev had initially been willing to overlook the affront of the U-2 flights, with its drastic violation of the Soviet passion for secrecy, and proceed with the summit meeting and President Eisenhower's visit to the Soviet Union, but was forced by a coalition of rivals within the Party apparatus to take a stiff line. According to this view, he was actually enjoined to read to the Paris press conference a statement prepared for him in Moscow, while the Minister of Defense, Marshal Malinovsky, sat beside him to make sure that he did not deviate from the text!

Undoubtedly, a genuine struggle for the succession took place after Stalin's death. The arrest and execution of Beria was an important step in the downgrading of the power of the secret police which had been used by Stalin for many years—at least since 1934—as a personal instrument of terror against the Party. And the political police had undoubtedly used its rôle to dominate Stalin by playing on his many fears and phobias. The demotion of Malenkov, in January 1955, and the dismissal of Malenkov, Molotov and Kaganovich in June 1957, served to consolidate Khrushchev's control. The gestures that Marshal Zhukov made toward promoting his own political prestige and his own control over the army were followed by a swift downfall, in October 1957. Probably the decisive building up of Khrushchev's domination over the Party's instruments of power took place approximately between mid 1954 and late 1957. A decisive stage in this process was marked by his famous denunciation of Stalin's arbitrary and cruel rule over the Party, at the Twentieth Party Congress in February 1956.

Basically Khrushchev's structure of rule is very similar to Stalin's, but his "style" of administration differs from Stalin's in some important respects. Like Stalin, he has and uses his full power to appoint and remove the members of the Party Presidium, the central drive-wheel of decision-making, as well as the members of the Central Secretariat. It is clear, at least since late 1957, that Khrushchev's choice of this body of close collaborators is entirely his own; it is not determined by any factions or cliques operating outside his control. He has strengthened the Party's, *i.e.,* his own, control over the military establishment and the secret police. Similarly, through appointing a long roster of Party Secretaries in the various Republics and oblasts, Khrushchev has established securely his control over the Party machinery. Through the Party's regional machinery he also determines the composition of the Party Congresses, and it is his handpicked Party Presidium that selects the membership of the Central Committee of the Party. Whether he has reverted to Stalin's single-handed manipulation of the secret police, or whether he shares control over it with the Presidium, remains obscure. In any case, neither the Presidium nor the secret police is likely today to offer any foothold to would-be challengers to his leadership.

If the structure of control remains basically unchanged, in what ways and why has Khrushchev changed the style or atmosphere of Soviet rule? Clearly Khrushchev allows a much freer expression of views within his entourage, and genuine discussions now take place on many issues before he hands down his decisions, as illustrated in the discussions of agriculture in the January 1961 session of the Central Committee. In this respect Khrushchev has apparently reverted in fact, as he claims, to a more Leninist style of work. New and important decisions, such as those on reducing the size of the armed forces, on raising the rate of investment in agriculture, on changing the requirements for admission to higher education, are often preceded by fairly open discussions and disputes in public channels, even though the basic work of decision-making is carried on within the Party Secretariat, the Council of Ministers and the Party Presidium, all of which are ultimately appointed by and responsible to Khrushchev.

Does this somewhat enlarged tolerance or even encouragement of more detailed and more frank discussions of ways and means of implementing Soviet purposes and programs mean, as some analysts have stated, that Khrushchev has allowed the reins of power to slip from his hands? Or that decisions are now made by counting votes within the Presidium? Or that Khrushchev can be outvoted by colleagues whom he has appointed? Or that members of the Presidium are free to trade votes on various issues and to form alignments or factions for and against Khrushchev? In the absence of firm information on this highly secret sphere of Soviet inner politics, many shaky assumptions have been given wide currency. Sometimes, it is Suslov, supposed guardian of ideological purity, who is touted abroad as leader of an anti-Khrushchev, Stalinist intrigue. Sometimes other names, such as Marshal Malinovsky's, are mentioned as potential rivals even though Malinovsky is not even a member of the Presidium.

As an absolute ruler Khrushchev needs frank discussions of ways and means to achieve his purpose. But as head of the Soviet party, he certainly knows how to suppress "factions" just as effectively as Lenin and Stalin did. Unlike Stalin in his later years, Khrushchev has seen the need to lay down broad purposes and then to leave the details to his principal subordinates, subject to his constant threat to check on their performance. But to assume from this useful and necessary subdivision of labor and partial delegation of operating responsibilities that he has carelessly let the reins of control slip from his hands and has somehow become a puppet buffeted by contending factions is clearly to underrate his experience and his willpower, and to underestimate the power that he wields. It can also lead to underestimating the skill and determination with which he is pursuing Soviet aims abroad.

The notion that Khrushchev's power is far from absolute or secure has been zealously spread abroad by Soviet emissaries, in supposedly confidential talks. "Our leader faces strong opposition at home in his effort to bring about a relaxation of tension with America" (or Great Britain, or France, as the case may be). "He needs something concrete to prove that he is right and the Stalinists wrong." From this it is but a step to implying that the West can safely abandon some of its positions and programs—West Berlin, the plans for strengthening NATO, Formosa—in order to assure the political survival of the "coöperative" Mr. Khrushchev and forestall the rise to power of some unnamed and supposedly more militant rival.

In the past, whenever a genuine struggle for power has been taking place within the Kremlin hierarchy, Soviet spokesmen abroad have been the last to refer to this dangerous subject. In those uneasy circumstances they have tiptoed about, avoiding tête-à-têtes without witnesses, and strongly denying all signs of dissension at home. The recent whispering campaigns seem designed to pave the way for one-sided concessions by the West, rather than representing an unprecedented rending of the veil of Soviet secrecy. The versatility displayed in this new tactic is, I believe, a sign of stability and great self-assurance. Only a very strong and confident Soviet leader can afford to turn to his profit self-launched rumors of his political vulnerability at home.

II

One beneficial feature of Khrushchev's new style of rule has been a greatly lessened reliance on the day-to-day use of political terror. Khrushchev has gained great popularity, within the ranks of the Party apparatus and among the Soviet population at large, through the greater sense of individual security and the spreading expectation of a somewhat more impartial justice. From this, however, there is a long jump, which many commentators in the West have not hesitated to take, to assuming that the system of political pressure and even of repression has simply disappeared. In this over-optimistic view, there are now no obstacles to a continuous evolution of the Soviet system toward a status of full freedom of person and opinion and, eventually, of active political liberty. Does this idyllic picture correspond to reality?

Today, factory managers, collective farm chairmen, artists and writers, Party officials of many ranks no longer fear sudden disappearance, whether through imprisonment or execution or exile to labor-camps or to forced residence. To a great extent the atmosphere of terror has been lifted. Some important improvements have been made in the administration of justice. To a considerable extent, the reforms of the past two years have separated the functions of investigation, prosecution and trial. Instead of being investigated, arrested, tried and sentenced by the secret police, an ordinary citizen can now expect that the evidence gathered by the police, secret or conventional, will be examined by a separate prosecutor's office, which decides whether to bring him to trial. And the trial will be conducted usually by courts which are separate in administrative "line of command" from the police and the prosecutor's office. Of course, all three arms of justice are controlled by the government, under the direction of the Party apparatus; all three are subject to appointment and removal from above. All three are responsive to the Party's demand for "vigilance," whether against hoodlums, embezzlers, speculators in *dachas* or cars, or disseminators of "Western propaganda."

Although the defendant is entitled in theory to the services of counsel, these may or may not be available in practice and defense attorneys are sometimes punished by the Party for an excess of zeal in defending their clients. Outside the system of state courts, the military tribunals are still empowered to judge cases in complete secrecy. Sentences are seldom published, except as a public warning to other potential offenders. Still, with all these defects, intolerable in a true system of law, the new conditions of justice offer a vast improvement over those of Stalin's days, especially for nonpolitical offenders.

In the past, a number of well-run autocracies, without a trace of democratic ideology, have also endeavored to provide their subjects with a regular and safeguarded system of justice, for injustice is a source of serious waste to the state itself. Each person wrongly condemned constitutes a direct loss of resources to the state. And the dread of unpredictable punishment brings with it many other losses, such as fear of taking responsibility, widespread resort to deception, apathy among the people and corruption within the government apparatus.

The new Soviet leadership has not, as many abroad prematurely assume, laid down its "punishing sword." Its secret police are still active.

"They" are still watching and writing things down. The ordinary Soviet subject, especially anyone over 35, can recall earlier periods when police pressure, but not police vigilance, has been relaxed. And he knows that seemingly innocent remarks and even imputed motives can be brought up against him at a later time, when the pendulum has swung back toward renewed "vigilance."

In the past two years the Soviet state has unsheathed a new weapon against those whom it regards as "anti-social" elements. By the vote of a neighborhood or block meeting assembled and dominated by Party members, any "unproductive" member of society can be expelled from his place of residence and ordered to live at a distance of not less than 100 kilometers. In recent months, newspaper articles and letters have been demanding the more frequent application of this form of "vigilante" law. Apparently, this type of "exile by popular decree" is designed to supplement the specific provisions of the code by holding the threat of ostracism over socially "undesirable elements" and dissenters. The picture of a Soviet system that has chosen, or been driven—by what forces?—to abandon its police controls and to leave the way open to all kinds of initiatives welling up from below is a most appealing one, but one that can hardly stand the light of Soviet day.

III

But, it is frequently argued, the steady if unspectacular rise in the Soviet standard of living is bound, sooner rather than later, to undermine the dictatorial character of the régime. As people become more prosperous and better fed, housed and clothed, they will raise their spiritual demands. They will exact a right to form their own opinions and eventually to tell the authorities what to do.

The rise in Soviet living standards since 1953 is an important and highly desirable development. Since Stalin's death there has been a very substantial improvement in the supply of food. The enormous waste of time through waiting in line has been reduced. Above all, the Soviet housewife is now confident that she will find in the shops the wherewithal to feed her family. Food costs remain high in relation to average earnings, and the variety and quality are poor in relation to Western standards and Soviet desires. In the major cities clothing is available in relative plenty, and prices, though still high, have been reduced almost by one-half; the quality has also been improved, in large part through importing superior goods from China, East Germany and Czechoslovakia. In Moscow a customer can now shop around for quality and style instead of taking whatever is offered. Mark-downs and bargain sales, once decried as examples of inferior capitalist management, have been instituted in some lines, such as TV sets, radios and shoes.

Housing, long a blight on Soviet comfort, is being built on an impressive scale, especially in some 150 principal industrial cities. At last, under the program instituted in 1957, millions of citizens are being moved from old, dilapidated housing, and from a one-room-per-family standard, to new and clean if not very elegant apartments of two, three and even four rooms. Nothing can give greater satisfaction and pride than to see and participate in these benefits.

Soviet people are enjoying their increased purchasing power to the full. The peasants receive a much larger cash income and are demanding more good things to buy. A reform instituted in 1956 has given old-age pensioners, formerly condemned to slow attrition, an adequate basic income, buttressed by nominal rents and free medical care. A parallel measure to raise the minimum wage to 300 rubles (30 new rubles of 1961) has, it is estimated, improved the purchasing power of almost one-third of the employed urban population. On the other hand, successful collective farms are still pressed to share their profits with weaker neighbors, and there have been few major reductions in prices since 1955. Still, Soviet incomes on the average are rising markedly and will continue to do so as personal income taxes are gradually eliminated—though not the much more onerous sales taxes. All this can only bring rejoicing that the Soviet people, hard pressed so long and bitterly tried in a very destructive war and its aftermath, are now enjoying a larger share of the fruits of their labor and their forced savings for investment.

For the outside world, however, one major question still remains: Will the improved standard of living build up pressure on the Kremlin to modify its general line of policy, at home or abroad? Will it cause it to abandon its international ambitions, which have been restated so eloquently in the Declaration of 81 Parties, in December 1960, and by Khrushchev in his program speech of January 6, 1961?

Soviet resources are subjected to multiple and conflicting demands, and since 1953 the Kremlin has given a bigger though modest cut of the pie to the needs of the people. Following his tour of the United States in 1959, Khrushchev promised substantial increases in the allocation of capital for the production of consumer goods; he also announced larger allocations in January 1961. These additional resources, human and material, can be found only by making adjustments in other sectors of the plan, for example in heavy industry, in military programs or perhaps in the still modest program of foreign economic aid. It must not be forgotten, however, that light industry is growing more slowly than heavy industry.

In 1960 a Soviet newspaper took the unprecedented step of printing a "Letter to the Editor" which asked if it would not be better to spend less on sputniks and more on housing. Of course, the propaganda machine denounced the unnamed author and denied that there was any conflict. Soviet citizens, having received first installments of the long-promised good life, are eager for the day when the Soviet living standard will, as Khrushchev assures them, overtake that of the United States. Indeed, they would be more than pleased to see it equal that of West Germany or even Czechoslovakia. "Prosperity" and "peace" are powerful slogans in Soviet society as elsewhere, but the effect of their popularity seems quite different there than in countries of free and representative institutions.

One obvious result of the improvement has been to raise Khrushchev's popularity to a peak Stalin never knew. His eagerness to go out among the people, his willingness to explain his policies frequently and at length, his "folksy" manner, are all valuable assets. A further consequence has been to increase enormously the credibility of Soviet propaganda among the people generally. Formerly, when Stalin proclaimed that the Soviet Union enjoyed one of the highest standards of living in the world, his subjects were instinctively on the alert for new sacrifices or new pressures. Aside from the steady rise of the professional and managerial groups to a distinctly superior way of life under Stalin, most of the people saw no evidence to confirm these lofty claims, and their skepticism about domestic propaganda often carried over to the sphere of international politics.

In general, so public opinion analysts tell us, people are best informed about events in which they participate or which they observe at first hand. They find it somewhat harder to form independent judgments about national affairs. And, except in countries where they have access to a continuing and abundant flow of authentic and contradictory information, they find it still harder to form reliable opinions about events and problems in the external world. The increased confidence with which ordinary Soviet people now accept the leader's word in domestic affairs seems to have a strong carry-over in the enhanced faith with which they accept his picture of world events. Far from raising a stronger demand for freedom of information and opinion, the rising standard of living seems, from personal observation by many visitors, to have raised the level of popular trust in the Party's propaganda. It has positively enhanced Khrushchev's ability to mobilize his people's energies and loyalties behind his foreign as well as his domestic programs.

IV

If the effect of the slow but steady spread of greater material satisfactions has been to relax one of the major sources of tension between the leaders and the led, will not the ideological grip of the Party be gradually undermined by the remarkable spread of middle and higher education to more and more layers of Soviet society? Some analysts have asserted that the Soviet régime is thereby "digging its own grave." The expansion of education will, they believe, not only equip its beneficiaries to serve the system better but will "inevitably" give rise to a spirit of questioning, independent reasoning and critical judgment that will sooner or later destroy the Party's ideological control.

Certainly there have been some signs, visible even through the strictly regulated Soviet press, of some stirrings of skepticism and dissent. Apparently, many students—at least in Moscow and Leningrad—were shaken by the events of 1956 in Hungary. Some expressed doubts of the Government's explanation that the popular uprising had been provoked solely by "imperialist intrigues." The much freer interpretation of Marxism within Poland has not been without some echoes within the Soviet Union. In the largest cities foreign delegates and tourists are now a commonplace sight. Officially sponsored channels of information, such as the Polish Art Exhibit and the American Exhibition of 1959, have had a wide impact, despite the official effort to discredit the Sokolniki display even before it opened.

Khrushchev's outburst of November 1958 against doubting or dissident students was surely not without cause, and he is not unmindful of the tendency, especially within a part of the younger generation which has grown up since the last period of purge and repression, to press beyond the permitted framework of official dogma. Very often students have shown their boredom with the Party's ideology and their eagerness to seek information through other than official channels. Khrushchev's demand, in 1958, that all students should have a two-year period of productive labor in a factory or on a collective farm, before proceeding to their higher education, was only one expression of his resentment and alarm at the attitudes of a part of the students. However, by the time his proposals were transformed into practice, beginning with the academic year 1959-60, the labor requirement was pretty much waived for students of engineering, pure sciences and medicine, as well as for technologists of all kinds.

The full impact of the new barrier has fallen on those seeking admission to higher training in the ideologically sensitive fields—social sciences, humanities, law and journalism. The most important provision of the new rules is, of course, the requirement that each candidate, after working "at production" for two years, must present a political recommendation by a "social organization," meaning the Party or its Young Communist League. As Khrushchev exclaimed in 1958, any student who is dissatisfied with the Soviet system ought to be expelled, so as to make room for the son or daughter of a peasant or worker who will value to the full the state-conferred benefit of higher education.

A spirit of inquiry, dissatisfaction or even dissent can arise even under a totalitarian system, for the demand for individual judgment, for sincerity, lies deep in each individual. This urge may stem from many causes, including boredom, family memories, the influence of Russia's great literature, or the impact of injustices. But the problem of harnessing scientific progress with ideological conformity is not a new one for the Soviet régime. It has persisted, in varying forms, from the beginning. The Party and its instruments have developed many ways of shepherding the young toward productive and orthodox careers well rewarded by the state, and away from dangerous thoughts. The controls can never work perfectly, and repression of potential dissent exacts its price today, even though that price is probably far smaller than in Stalin's time. The problem of making a uniform and "non-discussable" propaganda interesting or even palatable to young people after it has lost its initial savor of scientific infallibility is a continuing one, as witnessed by the Party's long and boring decree on propaganda, issued in January 1960.

By and large, foreign observers are left with the impression that any substantial spread of intellectual questioning is pretty much confined to a few major cities, and primarily to the sons and daughters of fairly well-placed and responsible Communists. It often takes the form of wanting to read everything and examine everything for themselves. It reflects a growing suspicion that the Party's choice of information may not be very complete or intelligent. For some it takes the form of wishing for more variety and color in a drab way of life, or of a fascination with the far wider range of literary, artistic and intellectual stimuli available in the West and even in such "friendly" states as India. For others it takes a less attractive form among the post-adolescent *stiliagi,* or "teddy-boys," who attempt to ape the manners, dress and haircuts of their Western contemporaries of a few years ago. Naturally, Soviet propaganda tries to equate all interest in the West with the fads and fashions of the *stiliagi,* and then to lump the latter with "hooligans," an American word which has long since been naturalized in Russian as "khuligany."

With the extreme official and popular emphasis on conformity—extending even to local puritanic attempts to forbid bright-patterned sport shirts and women's slacks on the otherwise fashionable promenades of Sochi—it would be strange if some high-spirited youths did not assert their "differentness" in various ways, some of them more intellectual than others. On the whole, however, Soviet youth seems highly conformist. For one thing, the college-level study of politically dangerous subjects, such as history, economics and law, is confined to a relatively few and carefully supervised students. The great majority of students, and often the ablest, are attracted by good stipends and promising careers into technical and scientific fields. For them, the study of world history or foreign literature, even in its carefully selected doses, ends at about 15. What goes by the name of "social studies" after that is simply Party history, Party theory and the current Party program of "do's" and "don't's." The widely noted apathy on the part of youth toward the cramming of Party ideology into their heads by dull propaganda hacks is probably far more serious than any conscious dissent.

The system of controls and incentives through which the Party promotes conformity with its views and goals is reinforced by a strong sense of national pride, even chauvinism. Soviet students are amazed when told that the Moscow subway was not the first one ever built. They assume that the sputniks have "proven" the superiority of the Soviet system. Most Soviet citizens accept as natural and desirable the extension of the Communist system to other countries, and they are unaware of the methods of control that have been applied or the deep-set hatreds those methods have implanted. They cannot imagine other systems, for example those that allow a genuinely free choice. While often displaying a greedy envy of Western comforts, gadgets and cars, they proclaim with full sincerity the superiority and inevitable triumph of the Soviet system. Needless to say, they are well briefed on American defects, such as economic fluctuations and unemployment, unequal access to higher education, and regional resistances to equal status for citizens of Negro descent. But they seem totally unequipped to reason critically about possible defects in the Soviet system; those that exist have either been removed by the post-Stalin régime or are bound to disappear with the spread of material plenty.

If anything, the slightly widened access to Western information and the presence in their streets of Western tourists makes ordinary Soviet people less aware than before of being cut off from contrary or thought-provoking information. Even the flow of casual foreign sightseers appears to confirm their confidence that Khrushchev is doing everything he reasonably can to reduce tensions and strengthen the prospects for peace.

Despite occasional outbursts of fear and resentment, as in the case of Pasternak's "Doctor Zhivago," the Soviet system of control seems confident of its ability to identify, contain and, if need be, repress such expressions of doubt or dissent as appear among a small minority of its youth. In handling a problem that has plagued it throughout its existence, the Party is alert but not unduly alarmed by its newest manifestations. Unlike some wishful analysts abroad, it is confident that it can train a very large part of its youth to serve the state, especially in engineering and the natural sciences, without letting many of them stray from the approved paths of ideological orthodoxy, reinforced as it is today by national pride and arrogance.

V

What does all this add up to? First, that the Soviet system with which the West will be dealing in the 1960s is likely to retain a high level of political stability, based on premises and methods very different from ours. The dictatorship is not likely to be torn to pieces by internecine struggles at the top, to lose control over its people or to surrender its ideology. The Party structure is better equipped today to ride through a new succession crisis than it was in 1953. No doubt, names and labels will change, but the concept of a single party, justified in its absolute rule by its monopoly over "truth" and foresight, has been strengthened.

Second, the Soviet leadership will not abandon its ultimate power of life and death over its subjects, even though it now exercises this power with new moderation. Its leaders will resort to terror again if they find that necessary to their aims, but they doubt it will be necessary. The farther the Stalinist brand of terror recedes in memory, the more active the confidence and the more energetic the coöperation they can hope to elicit from their people. Any minor movements of dissent can be contained by partial relaxation of controls over intellectual life, combined with methods of repression less cruel than in the past.

Third, the shared desire of the Party and the people to raise the standard of living is relaxing very old tensions between the two, is lessening the contrasts between life in Russia and in the West, and is likely to evoke ever greater individual efforts to share in the enlarged rewards offered by the régime for hard work and "right-thinking" loyalty. Finally, the spread of education may create some annoying worries for the ideological purity of the new generations, but it is not likely to endanger the stability of the régime or its ability to pursue the goals which its leaders set for the Soviet people at home or abroad.

It would surely be comforting if an analysis of the evolution, recent and prospective, of the Soviet system could lead us to a confident conclusion that it contains the seeds of inevitable and desirable changes, and that we have only to fold our hands, lower taxes, buy a third car and wait for this development to occur in the fulness of God's time. Unfortunately, such is not the prospect. During the decade of the 1960s we shall, under present prospects, be dealing with a Soviet system that is growing rapidly in economic, scientific and military strength and which will have fewer rather than more difficulties in preserving political stability and an adequate measure of ideological uniformity. These growing strengths, not offset by equivalent new weaknesses, will enable its leaders to devote greater rather than smaller resources and political determination to achieving the world-wide purposes that have been proclaimed in an evolving pattern of interpretation by Lenin and Stalin and now by Khrushchev.

PARTY platforms, like Fourth-of-July addresses in pre-automobile America, tend to have primarily symbolic or rhetorical value in American politics, in which the struggles, vehement as they are, turn mainly on whether to do more of this or less of that. In countries seeking paths to modernization, as Russia or China were in the early decades of this century, ideological disputes, however difficult to decipher through their veil of phraseology, have a more fundamental purpose, that of charting a highroad to the future.

A Communist régime or party must attach basic importance to defining "correctly" the situation in which it operates and deciding "correctly" the next major steps toward the long-term goal as described in its ideology. A Communist leadership must justify its claim to exercise total force by "correctly" foreseeing the future and transforming predictions into reality by all the power it can muster. A Communist régime is, by self-definition, an "ideocracy," for it rejects the legitimacy provided by traditional institutions, as in a monarchy, or by a genuine consultation of the popular will, as in a representative democracy. This factor, among others, makes the pursuit of "correct" ideology a very grim struggle within Communist parties and between them, so long as it cannot be overcome or suppressed. It likewise injects an additional element of ideological violence into disputes that arise between two independent Communist centers of power, as Moscow and Peking are today.

The interplay of ideology and politics in the Sino-Soviet conflict has been analyzed with great subtlety and insight by Zbigniew Brzezinski in "The Challenge of Change in the Soviet Bloc" (April 1961), in which he also recommends important changes in the posture and methods of U.S. foreign policy. Professor Brzezinski, Director of the Research Institute on Communism and a member of the Russian Institute at Columbia University, has also been an Associate of the Russian Research Center and the Center for International Affairs at Harvard University. He is the author, among other studies, of "Ideology and Power in Soviet Politics" (1962), "The Soviet Bloc, Unity and Conflict" (rev. ed., 1961), and "The Permanent Purge; Politics in Soviet Totalitarianism" (1956).

441

THE CHALLENGE OF CHANGE IN THE SOVIET BLOC

By Zbigniew Brzezinski

THE declaration issued by 81 Communist parties in Moscow last December 6 marks a seminal date in the history of international Communism. For the first time in the history of the Soviet bloc a conference of Communist leaders ended not merely with the usual "unanimous agreement" but also with a silent agreement to disagree. For the first time in about 35 years the general strategy of the Communist parties scattered around the globe is no longer to be set purely in terms of Soviet estimates of what will most benefit the interests of the Soviet Union. Cast aside is Stalin's categorical dictum that "a revolutionary is he who, without arguments, unconditionally, openly and honestly . . . is ready to defend and strengthen the U.S.S.R. . . ." What is good for the Soviet Union is no longer automatically also good for the Soviet bloc and for international Communism.

The Moscow conference thus highlights a process of transformation of the Soviet bloc into a Communist one. This process was inherent in the shift of Soviet power beyond the Soviet frontiers. However, Stalinism, with its insistence on absolute centralization of power in Moscow and on Soviet ideological infallibility, involved a conscious effort to prevent such a transformation. In fact, Stalin did not fear only national Communism—he even rejected its much more subdued variant, "domesticism," *i.e.,* the effort to make some domestic adjustments while accepting the principle of bloc unity and absolute Soviet leadership.

The Jugoslav break in 1948 was the first signal that an international Communist system could not work effectively merely by applying Stalinist domestic practices to the new Soviet bloc. The change became more rapid after Stalin's death. Several factors prompted it. The new ruling Communist élites in East Europe gradually—and not everywhere at first—became somewhat more confident of their ability to

build "socialism," especially if given sufficient leeway to make some
domestic adjustments. The presence of an indigenous and independent
Communist régime in China "objectively" (as the Marxists would put
it) strengthened the case of those within the ruling élites who felt that
perhaps Stalinism should be viewed as a transitional phase leading to a
more genuine Communist internationalism rather than as an enduring
prescription. Another factor prompting change was the accumulated
tension of popular, national reaction against Soviet domination—a sentiment which local Communist leaders could not afford wholly to ignore.

In response to these pressures, the post-Stalin Soviet leadership, particularly from the time of Khrushchev's ascendancy, began to search
for a new formula for unity of the Soviet bloc. The years 1954-1960
can be said to have been dominated by this search. Khrushchev and
Bulganin were the first Soviet leaders to visit China, where they sought
to warm the frigid relationship created by Stalin's reserve. Later, the
Soviet leaders attempted to repair the break with Jugoslavia. They
talked of "many ways to socialism." However, the search for unity
clearly did not mean that the Soviet leaders were prepared to preside
over the dissolution of the bloc. It is evident in retrospect that
Khrushchev hoped the bloc could be transformed into a comity of states
led by the U.S.S.R. but not terrorized by it. Marxist-Leninist ideology
would be the common bond and the source of unanimity.

These efforts were opposed at home and abroad. Some of Khrushchev's
colleagues felt that Soviet leadership would be undermined. Others
warned that too rapid reform could lead to crises. The vacillations
in Soviet policy during this period reflected these conflicting assessments
and the sudden pressures of unexpected events. The change in Poland,
the eruptions in Hungary, Khrushchev's realization that Tito was not
interested in shoring up the Soviet bloc but in sharing in its leadership,
all resulted in hesitations and often in retrogressive steps. The secret
circular letter in August 1956 warned the other parties not to follow
the Jugoslav path, and after the Polish and Hungarian outbreaks the
Soviet leadership began to seek some organizational device to substitute
for the Cominform, which had been abolished in 1956 because it was
thought to be outmoded.

From 1957 on, the focus of the problem increasingly shifted eastward.
The Chinese leaders shared Khrushchev's desire to create a healthier
camp. Just a year earlier they had encouraged the Soviets to improve
their relations with the Poles, even while recommending the suppres-

sion of the Hungarian revolution. Subsequently the Chinese joined Khrushchev in containing Polish diversity and in November 1957 they helped Khrushchev obtain Polish recognition of Soviet leadership of the camp. Mao Tse-tung personally insisted that Communist unity required an affirmation of Soviet leadership. Yet helping to consolidate the bloc did not mean to the Chinese that they should remain silent on the various issues facing it. On the contrary, in the course of helping Khrushchev, they appear to have become convinced that the post-Stalin leadership needed further advice from experienced revolutionaries like themselves. Liu Shao-chi alluded to this last year when he is reported to have stated that Peking had been concerned for some years with the indecisiveness and vacillations of the Soviet régime since Stalin.

In the fall of 1957 an event occurred which quickly assumed overwhelming importance in the Chinese perspective on world affairs and which colored subsequent Sino-Soviet relations. The successful Soviet firing of the I.C.B.M., followed by the launching of a sputnik, was interpreted by the Chinese as signalling a decisive shift in the balance of military power between East and West. The east wind was prevailing, Mao Tse-tung proclaimed. In his view the Soviet Union now had the means to effect further revolutionary changes in the world, in spite of the militarization of imperialism. But if the means were available in Moscow, the will seemed strangely lacking. The Chinese, therefore, felt duty-bound to infuse international Communism with the will to prevail. Bloc unity was the essential point of departure but still a means and not an end. Nothing could be done without unity, but unity should not become a substitute for action. Indeed, vigorous action against the common enemy could forge even greater unity than reliance on increased Soviet economic aid to the various Communist régimes or the elimination of the more obtrusive signs of Soviet domination. The almost simultaneous shift in intra-party politics in China in favor of a more radical wing and the great leap forward provided the domestic underpinning for these views of the international scene.

The Chinese did not desire war *per se,* but they were convinced that increased pressure on the West, including that of local wars, was justified and that the West would yield step by step. Furthermore, the Chinese feared that fear of war would inevitably lead to the fear of revolution and hence to the extinction of revolutionary zeal in the international movement itself. As a result, they did not hesitate in 1960 to characterize the conception of "a peaceful transition to socialism," propounded by

Khrushchev in 1956, as "stupid." They felt that continuous pressure by the militarily superior Soviet bloc would encourage revolutionary upheavals, particularly in the colonial areas. The disintegration of imperialism would soon follow.

The Soviets welcomed the Chinese aid in reconsolidating the bloc. However, in assessing the nature of the present phase of world history, the Soviets tended to see their opportunities in a somewhat different light. Their acquisition of nuclear weapons, and particularly of a delivery capability, forced them to rethink their earlier military assumptions and gave them a greater appreciation of the dangers of mutual annihilation. As a result, the Soviet leaders very carefully abstained from repeating Mao's claim that they had reached a turning point; they have merely reiterated that there is a definite shift in favor of "socialism." In their view, the military balance of destructive capabilities is in itself a new and important step forward. It makes possible the encouragement of revolutionary trends in Asia, Africa and Latin America and the deterrence of Western counter-actions in these areas. At the same time the I.C.B.M.s could be exploited politically: in recent years the Soviet Union has threatened nuclear destruction against its neighbors on at least 40 different occasions. In addition, under the protective shield of military power, the Soviet bloc could now bring to bear a new and vitally important factor—its economic strength and technical skill. The combination of mutual military paralysis, political revolutions and Communist economic power would prevail, without the risk of provoking a desperate reaction from the West.

These basic disagreements were reflected in a host of specific issues. In 1958 China urged a more aggressive attitude in the Middle East crisis and later ignited a new campaign for Taiwan; in 1959-60 there were agitated ideological debates on the significance of the Chinese pattern of revolution as a model for other nations; in 1960 China showed a distinct lack of enthusiasm for Soviet participation in disarmament talks; during 1958-60 there were growing divergencies concerning "revisionism" and its implications. Many of these conflicts were veiled in euphemistic terms, but it required no exegesis to recognize their meaning. They were accompanied by a marked decline in Chinese-Soviet cultural exchanges, and there were even hints of some uncertainties on the subject of the Sino-Soviet frontier.

It is obvious that different degrees of alienation and involvement in international affairs, the disparity in stages of economic, social and revolutionary development, as well as such specific matters as unsatisfied territorial ambitions (*e.g.,* Taiwan) provided the environmental background for such differences. Furthermore, it is very important to realize that the conscious commitments of the two régimes to a jointly shared *Weltanschaung* makes any disagreement between them even more intense. The purposeful effort to define reality and stages of historical change makes consensus more difficult, especially in the absence of a powerful arbiter such as Stalin. In the Communist outlook, general questions of interpretation are usually the points of departure for more specific strategies and tactics. For that reason it is more difficult in some respects for Communist parties to reach consensus, once they are able to assert their independence, than for Anglo-Saxon nations whose approach is pragmatic and not so concerned with conceptualization or long-range goals.

At the same time these disagreements over appropriate strategy and tactics operate within the framework of a larger agreement—namely a mutual method for assessing reality and a common objective. In effect, the common ideology, which defines mutual ends and selects common enemies, and which can be a source of intense friction, also serves to limit the dispute and prevents it from erupting into an open split. In the case of the Sino-Soviet divergencies of the last three years, it would appear that the dispute was confined by three limits, consciously observed by the parties involved: 1) Both sides have recognized that both would lose by an open split, hence that unity must be preserved; 2) each realized that the other's leadership is firmly entrenched and that, for better or for worse, Khrushchev would have to deal with Mao Tse-tung and vice versa, a situation quite unlike the one which prevailed in 1948 when Stalin calculated that Tito would fall from power after an open split; 3) the Chinese, for the time being at least, have striven to reassure the Soviets that they are not trying to displace them as leaders of the bloc but are merely anxious to persuade them to adopt a different strategy. The Chinese presumably realized that they could not, at this stage, replace the Soviets as leader since they do not possess the means to enforce such leadership.

The foregoing limits, however, have tended to make the weaker party stronger and the stronger weaker in as much as the partner who is better able to demonstrate overtly his disregard for unity has the advantage of initiative. The burden of responding in kind, thereby further straining unity, or of compromising, rested on the more passive of the two. Furthermore, it can be argued that subjectively the Soviet Union stands to lose more by an open split than China since so much of the international prestige of the Soviet Union and the internal strength of the régime rest on its rôle as leader of a united bloc of one billion people marching together toward Communism. Indeed, with two partners desiring unity, the one who can appear to be less cautious about preserving it might well gain the upper hand. Thus in the internal bargaining that has recently gone on between the two parties, the immense military and economic preponderance of the Soviet Union has probably not been decisive. China has been able to persist in her views and even to voice them openly. At the Moscow conference of November-December 1960 and also at the earlier July session in Bucharest, the Chinese delegation openly assaulted Khrushchev's policies, despite obvious Soviet displeasure.

The Moscow conference, however, was not a Chinese victory. If, in terms of the crucial issues, the statement issued by the 81 parties is carefully compared with earlier Soviet and Chinese pronouncements,[1] one finds that by and large the Soviet formulations have prevailed, with some adjustments to meet Chinese objections. It may be surmised that the somewhat greater emphasis on the dangers of war and on the aggressiveness of American imperialism, on the relevance of China to the revolutions in Asia, Latin America and Africa, on the militant character of national liberation struggles, and the direct condemnation of Jugoslav revisionism, all involved adjustment to the Chinese point of view. But on a larger number of issues the statement bears greater resemblance to earlier Soviet positions. This is so with respect to such matters as: the decisive character of economic development and the rôle of the "socialist world system" in shaping our age; the destructiveness of war (its horrors were explicitly reiterated); the significance of peaceful coexistence and the possibility of the prevention of war; the importance of the 20th and 21st C.P.S.U. Congresses, and the universal relevance of Soviet experience; the peaceful transition to socialism, the character of "national democracy" and the evils of dogmatism. This impression is corroborated by the unusually frank account of the conference pro-

[1] For instance, O. V. Kuusinen's important work, "Foundations of Marxism-Leninism," published early in 1960, and Soviet and Chinese statements on the occasion of Lenin's anniversary last year. The Moscow statement itself was apparently prepared originally by the C.P.S.U. This preliminary draft was then reviewed in October by an editorial commission representing 26 parties (including all 12 from the bloc) before submission to the conference as a whole.

vided by Walter Ulbricht's speech printed in *Neues Deutschland* of December 18. In it he indicates clearly what the controversial issues were and how the various points were resolved.

There appears to be a twofold reason for the relative Soviet success. The first is rooted in the nature of the Chinese position; the second involves the bargaining process in the meeting itself. Because China is more radically hostile to the outside world, her freedom of action is more limited, even if initially the Chinese succeeded in putting the Soviet leadership on the defensive. Given their impatience in dealing with the West, the Chinese leaders would probably shrink from actually splitting the Communist bloc, since in their minds the chief beneficiaries of such a split would be the United States and "imperialism" in general. Thus the range of their bluffing is limited. Furthermore, since their overt support consisted only of the Albanians and a few of the non-ruling parties, a split, or even the threat of a split, could not bring about the desired Chinese objective: a change in the line pursued by international Communism.

The Moscow conference thus had the important effect of articulating a common line for the various parties, and of narrowing somewhat the cleavage between the Soviets and the Chinese. Explicit limits to unilateral action by any one party were adopted and the principle of interference in the internal affairs of member parties for the first time was formally established. Unlike the November 1957 statement of the 12 ruling parties, which stressed "non-interference in one another's affairs," the 1960 declaration states: "When this or that party raises questions about the activity of another fraternal party, its leadership turns to the leadership of the party in question and, when necessary, meetings and consultations are held." It goes without saying that the principle of interference is likely to benefit the stronger rather than the weaker parties. In his report on the conference, Ulbricht apparently alluded to the Chinese when he stated that "there were objections to the formulation 'general line.' However, if we abandon this principle of 'general line,' vacillations may occur in complicated situations, such as in border problems."

At the same time, the length of the conference and the apparently calculated ambiguity of some parts of the statement suggest clearly that while the Sino-Soviet relationship remains based on common, conscious emphasis on unity, an element of divergence is inherent in the fact that both parties are independent and organizationally distinct. While it is likely that henceforth disagreements between them will be more muted and harder to detect, the relationship of divergent unity between them is likely to persist and could easily erupt anew into an open dialogue. The different emphases put on the Moscow statement by subsequent commentaries in *Pravda, Trybuna Ludu* or *Neues Deutschland,* on the one hand, and in *Hsinhua* or *Zeri I Popullit,* on the other, portend continuing dissension.

II

The changes that have taken place, and are continuing to take place, within the Communist world have important policy implications for the West. In analyzing these changes, we should abandon the tendency to operate in simple and extreme terms. The bloc is not splitting and is not likely to split. Talk of a Sino-Soviet conflict, of even a war between them, merely illustrates a profound misconception of the essence of the historical phenomenon of Communism, which, while affected by traditional national considerations, has from its very beginning reflected a conscious emphasis on supra-national perspectives. Similarly, a change within the Soviet bloc should not be viewed as presaging its disintegration or, conversely, its soon becoming one Communist state. The tendency to see the bloc in terms of such extremes simply obscures the important, if less dramatic, changes within it.

For years the Soviet bloc was in effect an international system run by one national Communist party. Today, it is becoming a Communist camp, with the various member régimes participating more actively in the important process of defining the camp's "general line." The events of 1956 served to reassure the Communist chiefs that the West was either unable or unwilling to challenge their domestic power, while the Sino-Soviet "divergent unity" achieved within the bloc meant that opportunities have now been created for more manœuvre, without running the risk of expulsion or condemnation as a deviationist.

The last Moscow conference, as well as subsequent events, bear this out. The leaders of the smaller parties, as for instance, Gomulka, played a more active rôle than ever before and have been reliably credited with strongly influencing the Soviet course. Some leaders, like Togliatti, could afford to show their misgivings about the conference by staying away from it. Some of the Latin American representatives offered amendments to the draft of the conference. Others, like the Albanians, could choose to defy the Soviets, even at the risk of incurring the wrath of pro-Soviet parties. It is symptomatic of the new conditions that Ulbricht broke all precedents to accuse the Albanian party leadership in public and in print, of "sectarianism" and "dogmatism." Yet both Albania and East Germany remained bona fide members of the bloc. Similarly, on the occasion of the Chinese anniversary, the Chinese sent the Albanians greetings that were both warm and personal—qualities missing from similar messages to Moscow and elsewhere, and notably lacking in Moscow's New Year's message to the Albanians. Similarly, in the course of the recent Albanian Party Congress, the C.P.S.U. refrained from greeting Enver Hoxha, while the Chinese heaped praise on the Albanian leader. Still, the Soviet boycott of the Albanian party chief took place *within* the framework of the camp. The prolonged and successful defiance of the most powerful party by one of the smallest could have infectious consequences, irrespective of the specific issues involved in this case.

Apart from the more overt sympathies of some parties for Moscow or Peking, there are now pro-Soviet or pro-Chinese factions within most parties. Also, for the first time in the history of the bloc, the various national leaders can quietly exercise options within the bloc itself, rather than having either to choose unity, *ergo* subordination, or a split. In effect, the smaller parties can take advantage of the implicit agreement of the two major ones to disagree.

As a result, relations between the Soviet Union and the Communist states and parties vary greatly. In the past one pattern generally prevailed: close subordination or open hostility (*e.g.,* Jugoslavia). Now, there is far greater diversity. In the Soviet-Polish relationship, state and party ties are good, while the Poles enjoy some domestic autonomy. On the other hand, East Germany and Czechoslovakia are completely subordinate to the Soviet Union, while state and party relations are also excellent. State and party ties with North Viet Nam are good despite its earlier dependence on China. With China itself there are good state relations but disagreements between the ruling parties. Finally, with Albania, there are correct state relations but apparent frigidity in party relations.

Perhaps the most dramatic illustration of a further change was the reversal of the Soviet attitude toward some organizational expression of unity, like the Comintern or the Cominform. Previously the Soviet leadership desired such an institution as a means of strengthening its hand.

At the conference Khrushchev is reliably reported to have opposed the very thing he earlier promoted—precisely in order to protect Soviet leadership! In the days when Soviet freedom of initiative was almost unlimited—particularly in the international arena—a Cominform type of organization was useful in ensuring that the other parties followed loyally. The protracted discussions in Moscow made the Soviet leaders sensitive to the possibility that today such an organization could limit their freedom of manœuvre. They thus preferred to rely on ad hoc multilateral meetings of party chiefs, meetings which need not be called regularly and which would be less likely to interfere with Soviet international activity.

Furthermore, if Khrushchev's version of the conference can be trusted, it was the Soviet delegation which suggested that the conference no longer refer to the Soviet party as the leader of the camp. In 1957, the Soviets, supported by the Chinese, had insisted on this designation since the status of leadership helped to ensure automatic support for any Soviet initiatives. But today, as Khrushchev put it, "the fact that we are called the leader gives no advantages either to our party or to other parties. On the contrary, it only creates difficulties." One may surmise that the elimination of such a reference could forestall any Chinese claim to co-leadership of the camp. In fact, the Soviets might be arguing that if the Chinese want a united, militant bloc, they should respect in practice the Soviet line. Another difficulty which Khrushchev might have had in mind was the danger that the other parties could claim that the formal status of leader puts the C.P.S.U. under special responsibility to its followers, and perhaps Soviet freedom of action would be greater without such a formal designation. Finally, the status of leader implied responsibility for actions which the Soviets could not control (*e.g.,* China towards India). In any event, the Kremlin could be certain that parties fully loyal to it would continue to do its bidding. The East Germans, for instance, have continued to make references to Soviet leadership even though the conference used the vaguer term "vanguard" to describe the rôle of the C.P.S.U.

This rôle should not be minimized. As Khrushchev put it in his January address: " . . . the Communist parties must synchronize their watches. When someone's clock is fast or slow, it is regulated so that it shows the correct time. Similarly, it is necessary to check the time of the Communist movement . . ." The emphasis in the statement of the conference on the fundamental importance of the C.P.S.U.'s experience left no doubt that its clock was to be the Greenwich Mean Time of international Communism. None the less, the absence of a formally designated leader, capable of acting as arbiter, is bound to complicate further the internal situation in the Communist world, even if abroad it makes the camp look more "democratic." While bringing to bear on any issue its own power, the Soviet leadership must now, to a far greater extent, anticipate the reactions of its followers, especially in view of some of the available options.

The Moscow conference may thus be the end of Khrushchev's search for a new relationship with the bloc. But he did not find what he sought. Indeed, there appears to be a curious and striking parallel between the Eisenhower and Khrushchev records. Both men strove to bolster the power of their countries by making more stable alliances. Yet, in spite of their efforts, or perhaps because of them, they each appear to have presided over a decline in the independent power of their respective nations. Nor did the conference fulfill Chinese hopes. Instead of achieving united militancy, they have contributed to greater heterogeneity within the bloc.

This heterogeneity involves both advantages and liabilities. By appearing less autocratic and more flexible, the Communist camp can now support more effectively the pseudo-Marxist régimes in Cuba or Guinea and encourage others in a similar direction. Thus a new type of expansion—indirect—may replace the old, direct type. Many of the new nations throughout the world are not only nationalistic in the nineteenth century sense; they are ideologically oriented and think in social and economic terms similar to those of Marxists. They use words like "imperialism" and "capitalism" much as the Soviets do. And modernization, which they seek, does not mean to them political democracy. The relationship of the Soviet Union and of the other camp members to these new states is already one of courtship and not of Stalin-like domination. In this relationship, the Poles, the Czechs, the East Germans, can be of great help to the Communist cause. They civilize Soviet Communism, their social and cultural level makes it more appealing, while the greater internal diversity within the camp makes Communism seem less threatening to the newly independent states.

At the same time, the new external strategy is likely to further the internal processes of change within the camp. One may increasingly expect Soviet allies helping to court a Cuba or a Guinea to seek a "most-favored-nation clause" from the Soviet Union, much the way the East

Germans did when the U.S.S.R. was courting Gomulka's Poland in 1956, or the way that Latin American states have recently done with the United States, after watching our Marshall Plan aid going to Europe. This is all the more likely because of the new opportunities created for internal manœuvring by the various parties. And these opportunities will probably increase when China acquires a nuclear capability.

From a Western point of view, a prolonged situation of formal Sino-Soviet unity with some degree of divergence is distinctly preferable to an open rupture. A thoroughgoing split would bode ill for the world. The Soviet Union can afford to tolerate within the camp a dissident but lonely China. Thus a break involving expulsion from the bloc could occur only if China were sufficiently strong to threaten Soviet leadership and to carry with it a significant number of Communist parties. A China capable of unilateral action could be very dangerous. The danger is no less if China should feel strong enough to leave the bloc on its own initiative. Presumably it would do so only if its leaders felt confident of their ability to go it alone and to influence the course of events more effectively outside the bloc.

In either case, the Chinese would be in control of a significant portion of the international Communist movement. They could thus effectively develop a more actively militant line and presumably back it with their own resources. The Western reaction would necessarily involve a more militant posture also, perhaps the use of force, certainly higher military budgets. Under those circumstances, the Soviet Union would have to follow suit, lest the West gain an over-all military preponderance. Furthermore, the C.P.S.U. would inescapably be forced to condemn Western countermoves to Chinese initiatives, for not to do so would involve an insupportable loss in Soviet revolutionary prestige and probably precipitate further defections to the Chinese side. Hence, a break in the partnership would gradually push the Soviet Union toward more radical attitudes in an effort to regain leadership of the Communist camp. In a world polarized in open hostility between the United States and China, the Soviet Union could not afford therefore to be neutral, and certainly could not side with the United States.

The most advantageous situation from the Western standpoint is one which involves a gradual adjustment of the common Marxist-Leninist ideology to the divergent perspectives of its various subscribers. The existence of the Sino-Soviet dialogue has already forced the Soviet leaders to think through what was formerly only a generalized statement that a war would be disastrous; it has contributed a great deal to increased Soviet sophistication on the subject of nuclear weapons. Unanimity is often a shield for ignorance and, if for no other reason than to argue with Liu Shao-chi, Khrushchev probably had to read some RAND studies! In his emphasis on the destructiveness of a nuclear war he has come close to admitting that a purely subjective factor, such as someone's decision to start a war, can possibly interfere with an immutable historical process. This necessarily involves a gradual relativization of the formerly absolutist ideology.

Furthermore, divorced from a single power center, this ideology is more and more stretched to embrace the diverse experiences and perspectives of élites, whether on the banks of the Elbe or the 38th Parallel. Increasingly each party becomes confident that its interpretation of the common doctrine is the correct one. Ulbricht highlighted this dilemma when he stated in his account of the Moscow conference that "somebody has raised the question as to who is the one who determines what is truth, and what complies with the principles of the Marxist-Leninist doctrine." There is no easy answer. Stalin was once the ideological arbiter and he possessed the power to enforce his interpretations. Today, the alternative to splits between the parties is some form of adjustment. Yet such adjustments mean that the formerly absolutist ideology is becoming increasingly a relative one.

The Communist leaders are aware that relativization could lead to dangerous erosion. To counteract it they are promoting closer economic ties and integration of the various members of their camp. In his speech of January 6, Khrushchev gave special attention to the problem of unity, insisting that all parties must continuously strive for it and asserting that the C.P.S.U. has made "every effort" to maintain unity with the Chinese. The Communist leaders are seeking rapid external victories to keep afire the sense of an inevitable and world-wide triumph. But the changes that have taken place within the Communist world were inherent in its expansion and can be viewed as part of the process of differentiation which all large-scale social organizations experience. The West had little directly to do with the emergence of these changes and precipitous moves overtly designed to promote splits will only push the Communist régimes together.

The West can, however, strive to create favorable conditions for the further growth of the diversity which has developed within the Communist camp. We should, for instance, explore the possibility of recognizing Mongolia, thereby encouraging the growth of a sense of independent statehood which almost certainly would lead to more assertive nationalism. We should reëxamine critically our policy of non-recognition of the Oder-Neisse line, since this policy helps to inhibit any Polish régime from "playing the game" of using the Sino-Soviet divergence for the consolidation of its domestic autonomy, and instead forces it to bolster its patron and only source of security, the Soviet Union. We should encourage some of our allies to exploit more the traditional bonds of friendship which have existed between them and some of the nations presently within the Communist camp. We should continue to address ourselves directly to the Communist-controlled peoples, thereby encouraging domestic pressures for change which each régime must now consider, given the greater flexibility of the camp. Finally, we should not make concessions to Khrushchev on such issues as Berlin, in the mistaken hope of bolstering him, but in effect depriving him of the argument which he has used against the Chinese—namely, that excessive pressure on the West might lead to a dangerous war. We should consider all these measures, and more. But perhaps it would suffice to note that the Soviet bloc is not immune to the flow of history in the name of which the Communists claim to act. The prophets of history may be gradually becoming its prisoners—and the time has now come for the West to prod history along.

SEVERAL of the major swings in Soviet policy over the past 45 years have been directed to the twin purposes of building up a more productive agriculture, and reshaping the stubborn traditions of the peasantry. In the midst of World War II, Stalin confided to Churchill that the struggle to collectivize the villages had been ever more difficult and uncertain than the battle against Hitler. Apparently some of Stalin's closest subordinates felt, even in his lifetime, that his methods were not bringing the goal any nearer and that new expedients must be found to overcome the inefficiency and apathy of the collectivized peasantry. For no sooner was the old dictator laid to rest than his successors embarked on a series of new and ever more costly programs to strengthen the agricultural basis of the top-heavy Soviet economy. The solution is not yet in sight.

Soviet agriculture is still suffering from several decades of exploitation for the needs of industrial growth, defense and a very costly administrative apparatus. To make it produce efficiently vast expenditures of capital and managerial skills are required. What has been mined out of the soil must be returned to it sooner or later. What has been mined out of the stamina and will-to-work of the collectivized peasantry must be restored to it in the form of material, cultural and perhaps political satisfactions. The basic dilemma of the dictatorship has been that it has striven since 1929 to transform agricultural labor into a form of industrial labor, whereby the ownership of livestock and the use of individual plots of land will disappear and the farmer will live solely from his work for the collective. Yet each time the Party moves toward this ideological and political goal, which would also make the collective farmers totally dependent on higher authority for their daily bread, it opens up a vast reservoir of suspicion, ill-will and downright malingering.

In "Soviet Agriculture Marks Time" (July 1962), which is based on two decades of research and on recent observations and discussions with planners and managers in the Soviet Union, Alec Nove sums up Soviet policies and prospects in this field. Reader in Russian Social and Economic Studies at the University of London, Mr. Nove is the author of "The Soviet Economy" (1961) and numerous other studies.

456

SOVIET AGRICULTURE MARKS TIME

By Alec Nove

NINE years ago, Khrushchev addressed the first "agricultural" plenum of the Central Committee since Stalin's death. His frank exposure of the poor state of Soviet agriculture was followed by action along a wide front. Prices paid by the state for farm produce were substantially raised, investments in agriculture increased, peasant incomes showed a much needed and rapid rise from very low levels. Tax and other burdens on the private activities of peasants were eased, to the benefit of all concerned; for example, in five years the number of privately owned cows increased 25 percent. In 1958 a major organizational weakness was corrected: Tractors and other machinery formerly owned and operated by the Machine Tractor Stations (M.T.S.) were sold to the collective farms which the M.T.S. had previously "serviced" (and also supervised). In 1958, too, the government dropped its complex multiple-price system, under which farms received a low price for a quota of produce and a higher one for deliveries in excess of their quota; this was replaced by a single price for each product, with zonal variations.

The period 1953-58, then, was one of reform, of higher incomes, of large investments, of new methods. It was also one of higher production. The 1958 grain harvest set an all-time record. Sugar beets and cotton also did very well. Milk yields benefited from the improved diet of the cows. According to the official statistics, the *annual* rate of growth of gross agricultural output in the five years 1953-58 was 8.6 percent. This would be a remarkable achievement, if the statistics were reliable, but there are ample grounds for suspecting some degree of exaggeration. Even so, no serious observer doubts that a substantial advance was recorded in these years.

No doubt inspired by the figures with which they were supplied,

Khrushchev and his colleagues projected an even more rapid growth of agricultural output in the Seven Year Plan (1959-65), and onward through 1970. Extremely ambitious plans were envisaged for meat production, in particular, and for other scarce items such as fruit and vegetables. Yet for three consecutive years since 1958 the figures have shown no appreciable change, merely some fluctuations reflecting better or worse weather. Indeed, grain harvests have been below the 1958 record (see table on p. 460). How far performance lags behind plan can be seen from the following table (totals are in millions of tons):

	1961 plan	1961 performance
Grain	155.2	137.2
Meat	11.8	8.8
Milk	78.4	62.5

SOURCE: Khrushchev, *Pravda*, March 6, 1962.

Allowance for statistical inflation of output would make the shortfall even greater. There is no doubt that Khrushchev is alarmed, because he has admitted as much at great length, and has proposed a number of remedies.

It is the purpose of this article to examine the reasons for the difficulties in which Soviet agriculture finds itself, and to assess the likely efficacy of the measures proposed to set matters right. But before doing so it is important to repeat that there has been a sizable advance since the death of Stalin, and that the crisis in Soviet agriculture is essentially to be seen as a failure to expand, a failure to measure up to very ambitious plans, rather than as a collapse. Various foods are in short supply in many cities at different times of the year, but there is some truth in Khrushchev's assertion that the shortage has been exacerbated by an increase in personal incomes (with retail prices broadly unchanged).

In considering the problems of Soviet agriculture, it is necessary to distinguish several types of difficulty, and, correspondingly, different kinds of policies or remedial measures. There is, first, the complex of problems related to soil utilization, agricultural techniques, equipment and the like, which may be called problems of production. Secondly, there are questions connected with the peasants, with their private interests, incomes, incentives. Finally, there are the many problems of agricultural planning, administration and control. These are all to some extent interconnected, as when, for instance, an administrative measure designed to improve technique affects the peasants' private activities. None the less, it remains true that these various matters are to some extent distinct and can be separately analyzed.

II. PROBLEMS OF PRODUCTION

One of the principal objects—though not the only object—of Soviet farm policy is to increase production. Under any political system, this would involve overcoming serious obstacles, for a large part of Soviet territory is unsuitable for agriculture. Where the soil is fertile there is usually a high risk of drought, and where rainfall is adequate the soil is generally poor. Two of Khrushchev's principal remedies—designed to provide more crops and especially more grain for human and animal consumption—were the virgin-lands and the corn campaigns. The first involved enlarging the area of extensive farming, the second was an attempt to intensify farming. Both have now been running for six years or more, and so some assessment of their effectiveness is possible.

The virgin-lands campaign was a truly formidable undertaking. It added to the farmland of the Soviet Union an area equal to the cultivated land of Canada. Between 1953 and 1956, the total sown area rose from 157 to 194.7 million hectares. So great an expansion in so short a period has no parallel in agricultural history. It was achieved through a major diversion of machinery and with a minimum number of permanent settlers, reinforced at harvest time by migrant labor (volunteers or "volunteers," probably both). The areas brought under cultivation were in the northern half of Kazakhstan, in parts of west and central Siberia and in the territories east of the lower Volga and the southern Urals. The principal crop was grain, largely spring wheat. The following table gives the official production figures (in millions of metric tons) for the total grain harvest in the years 1953-1961, with a breakdown showing that part of the total harvested in the virgin lands, of which Kazakhstan (shown as a further subtotal) is one region.

	1953	1954	1955	1956	1957	1958	1959	1960	1961
Total Grain Harvest	82.5	85.6	106.8	127.6	105.0	141.2	125.9	134.3	137.3
Harvested in virgin lands	27.1	37.6	28.0	63.6	38.5	58.8	55.3	59.1	n.a.
Harvested in Kazakhstan	5.4	7.7	4.8	23.8	10.5	22.0	19.1	18.8	14.8

SOURCES: for 1953-60, *Narodnoe khozyaistvo* S.S.S.R. v. *1960 godu*, p. 440-1; for 1961, *Pravda*, March 6, 1962.

Clearly, grain production did increase greatly through 1958. In 1954, the first year of the campaign, yields were good but little had yet been ploughed. In 1955, on the other hand, drought ruined the crop; in Kazakhstan, for instance, yields in that year averaged a mere 3.8 quintals per hectare, against a nation-wide average of 8.5 quintals in a not very favorable year. In 1956 the harvest was very good—the best to date in the areas with which we are concerned. The 1957 crop was a poor one. Since 1958, a good year, no further progress has been made, and the figures for Kazakhstan, the territory with the highest drought risk, have shown an alarming downward trend.

The difficulties encountered have been of the following kinds:

1. The nature of the campaign itself caused the ploughing up of some land with unsuitable soil, or with excessively sparse rainfall. The causes of such errors will be discussed when we come to analyze administration.

2. A surprisingly high proportion of the machinery is not kept in good repair and cannot be used, owing to lack of spare parts, skilled mechanics and workshops. The situation has been getting steadily worse; thus there were 32,000 combine-harvesters inactive in Kazakhstan in 1959, but 60,000 were in disrepair at the start of the 1961 harvest.[1]

3. The right kind of rapidly ripening seed is seldom available. This, in combination with the shortage of working machinery, delays the harvest, and, in this area of early frosts, heavy losses result.

4. Lack of amenities has driven away some of the permanent labor force, despite repeated criticisms of this state of affairs by Khrushchev and by many lesser officials.

5. The land has been misused. Spring wheat has been sown year

[1] These figures are taken from the remarkable speech by the Premier of Kazakhstan, Sharipov, in *Kazakhstanskaya Pravda,* Dec. 24, 1961.

after year, although there was no lack of warnings as to the consequences. Weed infestation, soil erosion, reduced natural fertility are all
named as causes of falling yields. No acceptable system of cultivation
and crop rotation has yet been agreed upon.

Despite these difficulties, the campaign to date has paid good dividends.
It was clear from the start that there would be some bad years, and,
whatever discount is made for statistical exaggeration, it is surely true
that a substantial contribution has been made to Soviet grain supplies,
which could not otherwise have been obtained so quickly. Moreover, poor
weather conditions in the Ukraine have often coincided with good ones
in Kazakhstan, so that one effect of the campaign has been to spread
the risks somewhat.

The future, on the other hand, looks much less satisfactory. It is
known that some of the newly opened lands are of good quality, while
others appear to have been ploughed up on orders from above and
against the better judgment of local experts, but we do not know how
much land may be in each category. Nor have we the means of assessing
the extent of damage done by prolonged monoculture, or wind erosion,
though these factors have certainly contributed to the steady drop in
output and yields in Kazakhstan, where the bulk of the least suitable
lands happens to be situated. Probably some of the ploughed-up land will
have to be abandoned. Remedial measures at present being discussed
may well run into administrative difficulties, because of Khrushchev's
strong distaste for fallow and grasses, which presumably should be extended in some areas if the land is to be saved. Increased application
of fertilizer is unlikely to provide a solution because of lack of moisture.
(Very little is used on the somewhat similar Canadian prairies, though
rainfall there is slightly higher.) In all the circumstances, it would be
sensible to assume that a bigger contribution will be needed from traditional agricultural areas, and that the Soviet Union will be fortunate
if means are found to maintain average yields in these marginal lands at
the modest levels of the last few years.

Khrushchev was conscious from the first of the need to increase substantially the output of fodder, particularly fodder grains, in the "old"
cultivated areas. This was the primary object of his corn campaign,
which was facilitated by the growing of so much wheat in the virgin
lands. Corn had been neglected, and its acreage in 1953 was actually
somewhat lower than in 1940 and 1950. To enforce a rapid change,
Khrushchev had recourse to continuous propaganda and administrative

pressures. As a result, the area under corn rose rapidly from 3.5 million hectares in 1953 to 19.7 in 1958 and 28.2 in 1961. With strong pressure to sow corn on good land and to give it a large share of the available fertilizer,[2] yields rose also, as the following table shows:

	1953	1958	1959	1961
Total corn harvest (millions of metric tons)	3.7	16.7	12.0	24.0
Yield (quintals per hectare)	10.6	20.6	13.8	18.2

However, these official averages conceal vast regional variations. Thus in some areas in which corn was sown "by order," yields were exceedingly low; these include the Volga area and the Urals, where average yields for the period 1957-59 were respectively 5.1 and 4.5 quintals per hectare. This represents utter failure.

None the less, as in the case of the virgin-lands campaign, the underlying idea behind Khrushchev's corn plan was sound, and the substantial increase in silage supplies (from 32 million tons in 1953 to 186 million tons in 1960, largely due to corn) certainly helped in raising milk yields and providing a better diet for an expanded livestock population. The trouble, as in the case of the virgin-lands campaign, has been the "campaigning" methods themselves, which caused rapid expansion under conditions which were often unsuitable. (Khrushchev has repeatedly claimed that corn can grow even as far north as Archangel.) Orders from the center demanded that all corn be sown in "square clusters," although, as several local agronomists sought vainly to point out, it is often more convenient to sow in rows.

Khrushchev has also set unrealistic goals. Thus whole provinces in the Ukraine were expected to achieve a yield of 50 quintals of corn per hectare in 1961, whereas American yields, with more suitable soils and warmer climate, averaged around 32 quintals. Even though the 1961 harvest in the Ukraine was an all-time record, with excellent weather conditions, no province came within 15 quintals of this target. Instead of learning his lesson, Khrushchev has repeated his demand for 50 quintals per hectare in 1962. One is left wondering which would do more harm: failure (with or without simulation of success), or success bought

[2] Perhaps this is why potatoes, which "compete" for scarce fertilizer with the more fashionable corn, have been doing badly of late.

at the cost of neglecting all other farming needs of the Ukraine; presumably the former. It is this chronic tendency to overdo a good idea, to impose it by decree, which ruins its application and does so much harm to Soviet agriculture. More will be said below about the causes of such practices.

Meanwhile we must turn to consider the latest of Khrushchev's campaigns—to plough up meadows and reduce the area of sown grasses. Its motive, like that of the corn campaign, was the need for fodder, more in quantity and more diversified in type. This called for a further intensification of agriculture, which, as Khrushchev rightly saw, was inconsistent with the previously fashionable *travopolye* (rotational grass) crop system, associated with the name of Vilyams (Williams) and imposed under Stalin on all parts of the Soviet Union, regardless of local conditions. While grass could be a valuable source of fodder in the Baltic States or the northwest, in central and south Russia it grows poorly and provides little hay. Consequently there was much to criticize in these cropping practices. Khrushchev attacked the indiscriminate enforcement of *travopolye* in 1954, but agronomists had been trained in this way of thinking, officials were used to it, and those experts who had opposed it in Stalin's day had been punished or demoted. Consequently, little change actually occurred.

Khrushchev launched an all-out assault on *travopolye* in 1961—in speeches in many parts of the country and at the Twenty-second Party Congress. He pointed to the vast areas of sown grasses, of meadows, of low-yield crops such as oats. He ridiculed those provinces, including Leningrad and Moscow, where 50 percent or more of all arable land consisted of grasses and fallow. He demanded that such crops as corn, peas, beans and sugar beets be sown instead, in virtually all parts of the country. Only by intensification of agriculture of this kind, he asserted, would it be possible to produce sufficient fodder. Agricultural experts or officials who did not see this would have to be reëducated or removed. Crop rotation, too, must be drastically altered forthwith.

Again, as in the case of the virgin-lands and corn campaigns, Khrushchev appears right in general principle, but the method of enforcing his ideas almost ensures that very serious errors will be made in some parts of the country. The new system will not be understood. New crops will be grown by order in areas where soil conditions or labor shortage or the lack of necessary machinery or fertilizer will make it impossible to apply the directive effectively. For example, in parts of the Baltic States or in the Leningrad province it may well be rational to grow grass, because, although it would certainly be possible to produce more fodder per hectare by planting, say, beans, it would not be worth the extra labor involved. Incredibly enough, Khrushchev hardly mentioned that additional inputs would be necessary; all he declared himself concerned about was the amount of fodder produced. Of course, Khrushchev was careful to warn against excesses; grass was not to be universally banished, fallow might be necessary here and there, and so on. But the general sense of his instructions was such that they are bound to be followed by orders to plough up grass, to ban fallow and sow beans, corn, etc., regardless of circumstances. Thus the Premier of Latvia mentioned that some of his colleagues in the Baltic States were already treating clover as a "forbidden crop." [3] Khrushchev must know all this. Yet presumably he can see no other way of breaking up existing irrational farm practices, since his only available weapon is the party machine, and this is the sort of way it works. In his impatience with low yields and general inefficiency, these crude administrative methods must appear to him as irreplaceable.

One cannot envisage a rapid advance of Soviet agriculture by such methods—the more so as the agricultural machinery industry has been undergoing a painful period of readjustment. Production of some vital items has fallen drastically. Khrushchev himself cited with dismay the fact that output of corn silage combines, urgently needed as a result of the expansion of the corn acreage, actually fell from 55,000 in 1957 to 13,000 in 1960.[4] Other sources confirm that the new system of industrial planning has caused much confusion in farm machinery factories.[5] The chronic shortage of spare parts continues, and decrees about expanding their output and making them available to farms on free purchase (as distinct from administrative allocation) have remained on paper.[6] Finally, fertilizer production and output of other important agricultural chemicals (sprays, weed-killers, etc.) are far behind schedule. Khrushchev contrasted the Seven Year Plan target for mineral

[3] Y. Peive, *Ekonomicheskaya gazeta,* March 5, 1962, p. 5.

[4] *Pravda,* March 6, 1962. Khrushchev there cites other examples.

[5] See in particular the article by the director of the Tula farm machinery factory, *Ekonomicheskaya gazeta,* Jan. 15, 1962, p. 8.

[6] A 1961 decree provides for severe punishment for allowing farm machinery to deteriorate, but often enough the cause of the trouble is lack of spare parts, or of materials with which to build shelter and storage space.

fertilizer—an increase from 12 to 35 million tons—with the "achievement" of an increase of a mere 2.9 million tons in three years. New capacity is being delayed, and the completion plan for the three years is only 44 percent fulfilled.[7] No wonder the Ukrainian party leader, Podgornyi, complained that fertilizer supplies were inadequate: "For instance, deliveries to the Ukraine of fertilizer for sugar beet growing, per unit of land, has actually diminished in the past few years." He also deplored serious difficulties in supplies of timber, vehicles, tires and metal.[8] These are products of obvious importance to agriculture. The adoption of even the best techniques cannot bring results if the required machines are not available, or if they break down and cannot be repaired, or if, as in some areas, farms do not even have carts or trailers to move into the fields the fertilizer which they do have available.

One purpose of the party's recent declarations may be to restore a high priority to the industrial sectors which serve agriculture, and surely some improvements are both possible and likely. However, these shortages, which hamper agriculture even with existing cropping arrangements, must greatly hinder the application of the anti-*travopolye* policies, which call for much increased utilization of both machinery and fertilizer. If this call cannot be met, the result is likely to be a large additional expenditure of peasant labor without sufficient return.[9] It should be added that, as a consequence of the ploughing up of grasses, private livestock may be deprived of pasturage, to the further detriment of production and peasant morale. (When the corn campaign was launched, the peasants were promised part of the corn for their animals; but no such promises are being made at present.)

III. THE PEASANTS

By the end of 1957, many collectivized peasants must have felt considerable grounds for satisfaction. Cash distributions from the farms had risen almost fourfold in five years. They were about to be freed from all delivery obligations to the state from their private holdings, and their private livestock was expanding at a fairly impressive rate. It is true that work discipline was being tightened. But clearly things were improving.

[7] *Pravda,* March 8, 1962.

[8] *Pravda,* March 7, 1962.

[9] The burdens on the labor force which present policies impose were stressed at the Central Committee plenum by P. Abrosimov (*Pravda,* March 8, 1962).

In the past four years, the peasants have been in a much less satisfactory situation. Space precludes anything like a full analysis of the many factors involved. The following is a summary of unfavorable developments:

1. Attempts, sometimes encouraged by the authorities, to pay collective farmers a guaranteed minimum "wage," instead of in "workday units" of uncertain value, have broken down in many areas [10] because there is still no financial basis for any regular payment for work done, except on the richer farms. For seven years the press has been publishing articles and letters insisting on the necessity of earmarking a fixed share of farm revenue to pay the peasant members. Yet nothing effective has been done.

2. The 1958 reforms had the unintended consequence of increasing disparities in income between rich and poor farms. This was because, until that year, the more fertile areas were charged a kind of disguised differential rent by having to pay more for work done by the M.T.S. and by being compelled to deliver a bigger quota of produce at low prices. The abolition of the M.T.S. and the unification of delivery prices eliminated these methods. It is true that the unified delivery prices are lower in fertile areas, but the difference is quite small.

3. Peasant income from collective farms appears to have declined since 1957. The evidence for this lies, first, in the fact that there has been statistical silence since 1957, which usually indicates that the figures look bad. Second, two Soviet scholars have used regional and/or sample data to show a fall in distributions to peasants since that date; one of the writers, citing a 15 percent reduction between 1957 and 1960 in the province of Rostov, lists a number of other areas in which "the situation is broadly similar." [11] This happened despite a rise in gross revenues, and appears to have been due to pressure to spend large sums on investment, to exorbitant charges for repairs in state-run workshops, and the need to pay black-market prices to obtain desperately scarce tires, building materials and spare parts.[12]

4. Restrictions have been imposed on private activities of peasants, and the number of privately owned cows has declined sharply since the end of 1957. In consequence, and also because of a decline in free-market

[10] See evidence in A. Kraeva, *Voprosy ekonomiki*, No. 8/1961, p. 74.
[11] *Ibid.*, p. 77, and E. Kapustin, *Ekonomicheskaya gazeta*, April 9, 1962, p. 8.
[12] *E.g.*, see articles in *Ekonomicheskaya gazeta* by M. Semko and A. Severov, respectively March 5 and March 19, 1962.

sales, peasant incomes in cash and produce from their private plots have fallen too. Thus there is evidence of a significant decline in peasant living standards, which must affect incentives.

Several measures have been taken to ease the financial burdens of the collective farms: prices of some items which farms must purchase were reduced in 1961, credit terms were eased, and payments for produce were made in advance. Also, nearly two million collective-farm peasants have been converted to state-farm status since 1957, making them regular wage earners (though the wages are low). However, possibly because of financial stringency, the government has done little indeed to improve peasant incomes, and must have caused much irritation by its measures against private livestock.

Perhaps the renewed restrictions on private activities of peasants are designed to persuade them to work harder for the collectives. Certainly, it could be shown that millions of man-hours are dissipated on private landholdings and millions more on taking produce to market. The Soviet leaders could well argue that these are not efficient ways of using labor. Yet, in existing circumstances, the private plot and the free market are indispensable, both for the peasants and for urban consumers of foodstuffs. In the first place, the private holdings, though primitively cultivated, are often much more productive, per unit of land, than collective or state farms, due partly to hard work and partly to the concentration of manure on a small area. To take a particularly striking example, in 1959 a hectare of potatoes on private holdings yielded 11.6 tons, as against 6.6 on state and collective farms.[13] Second, particularly in small towns and in rural districts, the state distribution network is utterly incapable of coping with food supplies, except for a narrow range of staple items. In this situation a cut in the number of private cows may create serious shortages.

Why, since milk production on state and collective farms has fully offset the decline in private output, does this situation occur? Some would point to exaggerations in the reporting of milk production, asserting that output has in fact fallen. This may well be so. But there is another and simpler reason. To distribute milk in a "modern" manner is a complex affair. It requires storage, refrigeration, specialized transport, bottles or cartons, and so on. All these are lacking, outside of a few

[13] Calculated from detailed figures given in the statistical compendium, *Selskoe khozyaistvo S.S.S.R.* (Moscow, 1960).

big cities. In these circumstances, even if milk does exist on some farm 30 miles away, it is impracticable to distribute it, and so the local woman and her one private cow are irreplaceable. In villages, except in a very few showplaces, the private plot is almost the sole source of milk and vegetables for peasant families. Given the present structure of Soviet farming and food distribution, measures against the private sector must have unfortunate results, and the quickest way of ensuring an increase in production of many much-needed items is to permit some enlargement of private farming activities. It is extraordinary that Khrushchev, who so strongly criticized the measures taken under Stalin against private plots, should be adopting his present policies—or permitting them, since it is not impossible for the party machine in the villages to take some initiative in these matters. Surely he must know better than anyone that such interference damages not only the supply of food from the private sector but also the morale of the peasants and their work for the collective and state farms. Yet only recently it was proposed that private plots on state farms be done away with and that communal vegetable-growing be substituted.[14] One can imagine the unpopularity of such imposed measures. Here ideology and administrative habit seem to stand directly in the way of increasing production.

IV. ADMINISTRATION AND PLANNING

The Soviet leaders must surely be fully aware that agriculture does not take kindly to centralized planning, that local initiative is vital. Yet ever since collectivization they have interfered with farming operations. This is to some extent explained by the fact that collectivization itself was imposed by the Party, and it has required constant vigilance to maintain collective farms and to "protect" them from their peasant members. Party watchdogs must also supervise the party-nominated "elected" chairmen who were often peasants themselves and therefore liable to give priority to the farm's needs rather than the state's. Low prices, which helped to finance industrialization but offered no financial incentive, made it necessary that the coercive apparatus of Party and state be mobilized annually to enforce deliveries to the state. For many years the principal task of the local party officials in rural areas, and of the political officers within the M.T.S., was to squeeze out produce for

[14] V. Grishin, the "trade union" chief, *Pravda*, March 10, 1962.

the state from reluctant and potentially backsliding peasants, who had to be restrained from spending their time on their private holdings. Farms could not be allowed to pursue the principle of maximizing revenues, since the price system was (and still is) geared to other objectives. The existence of a free market exercised a particularly distracting influence. Thus collective farms have been accused of marketing vegetables in distant cities at high prices, or growing sunflowers instead of sugar beets because they could sell sunflower seed in the free market at a profit,[15] or even—in the case of a state farm in 1961—growing grass instead of grain because, as a surprisingly honest director told Khrushchev to his face, grass does not need to be delivered to the state and grain does.

Consequently, the habit developed of controlling agriculture from above, and of so organizing farms and planning as to facilitate this control. To some extent the amalgamation of collective farms, which has more than quadrupled their average size since 1950 (and which is still going on), is explained by the greater convenience in exerting control from above, rather than the convenience of management. From the latter's standpoint, most state and collective farms are much too big. This tendency to very large size is also explained in part by the traditional Marxist belief that there are substantial economies of scale in agriculture.

When, in 1953, the appalling state of Soviet farming called for drastic remedial measures, Khrushchev showed himself very conscious of the harm done by inefficient central planning. The Soviet press printed a long series of articles criticizing the stupidity of inflexible production plans passed down the administrative hierarchy to farms for which they were quite unsuitable. Khrushchev and others declared that this must cease. In 1955, a decree was adopted freeing the collective farms from having production plans determined for them; they were to be given delivery quotas, and were to be free to decide their crop and livestock plans, so long as these were consistent with the quotas. It was repeatedly asserted that farm management and agronomists should be free to decide their own methods in the light of the very varied circumstances which always exist in agriculture.

In practice, since prices of neither output nor inputs reflected either needs or scarcities, direction from above had to continue. The period 1955-61 was one of experiment and frequent change in administrative

---

[15] I. Bodyul, *Ekonomicheskaya gazeta,* March 5, 1962, p. 6. Many similar examples could be cited.

arrangements. The Ministry of Agriculture was gradually shorn of its powers, part of which were transferred to *Gosplan* (the central planning agency) and part to a new body responsible for supply and utilization of farm machinery and fertilizer (*Sel'khoztekhnika*). A number of changes in purchasing arrangements culminated in the setting up, in 1961, of a Procurements Committee with local organs in close touch with farms, whose production programs they were supposed to influence. But production planning was also supposed to be the responsibility of the provincial agricultural department, while state farms came under a provincial trust which took its orders from organs of the individual republics.

The result was confusion. Everyone was to some extent responsible, therefore no one was. In practice, the local party organs at provincial (*oblast*) and district (*rayon*) levels exercised the most effective control over collective farms (and to a lesser extent over state farms). They issued orders on a variety of topics, they could and did dismiss the "elected" chairmen of farms and "recommend" others. But the responsibilities of the local parties, and the pressures to which they were subjected, gave rise to an administrative disease which is worth analyzing more closely.

A rural party secretary has always spent the bulk of his time dealing with agricultural problems. His promotion, or dismissal, depends on his success in coping with them. But how is his success or failure to be determined? The answer in practice has been: by his ability to report the fulfillment of plans to his superiors, if possible ahead of time. These plans tend to be very ambitious, and Khrushchev has systematically encouraged party secretaries to "compete" with one another by offering to overfulfill them. The plans in question are of many different kinds: they might concern grain procurement, meat deliveries, milk production, the completion of sowing by a certain date, the quadrupling of the corn acreage, the use of some fashionable method of harvesting, and so on. Almost invariably, the plans are either impossible of fulfillment, or (and this is the cause of much trouble) can be fulfilled only if other agricultural activities, which may be important but not at the moment the subject of a campaign, are neglected. Party secretaries are therefore repeatedly placed in an impossible situation. They are, of course, told to administer their areas efficiently, to take into account all the multifarious needs of agriculture. But they simply cannot do this while they are being cajoled to fulfill plans which, in the circumstances, are inconsistent with a healthy agriculture.

By long training, party officials have tended to adapt their behavior to the need to report success in the current campaign. Therefore cases like these recur repeatedly (all the examples are genuine and could be multiplied) : seed grain is delivered to the state to fulfill delivery plans, and later other grain, unsorted and unsuitable, has to be returned for seed; farms are ordered to sow before the ground is fit for it, and/or to harvest by a fashionable but, in the given circumstances, unsuitable method; meat quotas are met at the cost of slaughtering livestock needed in the following year; to fulfill the procurement plan the local party boss orders the state elevators to receive what Khrushchev (in his speech at Novosibirsk) described as "mud, ice, snow and unthreshed stalks," which damaged the elevator's equipment. Party officials have repeatedly broken up established crop rotations to compel the adoption of whatever was the subject of the current campaign; if they understood the long-term damage which this might do to the soil, they would, in any case, probably be in charge of some other area by then. Other party secretaries inspired or condoned large-scale falsification of plan fulfillment, by such methods as instructing farms to buy butter in retail stores for delivery as their own produce (note that the cost of this operation falls on the peasants), or more simply by "writing in" non-existent figures (*pripiski*). They did not do these things because they enjoyed cheating or damaging the farms of their area, but as a response to pressures to achieve the impossible.

It is interesting to speculate why agricultural plans are so much less realistic than industrial ones. The uncertainties of the weather constitute one reason, but another is surely the habit of "campaigning," which is of such long standing, has done so much damage to sound farming and which still continues. A campaign must have clearly defined objectives, priorities and dates on which achievements are to be measured; it must involve strain and effort to achieve success, and must lead, therefore, to neglect of other considerations. But in agriculture this does great harm.

Given these administrative habits, it followed logically that the planning autonomy granted to collective farms in 1955 could never be a reality. It is also easy to understand why all decentralization measures were doomed to failure. Devolution of authority in the existing setting meant in practice devolution to party secretaries, who alone were in a position to enforce decisions, and this led to the systematic neglect of anything for which there was no pressure from the center. In a genuine effort to encourage local initiative, Khrushchev announced in 1958 that only grain-surplus regions were to be given grain delivery quotas. The idea was to encourage other regions to meet their own needs from their own resources, and in particular to concentrate on fodder grains for their livestock. What happened was that both grain acreage and production fell sharply in the areas freed from delivery quotas. In returning to centralized procurement planning in 1961, Khrushchev himself explained the reason: party secretaries, finding themselves no longer under pressure to deliver grain, instructed "their" farms to pursue other objectives in which the center seemed more interested; consequently, the fodder shortage was accentuated.

It is in the light of all this that one must assess Khrushchev's latest administrative reforms. There were two possible ways out: either to grant much more autonomy to farm management, or, on the contrary, to attempt to organize a more streamlined and flexible machine of central control. He chose the latter. Given his own background and the traditions of the party, he could hardly have done otherwise.

A completely new hierarchical pyramid of control has been created in 1962. A new All-Union Committee on Agriculture is to be headed by a deputy premier, and is to include the head of the agricultural department of the Central Committee of the Party, and the heads of other relevant organizations, which retain their identity within, or alongside, the new structure: the Procurements Committee, *Setl'khoz-tekhnika*, the Ministry of Agriculture (reduced to purely research and advisory functions), plus representatives of the planning agencies. This new committee will apparently not be a policy-making body (Khrushchev would have headed it if it were); it is merely to ensure that party and state directives for agriculture are carried out. But below the all-union level the situation is different in one all-important respect: the heads of the agricultural committees in republics and provinces are to be the first secretaries of the republican and provincial parties. At provincial level and below, the tasks of procurement as well as production planning, for collective farms and state farms, will be unified under the new committee within a provincial agricultural department. The basic unit of agricultural planning, operating on the instructions of the provincial committee, will now be a new "territorial state and collective farm administration," which, as a rule, will group together several districts (*rayony*). In each of these territorial administrations there will be a "party organizer" deputed by the republican or provincial party organization.

This new hierarchy is to have authority to plan production, to issue directives as to methods, crop rotations, procurements, and in general to be in charge of both state farms and collective farm operations. "Inspector-organizers" employed by the territorial administrations will work within the farms and "will decide on the spot questions of production and procurement." The large number of workshops and other minor enterprises carried on jointly by two or more collective farms will be placed directly under the territorial administrations. An end is finally made of the doctrine, so often disregarded in practice, that collective farms are autonomous coöperatives governed by their members.

The reorganization marks a drastic alteration in, and a tightening of, the entire system of administration. Within it, the rôle of territorial party officials has undergone an important change. Hitherto, however frequently these officials interfered with plans and operations, they were not directly in charge of them. Their job was supposed to be to ensure that the relevant state organs did their job, to act as political commissars and not as army commanders, so to speak. It is true that they did in fact frequently issue commands, but—and this point was made several times—they could and often did dodge responsibility by putting the blame on one or more of the state officials whose formal duty it was to plan this or that aspect of agriculture. Now, the most senior party secretaries at the republic and provincial level have been put in direct command over farming in their areas, have been given full powers to issue orders to ensure that the agricultural plans are fulfilled. The state organs at their level, and beneath them, are at their command. The most powerful man in the new basic territorial controlling organs will be the "party organizer" whom they will appoint, and even the nominal chiefs of these organs will clearly be party officials for the most part, certainly not professional agricultural managers; both Khrushchev and Voronov warned against appointing farm managers to these posts.[16] One category of party official loses—the district (*rayon*) secretaries—and protests from them were mentioned by Khrushchev. (They will sit on a council which will be attached to the territorial administrations, but so will farm managers and other lesser

---

[16] Voronov in *Pravda*, March 28, 1962. The big rôle played by Voronov in carrying out this reform is surely a significant pointer to his rapidly increasing position of power in the U.S.S.R.

lights.) Apparently their behavior vis-à-vis the farms is regarded as having contributed to past distortion, which is true enough. Khrushchev appears to believe that the past failures of party control were due to the fact that it was unsystematic, spasmodic, with many overlaps with various state organs which in turn confused one another and, as he put it, left the farms "undirected." Presumably he imagines that, if a party secretary knows he is personally responsible for all agriculture in "his" province, he will no longer concentrate only on the immediately current campaign, and the many defects of party activities in rural areas will thereby be corrected.

But will they? If our analysis is correct, then the essential weakness arises not from irregularity of their interference but from the overambitious nature of the plans which, willy-nilly, they have to force down the throats of their subordinates, and from the contradiction between these plans and the self-interest of farms and peasants. Party officials will surely continue to try to please their superiors and to organize matters so as to be able to report what these superiors wish to hear. While it is true that a more logical administrative structure has been achieved, it lessens the effective powers of farm managements and farm agronomists. It is on the farms that crops are grown, and it cannot be right to diminish the range of choice open to those who can actually see the crops growing, who bear formal responsibility for farm operations and, in the case of collective farms, for the incomes of the labor force.

V. CONCLUSION

Soviet agriculture is indeed marking time. The liberal post-Stalin policies did produce quick results, but since 1958 the growth rate has been negligible, for a number of interconnected reasons which I have endeavored to analyze here. It clearly does not follow that growth cannot be resumed. If more investment funds can be made available for the fertilizer and farm-machinery industries, for instance, then the very low crop yields in the naturally unfertile lands of the center, north and west of European Russia can be increased. Success in agriculture tends to reinforce itself (higher yields of fodder grains, more livestock, more manure, higher yields, higher productivity, increased incomes, more incentives, therefore still higher productivity, etc., etc.). None of this is impossible, despite the adverse natural conditions under which Soviet agriculture operates. The trouble is that policies toward the peasant and the organizational arrangements of the régime seem inconsistent with the great advance in food production which Khrushchev desires with evident sincerity. And paradoxically, his impatient urgings, and their organizational and "campaigning" consequences, are among the principal obstacles to soundly based progress. Although we should expect to see some increases in production, there can be no question of fulfilling— or anything like it—the plans for 1965 and 1970, to which so much publicity has been given in the Soviet Union.

Finally, it is only right and fair to emphasize that there is no easy solution to the problems with which the Soviet leadership is wrestling. It is easy to criticize the price system, but it ill behooves us to lecture Khrushchev about the virtues of a free price mechanism when not a single major Western country permits it to operate in the agricultural sector. Difficulties arise in ensuring even modest efficiency in traditional peasant farming in many non-Communist countries, and agricultural plans have a regrettable habit of going awry in places well to the west of the Soviet border. Thus at the moment of writing there is an acute potato shortage in England, due largely to the fact that the Potato Board restricted plantings in the incorrect expectation of favorable growing weather; if there were a 1962 sheep plan in Scotland it would be a failure, since so many sheep have been killed by the severe winter. It is also not to be forgotten that, seen historically, Soviet agriculture has served as a means of financing and sustaining industrialization and has suffered in consequence. This is a disadvantage unknown to farmers in developed Western countries.

Yet it remains true that the huge farms of the Soviet Union have been inefficient in the use of resources and have shown a deplorable lack of flexibility and a failure to mobilize necessary human ingenuity. It is also significant that the only country in the Communist bloc which fulfills its agricultural plans is Poland, where most farms are privately owned and privately run. One reason for this is that Polish plans are reasonable: had Gomulka been so foolish as to promise to treble meat production in five years, he too would have "failed." Polish farming has its own weaknesses, and it is surely impossible on practical as well as ideological grounds to apply the "Polish model" to the Soviet Union. Yet, Polish experience underlines a fact too often overlooked: that with all the familiar inadequacies of small-peasant agriculture, it possesses advantages which Marxist theory has failed to recognize and Soviet practice has yet to find a way of emulating. Khrushchev is making an all-out effort to seek efficiency within the basic institutional and political framework of the Soviet system, and has mobilized the Communist Party machine for this purpose. The next few years will show whether a breakthrough can be achieved under these conditions. Much depends on the outcome—perhaps Khrushchev's political standing, probably also the influence of the Soviet Union on other peasant countries, within and outside the Communist bloc.

THE Soviet Union emerged from World War II as one of two super-powers, in control of a greatly enlarged sphere of domination in East Central Europe and with vastly expanded political ambitions. The course of events in Asia added to the Communist imperium the most populous nation in the world, a potentially great world power, as well as North Korea and North Viet-Nam. The Soviet Union also made a remarkably rapid recovery from its wartime devastation and has since shown a high rate of industrial growth. Soviet scientists and engineers have made tremendous advances in developing nuclear bombs and long-range rockets, thus largely neutralizing the single greatest strategic advantage the United States had possessed in the first decade after the war. If only because of the great power it wields, it is extremely important to understand how the Soviet leadership analyzes the present unstable situation in world politics and how it defines the goals of its policy.

The new Program of the C.P.S.U., the second to be promulgated over its first 45 years of rule, states the purposes of the leadership with remarkable precision and frankness. Of course, it will regulate the pursuit of its goals and the level of risks it will assume in accordance with its estimates of the expediency, at home and abroad, of this or that concrete policy. Having given its people new rewards for hard work and sacrifices, and having promised them a rapid advance in material and cultural goods, the Kremlin has to weigh a difficult range of choices even in allocating its expanding resources.

In pursuing his plainly stated goals of world policy, Khrushchev must also weigh a wide variety of external factors as he faces each decision. Will this or that step bring gains commensurate with the costs and the risks? Will immediate gains provoke highly disadvantageous reactions and counteractions in the outside world? Here the strength and clarity of purpose of the non-Soviet countries, primarily of the United States and its allies, are of decisive significance. The 1961 Program suggests how poorly equipped the Soviet leadership is to understand any system of power except its own. It also lays down the basic goals that the Soviet leadership intends to achieve in a more or less prolonged era of "peaceful coexistence." Both goals and strategy of Soviet policy are discussed by Philip E. Mosely in "The Meanings of Coexistence" (October 1962).

477

THE MEANINGS OF COEXISTENCE

By Philip E. Mosely

IN the deeply divided world of today, one main obstacle to achieving a genuine state of peaceful coexistence is the gap in the meanings attached to these two words in different societies and political systems. The gap is, of course, just one additional example of the estrangement of vocabularies that besets every effort at direct and sincere exchanges of ideas across or through the ideological and psychological barriers. Words like "democracy," "freedom," "progress" are, as we know only too well, employed in very different and even opposite senses in the two worlds.

Another obstacle lies in the confrontation of absolutes, the insistence on the total good of one ideal and the total evil of the way of life that it seeks to displace and destroy. This sense of serving as a mere instrument of History justifies, in the minds of its champions and supporters, a vast arrogance of self-righteousness. To them, the adversary is not only doomed but is morally wrong in his every act and thought.

Finally, the ideological armor that encases the Communist leaders is wrought of that contradiction in terms, "scientific revelation." Its theoretical bases, which were laid down over one hundred years ago at the beginning of the industrial era, must be proved to be uniquely correct and infallible today; and therefore those who dare re-examine or question any part of its fundamentalist dogmas must be silenced or destroyed.

The most recent and most authoritative statement of Communist dogma is, of course, the new Program of the Communist Party of the Soviet Union, unanimously adopted by the Twenty-second Party Congress on October 31, 1961. Despite its repetitious length and its many internal contradictions, it was carefully designed to serve as the main guide to Soviet thought, policy and action over "the next historic epoch." In the ten weeks between the publication of the draft program and the convening of the Congress, it was "discussed" in tens of thousands of meetings; since the Congress, it has been distributed in millions of copies

478

printed in scores of languages. Hence, its statements on the nature and purpose of coexistence must be studied seriously. First:

Peaceful coexistence of the socialist and capitalist countries is an objective necessity for the development of human society. War cannot and must not serve as a means of settling international disputes.[1]

Excellent! All reasonable people can welcome this position as a basis for a lively and earnest give-and-take discussion on how best to guarantee mankind against the danger of a new and terrible war and especially on how, in practical terms, we can concert our actions so as to diminish, contain or eliminate some or all of the conflicts that threaten to escape our control and balloon into a total struggle.

Here, however, the Program brings its non-Communist partners-in-dialogue up sharp against a flinty dogma of Communist fundamentalism:

Imperialism is the only source of the war danger. The imperialist camp is making preparations for the most terrible crime against mankind—a world thermonuclear war that can bring unprecedented destruction to entire countries and wipe out entire nations.

Here dogma, as so often, takes precedence over reality. After all, the Soviet Union has also been hard at work constructing horrendous weapons systems. Its leaders have, indeed, addressed blackmail notes to more than 30 governments, in which it has threatened their peoples specifically with nuclear destruction unless they abandon certain policies and postures of which Moscow disapproves. Semantically, the Kremlin, like its opponents, argues that it is not preparing for "aggression" but "to deter aggression." The distinction rests in the degree of faith or confidence in the government that makes the threat. Today any nuclear threat raises the level of international tension. This is all the more its effect when the Kremlin stretches the concept of "self-defense" to include the demand for Communist control over West Berlin and for the breaking up of alliances that Moscow views as obstacles to the extension of its own power.

The completely one-sided nature of the Communist interpretation of world politics appears in one small but interesting correction that was inserted in the final version of the Party Program. The draft of August 5 referred with approval to ". . . a growing number of countries that

---

[1] This and subsequent translations of excerpts are official ones, reproduced in "Soviet Communism: Programs and Rules," edited by Jan F. Triska (San Francisco: Chandler Publishing Company, 1962). Orthography and punctuation have been adapted slightly.

adhere to a policy of neutrality and strive to safeguard themselves against the hazards of participation in military blocs." This wording apparently gave too strong praise to non-alignment. At bottom, Communists are bound by dogma to view non-alignment as a way-station to joining their own power bloc. The words of the draft program might even imply an endorsement of Tito's posture, were it not for his heresy of claiming to be both Communist and uncommitted. And some Communists might have wondered why Khrushchev had used his tanks and artillery, in October 1956, to put down the attempt of the Imre Nágy government to declare Hungary neutral.

The drafters of the final version caught this awkward ideological ambiguity and changed "participation in military blocs" to "participation in aggressive military blocs." Since "aggressive" is an adjective that is applied only to "imperialists" and never to "the countries of socialism," the revised wording modifies the Kremlin's praise of non-alignment and leaves the gate open for presently uncommitted countries to commit themselves later to the "good" military bloc of "socialism."

The pursuit of "peaceful coexistence," in Moscow's view, must not lead to any slackening in the effort to reshape the rest of the world to the Communist pattern. On the contrary, the struggle for the triumph of Communism must be pressed even more vigorously and with the wider and more varied arsenal of instruments that is now available:

> Peaceful coexistence serves as a basis for the peaceful competition between socialism and capitalism on an international scale and constitutes a specific form of class struggle between them. As they consistently pursue the policy of peaceful coexistence, the socialist countries are steadily strengthening the positions of the world socialist system in its competition with capitalism. Peaceful coexistence affords more favorable opportunities for the struggle of the working class in the capitalist countries and facilitates the struggle of the peoples of the colonial and dependent countries for their liberation.

The Program specifically warns Communists everywhere against pinning to a new world war their hopes for their world-wide triumph. Indeed, the expectation of victory through cataclysm might lead them to relax their efforts and to slacken their discipline. However, in accord with a long Leninist tradition, the Soviet leadership is not against all types of wars:

> The C.P.S.U. and the Soviet people as a whole will continue to oppose all wars of conquest, including wars between capitalist countries, and local wars

aimed at strangling people's emancipation movements, and consider it their duty to support the sacred struggle of the oppressed peoples and their just anti-imperialist wars of liberation.

This reservation leaves a wide range of military actions open to Soviet arms, for the Kremlin reserves to itself the right to decide what peoples are "oppressed" and which wars are "wars of liberation." Despite the great risks that may accompany its participation, direct or indirect, in a variety of wars, the Program affirms the self-confident belief of the Soviet leadership that it can achieve complete victory without becoming involved in a nuclear war:

The growing superiority of the socialist forces over the forces of imperialism, of the forces of peace over those of war, will make it actually possible to banish world war from the life of society even before the complete victory of socialism on earth, with capitalism surviving in a part of the world. The victory of socialism throughout the world will do away completely with the social and national causes of all wars. To abolish war and establish everlasting peace on earth is the historic mission of Communism.[2]

In the Soviet view, "peaceful coexistence" is the correct policy in "an epoch," more or less prolonged, during which "capitalism" (the label the Kremlin attaches to those who resist its embrace) is to be compelled to retreat from one position to another until it finally gives up the ghost. The means for enforcing each such retreat are to be varied according to the local and international balance of power.

In some countries the transition to socialism (i.e., to rule by the Communist Party) may take place by peaceful, in others by "non-peaceful," means. Of course, even if "the working class" (those who obey and support the Communist Party) manages to ". . . win a solid majority in parliament . . . ," it must also ". . . launch a broad mass struggle outside parliament, smash the resistance of the reactionary forces, and provide the necessary conditions for a peaceful socialist revolution." Since the Communists would then hold the monopoly of force, they would also be able to define "the reactionary forces" to suit their own interests. In any case they would have no further interest in providing conditions of "peaceful coexistence" with any groups or individuals that they considered hostile or recalcitrant to that monopoly of power.

The Program emphasizes that the struggle must be waged untiringly

[2] I read the Russian original to mean "the historic mission," rather than "a historic mission."

and relentlessly, with a rapid succession of tactics, in order to keep the various opposing forces off balance and disunited:

The success of the struggle which the working class wages for the victory of the revolution will depend on how well the working class and its party master the use of all forms of struggle—peaceful and non-peaceful, parliamentary and extra-parliamentary—and how well they are prepared to replace one form of struggle by another as quickly and unexpectedly as possible.

In the end, of course, all roads lead to Rome, to the dictatorship of the proletariat, *i.e.,* of the Communist Party:

. . . whatever the form in which the transition from capitalism to socialism is effected, that transition can come about only through revolution. However varied the forms of a new people's state power in the period of socialist construction, their essence will be the same—dictatorship of the proletariat, which represents genuine democracy, democracy for the working people.

It is essential, of course, for the main center of the Communist movement to assure the unquestioning unity of "the working class," in order to lead a well-orchestrated offensive against "capitalism." In recent years this has not proved easy or simple even within those countries and Parties that acknowledge Moscow's hegemony. In fact,

Revisionism, Right opportunism, which is a reflection of bourgeois influence, is the chief danger within the Communist movement today. The revisionists, who mask their renunciation of Marxism with talk about the necessity of taking account of the latest developments in society and the class struggle, in effect play the role of pedlars of bourgeois-reformist ideology within the Communist movement.

However, "dogmatism and sectarianism, unless steadfastly combated, can also become the chief danger at particular stages in the development of individual parties."

Finally, who is to define "revisionism" and "dogmatism"? Obviously Khrushchev is determined to keep this "lever of power" in his own hands. He demonstrated this most dramatically at the Twenty-second Party Congress where he made his famous attack on the Albanian Party leaders, only to be rebuffed by Chou En-lai, who protested the bringing into the open of this bitter inter-party quarrel, and then departed for Peking. The Chinese leadership could, had it been so minded, have cited the very words of the Soviet Party Program on this crucial point:

The Communist Parties are independent and they shape their policies with due regard to the specific conditions prevailing in their own countries. . . . The Communist Party of the Soviet Union . . . regards it as its internationalist duty to abide by the appraisals and conclusions which the fraternal parties have reached jointly concerning their common tasks in the struggle against imperialism, for peace, democracy and socialism. . . .

Apparently the Soviet leadership has been unusually sensitive to the accusation that it dictates its policies unilaterally to other Parties, for it inserted a significant rewording in the final version of the Program. The draft of August 5 stated:

The C.P.S.U. will continue to strengthen the unity and cohesion of the ranks of the great army of Communists of all countries.

This could be read to mean that the C.P.S.U. will, by its direct action within or upon those Parties, strengthen their "unity and cohesion" and assure their obedience to Moscow. In the final draft this slip of the drafters was softened:

The C.P.S.U. will continue to direct its efforts to the unity and cohesion of the ranks of the great army of Communists of all countries.

Indeed, it is becoming increasingly difficult for Khrushchev to exercise over a wide diversity of régimes and Parties Stalin's "internationalist discipline." As the Program states in another context: ". . . not only the big states, but also the small ones . . . are in a position, irrespective of their strength, to pursue an independent foreign policy." The forces of division seem to be working within "the camp of socialism" as well as beyond its bounds. The impact of fissiparous trends may be all the more serious for Khrushchev's policy just because these tendencies run directly counter to Communist dogma as well as to Soviet ambition.

II

It is important to know the new Party Program. It is not mere rhetoric or a pious affirmation of hopes or aspirations. Lenin and his successors have prided themselves on "the unity of theory and practice," and since the new Program, despite Peking's carpings, is genuinely Leninist, it lays down not a theory but a set of comprehensive and coherent guidelines for action.

Modern practices of scientific analysis also affirm "the unity of theory and practice," but this means something quite different to the West. Under conditions of free inquiry it means that theories are formed on the basis of carefully examined facts for the purpose of giving order to larger and more complex bodies of facts. Then, when new or previously un-examined facts can no longer be explained or contained within existing theories, these comprehensive concepts must be revised, sometimes radi-cally. Thus, the generalizing role of theory in a system of free inquiry means that all theories have a utility value rather than a moral value, that many theories are competing to establish their validity as scientific tools, and that they are basically tentative rather than absolute in character.

Despite the recent and modest enlargements of the sphere of inquiry in Soviet scientific thought, the fundamental duty of the political leadership to define the limits of inquiry and to state in advance the conclusions it must reach has been strongly reaffirmed in the 1961 Program:

> The investigation of the problems of world history and contemporary world development must disclose the law-governed process of mankind's advance toward communism, the change in the balance of forces in favor of socialism, the aggravation of the general crisis of capitalism, the break-up of the colonial system of imperialism and its consequences, and the upsurge of the national-liberation movement of peoples.

In Soviet theory and practice, what is desired is stated as already proved "scientifically." The only purpose of inquiry is to prove again what has already been affirmed by political authority to be "true." The Soviet insistence that new data, or facts that cannot be fitted to the only valid theory, are "non-facts" is a continuing obstacle to any genuine freedom of discourse. The habit of raising each disagreement to a quarrel between "sin" and "virtue" also remains strong. This means that the examination of new or unwelcome facts is regarded, not as an interesting exercise in scientific skill, but as another form of political combat.

The rigidities of Communist thought make it very difficult (outside the natural sciences and technology) for the shapers of policy to have avail-able the findings of objective research. Nevertheless, the range of useful investigation is definitely wider today in domestic policy than it is in the analysis of world affairs. The Soviet leaders have made numerous adjust-ments in their domestic economic policy: breaking up the machine-tractor stations, cutting back long-range investment in hydroelectric power plants in favor of more numerous and less costly thermal plants, and so forth.

The quality of rational inquiry has been improved substantially in those fields where its validity is of direct advantage to the decision-makers. Unfortunately, even in this area of policy many of the major decisions seem still to be based primarily on deeply rooted prejudice. What will the Soviet people do with all the steel that has been promised by 1980? What can it do with a vast flow of petroleum if the output of private cars remains as low as is planned? Can agriculture possibly meet the growing and more varied needs of the Soviet people without a far larger investment of resources?

In the study of foreign countries and world politics, on the other hand, there has been almost no relaxation of political rigidities. Everything is painted in black and white. On one side, angels; on the other, devils. If dialectical materialism can provide a scientific basis for analysis, it should make it possible for Soviet experts to examine more objectively than they now do the causes of the high rate of growth in several of the free-world economies. It should actually encourage them to state calmly and without indignation why other systems operate differently from the Soviet one. A strong and powerful country needs objective information and conscientious analysis, and its rulers should not be afraid to permit the full use of scholarly inquiry if they want to be well served.

Because "science" had become a magic word in his time, Karl Marx baptized his theory of economic history with the name of "scientific socialism," and the same honorific adjective has been claimed by Lenin, Stalin and Khrushchev for their political programs. In practice, however, many of the judgments made by Soviet leaders have chiefly reflected ingrained ideological prejudices and strong political ambitions. As often as not, Soviet appraisals have fallen wide of the mark.

By the late 1920s the Comintern, along with some "bourgeois" economists, was predicting the onset of an economic crisis in Western Europe and North America. On the other hand, the first Five Year Plan was drawn up on the assumption that world prices of foodstuffs and raw materials, Russia's main exports, would remain stable. Moscow's oracles insisted, in the face of obvious facts, that the depression of 1929 was driving the United States down the path of fascism. In 1941 Stalin assumed that, if Hitler attacked the Soviet Union, Britain would make a compromise peace with him because of common "class interests." Fortunately for the people of the Soviet Union, Churchill and Roosevelt had already concerted a policy of alliance with Russia against the common enemy. In 1948 Stalin thought he could take West Berlin by a cruel blockade, and since 1958 Khrushchev has made several misjudgments of the Berlin question. Until recent months Soviet spokesmen have had little or nothing to say about the rapid steps that Western Europe has been taking toward economic unification; the "law" of capitalist competition made this historic process, in Moscow's eyes, an absurdity. The record of Soviet predictions suggests that it is more faith or habit than practical performance that supports the Kremlin's claim to possess the sole "scientific" and "infallible" instrument for predicting the future course of events.

III

Since 1953 many things have changed for the better in Soviet life. The improvements in food, housing, clothing and household conveniences have been widespread and substantial. In literature new themes of individual love and suffering, together with a cautious criticism of recent Stalinist "excesses," have become almost fashionable. More than at any time since the early 1930s the Party and the press seem to be trying to remedy some of the most callous features of Soviet administration and to improve the workings of Soviet justice.

All this is extremely welcome. The people of the Soviet Union, as they approach the forty-fifth anniversary of the October Revolution, have earned over and over the right to a modest return for their vast sacrifices and patience. Through this long travail they have preserved many fine qualities of friendliness, hospitality and patriotism. The modest comforts many of them have now attained, the pride in the scientific and material achievements of their country, and a burning memory of the Second World War combine to make them deeply and genuinely eager for peace and coexistence. They are now confident of the good intentions of their new rulers toward themselves, and therefore they accept more readily the Kremlin's protestations that only Soviet policy is "peace-loving" and that the sole risks of war now arise from the "imperialists" and their conspiracies.

"Making a peace treaty" with East Germany, "putting an end to the occupation régime in West Berlin"—all this sounds very reasonable to Soviet people. They are not aware that the people of West Berlin regard the token garrison as their protector and that they resent profoundly Ulbricht's insistence on "liberating" them from their hard-won freedom and prosperity. If people in the Soviet Union did know this, with whom could they discuss it? All they can do is hope that Khrushchev, who seems to them a human sort of man, knows what he is about and will, as he promises, safeguard peace.

The same old attempt to maintain a low level of strain at home and a high level of tension abroad has again been standard Soviet tactics in recent years. For many months Soviet readers heard all about the 400 or so American military advisers in Laos and the supply of American military matériel and economic support. It was many months before one relatively obscure Soviet newspaper gave one solitary hint that Soviet supplies and planes were engaged on the Communist side. Even now Soviet readers have no inkling that in Laos a major part of the fighting has been conducted by North Vietnamese units. Similarly, after the Soviet Government had announced on August 31, 1961, the forthcoming renewal of hydrogen bomb tests, it gave no further informaiton to Soviet readers for some six weeks. Even so, the news apparently spread rather widely, at least in the major cities, and gave rise to a good deal of muted anxiety.

A fierce patriotism, a defensive resentment of any condescension on the part of foreigners, a strong pride in Soviet strength and achievements— these emotions are widely shared. They make it easy for many Soviet people to accept a messianic ideology of Russia's unique mission, without thinking very much about the historic foundations of this notion or about its intellectual inconsistencies. The extreme self-righteousness of the Kremlin's boasts and demands is more troubling to many thoughtful Soviet people. Sometimes they wonder whether there is not a contradiction between Russia's being "the strongest power" in the world, as Khrushchev often claims, and the strenuous effort to protect its people against all but carefully screened and denatured information about the "imperialist" world.

Coexisting on the same globe with a one-eyed and angry giant is dangerous rather than exhilarating. In one breath he demands "friendship" and describes the many achievements, mainly material, that he admires in American life. In the next, he explains with "scientific" certainty why Communism will inevitably "bury" this much envied America. Even without benefit of Freud, it is not hard to see the power lust bursting out from behind the appeals for "peace and friendship."

We must, nevertheless, deal with the world as it is, and two of the facts of the world are the Soviet messianic fantasy and the power the Soviet leaders wield. It is, of course, a sign of good judgment that the Soviet leadership recognizes the mutually suicidal character of a nuclear war, and we must welcome its stated intention to contain the conflict within a rather elastic definition of "peaceful coexistence." As the Soviet spokesmen have made clear at Geneva, however, the Kremlin is not actively interested in bringing nuclear arms under control, and it believes it can gain more political advantages by continuing the arms race at a high pitch.

Moscow regards the present period of "peaceful coexistence" as a prolonged contest in which it must exert its full strength and will in order to make decisive gains by all means short of nuclear war. By the leverage of its strategic, political and economic power it hopes, within a few years, to bring about a great shift of political power in its favor. In contrast to Stalin's cautious peripheral probings, Khrushchev's declared ambitions, and the current Soviet programs of action, now extend to all continents except, perhaps temporarily, Australia. Since Soviet military and economic strength will be growing rapidly in coming years, it is not going to be enough for the countries that cherish freedom to repeat old and tried formulas that have served them well in previous crises. They must seek actively for new ways to bring their great political, economic and strategic resources to bear in the balance if they are going to survive in freedom the multiple challenge that is posed by Khrushchev's program of "peaceful coexistence."

INDEX

489

DEFENSE OF THE MIDDLE EAST: Problems of American Policy (Revised Edition), by John C. Campbell.

COMMUNIST CHINA AND ASIA: Challenge to American Policy, by A. Doak Barnett.

FRANCE, TROUBLED ALLY: De Gaulle's Heritage and Prospects, by Edgar S. Furniss, Jr.

THE SCHUMAN PLAN: A Study in Economic Cooperation, 1950-1959, by William Diebold, Jr.

SOVIET ECONOMIC AID: The New Aid and Trade Policy in Underdeveloped Countries, by Joseph S. Berliner.

RAW MATERIALS: A Study of American Policy, by Percy W. Bidwell.

NATO AND THE FUTURE OF EUROPE, by Ben T. Moore.

AFRICAN ECONOMIC DEVELOPMENT, by William A. Hance.

INDIA AND AMERICA: A Study of Their Relations, by Phillips Talbot and S. L. Poplai.

JAPAN BETWEEN EAST AND WEST, by Hugh Borton, Jerome B. Cohen, William J. Jorden, Donald Keene, Paul F. Langer and C. Martin Wilbur.

NUCLEAR WEAPONS AND FOREIGN POLICY, by Henry A. Kissinger.

MOSCOW-PEKING AXIS: Strengths and Strains, by Howard L. Boorman, Alexander Eckstein, Philip E. Mosely and Benjamin Schwartz.

CLIMATE AND ECONOMIC DEVELOPMENT IN THE TROPICS, by Douglas H. K. Lee.

WHAT THE TARIFF MEANS TO AMERICAN INDUSTRIES, by Percy W. Bidwell.

UNITED STATES SHIPPING POLICY, by Wytze Gorter.

RUSSIA AND AMERICA: Dangers and Prospects, by Henry L. Roberts.

STERLING: Its Meaning in World Finance, by Judd Polk.

FOREIGN AFFAIRS BIBLIOGRAPHY, 1942-1952, by Henry L. Roberts.

AMERICAN AGENCIES INTERESTED IN INTERNATIONAL AFFAIRS, compiled by Ruth Savord and Donald Wasson.

JAPANESE AND AMERICANS: A Century of Cultural Relations, by Robert S. Schwantes.

BRITAIN AND THE UNITED STATES: Problems in Cooperation, by Henry L. Roberts and Paul A. Wilson.